CONTEMPORARY SOCIAL THEORY

General Editor: ANTHONY GIDDENS

This series aims to create a forum for debate between different theoretical and philosophical traditions in the social sciences. As well as covering broad schools of thought, the series will also concentrate upon the work of particular thinkers whose ideas have had a major impact on social science (these books appear under the sub-series title of 'Theoretical Traditions in the Social Sciences'). The series is not limited to abstract theoretical discussion — it will also include more substantive works on contemporary capitalism, the state, politics and other subject areas.

Published Titles

Tony Bilton, Kevin Bonnett, Philip Jones, Ken Sheard, Michelle Stanworth and
   Andrew Webster, *Introductory Sociology* (2nd edition)
Emile Durkheim, *The Division of Labour in Society* (trans W.D. Halls)
Emile Durkheim, *The Rules of Sociological Method* (ed. Steven Lukes, trans.
   W.D. Halls)
Boris Frankel, *Beyond the State? Dominant Theories and Socialist Strategies*
Anthony Giddens, *A Contemporary Critique of Historical Materialism*
Anthony Giddens, *Central Problems in Social Theory*
Anthony Giddens, *Profiles and Critiques in Social Theory*
Anthony Giddens and David Held (eds), *Classes, Power and Conflict: Classical and
   Contemporary Debates*
Geoffrey Ingham, *Capitalism Divided? The City and Industry in British Social
   Development*
Terry Johnson, Christopher Dandeker and Clive Ashworth, *The Structure of Social
   Theory*
Douglas Kellner, *Herbert Marcuse and the Crisis of Marxism*
Jorge Larrain, *Marxism and Ideology*
Gerry Rose, *Deciphering Sociological Research*
John Scott, *The Upper Classes: Property and Privilege in Britain*
Steve Taylor, *Durkheim and the Study of Suicide*
John B. Thompson and David Held (eds), *Habermas: Critical Debates*

Forthcoming Titles

Martin Albrow, *Weber and the Construction of Social Theory*
Ali Rattansi and Dominic Strinati, *Marx and the Sociology of Class*

CONTEMPORARY SOCIAL THEORY

General Editor: ANTHONY GIDDENS

Theoretical Traditions in the Social Sciences

This series introduces the work of major figures in social science to students beyond their immediate specialisms.

Published Titles

Forthcoming Titles

Introductory Sociology

Second Edition

Tony Bilton, Kevin Bonnett, Philip Jones,
Ken Sheard, Michelle Stanworth and
Andrew Webster

MACMILLAN

First edition 1981
Reprinted 1982 (twice, with corrections), 1983 (twice), 1984, 1985,
1986, 1987
Second edition 1987
Reprinted 1988 (twice), 1989

Published by
MACMILLAN EDUCATION LTD
Houndmills, Basingstoke, Hampshire RG21 2XS
and London
Companies and representatives
throughout the world

Distributed in the United States of America by
Sheridan House, Inc.
145 Palisade Street,
Dobbs Ferry, NY 10522

Printed in Hong Kong

ISBN 0-333-44517-1 (hardcover)
ISBN 0-333-44518-X (paperback)

For our families, friends and students

Contents

Foreword

Sociology is a subject that has undergone some major transformations over the past decade or so. Both on the level of social theory and in terms of the expansion of empirical research, sociology has developed along many fronts. The task of incorporating the main elements of these developments within an introductory textbook is a formidable one. But it is a task that the authors of *Introductory Sociology* have accomplished in a very impressive fashion. This book, in my opinion, is simply the best and most comprehensive introductory text currently available. Its virtues are several. All of the chapters are written in a clear and cogent style, but manage to initiate the reader into debates of a complex character. The authors are particularly concerned to emphasise that sociology is an inherently controversial subject, and try to summarise several different competing views on the major topics that are analysed. The book includes reference to the latest empirical studies, and at the same time has lengthy sections dealing with problems which have rarely figured in introductory texts previously (e.g. sexual divisions in society). Not least important, the authors show themselves to be sensitised to contemporary trends in social theory: the 'sociological theories' chapter presents an exemplary discussion, accessible to the beginning reader, of basic theoretical issues that anyone studying sociology today must confront. Like several of the other chapters in the book, it is an independent contribution in its own right. The first edition of this book deservedly became one of the standard introductions to sociology in schools, colleges and universities, and this new edition can only add to its already substantial reputation.

King's College ANTHONY GIDDENS
Cambridge

Preface to the First Edition

In many ways this has been a difficult book to write. We have tried to meet the varying requirements of students approaching sociology for the first time at different levels of study. Moreover, we have been especially concerned to produce a book which is not only comprehensive in its coverage of substantive areas in sociology but which locates them firmly within theoretical perspectives and debates.

We hope we have been able to do justice to these objectives. Our experience of teaching at both GCE Advanced level and degree level allows us to appreciate the varying needs and expectations which students bring to a sociology textboook. Furthermore, while each of us teaches all the topics covered in the book at A level, the fact that we specialise in different areas at degree level has enabled us to draw upon specific expertise for the separate chapters.

Our objectives — of comprehensiveness, theoretical rigour and substantive depth — ruled out the possibility of a small introductory monograph. But students need not feel compelled to read the book at one sitting from cover to cover. The book is structured in such a way that each of the chapters can be read as a self-contained entity. The discrete nature of each chapter has required the occasional repetition of material, but such repetition has been kept to a minimum and, particularly through the use of cross-referencing, helps to ensure continuity of discussion.

At the same time, some chapters can be usefully combined and treated as a unit. Chapters 2, 3, 4 and 6, on 'Patterns of Inequality', 'Forms of Subordination', 'Power and Politics' and 'Sexual Divisions in Society', can be approached in this way, as can Chapters 5 and 6, on 'The Family' and 'Sexual Divisions'. In particular, Chapters 12 and 13 — 'The Production of Sociological Knowledge' and 'Sociological Theories' — were written as a pair and designed to read together. Our general objective has been to achieve a balance in the level at which the chapters are pitched; however, Chapters 12 and 13 tackle very complex methodological and theoretical sociological issues, and students are more likely to understand them fully after they have immersed themselves fairly extensively in the rest of the book.

References included in abbreviated form in the body of the text are reproduced fully at the end of each chapter. These are not meant to be a comprehensive list of the major contributions in a particular area of sociology, nor should students feel it necessary to read them all. The relative importance of particular books or articles should be clear from their prominence within the chapter in which they appear.

Writing this book has certainly helped us clarify and order our ideas about sociological issues and has reinforced our conviction that studying sociology can be an exciting and stimulating experience. We hope that after reading the result of our efforts you will share this belief.

ACKNOWLEDGEMENTS

While the writing of this book has involved the collective efforts of six authors, its successful completion would not have been possible without the assistance and advice of a large number of other people.

We are particularly grateful to John Winckler at Macmillan. He has proved a most reasonable and encouraging publisher, bearing our enthusiasm and occasional frustration equally calmly and consistently sharing our commitment to this book. We are very grateful to Tony Giddens, who (besides offering many useful suggestions and criticisms on individual chapters) did much to help us view the book as a whole at the crucial stage of final editing. We would also like to thank Louella Hodgson for her part in the book's early stages, and Graham Day, Eric Dunning and David Held for constructive comments and criticisms on particular sections of the manuscript. Needless to say, only we are responsible for any weaknesses the book may have.

Keith Povey performed the monumental task of copy-editing with exceptional thoroughness and efficiency. His work would have been even more difficult had it not been for the considerable typing and deciphering skills of Sue Barnard, Jenny Connor, Rosemary Leach, Rosemary Jolley, Deborah Allsop, Lynn Dopson, Ola Holasz, Barbara Sporne and Verna Cole. Our thanks go, too, to Ron Stellitano for the cover photograph.

Finally, we would like to thank all our sociology students at the Cambridgeshire College of Arts and Technology, past and present, whose stimulation and friendship have not only made teaching sociology here so enjoyable but have also contributed in no small measure to the writing of this book.

Cambridgeshire College of   Tony Bilton
Arts and Technology   Kevin Bonnett
1981   Philip Jones
                                   Ken Sheard
                                   Michelle Stanworth
                                   Andrew Webster

Preface to the Second Edition

In revising this book we have attempted to retain the basic objectives
and rationale of the first edition in terms of comprehensiveness, theoretical
rigour and substantive depth. We have, however, felt the need to make
a number of changes which go beyond the mere updating of empirical
material. A completely new chapter on the dynamics of inequality has
been produced for this edition, and a number of the chapters have been
extensively revised and rewritten. These changes take account of shifts
and developments in certain areas of debate within sociology and of
extremely useful suggestions made by colleagues, both known and
unknown, teaching in sociology, as well as remedying limitations which
we ourselves came to perceive in the first edition. We have also revised
the presentation of the text — notably through the use of 'boxes' — to
highlight important themes and debates.

ACKNOWLEDGEMENTS

A major driving-force in the production of this second edition has been
Steven Kennedy at Macmillan — a stern taskmaster, but someone with
whom we have enjoyed working. Tony Giddens again gave us useful advice
at the stage of planning, and Keith Povey's vigilant copy-editing was yet
again greatly appreciated. Ron Stellitano's photographic skills in
attempting to conceal the effects of the ravages of time on six authors
are again displayed on the back cover.

   We have greatly valued the many unsolicited comments and suggestions
from those who have used the first edition as a teaching aid, and the views
of our local colleagues, Roddy Gallacher, Lyn Brennan and Fenella Butler,
as well as those of our students, have been particularly welcome in this
respect.

Cambridgeshire College of   Tony Bilton
Arts and Technology   Kevin Bonnett
1987   Philip Jones
          Ken Sheard
          Michelle Stanworth
          Andrew Webster

Acknowledgements

The authors and publishers wish to thank the following who have kindly given permission for the use of copyright material:

Associated Book Publishers (UK) Ltd for material from *Power Without Responsibility* by J. Curran and J. Seaton, Methuen & Co.

Basil Blackwell Ltd for a table from 'The British Upper Class' by J. Scott from *A Socialist Anatomy of Britain* edited by D. Coates, G. Johnston and R. Bush, Polity Press, 1985.

The Open University Press for an extract from 'The professional stranger: some methodological problems encountered in a study of the Reverend Sun Myng Moon's Unification Church' by E. Barker from *D207: Media Booklet, An Introduction to Sociology*. Copyright © The Open University Press 1981.

BSA publications Ltd, T. Pinch and C. Clark for an extract from 'Patter Merchanting', *Sociology*, vol. 20, no. 2, May 1986.

Cambridge University Press for a table and diagram from *The Wealth of the Nation* by J. Revell; and for a table based on 'Men of Property' by Rubinstein from *Elites and Power in British Society* edited by Stanworth and Giddens, CUP 1974, and *The Upper Classes* by J. Scott, Macmillan, 1982.

Heinemann Educational Books for tables from *Class in a Capitalist Society*, edited by Westergaard and Resler.

The Controller of Her Majesty's Stationery Office for tables and data from Crown copyright material.

Unwin Hyman Ltd as The Free Press for an extract from *Doing Sociological Research* by Colin Bell and Howard Newby, 1977.

Every effort has been made to trace all the copyright-holders, but if any have been inadvertently overlooked the publishers will be pleased to make the necessary arrangement at the first opportunity.

1

Sociology: Themes and Issues

1.1 INTRODUCTION

All academic disciplines or areas of study are faced with the initial problem of providing the layperson or newcomer to the discipline with some idea as to what their subject 'is all about'. Most people feel that they have some understanding of the focus of disciplines like History or Physics, but are less familiar with Sociology. For sociologists the question 'What *is* Sociology?' frequently poses an awkward and embarrassing problem; indeed they may feel tempted to reply 'History', 'English' or 'Economics' when asked what they teach or study in order to simplify conversations with strangers! Offering a single-sentence, short-hand definition such as 'Sociology is the study of human society and human social behaviour' may seem rather vague and uninformative (though being essentially accurate), or not sufficiently precise as to distinguish sociology from other disciplines such as psychology.

Sociologists may attempt to improve on this by detailing specific *areas* of behaviour in which they are interested: how people behave in families, why some people are involved in crime, why some children perform better at school, and so on. Such brief 'thumb-nail' sketches do give some indication of the essence of sociology, but ultimately it is both necessary and perhaps more fruitful to emphasise that the most important and distinctive feature of sociology is not so much *what* is studied but *how* it is studied, i.e. it is important to indicate what is the particular *perspective* of sociology, its distinct *way of looking* at the individual and society.

Collectively, the population of Britain perform millions of acts every day during their waking hours, yet the net result of all this is *not* chaos and confusion, but a reasonable approximation of *order*: motorists drive on the left-hand side of the road, not on the right; shoppers offer coins and banknotes, cheques and cheque cards in exchange for goods and services, not goats and chickens or nothing at all; love-making takes place indoors in bedrooms, and not outside on the pavement. In short, behaviour occurs in more or less co-ordinated, regular sequences and patterns: social life involves patterned regularities. The sociologist would also suggest that these *patterned regularities* in social life mean that social behaviour is predictable, i.e. that one can safely say that individuals in similar social situations will behave similarly. Furthermore, the sociological perspective

1

maintains that these patterns in behaviour are the products of specific social 'forces' or factors, and more specifically are the consequence of the *social relationships and experiences* which go to make up human social living.

Developments within sociology

In order to appreciate fully the emphasis of a sociological perspective, it is important to realise that sociology as a discipline arose within distinct historical, intellectual and social contexts, and that is the product of a particular era in particular societies. Major questions about the individual and society have preoccupied thinkers in all periods of history: the philosophers of Ancient Greece and Rome reflected upon the way society operated and/or should operate, and for centuries afterwards social and political theorists and philosophers applied themselves to similar questions. But these 'philosophical' analyses of society were essentially based on speculation, on dubious and untested assumptions about the motives of human beings in their behaviour, and on undisciplined theorising, and they lacked *systematic* analysis of the structure and workings of societies. Philosophers and thinkers frequently constructed grand models and schemes about humans and their societies without looking at how societies *actually worked*.

However, from the eighteenth century onwards in Western Europe, important changes took place in perspectives on and understanding of society and the individual's place in it. Many considerable advances were taking place in scientific discovery with regard to the structure and composition of the physical world surrounding human beings, and with regard to the physical nature and make-up of human beings themselves. The natural sciences, though essentially in their infancy, were beginning to develop systematic methods for studying the physical world and the individual's part in (and relation to) it, and they were being increasingly recognised and valued for providing this more 'certain' knowledge. Could such a scientific, 'rational' approach also be applied to the analysis of humans' social worlds, their relationships, experiences and behaviour within it?

Alongside these developments there were also extensive social, economic and political changes which had and were to have profound effects on societies in Western Europe and elsewhere. Scientific and technological advances laid the foundations for the transformation from a predominantly rural, agricultural, 'manual' way of life to an urban, industrial, 'mechanised' pattern of living. New inventions and developments in methods of production, transport, etc., changed the scale and location of production at work from the land and small enterprises to the town and city and larger-scale enterprises like factories. A greater variety of occupations emerged.

These extensive changes integral to the process of industrialisation involved, moreover, a major paradox, in that they brought a 'new' society with great productive potential and more sophisticated and complex ways of living, while at the same time generating extensive disruptions in traditional patterns of life and relationships, as well as creating new material problems of overcrowded and unpleasant urban conditions, poverty and unemployment.

Sociology as a distinct discipline emerged against the background of these intellectual and material changes in the second half of the nineteenth century. The early sociologists were greatly influenced by the changes in patterns of life which they saw going on around them as industrialisation proceeded, and they were often deeply disturbed by what they saw. It is important to stress at this point that these early sociologists were *not* intensely 'radical' individuals, but rather could frequently be more accurately labelled as 'conservatives' made uneasy by the changes they were observing in society. Nevertheless, they were greatly concerned with the idea of obtaining exact knowledge of the workings of society, and, living in a period when the natural sciences were making real strides in knowledge, felt that the application of natural science methods to the study of society might produce similar advances in understanding. Thus, from the very beginning, there was a great emphasis on the need to analyse social life scientifically. Auguste Comte, the so-called 'founder' of sociology, who stressed the adoption of a scientific method of analysing society so that we might improve society through a thorough understanding of it, summed up in his famous phrase, 'To know, to predict, to control.' This early emphasis on the 'scientific' analysis of social life was to have (and still has) considerable implications for the subsequent development of the discipline, as we shall see in Chapters 12 and 13.

Although we have located the beginnings of sociology in Western Europe in the second half of the nineteenth century, its development and acceptance as an academic discipline was not a uniform and uncomplicated process. Sociology became firmly established in universities in France and Germany earlier than in Britain. British universities for a long time were relatively much more interested in the anthropological investigation of so-called 'primitive' societies in the more remote areas of the world, and British sociology constituted a relatively minor discipline, centred mainly on the London School of Economics. The focal points of British academic life were, of course, the universities of Oxford and Cambridge, traditionally the cornerstones of the established social elite, and the critical examination of British society (in such areas as inequality, the distribution of power, the basis of industrial conflict, and so on) was perhaps a less acceptable enterprise than the socially and politically 'safer' study of unfamiliar cultures.

The early classical works in sociology of the late nineteenth and early twentieth centuries were produced in France and Germany, with Emile Durkheim in France and Karl Marx and Max Weber in Germany as the outstanding figures. As Chapter 13 will testify, the work of these 'classic' sociologists still occupies a position of profound importance in contemporary theoretical debates. Sociology developed markedly in the USA too, and received more widespread acceptance there than in Britain: in many ways the USA early this century was ideal sociological material – a rapidly expanding and industrialising, cosmopolitan, immigrant-based society which was experiencing a wide range of social changes. Some sociology in the USA was therefore understandably characterised by detailed empirical studies of a variety of areas (particularly the more 'seamy' side) of American social life – of delinquent gangs and neighbourhoods, of particular ethnic minorities etc. – though other work, led by Talcott Parsons, involved theorising in the traditional grand manner.

As an established discipline, however, sociology is a relatively new arrival on the academic scene, and the real expansion in its popularity has occurred in the post-war period. We can point to some factors which have influenced this expansion:

(i)   In the post-war period there has developed a rather more critical awareness of how societies operate: fewer people simply sit back and accept their societies unthinkingly – they see that alongside the many technological and social advances that have been made there still exist problem areas like over-population, poverty and crime.

(ii) Alongside this, there has developed an increasing concern with social reform and the reordering of society, accompanied by the belief that in order to make such reforms effective and soundly based, knowledge about society and its members is needed.

(iii) There has also developed an increasing awareness of other societies and ways of life as a result of better systems of communication in travel and the mass media.

(iv) Increasingly, it has been claimed that people who work in government, industry, the social services, etc., ought to have some sort of specialist knowledge of society on the grounds that they will be better equipped to meet the demands of their work.

As a result, during and since the 1960s, sociology degree courses have increased considerably, sociology has found its way into schools, sociologists have been increasingly recognised and consulted by various organisations, from national government downwards, in research programmes, policy planning, etc., and some sociologists have also found fame in the national media.

Sociological versus non-sociological explanations

Despite all this, there remains a widespread ignorance and rejection of a sociological perspective when people think about human behaviour. Other, more familiar, 'common-sense' perspectives predominate in people's minds. They may, for instance, employ a *biological* perspective in attempting to explain family and marital arrangements: 'women rear children because they have a maternal instinct (biologically determined) for this task'. Similarly, they may use a pseudo-*psychological* perspective in explaining suicide ('People commit suicide when they are mentally unbalanced'), or a *moralistic* perspective in explaining crime ('Criminals are people who have not developed a conscience regulating their actions'). Because ordinary people are more familiar with these kinds of common-sense perspectives in their everyday lives a sociological approach does not come easily to them. This is further compounded by a deeply held commitment to the idea that we are all individuals, unique beings with our own special qualities and idiosyncracies, which sociologists deny, preferring to 'put people in boxes' without regard for their individuality.

Sociology, however, insists on a willingness to reject what is 'obvious', 'common sense', 'natural', and to go beneath the surface of such understanding of the world. As Berger (1966, pp. 32-4) puts it:

> The fascination of sociology lies in the fact that its perspective makes us see in a new light the very world in which we have lived all our lives . . . It can be said that the first wisdom of sociology is that – things are not what they seem.

Sociologists emphasise that what is 'common sense' or 'natural' may be by no means universal or eternal, but is frequently relative to particular societies or to particular periods in time. We can illustrate this by reference to a basic and familiar area of human social experience, courtship and marriage.

The common-sense view of differences in behaviour between men and women in the family in our society tends to assume that because there are biological and physiological differences between men and women, certain aspects of their behaviour are therefore 'natural'. For example, it is often argued that it is common sense and natural that women will engage in child-rearing and domestic tasks and that men will make sexual advances and will work outside the home. Mead's study of New Guinea, *Sex and Temperament in Three Primitive Societies* (1935), revealed the partiality of such common-sense interpretations of behaviour patterns. Among the Arapesh, she found very few 'natural differences' in men's and women's behaviour, with neither sex exhibiting aggression: women did the heavy carrying (because of their supposedly strong foreheads), and the men lay with their wives during and after childbirth, 'sharing' the pain and strain. Among the

Mundugamor, both sexes were aggressive, children were treated brusquely by both parents, and love-making was rather like a pitched battle. Among the Tchambuli, yet further variation occurred: men adorned themselves, gossiped, made things for trade, while women selected their partners, made the sexual advances, did all the trade, and were the more aggressive sex. Obviously, we cannot explain these very striking variations in behaviour via biology, since the people in the various societies were all the same biologically.

In the realm of courtship and falling in love, sociology further questions common-sense notions. In Western societies, men and women are popularly said to choose marriage partners by the uniquely personal act of falling in love – love strikes willy-nilly, 'across a crowded room', in a 'magical chemistry', etc. Sociologically speaking, nothing could be further from reality. As Berger (1966, p. 48) says:

> As soon as one investigates which people actually marry each other one finds that the lightning shaft of Cupid seems to be guided rather strongly within very definite channels of class, income, education, racial and religious background.

That is, falling in love is regulated and constrained by very powerful social factors: the odds against HRH Prince Edward falling in love with Elsie from the Tesco supermarket are very high indeed. Numerous other examples abound. For instance, to the Hopi Indians of North America it is 'common sense' that rain-clouds are gods and must therefore be enticed to rain by rain-dances, a view not entirely consistent with that of the Meteorological Office. Similarly, in medieval Europe, it was 'common sense' that one could determine the guilt or innocence of an accused person through 'trial by ordeal', e.g. accused people carried a red-hot iron bar for ten paces, and if their wounds were healed after x days they would be declared innocent – again, this method is noticeably absent in modern trials!

The essential point, then, is that one person's 'common sense' is somebody else's nonsense, and there are numerous examples of sociological and anthropological investigation questioning and exploding many common-sense notions about behaviour.

Although the use of everyday common-sense beliefs is usually not only unsystematic and inadequate but also often contradictory, if we look more closely at common sense it is likely such explanations of the world are based on what we shall call here 'individualistic' and/or 'naturalistic' assumptions. What do we mean by these labels?

An individualistic explanation of some event or phenomenon assumes that the event can be readily understood and explained solely through reference to the behaviour of the individual(s) involved in it. There is no attempt to understand or explain the phenomenon in terms of wider *social* forces. A naturalistic explanation of behaviour rests on the assumption that one can readily identify 'natural' (or sometimes 'God-given') reasons for behaviour, such that, for example, it is 'only natural' that two people should fall in love, get married, live together, and raise a family.

Both types of explanation are rejected as inadequate by the sociologist: the individualistic because it does not recognise the importance of wider social forces acting on the individual which he or she cannot control; the naturalistic because it fails to recognise that behaviour patterns are not primarily biologically determined but rather reflect social conventions that have been learned by individuals as members of social groups or, more generally, society.

In Tables 1.1 and 1.2 are presented an outline of the major differences between the everyday and sociological explanations of phenomena. Table 1.1 contrasts the accounts of poverty, industrial conflict, and suicide as provided by the individualistic and sociological approaches.

The reader may be familiar with aspects of the individualistic account sketched in Table 1.1: in particular, you may have noticed similar explanations of poverty or industrial conflict in the press or on television. Inasmuch as the media does reproduce such accounts it sustains the status quo, since

TABLE 1.1

Explanation of:	Individualistic	Sociological
Poverty	People who are poor are so because they are afraid of work, come from 'problem families', are unable to budget properly, suffer from low intelligence and shiftlessness.	Contemporary poverty is caused by the structure of inequality in class society and is experienced by those who suffer from a chronic irregularity of work and low wages.
Industrial conflict	Industrial conflict is caused by the interference of influential individuals or 'agitators' in the work-place.	Industrial conflict only occurs and is only sustained because of the existence of widespread grievances among the work-force.
Suicide	The most individual of all acts committed by a person of unsound mind.	The frequency, location, and type of suicide is governed primarily by social factors such as religion, family and marriage patterns and not individual factors.

'the problem' is said to lie within the individual and not wider social processes, implying that a solution comes through changes in the individual rather than in society. The predominance of the individualistic perspective in our everyday life is not difficult to understand: the birth of modern capitalist society was accompanied by a philosophy of individualism, the belief that individuals were free to choose their rulers, their employers, and their religion. At a time when structural unemployment means that many – particularly the young – will be out of work for long periods of time, the old individualistic idea that 'all we need is a bit of enterprise and motivation' seems to get stronger the more inappropriate it becomes.

We can repeat our exercise and briefly characterise the divergence between the naturalistic and sociological explanations, this time through reference to marriage and the position or role of women in the family (Table 1.2).

TABLE 1.2

Explanation of:	Naturalistic	Sociological
Marriage	It is only natural that a man and woman should live together for life because they fall in love and want to raise children.	Monogamy is only one form of marriage, predominant in Western society. For example, polygyny (a man with more than one wife) and polyandry (a woman with more than one husband) also exist in other societies. Marital patterns depend on a variety of economic and social factors. The eligibility of marriage partners depends on the class and status position of the individuals.
Woman's role	It is important that the woman should be at home to raise her children because this satisfies her maternal instinct and the children's need for a mother.	Women stay at home because it is a widespread social expectation that the home is the correct place for them to be and because of limitations on the opportunity to do otherwise. Socialisation of children is just one function of the institution of the family which could be performed in non-familial contexts.

That there is nothing 'natural' about our marriage pattern or the role of women in society is clear from the sociological account. However, the naturalistic account should not be rejected on the grounds that it is inadequate, as though it could be polished up a bit and made more acceptable: rather, it should be dismissed because it presents an entirely *distorted* picture of social reality. That marriage forms and the role of women in society are not 'God-given' is clearly demonstrated in Chapter 7 on the family and Chapter 5 on sexual divisions in society. These show how what is taken for granted in one society would be looked upon as being not only strange but perhaps also immoral in another society. We are not then just talking about the French eating frogs' legs and the English black pudding: we could eat frogs' legs in England without affecting our social structure. Eating habits are simply a matter of fashion and individual taste. But if marriage patterns were to be drastically altered, significant changes in the social structure would occur. In short, it is sociology's comparative perspective, its cross-cultural vision, that provides its strongest refutation of the naturalistic explanations or accounts outlined above.

Sociology reveals the rich variety of human societies, the vast differences between cultures, both in the past and in the present. What would be considered to be 'human nature' in one society might appear to be positively extraterrestrial in another: quite simply sociology tells us that there is no such thing as *the* 'Human Nature'. We *learn* to become members of a particular society and the most important forces involved in this process are *social*, not biological or instinctual. Let us look at what this means in more detail.

Sociological perspectives

Earlier we stressed how sociology's development as an academic discipline has not been uniform all over the world. One important implication of this must be emphasised, which we have glossed over until now: in the same way that there is no single pattern of development of sociology, so there is *no single* sociological perspective.

Rather there are a *variety* of perspectives which do share the common emphasis of viewing social behaviour as the product of social arrangements, social forces and conditions, etc., but which may differ in the relative emphasis which they assign to certain specific factors or variables for explaining that behaviour. Put more simply, sociologists themselves often disagree in explaining society and social behaviour because they may start with different 'background assumptions'. Though the existence of a variety of competing perspectives in sociology can sometimes be confusing and a little frustrating to the new student, he or she must recognise that there simply is no nice, neat package of 'sociology' which is universally accepted and which provides all the answers.

Sociology is a subject which consists of competing theories about what social life is and how it should be explained.

Some sociologists – *Structural* theorists – are interested in society as a *whole*, in how it is *structured*. Others – *Social Action* theorists (sometimes called *Interpretive* theorists) – are more interested in *individual pieces of social interaction*, and how the parties to them make them work.

Within the structural camp there is an important distinction to be made too: between *Structural–Consensus* theorists, who think that *the structure of a society's ideas and beliefs* is what sociology should primarily concern itself with, and *Structural–Conflict* theorists, who think that a society's *structures of advantage and disadvantage* and its *relationships of domination and subordination* are more important to concentrate on.

We shall look at the differences between these theories in detail in Chapter 13. In this introductory chapter we need not complicate things too much; it will do to simply identify the distinctive interests of each of these kinds of sociology – consensus theory, action theory and conflict theory – in turn.

Structural theories: society as constraint

It is a fundamental assumption for structural sociology that when we are born we are confronted by a *social* world which is just as real – at least in its consequences for our behaviour – as other realities which we also confront. What we are as individuals is decided by the particular society in which we live, and by the particular social groups to which we belong. This is so because the world around us – including the social world – channels our actions, *constraining* us to act in particular ways. As a result, regularities and patterns can be observed in the behaviour of different individuals. Let us look at a simple example.

If I want to leave a room, I must do so by the limited number of means available to me, which will be by the door or the windows; if they are locked, I cannot leave. I have a strictly limited choice of action, and the extent of the choice is determined for me by the constraints of my physical environment. Other sorts of things can constrain my actions too, of course; I may not be able on my income to afford a Ferrari. So I am constrained by my material world – the practicalities of my material circumstances – just as much as by my physical world.

(As we shall see, it is members of the conflict theory camp that concentrate on the structure of these material constraints on behaviour.)

Yet there are other aspects of my world which exercise similar constraints over my behaviour. Having bought my car, if I want to travel from A to B in Britain I have to do so by travelling on the left-hand side of the road. What sorts of factors constrain me to do so?

First of all my physical world constrains me in so far as every other car will be travelling on the left-hand side and my progress might be somewhat impeded if I chose otherwise; secondly, it is a *rule* that is being followed by every driver. Like every rule, it has means by which it is enforced; in this case, if I break the rule of driving on the left-hand side of the road I can be prosecuted under a law of the land. Now although such a rule is not part of my physical or material world, its existence constrains my action just as effectively as they do; we can call this a constraint of the world of ideas.

However, not every social constraint has a law to back it up. In fact most of the rules we follow in our social lives are not legally enforced, but they are rules nevertheless. For example, if I had all the money in the world I could quite easily buy a hundred Ferraris if I wished. But I might *not* wish to do so because I might believe it to be wrong to buy an Italian car for one reason or another. Now what is constraining my action here? Of course, it is my belief about what is right or what is wrong; if I believe something to be right, I am prepared to do it, whilst if I believe it to be wrong I am not. So my beliefs constitute an extremely important constraint on my behaviour and, bearing in mind that what we believe to be right or wrong is, to a large extent, *learnt* behaviour, that we do not *inherit* such beliefs, it is obvious that the *source* of these beliefs has to be seen as a major constraint on, and determinant of, our behaviour. Clearly, this source is society and the particular social groups within it.

The ways in which ideas and beliefs in societies constrain the behaviour of their members is the main concern of consensus theory.

1.2 CONSENSUS THEORY: CULTURE AND SOCIALISATION

Culture and socialisation are the key concepts in consensus theory. This is how they are employed to explain social life.

Culture

Learned behaviour in any particular society includes those ideas, techniques and habits which are passed on by one generation to another – in a sense, a *social* heritage – and which are virtually a set of solutions to problems that, in the course of time, others have met and solved before. This learned behaviour, or social inheritance, of any society is called its *culture*.

It is the possession of a common culture and the ability to communicate and pass it on to others that distinguishes the human being from other animals. Humans are human *because* they share with others a common culture, a culture which includes not only the artefacts of its living members but also those of members of past generations. This is the heritage awaiting those as yet unborn. Human beings are able to develop and pass on their culture by means of language, which is, of course, itself a product of culture. Language has to be learned in the same way as other elements of a culture and, once this had been accomplished, the individual can acquire the rest of his or her culture. How is this done?

Socialisation

The process by which we acquire the culture of the society into which we are born – the process by which we acquire our *social* characteristics and learn the ways of thought and behaviour considered appropriate in our society – is called *socialisation*. When individuals, through socialisation, accept the rules and expectations of their society that make up its culture and use them to determine how they should act, we say they have *internalised* society's cultural rules.

Now, in a very real sense socialisation can only be properly understood as an aspect of *all* activity within human societies. In the course of our social lives we are constantly learning about ways of thinking and behaving considered appropriate by those other members of society with whom we come into contact (as well as those considered inappropriate by them) and this learning process only ceases when social life itself ceases – on death. However, despite recognising this fundamental general and continuing character which it possesses, we can nevertheless identify specific vehicles, or *agencies* of socialisation. In particular, since the socialisation undergone by a human being in the early years of its life will obviously be of crucial influence in affecting the attitudes and behaviour of the social adult, then the *family*, as the first human group an individual in any society usually belongs to, is clearly a socialising agency of major importance.

Most of the influence of the family in this initial stage during the socialisation process is unintended, and takes place informally, as a product of social interaction between people in extremely close physical and emotional proximity to one another. In such a setting we learn as much through observation and experience as we do through deliberate instruction or training. Thus, though our parents tell us not to stare at strangers, not to speak with our mouths full, etc., they unintentionally teach us much more besides. For example, it is in the family that we first encounter the way in which people who have authority behave, and the differences in the way men and women behave.

Despite the primacy of its influence, socialisation in the early years of life is not confined to the family, however. As the child gets older, other agencies get in on the act. For example, other children with whom a child comes into contact – friends, playmates, and so on – can have a significant socialising influence. This agency, called the *peer group*, is probably the first means by which children encounter ideas and ways of behaving different from those at home.

Then, of course, the whole process of formal *education* is a crucial socialising agency. In complex and highly differentiated societies there is such an abundance of different sorts of skills and knowledge which one might learn that a reliance on informal means for their successful acquisition would be useless. The more complex a society and the more varied the skills possessed by its members, the greater the need for institutions deliberately designed to effect the formal dissemination of specialised skills and knowledge – educational establishments like schools, colleges and universities.

From a sociological point of view, however, such places are 'learning' establishments in a much broader sense than most people would ordinarily recognise and, as such, have to be seen as major agencies of socialisation.

When a child goes to school he or she is not only confronted with the traditional school subjects, but also with codes and practices governing behaviour. The pupil has to learn not only history and geography, but also how to relate to teachers and fellow students: for example, when it is acceptable to claim the attention of the teacher and to ask questions, or when conversation with friends is allowed. He or she also has to learn which strategies are acceptable in which classroom, since teachers' demands will vary.

Research seems to indicate that pupils are evaluated on their mastery of this 'hidden curriculum' just as they are evaluated on their mastery of the formal syllabus. In some cases mastery of the 'hidden curriculum' can almost compensate for lack of ability. Jackson (1968, p. 34) draws attention to this in his study *Life in Classrooms*:

> What do teachers mean when they say a student tries to do his work? They mean in essence that he complies with the procedural expectations of the institution. He does his homework (though incorrectly), he raises his hand during discussions (though he usually comes up with the wrong answer), he keeps his nose in his book during free study periods. He is in other words a model student though not necessarily a good one.

The socialisation process pupils encounter in schools therefore involves not only the acquisition of formally defined skills, but also the gaining of many other social skills, such as learning how to live in a group and how to respond to those in authority.

So, in the classroom, as in the family and the peer group, socialisation largely takes place as an unintended consequence of the interaction of its members. Much of *adult* socialisation is equally informal and unintentional, deriving from informal norms developed within groups.

Social groups are often deliberately set up for a purpose. Their goals cover an infinite range, from the manufacturing of nappies to campaigning for free abortion. Of equal sociological interest, however, is that any group, whatever its purpose, will always unintentionally develop distinctive *patterns* of behaviour. Members of the group will come to expect one another to conform to these patterns if they wish to remain members of it. This group pressure for conformity may often override values imposed from outside: for example, the child may refuse to 'tell tales on his or her friends' despite demands from the teacher, or soldiers may infringe Queen's Regulations rather than be disloyal to their comrades in the platoon. Groups evolve expected ways to behave which their members must normally obey.

So far we have identified specific group agencies of socialisation, but it is obviously a mistake to restrict our definition of the concept to a process taking place only in these settings. In effect, since socialisation is present as part of all social relationships, whether the parties to the relationship are aware of it or not, it is clear that it is a much more subtle, complex and pervasive process than it might at first appear and that we can only properly understand it as an aspect of *all* human activity. Moreover, since our involvement in social relationships and membership of social groups only ends when our social existence ends (at death), socialisation must be seen as an inevitable and a lifelong process. Even at the point of death we are nevertheless still members of a social group – be it a family, a hospital ward, a platoon of soldiers, or whatever. As a consequence we are still constrained to conform to standards of behaviour expected of us by the group. Where death is a normal occurrence – in a hospital ward, for instance – this constraint on us to behave in ways determined by our interaction with others will extend even to the actual process of dying itself. This has been well documented in Sudnow's book *Passing On* (1967).

Some socialisation takes place on an extremely particular level: for example, individual families will in many respects differ from each other and as a result the content of much of the socialisation characteristic of each will be correspondingly variable. In contrast, socialisation can be much more general. This is so where the structure and organisation of social groups and collectivities is fairly precisely defined by some overall set of rules, as, for example, in the armed services, or in other bureaucratic organisations like local government departments, the Civil Service, ICI, or in similarly organised work groups (for instance in the coal or motor industries).

Less deliberately structured groupings can exhibit similar patterns of socialisation, too. In British public schools, for instance, not only are the majority of pupils deliberately drawn from that small section of British society committed to the standards which the public school promotes, but teaching staff are similarly rigorously selected, not merely on the basis of academic competence, but also on the basis of the extent to which they have successfully internalised the standards they are expected to foster among their pupils. (In fact, this is really an example of intentional and deliberate socialisation in education, since one of the self-conscious functions of the British public school is the perpetuation of that distinctive life-style by which the elite marks itself off from the rest of society.)

The *most* general level at which socialisation takes place will obviously be where it is common to the society as a whole. The principal agency at this level is the *mass media* in all its forms: books, magazines, newspapers, cinema, theatre and television are all influential mechanisms for the dissemination of ideas and of particular sets of values and beliefs. (This book is itself an instrument of socialisation.) As we will examine in more detail in Chapter 10, the mass media can in a very important sense direct the way we look at the world and the questions we ask about it. In effect, it can along with other phenomena, structure reality for us.

The effects of non-socialisation

From what we have said so far, it should be clear that socialisation is a crucial concept for sociology, since it directs attention to a key element in the process by which the individual becomes social and acquires those qualities usually referred to as 'human'. In fact, proof of this can be seen by examining some of the available evidence concerning human beings who have failed to be 'made social' via socialisation in the way we have been describing. Such people manifestly lack those human characteristics a society both produces in its members and relies on for its continued existence.

There have been a number of recorded cases of children living in the wild and presumed to have been nurtured and reared by animals; such children are often referred to as feral (wild) children. Some of the better-known cases include the 'wild boy of Aveyron', found in a French forest in 1799, Amala and Kamala, two sisters found in a wolf-den in 1920, or the recent case of the Indian boy, Shamdev, found playing with wolf cubs near the Musafirkhana forest.

It has still to be proved conclusively that these children were reared exclusively by animals, but it is clear that they all had minimal human contact. Descriptions of their behaviour show how many of the character-istics which are considered natural or essentially human are not instinctive but learnt, indicating the necessity of human contact and care for the development of social behaviour and for the development of fundamental human faculties.

Consider how Shamdev first behaved when rescued from the forest at the age of about 5:

At first Shamdev cowered from people and would only play with dogs. He hated the sun and used to curl up in shadowy places. After dark he grew restless and they had to tie him up to stop him following the jackals which howled around the village at night. If anyone cut themselves, he could smell the scent of blood and would scamper towards it. He caught chickens and ate them alive, including the entrails. Later, when he had evolved a sign language of his own, he would cross his thumbs and flap his hands: this meant 'chicken' or 'food' (*The Observer*, 30 August 1978).

Although such behaviour corresponds closely to the descriptions of other feral children, it is impossible to know whether these children might have developed similar patterns of behaviour even if brought up in greater contact with people, and it has been suggested that feral children might have been abandoned by their parents *because* of their behaviour problems. However, another case of a child brought up in semi-isolation illustrates how unusual behaviour patterns would seem to be the product of minimal socialisation rather than the result of any inherent deficiency or abnormality. Isabelle is a case referred to by Kingsely Davis. She was an illegitimate child who spent most of her first six years of life in a darkened room with a deaf mute mother. When found, her behaviour was such that she was thought to be mentally deficient:

> Her behaviour towards strangers, especially men, was almost that of a wild animal, manifesting much fear and hostility. In lieu of speech she made only a strange croaking sound. In many ways she acted like an infant ... At first it was even hard to tell whether or not she could hear, so unused were her senses. Many of her actions resembled those of deaf children (Davis, 1970, p. 206).

In addition she was unable to speak or walk properly. What is interesting about Isabelle's case, though, is that after two years of rehabilitation and skilled training she covered the stages of learning that would normally require six years. It would seem in this case that her unusual behaviour patterns and impaired development were not a product of personal inadequacy, but were due to her restricted early experiences and minimal human contact.

From these examples it is clear that the acquisition of fundamental human characteristics does not occur instinctively; indeed, such behaviour is predominantly shaped by an individual's immediate social environment. Socialisation is essential for a person to develop into a social being.

Status, role, norms, values, sanctions

It is the process of socialisation into cultural rules that consensus theory concentrates on in order to explain both individual social behaviour and order in society as a whole. Through learning the same rules that constitute our culture we agree about appropriate behaviour and belief; this *consensus* ensures that we are able to live ordered lives together.

Because of socialisation it is only rarely that we have to puzzle out a meaning for an action which we come across in our normal social encounters – most actions seem perfectly intelligible to us the moment they occur – because we have learnt the *rules* by which others are playing the 'game'. To put this another way, we can predict what is going to happen in most of the situations in which we find ourselves because we have expectations that certain rules will be followed. For example, we would be surprised if the police did not wear a particular uniform or if a traffic warden did not book us for parking on a yellow line. Furthermore, we utilise such expectations about the way an individual in a particular position should behave, *irrespective* of whether we know that individual personally. All of us know how the police and traffic wardens behave, whether or not we actually *know* police or traffic wardens. The social position that a person occupies we call a *status* and the behaviour that we expect from a person occupying that position we call a *role*.

A social role is rather similar to a role played by an actor: people occupying certain positions or statuses in society are expected to behave in certain predictable ways, as if 'scripts' had been prepared for them. For example, if we go to the doctor, we expect him or her to behave in a particular way, to ask questions about our illness and symptoms, possibly to examine us, to make a diagnosis and perhaps write a prescription. Any other behaviour, such as suggesting a game of cards, would surprise and confuse us, as it would not conform to our notion of the appropriate role that someone occupying the status of doctor should perform.

Furthermore, we would expect *any* doctor, not just our own, to behave in the 'proper' manner, in the same way that we expect the same sort of behaviour from all shop assistants, or all priests, or all fathers. But the expectations involved in roles are not simply one-directional; it is not merely the case that a person is expected to play a role in certain typical ways. Rather, that person is also entitled to expect others to behave towards *him* or *her* in certain ways. Doctors can ask us all sorts of intimate questions and expect honest answers; in return, we expect them to treat this knowledge confidentially and not to gossip about the state of our health. A social role thus involves *mutual* expectations.

Social roles, therefore, are not just a matter of the way people can be *observed* to behave (in the usual run of things) but concern the way it is thought that people *ought* to behave. Ideas about what people *should* do, about what behaviour is 'proper' or 'fitting', we call *norms* and *values*. The most important expectations surrounding social roles are not just statements about what *actually* happens – about what a person *will* do, out of habit and so on – but are norms outlining things which a person occupying his or her status is *obliged* to do. That is, roles are *normatively defined*: the expectations are about an *ideal* pattern of behaviour to which actual behaviour only approximates.

Values are rules which are not attached to particular roles but are more general standards concerning worthy behaviour; for example, injunctions like 'Uphold the Law', 'Respect Private Property', 'Work Hard', 'Protect Family Life', etc. reflect the kinds of values typical of Western industrial societies.

Consensus theorists allocated a very important role to values; whatever differences in expected behaviour there may be between different groups within a society they consider that a general consensus on the most significant values – central values – must exist for any society to operate satisfactorily.

The relationship between norm and values and socialisation is plain. While norms and values define society's rules, it is through socialisation that individuals come to embrace as their own the norms and values of others and learn to regard the rules and traditions of their society as rightful.

However, there is something else to consider. Knowledge of the rules, the standards required of us, does not *necessarily* ensure that they will always be kept, for we still have the *choice* of breaking them if we wish. So, even though internalisation does in large measure explain the remarkable degree of conformity exhibited in social life, we have to recognise that there is another reason for this. Suppose you sometimes feel tempted to drive faster than the allowed speed limit, perhaps because you are in a hurry or because you decide that it is quite safe to do so and that the speed limit is unnecessary. Do you therefore automatically break this legal rule? Only with great care, of course, because you know that if you are caught breaking the limit by the police, the consequences will be unpleasant – a summons, a court case, a fine, perhaps an endorsement. That is, the rule – in this case, a legal one – is backed up or underwritten by *sanctions* – in this case, legal ones – designed to ensure compliance with it. All of society's rules have sanctions of one sort or another backing them up, although most are non-legal since most of society's rules are not legal ones. However, sanctions do not always work to ensure conformity by constituting a *threat* of some sort or another, for some encourage conformity instead by offering *inducement*.

There are two broad types of sanctions: *positive*, or rewarding, sanctions; and *negative*, or punitive, sanctions. The constraint of positive sanctions really refers to the general way in which the desire to seek the approval of others (though, sometimes, their disapproval) can influence our behaviour.

In contrast negative sanctions operate by encouraging behaviour designed to avoid the *disapproval* of others. These can be more or less *organised*. The most obvious example of such a sanction, of course, is the action taken by a state against those who break its laws. Less organised, but equally important, are those sanctions which involve the mobilisation of public disapproval in a more *diffuse* way against those who break society's non-legal rules. Thus, by the use of gossip, ostracism, satire, and, probably most important of all, ridicule, offenders against society's standards are punished for their transgressions. In small-scale and closely knit communities, where self-respect is very closely tied up with the esteem in which one is held by one's fellows, any sanction of this sort designed to erode it is likely to be particularly effective. Thomas Hardy shows this very clearly in his description of a 'skimmity ride' in his novel *The Mayor of Casterbridge*. He describes how Michael Henchard, the disgraced and bankrupt former mayor of the town, and his one-time mistress are publicly villified by an informal gathering of some of the townsfolk (complete with hideous effigies of the couple swaying drunkenly in a horse-drawn cart) outside the mayor's house. The shame of having her 'dirty linen' ritually washed in public in this way by representatives of the community is too great for the woman and she suffers a stroke from which she dies shortly afterwards.

Similar customs to this, all designed to hold up social miscreants to public ridicule, can be found in many different sorts of small-scale societies. Often such societies lack legal machinery, as they lack state institutions generally, and so this sort of diffuse sanction can be the most important means of punishing offenders against society's norms.

With all these formal and informal constraints, we can see that pure freedom for the individual actor is very unlikely; considering all these expectations and controls that surround us, Berger's portrayal of society as a prison begins to seem plausible: 'Our considerations of the sociological perspective have led us to a point where society looks more like a gigantic Alcatraz than anything else' (Berger, 1966, p. 107). But unlike ordinary prisons, members of most societies conform freely and willingly – they actually *want* to do what they are expected to do. As Berger (1966, pp. 140–1) graphically describes it:

> Society penetrates us as much as it envelops us. Our bondage to society is not so much established by conquest as by collusion ... we are entrapped by our own social nature. The walls of our imprisonment were there before we appeared on the scene, but they are ever rebuilt by ourselves. We are betrayed into captivity with our own co-operation.

Functionalism

So far we have been describing the ways in which the processes of socialisation and internalisation come to bind societies together and reproduce practices and institutions. In the structural consensus view, these processes are vital, for they are the means by which to achieve *social integration* and *moral regulation* in society. Let us imagine a society where social integration and moral regulation are perfect, and exist throughout society. There would then be complete agreement – consensus – on the rules of behaviour governing people as they occupy different social positions. Social expectations would cover all circumstances and problems perfectly. All members of society would be efficiently socialised into a complete acceptance of the social rules, perhaps leading to complete internalisation of the rules. Social harmony and peace would prevail as everyone would have their range of roles to play and would know how to play them. All would be committed to common goals and values, but they would 'know their place' and accept the ration of power and advantage deemed suitable for their social position.

Unlike some politicians who cling to mythical notions of a past golden age, no sociologist actually believes that society is, or could be, really like this. However, many, beginning with Emile Durkheim, believe that society approximates to this model. Durkheim and his followers have been concerned with consensus theory's one basic and overriding preoccupation – how society can continue as an integrated whole and not collapse into a mass of warring individuals. Their answer to this 'problem of social order' is in terms of socialisation into a consensus of norms and values. For them the key to societal continuity is conformity due to learnt rules of conduct. Individual people may come and go, but society carries on continuously – because it can shape the incoming individuals to fit the existing state of affairs.

From this point of view, societal characteristics cannot be explained as the product of actors' choices, since these choices are themselves the product of socialisation. If this is so, how do societies come to be organised in the way they are? For most consensus theorists, the answer lies in a theory of social structure made famous by Durkheim in the nineteenth and early twentieth centuries and developed to such an extent by Talcott Parsons and his followers in the USA between the 1930s and 1950s that during these years it came to be seen as *the* sociological theory. This theory is called *Functionalism*.

For the functionalist, the answer is that societies have *built-in* tendencies towards harmony and self-regulation, analogous to biological organisms or machines. In the same way that the human body, for instance, is an integrated whole whose individual parts serve particular 'needs' of the system (for example, the heart performs the function of pumping blood around the body, the bowel functions to collect and evacuate solid-waste products, and so on), so society comprises a system of interdependent institutions each with a contribution to make to the overall stability and continuity of the whole. According to the functionalist, then, to explain the existence of a social institution we must not look for purposive intention on the part of individuals but, rather, we should investigate the fact that the social system as a whole requires its needs to be satisfied.

Examples of functionalist analysis can be found throughout this book. In particular, the functionalist analyses of stratification in Chapter 2, of youth cultures, poverty and global development in Chapter 4, of the family in Chapter 7, of education in Chapter 8 and of the professions in Chapter 9 all clearly demonstrate the characteristic interests of this kind of sociological theory.

Of course, such sociologists do not agree with this model entirely. As it stands, it gives a picture of a society that is totally static, without change, and totally without conflicts between opposed social groups. Any sociologist has to accept that there are some differences in values between separate groups in society and that people must adapt and innovate to cope with changing social circumstances. But the functionalist starting-point is still the idea that people are socialised strongly into conformity and that social phenomena can be explained in terms of the functions they perform. This view remained dominant for a long time in sociology, but more recently other sociologists have become reluctant to view people as happy robots, acting out predetermined roles.

For one thing, they feel the functionalist approach does not only neglect change and conflict but tends to 'reify' society – to treat it as a thing – by attributing to social structures capacities for thought and purposive action which only humans can possess. To explain the existence of institutions in society not in terms of individual intention but in terms of societal need ultimately implies that societies are capable of *deciding* what they need. But, of course, societies do not think, only people do. Furthermore, some critics feel the functionalist approach overemphasises the determining nature of the socialisation process, which leads to a false and oversimplified view of human personality and human action. These sociologists belong to the *Social Action* camp of theories.

1.3 SOCIAL ACTION THEORY: THE INDIVIDUAL AS A CREATIVE SOCIAL ACTOR

Structural perspectives emphasise the important truth that societies exist and persist as solid, real entities. For any individual, society is a massive external reality, and it is necessary to emphasise this simply because we tend to take for granted these social arrangements as natural, immovable and inevitable. This is less so today in rapidly changing societies where great efforts are made to adapt and modify social institutions; indeed, it is plausible to suppose that the roots of sociology lie in the experience of rapid and far-reaching social change. However, even in modern Western societies, most people live within their culture as a given 'natural' world. In contrast, the sociologist is forced to recognise the *precariousness* of social existence. This is not just because of the threat from disease, famine or a self-inflicted nuclear holocaust; all social worlds are precarious in a deeper sense. This is because social arrangements are to some extent *arbitary* ways of organising human life – there is an apparently endless range of variations in social rules, ideas and conventions.

Social action theory emphasises these features of social life. 'Social action theory' is a general term within which several different approaches can be identified. These range from *Weber*'s micro-sociological work (though Weber was by no means just an action theorist), to *symbolic interactionism*, on to the most recent, and radical, action approaches – *phenomenology* and *ethnomethodology*. We will examine the differences between these action theories in Chapter 13.

Action theorists pay close attention to the ways in which 'definitions of reality' are used and sustained by actors. They show how these definitions may be disputed by individuals or groups, and how actors *negotiate* shared rules and ideas.

What this implies is neatly summed up by a famous saying of W. I. Thomas (1966): 'If men define situations as real, they are real in their consequences.' Thomas is emphasising that the social behaviour of human beings is a product of what *they decide* is going on around them, of what they take the behaviour of others to *mean*. Whether or not these definitions are correct, *every* social encounter involves a process of interpretation on the basis of available evidence, whether this is self-conscious or not.

At the simplest level this means deciding that someone wearing, say, a skirt in our society is female and acting on the basis of this decision, or deciding that someone shouting at the top of his or her voice is excited or angry and acting accordingly. The 'female' *could* be a female impersonator, or someone in disguise, or an actor on the way to a theatre; the 'angry' or 'excited' person could be deaf, or someone calling out to a friend some distance away. But the 'truth' is not the point at issue; what matters is that as human beings we necessarily engage in an interpretative process when we encounter others, as they do with us. From this point of view society is an aggregate of such activities; social order is negotiated order.

The emphasis here is on the individual's capacity to understand and interpret what other individuals *mean* by their social actions. The most distinctively human aspect in this respect is the capacity to communicate verbally: language is the principal medium by which humans exchange meaning. Although other vehicles are available – gesture, touch, dress, etc., all sometimes speak as loudly as words – for action theorists the capacity to give meaning to the world through a shared language enables people to interact socially and to create a social order.

In contrast to the functionalist, then, who sees the capacity of the human being to communicate as simply a vehicle for the 'activation' of imposed cultural rules, for the action theorist this capacity is the essential creative ingredient in social life. From this viewpoint cultural rules are not given determinants of individual action but are continually built up and broken down as the result of individual choices and decisions.

Although the negotiation of rules is a constant process, this does not completely undermine the power of socialisation. Societies are still largely reproduced through this proces. However, from a social action perspective socialisation can never be simply a matter of internalisation of fixed social rules. Socialisation is, by its nature, a means to create *change* as well, because human behaviour is learned rather than imprinted. Human cultures can change rapidly because cultural innovation is infinitely faster than biological evolution. Patterns of social life can change radically and still be passed to the next generation, and so adaptation and innovation can be rapidly institutionalised. This is the key to the human being's evolutionary break with other species. Culture and symbolic language, once developed through evolution, allow humans to race ahead.

These elements distinctive to humans were emphasised in the work of G. H. Mead, C. H. Cooley and W. I. Thomas, three of the early American symbolic interactionists who contributed to social action theory. They demonstrated the importance of early socialisation for the development of social and mental skills in the individual. Symbolic language, and the concepts and shared meanings embodied within the use of language, can only be learnt through socialisation. However, Mead, Cooley and Thomas also recognised that socialisation is not a simple one-way process, and that potential for change is also generated *within the individual*. There is a close connection between the learning process and the development of a thinking, reasoning *self*. This self has an individual identity and an individual capacity for reflexive thought: that is, actors can reflect on their own actions and *the way others respond to them*. For Mead, the actor was shaped by these responses from others, so that the self was a social product. But at the same time, the self was complex enough to initiate actions and innovate new ideas. The mature actor is self-conscious, and so begins to learn rules and expectations in a less passive way. As we take on new roles – plumber, teacher, mother, shop steward, etc. – we are partly aware of the demands and constraints involved and we can exercise choice. It may be that some of our roles conflict (e.g. parental responsibilities might conflict with commitments at work) or different groups might impose conflicting expectations in relation to one particular role (e.g. in a man's role as shop steward the managers might expect him to calm disputes while his work-mates might demand that he never compromise with the bosses). In either case, the individual must make choices, innovate, and if necessary abandon a role altogether.

Equally important, the whole notion of set role behaviour may come to seem problematic. In many situations, actors are faced with no clear rules for action, or the action may be hard to sustain. First of all, a 'frame' or definition of the situation must be established – 'is this an intellectual conversation between colleagues or an attempt at flirtation?' – and the situation might waver between definitions or be both at once. This means that social interaction requires mutual effort by the actors as they attempt to establish the definition of the situation for each other and negotiate appropriate behaviour for themselves and for the other. Much of the time the problem is eased by set rules for encounters and by rituals. (e.g. the polite formality between bank manager and client) but there is *always* some scope for challenging and redefining these and hence helping to redefine rules of appropriate behaviour.

The general social action approach thus emphasises fluidity and change in social interaction; it has a conception of the individual that emphasises people's creativity and capacity for innovation. For social action theory socialisation is a complex process running throughout life and roles arise from practical interaction; they do not derive from some static central value-system.

> Examples of action theory applied to social behaviour can be found in Chapters 8 (Education), 12 (The Production of Sociological Knowledge) and 13 (Sociological Theories) and, particularly, in Chapter 11 (Deviance).

As a general approach, this presents a very attractive picture of human beings, but we must not, on the other hand, allow this to distract us from the pressing reality of society as an institutionalised, patterned, constraining system. We *are* creative, innovatory individuals but only by virtue of socially created selves, and our actions all take place in the context of patterned social relationships with others. Social action can never be separated from *practical constraints* or from *social control*.

Practical constraints

We must never forget that people do not act and make choices in a vacuum. The factors influencing their choices can be understood, and these influences lie at two levels. The first level is that of the values and beliefs they have learnt through socialisation. For example, a couple might choose either to limit family size and have more money, or instead to maximise the number of children. The choice they make will depend in large part on their learnt values, but there is a second level of explanation, concerned with influences we mentioned earlier (p. 10) – *practical constraints* on action. In choosing family size, the couple's decision will be affected by factors such as the unemployment of the father, or government banning of contraceptives. In addition, the desire to keep up a respectable level of income or the desire of the woman to have a job or career, may lead to the woman going to work. At the same time there may be little provision of help in child care, and so the couple will have to organise their lives accordingly. Possibly this will mean changes in behaviour (such as the role of the man in housework) which violate the norms and values into which they were socialised. On the other hand, if they were sufficiently wealthy they might be able to afford a nanny or a private nursery school. This illustrates the crucial point that practical constraints affect people in differing degrees, depending on their level of material advantage. Power and reward are distributed unequally in most societies, and so the privileged will be much freer. They are relieved of many practical constraints on action. Thus even individual choice cannot be understood in isolation from the wider social structure.

This example demonstrates what we mean when we say that choices are never totally 'free' but are influenced in complex ways by the socialisation process and by practical constraints. In addition, we should consider whether there might be a link between the *dominant ideas* transmitted through socialisation and those people who benefit from the existing distribution of power and reward. In other words, we should always look for the *origin* of social norms and consider whether the values and expectations reproduced through socialisation serve the interests of any particular group or class. If they do, then we may wish to explore this issue of *ideology* to see whether socially dominant groups use their power to *impose* ideas and patterns of behaviour on their subordinates.

It is *conflict theory*, much of it derived from the classic structural and historical writings of Marx and Weber, that is principally interested in these kinds of issues.

1.4   CONFLICT THEORY: SOCIAL CONTROL, POWER AND CONSTRAINT

Dominant values

In exploring the origins of norms, it is important at this stage to distinguish two sources of change. One is the innovative adaptation by people to changed circumstances; the other consists of conscious, concerted attempts by groups to influence behaviour. For an example of innovative action in relation to norms we can return to the couple we met earlier. In the end, they make the same decision as most others and decide to go ahead and have children, and to try to reconcile this with their material aspirations. Therefore, they produce two or three children and the mother goes out to work. To cope with this, the father has to take a very active part in housekeeping and child-rearing, violating traditional conceptions of gender roles. However, these traditional role expectations prove weaker than the pressure of the other goals and practical constraints, and so the gender role is modified. As more people find themselves in the same position, men stop mocking each other for doing housework and mothers-in-law cease criticising their sons' wives about going out to work. Their expectations have had to change.

At the same time, there are other groups operating at the second level of influence on norms. Traditionalist 'defenders of the family' may actively attempt to influence behaviour. After the Second World War, fears of a decline in family size led to a fashion for theories of 'maternal deprivation' which, together with more direct exhortation, encouraged women to refrain from paid employment (see Chapter 7.)

It might be argued, in addition, that there is a further level of influence, where the unanticipated effects of communication became important. This may be seen as very significant today when we consider the way that advertising and women's magazines continue to portray women as finding all their fulfilment in the home. The role of woman as employee is systematically ignored, and this may unintentionally help to maintain a situation where women form a docile and cheap work-force.

We can see, then, that there are many elements and factors in this change in gender roles. One aspect is the spontaneous adaptation by members of society to new circumstances; another is the level of open attempts by groups to influence behaviour; a third is the whole range of unintended consequences which benefit different groups unequally.

This idea of unequal benefit links crucially to the point that competition for influence over behaviour is itself very far from free and equal. Conflict sociologists would argue that privileged groups are able to sustain a system of dominant values which helps to maintain the social structure. This social structure is itself unequal, and works to the benefit of this dominant group. We can see this system of dominant values as operating in two main ways. First, these values may limit conflict in crisis situations. For example, some historians have argued that Methodism and other non-conformist sects were deliberately encouraged by employers in the nineteenth century in order to placate the workers and persuade them to look for salvation in the next world rather than in this. This was perhaps successful in moderating opposition to the new industrial social order. In more normal times, however, we may see a second effect of dominant values. This strategy is simply to defend existing institutions and social relations as naturally right and inevitable. As long as things remain the same, the privileged will automatically retain their privilege. This concept of dominant values will be discussed more fully in Chapter 10; here we can simply note the role of such values in securing the acquiescence of the subordinate and less privileged members of society.

The behaviour of members of society is also directly affected, as we saw earlier, by *sanctions* designed to ensure compliance to its standards, that is, by *social control*. There are plenty of examples of such a control being effected by the use of *coercive* sanctions in the world today – from the killing of real or imagined enemies by despots to the widespread use of torture and incarceration in prisons and camps in many different countries. (In fact, it might be said that the use of torture in the 'civilised' world today is more widespread and certainly much more sophisticated than was the case in the 'barbaric' Middle Ages.) However, direct coercive sanctions require continuous effort, and may in fact be a rather brittle form of social control, so we should not expect dominant groups in different societies to rely wholly and simply on such crude means of retaining their power and privilege, especially where their position has long been entrenched. Since the downfall of military regimes in South America and elsewhere provide clear evidence that no political structure relying solely on coercion can hope to survive for long, we should not be surprised to find that the most effective form of social control involves attempts not to crush opposition but to stop it arising in the first place: that is, by the control of people's ideas, rather than of their actions.

We can see, then, that dominant values can make life easier for rulers. If the subordinate members of society can be persuaded to believe that those who dominate have a *right* to do so, and that those who have great material advantage have a *right* to it, then they are very unlikely to challenge or threaten the privileged. Thus ruling groups are likely to attempt to 'engineer the consent of the ruled' so that they accept their own subordination and disadvantage. It must be said that this has apparently been achieved with a good deal of success in many societies in many different periods.

Powerlessness and constraint

It may be, however, that the acceptance of dominant values is not as great as it might seem – we should not assume that actors conform because they wish to (even if these wishes were manipulated). Much more pressing considerations may produce a sullen acceptance of the existing social order which entails no strong commitment to the status quo. As we shall see in Chapter 6, much conformity may be explained by *powerlessness* in the face of social circumstances, where the actors recognise their inability to change things, and so resign themselves to making the best of it. This resigned attitude is an understandable response if individuals suffer subordinate positions in many of their social relationships. People may have little chance to argue with their foreman at work, with the council housing department, with the teacher of their child, or with the police officer who forces obedience to the law. All these figures of authority act in some degree as agents of social control, making decisions and issuing instructions which will bind those dependent on, or subordinate to them. Conflict theorists emphasise that most areas of our lives involve us in institutionalised power relationships, and most of us are subordinate most of the time. We know that if we really step out of line, then the police or the armed forces may step in with their right to use legitimate violence to force our conformity. As we show in Chapter 6, all patterned social relations involve relations of power and dependence, domination and subordination. Very often we conform because we know we dare not risk the consequences of non-conformity.

If power is distributed unequally in patterned ways, it is even more obvious that material resources are spread unequally. Sartre is reported to have said that he did not feel free without a thousand francs in his pocket; this is clearly a freedom which can only be enjoyed by a few. Chapter 2 will document the gross material inequalities which exist in wealth and income – and also in basic benefits such as health and job security. It is perfectly obvious that the choices made by creative social actors are limited by the practical resources available to them. What needs to be explained is the *origin* of concentrations of wealth and security or of poverty and deprivation. As we shall see in Chapter 2, we can distinguish different types of social structure which systematically generate unequal distributions of power and reward. Poverty and dependence are the result of particular systems of social relationships, which means that we can never understand the actions, choices and motives of actors unless we relate them to the position of the actor in the social structure. Knowledge, power and economic resources are the raw materials of social action, and they are all unequally available.

Among the examples of conflict theory to be found in the book, the discussions of Marxist perspectives on class (Chapter 2), on poverty (Chapter 4), on power (Chapter 6), on the family (Chapter 7), on education (Chapter 8) and on deviance (Chapter 11) clearly demonstrate this kind of approach.

All of this seems to have painted a rather gloomy picture. Our ideas are shaped by the pressures of socialising agencies, our actions are regulated by forces of social control, and society limits the resources available to us. Everything seems to indicate that we should accept the inevitable and just lie back and be happy robots. Needless to say, most sociologists are reluctant to relax into this supine position – and with good reason. Societies *do* change, and their social institutions are *not* immune to innovation, reform or rebellion. Although social arrangements constrain and control us, they are still constructed and reproduced by human action. People, especially when acting collectively, can come to break these barriers, overcome these constraints and reconstruct their social world. Many sociologists feel that their body of knowledge has a central contribution to make towards such reconstruction.

1.5 THE PRACTICE OF SOCIOLOGY

Sociology and social policy

A concern with social reform was an integral part of sociology from its beginnings. Many of the early sociologists were anxious about the social changes occurring around them and wanted to establish sociology as a comprehensive scientific discipline, charged with discovering sociological laws of behaviour and constructing social policy based on these laws. In other words, a scientific sociology was to be used for the reorganisation of society.

A similar conception of the role of sociology (though with a more 'radical' political orientation) is held by certain contemporary sociologists who want sociology to be not simply a discipline which analyses and explains social life but rather a vehicle for changing society, a discipline committed to the extensive alteration of existing social structural arrangements. At the opposite end of the pole there is the view of sociology as a completely objective, non-evaluative discipline, a way of looking at societies and developing knowledge about social behaviour, in which opinions or perspectives on policy-making, the solution of problems, and so on have no place.

Though these different perspectives on the role of sociology have been and still are the source of much debate among sociologists themselves, for the layperson no such complications exist: that is, many people understand sociology as being only concerned with social problems, social policies and social reform. While it is undoubtedly the case that sociology does attract people with a strong concern over social issues and problems, such preoccupations do not exhaust the subject-matter of the discipline.

Sociologists are interested in *sociological* problems. Any social phenomenon, be it 'nice' or 'nasty', that requires explanation is a sociological problem. *Social* problems (i.e. something identified as harmful to society and needing something doing about it) are merely one type of sociological problem.

However, the fact remains that demands are made on sociology to 'pay its way', to produce practical returns which can be utilised for policy purposes. There has been a considerable growth in the demand for applied social science from industry and, particularly, government, reflecting the increased willingness of governments to intervene in society (whether their own or someone else's), so that sociologists are being increasingly consulted in respect of certain problems ranging from population control to terrorist control. Even if sociologists do not actually provide a solution themselves, their data are often used in the formulation of policy by others.

Such a task for sociology may appear reasonable and innocuous, particularly in societies which embrace a commitment to the principle of using knowledge for practical purposes and not to any principle of 'knowledge for knowledge's sake'. Some would say that there is nothing remarkable or wrong in working for some group and being paid to answer some question that the group regards as important. But a whole host of questions are raised by the demand that sociology be geared towards assisting in the solution of social problems, policy formulation and social reform. In particular it is vital to remember that the recommendation, provision and implementation of social policies and reforms involve *political* questions and decisions – after all, who is to decide what is an 'appropriate' social policy, a 'desirable' social reform, an 'effective' solution to a social problem? As Bottomore (1962, p. 319) says:

> Every solution of a problem and act of policy is a political decision. It expresses the resolve of a social group to maintain or change a particular way of life, and to act in accordance with certain ideals. The sociologist may supply information, elucidate the context of problems, point to causes or conditions, indicate the advantages and costs of alternative courses of action ... But in the last resort, political decisions rest upon judgement, or political wisdom, and upon interests.

It cannot be assumed, either by the sociologist or by anyone else, that particular policy measures are in any way neutral instruments which are somehow divinely 'right' for the particular society concerned. Policies inevitably reflect ideologies, frameworks of values, either hidden or overt, and the sociologist employed on work in particular policy areas is inevitably bound up with these frameworks of values. Sociologists who lend their names or their work to a particular social policy are engaging in a political act; they cannot escape by saying that the use of their work to *justify* a particular social policy (even if they did not advocate that policy) is not their concern. The sociologist as a 'citizen' has to ask about the uses to which his or her work is to be put (see, for example, the discussion of Project Camelot in Chapter 13).

What *has* been the contribution of sociologists to social policy and reform, and what can they realistically expect to do in these areas? Probably the major contribution has been and will continue to be to encourage a more realistic and informed approach to social problems and matters of social policy. Sociology has an important role to play in exploding myths and misconceptions about social phenomena and institutions, and in providing a context in which controversial issues can be examined critically and analytically. Hence, sociological analyses of race relations, crime and the treatment of offenders, poverty and the like have helped to bring 'hot' issues out into the open and to clarify understanding of these areas. A good example of this can be seen in the area of educational research: before 1944 in England and Wales, education at a grammar school was predominantly the preserve of middle-class children whose parents had the ability to pay, with only a minority of 'free-place' pupils attending. The 1944 Education Act claimed to eliminate such inequality of opportunity by making entry to grammar schools the result of an examination open to all via the competition of the '11-plus'. The inadequacies of such a claim were starkly illustrated by subsequent sociological investigations in educational achievement (see Chapter 8 on education) during the 1950s and 1960s, which revealed sharply unequal chances in grammar school entry between middle-class and working-class children. Not only did these investigations reveal the fallacy of the claim about equal opportunity in the selective system, but they were also highly influential elements in the ammunition of the campaigners for the abolition of this system and the introduction of comprehensive education. The comprehensive system itself remains subject to similar investigation.

In a real sense, then, sociology can be seen as having an important 'critical' role to play in monitoring and assessing the impact of social policy, and in questioning accepted assumptions in these areas. A major contribution here has been to demonstrate that such social problems are the product of *social structural arrangements* and not the consequences of individual or personal qualities (see above on individualistic versus sociological explanations). Sociological studies have emphasised the need to investigate fully the complexities behind social problems, the need to reject the inadequate, simplistic, monocausal explanations of these phenomena often suggested by laypeople, politicians and the media. Sociologists have also strongly questioned the fallacy that social problems are necessarily the product of 'bad' things. Such problems may well be the product of social arrangements which are regarded as 'good', 'right' and 'desirable'; for example, high divorce rates may be the product of the high expectations and demands centred on monogamous marriage.

We must also underline a further dimension of sociology's 'critical' role in examining social problems. A major contribution of the discipline has been to emphasise how the identification and designation of a particular phenomenon or pattern of behaviour as a 'social problem' is not an unambiguous matter, but a process of *social definition*. Hence, for many sociologists, what is frequently most interesting is *why* a society defines a pattern of behaviour as a 'problem' and the process by which it *becomes* a 'problem'. As we shall see in Chapter 11 on deviance, the activities of groups with fewer power resources are much more likely to be labelled as 'social problems' and be given greater publicity than are those of the more dominant social groups in society. For instance, the use of cannabis by the young is far more likely to be branded as 'drug-taking'/'drug addiction' and hence a 'social problem' than is the consumption of thirty cigarettes a day by adults or half a bottle of brandy by middle-class businessmen. Thus 'social problems' are problems defined as such by the powerful; sociological problems concern the understanding of social life.

Sociology and social change

If it is necessary to draw a clear distinction between social problems and sociological questions then it follows that sociology must maintain a critical distance from the ideas – whether dominant or otherwise – of any particular society at any particular time. Any form of scientific endeavour must attempt to transcend its time and place to sustain an independent, doubting stance. This is obviously a pressing necessity – and source of difficulty – for sociology. Sociologists are only too well aware that ideas arise in particular social climates and contexts, and yet they have to seek a way of standing apart from society and analysing it objectively. The very project of sociology assumes the possibility of such knowledge, and implies that this knowledge should be made available to guide human action. If sociology produces more exact information, more rigorous analysis and new concepts to illuminate social life, then this knowledge can be used by people in society. All social action has to take place on the basis of ideas, assumptions and information, however false and mistaken these may be. Thus, whether individual sociologists like it or not, the fact that they produce knowledge is a significant contribution to the changing flux of social life. Some degree of influence cannot be avoided, and in fact many sociologists would now argue that the sociologist has a definite *responsibility* to disseminate this knowledge in order to criticise delusions and misconceptions. In this sense, sociological findings can be a resource available to all, to be used for whatever purpose the user decides. In this view, the social scientist produces neutral science and takes no responsibility for the ways in which it is used.

The simplicity of such a view disguises its danger. Is it really acceptable for knowledge to be used for any goal? Has science got no connection with the pursuit of human fulfilment and liberation? Certainly, many powerful groups with an interest in preserving the existing order do see sociology as threatening. They resent the disclosure of inconvenient truths, but above all they fear the disclosure that things need not be the way they are. The diversity and changeability of social structures is a central theme in this knowledge, together with the revelation that human action can recast social relations and institutions. If sociology reveals the extent of constraint and deprivation in societies, it also reveals the human potential for liberation and creative social reconstruction. If this knowledge is disseminated widely, and not restricted to already powerful groups, sociology can and must aid members of society to act more knowledgeably, more rationally, with more self-understanding; it will be a tool aiding people to build themselves a better society.

REFERENCES TO CHAPTER 1

Berger, P. (1966) *Invitation to Sociology*, Harmondsworth, Penguin.
Bottomore, T. (1962) *Sociology*, London, Allen & Unwin.
Davis, K. (1970) *Human Society*, London, Macmillan.
Jackson, P. (1968) *Life in Classrooms*, New York, Holt, Rinehart & Winston.
Mead, M. (1935) *Sex and Temperament in Three Primitive Societies*, London, Routledge & Kegan Paul.
Sudnow, D. (1967) *Passing On*, Englewood Cliffs, N.J., Prentice-Hall.
Thomas, W. I. (1966) in M. Janowitz (ed.), *Organization and Social Personality: Selected Papers*, University of Chicago Press.

2

Patterns of Inequality

2.1 INTRODUCTION

Inequality of power and advantage has been an extremely common, if not universal, feature of human societies, even if the degree of inequality has varied very greatly. It has almost always been the case that some group or groups have controlled and exploited other groups. At some points in the history of a given society people have rebelled and challenged this inequality; at other points they have meekly accepted their subordination; but probably most of the time people adopt a posture midway between these two extremes.

In this chapter we are not concerned with these responses of the oppressed – they will be discussed in Chapter 6 on power. Instead, the main task here is to understand the systems of stable inequality which have existed in different types of society. This chapter begins a detailed exploration of the issue of stratification, in particular stratification according to class. The chapter examines different theories of stratification and then goes on to present a full account of the facts of class inequality according to income, wealth, and so on. The reader is then invited to explore the 'living world' of class in Chapter 3 on the dynamics of class. These two chapters should, therefore, be seen as being theoretically and empirically linked. Inequality is not something which is randomly distributed between individuals in society. The sociologist is concerned with the way different *groups* are in an unequal relationship with other groups. Members of a given group will have features in common and will usually see their unequal position passed on to their children. The concept of *stratification* refers, then, to the idea that society is divided into a patterned structure of unequal groups, and usually implies that this structure tends to persist across generations. Now the actual nature of these groups, and the relationships between them, varies enormously. In this chapter we shall examine only some of the more important types of stratification structure.

The issue of inequality is absolutely central for sociology, not only because of the moral and political implications, but also because of the crucial place of stratification in the organisation of society. Every aspect of the life of every individual and household is affected by stratification, whether they realise it or not. As we shall see in the discussion of evidence from Britain, opportunities for health, long life, security, educational success, fulfilment in work and political influence are all unequally distributed in systematic ways.

Since stratification is so important, it is vital that concepts and explanations are employed in a clear and unambiguous way. Unfortunately, the very fact that the study of inequality is the central issue means that there have been a great variety of competing theories and concepts attempting to describe and explain it. This diversity is closely linked to the political importance of inequality. Different theories have been linked to different ideas on the value or otherwise of inequality, and also, as we shall see later, to different views on society and its future.

We described stratification earlier as a stable structure of inequality between groups which persist across generations. However, it is clear that we still need to distinguish between different advantages which can be distributed unequally. There are three basic forms of advantage which privileged groups may enjoy:

(a) *Life-chances*: that is, all those material advantages which improve the quality of life of the recipient – this may include not only economic advantages of wealth and income, but also benefits such as health or job security.

(b) *Social status*: that is, prestige or high standing in the eyes of other members of the society.

(c) *Political influence*: that is, the ability of one group to dominate others, or to have preponderant influence over decision-making, or to benefit advantageously from decisions.

Now it may well be that privileged social groups tend to be advantaged in all three areas, while subordinate groups normally enjoy poor life-chances, low status *and* little political influence. But we cannot assume that this is always the case. It is important to keep the three elements conceptually distinct, especially when trying to explain the basic nature of a given type of stratification structure. Inequality in one of these areas may be the root cause of inequality in the other spheres – caste society, as we shall see, appears to be based on *status* differences. Other inequalities follow as a result from this.

Furthermore, we must be clear on the differing nature of these types of advantage. Life-chances are *facts*. They describe the actual material benefits and opportunities of a group, whether or not the members of the group recognise these facts. Thus we can call these *objective inequalities*, which can be measured objectively by the sociologist. In contrast, inequalities of social status only exist by virtue of the fact that status differences are *constructed* and *recognised* by members of social groups. The basis for status may vary: it may be anything a social group claims as giving superiority and which is recognised by other groups – examples might include wealth, religious purity, political position or sexual prowess. Whatever the basis, status can only be sustained by conscious social action – groups claim status, and others actively defer to their 'superiority'. We can term this *subjectively based inequality*. Finally, inequality in political influence can normally be seen as deriving from either material advantage or high status, but it may be that political office may independently form the basis for gaining status and/or privileged life-chances. This can be termed *politically based inequality*.

> Structures of inequality may be based on any one of three types of advantage: the root of inequality may lie in economic relationships, in status relationships, or in relationships of political domination.

However, most industrialised societies today have stratification systems that strongly reflect economic relationships. Inequalities in material life-chances are fundamental; status differences and differences in political influence tend to be dependent on material life chances. Structures where economic relationships are primary we call *class societies*, and in these we refer to the different unequal groups as *classes*. There is considerable dispute over the precise definition of this term, but we shall use *class* to refer to *a group sharing a similar position in a structure of objective material inequalities, produced by a particular system of economic relationships characteristic of a particular mode of production.*

This means that the class position of a given group is determined by its relationship to other groups in the way production is organised. Different societies have different ways of organising production, and this creates different kinds of classes. For example, agricultural production might be organised on the basis of the *master-slave* relationship, as in Ancient Rome or in the southern states of the USA, or based on the *lord serf* relationship, as in feudal Europe, or on the *capitalist–proletarian* relationship, as in modern Western societies. Each of these economic relationships, which will be explained in detail later in this chapter, forms the basis for a totally different *class structure*. In each case, these economic relationships create inequality as one class dominates and exploits the other. This is not to say that economic relationships always constitute the main bases of inequality in a society.

2.2   CASTE AND AGE-SET STRATIFICATION

In a *caste* stratification system – traditional India provides the most complete version – an individual's position totally depends on those *status* attributes ascribed by birth rather than on any which are achieved during the course of one's life. This is not to say, as we shall see later on in this chapter and elsewhere in the book, that there is not a strict and systematic constraint on achievement imposed by ascribed status attributes in class societies too: those of race and gender are particularly significant ones in our society, for example. However, status attributes ascribed by birth in a *caste* society define an individual's position in the stratification system much more completely and securely than they do in a class society. The difference is clearly seen by comparing the ideologies of mobility held by the mebers of the two sorts of system. Thus, in a class society members typically believe that mobility is easily available and secured on merit. Though this chapter will demonstrate that this is questionable in practice, this belief still contrasts with that underlying caste inequality. The social position into which individuals are born here is the one in which, theoretically, they are bound to remain for the rest of their life. In reality, individuals, families and even groups can change position, although it is far from usual.

In traditional India, each position in the caste structure is defined in terms of its *purity* relative to others. The underlying ethos of the allocation of such status is that those who are most pure – the Brahmin or priest caste – are superior to all others, whilst those who are least pure – sometimes called the untouchables – are inferior to all other castes. (The traditional castes, or Varna, also included the Kshatriyas, or warriors, the Vaishyas, traders, and the Shudras, servants and labourers.) According to the ideology, such relative purity can only be retained by the ritual avoidance of contact between members of the different castes and as such determining the extent to which one can enter into any sort of activity or relationship. Here, then, we have a stratification system whose strata are defined in terms of ascribed status attributes and which is legitimated by religious values.

Another stratification system based just as exclusively on ascribed status attributes is characteristic of what are known as *age-set* societies. All socities differentiate and, to a greater or lesser extent, allocate unequal rewards on the basis of age. This age-based inequality in our society is most marked in the years of youth and early adulthood: thus, in British law, 16 is the age of consent, 18 is the age at which one can vote and drink in a pub, and so on.

In primitive societies the fact that as people get older they pass through socially recognised statuses is usually of much greater *structural* significance than in our society, and as a result is usually symbolically recognised by what van Gennep called *rites de passage*. In our society, such ritual celebrations of changes of status through ageing are now restricted to religious occasions like baptism, confirmation and burial, though 'coming-of-age' parties amount to the same thing. The process is much more serious for primitive society, however, for getting older in this sort of world is not just a question of securing certain basic legal rights as it is for us, but is fundamentally concerned with acquiring prestige. And this remains throughout life, for the old occupy a much higher status in primitive society than they do in societies like ours. A particularly crucial stage of status acquisition occurs when an individual enters social adulthood and is allowed to do things only an adult can, like marry and fight and so on. The *rite de passage* celebrating this change of status typically involves, for boys, circumcision.

In *age-set* societies, the changes in status involved in getting older are institutionalised to such a degree that they often constitute the very basis of political organisation. In such societies, those males who are initiated together – between the ages of, say, 13–18 – constitute an *age-set* and the members of each set together pass through a series of *age-grades*. Different sets perform different political tasks. Typically there will be a warrior set, composed of those of the suitable age for fighting, while beneath them, in both age and status, will be a set of initiates. Above them will be the set of newly retired warriors, while above this set will be sets of elders, their relative status depending on their social ages, who will be responsible for internal political and legal matters and perhaps for communicating with the gods.

A person's social development is thus crucially linked to the physical fact of ageing: no one can be fixed in a low position, but must eventually succeed to the highest status, simply by staying alive.

2.3 SLAVERY

Of all patterns of social stratification, it is the system of slavery which draws the most rigid legal boundaries between members of one class and those of another. In this system, some human beings are regarded as chattel, or items of property, belonging to another individual or social group.

Slavery has taken different forms, depending in part on the particular economic use to which slaves have been put. In the fifth and fourth centuries B.C. in Greece, for example, slaves, acquired through conquest and trade, were a recognised form of investment for well-to-do citizens. Rich Athenians set up small factories in which the chief, but not the sole, source of labour was slaves. These factories, which produced a range of goods from shoes to armour, brought in a regular profit for their owners, but the reliance on slave labour had disadvantages from the owners' point of view; the market for industrial goods was uncertain, and in slack times, when it was difficult to sell the products from the workshop, slaves still had to be fed and housed, even though their labour brought no immediate return for the owner. Consequently, most such factories employed free labourers, as well as slaves, who could be laid off in slack periods.

As well as working in factory production, slaves were often responsible members of wealthy households, entrusted with keeping accounts, tutoring children and protecting the family while the master was away on military excursions; slaves were frequently trained as craftsmen, and occasionally acted for wealthy owners as captains of ships, managers of banks, or directors of small workshops. Since the value of these slaves to their master lay so often in the slaves' intelligence, initiative and skill, incentives (such as the possibility of purchasing freedom) were used more consistently than physical coercion as a means of persuading slaves to accept their inferior status.

But many workers found their enslavement to be a virtual death sentence. In the silver mines of Laurium, where about 10,000 Greek slaves were employed, slave labour completely replaced wage labour. The profit from mining was so immense that owners could afford to treat slaves – their only major capital investment – as expendable; the treatment of slaves in these mines was brutal in the extreme, and many were literally worked to death.

Slavery is, then, under certain conditions, a highly profitable system of exploitation. In North America, where the enslavement of Africans and their descendants continued until the last quarter of the nineteenth century, this exploitation was 'justified' by beliefs about racial inferiority, and reinforced by a form of Christian preaching which emphasised to slaves the virtues of humility and submission. Furthermore, the harsh treatment of slaves was fully supported by the legal system. Slaves in North America had few civil or property rights. They were forbidden to enter into contracts, and consequently the marriage of two slaves was not considered legally binding; the slave owner could, if he wished, separate husbands from wives, and parents from children. Strict laws regulated every aspect of slave behaviour, restricting the slave's right to travel, to defend himself against attacks by whites, and to use as he might wish what little leisure time was available. The penalties for breaking the regulations were severe, including beatings and death. An important aspect of the slave's position was the perpetual nature of slavery – slaves were destined to occupy this status throughout their lives, and their children in turn because they were the property of the owner. Slaves, as property, were under the absolute power of their owners; they could be bought, sold or traded at the whim of the master, and were occasionally awarded as prizes in lotteries, or wagered at gaming tables.

The economic significance of slavery, both for the North American colonies and for European capitalism, is too important to be overlooked. Exploitation of the rich natural resources of the new world required far more labour power than European colonists themselves could provide. Approximately 20 million healthy young Africans were forcibly transported as slaves to the 'new world' between the sixteenth and mid-nineteenth centuries, and this had a critical effect on Africa's own development.

2.4   FEUDALISM

Feudal societies established in Europe a social structure where states were underdeveloped and hence unable to exercise direct control over the population. Political power was decentralised in the sense that warriors were able to claim rights over a local territory and enforce their own brand of justice by means of military might. Unarmed peasants were unable to challenge the power of a warrior (or noble) who had personal supporters with horses and weapons. Military power was linked to wealth, which meant, in this case, agricultural land. The greater a noble's military power, the more land he could control; and the larger his estates, the more warriors he could support in order to secure his domain.

Wider patterns of trade were common before the emergence of feudalism, but when these were disrupted by wars and invasions, local communities became virtually self-sufficient. Productive activity was carried out by peasants, who lived on and cultivated the land which was controlled by the feudal lords. The lords compelled the peasants to hand over a considerable portion of the agricultural goods that they produced as tenant farmers on small strips of land, and also to perform customary services directly for the benefit of the lord.

In early periods of feudalism, the link between a noble and his peasants was maintained in the form of a personal agreement which ended upon the death of either party. (The same was true initially of the oath of allegiance linking lords to other, more powerful nobles through rights to the use of land and military alliance.) But eventually the servile condition of the peasants (and the privileged status of nobles) became hereditary, passed down from one generation to the next. Serfs were tied to the land which they cultivated, with little opportunity of changing or improving their position. They became, in a sense, a captive labour force; those who tried to escape from the land to neighbouring towns could be forcibly returned or punished. Most serfs lived in miserable poverty, although the communal traditions of medieval villages went some way towards alleviating the worst forms of hardship.

The nobility and the serfs emerged, then, as two of the distinct strata in feudal society. However, the clergy formed a third stratum in feudal society. The Catholic Church had enormous secular (as well as spiritual) power, since it possessed the right to income from vast expanses of land. Like nobles, powerful clergymen had access to estates, which were cultivated by serfs and guarded by armed retainers. To some extent, the Church was an independent force in feudal society, in competition with the nobility and the king. However, as 'men of learning', clergymen were able to promulgate a view of the world which was taken for granted by most of the population, a world view which included the notion that the supremacy of the king, the privileges of the nobility and the lowly position of serfs were all ordained by God. Thus the power of the Church was used to legitimate the system of social inequality.

In Europe from the twelfth century onward, feudal society was affected by the gradual transformation of local markets into permanent towns, with important implications for the emergence of a fourth stratum. Eventually the townsmen (or burgesses), using wealth acquired from trade, purchased considerable freedoms from feudal obligations. Their newly acquired rights (to come and go as they pleased, to own and dispose of property, to buy and sell goods) contributed to the growth of trade and also strengthened the economic power of the burgesses in relation to that of the nobility.

Thus feudal society came to comprise four distinct social strata: the nobility and the clergy, who controlled most of the land and enjoyed the agricultural surplus; the serfs, who cultivated the land and were bound to it; and the burgesses. These classes were, by and large, closed; access to the nobility or the peasantry was determined by birth, though occasionally peasants could escape from feudal bondage to the towns, and rich merchants were sometimes able to purchase titles and estates. The clergy was, of course, an exception to the rule of hereditary classes; since clergymen were (in theory at least) celibate, they had no legal heirs, and so the lower ranks of the clergy were open to the younger sons of noblemen or, more rarely, to commoners.

The burgesses constituted a growing challenge to the social relations of feudalism. Expansion of their wealth depended upon drawing serfs away from the land to labour in the towns (thus serfs who could remain hidden within town walls for a year and a day gained freedom from the land) and on undermining those aristocratic privileges, such as control over roads, which inhibited commercial activity. The challenge of the burgesses paved the way for the eventual emergence of a large class of landless labourers with no means of livelihood other than the sale of their labour for a wage; this was, therefore, one of the conditions for the development of capitalism.

2.5 THEORIES OF STRATIFICATION

Marx (1818–83)

Marx's general approach

Karl Marx has provided modern sociology and politics with one of its most wide-ranging and powerful theoretical approaches. At the same time, his account of society has been one of the most bitterly contested of all social theories, for it is not only a sociological theory, but also a philosophy of man and a programme for revolutionary change in society. A large portion of the world's population sees Marxism as an illuminating and liberating body of thought; our own area of the globe in the West sees Marxism as a false and dangerous dogma.

Different sociologists have adopted these different views, and others fall in between, but it is certain that any theory of stratification owes a great debt to Marx's account of classes, even if the sociologist ends up rejecting Marx as mistaken or overtaken by history. The reason for debt is that Marx's theory of society is principally based on the study of economic relationships, and these economic relationships form the basis of *classes*. Class relations, for Marx, are the key to all aspects of society. According to Marx, all non-Communist societies are *class societies*. Economic reward, political power and social prestige all flow from the structure of classes. These classes are more than 'income groups', they are created by the way in which production is socially organised. In the Marxist view,

> mankind must first of all, drink, have shelter and clothing, before it can pursue politics, science, art, religion, etc.; and therefore the production of the immediate material means of subsistence ... forms the foundation upon which the State institutions, the legal conceptions, art, and even the ideas on religion, of the people concerned have been evolved (F. Engels, speech at the graveside of Karl Marx).

The production of material goods is the primary activity of humans, and it must come before all other activities. As soon as a society is able to produce more than the bare minimum needed for survival, it is possible for classes to emerge. One class (the majority) does the productive work, while a minority class dominates them and seizes all the surplus produced. Any class society is founded on this relationship between the exploiters – those who take the surplus and rule the society – and the exploited – those who actually produce through their labour.

The history of 'civilised' society, for Marx, has been the history of different forms of class exploitation and domination. It is the form of class domination present which determines the general character of the whole social structure. It is crucial to understand that this class relationship is a *social* relationship which is not automatically and directly produced by specific techniques of production. For example, the growing of wheat using traditional, non-mechanical techniques is compatible with a wide range of social relations of production. A Roman citizen often owned slaves who worked his land growing wheat; a feudal lord would seize the surplus wheat grown by the serf on the lands of medieval Europe; the early capitalist farmers began to employ landless labourers to do their manual work for a wage which was less than the total value of the product which they created. In each case, wheat is grown on land by the labour of men and women, but the social arrangements are *totally* different. There are *totally* different class relationships, leading to *totally* different forms of society: ancient, feudal and capitalist. The only thing that unites these three arrangements is that in each case a minority class rules and takes the surplus away from the producers.

Each society, says Marx, embodies class exploration based on relationships of production. It is this that Marx calls the *mode of production*. The key to understanding a given society is to discover which is the dominant mode of production within it. We then know the basic pattern of social and political relationships, and can appreciate what conflicts and potentials for change are built into the society.

The capitalist mode of production, for example, developed in Britain prior to industrialisation. Capitalist economic relations were established in the countryside through the 'enclosures', where land became the private property of landowners and the rural work-force was stripped of the land-use rights that gave them an independent source of subsistence. The workers, replaced by sheep and by mechanised farming techniques, were forced to become landless proletarians, dependent on employment in a labour market. The machine-breaking resistance of the Luddites against these changes was only one sign of the growing class conflicts to come. In later stages, cottage and craft industries were moved into factories, which then led on to the development of 'machinofacture' (mechanised production) through technological innovation. This quickened the growth of an urban proletariat in the mid-nineteenth century, which gradually came to develop the collective organisations (unions and political parties) necessary to struggle against exploitation. Quite apart from the class conflict endemic in capitalism, the economic system itself is beset with instabilities. Periodic slumps occur when trade and investment collapse and unemployment rises. Capital then emerges again more efficient, but concentrated in larger firms – the successful absorbing the weak. This eventually results in 'monopoly capitalism', where economic power is concentrated in the hands of a few very large enterprises. In Marx's view there are also longer-term threats to the survival of capitalism, especially through the tendency for the rate of profit to fall. When Marx tells us in the *Communist Manifesto* that 'all history is the history of class struggles', he is claiming that all conflict and change in societies can ultimately be traced back to the underlying class conflict, based on the opposing class interests arising from exploitation. These fundamental economic relations shape, in addition, all other aspects of the social structure. The state, laws, and even religion come to reflect and justify the basic class relations. The 'superstructure' of ideas and social institutions comes to reproduce the economic base: 'the ideas of the ruling class are the ruling ideas in every epoch', Marx claimed, and 'the state is but the executive committee of the whole bourgeoisie'.

However, this 'integration' of different institutions can never be perfect. There is always some potential for opposition and change; this comes to a climax in periods of revolutionary social transformation.

According to Marx, revolutions can only occur on the basis of appropriate material conditions, where economic development is being *held back* by the existing social relations. For example, the 'enclosures' concentrated land and allowed new techniques, but only through completely disrupting the social relations existing in the countryside. Thus, relations of production are transformed in a revolution. Secondly, people must become conscious of the opposed interests and fight them out through political struggle. Some historians regard the English Civil War of the seventeenth century as a crucial transition period where an emerging bourgeoisie removed old political barriers to its development – it was a 'bourgeois revolution'. The triumph of a new ruling class goes together with the eventual emergence of a whole new social structure based on the new mode of production.

For Marx, the final revolution will be made by the proletarian class. Unlike earlier revolutions, there will not be a new exploiting class, for rule by the proletariat means self-government by the working-class majority. Thus, class society is abolished, with all its evils, and a new realm of human freedom begins in Communist society. Here at last, people have an abundant society where all benefit and all are free to live and work in a flexible, creative way. Humanity comes to control its own destiny and 'make its own history'. Equality brings emancipation: according to Marx it will be 'possible for me to do one thing today and another tomorrow, to hunt in the morning, fish in the afternoon, rear cattle in the evening, criticise after dinner, *just as I have a mind* without ever becoming hunter, fisherman, shepherd or critic'. Thus, only here in Communist society can people fulfil their potential for creativity and goodness.

Marx's account of the capitalist mode of production

Some sociologists have tried to describe the general features of 'industrial society' or even 'modern society', arguing that 'industry' imposes a special pattern on society and social institutions. Marx could never have accepted such a view. It was not only industry that gave advanced European nations their character, but the way in which industrialisation took place, developing the growth of capitalist social relations. For Marx, the growth of industry promised wealth and abundance for all, but because industry had so far developed in a capitalistic way, the new-found wealth was monopolised by one class, while the mass of the working people were made poorer, not richer, by the advances in production.

Let us examine the class relations of capitalism, as Marx describes them. The key classes in the capitalist mode of production are the bourgeoisie and the proletariat, or capitalists and landless wage labourers. While Marx recognises that (as we shall see later) there are other classes, the fundamental class division is between this pairing of exploiter and exploited. The bourgeoisie derive their class position from the fact that they own productive wealth. It is not their high income that makes them capitalists, but the fact that they own the means of production (i.e. inputs necessary for production – factories, machines, etc.).

Indeed, the ability of workers to work (labour-power) itself is a marketable commodity, bought for the least cost to be used at will by the capitalist. There is a general tendency, Marx claimed, for wages to stick at a general exploitative level, except when some skills are temporarily scarce. In addition, the capitalist owns the product and will pocket the difference between the value of the labour and the value of the product – 'surplus value' as Marx called it – purely and simply by virtue of his ownership. His property rights also allow the capitalist the control of the process of production and the labour he buys. The proletariat, in contrast, own no means of production whatever.

Before capitalism, the worker had rights of use over some land, and had enough tools to grow some food and have some produce left to barter for other goods. Additionally, some of the worker's surplus was seized by the feudal lord. In the capitalist mode of production, however, the workers are landless and have no independent means of subsistence. They have to sell their labour-power in order to live and so labour-power becomes a marketable commodity, apparently no different from any other exchangeable object. Thus, the crucial division between classes is based on *property* ownership or non-ownership of the means of production.

Nevertheless, it might seem that the workers must get their just reward under capitalism, for they are free to work for whom they like, and to bargain for their wage. However, this can never be a free and equal contract, because the individual worker must have work at any price simply in order to survive, while the capitalist (though needing workers) can employ or sack any individual he chooses. The employer could even suspend production and live off his wealth for some considerable time.

This process of exploitation is not so obvious as the direct payment of tithes or forced labour under feudalism, but it is still, according to Marx, economic exploitation. Thus the capitalists have economic power, controlling and exploiting the worker, and this also gives them political power as well. The only ultimately effective way the worker can resist is through collective class action to overthrow the capitalist mode of production. More limited forms of resistance such as normal trade union activity do not alter the fundamental relationships of class inequality in capitalist society. The revolution, however, will not turn the clock back and abolish industry. Instead, it will reorganise industry on the basis of equal power and reward, spreading wealth throughout society and abolishing the ownership of productive property by a minority.

In his massive work *Capital*, Marx analyses the strains and disruptive tendencies built into capitalism. He argues that class conflicts and economic crises are built into the way the economic system works, and they cannot be avoided. The capitalists are themselves forced continually to maximise profits and maximise exploitation of the workers, because they are under pressure of competition and hit by economic crises. These and other pressures keep the worker in poverty (at least relative to the capitalists), but other forces will also create, Marx claimed, the conditions for revolt.

The urbanisation of workers and their employment in ever-larger factories break down old barriers of skill and status among the workers, and bring about a realisation of collective class identity and shared interests. In addition, the economies of the most advanced capitalist nations would advance to a point where any further development of production would be held back by the crises of capitalism and by the desire to produce for profit rather than the general good. The material conditions for revolution would evolve and the working class would develop into a revolutionary class ready to seize their opportunity. With this successful revolution, there would be the construction of the Communist Utopia, 'where society inscribes on its banners: "From each according to his ability, to each according to his needs!"'

Can Marx's analysis be applicable today?

It is obvious that there are some serious problems in Marx's account. Revolution has occurred in nations on the verge of entry into capitalism, not in societies which are mature and 'ripe' for change. The working class in capitalist societies has enjoyed, in the long term, a rise in the standard of living, and labour movements have won enough welfare concessions to ease the lot of many of the poor. By no means all Western societies have strong Communist parties. In addition, the growth of the new middle class of managerial, professional and clerical workers appears to contradict Marx's view that divisions among those without wealth would disappear. Western economies are certainly prone to crises, but the state seems able to keep them in check.

Generally, then, Marx's ideas seem to many people to have been 'disproved' by twentieth-century developments. In fact, however, this is a rather limited view. The real issues are firstly whether Marx's general perspective on stratification was sound, and secondly, whether contemporary Western societies are still capitalist in the general basic character of their social relations. The first issue is important because Marx provides an account of stratification which is significantly different from that of many other social theorists. Very often today, sociologists see classes as merely groupings of people with similar attributes such as income, type of occupation, and so on. Marx, in contrast, saw classes as systematically linked in a particular structure of social relationships. An *explanation* of inequality is given through the analysis of the mode of production. Marx points out the deeper class relations and potential conflicts below the surface of society. This strength, however, is linked to a crucial failing in the eyes of many sociologists. They argue that Marx's class analysis is too simplistic to account adequately for the complexity of social inequality. For them, Marx's overwhelming emphasis on the ownership of productive wealth leaves us unable to explain adequately all the differences in rewards and in consciousness within the mass of the population who are not capitalists. Every middle-class employee is certainly not a member of the bourgeoisie, but most sociologists would also feel that the middle class are not true proletarians either, even though they own no wealth. In order to cope with these problems, the ideas of Max Weber have often been employed in addition to, or instead of, those of Marx, and we will examine Weber's approach shortly. Before that, however, we must address the question of whether contemporary Western societies are still capitalist.

Quite clearly, the Western economies are vastly changed today in comparison with Marx's time. There is far more economic intervention by the state in most societies of the West, and state employees of one kind or another form a large part of the work-force (a quarter of all workers in Britain). Nationalisation and the frequent replacement of individual owner-managers by shareholders and managerial bureaucracies have both changed the structure of industry. However, as is indicated elsewhere in this chapter and in Chapter 6, it can still be argued that private ownership of the means of production is the basis of economic power and wealth, and that the labour market is still the prime determinant of wage levels. The worker is still in a subordinate position in the work-place, and the incomes of workers are still very low *in comparison with* those who control them. Other interpretations are possible: it is commonly argued, for example, that the West has 'mixed economies' which work in everyone's interest, but in our view this is mistaken.

But it is just such a view that could be said to lie at the heart of a second major theory of social stratification that has emerged more recently in sociology: the functionalist theory of stratification. Let us now turn to this very different approach.

The functionalist theory of stratification

As we have seen, the Marxist perspective on stratification and inequality envisages a time when class inequality can and will eventually disappear, after the destruction of capitalism and its replacement by a new socio-economic order. Such a view contrasts starkly with that of functionalist theorists which see stratification and inequality as permanent, necessary and inevitable features of human societies.

The functionalist approach in sociology rests on two major assumptions:

(i)   social phenomena exist because they have some positive function to perform in society;

(ii)   if societies are to be viable, a number of basic conditions have to be achieved – a number of 'functional prerequisites' must be effectively satisfied (e.g. reproduction of the species, socialisation of the young, etc.).

Functionalists emphasise that inequality has been a prominent feature of past human societies and continues to be so in contemporary societies of West and East. It would appear, then, they argue, that stratification and inequality perform some necessary and positive function for society. Such assumptions are an integral part of the theory formulated by Davis and Moore (1945). Two extracts from this article confirm the essence of their arguments:

> Social inequality is [the] device by which societies insure that the most important positions are conscientiously filled by the most qualified persons. Hence, every society, no matter how simple or complex, must differentiate persons in terms of both prestige and esteem, and must therefore possess a certain amount of institutionalised inequality (Davis and Moore, 1945, p. 243).

> As a functioning mechanism a society must somehow distribute its members in social positions and induce them to perform the duties of these positions. Inevitably, then, a society must have some way of distributing these rewards differentially according to positions. The rewards and their distribution become a part of the social order and thus give rise to stratification (Davis and Moore, 1945, pp. 242–3).

The functionalist argument can be summarised briefly:

(i)   some positions in society are functionally more important than others (i.e. vital to the continued existence of society) and require particular skills;

(ii)   not everyone in society has the talent to fill these positions;

(iii) the exclusive few have to have 'raw' talent converted into specialist skills by a training period which involves their making sacrifices;

(iv)   the talented will only be induced to train for these socially vital positions if sufficient rewards are attached to their future positions;

(v)   there must exist, therefore, a system of unequal rewards built into a hierarchy of positions in society.

So, according to Davis and Moore, stratification and inequality are both positively functional and inevitable in human societies, because societies have to fill a number of 'key' positions with the 'right' people, and this can only be achieved by allocating unequal rewards to these positions.

This theory has been heavily criticised from various theoretical standpoints, and notably by Tumin (1953). His points have been taken up and expanded by others.

Much controversy has centred on the concept of 'functional importance'. Critics argue that it is a highly value-laden term: deciding which positions are functionally more important than others cannot be done objectively, but will inevitably involve arbitrary value-judgements. How does one decide whether company directors are functionally more important then their workers, and if they receive five times as much as workers, does this mean they are five times more important? The problems involved in assessing 'functional importance' render the concept highly dubious sociologically.

Many critics have questioned the functionalists' emphasis on the limited availability of talented people in societies. Are sufficiently talented people as few and far between as functionalists suggest? There is much evidence to suggest (as we have indicated in Chapter 8 on education) that considerable potential talent is wasted, and that it is the *stratification system itself* which restricts the development of potentially talented members of society from the lower orders. The unequal distribution of resources in stratified societies enables the better-off to obtain privileged access to educational facilities to have their talent developed, while at the same time disadvantaging those at the bottom.

The theory wrongly assumes the existence of a 'meritocracy' – that there is equal opportunity for all to develop their talent: public schoolboys in Britain and white South African children, for example, do *not* start alongside their age-peers in an equal contest. As Tumin (1953, p. 389) points out, the very reverse is so: 'Smoothly working and stable systems of stratification tend to *build in* obstacles to the further exploitation of the range of available talent.'

It is by no means certain that material rewards are the *only* means by which societies can induce their members to fill social positions, as the theory seems to suggest. People may be, and frequently are, motivated to take up certain occupations by the prospect of intrinsic satisfaction from the job, by altruistic motives such as giving service to others, or by feelings of social duty or sense of mission – motives frequently unconnected with material wealth, status or power.

The functionalist theory also justifies high rewards for the occupants of certain positions partly as a compensation for the 'sacrifices' of loss of earning power and cost of training during the period of preparation for functionally important positions. Many critics regard this line of argument as dubious or, at best, misleading. The loss of earning power experienced by such as doctors, lawyers, etc., can be recouped fairly quickly after training (Tumin and others have estimated that no more than ten years is generally required), and is more than compensated by higher rewards after this time. The cost of training is generally the responsibility of parents or the state and not that of the trainees themselves.

Furthermore, the training period may be an attractive rather than depriving experience, offering gratification and stimulation to elite trainees which are not available to their age-peers working in less interesting jobs. The elite trainees may frequently enjoy higher prestige ('Our son Justin is training to be a doctor' sounds far more impressive than 'Our lad Jim's a barrow-boy'). Further, they have greater opportunities to develop their minds and personalities (the atmosphere of a university campus is more stimulating than that of an assembly line), and greater autonomy in deciding how they will organise their work and leisure time.

Functionalist theorists have also been attacked for their emphasis on the functional nature of stratification. Even in terms of their own theoretical approach, it is surely obvious that in many respects stratification is *dysfunctional*, producing many negative and damaging social consequences. We have already pointed to the way in which stratification may well inhibit the full development of talent in a society as a result of inequality of opportunity, which inevitably means that a stratified society is not utilising its talent resources fully. Furthermore, a stratified, hierarchically divided society may well generate conflict and antagonism among the various strata, rather that provide social integration (which Marxist explanations recognise and rightly emphasise). Functionalists fail to acknowlege that social institutions do not operate 'magically' in the interests of all but frequently work to the benefit of some at the expense of others.

The functionalist explanation of stratification appears especially naive in its emphasis on 'functional' importance as the determining factor in inequality of reward, at the expense of other crucial influences. Certain groups are better rewarded, *not* because they are functionally more important than others, but because they are well organised in trade unions or professional associations, having developed and used strategies and ideologies which further their claims for differential rewards effectively. Similarly, some people have access to unequal reward, not because of any talent or functional importance, but by accident of birth. Family inheritance is a crucial factor in sustaining inequality, quite simply because families are able to hand on both material and social advantages.

This is at the crux of one of the two major criticisms which Parkin (1971) makes of the functionalist theory.

First, Parkin argues, whilst a hierarchy of material reward does indeed usually represent the unequal distribution of 'marketable skills' in a society, it is illegitimate to extrapolate from this, as the functionalists do, and assume it *also* represents the distribution of these skills, as an innate quality amongst society's members. We must also consider the opportunity that some occupations have for deliberately restricting access to the acquisition of the skills needed to do the job, thereby keeping down their distribution amongst the population, and enabling them to claim higher rewards in the market place. Such a strategy, says Parkin, is adopted by professions like law and medicine, where long periods of training, very often only marginally relevant or even unnecessary to the actual performance of the job, restrict the numbers of those prepared, or able to afford, to forgo the rewards of an occupation for a long period. (This willingness to delay seeking rewards is sometimes called 'deferred gratification'.)

Parkin secondly criticises the use which functionalists make of evidence which seems to indicate a consensus about the prestige ranking of occupations. A whole series of studies, he admits, appear to demonstrate that there is a broad agreement concerning the relative worth of different occupations, which apparently supports the functionalists' contention that it is possible to identify those positions which are most important in society. However, although people *seem* to agree on a hierarchy of symbolic rewards, this apparent consensus is not the sum of people's *personal* evaluations regarding the relative importance of different jobs, but a reproduction of what they have been socialised into accepting and which, when asked, they reproduce as though this sort of thing is a matter of fact. Thus, for example, although a miner might not *personally* believe that a university professor teaching three hours a week for 25 weeks of the year is doing a more worthy or important job than himself, he will nevertheless rank this occupation above his own in the construction of a prestige hierarchy because he has learnt that 'professors are more important than miners'. So, argues Parkin, this apparent consensus is, in fact, an *expression of the particular system of dominant values* which operates in such societies. It represents the capacity of those in dominant positions to persuade the rest of society that the attributes *they* consider admirable, and *their* evaluations of worth, are somehow the 'right' ones. Indeed, Parkin goes on to suggest that the functionalist theory of stratification itself is an expression of the same value-system: no more than a rather sophisticated mechanism for providing a justification of unequal rewards. In his view, then, the functionalist approach to *inequality* is nothing else than an ideology designed to legitimate this same inequality.

This criticism echoes our general argument in this chapter. Any explanation of structured inequality which concentrates on normative factors to the exclusion of material ones is inadequate. The failure of the functionalist theory of stratification is ultimately its failure to locate normative and cultural dimensions of stratification within a framework of material inequality; indeed, this reflects the complacent neglect of relations of domination and subordination characteristic of functionalist theory generally.

The fundamental disagreement between functionalist and Marxist perspectives has not been limited to the debate over stratification outlined above. It is also evident in their respective analyses of the family (see Chapter 7) and education (see Chapter 8).

It should be clear now that whereas for Marx it is one's economic *class* position (crucially how one relates to productive property) that determines much else in one's life, for the Functionalist it is the *status* one has established through developing marketable skills and the value put on them by society that determines one's life chances. There is, however, a third approach to stratification that in many ways adopts a position that places equal emphasis on property relations and marketable skills and that is the theory developed by Max Weber, which actually predates the functionalist view.

Weber (1864–1920)

Weber's general approach

Weber's ideas differed from those of Marx in a variety of ways. His political goals were quite contrasting – Weber had no objection to seeing his native Germany develop as a capitalist state overseen by a parliament. He rejected the goals and policies of the German socialists and regarded communism as an unattainable Utopia. More generally, Weber rejected the idea that sociologists could generalise about social structures by using the analysis of modes of production. For Weber, every society was historically unique and complex. Above all, he rejected the Marxist view that economic relations were always the explanation of social structure and the prime mover of social change. He believed that religious ideas had an independent historical influence, and that the realm of politics was usually the crucial controlling force in social change. This led him to reject Marxism as a one-sided sociology, unable to deal adequately with the full complexity of society and social change.

Weber's approach to inequality was to present a range of descriptive categories that could be used to describe it in any given society. He gave no priority to any particular relationship of inequality: for example, he believed that the relation between money-lender and debtor might be as significant as a basis for class as that between workman and employer. A wide range of economic bases for class could therefore be found. Additionally, Weber emphasised in his essay 'Class, Status and Party' (see Gerth and Mills, 1948) that inequality in society might not be based on economic relations at all, but on prestige or on political power, mobilised through a party. Thus, unlike Marx, Weber did not see every unequal social structure as a class society – caste, for example, was based on status differences, grounded in religious ritual.

Indeed, Weber emphasised that 'economic power may result from the possession of power which rests on other foundations'. Social status, or prestige, may derive from economic power, but this is not necessarily the case; Weber cites the case of the newly rich businessman who does not possess the education or 'culture' to command high status. Also, status may form the basis of political power – Weber saw this as especially relevant in the case of the German Junker aristocracy, who were economically weak but still held the reins of political power. For Weber it was a matter for social and historical analysis to discover the real basis of inequality in a particular society.

In spite of these considerations, Weber certainly did regard capitalism as a class society – economic relations form the basis of inequality. We might suppose from this that Weber is merely echoing Marx's theories, but in fact Weber emphasises the importance of the *market* as the economic basis for class much more than *property*. For him, the primary cause of inequality in capitalism is *market capacity* – this is the skills brought to the labour market by the employee. Differences in reward between occupations result from the scarce skill held by the occupational group. If the skill is in demand, the reward will be high.

A good contemporary example can be seen in the typographers who work for British newspapers. These skilled workers have controlled entry to their craft of type-setting, and hence 'kept themselves scarce'. As a result they have traditionally commanded higher wages than most other manual workers. Unfortunately for them, however, the computer technology is rapidly replacing antiquated machines, resulting in a great cut in demand for the old craft skills. The strong market capacity of the typographers is now undermined, and they are likely to suffer a fall in *life-chances*. This concept is Weber's term for all those rewards and advantages afforded by market capacity. Life-chances include income, perks and pensions, together with less tangible benefits such as security or good working conditions. We can therefore distinguish groups with similar market capacity, and these can be termed 'classes'. We can see, then, that Weber agrees with Marx that the crucial economic features of capitalism are private ownership of the means of production, and markets for goods and labour. The crucial difference is that Marx emphasised the first element, while Weber emphasised the second.

Sociologists are often attracted by Weber's account because it gives an explanation for the distinct differences in life-chances between different strata in contemporary capitalism. We can see that there is a broad division in life-chances between manual and non-manual workers; the skills of the non-manual employees, especially professionals, give this class significant advantages in market capacity and hence in life-chances. At the same time, we may distinguish unequal strata within a class. The working-class occupations may be divided into skilled, semi-skilled and unskilled strata, and life-chances broadly differ according to the skill level. Normally, though, sociologists have argued that these three strata have enough in common to make them components of one class, because they are all divided by a considerable gulf from the non-manual middle class, which contains its own strata.

Weber's consideration of the capitalist market therefore appears to give an explanation of the hierarchy of occupational reward found in capitalist societies, and gives us the means to describe sociologically the complexity of inequality in reward and advantage.

Evaluation of Weber's theory

There are, however, a number of problems in Weber's account. One problem is that we may have no clear criterion for dividing up the work-force into classes and strata. In other words, taken to its logical conclusion, Weber's analysis of market capacity would put *each person into a separate class* because each individual would have a minutely different skill from everyone else. (In fact, Weber himself tended to use much broader class categories in his own empirical research.) More importantly, Weberian approaches tend to concentrate on occupation and neglect *wealth* as a crucial element in the class structure. If we are concerned with concentrations of economic advantage and power, we cannot neglect that small minority – Marx's bourgeoisie – who monopolise the ownership of the means of production. As this chapter will go on to show, a small economically dominant class undoubtedly does still exist in Western societies.

Theories of stratification: conclusion

We have seen that both Marx and Weber see contemporary Western societies as capitalist, and both agree that the crucial distinctive features of this are private ownership of the means of production, and a market for labour. If we wish to understand the structure of objective economic inequality in capitalist society, we must understand both of these economic relations and see both as producing distinct social classes. The functionalist approach seems to be inadequate on both counts. That is, it totally fails to consider the persistence of power through property ownership; moreover, its conception of the labour market ignores those factors which determine whether or not one's skills are perceived as marketable, and whether some groups, for example the professions, have the power to establish the view that their particular skills *are* valuable.

We can therefore conclude that the ideas of Marx and Weber can, for our purposes, be partly combined to produce a three-class model of contemporary capitalist societies (see Figure 2.1).

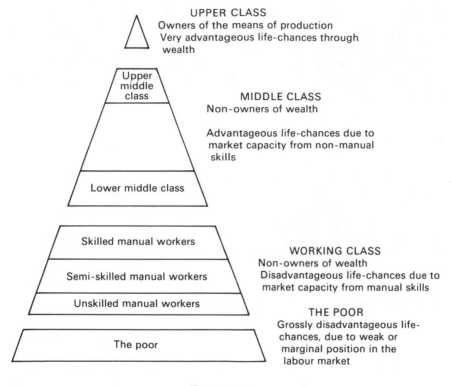

UPPER CLASS
Owners of the means of production
Very advantageous life-chances through wealth

Upper middle class

MIDDLE CLASS
Non-owners of wealth

Advantageous life-chances due to market capacity from non-manual skills

Lower middle class

Skilled manual workers

WORKING CLASS
Non-owners of wealth
Disadvantageous life-chances due to market capacity from manual skills

Semi-skilled manual workers

Unskilled manual workers

THE POOR
Grossly disadvantageous life-chances, due to weak or marginal position in the labour market

The poor

FIGURE 2.1

Thus, we can see that we can distinguish three main classes in contemporary capitalist society. The small 'upper class' consists of those with substantial holdings of productive wealth. This class – only a small percentage of the adult population – has succeeded in preserving and expanding its wealth, and has developed effective means to ensure that both this wealth and the accompanying social attributes are transmitted across generations. The ownership of productive property defines this class and separates it from the rest of society. This class coincides with Marx's bourgeoisie. The non-owners of the means of production, however, cannot all be described as proletarians. Many managerial positions involve the employee being both a representative of the capitalist *and* a worker who is in some degree exploited. These positions have been labelled by Wright (1978) as 'contradictory class locations'. They contain elements of both worker and bourgeois class positions. Generally, however, we can divide up those below the upper class on the grounds of life-chances, based on market capacity. Broadly speaking, the working-class/middle-class division still reflects crucial differences in life-chances between manual and non-manual workers, and so we are justified in seeing non-manual workers as members of a distinct class. A wide range of differences in attitude and life-style are associated with these objective economic differences between middle and working class, and these are examined more fully in Chapter 3.

However, it is not these differences in behaviour which form the *basis* of the class structure; rather these differences are an indirect reflection of objective economic inequalities.

2.6   THE OWNERSHIP OF WEALTH

Just as every citizen has the right to enjoy a meal at the Savoy Grill, so every individual has the right to become a millionaire. As we shall see, however, the enormous and persistent inequality in the distribution of personal wealth is one of the most important features of capitalist class structure. The question of changes in patterns of inequality in the distribution of wealth must therefore be considered in detail; our empirical evidence will relate to contemporary Britain.

What is wealth?

The distinction between income and wealth is not entirely rigid. We can say, though, that income is a flow of disposable (spendable) money, while wealth refers to fixed assets such as land, shares, buildings or durable possessions. Wealth thus seems to mean the same as 'property', but 'property' is a term commonly used to refer to anything from Henry Ford II's car company to the clothes you are wearing. Both of these count, in legal terms, as private property, and the individual owner has the right to buy, sell, control and even destroy personal wealth. (These rights, we might note, are specific to capitalist society. Ownership of land in many pre-industrial societies meant 'rights of use' and not complete personal control.) These rights of control over one's own possessions are valued rights – we would not want our shirt to be stolen, torn, or dyed by someone else – but this all-embracing idea of 'property rights' conceals a crucial difference between different forms of property. We must distinguish between *consumption property* and *production property*. Property for personal consumption includes consumer durables (e.g. washing-machines, motor-cars) and family homes which are owner-occupied. Productive property is significantly different, for this includes factories, farming or building land, and stocks and shares. This kind of property is *capital* and yields income through profit on the productive use of property. It is a defining feature of capitalist society that the productive wealth of the society (on which the whole population depends for employment and products) is privately owned and controlled. Private productive property provides massive unearned income, and also frequently forms the basis of economic power. Unearned income derives from:

(i)   rent on buildings or land;
(ii) dividends paid from profit of firms to shareholders; and
(iii) interest on monetary investments such as deposit accounts or government securities.

In addition, the right to buy and sell property provides *capital gains*: where the market value of an item of property has risen, this provides a profit on its sale. This is the basis for property speculation and investment in antiques or works of art. In the latter cases, capital gains are being made from what might be termed special kinds of consumption property, only available to the rich.

It is crucial to note that 'wealth begets wealth': that is, productive property provides a return which may itself be reinvested to provide further return. Indeed, the more you possess, the faster this wealth begets more. Those whose income wealth exceeds their consumption must always get richer, and hence the gap between the property-owner and the propertyless must always widen (unless there are countervailing measures such as wealth tax). The dynamics of capital accumulation thus ensure that property is distributed unequally, and that it remains so. We shall see that this concentration of productive wealth creates a propertied upper class, which can also be regarded as an economically dominant class.

The distribution of wealth in Britain

The statistical description of the distribution of wealth is by no means straightforward. One reason is that the distinction we have made between productive and consumption property is not always maintained, or it is applied in differing ways. Sometimes income gets included as well – for example, should the contents of current accounts in banks or building societies be included as wealth? In addition, most information comes from official statistics, especially from the Inland Revenue, deriving from tax returns and death duties. These sources are neither totally reliable, nor do they always provide the information required. The records typically under-state the concentration of wealth, for they rely on individual declarations which are manipulated and presented so as to minimise apparent wealth holdings. There is, therefore, a great need for interpretation and adaptation of the figures which in turn gives rise to conflicting views among different researchers.

This account draws upon the important recent contributions of Scott (1982, 1985), Atkinson (1974), Westergaard and Resler (1975), Revell (1967) and the Diamond Commission (1979).

In asking the question 'who owns Britain's wealth?' it is not immediately obvious that we should focus on individuals.

After all, the state owns many buildings and assets, and much emphasis has been put on the institutional shareholdings of insurance companies and pension funds. It is true that personal ownership of some kinds of wealth is declining – but our focus is on assets under the control of individuals so that we can understand the effects of wealth on class position. Indeed, official figures on wealth includes a whole range of marketable assets such as savings, owner-occupied homes (net of mortgage borrowing), plus cars and other consumer durables. Of course, if wealth is defined in this very broad way, then we would expect very many people to possess some; in fact the most recent figures still show very striking inequalities in wealth distribution.

Estimates for United Kingdom adults in 1983 (*Social Trends, 1986*) based on tax data show that:

(i)   78 per cent of personal assets are owned by 25 per cent of adults, so that 75 per cent of the population share the other 22 per cent.
(ii)   54 per cent of assets are owned by 10 per cent of adults.
(iii) 40 per cent are owned by 5 per cent of adult.
(iv)   27 per cent of personal assets are owned by 2 per cent of the adult population.
(v)   The lower 50 per cent of the adult population share amongst them 4 per cent of personal assets.

The concentration of wealth

Since the total personal assets amounted to £745,000 million, and there were roughly 40 million adults in the UK in 1983, this means that the top 2 per cent of adults share between them £201,150,000,000 of wealth. These 400,000 people range from the super-rich to the merely wealthy, but an equal shareout amongst them would give them about £500,000 each. Meanwhile the poorest 50 per cent of the population have an average of £1490 in marketable assets.

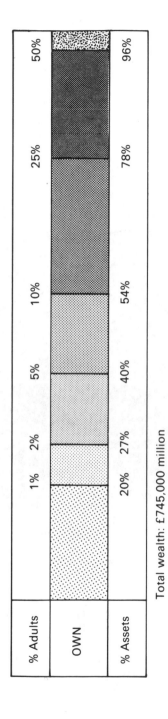

Total wealth: £745,000 million

Source: Derived from *Social Trends, 1986.*

FIGURE 2.2 *Distribution of personal marketable wealth, 1983, UK*

The distribution of these wealth shares is shown in Figure 2.2, while the composition of the assets held is shown in Figure 2.3. The diversity of this wealth is obvious, with nearly half composed of homes and consumer goods. In addition, it is hard to tell how much of the cash and savings comprise everyday cash-flow rather than investments for income or gain. Although householders may make money on their home, the great bulk of these assets clearly relate to commonplace forms of consumption property. Only a part is production property which yields high income and only some of this confers economic power over others.

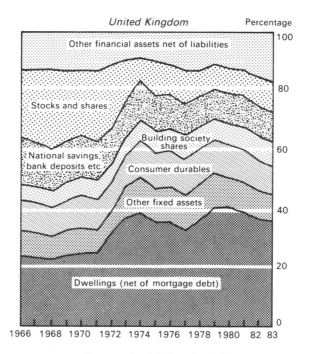

Source: *Social Trends, 1986.*

FIGURE 2.3   *Composition of net wealth of individuals*

It is clear, though, that there remains a very wealthy minority who cannot reasonably be regarded as 'middle class'. Certainly, professional and managerial groups enjoy higher levels of consumption property, but the bulk of them fall well below the top 5 per cent who own 40 per cent of assets. No doubt some top managers and self-employed professionals shade into this category – with salaried company directors being particularly likely to own production wealth.

Increasing Income Inequality

In 1979, the 20 highest paid company directors received as much as 454 average male manual workers. By 1983, they got £5.5 million between them – as much as 722 such workers.

David Sainsbury, finance director of Sainsbury's food stores, was paid over £5.5 million in salary and dividends on shares in 1983. Among British directors in 1983, 179 had salaries over £100,000.

Source: *Labour Research.*

People with very high salaries can obviously save and invest, hence accumulating wealth, and joining an upper class of businessmen, financiers, landowners or inheritors of wealth.

The economic and social position of this upper class is determined by their ownership of productive wealth, and the substantial incomes they gain through such ownership. The vast majority of the population, even if they do own some consumption property, certainly have little access to income from productive assets.

Land and shares as productive wealth

Rent from landownership and shares in the profits of companies have been the twin foundations of the wealthy upper class. The 'aristocratic' character of landowning has been a central basis for social status and political power in Britain for centuries, and the divisions of interest between land and industry have been fundamental to the political development of the upper class. Scott (1982) provides a fascinating overview of its changing character. He emphasises the way that the titles and trappings of monarchy and landed aristocracy help to disguise the capitalistic nature of ownership and aid the integration of many of the wealthy into a closed status group. Such boundaries of status and social closure, working through kinship, elite education and commercial networks, serve to sustain the British upper class as a clear social entity with special access to power and social influence.

The pattern of shareholding in companies is changing rapidly, with a declining role for individuals, but even so, Scott has shown (1985, p. 77) that 43 out of the top 250 British firms are still controlled through personal shareholding. There are still clearly identifiable wealthy families, even if their assets are spread across different holdings and various forms of investment.

The changing trend of shareholdings was clear until 1981 – individuals were owning far less compared with insurance companies, pension funds and trusts. The proportion held by individuals fell from 54 per cent in 1951

Landed estates – a few examples

Owner	Acreage: 1873	1967
Duke of Devonshire	138,500	72,000
Duke of Northumberland	186,300	80,000
Earl Spencer	27,100	15,000
Duke of Westminster	20,000	18,000
Earl of Iveagh	—	24,000
Viscount Leverhulme	—	99,000
Viscount Cowdray	—	17,500

The first two examples here show long-established aristocratic families, while the Duke of Westminster (with Lord Cowdray among the richest men in Britain) has most wealth in smaller acreages of Mayfair. The last three names are examples of successful businessmen (Guinness, soap and general commerce) who have acquired the status symbols of title and land to confirm their elite standing (data from Perrott, 1968).

In Scotland, there are six estates of over 100,000 acres, and the top 34 estates own between them 2,592,000 acres – a sixth of the total (Scott, 1982).

Britain's wealthiest families (not including land)

Family	No. of half-millionaires in last 150 years	Origins of family fortune
Rothschild	21	finance
Wills	21	tobacco
Coats	16	textiles
Colman	10	food
Palmer	10	food
Morrison	9	commerce
Ralli	9	commerce
Gosling	7	banking
Baird	6	iron
Courtauld	6	textiles
Garton	6	sugar
Guinness	6	brewing
Joicey	6	coal
Pilkington	6	glass
Ratcliff	6	brewing
Reckitt	6	starch
Tate	6	sugar
Watney	6	brewing
Wilson	6	shipping
Sebag-Montefiore	6	finance
Dukes of Northumberland	6	coal/land

Source: Rubinstein, cited in J. Scott, *The Upper Classes*, London, Macmillan, 1982, p. 122.

to 28 per cent in 1981 (Stock Exchange, cited by Scott, 1986). Recent asset stripping by government ('privatisation') has transferred nationally-owned firms to private shareholders. The Stock Exchange estimates that about 6 per cent of adults own shares, with a third of these deriving from the sale of British Telecom (*Guardian*, 10 May 1986). Substantial shareholdings remain in very few hands.

Changes in the distribution of wealth

Evidence on shares of wealth seem to show a substantial reduction in the degree of inequality – even if we are very far away from equal shares. It is undoubtedly true that consumption wealth has become much more widespread as a result of general economic growth. In addition, social and economic changes during and after the two world wars diminished some of the concentration of landholding and investments. Taxes on wealth at death have declined in effectiveness, but they did have some impact; just as important were crashes in land prices in the 1930s and liquidation of foreign investments to finance war.

It is certainly not true, though, that the rich have been 'soaked' to finance the welfare state. Much of the redistribution shown in Table 2.1 results from the spreading of wealth among family members through trusts.

TABLE 2.1

Groups within adult population owning wealth

Groups within adult population owning proportions of wealth	Estimated proportion of total personal wealth						
	1911–3 (%)	1924–30 (%)	1936–8 (%)	1954 (%)	1960 (%)	1971 (%)	1983 (%)
Richest 1% owned	69	62	56	43	42	31	20
Richest 5% owned	87	84	79	71	75	52	40
Richest 10% owned	92	91	88	79	83	65	54
Richest 1% owned	69	62	56	43	42	31	20
Next 2–5% owned	18	22	23	28	33	21	20
Next 6–10% owned	5	7	9	8	8	13	14
95% owned	13	16	21	29	25	48	60
90% owned	8	9	12	21	17	35	46

Sources: J. Westergaard and H. Resler, *Class in a Capitalist Society*, London, Heinemann (1975, p. 112); J. Revell, *The Wealth of the Nation*, Cambridge University Press (1967); *Social Trends 1986*. The series is on a new basis in both 1971 and 1983. Falls in share prices in the 1970s diminished the assets of the wealthiest for a time. Increases in home ownership raise the share of less wealthy groups.

Consequently the top 1 per cent appear to lose wealth while the next richest band gain. This is clear from Figure 2.4. It is important to bear in mind that these statistics are collected on a changing basis, even though all derive from taxes at death; they cover both consumption and production property.

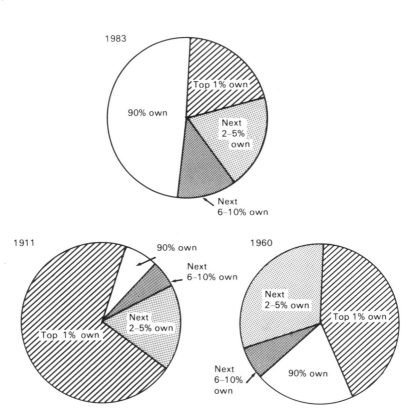

Source: J. Revell, *The Wealth of the Nation*, Cambridge University Press (1967); *Social Trends, 1986*.

FIGURE 2.4   *Changes in proportion of wealth owned by different groups*

Summarising these data:

(i)   The share of the richest 1 per cent has dropped from 69 per cent in 1911–13 to 42 per cent in 1960, and now to 20 per cent.

(ii)   The share of the next 2–5 per cent increased from 18 to 33 per cent in 1960, but now is recorded as 20 per cent.

(iii) The share of the next 6–10 per cent has risen steadily.

(iv)   The share of personal assets owned by the 90 per cent below the richest 10 per cent has dramatically increased from 8 per cent in 1911 to 17 per cent in 1960, and on to 46 per cent in 1983.

Although it is hard to know how valid these comparisons are, it is clear that ordinary people in Britain have far more possessions and assets than they did in 1911. The figures on relative shares then become highly variable, depending on factors such as share prices and house prices. Between 1971 and 1974, Britain apparently became more equal because share prices fell while the homes people occupied boomed in price. The relation between statistics and reality is, as ever, problematic.

Conclusion: the propertied upper class

The importance of inheritance, and the barriers to gaining substantial wealth through saving or employment mean that the upper class has maintained a considerable degree of social closure. That style of life and demeanour characteristic of Britain's dominant class is a result of its peculiar history. Unlike many other European countries, the ancient British aristocracy has managed to preserve and transmit its wealth through judicious marriage and inheritance. Marriage to foreign heiresses – German in the last century, American in this – helps to maintain the financial standing of noble families. Far more important, however, has been the merging of the new bourgeoisie with the traditional aristocracy.

The landed rich became economically active, especially in the eighteenth century, through the rise of commercialised farming, banking, and trade with the colonies. When the new class of bourgeois manufacturers and traders arose in the nineteenth century, it was able to merge with the commercialised aristocracy through marriage, and through the newly reformed public schools and universities. Old values and class patterns of behaviour became grafted on to a new economic class. The rise of the Empire and British trading dominance allowed a gentlemanly upper class of senior colonial administrators and City financiers to sustain and nurture distinctively upper-class characteristics. The continued dominance of City and Civil Service elites has often been seen as a barrier to dynamism in British industry; in fact, it has merely been one aspect of a secure and integrated dominant class, linked by kinship, ownership of wealth and distinctive patterns of education.

2.7 THE DISTRIBUTION OF LIFE-CHANCES

In the previous section we described and accounted for the unequal distribution of wealth in Great Britain in terms of the ownership and control of forms of private productive property. We argued that the ownership of this form of property and its effect – wealth – is the defining feature of the dominant or upper class. In this section, we shall shift our attention to the two remaining strata of our model, the middle and working classes. Rather than the result of differential access to productive property *per se*, the inequality between these two broad *occupational* strata can be explained in terms of Weber's emphasis on their different *market capacities*. Market capacity generates its own effects which are expressed in terms of different material rewards, conditions of work, health, housing, and education. In general, one can distinguish between the fundamental conditions of any capitalist system which *explain* its continuation – private property and market capacity – and the *resulting* inequalities of wealth-ownership and life-chances.

The market capacity of the individual depends on the sort of skills that he or she can bring to the labour market as an employee. Clearly, given inequality of skills – primarily caused by an unequal opportunity between classes to obtain such skills – inequality of reward is inevitable. The crucial point is that rewards are important in determining an individual's life-chances; in other words, inequalities of reward are accompanied by and produce inequalities in all areas of life: conditions at work, health, housing, education, mortality, and justice.

Material rewards

Income distribution

Social commentators of the 1950s and early 1960s claimed that with the burgeoning of the 'affluent society' the major class inequalities of industrial society were a thing of the past. We have seen that any such claim about the distribution of wealth could not have been and cannot today be legitimately sustained. What then of income?

One way of gaining a crude overall view of the pattern of income is to look at the current pay attached to a range of jobs in Britain. Figure 2.5 lists the earnings enjoyed by male workers in a number of familiar occupations.

A glance at these figures clearly indicates that in Britain today there are major differences in earnings. The actual differences between the highest paid and the lowest paid have in fact changed only marginally in the past thirty years, and it is still broadly true that the richest 1 per cent of income earners enjoy a gross pay which is about four times greater than they would receive if income were to be equally distributed among the total working population. But even then, such estimates do not take into account certain types of income which must be included for an accurate picture. These are employers' national insurance contributions, employees' superannuation contributions, benefits in kind as provided to all by the state (e.g. hospitals, schools, etc.) and finally, benefits received in the form of expense-account living. The latter benefits have become increasingly important for top wage earners as a means of 'topping up' salaries.

If we now move away from regarding income distribution in terms of the relative amount received by different groups of 'income units' to that

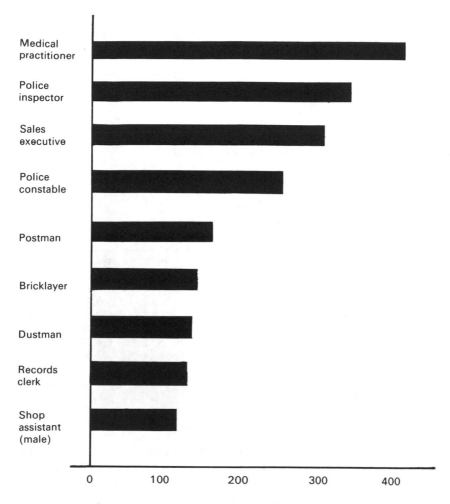

Source: Adapted from *New Earnings Survey*, October 1985.

FIGURE 2.5   *Weekly gross average earnings of males in selected occupations (1985).*

received by different occupational strata, we gain a much more concrete indication of inequality. Dividing the strata into two broad bands – the male non-manual and the male manual workers – Table 2.2 demonstrates the degree to which the distribution of earnings between them has remained relatively constant over the past fifty years.

Furthermore, as Table 2.3 shows, within the broad non-manual/manual categories inequalities of reward between the sexes are very much in evidence. Table 2.3 describes the broad occupational and sexual hierarchy of reward in Britain in descending order over the past fifteen years. For

TABLE 2.2

Indices of earnings – occupational group average expressed as a percentage of average for all men in the same period

	1935–6	1955–6	1985–6
Non-manual workers	152	144	140
Manual workers	85	83	80

Source: J. Westergaard and H. Resler, *Class in a Capitalist Society*, London, Heinemann (1975, p. 74); *New Earnings Survey* 1985.

TABLE 2.3

Average gross weekly earnings of full-time workers by sex and occupational strata (GB) (including overtime, shift premium payments and excluding fringe benefits)

	1970 (£)	1975 (£)	1978 (£)	1984 (£)	1985 (£)
Male non-manual (21 +)	35.8	68.4	100.7	200.7	225
Male manual (21 +)	26.8	55.7	80.7	152.7	163.6
Female non-manual (18 +)	17.8	39.6	59.1	124.3	133
Female manual (18 +)	13.4	32.1	49.4	93.5	101

Sources: Adapted from *Department of Employment Gazette*, October 1975; *New Earnings Survey*, October 1985.

both occupational strata female employees earn about 60 per cent of the wages of their male counterparts, and this discrimination against and exploitation of women's labour has only marginally decreased through legislation such as the Equal Pay Act of 1970. As Westergaard and Resler say (1975, p. 101), 'sex inequality in pay reinforces class inequality: it strikes hardest at the lowest levels of the occupational hierarchy'.

The marked inequalities between manual and non-manual earnings is even more significant when one considers the importance that overtime and similar variable payments play in the gross figures of Table 2.3. That is, if we exclude such payments, the manual sector – in particular the male manual worker – suffers a major reduction in average weekly earnings while the non-manual workers do not, since their gross wages depend on very little overtime. This fact is illustrated in Table 2.4.

The figures in Table 2.4 demonstrate the vital importance of overtime and other payments for the male manual workers' earnings (over 25 per cent) and their limited significance for non-manual workers. For some male manual employees in certain industries overtime and other payments are

TABLE 2.4

Average gross weekly earnings of male (21+) full-time manual and non-manual employees (all industries and services, April 1985)

	Manual (£)	As % of earnings	Non-manual (£)	As % of earnings
Average gross earnings	163.60		225	
of which overtime payments	23.80		8.6	
Payment by results and bonus or commission	12.40		7.4	
Shift work	5.60		1.9	
Remaining earnings	121.80	74	207.10	92

Source: Derived from *Department of Employment Gazette* (New Earnings Survey 1985), October 1985.

even more important in determining average earnings: for example, on average, 30 per cent of the wages of manual employees in the metal manufacture and mining industries is made up in overtime payments, etc. In other words, in general, manual workers have *to work more hours* per week to achieve a gross average wage which is *still about 25 per cent less* than that of the non-manual worker. Moreover, as mentioned earlier, the figures presented so far do not include a range of fringe benefits usually the privilege of non-manual employees which have a real income value: among these are luncheon vouchers, company cars, credit facilities (cheap company loans), and so on. There appears to be, then, no justification for the claim that manual and non-manual earnings are starting to overlap and becoming more comparable.

What of the distribution of earnings within the broad occupational and sex categories? Obviously, not every male manual worker earned the average of 163.60, nor every male non-manual worker £225 in April 1985. However, there were many more non-manual workers close to or above their average than was (and still is) the case for manual workers: low pay among non-manual workers tend to figure in low-level clerical, sales and nursing groups but to be spread across a much wider range of jobs in the manual sector of the labour market. The data presented so far, then do not support the view that there is a general level of earnings which 'most people' enjoy.

The life-cycle of earnings

People also experience radically unequal patterns of earnings over the span of their working lives as employees. For the majority in all occupational groups, earnings are roughly similar in the early years of employment, that is, between the ages of 20 and 25. But from age 25 onwards the earnings gap between the groups widens in favour of those in the non-manual sector. For the latter, those in the higher occupational categories, such as managers, professional employees, academics, engineers, scientists and technologists, earnings increase rapidly because of an incremental system of reward – a regular and progressive increase in earnings in addition to any pay awards negotiated – whereby earnings rise steeply up till their late forties. At this stage in their careers employees enjoy salaries which are about twice that received in their early twenties (i.e. referring to their 'real' earnings when allowance has been made for inflation, etc.). After this peak has been reached, their real earnings fall, but only very moderately. For manual workers, however, including skilled, semi-skilled and unskilled, wages increase only slightly over their working lives; wages increase on average by only 15 per cent, reaching their peak in the employee's mid-thirties. They then tail off to a level which, for the majority of the manual working population, is less than that enjoyed in their early twenties. This is due to many factors, one of the more obvious of which is that the cumulative physical demands of manual work may well affect the worker's health. Moreover, as a worker gets older, overtime, shift work and so on become less and less a physical possibility. Similarly, job-related sickness may mean that the ageing worker is more frequently unable to turn up for work.

Life earnings and life-style

Differences in life cycle of earnings clearly have a number of consequences: for example, they will be expressed in the consumption patterns of the two classes. Non-manual workers, given their greater security and better financial prospects, could, for example, make some provision for replacing their car once every two years, or afford to obtain and pay off a mortgage. Only those non-manual workers who engage in low-level clerical and sales work experience of life cycle of earnings akin to that of the manual workers. But even these may envisage some possibility of promotion to a sub-managerial or supervisory position, a prospect which is probably as far from the mind of the manual worker as it is from the reality of his or her employment situation. As Westergard and Resler (1975, p. 83) say, the difference between the classes in terms of their life cycle of earnings 'plays a large part in differences of approach to the management of everyday life, and of responses to the social order, between the classes'.

Differences in terms and conditions of work

In this section we are not so much concerned with how many pounds are 'in the pay packet', i.e. *what* is earned, but rather with the general conditions of employment experienced by the manual and non-manual sectors. Thus, one could consider such factors as hours, sick pay, pension schemes and holiday entitlements.

Hours worked per week vary considerably between the two broad occupational sectors. As was seen earlier, overtime plays a much greater role in pushing up the average gross weekly earnings of the male manual than of the male non-manual worker. For the former, the average working week in 1985 was forty-five hours, for the latter about thirty-eight hours. Besides being paid less per hour the majority of women employees in both sectors work fewer hours than their male counterparts. This is a result of a number of factors such as the much larger proportion of part-time work, the artificial restriction of female overtime by male-dominated trade unions, and social measures against women at work in general. (These factors are examined in more detail in our chapters on the family and sexual divisions.) In terms of historical change, manual workers of both sexes work today almost as many hours each week as they did in the late 1930s and early 1940s; this demonstrates the fact that, where available, overtime is a crucial necessity for the manual worker if he or she is to receive a wage at or above the 'average' for all manual occupations. In short, although the 'standard working week' has been reduced since the war, in reality the working week for the manual worker is much the same. Table 2.5 gives some of the relevant figures.

Hours of work are only one aspect of the conditions of employment: holidays, sick pay, the provision of pension schemes, penalties for lateness at work and so on are other conditions that reflect occupational inequality. Taking pension provision, for example, only 60 per cent of male manual workers are covered (1986) by an employer's pension scheme, and many of

TABLE 2.5

Average weekly hours and distribution of hours worked by sex and occupational strata (1985)

	Full-time males (21 +)		Full-time females (18 +)	
	Manual	Non-manual	Manual	Non-manual
Average weekly hours	45	38	38.1	37.9
of which overtime	5	1.3	1	0.5
Distribution of hours				
(% employed)	(%)	(%)	(%)	(%)
30–36 hours	3.1	7.3	16.6	14.4
36–40 hours	44	68	67.9	76.3
40–48 hours	28.3	20.5	12.5	8.5
48 + hours	24.6	4.2	3	0.8

Source: Derived from *New Earnings Survey*, October 1985.

these, unlike their non-manual counterparts, do not enjoy an enhanced or earnings-related pension at retirement.

Whatever the conditions of work are, they and the sort of work that is done are likely to be important variables affecting a person's health, as we can now see.

Illness and death linked to occupation

Working-class adults – particularly the unskilled – experience the physically damaging and mentally stultifying effects of a disadvantaged home and work environment. Specific occupational hazards, along with diet, poor housing and home environment, personal habits such as smoking, mental stress and relatively lower use of the health service result in a higher rate of illness and injury for manual compared with non-manual workers. Social class differences are most apparent at the extremes, i.e. between professional and unskilled occupational groups. The annual report of the *General Household Survey* provides information on the distribution of chronic illness by socio-economic group.

Mortality rates among the adult working population parallel the progressive incidence of illness that occurs as one moves down the social hierarchy. In 1982, the death rate for adult professional and managerial employees was 23 per cent below the overall average, while for unskilled workers the death rate was almost 40 per cent above the average. The gap between mortality rates for the two groups has in fact widened since the 1930s, when the rates were 10 per cent below the average for professional and managerial workers, and 11 per cent above for unskilled workers.

Patterns of poverty

The analysis of patterns of class based inequality that has been presented so far clearly indicates the existence of people who experience considerably disadvantaged life chances, those for example who are found among the lowest 20 per cent of income earners. Virtually all of these will be receiving Supplementary Benefit (SB) allowances to increase their disposable income. The level of income at which SB is received is widely accepted as a crude and basic measure of the 'poverty line', that point below which people may be said to be 'in poverty'.

Clearly, where the State decides to draw this line determines how many are officially recognised to be in poverty. The 1986 Conservative government argued that 'want – in the sense of absolute deprivation – has been largely eliminated'. Yet the 1986 figures from the Department of Health and Social Security suggest that almost 9 million, a sixth of the total British population are living on a wage which is on or below the SB poverty line. While none of these may suffer from 'absolute deprivation' (a term that is anyway difficult to define unless it is meant to refer to circumstances in which people literally have no food, shelter and clothing), clearly many are unlikely to be enjoying an 'average' or 'normal' standard of living. Poverty should then perhaps best be seen more realistically in terms of relative rather than absolute deprivation. This is the view taken by the eminent American economist Galbraith (1958, p. 252) when he says:

> People are poverty-stricken when their incomes, even if adequate for survival, fall markedly below those of the community. Then they cannot have what the larger community regards as the necessary minimum for decency . . . They are degraded for, in the literal sense, they live outside the grades or categories which the community regards as acceptable.

What is 'necessary' for a decent standard of living is a matter of social definition which may change over time. For example, as expectations have changed during this century, first indoor running water, then hot water, and finally an indoor fixed bathroom have come to be regarded as necessities.

The fact remains, however, that the poor are not simply at the bottom of the stratification hierarchy, but are almost, in a sense, *outside* the margins of that hierarchy. They form what some have called an 'underclass' in the stratification system. It is important to recognise that such a circumstance may have significant psychological implications for the *self-images* of the individuals concerned: not only do they have less than everyone else, but they may *feel* and *see* themselves as different – less significant, less integrated, almost outside the mainstream of society.

There have been a number of studies of poverty in the UK that have been made over the past twenty-five years that have consistently indicated that a substantial minority of people may experience serious relative deprivation. The most recent of these is that by Townsend (1979).

Townsend measures deprivation in terms of the inability or incapacity to participate in 'the activities and have the living conditions and amenities which are customary, or at least widely encouraged or approved' because of a lack of 'resources' (1979, p. 31). He measures the conditions and amenities considered to be 'customary' in terms of 60 indicators of an approved standard of living. According to Townsend's estimates, over half the people in Britain at some state in their lives may well experience relative deprivation to such an extent that they could be said to be 'in poverty' for those periods. Critics of Townsend argue that this is a spurious claim inasmuch as it depends on Townsend making very dubious judgements about what the social needs are of which people might be 'deprived'. Some people may not want to send Christmas cards or eat meat at least once a week (two of Townsend's indicators of conventional British life): the implication is that Townsend grossly exaggerates the incidence of poverty because he ignores the fact that people may choose to do without such things. However,

Townsend's response would be that true deprivation is indicated by the fact that choice in matters of style of living is an issue that does not arise among the poor: for example, three million people presumably do not choose *not* to heat the living area of their homes in winter (see Mack, 1985).

Studies by Atkinson and Kincaid in Britain, Harrington in the USA, and official government studies in both countries, reveal a persistent and significant section of the population living in poverty-stricken circumstances at any one time, to say nothing of the many others, who, at certain crucial periods of their life (e.g. the old, families with young children), may temporarily lapse into poverty. Such investigations indicate clearly and forcefully that poverty is still very much with us, and that any complacency about rising standards of living in the post-war period inevitably banishing poverty must be quickly dismissed.

Who are the poor?

It is apparent that certain social categories appear at greater risk of being poor than others. Those most vulnerable to poverty at present are the old; the sick and disabled; the large family and the single-parent (usually fatherless) family; the unemployed and the insecurely employed low-wage-earner. The latter are now the largest two groups that make up the numbers of those in poverty as Britain's economic decline (especially in manufacturing) becomes firmly established.

Let us look briefly at those most likely to experience chronic poverty.

(i) Despite reports of 'fabulous' wages earned by manual workers the receipt of low pay remains the fate of many workers in Western industrial economies. In a recent survey (Pond and Burghes, 1986) the low paid, or 'the working poor', represent the largest group in poverty today, 680,000 receiving wages below the official poverty line. If one combines those living below the SB line with those within 140 per cent of it – i.e. those 'on the margins of poverty' – low wages mean that 3.75 million people suffer serious deprivation. The problems of the low paid are further compounded by the fact that their jobs are also frequently *less secure*. Moreover, they frequently work in declining industries lacking effective union organisation and political representation, so that their prospects of escaping the low pay treadmill are slim indeed.

(ii) The period of so-called full employment of the 1950s and early 1960s prompted many to dismiss *unemployment* as a factor in poverty, yet all the British studies indicate the seriousness of even temporary unemployment for large numbers of families. The high unemployment of the 1970s and 1980s seems unlikely to be a temporary phenomenon: in fact many experts predict a persistent and probably increasing level of unemployment in Western economies for the rest of the century. So, prolonged unemployment for the principal breadwinners and their offspring is thrusting more and more families into poverty and threatens to do so for many years to come.

(iii) The *elderly* are particularly vulnerable to poverty. As life expectancy has increased and earlier retirement has become more widespread in the twentieth century, so the elderly have come to comprise an ever larger section of the poor. Thus, in a study by Abel-Smith and Townsend (1965), a third of the poor were the aged, and almost half the old-age pensioners in their study were living below the poverty line.

(iv) Though large families are less widespread in the twentieth century, the *large family* still remains vulnerable to poverty, if relatively less so than in the nineteenth century. The addition of subsequent mouths to feed merely compounds the problem, and this remains true despite the accompanying welfare state provisions of family allowance and so on. But even the *first* child can throw a low-income family into poverty.

(v) *Single-parent families*, whether the result of choice, death, desertion, or divorce, constitute a significant portion of the poor. Coates and Silburn's study (1970) showed that many of the poor were those without a male breadwinner, and Abel-Smith and Townsend's study found 10 per cent of the poor belonging to fatherless families.

(vi) The *sickness* or *disablement* of one parent, whether temporary or permanent, can have major implications for families near the poverty margin. In the St Ann's study, the sick and disabled constituted the fourth largest category of the poor.

While recognising the relative vulnerability of certain groups to poverty, it must be emphasised that they do share one crucial common feature, their *social class position*. The poor are an integral part of the working class, poverty is the *direct product* of the general pattern of class inequality. As Miliband (1974) says, 'Old age, disablement, low pay, unemployment, etc. become synonymous with poverty in so far as those involved are members of the working class.'

There is then plenty of evidence to indicate the existence of a firmly entrenched structure of class inequality in modern Britain, much like many other industrial capitalist societies. But how is the pattern of inequality influenced by the effect of taxation and the benefits provided by the Welfare State? Is class inequality in any ways reduced?

The redistributive effect of taxation and benefits

Taxation

Most people believe that the British tax system is highly progressive, that is, the more you earn the more you pay, and the routine chant of those who earn most is that they are over-taxed, that 'if taxes were reduced we'd have more incentive to work harder'. But just how progressive is the tax structure? What is the effect of the combination of direct *and* indirect taxes? What opportunities are there for people to avoid paying tax? Answers to these and other questions should allow us to develop a more accurate picture of the impact of tax on people's earnings and hence the extent to which it redistributes income within Britain.

All employees in 1986 earning more than £3640 p.a. (the individual's so-called 'personal allowance') are subject to an income tax at the basic rate of 29 per cent to a maximum of £17,200. Only that portion of income above this figure is taxed at a marginally higher rate. However, given that the majority of employees receive earnings which are below the £17,200 threshold, the 29 per cent rate is clearly imposed on a wide range of incomes, from the lowest to the relatively highly paid employee. Within this large sector of the population, therefore, income tax is virtually non-progressive, with the lower paid paying a disproportionately large amount of their earnings in tax compared with those in the higher income bracket. Indeed in terms of *marginal* rates of taxation, i.e. the proportion of any additional earnings that are taxed, those on below-average incomes may in fact suffer a rate higher than those on incomes in excess of £17,200. This is the so-called 'poverty-trap' of the lower paid: a small increase in earning takes them over a threshold, whereby they may lose certain welfare benefits and at the same time have to pay a disproportionately large increase in tax on their original income.

When indirect taxes – taxes such as VAT which are levied mainly on commodities purchased – are taken into account the tax burden on income is even less progressive. Indirect tax, sometimes known as 'expenditure tax', is generally *regressive*, i.e. it hits those with lower purchasing power the hardest.

Thus, in general, when all taxes, both direct and indirect, are combined the tax burden is for the most part far from progressive.

At the higher income levels the higher marginal tax rate encourages employers and their wealthier employees respectively to provide and seek forms of income that are untaxable or only slightly taxed. This had led to the development of top executives receiving not a salary but a 'total remuneration package' which includes a whole range of fringe benefits. For example, cheap mortgages supplied by employers are one important way in which higher income earners maintain real higher standards of living. However, such strategies have perhaps become less important for the very high income earners who, in recent years, have enjoyed a large reduction in the taxes they have had to pay following the reduction in the highest rates of income tax since 1979: for example, in real terms, those earning over £400 per week take home on average an extra £55 more in 1986 then they did in 1979.

Benefits

Given that the tax system is much less progressive in real terms than at first sight, what affect do welfare benefits have on the redistribution of income?

Benefits need to be seen in two ways: benefits in cash and benefits in kind. The former refers to payments such as pensions, supplementary benefit, family income supplement, child benefit, and so on. Some of these are available to all households (e.g. child benefit) while others are income or age related. Benefits in kind refer to the State provision of education, health care, travel subsidy, housing subsidy and other allocated benefits. How effective are welfare benefits as redistributive measures?

As part of the social security provision in Britain, the two largest cash benefits are for pension and SB payments. For those in households with a very low income such benefits are a vital source of support against 'absolute deprivation', though all of these people will still be in poverty: the benefit provision is not designed to lift people out of poverty. Such benefits are of course also received by households with the highest gross income (averaging £18,640 in 1983), though to a much smaller extent. The value of cash benefits to the poor should not be minimised or dismissed, but it does not mean that relative deprivation is removed. When benefits in kind are considered, the balance of the redistribution is in fact significantly in favour of the most prosperous households that typically enjoy more take-up of education through children staying on at school and more benefits with regard to health care.

In short, while there is a redistributive effect through benefits there is a much less progressive pattern to this than might be expected. This reflects the situation with regard to taxation as we saw earlier. Reflecting on this state of affairs Kay and King (1978, p. 56) have said that:

It is possible that although the politicians and administrators most closely involved know that the appearance of immense progressivity is a sham, they believe that this appearance will deceive others into thinking that such objectives are being achieved. It is hard to imagine that the deception is successful, and the explanation is not one which flatters either group. The hypocritical nature of the present situation reflects little credit on the British tax system or on the British political system.

2.8 SOCIAL MOBILITY

Introduction

Social stratification is, as we have seen, structured inequality in society, such that some strata have more power and reward than others. In many

societies this has been an avowed and recognised feature of social organisation – acknowledged and (usually) justified both by those who benefit and
those who are disadvantaged. Normally in such societies – for example, in
the form of castes or feudal estates – social positions are defined and fixed
by birth. Unequal power or benefit is inherited – 'ascribed' – and in theory
this position cannot be changed by the efforts of the occupant of such a
stratum. However good, however servile, the untouchable in India can
never make himself anything other than an untouchable (and equally
important, he accepts this fact). Thus social hierarchy is fixed, rigid, and
transmitted across generations in these societies.

For industrial societies, the position has often been portrayed in very
different terms. Many sociologists have assumed that social position is
gained by individual *achievement* rather than by birth – at least for the
majority of the population. Inequality, they argue, is attached to *positions*;
the crucial concern is, therefore, with how one gets into these positions and
how much movement there is across generations. Social mobility thus
becomes the focus of attention. It is accepted that individual positions are
unequally rewarded, but the questions of access and opportunity now
become central, and although Western capitalist societies do not claim to
be equal, they *do* claim to offer equal opportunity to all in the competition
for unequal positions. That is, they claim to be meritocratic.

As we have seen, the inheritance of wealth and educational advantage
make this ideology of 'free competition for unequal reward' a very dubious
claim, but in studying social mobility we are still comparing the actual
amount of social mobility with the ideal of totally free movement through
totally equal opportunity. In such a perfectly mobile society, the social
position of the individual need bear no relation to the social position of his
family of origin. The individual would move up or down according to
merit.

In comparing societies with this ideal, *open* condition, we can distinguish
two aspects of mobility:

(i)   Intergenerational mobility: that is, the son or daughter has a different
       social position (higher or lower) than that of the parents (for example,
       a miner's daughter might train to become a teacher). This is usually
       seen as the most important form of mobility today.
(ii)   Intragenerational mobility, where a person changes their occupa-
       tional level significantly during their worklife.

Social mobility can refer to any movement up or down the occupational
hierarchy, though sociologists often emphasise cross-class mobility. Here it
is important to establish the class categorisation and number of class
boundaries actually being used in the study. Otherwise we may draw
misleading conclusions about the movements across changing occupations
(for example, whether clerical positions are counted as middle class affects
our analysis).

Causes of the level of social mobility

In general, three causal factors affect the overall level of mobility:

(i)   The changing number of positions to be filled.
(ii) The methods of access and entry to positions.
(iii) The number of suitable offspring available to fill positions.

The most important causal factor in industrial societies has certainly been the sustained expansion of skilled positions in professional, managerial and technical occupations. This has been the constant trend, despite the fact that particular occupations may have been de-skilled in the process. While some jobs such as clerical work declined in reward and status, other groups expanded both through credentials and professionalisation. The change in the balance of occupations is real enough, as is the pressure on individuals to obtain educational credentials as a means of access to these jobs. The importance of qualifications held on entry to the labour market continues to increase, even if promotion and training at work still produce some social mobility. The consequence of all this is that there are considerable social pressures towards increased educational provision. The educational system was expected to produce a higher output of suitable entrants to professional and managerial employment; one aspect of this was the hope of tapping an unused pool of talent among those lacking educational opportunities. Thus educational policy was oriented both to perceived economic needs, and to broader social goals of equality of opportunity.

Does educational expansion increase mobility?

There is no guarantee that these increases in educational provision will actually benefit disadvantaged groups, or create more equality of opportunity (as functionalist arguments would assume). The post-war expansion of education was essential to facilitate the growth of the middle class occupations; but these opportunities have largely been taken up by middle-class offspring.

We shall see in Chapter 8 on Education that the race for credentials is a very unequal affair; one result of this is that chances of upward and downward mobility are very unevenly spread across social groups.

Routes for social mobility

It is generally assumed that the rise of more widespread educational opportunities has given children of working-class parents the chance to study for the qualifications necessary to enter middle-class occupations. At the same time, it is argued, the increasing demand for competitively gained qualifications means that children from middle-class families cannot assume that they will avoid downward mobility. Hence, those who enter an occupation holding few qualifications are, it is argued, less likely to achieve work-life mobility (i.e. intragenerational mobility), because qualified trainees will be recruited directly to these higher positions. Thus, these trends towards a greater stress on educational qualifications imply that intragenerational mobility within work caused through promotion becomes much less important as a route for advancement. Even so, worklife mobility is still of some importance; the Oxford researchers (Goldthorpe, 1980) found that many of the downwardly mobile men recovered their position of origin through this means.

Marriage has sometimes worked as a further route to mobility but the evidence for its significance is slim and inconclusive. Some have found considerable levels of cross-class marriage in the nineteenth century (Penn, 1985) and we might speculate that the concentration of female employment in the office brings women from diverse backgrounds together and blurs class lines as people seek partners. On the other hand, class divisions in residence, education and job opportunities remain sufficiently distinct to favour marriage between partners of similar origin.

Social mobility in England and Wales

Is Britain a closed, rigid society? Have reforms since 1945 created more fairness and openness? Can class barriers be broken down by educational reform? These questions have been central to recent studies and the answers may be unexpected. Current findings suggest a complex picture, where opportunity has increased, but the relative chances of success between classes have changed very little.

Rapid changes in the occupational structure, facilitated by educational expansion, have increased the overall chances of entering higher-ranking occupations. As a result, some working-class sons can move up, while many middle-class sons can avoid moving down. The result is that there is an apparent openness in the class structure, with very diverse backgrounds for people in middle-class jobs. At the same time, though, working-class people are more uniformly working class in origin than ever. In addition, there is still considerable social closure and self-recruitment at the very top of the occupational structure. The picture for women is strikingly different, with far less opportunity available to females whatever their class origin.

Mobility patterns for males

Mobility studies focus almost exclusively on males, so data on changes are partial and partly misleading. However, Table 2.6 shows the long-term trends, with upward mobility rising and downward moves declining,

TABLE 2.6

Social mobility percentages, males

Birth date	Pre-1890	1890–9	1900–9	1908–17	1918–27	1928–37
Upwardly mobile	16.5	23.3	23.2	19.9	24.5	30.5
Down	33.0	25.9	24.6	25.3	23.2	20.4
Total mobile	49.5	49.2	47.8	45.2	47.7	50.9

Source: A. Heath, *Social Mobility*, London, Fontana (1981), using data from Glass (1954) and Goldthorpe *et al.* (1980).

though the overall proportion of sons moving occupational level compared with their fathers remains fairly constant.

When Glass (1954) studied trends up to the 1950s, he found that although many men experienced mobility, most of this was short-range and across the middle levels of the hierarchy in a 'buffer zone'. Thus class divisions were not really disrupted by this movement. Those at the bottom rarely moved up, and nearly half of the sons of the upper-middle class stayed there.

The 1972 Oxford survey investigated how far these patterns had changed in the post-war period with all its economic growth and social reform. From their study of men aged between 20 and 64 years, they concluded that overall mobility was more widespread and often long-range. The primary cause was not reformed institutions, but instead the changes in occupational structure which expanded the middle class and shrunk the manual working class (see Table 2.7).

The result is that more working-class sons can move up while fewer middle-class boys need to move down; the middle-class boy still has four times the chance of getting a managerial or professional job compared with a manual worker's son. (We use the term 'middle class' here to exclude routine white-collar work; Goldthorpe uses the phrase 'service class' in the same way.)

TABLE 2.7

Male occupations, percentages

Males	1911	1951	1971
Managerial and professional	6.9	12.6	21.5
Intermediate occupations	11.9	13.3	14.5
Manual	73.6	68.4	58.8

Derived from J. H. Goldthorpe *et al.*, *Social Mobility and Class Structure in Modern Britain*, Oxford, Clarendon Press (1980).

For example, two-thirds of the sons of top professionals and managers stayed middle class – including 48 per cent who entered top level jobs like their fathers'. Meanwhile 58.3 per cent of the sons of non-skilled manual workers stayed working class, with only 10.7 per cent moving up into managerial or professional jobs. Between these groups came routine non-manual workers, supervisors, technicians and self-employed tradesmen. Their sons entered occupations evenly spread across the hierarchy.

There is, then, considerable movement without this giving equal opportunity to all groups. There are other real effects of the expansion in the middle class as well. Since the working class remains much bigger than the middle class, a small proportion of manual sons provides sufficient numbers to fill many of the higher-level vacancies. As a result, when we examine top professionals and managers, we find that 29 per cent come from working-class origins. Among lower professionals and managers, 40 per cent had manual fathers while only 23 per cent had middle class backgrounds – the rest having fathers with routine non-manual or intermediate occupations. These dry figures express a dramatic and significant social change. The British middle class is diverse in social origin, and so perhaps diverse in values. Coexisting within this category are people with a middle-class inheritance of culture and resources, coexisting beside others (including many managers, teachers and social workers) who owe their social advancement to state education and to state-sponsored growth schools, health services and local authorities. The experiences and perceived interests of these groups varies so much that generalisations about 'the middle class' become crude and misleading.

Meanwhile, other areas of the class structure are much less open. Only about 4 per cent of the sons in manual work had professional or managerial fathers, but 70 per cent had working-class origins. The working class is more uniform in origins than ever before because downward mobility has declined. Although many sons have moved up, the homogeneous character of manual workers' origins contrasts starkly with the middle class. At the very top of the hierarchy, elite recruitment shows the most social closure. Heath (1981) uses Oxford data to show that 47 per cent of proprietors of large firms had fathers who were owners of companies, and 40 per cent of self-employed professionals (e.g. barristers) came from upper-middle class homes. Even in 1970, public schools produced 62 per cent of top civil servants and 80 per cent of the top judiciary. Thus social closure is still real, and tickets to the top depend on property, connections or elite education. Indeed, the continued dominance of Oxford, Cambridge and the top public schools severely weakens the claim that educational reform has opened up British society. Any effects fall short of the most powerful and best paid positions, leaving the upper class intact.

Female social mobility

Data are extremely scarce, but Heath (1981) gives evidence to show how far women are disadvantaged by their limited opportunities in the labour market. Women are systematically excluded from top managerial and professional jobs, as well as from skilled manual labour. As a result, women are concentrated in routine non-manual work, in lower professions such as nursing and teaching, and in low-paid manual jobs (see Table 2.8 and Chapter 5 on Gender Divisions in Society).

TABLE 2.8

Female occupations, percentages

Females	1911	1951	1971
Managerial and professional	9.1	11.6	15.5
Intermediate occupations	9.9	31.0	38.6
Manual	76.7	44.2	43.0

Derived from J. H. Goldthorpe *et al.*, *Social Mobility and Class Structure in Modern Britain*, Oxford, Clarendon Press (1980).

The result is that 53 per cent of the daughters of professional and managerial fathers enter routine office work, while only 8.4 per cent enter top middle-class occupations. Women from manual origins have about a 1.5 per cent chance of a top occupation, though 10 per cent go into lower professional jobs; 48 per cent enter office work. Education can be a route to a narrow range of professions, but for most the prospects are poor. Considering this distinctive occupational distribution, it is difficult to apply the notion of cross-class mobility to most women. Goldthorpe has argued that this justifies studying only male mobility, but it can be argued that women's occupational position and chances are both important sociologically, and important to women and their families. This is so regardless of whether the occupation of the male (if any) in the household decisively shapes the class location of the household.

Social mobility 1972–83

The Oxford data on male mobility has been brought up to date using the 1983 General Election Study (Goldthorpe and Payne, 1986). The previous trends have continued, apart from three important changes. First, the relative chances of getting professional or managerial jobs have changed, reducing the relative disadvantage of manual sons. Previously, middle-class sons had four times the chance of manual sons; this now reduces to three times the chance. Secondly, downward mobility is less likely than ever – the chances (or risks) of entering manual work have become more unequal. Thirdly, mass unemployment has hit a significant minority, and the blow has fallen much harder on the working class. As Goldthorpe and Payne put it (1986, p. 17), 'mass unemployment has created a serious new risk of what can only be regarded as downward mobility – and . . . this risk is much greater for men in working-class positions, by whatever route they came into them, than it is for others'.

We might add that the same applies to working-class women. The net effect for men is that manual workers' sons diverged dramatically in their fate. By 1983, 23 per cent entered the middle class (16 per cent in 1972), while 11 per cent or so suffered unemployment instead.

Social mobility and class structure

It is important to realise that changes in the level of social mobility have no direct connection with patterns of inequality in society: movement between classes does not abolish objective class structures. *The structure of class positions is a separate matter from the recruitment of individuals to fill these positions.*

While these positions constitute the structure of objective inequalities, sociologists have often regarded stratification as including a broader range of features, including subjective aspects of inequality. We have seen that in capitalist societies, different classes exhibit differences in social characteristics, such as values and patterns of behaviour. If class membership is transmitted across generations (that is, if there is little social mobility) then it is more likely that these classes will become distinct social entities, differing in many ways in their social characteristics. Giddens (1973, p. 107) emphasises this idea with his concept of 'structuration': 'The greater the degree of "closure" of mobility chances the more this facilitates the formation of identifiable classes. For the effect of closure in terms of intergenerational movement is to provide for the reproduction of common life experiences over the generations.'

If, on the other hand, there is a constant flux, with high levels of social mobility, such sharp differences are less easily sustained. The upper class in Western societies have normally succeeded in maintaining a high degree of social closure, and show very distinct values and patterns of behaviour.

These partly result from their objective position – their concern with wealth and its management – but also from a sustained upper-class culture. Even when considering the middle and working classes, though, we must not forget that mobility levels are still low enough to sustain different class cultures, especially at the extreme 'ends' of these classes in the upper middle class and the unskilled working class. In any society, as long as objective classes remain, there will be different opportunities and experiences available to different classes, and these will be sufficient to produce differing ideas and behaviour. This is still most emphatically true of contemporary societies, where the class structures are far from fully 'open' and hence where the degrees of structuration remain substantial.

This concept of structuration provides a bridge between our static models of class and the complex dynamic reality of changing inequality. We need the models to make sense of structure, but we also need to examine how different dimensions of inequality interrelate. That alone makes the patterns in social relations more complicated, but in addition we must analyse processes of change to judge how far the character of these structures is being modified or even transformed. It is to these complex processes that we now turn in Chapter 3.

REFERENCES TO CHAPTER 2

Abel-Smith, B. and Townsend, P. (1965) *The Poor and the Poorest*, London, Bell.
Atkinson, A. B. (1974) *Unequal Shares*, Harmondsworth, Penguin.
Coates, K. and Silburn, R. (1970) *Poverty: the Forgotten Englishmen*, Harmondsworth, Penguin.
Davis, K. and Moore, W. E. (1945) 'Some Principles of Stratification', *American Sociological Review*, vol. 10, pp. 242–9.
Diamond Commission (1979) Royal Commission on the Distribution of Income and Wealth, *Report*, 1979.
Galbraith, J. (1958) *The Affluent Society*, London, Hamilton.
Gerth, H. and Mills, C. W. (1948) *From Max Weber: Essays in Sociology*, London, Routledge & Kegan Paul.
Giddens, A. (1973) *The Class Structure of the Advanced Societies*, London, Hutchinson.
Glass, D. (1954) *Social Mobility in Britain*, London, Routledge & Kegan Paul.
Goldthorpe, J. H. *et al.* (1980) *Social Mobility and Class Structure in Modern Britain*, Oxford, Clarendon Press.
Goldthorpe, J. H. and Payne, C. (1986) 'Trends in Intergenerational Class Mobility in England and Wales 1972–83' *Sociology*, vol. 20, pp. 1–25.
Heath, A. (1981), *Social Mobility*, London, Fontana.
Kay, J. and King, M. (1978) *The British Tax System*, Oxford University Press.
Mack, J. and Lansley, S. (1985) *Poor Britain*, London, Allen & Unwin.
Miliband, R. (1974) 'Politics and Poverty', in D. Wedderburn (1974).
Parkin, F. (1971) *Class Inequality and Political Order*, London, Paladin.
Penn, R. (1985) *Skilled Workers in the Class Structure*, Cambridge, Cambridge University Press.

Perrott, R. (1968) *The Aristocrats*, London, Weidenfeld & Nicolson.
Pond, C. and Burghes, L. (1986) 'The Rising Tide of Deprivation', *New Society*, 18 April.
Revell, J. (1967) *The Wealth of the Nation*, Cambridge University Press.
Scott, J. (1982) *The Upper Classes*, London, Macmillan.
Scott, J. (1985) *Corporations, Classes and Capitalism*, 2nd edn, London, Hutchinson.
Scott, J. (1986) 'The Debate on Ownership and Control', *Social Studies Review*, vol. 1, no 3.
Townsend, P. (1979) *Poverty in the United Kingdom*, Harmondsworth, Penguin.
Tumin, M. (1953) 'Some Principles of Stratification: a Critical Analysis', *American Sociological Review*, vol. 18, pp. 387–93.
Westergaard, J. and Resler, H. (1975) *Class in a Capitalist Society*, London, Heinemann.
Wright, E. (1978) *Class, Crisis and the State*, London, New Left Books.

3

The Dynamics of Class

3.1 INTRODUCTION

> Cheshire is rather upmarket. It's a well-known fact that in Knutsford the Fire-Brigade is ex-directory. In Holmes Chapel they take fish and chips home in briefcases, and if you want red cabbage in Macclesfield you get it through Interflora.
>
> Les Dawson

In Chapter 2 the broad pattern of class inequality was described and explained using a model that combined Marxist and Weberian theories of stratification. But in order to keep the argument as clear as possible we presented a fairly static picture of the class structure. But clearly, as society changes, so too may the patterns of inequality that prevail. Thus, while in Chapter 2 we were interested in exploring the theories of stratification and the evidence for class and related inequalities, here we are more interested in those processes that bring this class structure alive, what we call the dynamics of class.

This is an issue which encompasses important sociological debates about all three great classes outlined in our model in Chapter 2 (see p. 55). A key concern that runs through all these debates and to some extent actually inspired them in the first place is whether one can draw clear boundaries between the social classes. This in turn rests on how we define the distinctiveness of each class and how we think this is blurred or enhanced as a result of broad socioeconomic processes.

In order to make some sense of these debates about changing class boundaries, we look at each class in turn, and draw in our analysis on two highly useful concepts, the concepts of 'social closure' and 'social reproduction'. These two notions, which we shall explain shortly, have become increasingly important for current research on social mobility and social stratification, for both neo-Weberian and neo-Marxist sociologists (see e.g. Murphy, 1986).

The germ of both ideas can be found in the original writings of Marx and Weber: Weber, for example, speaks of the desire of advantaged occupational groups to 'increase their closure and economic security'.

Together, these two concepts of 'closure' and 'reproduction' demand that we integrate our understanding of economic processes that allocate people to certain *positions* in a hierarchy with an understanding that such positions

87

also depend on people's perception of class, their sense of class culture, the culturally perceived 'pecking order' – the higher reaches of which are humorously caught by Les Dawson's commentary that heads this chapter. Moreover, just as the empirical data on social inequality that were presented in Chapter 2 could be usefully explained through a *combination* of Marxist and Weberian theories, in this chapter, the concepts of closure and reproduction also help to bring Marxist and Weberian approaches together, this time for the analysis of the dynamics of class. Let us now examine these concepts in more detail.

Social closure

This refers to the sense in which any particular social class is 'closed off' from any other(s). Is, for example, the upper class easily penetrated by the upwardly mobile middle classes? If it is not, then we can say that the upper class enjoys a high degree of social closure relative to classes below. Alternatively, one could ask whether the working class *suffer* social closure inasmuch as its members find upward mobility into the ranks of the middle class exceptionally difficult. Social closure can then imply the capacity a class has to defend its interests (as for the upper class) or a condition of being 'enclosed' disadvantageously (as for the working class). Broadly speaking, the less social closure there is, the less cohesive the social class grouping will be.

Reproduction

This refers to the conditions which work to maintain the cohesion of classes over time, from one generation to the next. While closure refers to the relative degree of openness of different classes, reproduction refers to the *economic and cultural resources that classes use* to sustain themselves. Property inheritance, for new generations of the upper class, for example, is clearly a vital economic resource that is crucial to the reproduction of this class over time. A subordinate class, such as the working class will, by definition, be low on economic resources and this will reproduce its subordination; but it may also possibly generate a collective ethic to cope with adverse circumstances and so reproduce itself in this way according to a common cultural identity. Where the conditions for such cultural reproduction are missing, perhaps because the occupational and residential communities have been dispersed, then the social cohesion of the class becomes more difficult to sustain.

Broadly speaking, therefore, these two terms help us to define class boundaries and to see how they are sustained (or not) by the action of classes themselves within an economic system. This dynamic process of class reproduction is also known by the term 'class structuration', again an idea drawing attention to the fact that class exists by virtue of the creative agency of social actors as much as by any determination of the workings of the economic system. That is, structuration refers to the process by which classes become reproduced as real 'lived' entities, together with the way in which their structure is changed over time by social processes.

This chapter will examine the 'structuration' of the three principal classes in capitalist society. Some of this discussion will refer to the material inequalities between classes – income and wealth differences, for example – so the reader should bear in mind the very detailed evidence for this that was presented in Chapter 2. The terms social closure and social reproduction will be used to frame the debate in the following fashion: each class is examined:

(i)   In terms of its degree of social closure;
(ii) Its development as a class historically;
(iii) Its current reproductive capacity as a social group;
(iv) Its future prospects.

Specific debates about the character of class, class boundaries and changes in the class structure are contained within this framework.

It is, of course, of great social and political importance that we examine the constitution and reproduction of social classes. Many studies of voting behaviour, educational achievement, urban development and so on, have in the past reflected the reasonable assumption that the social boundaries between the classes have been fairly clear. They also, understandably, portrayed the British class structure as one which, despite evident inequality, had rested on a well-developed social consensus (see Parkin, 1971). This unequal but in general legitimated social hierarchy had depended on a healthy capitalist economy and benign, prosperous welfare State. But this past decade has seen fundamental changes in the British economic and political scene that have made the provision of social and economic resources more difficult: what affect could this have on the class structure?

The 1970s and 1980s have seen a series of fundamental economic problems beset not only British but also international capitalism. While capitalist states elsewhere have had to deal with high levels of inflation, balance of payment crises, low productivity and increasing demands put on State expenditure, Britain has had to respond not only to these problems but also to a decline in its manufacturing base: profits from industry have not gone back in sufficient volume to sustain the long-term investment in new technology that Britain has needed. As productivity declined and inflation rose, the State under Conservative rule responded with a monetarist policy, the effect of which over the period 1979–86 took unemployment from about 1.5 million to almost 4 million. More people were out of work in 1986 than in the worst years of the 1930s and long-term or 'structural' unemployment is increasingly common. The era of 'full employment' has clearly gone, and the economic depression is now reflected in the personal depression, anxiety and illness that unemployment is increasingly producing. Yet there is also evidence to suggest that those at work in solid middle class jobs are enjoying unprecedented high levels of pay.

This period has seen capitalism shake out labour in such a way as to decimate the working class, now much smaller, living in decaying urban areas, with little chance of upward mobility, and yet create the conditions for a relatively secure middle class. The social cost of these processes, added to by government policies, has been said to be the end of 'consensus politics' and a turning away from the notion that the social hierarchy can be perceived to be legitimate. The 1980s have seen an increasing North–South regional polarisation, a de-industrialisation of the old heartlands of British industry so great that one can understand why it has been said that the working class have a nostalgia for industry, a decline in welfare provision for those most in need, a redistribution of taxation in favour of the well-off and – as distressingly revealed during the miners' strike of 1984–5 – the growth of a national paramilitary form of policing acting on behalf of a government determined to weaken trade unionism while British capitalism restructures itself.

In this context what do the simple 'upper', 'middle' and 'working' class designations mean? If unemployment continues to rise will there be any working class left? What will de-industrialisation mean for other social groups? Can there remain any public consensus on the social structure if divisions between the well-off and the poor widen? With such questions in mind we can now look at the 'structuration' of each class in turn, starting with the upper class.

3.2   THE UPPER CLASS

Classes have their fullest social significance when their members share a sense of common social identity and 'separateness' from other social classes. The upper class has clear distinctive characteristics which give it such a sense of identity: not only its ownership of productive property (the fundamental and defining feature) but also its distinctive culture and status hierarchy. Indeed, the divisions within the class are as striking as the features which separate it from the middle class. The explicit status distinctions within it (epitomised in the ranks of peerages and titles) are central to upper-class culture and form part of its claim to special superior qualities.

Some might argue that there is a contradiction between our definition of the upper class (based on Marxist theory) and our use of Weberian concepts such as status and social closure. Despite Parkin's (1979) hostility to newer Marxist class theories, his elaboration of the nature and process of social closure seems compatible with basic Marxian economic class theory. We suggest through this chapter that the use of such concepts is essential for understanding the social processes through which classes are reproduced as social groups.

The dominant classes of different nations have their own unique histories and characteristics which are not simply reducible to the economic position they all have in common. No history of the 'peculiarities of the English' can be generalised to other bourgeoisies elsewhere, but a detailed account of this class will show the kind of analysis which could be applied to others. We shall see that the principal peculiarity of the English upper class is the survival of cultural and status characteristics from stages before industrial capitalism, and the continued dominance of non-industrial capital in powerful circles.

The reproduction of this integration and cohesion, despite all the changes in the upper class and its membership, will be the focus of our discussion.

The development of the upper class

The British monarchy, and the survival of aristocratic titles dating back to the Norman conquest lend a spurious sense of continuity to English history (if not to that of the other countries in the UK), suggesting that feudalism imperceptibly evolved into modern capitalist democracy. Institutions may retain the same appearance while transforming their character – a truism pertinent to both monarchy and parliament. This 'ancient heritage' may seem to be a purely ideological device – but it is more than just a myth. The very anachronisms of British institutions reflect some of the compromises that have shaped the British upper class.

The medieval class system was imposed on England by the Normans but this imposition of feudal ranks and hierarchies of allegiance was never complete and proved relatively shortlived. But the power of the feudal barons was real enough in military, economic and political terms; with no unified state controlling military power, competing armies could vie for control. The exalted status of peers such as the Duke of Norfolk is a faint echo of this power in the land.

At a relatively early stage in England – the Black Death in the fourteenth century is one marker – feudal relations in the countryside began to make way for wage labour and the beginnings of a market in land as a commodity. The land enclosures and dispersal of monastic estates during Tudor times hastened this commercialisation. Slowly there emerged the rural three-class system which reached its apogee in the eighteenth century: aristocratic landowners could live in civilised leisure from the rents of tenant farmers who in turn employed landless wage-workers.

The urban guilds and merchants steadily advanced in wealth and power, and began to spawn a top bourgeoisie of financiers and international traders who could help the landowners to invest their surplus capital profitably. By the eighteenth century the colonies and their associated slave trade, followed by greater investment opportunities at home, allowed the development of a highly wealthy and powerful establishment linking land, finance and commerce. Important families grew out of brewing, for example, linking agricultural production to the financial system which channelled the profits. This rapidly changing eighteenth-century upper class reaped the rewards of the political settlement hard-won in 1688 after civil war and the interregnum. Commercial and political freedom liberated the commercialised aristocracy and gentry to establish oligarchy in parliament and stately-home civility in the countryside. The symbols of lordly status were mobilised to cloak commercialism and to reinforce a hierarchy of status and power from major landowning Dukes down to the lesser gentry with smaller landholdings. A culture of gentility and manners was based on profit from rent and colonial investments. In no sense was this upper class anti-capitalist; but their values related to forms of profit far removed from the dirty details of production.

An inexhaustible debate surrounds the transformations of the upper class in the nineteenth century. From one angle, the expansion of Northern industry, the Repeal of the Corn Laws, the expansion of the suffrage to new well-off groups in 1832, and above all the rise of Liberal politics and competitive free-trade, all point to the predominance of industrial capital. But the relative decline of industry since 1870 in terms of its dynamism compared with international rivals, has prompted an opposite interpretation (see, for example, Hobsbawm, 1968 and Nairn, 1981, Ch. 1). On this view industry found itself subordinated to older sections of the upper class both economically and culturally. As Nairn put it, the late nineteenth century witnessed 'first the containment, then the defeat, of industrialism by an older, more powerful and more political bourgeoisie' (cited in Coates, 1984, p. 117). It is strongly argued by Rubinstein (1976) and others that establishment institutions revitalised themselves in this period to absorb and assimilate the new capitalists into older values and older structures of influence. Landowners invested in mining and railways, while industrialists bought land, secured lordly titles and sent their sons to the expanded public schools to be turned into gentlemen. All this aided, these writers argue, a merger of the three leading sections of the bourgeoisie – land, finance and industry. This occurred within firms through directorships and through families by intermarriage. The influx of new upper-class members underlying these changes led to social innovations such as published listings of the gentry and members of 'Society' (Scott, 1982, p. 90, citing Davidoff), which were a blatant example of social closure in their regulation of social acceptability and status among the propertied.

Rubinstein argues that the outcome of these processes, by 1914, was resolution of the competition for wealth, status and power by the collapse of the three old elites [land, finance and industry] and their merger into one elite, dominated by the South of England and finance, with its London-based associates of great influence in twentieth-century society, like the Civil Service and the professions, the familiar 'establishment' of fact and fiction (quoted in Coates, 1984, p. 117).

The fate of twentieth-century Britain has been shaped to a considerable extent by this economic and political dominance of financial capital, as we emphasise in Chapter 6 on Power and Politics. Even though the merger of these sections of capital has brought industry and finance closer together, especially through directors who sit on the boards of both industrial firms and financial institutions, the affect seems to have often been stultifying for the manufacturer. This effect may come partly through economic calculations not favouring risk-taking, and partly through the broader anti-entrepreneurial ethos of the upper class. Leys (1983) gives a clear analysis of Britain's problems in such terms.

These characteristics help to support popular notions of the upper class as 'the aristocracy' – landowners with titles ranked below the monarchy –or as an 'establishment' where elite individuals man (*sic*) core traditional institutions in order to effectively control the country. There is much residual truth in these popular conceptions and we shall find them useful, subject to some refinement. John Scott's clear and comprehensive studies of the upper class will form one main basis for our account (Scott, 1982); following him, we can regard the establishment as a dominant status group within the upper class which uses kinship links and social networks of contacts to retain its hold on social and political influence. As Scott argues:

> This status group – the establishment – emerged as an important social and political force during the nineteenth century and has been seen as a central element in the 'antique' or 'patrician' character of the British state ... [I]t facilitates communication amongst those who are familiar with one another, share a common background and meet in numerous formal and informal contexts (1982, pp. 158–9).

Scott lists the key institutions of this group as the Conservative Party, the Church of England, the public schools and ancient universities, the legal profession, Guards regiments, London clubs and country-house life (1982, p. 159). The core families are linked by intermarriage, private schooling and social contacts through business and leisure. Referring to the propertied as the 'business class', he illustrates how (1982, p. 149):

> The establishment has successfully monopolised the major positions within the state and the social institutions allied to the state, and it has exercised a pervasive influence over those outside its own ranks. The structuration of the business class as a whole has, to a considerable extent, been determined by the hegemony [dominance] within it of the establishment families. As a result the business class as a whole exhibits a high degree of integration and social cohesion ...

The preservation of a pseudo-aristocratic culture within the upper class has been emphasised by many authors as a source of Britain's weakness. Nairn (1981) and Weiner (1981) have argued from very different political positions that this culture together with the predominance of financial capital has undermined British industry. According to Nairn, the unequal merger of different sections of capital led to:

> the containment of capitalism within a patrician hegemony [ideological dominance] which never, either then or since, actively favoured the aggressive development of industrialism or the general conversion of society to the latter's values and interests (1981, p. 32).

It is important not to confuse this anti-industrialism with anti-capitalism; Britain's dominant culture could hardly be more imbued with capitalistic values of property and profit. Even so, Weiner provides a graphic account of the character of this dominant culture – the disdain for trade or manufacture, the cult of countryside and garden, the grip of Southern culture and conservative notions of historical 'heritage'. The myths of continuity and harmonious inequality all persist more comfortably well away from industry or the inner city. Current attempts to promote more energetic competition and entrepreneurial risk swim against the dominant tide of upper-class values, which continue to be reproduced.

Reproduction of the upper class

We can identify social mechanisms which secure the transfer of upper-class privilege across generations, transmitting both economic and cultural capital and perhaps also political influence. We saw in the previous chapter how productive property is inherited and distributed amongst kin, and how the patterns of wealth ownership have changed over time. This transfer of wealth forms the foundation for the other aspects we discuss here.

Control of kinship linkages lies at the heart of privileged class reproduction. Simple images of marriage as a matter for individuals, based on romantic love, are seriously misleading when property inheritance and class culture are at stake (Lupton and Wilson, 1959). There are powerful pressures for homogamy (marriage within the class or status group) for these reasons; equally, a strategic marriage can bolster aristocratic wealth or consolidate the status of new wealth. This high level of homogamy converts the upper class from a mere social category (albeit with an economic reality) into an intermarrying group aware of its own social boundaries. (Castes are another example of such closed status groups.)

The importance of reproducing cultural capital cannot be overstated. So long as recruitment to privileged positions depends upon connections, values and demeanour as well as formal qualifications, then elite education will play a key role. The evidence on the over-representation of public school old boys in elite positions is both familiar and overwhelming (e.g. Stanworth and Giddens, 1974). Their advantages come not just through enhanced examination success – the grammar schools achieved that. The social exclusivity of private education enables a distinct 'superior' culture to remain intact, and ensures that this world-view is displayed with the self-assurance and 'soundness' that is valued by those recruiting entrants to elite occupations (the elite-educated spies Burgess and Maclean are notorious for having exploited this trust). In addition it must be acknowledged that the public schools have adapted to the demand for scientific and managerial graduates by modernising their range of subjects and strengthening their science teaching. As a result their ex-pupils may compete better for those elite jobs which demand scientific credentials, while retaining the general socialisation we have described.

These privileges extend across a wide range of positions even outside the core institutions of the establishment. Whitley found that 'one-half of the directors of the largest industrial companies were former public schoolboys with one-sixth coming from Eton alone' (Scott, 1982, p. 173). Among clearing banks (the big high-street names) and insurance companies the proportion of public-school products among directors actually rose from half in 1957 to three-quarters in 1970. Among the judiciary, 52 per cent of judges had lawyer fathers and four-fifths attended public school (Scott, 1982, p. 171).

Otley found that a rising proportion of senior army officers had elite educational backgrounds. The qualities of leadership sought by selectors seem to be more readily identified among public-school candidates (Salaman and Thompson, 1978).

It is possible to question the force of such evidence – perhaps school has no independent effect and we are simply seeing a side-effect of class-biased recruitment. This is too simple, because elite education does shape its clients, especially the newer entrants to the class who need shaping into 'gentlemen'. All education has informal as well as formal content, and elite routes generate cultural capital through the 'social and cultural unity among those who possess superior life chances' (Scott, 1982, p. 162).

Weiner (1981, Ch. 2) provides a graphic account of the creation of a renewed public school ethos from the 1860s. This ethos was overwhelmingly aristocratic or professional in tone, denigrating economically 'productive' forms of knowledge in favour of the classics and civilising humanities subjects. Science subjects and laboratories were almost entirely absent, and applied science was the province of artisan workers, not gentlemen. The non-academic curriculum of sport and the arts, as well as the total immersion through boarding in an enclosed culture, were crucial in the broader socialisation that was wholly deliberate. New entrants to the upper class were made civilised and imbued with an ethos which extolled administrative and professional qualities rather than inventiveness or entrepreneurship. Weiner regards this as irrational and a root of Britain's weakness; in fact these values fit closely with the dominance of other kinds of capitalistic activity in land, finance and empire.

One final aspect of the reproduction of upper-class identity deserves mention. Part of the role of the monarchy is to head and legitimate a ranking of titles and honours which reflects and codifies degrees of status within the establishment. The honours system symbolises social superiority while also acting as a social discipline on upper-class members who wish to retain or enhance their standing (as with public employees seeking lesser honours). In addition, this system inserts a non-democratic forum – the House of Lords – into the heart of the state as a bulwark against radical change.

The changing nature of capital

Changes in the structure of economic enterprises and their patterns of ownership are two dimensions of the constant restless dynamism of capitalist economies. Structures of control and ownership are inevitably affected by the rise of giant corporations and by the growth of financial institutions such as investment trusts and pension funds. Not surprisingly, ownership has become less personal or familial, but this does not imply that enterprises have become any less capitalistic as a result. Nor does it mean that the new controllers are any less constrained by the pressures of markets and profitability than old-style entrepreneurs. Indeed, it is often claimed that some family firms preferred to avoid being profit-maximisers and take a safe return from past investments. Other family-run firms have remained dynamic (e.g. Marks & Spencer) but wealthy individuals today are more likely to spread their investments with the aid of financial institutions. By 1981, personal shareholdings held 28 per cent of the value of British enterprises, while financial institutions held 58 per cent. These institutions not only mobilise the assets of the wealthy, but also bring together the pension contributions and life assurance premiums of millions of others. (Scott, 1982, p. 78). Simultaneous with this is the trend toward control of companies through minority shareholdings; holders of minority stakes (including individuals, financial institutions and other companies) can potentially band together to form a controlling 'constellation of interests'. Scott's research show that among the top 250 British enterprises in 1976, 43 were controlled by personal shareholders, 71 by corporate owners, and 110 by a mixture (Scott, 1985, p. 77). Does this mean that the upper class no longer controls the wealth that it owns?

This question echoes the old debates over the so-called 'managerial revolution' (Burnham, Berle and Means) where salaried personnel were seen to take over the running of firms. Some extended the argument to claim that this produced a less capitalistic 'soulful corporation' (Kaysen).

Such arguments have serious weaknesses. Quite apart from the fact that managers do not dominate the board of directors in many firms, there is every reason to believe that corporate managers are under intense pressure (from the markets, and from the need to deliver profits) to behave capitalistically. It is also seriously misleading to lump together all managers as members of a 'technocracy' of experts and professionals. Those at the top, on or near the board of directors, may exercise strategic control over investment and planning of markets and products. These strategic positions are not filled by just another group of salaried employees. They act, in Scott's phrase (1982, p. 125), as 'internal capitalists'; even if they do not hold major shareholdings their rewards are closely tied to company profitability. In 1972, found Heller (1973), 45 per cent of the directors of Britain's top 200 firms owned substantial shareholdings in the firm. In addition, senior executives are largely drawn from the same narrow background as company directors.

The degree of social closure of the upper class is considerably enhanced by the extensive networks of interlocking directorships. Directors are especially valued if they are also on the boards of other organisations, and these interlocks bridge the worlds of manufacturing, banking and investment institutions. Such linkages facilitate business transactions and partly offset differences of interests between, say, manufacturers and banks. This commercial network is greatly strengthened by shared social and cultural identities – and the unity of the upper class is further reinforced as these links are utilised. Recent research has found that among the top 250 British firms, 77 have six or more interlocks to other organisations, while 112 have one to five interlocks. Out of the 2682 directors of these firms, 195 have two directorships and 87 have three or more. These 282 men are at the core of British capital (Scott and Griff, 1984, tables 2.7 and 6.3).

The future of the upper class

The most recent trends in British capital suggest that the economic basis for cultural unity within the upper class is being steadily undermined. The relentless pace of internationalisation in the economy has speeded up in the 1980s. Manufacturers based in the British market have generally been hard-hit; the penetration by foreign products and incoming foreign producers has never been greater. The financial world in the City of London has been transformed by the massive influx of foreign banks, together with the establishment of major new markets, especially in dollars. It is increasingly difficult for the establishment elites to retain dominance over all this new activity, even if they still have charge of the key institutions such as the Bank of England. It seems likely that the British-based institutions will do their best to retain their old class character whilst co-opting new expert personnel and new methods of operation in order to remain competitive

Some of the key linkages among the Directors of British companies are outlined in Figure 3.1.

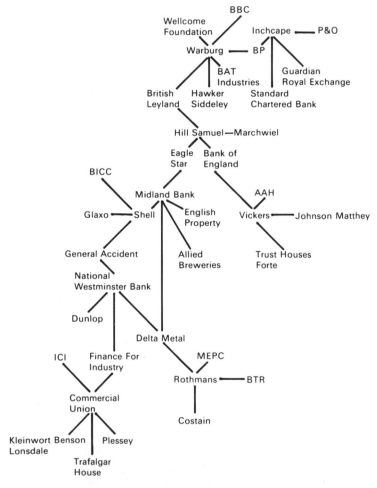

Source: J. Scott in D. Coates *et al.* (eds), *A Socialist Anatomy of Britain*, Cambridge, Polity Press. (1985) p.45.

FIGURE 3.1　*Interlocking directorships*

with the newcomers. Full assimilation of them into the old upper class would seem unlikely.

Whatever may be changing in the field of production and finance, the distinctive patterns of upper-class consumption, education and social contracts are thriving. If anything, the wealthy have become less shy of displaying their privilege in recent years. As we saw earlier, trends in elite recruitment show no sign of reflecting the increase in qualified candidates from outside the ancient universities and public schools. Even areas of influence beyond the core of the establishment – the media and advertising, for example, show clear signs of favouring privileged candidates for entry, and their patterns of ownership have many links to other areas of capital. Even if the rise of new politicians in the Conservative Party has displaced some elite 'grandees', they are overwhelmingly recruited from business and the professions, and still mostly have privileged origins.

Thus the upper class shows no sign of weakening culturally or politically, even if its economic base is once more in a state of change. In the absence of any serious challenge to the wealth and institutions that reproduce them, the upper class will survive, adapt and thrive.

Class boundaries and the upper class

The problem of defining a cut-off line (or boundary) between the upper class and the upper middle class has been a highly contested sociological topic. Of course, if it were simply a matter of agreeing on an arbitrary definition, there would be little problem. The issue really concerns whether we can capture the point where social reality actually alters so that people either side of that line have structurally different resources and social relations.

In our discussion of the classic class theories in the previous chapter, we argued that there was a degree of common ground between Marxist and Weberian approaches. They could both accept that the upper class should be defined, first and foremost, by its possession of productive capital. Much of the evidence cited so far in this section has derived from the research of John Scott, who adopts a self-consciously Weberian approach. The merit of this, as we have seen, is that we are led to examine the ways in which this 'objective' economic class comes to persist and reproduce itself as a self-consciously 'lived' social entity. Through this account we have found deliberate boundaries created by class members through their claims to status and their strategies of social closure. It is clear that the core of the upper class certainly do differentiate themselves from the broader middle class, even if it suits them to call themselves 'middle class' when asked. But there are significant areas of apparent overlap – what of highly-paid managers, or top professionals who amass personal property and perhaps own their firm or clinic? Criteria based on lifestyle and consumption begin to fail us, and the property/lack of property yardstick is hazy at the margin.

One solution to this problem of where to draw the boundaries between classes derives from recent neo-Marxist theories. Writers such as Carchedi, Wright and Poulantzas have been less concerned with culture or status and more concerned with objective economic relationships. That is, they stress the position of a person as producer rather than consumer, and in particular they emphasise the degree of control a producer has over other workers, and over the production process. We cannot go into detail on these various theories, but we can draw upon their emphasis on the 'functions of capital' performed by those with strategic control over the enterprise and significant control (directly or indirectly) over subordinate employees. Such top managers should be regarded as part of the capitalist class since their position is qualitatively different from other employees. The broader ranks of managerial and professional employees have a degree of autonomy in their work, a degree of decision-making responsibility, and a certain amount of control over others. But they are still highly circumscribed in their authority, and wholly dependent upon their salaried employment. For these reasons, Erik Wright (1985) regards the very top managers as having a class position among the capitalist (upper) class, while the managerial and professional middle class occupy 'contradictory class locations' combining some elements of capitalistic control with other elements of proletarian dependence.

Whatever the merits of this analysis of the structural location of people in production, these positions can only form a foundation for the processes of status, closure and reproduction which transform these structural relationships into a lived reality of social divisions. This is the process of 'structuration' which can be observed so clearly among the British upper class, as we have argued through this section. We can now move on to analyse the middle class and the varied strata within it in terms of this dynamic of structuration.

3.3   THE MIDDLE CLASS

Social closure

It is noted in Figure 3.2 that the social closure of the middle class is comparatively weak, especially compared with that of the upper class. The diversity of groups that make up the middle class has led some sociologists to speak of the middle classes. Indeed, we shall shortly be discussing some differences between the 'old' and the 'new' middle class and between the 'established' and 'marginal' middle class.

Nevertheless there is some sense of boundary, of a discrete class identity to the middle class: if there were not, we would be in the analytically weak position of saying that the middle class is simply made up of those who 'came somewhere around the middle'. We saw in the previous section that there is a qualitative break between the upper class and the broader middle class in terms of the former's access to, ownership of and strategic control over capital. Where, though, do we draw the lower boundaries of the middle-class'?

Distinctive aspects of the middle class

There are, broadly speaking, two distinctive dimensions of the middle class that mark it off from the working class.

First, there is a significant break, not merely quantitatively but also qualitatively, between the middle and the working classes, in terms of their respective levels of pay, its status as a 'salary' as opposed to a 'wage', the life-cycle of their earnings, work conditions and their respective ownership of marketable wealth holding (e.g. owner-occupied housing). These material advantages of middle class occupations are a precondition for (though not necessarily a guarantee of) its ability to reproduce itself as a class: we note later how the middle class can rely on an income transfer to its children to promote their careers and so retain the family's class position over time. This has been well documented by Bell (1968). Moreover, as Bain and Price (1972) have argued, the occupations of middle-class employees have or are associated with positions of authority: much non-manual work, even that which is fairly routine, is or is typically perceived to be superior to manual work and perhaps enjoys a 'staff' status. It is also the case that a typical feature of established middle-class work is that it embodies a 'career', a structure of occupational opportunities that imply promotion and increasing security in some sort of orderly progression. The work life-cycle of the working class is in contrast typically careerless and often disjointed reflecting vulnerability in the labour market.

Secondly, the middle class possesses significantly higher levels of training and education, its so-called 'cultural capital', used most effectively by the 'new' middle class, the professionals, administrators and managers. Halsey (1980) shows how from secondary through to further and higher education, the structure of opportunities for educational achievement and advancement favour the sons and daughters of the middle class. Educational expansion since 1945 has, it is true, benefited all social classes but, even during the comprehensive schooling programme of more recent years, a middle-class background was more likely than not to be a significant cultural resource for children.

Before we look at the problems of social closure and reproduction for the middle class we shall briefly examine its development, for in its history lie the reasons for its weak social closure.

The development of the middle class

One can trace the roots of the middle class back to the eighteenth century for it was from then that we see an acceleration of two processes crucial to the modernisation of British society, and thereby to the development of the middle class. These were the gradual emergence of a modern nation State and the onset of industrial capitalism. Both developments stimulated an evergrowing demand (especially during the eighteenth and nineteenth centuries) for people to work for the State as 'public servants', to work for industry as managers, administrators and supervisors, and to act as independent professionals – accountants, lawyers, engineers, medics, and so on – for both the emerging State and industry.

Those who occupied these positions did not come from as singular a source as their upper-class superiors. This was in part because there were as yet no evident social credentials for being respectably 'middle class'. So, for example, in the seventeenth and eighteenth centuries there was continual dispute about those who should be recognised as 'professionals', as experts who could advise clients. This was more true of some areas of work than others, medicine being a particularly good example of a contested occupational arena.

Broadly speaking, those groups who have over the last four hundred years come to deserve the title the 'established' middle class are those that have either managed to monopolise an occupational expertise and control its supply and regulate its demand (e.g. the legal or medical professions) or who have performed a senior managerial function for State or industry.

This established middle class can be seen to have grown in two distinct phases reflecting the changing demands of State and industry. The first phase, lasting, say, between the late seventeenth and nineteenth centuries saw the consolidation of what can now be called the 'old' established middle class by two broad social groups who came to enjoy considerable social status, high income and considerable political influence: these were the *traditional professions*, growing in size and importance as the demand for their services grew, and the new breed of *civil servants* administering the increasingly complex institutions of government. The increasing strength of the civil service meant that its members became less dependent on the particular government of the day for the security of their jobs. Public administration became, and still remains, a vital source of employment for the aspiring middle class. The growth of the civil service and the independent professions was helped from the mid-nineteenth century onwards by the public and private sectors' demand for skilled personnel in the colonies. Doctors, engineers and administrators were all needed in considerable numbers.

A distinctive cultural feature that unites these two wings of the older established middle class is their occupational claim that education has given them a 'trained mind' and sense of independent judgement. It is this claim that lies at the heart of the occupational ideology of professions who present themselves as groups in the 'service' of clients. The ideology of professionalism and the occupational strategies associated with it whereby a group strives after a collective upward social mobility are discussed in Chapter 9. What is important to note here is the *political* legacy that this orientation has created among the established middle class. Their putative independence or autonomy from their employers – the State or private business – has created an attitude amongst them of liberalism, social reform, fair mindedness and perhaps a charitable support for the less advantaged. At the same time, however, the established middle class has always sought to defend its territory, its degree of social closure, from usurpation or encroachment from below, from the working class. These potentially conflicting attitudes have historically been resolved among the middle class by its adoption of consensus politics, a social welfarism that supports the 'underdog' without harming its own interests. The result is that the class is most anxious to avoid social conflict, particularly during times of serious economic decline. The recent growth of the SDP/Liberal Alliance in Britain is indicative of this process, dominated as it is by the established middle class keen to check the confrontational politics of Thatcherism. At such times the appeal to a broad community of interest is made; witness the following clarion call to a 'tradition' of unity made recently in the quality British press:

> What are the essentials of that tradition? A citizenship based on a reciprocity of rights and duties. A commitment to reform without the pain of revolution. A belief in the progress of mankind, in harmony with the improvement of the individual ... A sense of public service as a moral responsibility, and so of the State and community as moral institutions. (*Times Higher Educational Supplement*, 1986)

This could have been written a century ago and has no doubt been heard time and again in middle-class circles.

The second phase in the development of the established middle class can be dated from the late nineteenth century onwards, with the growth of a range of new occupations in the non-manual sector as part of the growth of capitalist corporations and the emergence of new industries based on the development of science and technology (e.g. the chemical industry). There were not enough children from the older middle class to fill these positions. One reason for this was, of course, the demographic impact of the First World War: the war decimated a whole generation of middle-class off-spring serving as officers at the front. As a result, after the war we saw the consolidation and expansion of a 'new' middle class, that is new professional, salaried groups working in administration, banking or business recruited in part from an increasingly educated and mobile *working class*.

The post-1945 growth in the public sector gave further impetus to this process of creating this so-called 'new', established middle class. In addition, the post-war saw the rapid growth of a lower middle class of white-collar workers servicing industry and government in routine administration (see below). Many of these, too, have been recruited from the working class.

The middle class has become increasingly complex carrying within it the old and new established sections enjoying considerable material and cultural advantage along with a less secure, less favoured mass of white-collar workers many recruited from a working-class background. To these we should add the artisanal, self-employed group of workers – Marx's 'petit bourgeoisie' – the shopkeepers, skilled craftsmen and women in own business establishments, and so on, all of whom can be placed in a rather precarious position economically as they are marginal to both the primary labour market and the centres of capitalist investment.

Figure 3.2 gives a brief outline of the four main sections of the middle class.

	Old	New
Established	Traditional professionals	Modern salariat, senior management
Marginal	Skilled craft workers/artisans	Routine non-manual staff; self-employed

Source: Based on J. H. Goldthorpe, 'Comment', *British Journal of Sociology*, vol. 29(4). (1978).

FIGURE 3.2   *Who are the middle class?*

Reproduction of the middle class

We saw earlier that the reproductive capacity of the middle class and thereby its capacity for social closure depends on the material and cultural advantages that a relatively higher income and educational training bring. However, it is suggested that the middle class's ability to reproduce itself is constrained and thus so is its social closure. Why is this so?

While it is true that the growth of education and the expansion of non-manual jobs have favoured middle class offspring, the fact is that training and non-manual job opportunities have grown at a much faster rate than the supply of children from the established middle class. The traditional professions (doctors, lawyers, accountants, etc.) still recruit new members from solid middle-class families. Data show, however, that the massive post-war growth in administrative and managerial posts has called on a much wider recruiting base to include substantial members from the working class. And Goldthorpe (1972) has shown that many of these new middle class do not have the cultural capital typical of their more established peers.

These processes have two significant affects on the cohesiveness of the middle class. First, given the importance of education today for access to established middle-class positions, even though the educational system favours middle-class children, there is no *guarantee* that they will do well. Thus their failure may lead to downward mobility into a marginal middle class or even working-class position, despite the fact that they might still see themselves as solidly middle class. Secondly, the upwardly mobile children of the working class act to weaken the tendency towards the formation of a cultural, normative homogeneity throughout the middle class. The middle classes today do not enjoy sufficient social closure to ensure their 'cultural unity'.

Nevertheless, for both old and new members of the established middle class, the advantages of high income and professional status are translated into the trappings of solid middle-class respectability – the costly suburban semi, cleaning woman, childminder, new car or two, and so on. The residential area is typically quite separate from that of the working class or ethnic minorities. Their children will attend the local independent grammar or usually more distant public school except those whose parents – perhaps because they themselves work in public sector employment – are committed to a State education for their children.

The reproduction of this sector of the middle class is secure for the time being. There are increasing anxieties though about cutbacks in government expenditure since 1979 which have threatened and actually brought unemployment to senior personnel in the educational, scientific, medical and bureaucratic sectors of State employment. Similarly, cuts in educational provision at further and higher levels have created considerable problems for middle-class parents keen to ensure that their children have the opportunity to gain the cultural capital needed to secure a career in the salaried professions.

The marginal middle class: the proletarianisation of white-collar work?

While the established middle class can sustain itself effectively, the marginal middle class occupies a more precarious structural position in the social hierarchy of capitalism. What this position actually is has been a matter of considerable debate among sociologists: one key question is, have lower-level non-manual workers – clerks, secretarial staff, technicians, and so on – been subject to a wholesale downgrading, a collective downward mobility over the past such that their boundary with the working class is not merely blurred but actually broken. Have routine non-manual workers become 'proletarianised'? It is important to note that while in 1851 there were only about 60,000 clerks, all male working in small-scale 'professional' settings (merchant houses, banks, solicitors, etc.), by 1981 there were about 13 million clerks and associated office, retail and 'personal service' staff made up of both men and women and found in a wide range of work settings but particularly large scale, impersonalised office blocks attached to industrial enterprise (State and private) and the national Welfare State sectors of employment. Many of these workers are on relatively low pay, have little chance of a career and very limited cultural capital. To what extent are these 'marginal' middle class, 'really' no different from the working class?

Lockwood's (1958) now classic study of clerical work was the first to examine this question in detail. He argues that changes have occurred in some important respects. The most important of these is that the clerks' work situation has become bureaucratised: their tasks are now subject to impersonal, bureaucratic rules and conditions of service that can make their work routine and lacking in any responsibility. Nevertheless, Lockwood argues that clerks still enjoy a better status position and career potential and culturally have a strong identification with management. In short, he feels that this job has *not* been 'proletarianised'.

Lockwood's study has more recently been given support by Goldthorpe *et al.* (1980). They argue that there has been a large increase in routine non-manual work largely made up of clerical employees in administration and commerce, sales personnel and other rank and file staff. They also accept that many have much lower income than those in more senior posts and sometimes *lower* than some *manual* workers.

However, they argue that they have (i) high job security, (ii) enjoy 'staff' status and (iii) are 'functionally associated with but marginal to the established white-collar service class'.

Goldthorpe sees them as constituting part of an *intermediate class*, a 'white-collar labour force', in between the established service class and the working class. He argues then that they are not proletarianised and also notes that they are unlikely to form any clear class identity or consciousness, in part because there is considerable horizontal mobility within the wide range of jobs that make up this strata, and because it has a fluctuating membership as people may take this type of work for short periods or as part-time work.

Comment

There are at least three points that need to be made in response to Lockwood and Goldthorpe's position.

(a) As Kelly (1984) notes they have failed to take proper account of the growth of broad based trade unions which incorporate both blue *and* white-collar workers (e.g. NUPE, GMWU, etc.) which have a much stronger sense of class or at least occupational consciousness, particularly in the public sector, than Lockwood and Goldthorpe's analyses would envisage.

(b) While recognising the increasing number of women in white-collar jobs, both accounts fail to examine the *specific disadvantages* experienced by women – in terms of pay, career prospects, decision-making powers – compared with their male counterparts. According to Heath and Britten (1984) one finds that there are many women in routine non-manual jobs who cannot be differentiated from women in *manual* work in terms of pay security, conditions, etc. and so have to be seen as occupying a *'fundamentally proletarian market position'*.

(c) The strongest attack on Lockwood's (and by implication Goldthorpe's) position came from Braverman (1974). His basic thesis is that all work in capitalist society is subject to a process of *de-skilling* – an incessant lowering of workers skills, to cheapen their labour, make them easily replaceable, remove their control over the execution of their tasks allowing the increasing introduction of machinery. This process affects both manual and non-manual work. Thus, for Braverman, routine white-collar workers have joined the mass of unskilled employees 'assigned a series of simple unchanged operations'. As such *they are part of the working class, they are proletarianised.*

Braverman's ideas have received some support from studies by Crompton and Reid (1983) of the impact of computer technology on white-collar work and elsewhere by Poulantzas (1975) and Wright (1978). However, recent work, while sympathetic to some of his ideas, has challenged the accuracy of the claim that de-skilling is as extensive (or as necessary) a process in capitalism. For example, Crompton and Jones (1984) argue that there is not an 'immense mass of wage workers' in the clerical sector all subject to the same deskilling process: some are better placed than others (see also Chapter 9, pp. 362–7).

Conclusion

It would seem that in order to make sense of this debate we have to recognise that: (i) life-chances *have* worsened for routine clerical workers, and that (ii) this is particularly true for those in the part-time, cheap labour market; (iii) women are more likely to be subject to 'proletarianisation', but that (iv) even for these, they may not thereby display a strong sense of 'proletarian' consciousness.

The future of the middle class

In general terms, the future of the established middle class seems reasonably secure. There are, of course, anxieties about the current cutbacks in public expenditure which is now beginning to hit professional staff in the public service industries and academia. The 'rationalisation' of business – increasingly associated with mergers and take-overs – often leaves in its wake middle managers, redundant in their forties or fifties for whom similar employment is scarce. Nevertheless, it is likely to be the case that the advantages of the established middle class will be most clearly evident in such periods of recession: their material and cultural resources can be drawn on to stave off the threat of downward mobility that a declining economy encourages. Moreover, so long as educational credentials are important to an industrial society, the middle class will take every opportunity both to promote credentialism and to ensure its children are well-placed to obtain the necessary qualifications.

3.4   THE WORKING CLASS

The working class, and particularly the working-class community, have long been of interest to British sociologists. Much has been written about the 'traditional' working-class culture as well as about the 'new' working class – the more affluent, allegedly more middle class, skilled workers of modern industry. The latter have often been seen as a 'labour aristocracy', a relatively privileged section of skilled workers, developing out of the traditional, proletarian working class. In part this is linked to the debate about the so-called 'embourgeoisement' of manual work, a thesis which had a considerable airing in the late 1950s and 1960s but which, as we shall see, has been shown to be highly suspect.

Before we look at the ways in which sociologists have described and theorised the development of the working class we ought to bear in mind that it has no uniform or homogeneous nature. While the economic structure of capitalism will determine the broad life-chances of all manual work in a roughly equivalent way, the *experiences* of this work, the extent to which it enjoys 'skilled' status and the responses to it vary considerably and produce a richly diverse culture within the working class. Typically, this culture is a product of the experience of disadvantage and in certain circumstances, increasingly common, chronic deprivation.

The reproduction of the working class has two dimensions: first, the class is structurally located in the labour market such that there is little opportunity for it to escape its subordination in the social and material hierarchy of capitalism. Yet, secondly, the common experience of subordination can be a force that produces a whole range of cultural frameworks for interpreting and *drawing on* the experiences of working-class life in order to 'get by', 'make out', or adjust to the situation. Sometimes this may express itself as the culture of working-class 'respectability' (epitomised by the polished front steps), at other times perhaps by the 'masculinity' and toughness of the shop-floor (see Willis, 1979a). At one level such cultural responses act as forms of resistance to subordination, but at another they may well act ritualistically to reproduce that subordination. Let us now examine the development of the working class.

The development of the working class

One simple way of seeing the development of the working class is in terms of its changing leisure patterns, from the pub/music-hall and chapel of the Victorian and Edwardian era to the dance hall and cinema of the 1950s, to the TV and package holiday of today: a shift from a community centred discrete culture in the past to a mass commercialised culture now. This may exaggerate the degree to which working-class community culture has been dissipated, particularly in more ruralised village or town settings where employment and residence may have been relatively constant over the years. However, a number of social commentaries (e.g. Halsey, 1981) highlight this shift to a mass culture away from the 'traditional' values of the working class as the single most important change affecting the cultural reproduction of the working class. Some, such as Hoggart (1958) see this shift as a significant cultural loss: 'the replacement of an urban culture of the people' by a 'less healthy ... mass culture' (p. 24). However one evaluates this change, it is clearly based on the assumption that there was a relatively homogeneous 'traditional' working class which experienced such changes.

There have been a number of important studies of the so-called 'traditional' working-class community (e.g. Young and Willmott, 1962; Williams, 1961; Frankenberg, 1966). One of the most richly detailed studies was by Dennis *et al.* (1956), a survey of a traditional Yorkshire mining town, 'Ashton', that captured the work, leisure and family patterns of a male-dominated community. All the studies give a strong impression of the working-class community as compact, socially and geographically: a close-knit community living and working together. As an example, we can turn to Wild's (1979, p. 276) description of the Lancashire town of Rochdale:

> At the turn of the (20th) century most of Rochdale's occupied population worked in the textile or engineering mills of John Bright, Kelsall and Kemp, Tweedale and Smalley and numerous smaller concerns. The town was very much more compact than now: it centred around Kelsall's mill, the Wellington Hotel and the Town Hall square. The two main shopping streets, filled with mainly local family firms, stretched north and south from the centre. In a roughly circular area, about a mile wide, the majority of the population lived and worked.

Not surprisingly, in such towns most working people shared similar work and leisure experiences though these were usually divided along lines of gender. Yet the notion of a homogeneous working class fails to register the *economic divisions* among manual workers which have often led to bitter rivalry and dispute between sections of organised labour, particularly when there has been a strong demand for workers from local employers.

The view of the 'traditional' working class has been most strongly challenged by Penn (1985). Arguing in favour of a position that sees class and specifically the working class more dynamically, Penn provides evidence to show that there were (and are) divisions within the working class that result in a 'privileged position' for craftsmen in the manual work-force. As he says:

> Skilled manual workers have been separately organised, economically advantaged and permanently concerned with the battle for the continuation of the structural supports of skill which *actively* divides the manual working class at the point of production. (p. 188)

Thus, skill is a resource which manual workers use to actively exercise some degree of control over the labour process. They can, for example, resist management initiatives through ensuring the recognition of *apprenticeship* as an occupational requirement of 'doing the job' – even if the actual task may not require or draw on all that is learned during the period of training.

While divisions within the working class exist as such, Penn does not believe that the advantaged skilled workers constitute a 'new' working class, nor are they to be seen as the leading edge for a wholesale *collective* upward mobility of all the working class through a process of 'embourgeoisement'. Put another way, they have neither established a new discrete boundary for themselves nor do they herald a shift in the boundaries of the entire working class *per se*. Taking the first point, evidence shows that skilled workers *intermarry* with un/semi-skilled households, such that on a *social* level they remain firmly within the working class: as Penn says (1985, p. 189),

> The separate *economic* identity of skilled manual workers has not been translated into equivalent *social* boundaries. The evidence on marital endogamy suggest(s) that *their 'manualness' has been of greater significance for the determination of their social class situation than skill*. Skilled manual workers do not constitute a part either of the middle class or of the lower middle class: they represent a distinct stratum (at the top), of the British manual working class.

On the second point, as is evident in the quote, Penn argues strongly against the thesis that the well-paid skilled worker penetrates the boundaries of the middle class. This claim, strongly advocated as a central tenet of the embourgeoisement thesis, found one of its most telling critiques in the work of Goldthorpe *et al.* (1968) (see below).

The embourgeoisement debate and the affluent worker studies

During the twentieth century, changes in the nature of work (particularly the growth of new, light automated industries), real wage rises for manual workers (up 300 per cent in real terms since 1900), increasing educational opportunity, and a growth in consumerism led some US and European social scientists (e.g. Zweig, 1961; Halmos, 1964), to believe that the improving living standards of the working class were ending class divisions and promoting a collective upwards mobility.

Against this view, popular as it was among academics, politicians and the press, Goldthorpe *et al.* found that manual workers in modern industrial enterprises, though relatively well-paid, had to work exceptionally long hours in very unpleasant circumstances, had little interest in socialising with their middle class co-workers and had lifestyles that were very different from them. The evidence indicates that the overriding majority of the manual workers did not develop social relationships with middle-class individuals. Most associated either with kin or with individuals of a similar socioeconomic status, i.e. fellow manual workers. Only 7 per cent of the sample associated primarily with members of a middle-class status group. This lack of involvement in 'middle-class society' was also exemplified by the type of associations or organisations that the manual workers joined: working men's clubs, allotment associations, angling societies, etc., all noticeably lacking in middle-class membership. Most, in fact, had little desire to join associations likely to have a strong middle-class membership. In short, there was a strong degree of social boundedness between the middle and the working class.

What changes, then, have occurred in the life of the relatively affluent manual worker? The most important development has been the 'privatisation' of the worker and his family with home-centredness consequently amplified: the manual worker's family and its fortunes become his 'central life interest'. Secondly, although unionism is still strong, it expresses an instrumentalist rather than solidaristic orientation: that is, the newly affluent worker is likely to regard the union as the means to a particular end: e.g. he no longer sees union membership as the expression of a strong, ideological, working-class solidarity. Attracted to the Luton firms through higher pay, he joined the unions even though this was not compulsory. These two factors, privatisation and instrumentalism, encourage 'a more individualistic outlook' among the manual workers, with a simultaneous weakening of communal and kin orientations. But this has *not* led to any strong desire to attain and identify with the middle-class life-style and values of the white-collar workers.

Goldthorpe *et al.* argue that the cost to the 'affluent' worker for achieving these new features in his life is a tedious, mind numbing and less secure work task. Crucially, then, relatively high wages do *not* mean that embourgeoisement is occurring. We are reminded here of the point made earlier that one must not look at the level of income as the sole determinant of class membership – occupations carry with them conditions of work and work experiences that are just as important as indications of class position. And often it is the case that the work experiences of the working class leave a lot to be desired: as Willis (1979b) says (p. 185),

> What is the human meaning and actual experience that lies behind our easy use of cars, cosmetics, clothes and buildings? ... Is the meaning and pleasure of these things as they are consumed any more important than the meaning of the drudge of their production? It is often forgotten that the main reality for most of the people, for most of the time, is work and the sound of work – the grind of production, not the purr of consumption, is the commonest mark of our industrial culture.

Reproduction of the working class

In Figure 3.2 we indicate that there are two processes crucial to the reproduced subordination of the working class: these are educational disadvantage and poor material life-chances. We have already seen in Chapter 2 (Section 2.7) that there are major material inequalities in income, life-cycle of earnings, health and mortality rates across the social classes. Clearly, the limited occupational opportunities of the vast majority of the working class are a direct result of their low 'cultural capital': as we saw in our discussion of the middle class, qualifications are increasingly important credentials in society. So educational disadvantage and poor job prospects are linked.

In order to understand how this disadvantage occurs one has to go beyond the material inequalities in educational provision that can often lead to under-resourced schools in working-class catchment areas. We need too to recognise that culturally most schools favour a child from a middle-class background, for whom schooling is often an extension of pre-school family experience and tuition. Working-class children can and do overcome the cultural hurdles they confront: but many, as Halsey (1980) has shown, do not, even in supposedly progressive comprehensive schools.

There may also occur a process whereby social disadvantage is, in a sense, 'self-inflicted': thus, for example, children, in rebelling against 'the system' embark on a journey that takes them through a few years of adventure and excitement in school to end up in a lifetime of drudgery and low-paid work (see Willis, 1979b). For those in subordinate positions, the very means whereby their sense of 'freedom' from subordination is expressed can paradoxically help to reproduce the material and cultural circumstances that ensures their 'enclosed' subordination.

The actual response to the chronic experience of subordination will vary according to the situation confronting individuals and groups within the working class. For example, those in a more favourable position – say, skilled manual workers – will draw on their collective strength in an 'offensive' way to carve out an occupational monopoly. Ethnic minority groups on the other hand will perhaps engage in 'defensive' strategies to limit the damage of prejudice and discrimination against them in the labour market. They may have to organise along ethnic lines through neighbourhood based organisations to promote their interests. It is often though not always the case that because of racial divisions within the work-force, Asian and West Indian workers find that they cannot rely on their fellow white workers to support them in industrial disputes. This is because the more advantaged white manual workers want to protect their privileged position with regard to promotion and job opportunities. As Moore (1982) has shown, when this occurs, ethnic minority workers have to depend on their community rather than on fellow white workers and unions to fight their case. Clearly, there is a process of social closure at work here along ethnic or racial lines: white manual workers seeking to limit the degree to which the less advantaged black and coloured working class can improve their position. Because of this, some sociologists have argued that black people who suffer racial discrimination and prejudice form an 'underclass' in the social hierarchy, tantamount to a class *beneath* the working class (Sivanandum, 1982).

Whatever their response to subordination, there is a crucial condition that must hold for any reproduction of the working to occur at all: there must be a labour market for them. Thus, any changes in the structure of capitalism that threaten the labour market threaten the very survival and so reproduction of the working class. There are two processes at work which may well be doing this in Britain: the de-industrialisation of the economy and the de-skilling of labour.

De-industrialisation

There is a vast literature on this subject that debates whether or not Britain is in the throes of a long-term industrial decline with little prospect for a regenerated manufacturing base in the future (Gamble, 1985), or experiencing a restructuring of the economy that, while displacing mass manufacture to cheap labour countries of the Third World, is now building a new postindustrial 'Hi-tech' enterprise to take its place. The evidence so far suggests that the former is more likely to be correct: for example, between 1966 and 1981 employment in manufacturing fell by 3 million. Much of this has become long-term severe structural unemployment in Northern Ireland, Wales, Scotland and the North East. There is little to suggest that 'Hi-tech' industrial growth will provide alternative work for such numbers, even in the longer term. Critics of the Thatcher government argued that, while the decline has had a long history, the monetarist policies of her administration accelerated it without restructuring the economy for future economic growth.

De-skilling

The conventional view of industrial society is that there is a continual process of education and training to sustain and raise the levels of job skills and knowledge throughout the population: new technologies = new jobs- = new skills = new training needed. Against this view, as noted above (p. 107), Braverman, adopting a somewhat deterministic Marxist line, argues that capitalist profit can only be sustained by a long-term process of de-skilling the working class, since thereby are workers cheapened, controlled by management and susceptible to replacement by automated technology. Braverman's position requires that we accept that the working class will increasingly become less skilled, that skilled, craft labour will be decimated and that union power will be seriously undermined: the automation of production means that there will be less to bargain over – production is (literally) out of their hands. The 'scientific management' thesis of Taylor (see Chapter 9, Section 9:3) on the one hand, and the practice of Fordism on the other, were for Braverman the hallmarks of the modern capitalist enterprise. *If* skilled manual workers were to suffer such a sustained attack, one would expect to find an increasingly homogeneous mass of workers, with no real internal differentiation of the sort described earlier.

While many acknowledge the value of Braverman's thesis, there are many reservations which have been expressed, including:

(a)   The thesis underestimates the ability of the (skilled) working class to resist management controls through organised unionism (see Beynon, 1973);

(b)   The thesis fails to distinguish between skilled *workers* and skilled *tasks* – while some tasks may be de-skilled, new ones may be in creation (e.g. in association with electronics or biotechnolgy), or skilled workers may move to other skilled tasks available elsewhere;

(c)   In order to give an impression of widespread de-skilling, the thesis *overstates* the extent of skilled work in the nineteenth century;

(d)   Finally, the thesis tends to treat 'skill' as a self-evident technical accomplishment associated with the doing of a task: while craft skills in this sense are part of any labour process, the recognition of skill is also *socially* determined through the variable power of interested groups – say workers and managers – to define work as 'skilled'. Thus, the concept of de-skilling is much too much a mechanical view of the relationship between 'skill' and work.

Despite these important reservations, most agree (see Wood, 1983) that the process of de-skilling has occurred in the real content of some jobs but at an uneven pace and accompanied by the growth of new forms of skilled work.

One might think that de-industrialisation and de-skilling could not happen simultaneously for, while the former implies a closing down of industry, the latter implies a restructuring of industry such that it requires less labour. However, there is nothing mutually exclusive about these processes: thus, within different sectors of the economy or even within the same sector both may occur, as has happened in the British car industry. In Britain the effect of these two processes is rising structural unemployment, and long-term unemployment for large numbers of the working class. This creates major difficulties for the cultural and economic reproduction of that class: substantial sectors of the working class are no longer *working*.

The future of the working class

De-industrialisation and de-skilling weaken the organisational strength of working-class unions and erode the vitality of community life so important a part of the cultural reproduction of the working class. Structural unemployment, particularly among the young will mean that the culture of working-class work will mean little or nothing to the new generation of severely depressed areas, such as the housing estates of Belfast where unemployment among families now approaches 90 per cent.

The social hierarchy of capitalism with which we opened this chapter becomes increasingly polarised into 'Two Nations', the rich and the relatively well-off in work, and the low-paid or unemployed poor. There may well arise among the working class – again especially among its youth – a sense of alienation, distrust of government, public services (including education), and the police. The riots of the 1980s have been connected with the high levels of unemployment. Whether there is thereby any indication of working-class radicalism depends on one's view of politics: many would argue that class radicalism can only occur when class divisions are organised and drawn on by a radical political party – but the opposition parties of the late 1980s seem much more oriented towards a return to consensus rather than radical politics. If the Labour party is returned to office, the future for the working class is likely to improve as unemployment will be reduced, but it seems unlikely to involve a wholesale rebuilding of a British manufacturing base in the longer term: Marx's 'reserve army of labour' is likely to grow.

3.5 CONCLUSION

We began this chapter by saying that the two concepts of social closure and social reproduction have increasingly been regarded as useful analytical tools for understanding social stratification. We have drawn on them to help to make sense of the debates about changing class boundaries. Figure 3.3 presents a brief summary of the process of class structuration in light of these two concepts.

	Social closure	Reproduction across generations
Upper class	**Strong** Upward mobility from below limited through: (i) intermarriage (ii) elite education (iii) social networks (iv) elite recruitment	Two crucial resources: (i) property inheritance (ii) elite education: the most profitable cultural capital one can possess
Middle class	**Weak** Movement into and out of this class more possible because of: (i) access to occupations by education makes downward and upward mobility more likely (ii) 'traditional' middle class being outnumbered by new recruits (the new professionals) (iii) ambiguous position of routine white-collar	The middle class sustains itself by: (i) educational advantage (ii) transfers of income to children to aid career or lifestyle
Working class	**Ambiguous** Conflicting trends here since we see: (i) the emergence of a distinct economically 'enclosed' class, but (ii) the decline of communities with distinct identity and (iii) the growth of the culturally diverse ethnic urban communities outside of the 'traditional' working class	Reflects conflicting trends of social closure, i.e. reproduction promoted by: (i) educational disadvantage. (ii) Poor life-chances. Yet reproduction limited because of decline in cultural identity: lack of homogeneity

FIGURE 3.3   *The process of class structuration*

Figure 3.3 draws attention to the relative strengths of social closure, i.e. the upperclass's is said to be 'strong', the middle class's 'weak' and the working class's – here, there is some uncertainty, i.e. the class's closure is 'ambiguous'. This is because of the conflict between trends favouring its reproduction against those that do not. Another way of seeing structuration, therefore, is in terms of Figure 3.4, which enlarges on this theme of the degree of closure and hence strength of class boundaries of the three social classes.

	Class boundaries
Upper class	Fairly clear: ownership of productive property a defining feature; members occupy key positions on boards of directors
Middle class	Fairly clear at top: established and 'new' middle class professionals. Major question at base: what is the class position of marginal middle class, especially those in routine non-manual positions? What of low-paid *female* professionals? (See the proletarian section debate.)
Working class	Clear boundary for the 'enclosed' working-class base (the low-paid, the unemployed): manual work carries distinctive life-chances and working conditions; less clear about upwardly mobile workers. (See the *embourgeoisement* debate)

FIGURE 3.4 *Implications of structuration for class boundaries*

What this chapter has tried to do is to illustrate the dynamics of class as both an economic condition and cultural experience. This chapter is tied in with the theories and facts of inequality outlined in Chapter 2. But, while class has been and remains a crucial mechanism for reproducing unequal life-chances, it is not the only form of social stratification. Chapters 4, 5 and 6 examine different forms of inequality, such as race and gender, which, although typically tied to class divisions, have to be examined on their own terms.

REFERENCES TO CHAPTER 3

Bain, G. and Price, R. (1972) 'Who is a White-collar Employer?', *British Journal of Industrial Relations*, vol. 10, pp. 325–39.

Bell, C. (1968) *Middle Class Families*, London, Routledge & Kegan Paul.

Beynon, H. (1973) *Working for Ford*, Harmondsworth, Penguin.

Braverman, H. (1974) *Labour and Monopoly Capital*, New York, Monthly Review Press.

Clarke, J. *et al.* (1979) *Working Class Culture*, London, Hutchinson.

Coates, D. (1984) *The Context of British Politics*, London, Hutchinson.

Coates, D. *et al.* (eds) (1985) *A Socialist Anatomy of Britain*, Cambridge, Polity Press.

Crompton, R. and Reid, S. (1983) 'The Deskilling of Clerical Work', in S. Wood (1983).

Crompton, R. and Jones, G. (1984) *White-Collar Proletariat*, London, Macmillan.

Dennis, N., Henriques, F. and Slaughter, C. (1956) *Coal is Our Life*, London, Eyre & Spottiswoode.

Frankenberg, R. F. (1966) *Communities in Britain*, Harmondsworth, Penguin.

Gamble, A. (1985) *Britain in Decline*, London, Macmillan (2nd edn).

Goldthorpe, J. H. *et al.* (1968) *The Affluent Worker: Industrial Attitudes and Behaviour*, Harmondsworth, Penguin.

Goldthorpe, J. H. (1972) Oxford Occupational Mobility Study.

Goldthorpe, J. H. (1978) 'Comment', *British Journal of Sociology*, vol. 29(4)

Goldthorpe, J. H. (1980) *Social Mobility and the Class Structure in Modern Britain*, Oxford, Clarendon Press.

Halmos, P. (1964) *The Development of Industrial Societies*, Keele, Keele University Press.

Halsey, A. *et al.* (1980) *Origins and Destinations*, Oxford, Clarendon Press.

Halsey, A. (1981) The Reith Lectures, *The Listener*, BBC Publications.

Heath, A. and Britten, N. (1984) 'Women's Jobs do make a Difference', *Sociology*, vol. 18(4).

Heller, R. (1973) 'The State of British Boardrooms', *Management Today*, May.

Hobsbawm, E. (1968) *Industry and Empire*, Harmondsworth, Penguin.

Hoggart, R. (1958) *The Uses of Literacy*, Harmondsworth, Penguin.

Kelly, M. P. (1984) *White-Collar Proletariat*, London, Routledge & Kegan Paul.

Leys, C. (1983) *Politics in Britain*, London, Heinemann.

Lockwood, D. (1958) *The Blackcoated Worker*, London, Allen & Unwin.

Lupton, T. and Wison, S. (1959) 'The Social Background of Top Decision-Makers', *Manchester School*, vol. 27.

Moore, R. (1982) 'Immigration and Racism', in Burgess, R. (ed.) *Exploring Society*, London, British Sociological Association.

Murphy, R. (1986) 'The Concept of Class in Closure Theory', *Sociology*, vol. 20, May, pp. 247–64.

Nairn, T. (1981) *The Break-Up of Britain*, London, Verso (2nd edn).

Parkin, F. (1971) *Class Inequality and Political Order*, London, MacGibbon & Kee.

Parkin, F. (1979) *Marxism and Class Theory*, London, Tavistock.

Penn, R. (1985) *Skilled Workers in the Class Structure*, Cambridge, Cambridge University Press.

Poulantzas, N. (1975) *Classes in Contemporary Capitalism*, London, New Left Books.

Rubinstein, W. D. (1976) 'Wealth elites, and the class structure of modern Britain', *Past and Present*, vol. 70.

Salaman, G. and Thompson, K. (1978) 'Class Culture and the Persistence of an Elite', *Sociological Review*, vol. 26(2), pp. 283–304.

Scott, J. (1982) *The Upper Classes*, London, Macmillan.

Scott, J. and Griff, C. (1984) *Directors of Industry: The British Corporate Network 1904–1926*, Cambridge, Polity Press.

Scott, J. (1985) *Corporations, Classes and Capitalism*, London, Hutchinson.

Sivanandum, A. (1982) *A Different Hunger*, London, Pluto Press.

Stanworth, P. and Giddens, A. (eds) (1974) *Elites and Power in British Society*, Cambridge, Cambridge University Press.

Weiner, M. (1981) *English Culture and the Decline of the Industrial Spirit*, Cambridge, Cambridge University Press.

Wild, P. (1979) 'Recreation in Rochdale, 1900–40', in J Clarke (ed.)

Williams, R. W. (1961) *Culture and Society 1780–1950*, Harmondsworth, Penguin.

Willis, P. (1979a) 'Shop-floor Culture, Masculinity and the Wage Form', in J. Clarke. (ed.).

Willis, P. (1979b) *Learning to Labour*, Westmead, Saxon House.

Wood, S. (1983) *The Degradation of Work?* London, Hutchinson.

Wright, E. (1978) *Class, Crisis and the State*, London, New Left Books.

Wright, E. (1985) *Classes*, London, Verso.

Young, M. and Willmott, P. (1962) *Family and Kinship in East London*, Harmondsworth, Penguin.

Zweig, F. (1961) *The Worker in an Affluent Society*, London, Heinemann.

4

Forms of Subordination: Youth, the Poor, Race and the Third World

4.1 INTRODUCTION

The preceding two chapters examined the general features of stratification, particularly with regard to class inequality within contemporary capitalism. The dimensions of inequality were said to be best explained in terms of both Marxist and Weberian perspectives rather than through functionalist theory, which was shown to be both empirically unfounded and ideologically suspect. One of the principal deficiencies of the functionalist approach is its neglect of conflict and exploitation in society, partly derived from its assumption that *moral unity* is the basis of social life. Social phenomena are explained as being the result either of the 'needs of the social system' or of the 'shared values' held by a group.

The notion that the relationship between groups, that their relative economic, political and cultural place in society can be explained in terms of the particular values and attitudes that each holds, has, however, been adopted by a variety of social science theorists. This chapter examines four forms of subordination that popularly, ideologically and/or academically have been attributed to the distinctive 'cultural characteristics' of the subordinate groups concerned. The four patterns of inequality discussed are: (i) that generational division between young and old; (ii) that division between the poor and non-poor of society; (iii) that racial division between 'white' and 'black', and (iv) that international division between developed and undeveloped countries. We show that these four patterns of inequality have much to do with the general processes of stratification that we outlined in the first part of Chapter 2, and that any particular cultural phenomena which may be associated with these patterns can only be seen accurately in the light of such processes. Thus we argue that the subordinate position of groups in each of the four contexts cannot be properly explained by an emphasis on their values and attitudes which allegedly mark them off from the rest of society, or, in the fourth case, the developed world.

4.2   YOUTH CULTURES

Many sociologists and media commentators regard the idea of the existence of a 'youth culture' as reflecting and expressing the experiences, activities and values of young people. The idea of a 'youth culture' – or more accurately a 'youth subculture' – implies that the young are socialised into and committed to a special set of values, standards, expectations and behaviour patterns distinguishable from those of 'adult society', and at its most extreme it implies a fundamental rift between the two age categories – a 'war between the generations'.

Some have gone so far as to suggest that youth has developed as a separate 'class', subordinate to and cut off from the adult world, so that generational division may be an equally significant, if not more important, social barrier than social class, and, furthermore, one which reduces class divisions. Berger and Berger (1972, p. 227) maintain that 'To a considerable degree, the youth culture cuts across class lines ... [It] has created symbols and patterns of behaviour that are capable of bestowing status upon individuals coming from quite different class backgrounds ... The youth culture has a strongly egalitarian ethos.'

This popular idea of generational division as expressed in the form of a youth culture rests on an essentially functionalist or neo-functionalist perspective, involving a conception of a discontinuity between the *value-systems* of adults and youth. In this view the stable interaction of members of different age grades is essential for the working and continuity of the social system. Sugarman (1968, p. 71) maintains:

> The survival of society requires that as members go through this phase [adolescence] in their lives, many of them should work hard at acquiring certain knowledge, skills and values. Failing this, important roles that require great expertise and dedication will not be filled adequately. Yet at this phase of their lives the young are undergoing considerable strain ... and are exposed to the temptation of a youth culture.

These strains of adolescence, it is argued, mean that youth share common problems and interests in handling a difficult period of transition, and a youth culture with its own values and standards arises as a means of adjusting both to these problems and to imminent adulthood.

Age and membership of an age category, then, are seen as specific and fundamental variables, and generational conflict is the product of the complex and ambivalent socialisation processes at work in modern industrial societies, which are neither as integrated nor as coherent as in preindustrial societies. In the former 'Intergenerational conflict ("the generation gap") is a socialisation dysfunction, resulting from weak integration between society and age groups. Age is the basis of social and cultural characteristics of actors' (Brake, 1979, p. 25).

Eisenstadt (1956) provides perhaps the most extensive functionalist explanation of youth culture. For him, the problematic position of youth in industrial societies rests on the difficulties involved in the transition to adult roles. While the family is the basic socialising unit, the kinship system is not the basis on which adult roles are organised and allocated: the family is based on ascriptive and particularistic criteria and values, while adult roles (particularly occupations) rest on a foundation of universalism, achievement and impersonality. Thus, there exists a sharp cleavage in value-orientations and expectations between the family and the wider society, so that youth becomes a significant social category, and a youth culture emerges to alleviate this disjunction.

This division is said to be intensified by a number of specific features of industrial societies: the extended provision of education means that more young people for a longer period have to experience status insecurity and an ambiguous transition; a more complex and differentiated occupational structure with increasingly specialised division of labour means that meritocratic competition for occupation occurs increasingly, and following in parents' occupational footsteps is less likely; and increased social mobility and changes in leisure provision mean that each generation lives qualitatively 'different' lives. In Eisenstadt's view, primary and early secondary socialisation does not prepare individuals to adapt to all this, so that their values are not stable and their identity is insecure. The creation of a youth culture is the response to the discontinuities created by the failure of the family and school to effect the transition to adulthood. As Eisenstadt (1956, pp. 43–5) says:

> In universalistic-achievement societies . . . an individual cannot achieve full status if he behaves in his work according to the ascriptive particularistic criteria of family life: such behaviour would also prove a strain on the social system . . . There occurs in such cases a defensive reaction in the direction of age-homogeneous relations and groups . . . The individual develops need-dispositions for a new kind of interaction with other individuals which would make the transition easier for him.

Is there a distinct youth culture?

While the idea of a 'youth culture' has held considerable influence within the ranks of sociologists and the mass media, its accuracy in portraying realistically both youth-adult relations and the internal relations of youth has been seriously questioned. Essentially, the critique focuses on two basic and often interrelated themes: (i) that the differences between 'adults' and 'youth' can be easily overexaggerated; and (ii) that it is seriously misleading to see both young people and adults as simple homogeneous categories, since this over-emphasises the significance of age as a sociological division. Both these themes cast doubt on the existence of a 'youth culture'.

In the first place, the concept implies a homogeneous adult world, a *consensual* picture of 'adult society' which is sociologically inaccurate. As we saw in Chapter 2, inequalities of wealth, income, mortality, etc., *within* the adult population are considerable and persistent: the world of adults is as divided along crucial lines of life-chances as it is united by accident of age, so that an identity of interest and values is highly doubtful. This alerts us to one of the fundamental inadequacies of the concept of a youth culture, and one which more recent analyses of youth, from a neo-Marxist perspective, attempt to rectify. As Mungham and Pearson (1976, pp. 2–3) observe: 'Behind all the talk of "generation" and "generation gap" there is the forgotten question of the class structure of society. It is as if when youth are discussed that social class goes on holiday. But youth are not a classless tribe.'

The neo-functionalist view of youth seems to suggest (apart from the occasional nodding acknowledgement of class variations) that the young are suspended without other fundamental points of identity in a classless world of leisure, where differences in educational and occupational opportunities and experiences disappear. It is no coincidence that the idea of a distinctive 'youth culture' emerged most strongly at a time of alleged embourgeoisement and increasing dilution of class divisions and consciousness: a myth of affluent youth, with time and money on their hands for enjoying mass entertainment and fashion products, reflected the more general myth of working-class affluence. But, as numerous sociologists have stressed, Western societies are still capitalist class societies, in which class position is fundamental in shaping life-chances and life-styles.

Thus, while youth share certain disadvantages in common and are accorded minority-group status, their life-chances are markedly unequal and differentiate them internally more fundamentally and rigidly than any temporary 'unity' engendered merely by being young, minimising the likelihood of a common sense of identity and often generating mutual hostility. As Murdock and McCron (1976, p. 18) observe:

> Schools provide an obvious case in point. They are institutions not simply of age segregation but also of class domination. They operate not only to delay adolescents' entry on to the labour market and to reinforce their subordination to adult authority but also to reproduce the existing structure of class inequalities and class relations. Far from uniting youth as a single subordinate 'class', therefore, schools serve to remake and confirm the prevailing patterns of class divisions and antagonisms.

If some sections of society are given an inferior educational experience, are consigned to routine, unsatisfying work (or to no job at all) and to residence in anonymous estates lacking facilities, it is no surprise that they feel little or no identity with those living in residential suburbs and attending private boarding schools which give access to elite positions. The middle-class teenager (both male *and* female) is socialised towards educational and occupational horizons in which youth is seen as a stepping-stone to a burgeoning career, whereas for the working-class teenager it is a prelude to a humdrum existence and hence to be enjoyed 'while you're young' before harsh reality takes over.

The result is that middle-class and working-class youth tend to develop *distinct* and *separate subcultures* (for example, the Teddy Boys and the Beatniks of the 1950s and the Skinheads and Hippies of the 1960s and 1970s), which, even when they manifest 'oppositional' elements, constitute very different responses. For instance, both radical student protest among middle-class youth and racialist 'Paki-bashing' among some working-class youth were political responses to changing economic and socio-political circumstances in Britain, but they were of a very different order, reflecting less about youth *per se* than about the pressures and contradictions of capitalist class society experienced by *specific* subgroups within the two classes.

Not only are middle-class and working-class youth subcultures separate entities but they may also be antagonistic. Willis's (1978) 'bike boys' were highly critical of Mods and Hippies as being effeminate and weak in their involvement with drugs, and the hippy counter-culture (1960s) consisted mainly of students and ex-students, evoking little working-class response besides hostility. In fact, some writers suggest that one particular working-class youth subculture group, Skinheads, were to a large extent a reaction to middle-class hippy subculture,

> a reaction against the quiet introspective influence of flower-power; its most obvious symbol was 'bovver boots' . . . The Skins adopted a uniform which seems to be, at one and the same time, both a caricature and a reassertion of solid male working class toughness (Mungham and Pearson, 1976, p. 7).

From the neo-Marxist perspective, then, we must abandon the assumption of a homogeneous youth culture and recognise the basic importance of class inequalities in shaping responses. In this view we need to consider youth subcultures and their styles in relation to a system of class domination and to a dominant culture and ideology. Capitalist societies, as Marx stressed, are characterised by dominant and subordinate classes according to their relation to the means of production, and the existence of a dominant culture reflects the position and interests of the economically dominant class. This class attempts to maintain its hegemony (see Chapter 6) to some degree by achieving the consent of the subordinate classes by incorporating them into the key institutions and structures which support its authority.

But subordinate classes develop means of expressing a response to their position through their own distinctive subcultures, which help them to negotiate relations with the dominant class and its culture – that is, to 'win space' from them by virtue of subscribing to alternative cultural definitions and concerns which may reflect resistance, accommodation, pragmatic acceptance, or whatever. As Clarke *et al.* (1976, p. 4) say: 'The subordinate class brings to this "theatre of struggle" a repertoire of strategies and responses – ways of coping as well as resisting.'

Thus youth subcultures are to be seen as particular generational responses to wider problems experienced by their class, reflecting the common experiences of their members in education, employment and rewards, residential provision, neighbourhood and community relationships, and so on. For example, the dominant ideology suggests that Britain is a meritocracy with equal educational and occupational opportunity and political rights, and equality before the law. Black working-class youths on the dole since leaving school and on the receiving end of racist attitudes (at school, in work and in leisure) experience contradictions directly, so that a distinctive subcultural response on their part may be a meaningful attempt to express dissatisfaction at such inequality.

But class does not simply *replace* age as the major variable of analysis since.

> Clearly age is an important factor in structuring the social situation of young people. Some experiences, noticeably compulsory secondary schooling, are youth specific ... Age also plays a key role in determining the range of options and choices available within the leisure environment. It is not therefore a case of [simply] substituting class for age ... but of examining the relationship between class and age, and more particularly, the way in which age acts as a mediation of class (Murdock and McCron, 1976, p. 24).

Class and generation interact dynamically to produce a specific class-generational response: they *coalesce* to produce a distinct subcultural *style*.

However, while seeing youth subcultures as producing something distinctive, their relations with the parent culture – what is *shared* with this culture – cannot be ignored. Although many youth activities appear to be anti-adult, they often actually *exaggerate* aspects of the parent culture (as with the Skinheads).

Youth subcultures, then, constitute more micro-level responses to the changing macro-structural arrangements of capitalist society, particularly those of the post-war era. Changes in national economic patterns, from the relative prosperity of the 1960s to the recession and inflation of the 1970s, the erosion of the traditional working-class community and the development of housing estates, the impact of technological and organisational changes in the work environment on employment and skills, and the growth of mass consumption and mass entertainment industries, all have left their mark on the working class and have evoked some striking responses among certain sections of working-class youth, from the Teddy Boys of the 1950s to the Punkrockers of the 1970s.

For example, the Skinheads of the late 1960s adopted a 'model worker' dress of short hair, clean-shaven faces, industrial work boots, turned-up jeans with braces as a reassertion of working-class culture and values. Their overtly masculine style, their preference for pubs and beer over clubs and pills, their 'queer bashing' and dislike of student 'hippies', and their willingness to fight, re-emphasised their working-class origins. Their racist attitudes and 'Paki-bashing' and their commitment to the idea of territory ('Hackney Boot Boys Rule, OK?') reflected the sense of threat felt by many sections of the working class over immigration and changes in their community.

They were particularly renowned for their attachment to football teams and came to be seen as the stereotypical 'football hooligans'. The fierce commitment of young (and not so young) football supporters, their singing and chanting and occasionally violent behaviour – under the umbrella description of 'hooliganism' – has been a matter of increasing public and media concern and is often presented as being 'mindless' and spoiling the game for the 'true' spectator. But for a number of writers it classically exemplifies the youthful working-class response to the post-war changes in Britain to which we have referred.

Watching soccer has been traditionally a working-class leisure activity, providing a sense of excitement, pleasure and commitment to 'our team', in stark contrast to the indifference and alienation experienced in unsatisfying work and educational experiences. But, as Taylor (1971) and others have pointed out, in the post-war era – and especially since the 1960s – the game has become more 'bourgeois', more professionalised, more commercialised and less traditionally based in the working-class community. Clubs have attempted to cater for a new kind of spectator, the (classless) consumer of entertainment rather than 'the fan', with the introduction of more seating, of restaurants, and so on, so that the working-class supporters on the terraces, having been removed from their traditional neighbourhoods by urban redevelopment, find that the football team is no longer 'theirs'. Football hooliganism represents the working-class youth's attempt to win back control of his class's game and is 'an attempt to retrieve the disappearing sense of community' (Clarke and Jefferson, 1976, p. 154) in its emphasis on territorial loyalty and sense of common identity. As Robins and Cohen (1978, p. 137) observe: 'It's as if, for these youngsters, the space they share on the North Bank is a way of magically retrieving the sense of group solidarity and identification that once went along with living in a traditional working class neighbourhood.' This means, then, that passion-ate support of a football team *is* more than watching a game and being entertained: it is a collective response to problems of class experience and cannot be dismissed as mere 'mindless aggro'.

This *remains* a 'magical' solution, however, because it operates only in the harmless area of leisure. This is no solution for those unlucky enough to have monotonous, alienating, low-paid, demeaning jobs, let alone for those unemployed. Dull schooling, dull jobs and the inequalities they embody are not solved by ritual conflict with opposing fans who suffer similar life-chances. These youth subcultures thus constitute partial 'negotiations' with the dominant class culture rather than effective challenges to the subordination they experience.

Thus the phenomenon of youth subcultures illustrates the need for an analysis of institutions which recognises the central importance of *class*. Instead of seeing a universal 'youth culture' as the product merely of the problems of membership of an age category, as the functionalist perspective does, it seems more profitable to explore the ways in which the social relations of capitalist society produce distinctive class subcultural responses and how these are manifested in distinctive youth subcultures.

The 'invisibility' of girls

One of the most significant limitations of both Functionalist and neo-Marxist accounts of youth cultures and subcultures is the absence of any meaningful analysis of *girls*. In the vast majority of these studies, girls are either invisible or are depicted as shadowy background figures who appear in youth subcultural activity merely by virtue of their dependent relationship with young males and/or through their roles as 'decorative' sex objects. As Frances Heidensohn (1985, pp. 139–40) observes:

> Girls do flit through the pages of these books and articles, but ... they are perceived and portrayed through the eyes of the 'lads' .... In almost fifty years of theoretical and ethnographic work on deviant cultures from Whyte to Willis, *nothing* had changed. Skinhead girls in Smethwick, Sunderland or the East End were as invisible to contemporary researchers and as liable to be dismissed as mere sex objects as they had been in Boston.

It may well be that girls to occupy subordinate positions in youth subcultures, reflecting their subordinate position in the wider society. It may well be, as McRobbie and Garber (1976) have pointed out, that the invisibility of girls in youth subcultural analyses is attributable to the long-time monopoly of this field by male researchers, and it may also be the case, as these authors and others maintain, that distinctively female youth subcultures take a less public, less street-based form ('a subculture of the bedroom', for instance) as a result of the greater restrictions placed upon girls. Whatever the merits or otherwise of these observations, girls do need to be *included* in the analysis of youth subcultures.

4.3   EXPLANATIONS OF POVERTY

The prevalent conception of poverty prior to the nineteenth century was that it was 'God-given', part of the natural order of things. Such a view gave way in Victorian times to one of poverty as an individual problem, the product of deficient personal character and morality: the poor were seen as thriftless, lazy and undisciplined, lacking initiative and moral fibre. They were to be assisted in coping with their condition of poverty, but any alteration in this condition had to be achieved through their own efforts. Viewing poverty not simply as an individual but also as a social problem to be handled by systematic state action and provision of welfare services is essentially a relatively recent conception.

As in many other areas of sociology, controversies and disagreements exist as to the explanation of poverty. This particular area of controversy well illustrates how different explanations also often generate very different policy solutions. This can be seen by contrasting 'culture of poverty' explanations – which emphasise shared values, as in the functionalist tradition – and neo-Marxist explanations of poverty.

The *'culture of poverty'* thesis

This thesis suggests that the poor are poor because they have different values and way of life from the rest of society, a culture of their own – a 'culture of poverty' – which prevents them from achieving success and prosperity.

Oscar Lewis and the culture of poverty

A prominent exponent of the thesis is Lewis (1961, 1966). He maintains that the poor possess certain cultural features which mark them off from the rest of society and which are passed on from one generation to another, inhibiting those exposed to them from taking opportunities to escape from poverty.

Lewis identifies a number of 'core features' of this 'culture of poverty', including mother-centred families, a male preoccupation with being tough and masculine, fatalism, an inability to defer gratification, and a narrow perspective on the world, restricted to the immediate environment and condition. For Lewis, such features constitute a distinctive culture of poverty, preventing the poor from attaining the material standards common to the rest of society: in other words, because their way of life is different, they are poor.

The 'culture of poverty' thesis has found favour with politicians and governments in providing a foundation for policy programmes. In the USA in the 1960s a number of government reports (such as the 1965 Moynihan

Report) claimed that adverse socialisation of children by black families was the major factor in black poverty in the ghettos: the solution lay with changes in the blacks themselves, particularly in their (inadequate) social-isation and cultural practices. Hence, during the 1960s, American govern-ments emphasised the need for more social work but less direct economic aid for blacks.

Similarly, in Britain in 1972 the then Minister of Health and Social Security, Sir Keith Joseph, made a number of controversial statements which amounted to the view that 'inadequate' parents do not socialise their children properly in the skills, capacities and motivation necessary for taking up educational and job opportunities. A 'culture of poverty' is passed on, exacerbated, according to Sir Keith, by their 'unfortunate' breeding habits of producing larger numbers of children. So, social intervention is needed to change the behaviour patterns of the poor, particularly their child-rearing practices.

Critique

Lewis and other exponents of the thesis have been criticised for using evidence collected on *families* to construct a picture of a *culture*, of a whole way of life, i.e. for concentrating predominantly on attitudes and activities within households to the neglect of the wider social group. Furthermore, 'culture of poverty' theorists are accused of engaging in a purely *negative* analysis: by starting with a middle-class model of life, they have identified merely what is 'lacking' in the poor (e.g. family stability, future planning) without giving sufficient attention to the positive aspects of their way of life.

A more fundamental criticism suggests that differences between the poor and the rest of society have been overstressed at the expense of similarities which exist. One might ask, for instance, whether some of the 'core' features which Lewis identifies as constituting a 'culture of poverty' are entirely absent among the non-poor working class; certainly, emphasis on mascu-linity and a limited social outlook are by no means restricted to the poor working class. Furthermore, critics would argue that there is considerable evidence that the poor *do* subscribe to many of the 'normal' standards and values about security, steady employment, stable marriage, and so on.

The crucial point, however, may be that the *very fact of being poor* prevents the poor from putting these values and standards into action: for instance, poverty makes future planning and deferred gratification a remote if not unattainable luxury – poverty may necessitate fathers moving away to seek work, and so on. As Gans (1971, p. 160) says:

> Many poor people share the aspirations of the middle class, and yet more those of the stable working class. If they could achieve the same economic security as middle and working class people, they would quickly give up most of the behaviour patterns associated with poverty.

Gans and others stress that it makes far more sense to see that many of the features of the 'culture of poverty' identified by Lewis are not *chosen* ways of life but simply *realistic responses* to being poor, to the realities and pitfalls of an insecure and unpredictable economic existence. If a 'culture of poverty' exists, it is a consequence of poverty and not its cause, and the poor's cultural patterns are not the *source* of their poverty but its outcome.

The *neo-Marxist explanation* of poverty

The neo-Marxist approach has pointed to the important *ideological* implications of the 'culture of poverty' thesis, whereby emphasis on the apparent internal inadequacies of the poor suggests that their problems are of their own making. As Westergaard and Resler (1975) succinctly put it, 'The blame for inequality falls neatly on its victims.'

The danger in the 'culture of poverty' approach lies in its neglect of the impact of wider economic forces and relationships in shaping behaviour patterns and social structures. The 'culture of poverty' thesis presents poverty as a 'cultural' condition, a by-product of the inadequate culture embraced by certain social groups, rendering them less socially competent and lacking in initiative; the remedy, therefore is one of limited, localised 'social therapy', involving the re-education of the poor, with little attention or priority given to structural or economic change.

Gans (1971), Miliband (1974) and Westergaard and Resler (1975) reject the idea of viewing the poor as a distinct, culturally homogeneous group, because this is obviously false and because it involves a too narrow conception of the dynamics of poverty, diverting attention away from larger structures of inequality created by the stratification system, and providing wrong-headed solutions to poverty. These critics emphasise that poverty results from the economic arrangements and relationships of society which determine the distribution of material resources and power; in a society where wealth is still heavily concentrated, where speculators in shares and property can make big financial 'killings', where employers can pay low wages to individuals working long hours in unpleasant conditions, poverty for some will be a persistent fact of life.

Furthermore, the economic *ideologies* of our society do little to enhance the poor's position. Capitalist societies have long emphasised the importance of individual effort, self-help and initiative, so that an 'if you don't work, you don't eat' philosophy is strongly ingrained. The result is that we are not quite prepared to do everything we can for the poor: they receive assistance, but this stops short of relieving poverty completely. Nowhere is this better illustrated than in the operations of the Welfare State. The British Welfare State is widely regarded with great reverence, but the fact remains that the major benefits it provides (family allowance, old-age pension, supplementary benefits, etc.), while assisting the poor, do *not* lift them out of poverty: that is, the benefits are not sufficiently generous to guarantee an income above the official 'poverty line'. As Coates and Silburn (1970) say: 'The Welfare State has been no Robin Hood. It has taken little from the rich and given even less to the poor.' Behind the theory and practice of the Welfare State appears to be an anxiety about giving people 'too much' in case their moral fibre weakens and they become too dependent on help from others and abandon self-help.

The limitations of the Welfare State are compounded by the fact that many benefits to which individuals and families are entitled are simply not taken up. 'Serves them right, then' might be the response to this, but there are more powerful factors working against complete take-up of benefits than mere indifference to what is available. First, many people do not *know* what benefits are available to them, and some benefits are not widely publicised. The system rests on individuals *seeking out* benefits to which they are entitled, and not on 'automatic' provision by the state. Second, personal pride inhibits many eligible cases. Many people feel humiliated or embarrassed at accepting what they see as 'charity'. Again such attitudes demonstrate the powerful impact of Western economic ideologies (as well as the hangover from nineteenth-century notions of poverty), and accepting state aid is made no easier for the poor by the frequent outbursts of the mass media (and others) against 'scroungers', 'layabouts' and 'dole kings'. Third, claiming benefit involves problems and difficulties in procedure: entitlement to many benefits depends on a *means test* (i.e. providing information about personal circumstances in order to demonstrate *proof of need*), involving complicated contact with bureaucratic agencies, as well as the often degrading experience of having to divulge personal details to officials. Consequently, many people eligible for means-tested services do not apply for them.

Ultimately, poverty is a product of the unequal distribution of power in society: it is a condition of political as well as economic deprivation. As Miliband (1974) emphasises, although the poor theoretically possess the same civil and political rights as others, their circumstances do not enable them to be effective politically. The low paid, for instance, are often older, in smaller firms, in declining industries, with significant numbers of women workers – circumstances which do not encourage effective political organisation.

Here, then, we have a very different explanation of the existence and persistence of poverty from that of the 'culture of poverty' thesis, one which firmly locates it within the wider socio-economic structure and its patterns of inequality.

4.4 RACE RELATIONS

Theoretical issues

The problems of race and racism loom large in the modern world; in Africa,

America, Europe and Great Britain men and women have been, and still are, deprived of basic human rights and dignity because of their 'race'.

Many people see racial discrimination and racist ideologies as the result of blind and irrational prejudice against 'outsider' groups by individuals of intolerant or bigoted disposition, or, less severely, by groups who cannot cope with the 'strange' cultural characteristics of different racial groups. While both of these notions of prejudice may have some reality and engender forms of inter-racial conflict, and are therefore important issues for sociological analysis, they do not tell the whole story. Racial prejudice functions, as we shall see, in ways which indicate that it is inextricably locked into broader structural dimensions of inequality: racial disadvantage is a form of subordination that, like youth cultures and poverty, must be seen in the context of social stratification.

A number of recent sociological approaches to race relations have concentrated on the relationship between race and social stratification. Those who adhere to this position argue that race relations represent a form of class and status relations and that, accordingly, problems of race relations can be dealt with by existing sociological theories. According to this view, inequality in a class society can be traced to some basic structural fact such as the ownership or non-ownership of productive property or the possession of different market capacities. Racial differences, it is argued, may be viewed (in the same way as sex, age and religion) as complicating factors in the dominant system. Race or colour simply makes the groups in question more visible and more vulnerable to class exploitation. Writers as far apart on the political spectrum as the functionalist Parsons (1965) and the Marxist economists Baran and Sweezy (1966) would, in their different ways, support such an interpretation.

On the other hand some writers, such as Rex (1970) and Lockwood (1970), argue that the attempts to explain race relations in class and stratification terms ignore the unique problems raised by race. Lockwood, for example, gives two main reasons why theories of *class* cannot account for patterns of race relations. On the one hand, he says, racial protest movements involve unification across class lines *within* racial groups, and, on the other, certain moral, aesthetic and sexual connotation of colour are built into our language, and have no equivalent in class terminology. Similarly, Rex argues that stratification theories are unable to explain the part played in racial stratification by 'deterministic' belief systems. These beliefs 'explain' and justify the discrimination directed towards a particular race either in terms of its genetic/biological inferiority or in equally deterministic socio-cultural terms.

Against this points of view, Dunning (1972) argues that the distinctive character of race relations from a sociological point of view lies, not in the presence or absence of deterministic theories and beliefs, as Rex suggests, but that the degree of significance of such ideological constructs is a function of the power discrepancies which exist between groups in a society. Groups with a great deal of power are able to impose their definitions of a situation upon the less powerful, who (given their economic and social subordination) do not have the resources to challenge the way in which they are represented. Where there are vast discrepancies of power between groups, deterministic beliefs may arise which perform certain functions for the dominant group. This means that such beliefs are not restricted to the context of race relations; *class* differences, i.e. inequalities, have been rationalised in such terms. For example, in the eighteenth and early nineteenth centuries there were people who believed that the social classes were formed from different streams of heredity and that they possessed distinguishing physical characteristics that marked the superiority of one class over another. This ideology can be found in the context of race relations in South Africa. Whatever their specific form and context, such beliefs help to justify privilege and/or to handle the discrepancy between established practice and egalitarian values – where such values exist. For example, one way in which Christian slave-owners were able to handle the conflict between their beliefs and their actions was by defining black Africans as 'animals' and therefore as beyond the pale. In general, then, as Castles and Kosack (1973, p. 430) say:

> In reality, the relationship between discrimination and prejudice is a dialectical one: discrimination is based on economic and social interests and prejudice originates as an instrument to defend such discrimination. In turn, prejudice becomes entrenched and helps to cause further discrimination.

The capacity of subordinate racial groups to organise and resist exploitation and discrimination will be constrained by the sort of economic and political setting in which they are placed, and this may vary from, say, that of slavery to 'free' wage-labour. Furthermore, whatever general economic relationships hold, the success of resistance against exploitation is bound up with specific historical factors such as ease of communication (important for organisation), the ecological setting in which the groups are located (e.g. rural or urban), and the degree and type of interdependence associated with the division of labour. These factors will vary given different economic and industrial frameworks.

The different power balances which arise out of this complex intermeshing of variables will have potentially different psychological effects upon both oppressors and oppressed. Very unequal power balances are likely to have negative effects both upon the self-images and potential for political action of subordinate groups. Under such circumstances deterministic belief systems are likely to flourish. More equal power balances may create the conditions whereby subordinate groups can challenge, with varying degrees of effectiveness, their subordination and the hostile stereotyping to which they are subject. However, all these processes – their extent and efficacy – are constrained by the fundamental character of the economic system within which they operate. In the light of the discussion above, how can we portray race relations in Britain today?

The British case

Race relations in Britain are very different from those in, say, the USA. Unlike the USA and a number of other countries Britain did not have domestic slavery but, rather, a colonial system in which racist theories were used to rationalise and justify the privileges of whites; a hangover from this situation is that coloured immigrants are still thought of as subject 'races'.

The 'problem' of race relations is of relatively recent origin in Britain. It is only since the Second World War that there has been a sizeable coloured population in Britain, though blacks have been resident in England for more than four centuries. Many of these earlier residents will have experienced exploitation and discrimination of a kind not unlike that suffered by present-day blacks in Britain: in this sense the so-called race-relations 'problem' has existed for many years as an expression of the relative powerlessness of blacks as an economic and political group in the face of British capitalism, whether it be in the context of colonialism and slavery abroad or the exploitation of black wage-labour within Britain.

The immigration of coloured people from the British Commonwealth in the two decades after 1945 was only part of a broader phenomenon, in that over 350,000 white Europeans also entered the country between 1945 and 1957. In general, such immigration was a product of the chronic labour shortage in the period of economic expansion which followed the war. Most of the early Commonwealth immigrants came from the West Indies, but since 1961 the numbers of Indians, Pakistanis and subsequently Bangladeshis have also been growing. However, the scale of this immigration is frequently exaggerated by both press and politicians, and the notion that Britain is being 'swamped' with immigrants is completely false (concentration in particular urban areas given the impression of 'swamping'). In 1976 the resident coloured population was estimated to be 1.8 million, i.e. only 3.5 per cent of the total population. People from the West Indies made up 40 per cent of this total, Indians 26 per cent, Pakistanis and Bangladeshis 16 per cent, East African Asians 11 per cent, and Black Africans 7 per cent. Moreover, while 1,207,000 immigrants entered Britain between 1970 and 1977, more than 1,400,000 left. (Data from *New Society*, November 1979.)

By the time of the third PSI (Policy Studies Institute) survey into the British black population in 1982 New Commonwealth immigration had declined significantly – reflecting the various immigration legislation introduced since 1962 (see pp. 138–40) – and was almost entirely made up of dependents of people already settled here. The population with New Commonwealth origins had grown to about 2.2 million, of whom about four-fifths were black. The black population is now over 40 per cent British-born and over half of those who are immigrants have lived here for more than fifteen years (Brown, 1984). Estimates for the year 2000 do not expect that the population descended from the New Commonwealth migration of the 1960s and 1970s will then amount to more than 6 per cent of the population.

It should not be thought that coloured immigration from the colonies occurred haphazardly. These workers were *invited* and positively encouraged to come to Britain. For example, London Transport set up centres in the West Indies to recruit bus crews, and from 1956 the British Hotels & Restaurants Association recruited labour from Barbados. In India and Pakistan, Birmid Qualcast had agents to find workers for its foundries. Ironically, Enoch Powell was centrally involved in recruiting West Indians for the National Health Service.

Racial disadvantage

Most of the coloured immigrants have been recruited to fill lower working-class occupational positions and hence suffer the low-status, material and environmental disadvantages experienced by many white manual workers.

In this regard, Castles and Kosack argue that immigrant workers are part of the working class inasmuch as they occupy the same objective position within the capitalist mode of production as members of the 'proletariat' – they neither own nor control the means of production. However, they also argue that the particular hardship and exploitation experienced by immigrants mean that one should distinguish two 'strata' or levels within this proletariat: on the one hand the relatively better-off indigenous workers, and on the other the immigrants, 'who are the most underprivileged and exploited group of society' (Castles and Kosack, 1973, p. 477). Thus, immigrants fall into the same general category of subordination as 'the poor', who will, logically, including many immigrants in their number.

The disadvantages experienced by immigrants as *workers* are then multiplied through *racial* discrimination. It was suggested in Chapter 2 that the life-chances an individual enjoys are, for the majority of the population, determined by the 'market capacity' or skills that he or she can sell on the labour market, but there are unequal opportunities between groups to obtain such skills. In the case of immigrants racial discrimination not only accentuates disadvantageous life-chances for those without skills and qualification, but may also deprive those *with* skills and qualifications of the rewards enjoyed by comparable white workers (particularly in the non-manual strata). This is particularly true for Asians. As the Community Relations Commission (1977, p. 11) says:

> The job levels held by minority men are not equal to those of white men with the same level of educational qualification, even when allowance is made for a possible difference of standard between education in this country and in Asia.

As Smith (1977) has shown, even where coloured workers hold the same job levels as indigenous whites, from professional to unskilled manual, on average whites are paid more. Most coloured workers, of course, are concentrated in the manual occupational strata: whereas only 18 per cent of white males occupy semi- and *unskilled* manual positions, 26 per cent of East Africiam Asians, 32 per cent of West Indians, 36 per cent of Indians and 58 per cent of Pakistanis in Britain are to be found there. Many of these workers are not 'immigrants' in the strict sense of the word. The use of the term 'immigrant' can be misleading because a significant proportion of coloured people in Britain were born in the country and hence are citizens by birth. However, the statistics do not always enable us to distinguish between recent immigrants, long-term residents and other coloured people.

Income level is only one, albeit very important, factor determining life-chances for coloured workers. As the Community Relations Commission argues, a 'cluster of multiple deprivation' can be found. By way of example the Commission (1977, pp. 15–16) refers to Smith's finding that:

> Asians who speak little or no English were found to have low status jobs with few promotion prospects and low wages, to live in an extended family (which led to a high rate of dependents to wage-earners, and tended towards overcrowding in housing), and to occupy poor-quality housing with no, or shared amenities for which their payments in rent or mortgages were high.

Since the 1970s the most important changes in the overall position of coloured 'workers' in Britain has been the rise of unemployment rates among Asian and West Indian men and women to very high levels. Unemployment has been growing at a much faster rate among blacks than that among whites and has opened up an area of massive racial disadvantage that was absent in the 1970s. At the time of Smith's 1974 report the unemployment rate for both white and black people was around 4 per cent, although there was evidence that young West Indian men and all black women suffered a higher rate. Brown's 1982 survey reports that while the white unemployment rate has risen to 13 per cent for men and 10 per cent for women, over the same period the rates for West Indians have risen to 25 per cent and 10 per cent respectively, and for Asians to 20 per cent for both men and women. Brown's survey shows that although unemployment is particularly bad among young people this source of racial disadvantage has also affected older people and it is therefore accurate to identify unemployment as a major new factor of racial inequality for both young and old (Brown, 1984).

Why do coloured 'workers' experience multiple deprivation and, in particular, occupy such a vulnerable position in the labour market? Is there any evidence for the claim that coloured workers represent a convenient 'reserve army' of labour to be utilised or abandoned as the economy dictates? What, if any, is the role of racial prejudice in explaining racial disadvantages?

Racial prejudice against coloured workers by indigenous whites clearly exists, but is not the only factor behind racial disadvantages: it would be naive to suggest that racial disadvantages could be overcome by removing ignorance and language barriers between white and black. Nevertheless, prejudice, as acknowledged earlier, does play an important role in sustaining and legitimating racial exploitation. Prejudicial attitudes tend to be self-confirming, inasmuch as by encouraging discrimination against a coloured group members of this group are forced into subordinate positions which are then taken to be 'proof' of the group's inferiority. A similar process was seen to operate in the case of the poor. As Castles and Kosack (1973, p. 458) remark: 'This vicious circle helps to prevent the group from improving its situation and gaining equality with the dominant group.'

In general, Castles and Kosack argue that prejudice serves three functions: (i) it conceals and yet legitimates the exploitation of coloured labourers by asserting their racial inferiority; (ii) it helps to divert attention from the real economic destructiveness of capitalism that affects all by placing the blame on coloureds for, among other things, job scarcity; and (iii) it may be used by indigenous workers themselves to protect their position in the labour market – employers and government may be supported by indigenous workers in the implementation of discriminatory and exploitative measures against competing coloured workers, as has happened in both Britain and South Africa. In Britain, as in other countries, prejudice has been channelled into organised political movements usually of an extreme right-wing disposition: the National Front party is the prime British example. The Front promotes a fascist political programme through the ideological guise of a fervent British patriotism. It actively seeks the repatriation of all black workers and their families to keep Britain 'truly British'. Coloured workers are quite openly said to be 'inferior to British people', to be 'taking our jobs', or to be 'scroungers'. Such myths have unfortunately been believed by certain sectors of the electorate, in particular unemployed working-class youth, though recently support for the Front has declined because of the opposition from people of all classes, young and old, who want no truck with fascism.

Despite the opposition to groups like the National Front, and the inter-racial communication and perhaps solidarity this has generated, coloured workers in Britain still lack adequate support from fellow white British workers. Those coloured people who become low-paid workers concentrated in the public service, textile and foundary industries do so because of their economic and political weakness. However, coloured immigrants should not be treated as a homogeneous group: newcomers arrive bearing with them differing socioeconomic backgrounds and, as we shall see, enter on different legal terms. Those with qualifications and fluency in English have a better chance of gaining access to higher rewards than others (despite the fact that, as we have seen, the level of their rewards may be lower than that received by white workers in similar jobs). The majority of Commonwealth members, however, who enter Britain lack qualifications, knowledge of welfare rights, and all, since 1971, unless dependants of male immigrants already settled here, are denied 'immigrant' status, being treated now as 'migrant workers' even though they may hold a British passport. Moreover, a large proportion of coloured immigrants have been recruited to low-paid jobs in industrial areas which typically have had weak trade unions: in the textile industry, for example, they are concentrated in the combing and spinning sectors. Furthermore, in industries with tradi- tionally strong trade unions, coloured membership and representation has been relatively low. Trade-union officials and shop stewards are more likely to seek maximum earnings for their own – typically *white* – members. As such they have been able to organise and control the distribution of overtime and shift-work in the interests of their own members' pay packets, as well as using the principle of the closed shop against both white and black non-members.

Changes in the legal status of immigrants

In 1958 serious race riots in Notting Hill, London, and in other British cities were one factor behind the introduction in 1962 of an Act of Parliament restricting immigration from the Commonwealth. The distur- bances demonstrated that the economic benefits of importing cheap labour from the colonies or ex-colonies ('cheap' because the host country had not had to bear the expense of supporting or educating the labour force) had to be weighed against the social cost of political and industrial unrest among the indigenous labour force, certain sectors of which saw immigrants as a threat to their own employment and housing opportunities. The 1962 Act was a significant step in the process of redefining the status of the immigrant from that of Commonwealth citizen to that of migrant labourer. Banton (1972, p. 72) has pointed out that the British labour shortage did not need to be met by immigrants from Jamaica or the Punjab:

> They could have come from Turkey, Spain, Iran or Brazil. That they did not was due chiefly to the Imperial connection. Britain had given her citizenship to people overseas, conferring upon them the right to enter the mother country freely. They did not ask for this right. They were given it as part of a policy British governments chose to pursue.

The 1962 Act withdrew this right of entry for Commonwealth immigrants, as did subsequent legislation (1968) for black UK passport holders without parents or grandparents resident in Britain.

The 1971 Immigration Act finally put an end to any settlement and put all Commonwealth citizens on a par with aliens. Immigrants could only enter this country on a permit to do a specific job in a specific place for a period, initially at least, of not more than twelve months. The government had to give its permission before the original job could be changed, so immigrants were dependent upon employers' recommendations and were thus severely restricted in their industrial and political activities. Like any other foreigner, they might apply for UK citizenship after four years provided that they had been of good behaviour. However, it was also possible for the Home Secretary to deport them if it was 'conducive to the public good as being in the interest of national security or of the relations between the UK and any other country or for other reasons of a political nature'.

The 1971 Immigration Act introduced the concept of 'patriality' effectively changing the status of New Commonwealth citizens to aliens by insisting that only those with British passports born in the UK or whose parents were born here had the 'right of abode', and effectively putting an end to all new 'coloured' immigration.

In 1981 the British Nationality Act was introduced by the Conservative government, ostensibly to clarify the concept of British citizenship and to clear up administrative confusions. There are now three classes of British citizenship, with one of the important consequences of this being that UK citizenship is not automatically gained by birth and residence in Britain; if neither parent was born in the UK or was not lawfully settled here, then a child would not be able to obtain citizenship, until he or she could prove that they had not been absent from the country for more than ninety days in any one of the first ten years of their life.

So there is no longer such a person as a 'Commonwealth immigrant'. Those who came to this country from the Commonwealth before the 1971 Act came into force (January 1973) are not immigrants but 'black settlers'. Those who came afterwards are neither settlers not immigrants; they are simply migrant workers, and their position, correspondingly, is a very weak one.

The government was not just concerned with introducing legislation to curb immigration during this period, but also introduced anti-discriminatory legislation and policies designed to help integration. It has long been assumed that one cannot legislate against prejudice but that one can legislate against discrimination.

The first legislation designed to combat racial discrimination was the Race Relations Act of 1965, which also set up 'conciliation machinery' to deal with complaints of discrimination. This brought into existence the Race Relations Board. Under the terms of the Act the practice of discrimination was made unlawful in public places, e.g. in hotels, restaurants, places of entertainment or on public transport. It was also made an offence to place discriminatory restrictions on the disposal of leases on property, or to stir up racial hatred by means of speech or written matter.

The Race Relations Act of 1968 extended the provisions of the 1965 Act to cover a wider field, notably in the spheres of housing, accommodation and employment, forbidding discrimination generally in the provision of goods, facilities or services to the public.

Despite being motivationally well intentioned, government legislation against discrimination cannot overcome the disadvantaged position of the coloured population in Britain: the law implies that the 'problem' for blacks is racial prejudice, thereby reducing the cause of disadvantage to cultural, ideological or psychological processes. Certainly such processes exist in the form of prejudice, but they arise out of, legitimise and reproduce a structure of inequality that works against the objective interests of black British men and women. In theory, anti-discriminatory legislation gives everyone the legal right to an equal opportunity to be upwardly mobile; but equal opportunity does not imply equal chance (see also Chapter 8 on education). Hence those who adopt a radical perspective in sociology argue that state legislation is simply a cosmetic device designed to prevent unrest, that divisions within the working class between white and black work to the benefit of capital, and thus that racial harmony is impossible until class conflict has been resolved. One need not adopt this perspective to recognise the fundamental weakness of government action: it is frequently pointed out that the anti-discrimination Acts are unenforceable in practice. The coloured population, for example, may not be aware of their rights, may not recognise discrimination against them when it occurs, and if they do may be unwilling to enter into a lengthy complaints procedure through the courts. Furthermore, it is probable that the major source of inequality – disadvantageous life-chances – is likely to engender resignation rather than aspirations for upward mobility among blacks; where this acquiesence occurs, the true extent of the structural constraints on black life-chances remains concealed.

Legislation against discrimination is also proposed with a view towards 'integration' and 'assimilation'. But such notions need close scrutiny: Does 'integration' mean a process through which subordinate racial groups come to accept as legitimate the authority and advantages of the dominant group in society? Or does integration imply a coming together of groups culturally and economically through a process of adaptation, conflict, or competition? Perhaps 'integration', if it occurs anywhere at all, involves a combination of all these processes?

4.5 INTERNATIONAL SUBORDINATION: THE THIRD WORLD

As we have seen, racial discrimination is associated with the exploitation of cheap immigrant labour, a process that has some of its roots in the colonial past. While exploitation of coloured minorities has occurred in Britain and elsewhere in Europe, what about the countries they have come from, for the most part countries which are part of the group collectively known as the 'Third World'?

Just as we have noted that life-chances are unequally distributed within society, so there are unequal life-chances of an international order. The gap between rich and poor countries, once rarely discussed or examined in the popular media of advanced countries, is now regularly revealed for all to see on news broadcasts and documentaries. The global impact of 'Band Aid' should not be underestimated, although it is perhaps unfortunate that it has given the impression that severe impoverishment is a peculiarly African phenomenon: three out of every four people in the world live in poor countries found throughout the southern hemisphere. As in Africa, it is the children who suffer most from the deprivations of food and water: one in every four children in poor countries dies under the age of five.

The relative position of the Third World countries in the world's development hierarchy is normally assessed by comparing international rates of manufacturing and agricultural output, the proportion of the labour force employed in each sector, the level of technology, the development of education, the ratio of imports to exports, and the availability and distribution of consumer goods.

The evidence that we have available from authorities such as the United Nations and the World Bank indicates that there is a wide gap between rich and poor countries in terms of these broad criteria of 'development'. Nevertheless, there is also evidence that shows a remarkable growth rate in a few countries, the so-called 'newly industrialising countries' (NICs), i.e. Brazil, Mexico, South Korea, Taiwan, Hong Kong and Singapore, which some economists (e.g. Little, 1983) believe heralds a period of rapid industrialisation throughout the Third World. Brazil, for example, has had a growth rate approaching 10 per cent per annum since 1967, its exports are up, particularly in manufactured goods, and its oil production has increased fourfold since 1973 giving Brazil one of the highest Gross Domestic Products (GDP) in the southern hemisphere. Liberal, 'free market' economists, such as Little, argue that the reason why NICs have been successful is because they have adopted an export-oriented, 'free trade' policy which has attracted substantial overseas investment to promote dynamic, long-term growth.

However, while not underrating these achievements, there is good reason to be more cautious about the prospects for Third World development.

First, the NICs GDP may have grown but at considerable internal cost and without necessarily establishing an economic infrastructure conducive to sustained development. Foreign investment has been especially attracted to the cheap labour available in the NICs, and the low-paid workers – in the multinational subsidiaries – seem to have benefited little from their employment. In Brazil, for example, it is the richest 10 per cent that take 50 per cent of National Income while the share of the other 90 per cent actually fell between 1960 and 1986. Foreign ownership of manufacturing in Brazil means that while the Brazilian elite prosper, there is little 'trickling down' of income to the rest of the population. Moreover, capital returns or profits will be returned to foreign shareholders, while foreign companies increasing ownership of land has displaced many rural tenants and small farmers who can find little alternative work as the labour market is so limited.

Secondly, the vast majority of Third World countries have over the past two decades experienced little or no growth at all: this suggests that there is a limit to the number of Third World states that can attract the level of foreign investment and loan capital that the NICs have. Some of these poor countries of Africa and Asia are becoming not merely relatively but absolutely poorer.

Finally, the dynamism of the NICs seems itself to be draining away rapidly in recent years as their debts to international agencies such as the IMF and commercial banks increase.

Thus, in general, crude statistical measures of whatever GDP growth there has been in the Third World do not tell us anything about the *character* of this growth. The kind of industrial expansion in less developed countries is very different from that which occurred in the industrialisation of the first capitalist sector of the world economy. The simple presence of economic resources such as capital, technology and labour within a Third World country is a necessary but not sufficient condition for its development. The poor country needs to be able to *control* these through its state or class institutions: however, usually sufficient control (particularly over multinational corporations) is lacking, a factor which is one of the most important political aspects reproducing the subordination and stagnation of poor countries; it is, in part, an expression of *the weakness of both the dominant and subordinate classes within them.*

Does this weakness derive from an inherent incapacity of people in the Third World to develop their societies towards modern industrialisation? There is a popular view that Third World members lack 'planning' and 'know-how' and are unable to channel their energies into useful enterprise, apart from blindly producing more and more mouths to feed. Such a view, however, merely draws attention to superficial and somewhat caricatured features of the contemporary Third World. Despite its inadequacies, however, a more elaborate version of this popular thesis can be found within sociological theory itself.

Modernisation theory

There is a school of thought, known as 'modernisation theory', which claims that one of the principle reasons why the Third World is underdeveloped is that many of its countries have distinctive cultural characteristics that block or hinder economic growth and political stability. These societies have been said to be suffused by values of 'traditionalism' that promote backward-looking and fatalistic attitudes, attitudes that do not encourage innovation, enterprise or achievement. Modernisation theory puts forward the view that less developed societies can become more developed or 'modern' by being exposed to the values and norms of advanced societies, through communication, trade, and so on. Many development economists – such as Rostow – have argued strongly for the introduction and diffusion of Western economic, social and political institutions in the Third World as *necessary* conditions for growth. Rostow (1960) has claimed that the development of *all* societies can be understood in terms of a logical, continual progression through 'stages' of growth.

Other theorists, such as McClelland (1967) and Lerner (1964), who adopt a socio-psychological perspective, have gone so far as to suggest training courses for Third World elites to ensure that they develop the appropriate entrepreneurial values and attitudes. In general, this assumes that in the long term developing societies will inevitably become more and more like the already advanced industrial countries of the globe, as their institutions and values are reorganised and adapted to favour modernity.

Underdevelopment theory

Against this, now much criticised, theory there is another school of thought that argues that one cannot understand Third World poverty through identifying alleged deficiencies in poor countries' cultural make-up; instead, it is claimed that Third World underdevelopment is a socio-economic condition *brought about* by processes associated with the growth of North Atlantic countries over the past century and more. This position has been adopted by some neo-Marxist and radical economists and sociologists such as Frank (1971) and Griffin (1974). They see the development and underdevelopment of societies as simultaneously and mutually produced manifestations of the *same global* historical process. Not only does the modernisation thesis neglect the imperialism of the last few hundred years but it also seems to present development as a process that takes place within discrete, isolated, social systems. The decisive strength of the radical perspective is its *global* viewpoint. We now examine the historical analysis on which this perspective is based (see Webster, 1984, ch. 2).

The wealth of West European economies – particularly their mineral wealth – was as much the result of colonial exploitation (especially in southern Africa) as it was a reflection of the 'native wit' of the English, French or Dutch. By military and political domination the capitalist states established a monopoly of international trade that allowed 'merchant capitalism' to flourish and the 'primitive accumulation' of capital to ensue: profits were made by buccaneering on the high seas and the plundering of Africa, Asia and Latin America. This account implies the need to integrate into one historical analysis the development of capitalism that has taken place in the advanced sectors and the destructive consequences of this development for other sectors we now call 'the Third World'.

Colonialism exploited not simply natural but also human resources. The work of Williams (1972), Dumont (1966) and Rodney (1972) catalogues the colonial promotion of the slave trade in Africa. During the seventeenth and eighteenth centuries there developed what is known as the 'triangular trade' system whereby European (particularly British) manufactured goods (often of inferior quality) were exchanged at a profit in the colonies in exchange for African Negroes, who in turn were traded as slaves for produce in the Americas. It is important to note that profits were made at every stage of the triangular transaction and inevitably encouraged capital accumulation in England. It is estimated that between 1450 and 1870 nearly nine million male and female Africans between the ages of 15 and 35 were sold as slaves. This figure does not take into account the number who died in transit to the Americas on the slave ships. Clearly, the slave trade had a major demographic effect on Africa, draining the continent of its skilled labour power. British, French and Dutch mining in South Africa and the then Rhodesia complemented the drain on Africa's human resources: the gold and copper mines took able-bodied young men from the rural areas, which, consequently populated for the most part by older men, children and women, were unable to sustain any real level of agricultural productivity.

As might be expected, those regions that experienced the full force of European colonialism suffered economic *and* political distortion. Pre-existing tribal boundaries and trade routes in both Latin America and Africa were rapidly destroyed by the slave trade and by the establishment of coastal ports and towns by European merchants and settlers linked together by the shortest possible navigable route that paid little or no attention to tribal territories.

Typically, the colonies were very much administrative conveniences rather than self-determined nation states, even though prior to colonial expansion, the indigenous African, Asian and Latin American countries did have emerging political systems that were complex and advanced. As Worsley (1984, p. 3) says:

> When Europeans first arrived in Africa and the Americas, they often found themselves dealing with societies whose levels of economic development and cultural sophistication were superior or equal to anything Europe could show.

Their underdevelopment, today, is not a natural condition but an unnatural one, a social state which is the product of history; not a passive condition but the consequence of conscious action; not something that just happened, governed by the logic of an impersonal system, but something that was done to people by other people

Independence has done little to alter this state of affairs of control by the dependency on 'other people' whether these be ex-colonial powers, multinational corporations or the powerful financial agencies of the world. As we saw earlier, even the NICs are now beginning to experience major problems as their debts increase (e.g. Mexico's is over $100 billion today) and as the world international recession bites. There are only a handful of socialist state in the Third World that have had some degree of success in industrialisation and real GDP growth; the more important are China and North Korea. For the most part their success is based on their historical isolation from both colonialism and the world capitalist system, their resource endowment and their strong centralised States that have very effectively mobilised their countries' respective capital and labour to promote a growth which has benefited the population as a whole. There is little real chance of other, poorer Third World socialist states – such as Tanzania – emulating the Chinese or North Korean success (see Kitching, 1982).

The underdevelopment perspective does, then, point to the economic and political constraints that currently restrict Third World development. In many ways, one can regard the poorest Third World states – such as Burkina Faso and Ethiopia in Africa – as countries experiencing social closure at an international level; in a sense, their reproduced subordination is akin to the socially 'enclosed' position of the low-paid working class discussed in Chapter 3. Modernisation theory ignores the way in which this disadvantage is the product of a world system, referring instead to the traditionalistic orientation of Third World people. Modernisation is not dependent on the gradual unfolding of an evolutionary process of development or on the adaptation of cultural values (important though the latter may be). Rather, the underdevelopment theory's historical foundation lends strength to the view that development is more dependent on the access to, and use of, political and economic power. As this is denied most Third World societies, many of them will remain underdeveloped, and where development occurs it is likely to be highly distorted.

4.6 CONCLUSION

This chapter has examined four forms of subordination, distinct in their concrete expression but sharing a basic similarity by virtue of their being a product of the dynamics of social stratification. All four, as we have seen, have in varying forums, academic and non-academic, been inaccurately depicted as the result of subordinate groups' particular cultural orientation. Disadvantage, whether experienced by the young, the poor, immigrant minorities or Third World countries, will not be overcome simply by attempting to change these groups' *outlook*. Too often the problems of these groups are seen in this way and dealt with on a piecemeal, partial and fragmentary basis via welfare and aid agencies. Instead, a solution can only be social, national and international, a matter of re-assessing and reorganising social priorities, and ultimately dependent on basic changes in socioeconomic arrangements and ideologies.

REFERENCES TO CHAPTER 4

Banton, M. (1972) *Racial Minorities*, London, Fontana.
Baran, P. A. and Sweezy, P. M. (1966) *Monopoly Capital*, Harmondsworth, Penguin.
Berger, P. and Berger, B. (1972) *Sociology*, New York, Basic Books.
Brake, M. (1979) *The Sociology of Youth Culture and Youth Subcultures*, London, Routledge & Kegan Paul.
Brown, C. (1984) *Black and White Britain*, London, Heinemann.
Castles, S. and Kosack, G. (1973) *Immigrant Workers and Class Structure in Western Europe*, Oxford University Press.
Clarke, J. *et al.* (1976) 'Subcultures, Cultures and Class: a Theoretical Overview', in S. Hall and T. Jefferson (eds), *Resistance Through Rituals*, London, Hutchinson.
Clarke, J. and Jefferson, T. (1976) 'Working Class Youth Cultures', in G. Mungham and G. Pearson (eds), *Working Class Youth Cultures*, London, Routledge & Kegan Paul.
Coates, K. and Silburn, R. (1970) *Poverty: The Forgotten Englishmen*, Harmondsworth, Penguin.
Community Relations Commission (1977) *Urban Deprivation, Racial Inequality and Social Policy: A Report*, London, HMSO.
Dumont, R. (1966) *False Start in Africa*, London, Deutsch.
Dunning, E. (1972) 'Dynamics of Racial Stratification: Some Preliminary Observations', *Race*, vol. 13, no. 4.
Eisenstadt, S. (1956) *From Generation to Generation*, New York, Free Press.
Frank, A. G. (1971) *Sociology of Development and the Underdevelopment of Sociology*, London, Plato Press.
Gans, H. (1971) 'Poverty and Culture', in P. Townsend (ed.), *The Concept of Poverty*, London, Heinemann.
Griffin, K. (1974), *The Political Economy of Agrarian Change*, London, Macmillan.
Heidensohn, F. (1985) *Women and Crime*, London, Macmillan.
Kitching, G. (1982) *Development and Underdevelopment in Historical Perspective*, London, Methuen.
Lerner, D. (1964) *The Passing of Traditional Society*, New York, Free Press.
Lewis, O. (1961) *Children of Sanchez*, New York, Random House.
Lewis, O. (1966) *La Vida*, New York, Random House.
Little, I. M. D. (1983) *Economic Development*, New York, Basic Books.

Lockwood, D. (1970) 'Race, Conflict and Plural Society', in S. Zubaida (ed.), *Race and Racialism*, London, Tavistock.

McClelland, D. (1967) *The Achieving Society*, New York, Van Nostrand.

McRobbie, A. and Garber, J. (1976) 'Girls and Subcultures', in S. Hall and T. Jefferson (eds), *Resistance Through Rituals*, London, Hutchinson.

Miliband, R. (1974) 'Politics and Poverty', in D. Wedderburn (ed.), *Poverty, Inequality and Class Structure*, Cambridge University Press.

Mungham, G. and Pearson, G. (1976) 'Introduction: Troubled Youth, Troubling World', in G. Mungham and G. Pearson (eds), *Working Class Youth Cultures*, London, Rouledge & Kegan Paul.

Murdock, G. and McCron, G. (1976) 'Youth and Class: the Career of a Confusion', in G. Mungham and G. Pearson (eds), *Working Class Youth Cultures*, London, Routledge & Kegan Paul.

Parsons, T. (1965) 'Why "Freedom Now", Not Yesterday', and 'Full Citizenship for the Negro American', in T. Parsons and K. B. Clark (eds), *The Negro American*, Boston, Houghton Mifflin.

Rex, J. (1970) 'The Concept of Race in Sociological Theory', in S. Zubaida (ed.), *Race and Racialism*, London, Tavistock.

Robins, D. and Cohen, P. (1978) *Knuckle Sandwich*, Harmondsworth, Penguin.

Rodney, W. (1972) *How Europe Underdeveloped Africa*, Paris, Bogle L'Ouverture.

Rostow, W. W. (1960) *The Stages of Economic Growth*, Cambridge University Press.

Smith, D. (1977) *The Facts of Racial Disadvantage*, Harmondsworth, Penguin.

Sugarman, B. (1968) *Sociology*, London, Heinemann.

Taylor, I. (1971). 'Soccer Consciousness and Soccer Hooliganism', in S. Cohen (ed.), *Images of Deviance*, Harmondsworth, Penguin.

Webster, A. (1984) *Introduction to the Sociology of Development*, London, Macmillan.

Westergaard, J. and Resler, H. (1975) *Class in a Capitalist Society*, London, Heinemann.

Williams, E. (1972) *Capitalism and Slavery*, London, Deutsch.

Willis, P. (1978) *Profane Culture*, London, Routledge & Kegan Paul.

Worsley, P. (1984) *The Three Worlds*, London, Weidenfeld & Nicolson.

5

Gender Divisions in Society

5.1 INTRODUCTION

In Chapter 1, it was pointed out that many of our commonsense notions about 'natural' differences between the sexes do not stand up to scrutiny. The more informed we are about other cultures, and other periods in history, the more we are forced to recognise that men or women can be active or passive, aggressive or conciliatory, sexually voracious or sexually timid, depending upon the society in which they are born (and, to an extent, their position within that society). However, there are a number of important points to recognise about sexual difference and gender divisions.

First, we can clarify our thinking by adopting Oakley's (1972) distinction between *sex* and *gender*. Sex refers to the most basic physiological differences between men and women – differences in genitals and reproductive capacities. Gender refers, on the other hand, to the culturally specific patterns of behaviour, either actual or normative, which may be attached to the sexes. When speaking of *sexual* differences, we are distinguishing between males and females; when speaking of *gender*, between masculine and feminine. The content of the male/female distinction is genetically determined and largely universal; the content of the masculine/feminine distinction is culturally determined and highly variable.

Second, most societies do prescribe different activities and characteristics for males and females; these may come to be perceived as 'natural' by the people concerned. In this way the fairly limited range of biological differences between male and female are heightened, or compounded, by culturally prescribed gender differences. As Mathieu remarks, thinking of the French language which assigns a gender to objects such as books, streets and rocks, 'We must therefore try to understand that each society *uses* the biological sexes to construct a sexual grammar . . . just as arbitrary as the grammatical genders of the language' (1977, p. 2). One of the things we will consider later in this chapter is the way in which patterns of socialisation in our own society encourage females to become feminine and males to become masculine. The amount of attention paid to shaping the personalities and interests of males and females along lines deemed appropriate by our culture is in itself an indication that masculinity and femininity are socially constructed; as the angry girl in the cartoon (Figure

5.1) emphasises, if femininity were biologically induced, then much of the process of socialisation and social control would be superfluous.

FIGURE 5.1 *Cartoon from Liz Mackie, Jo Nesbitt, Christine Roche and Lesley Ruda,* Sour Cream, *published in 1979 by Sour Cream, 136 Florence Street, London N1*

Third, gender divisions cannot be subsumed under the question of gender differences. While masculinity varies – for example, tenderness is sometimes allowed, sometimes tabooed – in most societies, males, whatever their gender characteristics, have more power and more authority than women; more than that, they have power *over* women. Men and women are, then, not merely *different* but in a relation of subordination and domination. The structure of subordination and domination is called *patriarchy*. Although there is a great deal of controversy about the precise connotations of the term, at least it implies a hierarchy of social relations and institutions in which and through which men are able to dominate women (and other, more junior, men).

In Chapter 2 we saw that inequality is not explicable in terms of the individual attributes of property-owners or of workers. Stratification inheres in relations – to understand wage labour we have to understand capital. Similarly, the inequality of males and females is not something that can be explained by reference to the qualities of one or the other sex. Sexual inequality or oppression inheres in the relations between women and men.

5.2 THE SIGNIFICANCE OF FORMAL OR LEGAL EQUALITY

The campaign for social and political equality for women appears as one of the great success stories of the past one hundred years. Women gained full voting rights in 1928. A number of important legal rulings and administrative decisions restored or extended to women the right to hold public office, to enter the professions, and to own and administer property. Laws governing family life gradually circumscribed husbands' exclusive rights over wives and children, so that women were enabled, for example, to sue for divorce on the same terms as men. In the 1970s two important pieces of legislation – the Equal Pay Act (1970) and the Sex Discrimination Act (1975) – 'outlawed' certain categories of less favourable treatment to men or women on the basis of their sex.

'You've come a long way, baby!' quipped an advertisement for Virginia Slims in the 1970s, and (if we ignore the implication that cigarette smoking represents the ultimate in liberation) most people would probably agree. Yet the notion that the traditional domesticity and dependence of women in the nineteenth century yielded to complete equality with men in the twentieth century needs to be qualified in the light of sociological and historical evidence. On the one hand, the Victorian period may have represented a low point in the history of the relations of the sexes, and it may not be correct to characterise the Victorian situation as the 'traditional' one. It has been argued that three centuries earlier women enjoyed a more prominent position in public life; before the end of the sixteenth century women had, according to Sachs (1978, p. 37), 'voted in Parliamentary elections, acted as attorneys, held leading positions in trading guilds, and even occupied high military office'. A comparison of the sixteenth and nineteenth centuries should warn, therefore, against too readily accepting Victorian standards as representing the 'traditional place' of women. Such a comparison should also make clear that a view suggesting steady, progressive advance in women's position throughout the ages is unfounded; the history of the sexes is one of shifting balances of power, sometimes in the direction of greater equality, and at other times away.

On the other hand, the notion that there is complete equality between women and men today, even in the narrow sense of formal rights, does not stand up to scrutiny. Despite the high proportion of married women who have an income of their own (or who need one), the assumption that married women are not, and should not be, financially independent of their husbands continues to be a cornerstone of the administration of the welfare state. As described by Land (1976), this assumption has been used to justify different pension and disability entitlements for married women. It underlies the payment of the taxation subsidy for married persons specifically and exclusively to the husband. A most important consequence of the assumption that wives are dependent is that wives (and female cohabitees) are thereby not entitled to draw supplementary benefit in their own right, regardless of their financial circumstances or employment history; the self-fulfilling prophecy element of this regulation is neatly summarised by

Wilson and her associates (1974, p. 274): 'The Social Security scheme starts with the assumption that women are dependents of men. Because of this expectation, it almost forces them to be so.' Since the passage of the Sex Discrimination Act (1975) it is sometimes assumed that any remaining discrimination based upon sex is vestigial, and will fade away of its own accord. However, far from a situation of continuous movement towards equality, new legal and administrative distinctions in the treatment of women and men have been introduced *since* the Sex Discrimination Act came into effect. Under the provisions of the 1980 Immigration Rules, for example, many British women were denied the right to bring their foreign-born spouses to live with them in Britain, though all British men retained that right. This rule has in practice been particularly disadvantageous to black women; it is thus racist as well as sexist, and is an indication of the shortfall of legislative attempts to establish racial and sexual equality.

The impact of the Sex Discrimination Act (1975)

In an early assessment of the Sex Discrimination Act Coussins (1980) argues that the main impact of the law was educational: the Act provided an impetus for people to recognise that sexual inequalities are neither natural nor inevitable, but man- (and woman- ?) made. On the other hand, in terms of ensuring non-discriminatory treatment in employment, education and other spheres, Coussins describes the Act as 'feeble'; difficulties of proof and enforcement have limited its usefulness. In her view the crucial areas excluded from the Sex Discrimination Act demonstrate governments' *lack* of commitment to equality of the sexes:

> Tax, social security, pensions, nationality and immigration are the most important exclusions. The Government was clearly not prepared funda-mentally to challenge the position of women's dependency on men, whether it be for money or for status; and it did not intend to do anything which meant spending money on achieving equality (Coussins, 1980, p. 10).

It should be clear, then, that the legal status of women and men is far from equal; women continue to be regarded in many respects as adjuncts of their husbands. But formal or legal equality is in any case an inadequate index for assessing the structural position of different social groups; as we have seen in earlier chapters, manual workers have *legal* equality with others in our society, but this equality goes hand in hand with persistent and severe inequalities in life-chances and power. Before examining the distribution of income between women and men, a few points can be raised for consider-ation.

First, an assessment of movements towards or away from equality, and of the consequences, must not ignore the absolute condition of the groups being compared; in certain circumstances equality for women would involve a worsening of their life-chances. For example, women have at present certain protections in law which are not available to men; protective legislation, for instance, gives women and not men the possibility of resisting shift-work and night-work, while some women are entitled to retire and draw a pension five years earlier than men. Whether women's lot would improve or deteriorate by attaining equality with men on these issues depends largely on whether change involves removing the protections and earlier retirement eligibility from women, or extending similar protections and opportunities to men.

Second, it should be borne in mind that equal opportunities legislation *does not guarantee* equality of condition. Just as the freedom to dine at the Ritz rings hollow if you lack the money to pay the bill, so too the freedom to pursue a career is illusory unless appropriate training, encouragement and advice, and – in the case of those in charge of children – suitable help with child care are widely available. There is, for example, no legal disability which prevents women from assuming directorships in industry; yet a survey published in 1978 of the twenty largest firms in the United Kingdom (including BP, Shell, Unilever, ICI) revealed a total of 288 men on their boards of directors, and not a single woman (*Guardian*, 11 September 1978).

The third reservation to bear in mind is that formal equality tells us little about informal social relations between men and women, the sphere about which legislation is relatively silent. Having the vote, for instance, does not ensure that women will be treated as politically important or politically responsible. In fact, many discussions of the legal status of women contain an implicit assumption about the powerlessness of women, as when it is said that 'Women have been *allowed* to vote', or that 'Women have been *given* the right'. Such statements imply, perhaps unintentionally, that whatever rights women have are due to the goodwill of others – that women are not active political agents with the capacity to influence their own destinies.

Patterns of inequality: the male earnings advantage

The right to work does not guarantee earnings which most people would see as a living wage. According to the *New Earnings Survey 1985* (see Table 5.1), over 35 per cent of women in full-time employment (56 per cent of manual, 29 per cent of non-manual), but less than 8 per cent of men, were earning less in April 1985 than £100 gross per week. Women constitute a disproportionately large percentage of low-paid workers in Britain today.

Moreover, these data, concentrating as they do on full-time workers' cash earnings, underestimate the disparity between women's incomes and men's. Approximately 44 per cent of women in the labour force are employed on a part-time basis; they experience poorer prospects for training, greater insecurity and reduced fringe benefits, as well as lower hourly rates than full-time colleagues who might be doing identical work. Furthermore, like other low-paid workers, women are likely to be awarded less in the way of fringe benefits than those whose cash income is relatively high. If comparisons of male and female earnings included the value of fringe benefits, and took part-time as well as full-time workers into account, then the male earnings advantage would be even greater than it appears in Table 5.1.

The male earnings advantage

Our analysis in earlier chapters highlighted the fact that manual workers – women or men – are systematically disadvantaged in comparison with their non-manual counterparts. Yet, as can be seen below, there is greater similarity of earnings between workers of the same sex across the manual/non-manual boundary than there is between women and men within a single occupational class. In order of their average gross weekly earnings, the incomes of women and men (full-time employees only) in Britain in April 1985 were as follows:

Male non-manual workers	£225.00
Male manual workers	£163.60
Female non-manual workers	£133.80
Female manual workers	£101.30

The excess of men's earnings over those of women (the 'male earnings advantage') was £91.20 among non-manual employees, and £62.30 among manual workers. The relatively privileged women who are in non-manual jobs earn on average £29.80 less a week than male manual workers.

Why are women's earnings so much lower than those of men? In part this is due to longer hours worked by men; male workers are able to boost their basic rate earnings by overtime, as well as by shift premia and bonus schemes, to a far greater extent than females workers.

However, in April 1985, non-manual men earned £91.20 more than non-manual women, even though the men's working week was a mere two hours longer. Moreover, a look at gross hourly pay reveals that – even with the effects of overtime excluded – there is a male earnings advantage of £1.18 per hour (£1.04 among manual workers, and £2.15 among those in non-manual jobs).

The male earnings advantage is in large part accounted for by the segregation of women into occupations to which lower pay and status is

TABLE 5.1

Earnings and hours worked by women and men in April 1985: adult employees in full-time work whose pay was not affected by absence

	All women	All men	Manual workers		Non-manual workers	
			Women	Men	Women	Men
Average gross weekly earnings (before tax or other deductions)	£126.4	£192.4	£101.3	£163.6	£133.8	£225.0
Proportion whose gross weekly earnings were:						
less than £100	35.3%	7.7%	56.2%	9.7%	29.2%	5.4%
less than £120	55.2%	17.3%	78.0%	22.7%	48.5%	11.2%
Average hours worked per week,	37.3	41.9	39.5	44.5	36.6	38.6
of which overtime hours	0.8	3.7	1.5	5.4	0.5	1.6
Average gross hourly earnings, excluding overtime pay and over-time hours	332p	450p	253p	357p	358p	573p

Source: Department of Employment (1985) *New Earnings Survey 1985*, London, HMSO, Part A, Table 1, pp. A14–15.

attached, and by their concentration at the bottom end of the career structure within each occupation. The pattern of horizontal and vertical segregation will be examined in more detail in the next section of the chapter. But it must be recognised that the effects of sex segregation are crucial in explaining not only the male earnings advantage but also the very limited success of the Equal Pay Act.

The impact of the Equal Pay Act

An immediate effect of the Equal Pay Act was a significant narrowing of the male earnings advantage (see Table 5.2). Women's gross hourly earnings rose from being 63.1 per cent of men's in 1970, to 75.5 per cent in 1977. Since the late 1970s, however, women's full-time hourly earnings appear to have stabilised at a level 25 to 27 per cent lower than men's; if calculated on a weekly basis, the shortfall is 33 to 37 per cent. Most commentators agree that although the Equal Pay Act may continue to offer a legal remedy to a handful of women or men who experience discrimination in pay and conditions at work, it is unlikely to occasion equal incomes between women and men.

TABLE 5.2

*Women's earnings as a proportion of men's: full-time employees aged 18 and over,
1970–85*

	Average gross hourly earnings, excluding effects of overtime (%)	Average gross weekly earnings, including effects of overtime (%)
1970	63.1	54.5
1974	67.4	56.4
1975	72.1	61.5
1976	75.1	64.3
1977	75.5	64.9
1978	73.9	64.8
1979	73.0	63.6
1980	73.5	64.8
1981	74.8	66.7
1982	73.9	65.8
1983	74.2	66.6
1984	73.5	65.8
1985	74.0	

Source: Equal Opportunities Commission (1985), *Ninth Annual Report, 1984*, Manchester, EOC, Table 4.1 and Figure 4.1, p. 80 and Table 4.3, p. 82; Department of Employment, *Employment Gazette* (October 1985) Table 4, p.387.

The explicit aim behind the Equal Pay Act was to eliminate differentiation based on sex with respect to pay (or terms and conditions of employment) between women and men doing like work (or work judged to have equal value according to job evaluation) at the same or associated workplaces. Employers were allowed five years, until 1975, to ensure that their payment practices accorded with the Act.

The limited effectiveness of the Equal Pay Act is not surprising given that men and women, prior to 1970, had generally been discouraged from doing like work; in many firms, women are assigned to different jobs than men, so that there is no basis for comparison for a claim of equal pay. In addition, during the five-year implementation period, many firms (sometimes with the collaboration of trade unions) took steps to ensure that the earnings of male employees would continue to outstrip those of female work-mates. Snell (1979) documents several such 'minimising actions': introducing new job segregations by sex where previously there had been a mixed workforce; hiring a handful of men for very menial tasks at exceptionally low pay, so that it could not be claimed that women were earning less than the lowest-paid man in the firm (though they might be earning less than the vast majority of men); introducing new systems of grading which gave greater weighting to traits associated with 'male' jobs (e.g. lifting heavy loads) than to those associated with 'female' jobs (e.g. manual dexterity). The last minimising action raises the possibility that the classification of occupations according to 'skill' or similar criteria may tell us less about actual job content than about the power of different groups negotiating over the classifications. As Phillips and Taylor (1980, p. 79) explain:

> Far from being an objective economic fact, skill is often an ideological category imposed on certain types of work by virtue of the sex and power of the workers who perform it.

There are some general points worth noting about data on sex differences in earnings. First, women's average earnings may be small in comparison with men's, but they can not be regarded as 'pin money'. Setting out to challenge the 'myth of the male breadwinner', Land (1975) reported that in 1971 at least one household in six, excluding pensioner households, was dependent to some extent on a woman's earnings or benefits. The wages of women, then and now, often staved off poverty for their families. An analysis conducted by the Central Policy Review Staff (1980, para 6.14) indicates that the number of families with incomes below the official poverty line in 1980 would have been three to four times greater if it were not for the crucial contribution made by the earnings of wives.

Second, women themselves are more likely than men to experience poverty. Townsend's extensive study of poverty in the United Kingdom indicated that 57.2 per cent of those in households in poverty were women. The 'proportion of women in poverty', Townsend notes, 'was higher than of men at all ages except under 15' (Townsend, 1979, p. 285). Women are vulnerable to poverty in several respects: their earnings are, as we have seen, lower than men's; women live longer than men, and spend a greater proportion of their lives beyond retirement age, and yet are less likely than men to be entitled to occupational pensions. A survey carried out in 1982 found that 62 per cent of male employees, but only 32 of female employees, were covered by an occupational pension scheme (Ritchie and Barrowclough, 1983, Table 2.1); the male earnings advantage is likely, therefore, to be carried over into old age. But the factor that has contributed most to the 'feminization of poverty' (Scott, 1984) has been a rapid increase, mainly through divorce, in the number of women raising children on their own. The Finer report on one-parent families in 1971 identified the low wages available to women, and the lack of day-care facilities to enable single mothers to hold full-time employment, as the major factor perpetuating the poverty of one-parent families (Finer Report, 1974). One-parent families made up 58 per cent of families with children on supplementary benefit in 1981, and 95 per cent of them were headed by women (National Council for One Parent Families, 1981).

It should be added that assessments of poverty which rely on analysing family or household income undoubtedly underestimate the number of women who experience severe material deprivation, for such assessments make the often unwarranted assumption that the benefits of income are equally distributed among members of the household. This assumption has been challenged by studies which suggest that in many households, the lion's share of resources (access to meat, to expenditure on health, to money for leisure) goes to men (Pahl, 1985, ch. 3; Charles and Kerr, 1986; Delphy, 1984, ch. 3; Oren, 1974) and that the strains of ensuring that children in low-income households have the food, clothing and extras that they need often involve mothers, rather than fathers, in sacrificing their own standard of living (Land, 1972; McKee and Bell, 1983; Whitehead, 1981). As Graham comments, 'the presence of a high wage-earner does not guarantee a high standard of living for all the family. Money can be distributed in such a way that there is "poverty amongst plenty"' (1984, p. 22).

A third point concerns the implications of inequalities in pay for the autonomy of women. If women are less able than men to command a 'living wage', then they will also be more dependent on men for economic survival; and, of course, this is particularly true where women have primary responsibility for the care and protection of children. Thus the structure of income and reward reinforces the dependency aspect of marriage, and makes other options less viable for women than for men.

Any attempt to understand gender divisions must take us beyond a simple check-list of inequalities. It is necessary to examine the different structure of men's and women's lives, an examination which will touch upon the consequences of income (and other) inequalities and upon some of the institutions and practices that reinforce those inequalities. We have broken this discussion down into four areas, areas which overlap but which are analytically distinct: employment; domestic labour or housework; reproduction; and sexuality.

5.3 EMPLOYMENT

Some form of division of labour based upon sex has been a feature of virtually all societies and periods in history of which we have knowledge. But the characterisation of women as 'non-productive' homemakers is relatively specific to the later stages of industrial capitalism.

It is useful to put the return of married women to the paid labour force since the Second World War into some historical perspective.

As we shall see in Chapter 7, the existence of most families in Western history has been a somewhat precarious one. Before the changes wrought by the emergence of industrial capitalism, all the members of most households had to work. Whether they were engaged in agricultural labour, or cottage industry such as weaving or spinning, none but the very youngest children would be exempt from making a contribution to the economic survival of the family. Moreover, when families were forced to take factory employment because other forms of livelihood were curtailed, often the entire family of mother, children and father entered the factory together. The notion that only men should support the family – that they should provide the income for wives and children as well as for themselves – was not only impracticable (their earnings would not have been sufficient) but in many cases abhorrent, involving an unwelcome precedent.

However, as we know, many children and many married women were in fact gradually excluded from factory labour in the course of the nineteenth century. The notion that they thereby stopped working (leaving aside the issue of whether housework is work) is open to doubt. Probably the vast majority of single working-class women worked – in factories or sweat-shops, in domestic service, and so on. Many of them continued to contribute to family income even after the birth of children forced them to spend more time in the home; they took in laundry, for example, or did sewing, or made buttons and lace. Many middle-class women similarly worked in the family business, ran small lodging houses, or acted as governesses or nurses to the children of the well-to-do. As Land (1975) points out, much of the labour of these women was simply rendered invisible to official eyes by the practice of collecting census data in such a way that only the labour of male members of a household was classified as 'employment' or 'economic activity'.

The First and Second World Wars wrought vast changes in people's lives. During both wars, in the absence of male labour to run munitions factories and steel works, public services and engineerings firms, notions of a 'woman's place' were temporarily swept aside. Women were cajoled and instructed to enter these industries in vast numbers. To make it easier for women with family obligations to take up a job during the Second World War, nurseries and crèches were provided in abundance and British restaurants offered cheap meals. After the war, in spite of evidence that the majority of newly employed women wished to keep their jobs, these facilities were largely withdrawn; women were encouraged to return home 'where they belonged'. From this brief sketch it should be clear that the 'male breadwinner/female homemaker' dichotomy does not offer an accurate summary of the traditional division of labour between women and men; rather, it has the character of an assertion that obscures a complex reality, and justifies particular patterns of exploitation of women.

In the 1960s, during a period of economic expansion, women were again acknowledged by industry and by the state as a large reservoir of effort and talent, but by then women had already begun to re-assert their right to jobs and careers. However, women's rapidly increasing presence in industry and commerce (from 32 per cent of the labour force in 1951 to 41 per cent in 1984) did not mean the dismantling of the gender hierarchy which had been reinforced by the earlier denial to women of independent sources of income. On the contrary, some of the privileges accorded to men within patriarchal family structures were reproduced, with modifications, in the relationships of women to men in the workplace.

Gender divisions in employment

Gender is a fundamental feature around which the labour force of contemporary Britain is fragmented. In the first place, female workers tend to be concentrated in a relatively narrow range of occupations. Although eighteen occupational orders are listed in the *New Earnings Survey 1985* Part E, Table 135, pp. E100–105), over 70 per cent of full-time female workers (and an even higher proportion of part-time female employees) are contained in only three groupings: clerical work; professional and similar occupations in education, welfare and health; and personal services. Within these three occupational groups, female employees are further concentrated in jobs that have come to be defined as 'women's work'. In the category of professional and similar occupations in education, welfare and health, for example, the largest occupation for women is nursing. Women who are classified as 'personal service workers' are mainly domestic staff and school helpers (98.1 per cent are women); counter-hands and kitchen assistants (92.5 per cent female); or cleaners, road sweepers and caretakers (74.4 per cent are women) (*Census 1981, Economic Activity, Great Britain* (1984), Table A, pp. xviii–xx). Evidence such as this indicates that women are far more circumscribed than men in their choice of work, and that *horizontal segregation by sex* – the tendency for men and women to be allocated to qualitatively different types of jobs – is a persistent feature of employment patterns in Britain. The return of women to the labour force has not resulted in a fundamental challenge to demarcations between men's work and women's work, or in many women moving across the boundary into 'men's jobs'.

Second, *vertical segregation* by sex is also marked, with women overwhelmingly concentrated at the lower levels of the occupational hierarchy in terms of wages or salary, status and authority. As can be seen from Table 5.3, although women are more likely than men to be found in non-manual occupations, far fewer women than men are in the top stratum of professionals, managers and employers.

Moreover, Westergaard and Resler (1976, p. 163) point out that within the professions, the vast majority of women are located in the minor professions (such as schoolteaching, librarianship, or social work), while the majority of male professionals are found in higher-status professions such as dentistry, accountancy, architecture and law. Women comprised 90 per cent of nurses in 1980, but only 70 per cent of senior administrative nursing staff, 17 per cent of GPs, and 0.7 per cent of consultants in

TABLE 5.3

Socioeconomic class of men and women in employment, Great Britain, 1983

		Distribution (%)		
	Males	**Females**		
		Full-time	**Part-time**	**Total**
Professional, managers and employers	24	9	3	7
Other non-manual	17	61	43	53
Skilled manual	40	8	8	8
Semi-skilled manual	15	20	29	24
Unskilled manual	4	2	17	8
Total	100%	100%	100%	100%

Source: Office of Population Censuses and Statistics, Social Surveys Division (1985) *General Household Survey 1983*, London, HMSO, Tables 7.28 and 7.29.

specialisms like general surgery (Elston and Doyal, 1983, p. 41). An analysis of the location of men and women in the Civil Service (Administration Group) in 1984 provides a particularly compelling example of vertical segregation by sex. At the lower end of the civil service hierarchy in 1984, women comprised 76 per cent of clerical assistants and 68 per cent of clerical officers; at the top end of the scale, fewer than 5 per cent of under secretaries, and 4 per cent of deputy secretaries were women, and there were no women in the post of permanent secretary (EOC (1985) Figure 4.2, p. 81).

Vertical segregation by sex is characteristic of manual work as well as of non-manual occupations. As Table 5.3 indicates, women are heavily under-represented, compared with men, in skilled manual work; the jobs of part-time women workers, in particular, tend to be classified as 'unskilled', though, as Beechey and Perkins (1987) show, many of these jobs, especially in the social services, involve complex competencies and responsibilities. Furthermore, the concentration of women at the bottom of the occupational ladder appears to have become more acute in the course of this century: while the proportion of *unskilled* manual workers who are female increased (from 16 per cent in 1911 to 28 per cent in 1966), the proportion of skilled manual workers who are female declined dramatically, from 24 to 15 per cent, during the same period (Department of Employment, 1974, p. 22).

Paid work and child care

The patterns of employment described above help to account for the substantial gap in earnings between women and men; however, the analysis cannot stop here, for patterns of employment themselves require explanation. One level of explanation concerns the relationship between wage labour and child care. Although the number of years in which women are 'free' to take paid employment has increased during this century (due to lower rates of fertility and longer life-span), this does not mean that childbearing and childrearing have no impact upon gender divisions outside the family.

The 'understanding employer'

Women who attempt to combine paid employment with child care are particularly vulnerable to exploitation. As Freeman (1982) points out, employers and trade unions alike have often treated the problems women face in accommodating employment demands to children's needs as a personal problem, not an issue to be resolved by negotiating more suitable conditions. Consequently, many women have no option but to seek 'an understanding employer' – one who 'allows' women's work hours to deviate from the 'standard' working day, while often paying very low rates and not remunerating for shift work, unsocial hours, or overtime. Her analysis can be applied to part-time workers, who, as we have seen, typically have lower hourly rates, less security, and less opportunity for training or promotion, then full-time employees, even when the work they do is similar. The *Women and Employment Survey* confirms that 'the presence of children and the age of the youngest child are the major determinants of whether women work full or part time' (Martin and Roberts, 1984, p. 18).

A marginal group of (largely) female employees are the homeworkers, who machine clothes, assemble greeting cards or toys, or do routine clerical work on a piecework basis in their own homes, for an outside employer. A report by the Low Pay Unit (1979) revealed that there were at least 150,000 homeworkers in Britain, nearly half of whom earned less than 40 pence an hour; this was at a time when the average gross hourly wage of the poorest 10 per cent of female manual workers was £1. Moreover, homeworkers are rarely entitled to such basic employment rights as holidays (paid or otherwise), pensions and compensation for industrial accident. The vast majority of homeworkers are women with children or others dependent on their care, who see homeworking as the only way of supplementing income while being present in the home. But, as Allen and Wolkowitz (1986) point out in recent study of homeworking in Bradford, far from offering women a flexible type of work which can be readily combined with domestic responsibilities, there is for most home-workers a constant conflict between long hours of paid work in over-crowded surroundings, and the kind of attention to children and others that they might like to give. The authors of a study of homeworkers in north London conclude.

> The homeworker is a casual labourer exploited on the basis of her ascribed role as
> a woman/wife ... The economic and social situation of the homeworker is in
> effect an extreme instance of the situation of women in general (Hope *et al.*, 1976,
> pp. 103–4).

Child care is a social activity the major costs of which are borne by
individual families; within families the burdens as well as the pleasures
predominantly fall to women. The sweated labour of homeworkers demonstrates in an extreme form the way in which the assignment of child care to
women gives rise to multiple disadvantages; formal equality is a sterile
concept, it has been said, as long as women are left on their own, holding
the baby. A number of delicate issues are raised by the recognition that
women's exclusive responsibility for child care presents a stringent obstacle
to sexual equality.

First, there is the question of why women/mothers, as opposed to men/
fathers, are the ones who are assumed to devote themselves to child care on
a full-time basis – or, more often, to forge a precarious compromise
between child care and employment. There is no compelling psychological,
physiological or social reason why primary responsibility for the intimate
and long-term care of children should rest exclusively with women –
although ideologies of motherhood would try to persuade that either the
yearnings of women ('maternal instinct') or the needs of children (the
dangers of 'maternal deprivation') demand that the mother–child relationship be virtually full-time and relatively exclusive. An equal contribution
from the father would require drastic changes in the organisation of work
and home life which few employers – and as yet few male employees – seem
prepared to contemplate. At a TUC Conference, Anna Coote, speaking
from the platform, received a somewhat unsympathetic reception when she
argued that a commitment to sexual equality would have to embody
personal changes by male union members in the sexual division of labour in
their own homes. The issue of whether mothers and fathers accept mutual
responsibility for 'their' children is simultaneously a *personal* issue and a
public one.

A second issue concerns the absence of a material infrastructure which
would offer to women, and to men, a greater degree of choice by making it
feasible to combine a responsible involvement in child care with paid
employment, full-time study, or unpaid community service. This might
involve, on the one hand, the provision of viable forms of collective child
care – day nurseries, nursery schools, crèches in public places, children's
centres – for those who wished or needed them. The policy of the government in recent years has been to offer day-care facilities only to children in
dire need – and need has not been taken to include children both of whose
parents are employed.

In 1984, as Land (1986) points out, the provision of day care places in local authority day nurseries, registered nurseries, or with registered childminders, was sufficient to cover only 5.3 per cent of children aged 4 or less. The majority of employed mothers rely on unpaid assistance from relatives or neighbours; according to the *Women and Employment Survey*, only 9 per cent of women who make care arrangements for preschool children are able to use crèches, day nurseries or nursery classes (Martin and Roberts, 1984, ch. 4). The popular notion of 'dual career couples' – husbands and wives in elite occupations, drawing upon the services of nannies and live-in help – is punctured by Benenson (1984); using American data, he demonstrates that the vast majority of dual-earner couples are working-class or lower middle-class employees, whose joint incomes will not allow for costly privatised strategies to reconcile the demands of family, home and work.

A third issue confronts the organisation of work itself. Why should wage labour be structured in such a way that it is often impossible for adults of either sex to combine day-to-day involvement with child care with responsible and fulfilling employment? As Anne Phillips argues:

> One of the most dehumanising aspects of work today is that it does not acknowledge our needs as people. Men are expected to turn up for overtime, and no one asks where their children are . . . It is accepted as normal that people work twice as hard when they have children – no one suggests that this is precisely when they need most time off. Work is organised as if every worker (whether man or woman) has a full-time housewife at home . . . We need an hours strategy that admits the needs of children, which means not just shorter but more flexible hours, and a working pattern that acknowledges the times of nurseries and schools (1983, pp. 56–7).

Many developments stemming from the intensification of work patterns – the extension of shift-work, for example – raise this problem of the articulation of domestic life and work life in an acute form.

Misconceptions about women and employment

Many of the attempts to explain, or to justify, gender divisions in employment over the years have invoked essential differences between the sexes in abilities, interests or motivation as the major explanatory factor; such hypotheses rarely stand up to scrutiny. The evidence mentioned earlier about the importance of two wages for keeping family incomes above the poverty line puts paid to the notion that married women work only for pin money. But a more fundamental issue is why, where the combined incomes of wife and husband are ample for the family's needs, should it so often be assumed that it is the woman's job that is secondary to, or of lesser importance than, the man's? It could as easily be argued that the husband's income is for luxuries, and the wife's for essentials; or that both partners earn partly for luxuries, partly for basics. Gender inequalities in the sphere of work may encourage the view that married women's work is secondary; where women are allocated jobs with lower incomes and less responsibility than those of men, it is not surprising if they come to think of their careers as of lesser importance than those of their husbands – but, of course, lesser importance does not mean *no* importance. To use this as a basis for explaining gender divisions in employment is, however, a totally circular argument: women define their jobs as 'secondary' because they are lower paid and less secure, and women are given lower-paid and less secure jobs because they define their work as 'secondary'.

To argue that there are no obvious grounds for viewing women's work as secondary to that of men is not to imply that all women enjoy and cherish their jobs; many women find their work monotonous and regard it as drudgery – and so do many men. But with women, as with men, paid employment is often a necessity in two senses: first, it is almost the only route to financial independence; and second, in a society in which status and social participation are closely linked to occupation and earning power, a job is for most men *and* women important for social acceptance, involvement and respect.

But women are not as strong as men . . .

A common misconception is that the subordination of women in the labour force can be attributed to their inferior strength; a standard riposte to demands for women's rights used to be, 'Women will get equality the day they are prepared to work in the mines!' The reply to this is straightforward. First, women (and children) used to work in the mines, indicating that they are not incapable of doing so; the last of the 'pitbrow girls' retired in 1953. Second, the vast majority of men neither work down the mines, nor even consider mining as a career; moreover, men who work in other, particularly professional, occupations are higher paid and better rewarded in other ways than miners. This raises a more general point. Women's physical strength, their ability to lift heavy loads unaided, is on average less than that of men in our society, whether through genetic make-up or different physical training. However, the sort of 'sheer physical brawn' in which men excel is not generally a basis for superior reward in our society; one of the recurrent justifications for paying non-manual workers more than manual ones is that the latter 'merely' use muscle power, while non-manual workers allegedly use the more important qualities of intelligence, judgement and skill. The ideological nature of *both* assertions (about women, and about working-class people) should be clear.

Most of the other attempts to justify gender divisions in employment by reference to essential differences between women and men are equally contentious. For example, the claims that women are less reliable employees than men (that they are more prone to absenteeism, that they have higher rates of turnover) turn out to be unfounded when like is compared with like – that is, when the women who are chosen for study are in jobs as rewarding as those of the men with whom they are compared, or when the men who are studied have as many domestic responsibilities as the women. However, inaccurate as these views are, they still exert an influence, in so far as they are used by the state to justify the reduction of 'manpower' (*sic*) training schemes for women, or by employers to exclude women from appointment or promotion. Hartnett (1978, p. 83) concludes that these misconceptions 'are still espoused by "gatekeeper" males in personnel departments who are in a position to exert a powerful influence on selection and promotion procedures'.

It is not only men (and women) in authority but also some of those on the shop-floor and in the office who may resist attempts at radical improvement of women's employment opportunities. Men and women are sometimes in a competitive relationship in the labour market: that is to say, better promotion prospects for women may mean reduced promotion prospects for men, particularly in periods where the more attractive jobs are contracting. Sometimes it is said that by returning to the labour force in large numbers in recent years women have thrown men out of work; the implication is that a 'solution' to unemployment is the return of women to the home. A somewhat similar argument is that women, by 'agreeing' to work for lower pay, undercut men's wages, thereby leading employers to hire women in place of men, or forcing men to accept lower wages in order to remain competitive with women workers. How justified are these claims?

On the one hand, to the extent that women's jobs are segregated from those of men, the charge cannot be substantiated. Women cannot take 'men's' jobs; they take (and lose) jobs which are anyway specially reserved for women. On the other hand, it is clear that the competition between men and women workers is sometimes used in an exploitative way by employers. The availability of women workers (presumably at lower wage rates) means that it is possible to threaten male workers with possible replacement by women. (The same threat is of course used against women: 'If you ask for equal pay, you will price yourselves out of a job; in short, we will give these jobs to men'.) But the more crucial issue concerns the structural arrangements that cannot provide jobs for all who want or need them, and cannot guarantee a tolerable standard of living to all who are prepared to contribute to production. It is precisely these structural arrangements which are the subject of theoretical attempts to make sense of gender divisions in employment.

Dual labour market theory

Some economists and sociologists have suggested that capitalist countries like Britain or the USA give rise to not one, but two, markets for labour. The jobs available in the primary sector are relatively secure, well paid, and tend to have good long-term promotion prospects; those in the secondary sector are more precarious and less well rewarded. According to dual labour market theory, those workers who are preferred by employers (on the basis of certain personal characteristics) in the primary sector will tend to accrue greater rewards than those of identical ability or qualifications who are absorbed into the secondary sector. Moreoever, because of the nature of jobs in the secondary sector, those who enter there will, over the course of their working lives, receive less on-the-job training and be more frequently made redundant, so that their disadvantageous position in the labour market will be reinforced. Thus the likelihood of movement of workers from the secondary to the primary sector is small.

Access to primary-sector employment is controlled through the operation of internal labour markets: that is, training for jobs of skill and responsibility, and promotion to and selection for these posts, takes place not on the open market (e.g. through advertisements in newspapers, so that anyone can compete) but within firms themselves. Many firms take in young, relatively inexperienced workers (whether into manual jobs, or clerical/managerial streams) and train them to be good company men and women over a number of years. Those who appear most promising (and who are lucky enough to find themselves in a firm with good prospects in the first place) may be promoted to relatively high positions. Because selection and training takes place within the firm there is little workers can do when initially seeking employment to ensure their chances of ultimate success.

Now, it can be argued that internal labour markets work to the disadvantage of women in at least two ways. First, firms are less likely to recruit women to promotion-stream jobs in the first place, due to stereotypical beliefs about the unsuitability of women. Second, promotion streams have been structured over the years in ways that match the life experiences of men better than those of women. Thus workers are recruited fairly young; and the fundamental prerequisite for promotion is several years *continuous* service, in the late teens and early twenties. Women who leave for even a few years to have children find themselves out of the running for posts of responsibility when they return. Any rigid career structure which demands continuous application during the twenties will, in the absence of alternative child-care arrangements and generous maternity/paternity leave schemes, work to the disadvantage of women.

There has been heated argument over the applicability of this model to the British context. Barron and Norris (1976), drawing upon data from the early 1970s, analyse the characteristics of the social position of women in Britain – particularly dispensability – and confirm that this leads to their confinement to the secondary market. Blackburn and Mann (1979) add that the emergence of a dual labour market depends to some extent upon the maintenance of an institutional framework (a legal system allowing, or endorsing, discriminatory practices, etc.) which permits easier segregation of different sectors of the labour force. They too conclude that (1979, p. 284):

> Women manual workers, unlike any of the male groups we have considered, are probably a 'secondary' labour force in the sense of the dual and radical labour market theories. The internal labour market and other defences against insecurity exist on the backs of a secondary labour market, and in this country, that means largely on the backs of women.

The strength of this argument (and of the 'reserve army of labour' view that we will examine in a moment) is that it avoids two pitfalls common to discussions of women's disadvantaged position in the labour market. First, it avoids attributing divisions in employment purely to *individual* cases of 'discrimination' or 'predjudice' without specifying the institutional demarcations which make such discrimination advantageous in the first place. Second, it negates the assumption that better qualifications for women, or greater ambition, would automatically dismantle gender divisions in employment; this is a view which fails to give due attention to the facts that even women with the same qualifications as men are disadvantaged in terms of wages and promotion, and that although qualifications may be used as 'screening' devices by employers in choosing between candidates, such qualifications do not actually determine the structure of occupations or the number of rewarding jobs available.

There is, on the other hand, considerable debate as to the processes that give rise to dualism in the labour market. Emphasis is given in some theories to technological developments which encourage firms to train their own employees in relatively specific skills; under such conditions it is in the interests of firms to offer better-than-market rates and conditions in order to maintain a stable labour force, while other firms (or plants) can tolerate higher turnover. The 'radical' version of dual labour market theory emphasises instead the development of stratified labour markets (within the primary and secondary sectors, as well as between them) as an attempt by employers to counteract tendencies towards the homogeneity of the labour force – a strategy of divide and rule in order to inhibit the possibility of unified class action. Finally, the contribution of workers' collective efforts to protect themselves from the most damaging effects of labour market competition by extending areas of job security and improving wages is seen by some as a factor in the development of primary-sector employment (Rubery, 1978).

Reserve army of labour

Other analyses of gender divisions in employment, particularly those deriving from Marxist traditions of thought, identify women as a crucial constituent of the reserve army of labour. This theory suggests that, as capitalism develops, it has an inherent tendency to throw up a large and growing body of people who are available for work but who are only marginally incorporated within the main labour force. One source of the reserve army stems from the permanent and progressive decline in the size of the agricultural labour force – which 'frees' workers for employment in the industrial or service sectors. Another source is the mechanisation and deskilling of manual and non-manual jobs, deriving from ongoing attempts to intensify the labour process; mechanisation either throws people out of work, or pushes them into labour-intensive sectors where they may be under-employed or irregularly employed.

The creation of a reserve army of labour – of a body of people who, though available for work, are unemployed, under-employed or insecurely employed – is thus seen as a consequence of capitalist development, but also as a precondition for *continued* development. First, the reserve army can be drawn upon by prosperous firms in times of rapid expansion but can be expelled again when recession sets in and production and costs have to be cut. Second, more labour-intensive firms, whose fortunes are tied to those of the larger corporations and which are often engaged in providing cheap goods and services for the larger firms, can draw upon the reserve army, can pay these workers at lower rates, and can, as above, sack them in a recession, or when rising labour costs make capital investment a more viable proposition. Third, the existence of the reserve army of labour, unemployed or working for lower pay, helps to discipline other workers and to regulate wage demands. Thus, in this view, unemployment and under-employment are not accidental or pathological features of the industrial scene but more or less predictable by-products of the capitalist process of accumulation.

The reasons why women in particular become part of the reserve army of labour is a matter of continuing debate. There is a technical argument which suggests that the employment of *married* women lowers the 'value' of their husbands' labour power, and therefore cheapens the cost of labour to employers (Beechey, 1977). More simply, it has been suggested that women's suitability for the reserve army is a consequence of ideologies that locate women in the home, and therefore diffuse the political strains that arise from cyclical unemployment of women; moreover, the unemployment – at least of married women – can be disguised more easily than that of other workers. ('She's not unemployed, she has gone back to being a housewife.') Bland and her colleagues (1978) add that women in different circumstances may be vulnerable to inclusion in the reserve army of labour for different reasons: women of child-bearing age may, because of their reproductive life-cyle, experience periods of 'voluntary' unemployment; Asian and West Indian women, and unmarried mothers, may be among those women who for social and economic reasons are forced to take work when and where they can.

The reserve army of labour theory has been criticised for failing to take account of the distinct uses to which male and female labour is put. However, empirical support for the theory – or at least for that aspect of it which proposes that women would be expelled from production more readily than men – comes from a paper by Bruegel (1979). While acknowledging the severe difficulties in analysing unemployment figures for men and women, Bruegel notes that between 1974 and 1978 the official rate of unemployment among women rose three times faster than that of men. Moreover, in industries where there was a decline in levels of employment the decline was most acute for women; thus women appear to be more vulnerable than men to recession. A most important point is that the rate of employment decline for part-time women workers exceeded that for full-time workers of either sex: 'It is part-time women workers . . . who conform most closely to the model of women as a disposable reserve army' (Bruegel, 1979, pp. 18–19). On the other hand, Bruegel notes, women's overall employment prospects have not declined in recent years as rapidly as those of men because of women's segregation into the expanding service industries; had women workers been evenly distributed throughout industries, Bruegel argues, their overall employment prospects would have been further diminished compared with those of men. However, as the growth of the service sector ends, and as rationalisation – including the introduction of micro-processing – eliminates many of these jobs, female workers will increasingly be in danger of redundancy.

5.4 DOMESTIC LABOUR

The vast majority of 'housewives' – in the sense of persons wholly or mainly responsible for the running of a household – are women. Ann Oakley, writing in 1972 (p. 152), emphasised the extent to which housework is built into the feminine role in our society: 'One basic occupation in particular, that of housewife, is exclusively feminine. In Britain, 76 per cent of all employed women are housewives, and so are 93 per cent of non-employed women'.

There is no evidence to suggest that Oakley's claim would be far off the mark today. A national survey conducted in 1984 indicates that only a minority of married people (though somewhat more single people) think that household tasks should be equally shared between women and men; and the actual allocation of tasks is even more skewed towards a conventional household division of labour than these attitudes would suggest. It is mainly the man who undertakes repairs of household equipment in 83 per cent of married households, but women are primarily responsible for washing and ironing (88 per cent of households), preparation of evening meal (77 per cent of households), house-cleaning (72 per cent) and looking after sick children (63 per cent of households) (*Social Trends 16*, 1986, Table 2.12, p. 36).

Housework is indeed treated as a 'feminine' activity. Men do some housework, of course, particularly if they are living on their own. But when a woman enters the scene, it is assumed that she will take over many mundane tasks for him, freeing him to return to his 'proper' spheres. Many a wife has ben chagrined to see that when her husband goes away on business or pleasure, she is left at home, looking after the children and watching television; but when she goes away, her husband is besieged with offers of meals and assistance – it is assumed that he can not, and should not, cope on his own. Similar assumptions operate at the level of social policy. Whem women were drafted into war duties, for example, they could be excused if it were shown that they were the only woman in a household of men; in that case, it was assumed that their presence was required for housekeeping duties. Even in the early 1980s, the taxation regulations allowed a man without a wife to claim an allowance for a female housekeeper; a woman on her own could not make a similar claim. Barrett and McIntosh comment:

> Underlying this is the assumption that to keep house is a natural adjunct of femininity. Wielding a needle or a mop, changing a nappy or a bed, not running out of flour or into debt come easily to women, it seems. We are blamed if we cannot manage them, whereas men are praised if they can (1982, p. 61).

Oakley was one of the first sociologists to analyse the variety of skills and responsibilities lumped together under the heading of 'housework', and to argue that the frequent refusal to acknowledge housework as *labour* is both a cause and a reflection of the lower status of women in society. The 40 housewives Oakley interviewed described some aspects of housework, such as washing-up, ironing or cleaning, in terms reminiscent of assembly-line workers; in fact, they more often reported experiencing monotony, fragmentation and excessive speed in their work than had assembly-line workers in the 'affluent-worker studies' (Oakley, 1974, p. 87). Oakley analyses housework, then, in the same way that sociologists might analyse automobile assembly work, clerical labour, or teaching: as a set of tasks done by a particular group of people, within a particular set of social relations. These relations are crucial for understanding housework: domestic labour is usually not directly supervised; it is performed largely on the basis of personal, rather than contractual, relationships; and it is unpaid, with no fixed remuneration linked to the hours put in or the quantity of goods or services produced. All three of these conditions contribute to the fact that the effort expended in housework is largely undervalued and unrecognised; in particular, *unpaid* work is largely regarded as 'not-work'.

It's only natural ...

The supposedly 'natural' aptitude of women for housework is, in fact, constantly taught and reinforced, monitored and sanctioned. Media advertising seeks to remind women that their love for their family should extend to pride in a germ-free toilet, or to a hot meal with gravy at the end of the day. Domestic education in schools – even when extended to male pupils – has been treated as the concern of girls, and as embodying skills related not to self-reliance but to the servicing of men. Wynn (1977, p. 33) reports that candidates for the 1974 Metropolitan Examinations CSE practical paper in home economics were asked to place themselves in the following situation:

> You and your husband are going to spend a weekend with your parents. Launder a selection of your own and your husband's clothes: these should include a variety of fabrics and finishes. Name these fabrics with labels, when displaying your finished work. Prepare a meatless meal for the two of you, using up left-over cooked vegetables and stale bread.

And an important point is that this 'training' in women's obligation towards housework may affect not only women's expectations but also men's; husbands' expectations regarding wife's housekeeping are, according to Dobash and Dobash (1980) one of the three main triggers for episodes in which husbands beat their wives.

Moreover, the view that housework and child care are not work, but merely part of the feminine role, has tended to obscure the links between the division of labour in the home, and gender divisions in employment:

> In an economy in which a person's capacity to work is bought and sold in exchange for a wage, labour which is performed on the basis of personal relations rather than on the basis of monetary exchange is not recognised as labour. Consequently women's work in caring for children and husbands does not appear as necessary labour; it appears as a natural part of family life ... Since domesticity appears an inherent part of being a woman ... the inequalities facing women have appeared to be the inequalities they face when they enter the world of men; there has been no need to explain why this world is a 'man's world'! (Wainwright, 1978, p. 160).

Contrary to popular belief, the introduction of labour-saving devices into the home has not reduced the time spent on housework. Domestic appliances have eliminated some of the heaviest physical demands of housework, but standards of hygiene have risen along with expectations concerning the 'home beautiful' and 'creative homemaking'. The average time spent on housework by a sample of urban housewives (some of whom had paid employment) in 1971 was seventy-seven hours, compared with seventy hours in 1950 (Oakley, 1974, table 5.4). On the other hand, something which has not yet been fully explored is the extent of polarisation within the category of houseworkers. For example, widespread car ownership and the emergence of hypermarkets make it possible for *some* women to complete the bulk of the weekly shopping in one journey; the same development makes shopping much more difficult and time-consuming for those who have no access to a car, or who have insufficient cash to spare for a massive once-and-for-all expenditure.

The different demands of housework on women in different economic and personal circumstances is just one of the features of housework militating against a sense of solidarity among women. First, in our society, housework is a largely solitary activity. The design of houses, the location of laundry facilities within the home rather than at some community wash place, and so on, all mean that women spend a large part of their day isolated from one another. Even the act of meeting for political purposes may be inhibited by family responsibilities. Second, women are tied to housework through bonds that few other workers experience – the bonds of love and identification. It is easier to go on strike against a boss you hardly know than it is to refuse to get the children's tea. Third, most people like to feel they are reasonably 'good at their job'. Houseworkers are no exception. But often, in the absence of clear universal standards or praise from 'employers', women use other women as standards against which to judge their own performance in a competitive light. Hence, as presently organised, housework has a tendency to divide women rather than unite them.

The recognition that domestic labour is indeed *work* – and not simply a natural part of being a woman – has raised the question of why this aspect of the sexual division of labour persists. Often this question is posed in terms of asking who benefits from such an arrangement.

The first type of answer stresses the benefits which men of all social classes reap from sustaining a system in which women, regardless of other demands on their time, are expected to look after men, to take care of their daily needs, to soothe and comfort them. Men have to work hard to earn a living, it is argued; but they can expect not only an income but personal service as well, at a cost to themselves (in terms of maintenance of the woman) far less than the market value of the goods and services provided. Delphy, for example, argues that housework cannot be defined by the nature of the tasks involved (floors are washed, toilets cleaned, and chops cooked in paid employment, too), but only by the nature of the contract which enables husbands to 'appropriate' the labour power of their wives (1984, chs 5 and 6). Thus the marriage contract is in fact a labour contract, the terms of which only become fully apparent when it is alleged that a wife has failed to fulfil her side of the bargain. (Smart's 1984 analysis of marital law illustrates in a concrete way how judges and magistrates interpret the labour obligations of the marriage contract in cases of divorce.) Since men benefit from the services provided by their wives (or daughters or sisters or mothers), they have an interest in maintaining the sexual division of labour. They may express that interest in a variety of ways: by resisting (or failing to support) legislation that might truly give women equal opportunities outside the home; by supporting, through professional organisations and trade unions, protectionist policies which restrict women's access to rewarding occupations; by 'allowing' wives to go out to work, while insisting that the house be kept as efficiently as before; and, finally, by refusing to give more than a token gesture of help in the home.

A second view is that it is not men but the capitalist system that is the prime beneficiary of women's unpaid domestic labour. Attempts to trace the route by which capital appropriates domestic labour as 'surplus value' (the 'domestic labour debate') have been less than satisfactory. On the other hand, it is the case that women's domestic labour contributes to the maintenance of tolerable standards of living, and may therefore reduce political pressure for radical change. In periods when wages are rising more slowly than prices women's efforts and energies may stretch the household income that little bit further so that the drop in standard of living is not apparent to men. As a result, 'breadwinners' are less likely to be pressed to open revolt. (Of course, women also cushion the effects of falling standards of living by taking jobs, however poorly paid, to boost the family income.) Moreover, women expend much effort on housework and emotional support that rejuvenates their older children, their husbands, their fathers for each day's work.

Although the two approaches to explaining the persistence of the sexual division of labour are not wholly incompatible – in the second, for example women's efforts protect both men and the capitalist relations of production – the two versions do have different emphases. One limitation of the former (male-benefit) view is that it does not so readily encompass the benefits which female domestic labour offers to children, the elderly and invalids, as well as to men, while the latter version is less effective in explaining why *women* should be designated to these particular tasks.

5.5 REPRODUCTION

The single most far-reaching difference between men and women lies in their reproductive capacities. Genetic contributions from both a woman and a man, in the form of egg and sperm, are biologically necessary to begin the process of creating a human child. But only women have the physiological capacity to nurture the foetus through the months from conception to birth; only women can bear children.

This simple fact sometimes leads people to assume that the divisions between men and women in society are biologically determined: that 'biology is destiny'. Such arguments are sometimes developed by drawing analogies between women and the females of other species. The comparison between women and cows, for example, is explicitly drawn in this celebration from *The Imperial Animal* of the qualities of women:

> The human mother is a splendid mammal – the epitome of her order. Her physiology is more highly developed for suckling behaviour – with permanent breasts, for example – than any of her cousins, except domestic ungulates bred specially for milk-giving. But more than this, she is like any other mammal, emotionally programmed to be responsive to the growing child (Tiger and Fox, 1974, p. 86).

This quotation implies a direct continuity between the human and animal worlds which is unwarranted. Of course, humans, like other animals, reproduce; and women, like other mammals, bear the growing infant. But in the case of human beings all behaviour surrounding reproduction – from the decision to engage in heterosexual intercourse, to the forms of contraceptive knowledge available, from the taboos and obligations surrounding pregnancy, to the manner and place of birth – is meaningful in social (rather than biological) terms, and is heavily influenced by social custom and social structure.

There have been many societies in which child-bearing was regarded as the principal duty of women. They have been trained from infancy with this goal in mind, being discouraged from any pastimes other than those that would make them more pleasing wives and more devoted mothers. Married women who remained childless (whether through their own, or their husband's infertility) might be regarded as social failures, to be cast aside, divorced or replaced by other wives. Child-bearing was the only way in which women could gain a degree of security and acceptance in the community. In such societies there would be some truth in the statement that 'biology is women's destiny' – but the thing to notice is that the importance of biology in defining women's position rests up *social* mores and *social* structure which forbid women other sources of security and esteem, and not on natural laws.

The social conditions surrounding reproduction have changed dramatically in Western Europe in the past one hundred years. For example, the availability of more effective means of preventing or terminating unwanted pregnancies means that the proportion of women's lives which is devoted to pregnancy and early infant care has dramatically decreased.

> The typical working mother of the 1880s, married in her teens or early twenties, and experiencing ten pregnancies, spent about fifteen years in a state of pregnancy and in nursing a child for the first year of its life. She was tied, for this period of time, to the wheel of childbearing. Today, for the typical mother, the time spent would be about four years (Titmuss, 1958, p. 91).

And of course, that four years represents a considerably smaller fraction of a typically longer life-span.

One view of these developments is that medical and scientific advances, by enabling women to limit their fertility and by making childbirth safer, have given women more control over their own lives. However, this view takes insufficient account of the impact of changing social definitions of motherhood. While women today spend less time in pregnancy and breastfeeding than in the recent past, the care of children has come to be defined in a far more rigorous way; mothering involves responsibility not only for the physical production and maintenance of children, but for detailed attention to their psychological, social and intellectual development. Motherhood is seen, in a way it wasn't in the past, as a full-time occupation. Thus, mothers may be expected not to lavish as much 'care' on two children as they might have provided for six children in the past. And even if we limit our focus to childbearing, the notion that women are now free to choose whether or not to have children ignores the many ways in reproductive decisions continue to be constrained.

These constraints involve, firstly, the shortcomings of existing means of fertility control. For example, the pill and the IUD – heralded in the 1960s as instruments of women's liberation – appear now to carry significant health risks, and a range of distressing side-effects. The failure to develop safer and more acceptable means of birth control is not simply a technical problem; in part, feminists argue, it reflects a low priority given to women's health, and a tendency to disregard the symptoms which women themselves think are important (Weideger, 1978; Pollock, 1984). The extent to which most people are shocked by the satirical description of the 'Umbrelly' – a male contraceptive device which parallels the effects of the female IUD – is perhaps an indication of how far women are encouraged to take risks with their comfort, health and future fertility that men would not be expected to tolerate (see below).

Second, the way that access to means of fertility control is managed illustrates how women's experience of reproduction continues to be linked to their location in the social structure. Attempts have recently been made to restrict the access of younger women to contraceptive information and supplies. The injectable contraceptive Depo-Provera – a highly suspect drug whose marketing and manufacture was effectively banned by the American Food and Drug Administration in the 1970s – has been used extensively on Asian and black women in Britain and is widely marketed in

---

Breakthrough in male contraception

The newest development in male contraception was unveiled recently at the American Women's Surgical Symposium held at the Ann Arbor Medical Centre. Dr Sophie Merkin, of the Merkin Clinic, announced the preliminary findings of a study conducted on 763 unsuspecting male undergraduate students at a large midwest university. In her report, Dr Merkin states that the new contraceptive – the IPD – was a breakthrough in male contraception. It will be marketed under the trade-name "Umbrelly".

The IPD (intrapenile device) resembles a tiny folded umbrella which is inserted through the head of the penis and pushed into the scrotum with a plunger-like instrument. Occasionally there is perforation of the scrotum but this is disregarded since it is known that the male has few nerve endings in this area of his body. The underside of the umbrella contains a spermicidal jelly, hence the name "Umbrelly".

Experiments on 1,000 white whales from the continental shelf (whose sexual apparatus is said to be the closest to man's) proved the umbrelly to be 100% effective in preventing production of sperm, and eminently satisfactory to the female whales since it does not interfere with her rutting pleasures.

SCROTAL INFECTION
"Only 2 died"

Dr Merkin declared the umbrelly to be statistically safe for the human male. She reported that of the 763 graduate students tested with the device only two died of scrotal infection, only 20 experienced swelling of the tissues. Three developed cancer of the testicles, and 13 were too depressed to have an erection. She stated that common complaints ranged from cramping and bleeding to acute abdominal pain. She emphasised that these symptoms were merely indications that the man's body had not yet adjusted to the device. Hopefully the symptoms would disappear within a year.

One complication caused by the IPD and briefly mentioned by Dr Merkin was the incidence of massive scrotal infection necessitating the surgical removal of the testicles. "But this is a rare case," said Merkin, "too rare to be statistically important." She and other distinguished members of the Women's College of Surgeons agreed that the benefits far outweighed the risk to any individual man. (*Reprinted from East Bay Men's Centre Newsletter and The Periodical Lunch, Ann Arbor, Michigan.*)

Source: *Spare Rib*, vol. 93, p. 9 (April 1980).

Third World nations (Rakusen, 1981; Bunkle, 1984). In Britain, too, some West Indian women have been sterilised without their full consent, often as a condition of having an abortion (Savage, 1982). In spite of the 1967 Abortion Act which entitled women to legal abortion on medical and social grounds, access to safe abortion in many parts of the country depends on ability to pay; the bulk of legal abortions in Britain today are performed outside the NHS (Doyal, in Stanworth, 1987).

Third, the technical possibility of fertility control coexists with a power-ful ideology of motherhood – the belief that motherhood is the natural, desired and ultimate goal of all 'normal' women, and that women who deny their 'maternal instincts' are selfish, peculiar or disturbed. Evidence suggests that many members of the medical profession share this view (Barrett and Roberts, 1978). While many women wish to have children, the views of medical personnel are not simply a reflection of that fact; the idea of maternal instinct is sometimes used to override women's expressed wishes with regard to childbearing.

Who wants babies?

Some of the inconsistencies of medical ideology are revealed in Macintyre's (1976) study. She found that medical personnel and social workers tended to view pregnancy in healthy married women as a welcome and unproblematic event. Such pregnancies did not require explanation; women became pregnant because of their 'maternal instinct', their biologically-based desire to have babies. Evidence to the contrary was often disregarded. Women who wished to terminate the pregnancy, or who were ambivalent about it, were advised that their reaction was a temporary depression brought on by hormonal changes: 'Of course you want the baby'. On the other hand, *unmarried* women who wanted to keep their babies were often regarded with suspicion and dismay, and attempts were sometimes made to persuade them to accept an abortion or to have the baby adopted. Here the 'maternal instinct' of women was not invoked as an explanation for pregnancy; instead, explanations were sought in some disturbance which propelled unmarried women to become pregnant 'against their nature'. (One may wonder whether a man who time after time contributed to pregnancies would be regarded as having a strong paternal instinct!)

As Macintyre's research suggests, a belief in maternal instinct coexists with obstacles to autonomous motherhood – obstacles, that is, to mother-hood for women who are not in a stable relationship to a man. The much-publicised techniques of *in vitro* fertilisation and artificial insemination by donor, for example, make it possible for women to bear children without heterosexual intercourse. But the Warnock Report (1985) recommended that the use of these techniques be restricted to women who are married, and have the full consent and co-operation of their husbands. According to ideologies of motherhood, then, all women want children; but single women, lesbian women (and disabled women) are often expected to forego mothering 'in the interests of the child'.

Fourth, pregnancy and childbirth – undoubtedly significant events in many women's lives – have been in the course of this century increasingly medicalised. This involves, on the one hand, a dramatic increase in the proportion of babies born in hospital (from 15 per cent in 1927, to 98 per cent in 1980), and a proliferation of medical techniques for monitoring pregnancy, for intervening in childbirth and for care of newborn infants. On the other, it involves the use of a medical frame of reference to make sense of pregnancy and childbirth – a frame of reference which sees pregnant women as 'patients', pregnancy as an illness, and successful childbearing in terms which de-emphasise its social and emotional aspects. In some respects, the medicalisation of childbearing may have made the process safer for women and their infants (though researchers point out that medicalisation has also brought new dangers in its wake – Oakley, 1981, ch. 9, and Oakley, 1987). However, as the management of pregnancy and childbirth has passed into the hands of medical professionals, the majority of whom are men, many woman are left with a sense of being mere onlookers in the important process of giving birth.

Thus, medical and scientific advances in the sphere of reproduction – so often hailed as the liberators of twentieth-century women – have, in fact, been a double-edged sword. On the one hand, they have offered women a greater technical possibility to decide if, when and under what conditions to have children; on the other, the domination of so much reproductive technology by the medical profession has enabled others to have an even greater capacity to exert control over women's lives. Moreover, the 'technical possibility' of choice is only a small aspect of reproductive freedom; for some women, motherhood remains their only chance of creativity, while economic and social circumstances compel others to relinquish motherhood altogether.

In addition, the state always has an interest in the number of children born and in the manner in which they are raised, and policies fostered in this regard have their most direct impact on women. An interest in lowering the birth rate has involved policies as diverse as the seemingly compulsory sterilisation programme pursued by Indira Gandhi, and the recommendation by Robert McNamara, the then President of the World Bank, that the governments of developing countries could, by raising the status of women, encourage them to limit their family size. Where the aim is to increase the birth rate, incentives such as family allowances or medals for fertile mothers have sometimes been offered, and abortion and contraceptive facilities have been restricted to the well-to-do. Eugenicist policies (encouraging births from favoured groups, discouraging those from the poor or from ethnic minorities) have frequently been recommended, though fortunately less frequently implemented. Nevertheless, selective breeding programmes were used on a compulsory basis in Nazi Germany, and some sociologists argue that policies of the American government, which resulted by the 1970s in the surgical sterilisation of over one-third of all Puerto Rican women of childbearing age, have been eugenist in intention and effect (Davis, 1982, ch. 12). These sober considerations remind us that 'technological' or 'scientific' knowledge is seldom neutral either in its usage or its consequences. The state may use the withdrawal or provision of reproductive technologies as an instrument of policy, but may thereby curtail, in dramatic ways, women's control over their own destinies.

5.6 SEXUALITY

The dominant assumptions about male and female sexuality in contemporary society emphasise the different sexual needs and desires of women and men, with women generally seen as the more passive partners and men the more active. Men, it is believed, *have* more sex because they *need* more sex. Specifically, the male sexual drive is seen as stronger and less easy to control than the female, so that it leads men to make sexual initiatives, while women's sexual urges are reactive, aroused primarily in response to advances from men; male sexuality is thought to involve a more indiscriminate need for gratification, while women's sexual needs are allegedly more closely governed by their total relationship with a particular partner; men, it is assumed, seek sex primarily for the intrinsic pleasure, while women are more likely to use sex as a means to an end – a route to winning affection or specific favour from a man.

McIntosh (1978) argues that there is little evidence to support these assumptions about the specificity of male sexual needs, but she points out that such assumptions are implicit, none the less, in many analyses of such phenomena as prostitution. Often, for example, female prostitutes are seen as serving a necessary social function in catering for the sexual needs of unattached or unattractive men; but female sexual needs are not seen as requiring an analogous institution. Moreover, many writers find it puzzling that female prostitutes are able to engage in a casual sexual act, apparently without emotion; but no surprise is expressed at the ability of their male clients so to do. The implication is that sex outside an emotional relationship is in keeping with the masculine character but not with the feminine. Hence, McIntosh argues, the ideological assumptions about differences in male and female sexuality underlie, and reinforce, a double standard of sexual morality.

Any notion that the assumptions about male and female sexuality prevailing in our culture are universal must be rejected in the face of comparisons with other cultures and other historical periods. Albert reports that among the Zuni Indians of North America, women are expected to be sexually aggressive, and men sexually timid. It is men, and not women, who approach their wedding night with trepidation. Henry describes a tribe in the Brazilian highlands where both males and females engage in 'open, ribald and aggressive onslaughts' on members of the other sex, and both sexes take precautions to avoid rape (cited in Oakley, 1972, p. 55). In Europe a frequent male complaint in the seventeenth century was, according to Rowbotham (1974, p. 6), about the 'sexual insatiability' of women; popular folklore retained the notion of the sexually voracious female through to the nineteenth century.

These examples demonstrate the pitfalls of attempting to draw generalisations about the 'essential' or 'fundamental' sexual natures of men or women by examination of contemporary sexual practices. They also illustrate the necessity of trying to understand how assumptions about sexuality, and different sexual practices for men and women, are created and reproduced.

In contemporary society heterosexuality is defined as an important part of gender; men and women whose primary sexual relationships are with members of their own sex are severely sanctioned, and it is often implied that they cannot be seen as 'real men' or 'real women'. To a lesser extent, a similar attitude is taken towards those who are celibate. The sanctions against people who are not in a socially approved heterosexual relationship indicate just one facet of social control over human sexuality in contemporary society.

Control over heterosexual relations tends to incorporate the double standard of morality referred to above: the assumption that sexual 'promiscuity' is natural and even laudable in boys and men (sowing their wild oats), but shameful, 'unfeminine' and disruptive of social order in girls and women. These social controls can be seen to operate at two levels, as Smart and Smart (1978) suggest – the level of informal group processes, and the level of institutional procedures.

Informal group processes include the social pressures which are brought to bear by neighbours, family and peer groups on males and females who appear to deviate from the usual gender roles. In *Learning to Labour*, Willis (1977) describes the centrality of the double standard for 'the lads' – working-class boys who evolved a distinct counter-school culture – and highlights the effects this has on their perception of girls. A hallmark, Willis says, of being one of the lads is 'to have either sexual experience or at least aspirations which are exploitative and hypocritical. Girls are pursued, sometimes roughly, for their sexual favours, often dropped and labelled "loose" when they are given' (p. 146). The lads expect to be 'promiscuous', but 'promiscuous' girls are despised:

'The lads' are after the 'easy lay' at dances, though they think twice about being seen to 'go out' with them. 'The girlfriend' is a very different category from an 'easy lay'. She represents the human value that is squandered by promiscuity. She is the loyal domestic partner. She cannot be held to be sexually experienced – or at least not with others (Willis, 1977, p. 44).

It is not only boys who penalise sexually active girls; Wilson (1978) reports from her study of teenagers' sexual codes that the girls regard sex as acceptable only when it takes place in the context of a steady relationship; girls who have sex without proclaiming their love for the man are regarded as 'lays'. But while 'lays' were ostracised and penalised, 'promiscuous boys apparently did not suffer any loss of prestige or status' (Wilson, 1978, p. 71).

Sexual abuse and social control

The pervasiveness of the double standard implies that open sexuality is acceptable for girls, even in the 'permissive society', only in the context of love and domesticity. For boys, overt sexuality is part of the process of 'being a man'. Even our language enshrines this double standard; against the dozens of insulting names for sexually active females, are laudatory terms for sexually active males. Lees (1986), interviewing 15- to 16-year olds in three London comprehensives, documents the significance of sexual reputation in the experience of adolescent girls. To be branded as a 'slag' has severe consequences, and girls are wary about behaving, dressing or speaking in a manner that might attract this dangerous label. But the way that the term 'slag' is used suggests that it is 'about' a girl's relationship to men rather than about sexual activity *per se*; a young woman who is unattached (regardless of whether she is sexually active or not) is more likely to be called a slag than one who sleeps with a regular boyfriend. The term slag functions, Lees suggests, as a form of social control, which steers girls into 'acceptable' sexual behaviour – into steady heterosexual relationships, followed by marriage.

At the more formal levels of social control over sexuality, assumptions of male–female differences in sexuality are reproduced and, sometimes, reinforced. The more enlightened and open discussions of sexuality which are said to characterise modern schooling still often represent female sexuality as essentially reproductive (about having babies, rather than having pleasure) and as submissive:

> Of course things have changed over the years; we don't just endure sex any longer. It has been converted into a wonder of the world ... 'It's the most beautiful thing that can happen to you', said one of my teachers. Precisely, it happens to you. You don't do it, it's done to you (Campbell, 1974, p. 102).

Again the ideology of male needs (and of girls' responsibility for controlling them) is explicitly endorsed in a 1977 report on health education from the Department of Education and Science:

Girls should understand that they may inadvertently impose great stress on boys by arousing sexual reactions in them which they do not fully comprehend and may not be able to control (cited in Rance, 'Going all the Way', *Spare Rib*, October 1978, no. 75, p. 15).

The schools help to transmit certain attitudes towards sexuality, but the courts and judicial authorities take a more direct part in enforcing the prevailing definitions of male and female sexuality. In studies of delinquent behaviour it has been suggested that the courts take an interest in the sexual record of girls brought before them for other offences, while generally considering that the sexual behaviour of delinquent boys is immaterial. As Shacklady Smith (1978, p. 82) found, 'there is every reason to suppose that offences by girls are sexualised, in fact non-sexual offences are overlooked in favour of sexual (mis)-behaviour'. This has two implications: first, that girls are penalised for acts which are considered unworthy of attention when committed by boys; second, that the complexity of female deviance is disguised by an undue interest in the sexual content of women's lives.

Our emphasis so far has been upon adolescents, but one area where strong societal control of sexuality is asserted over women and men of all ages is in the area of social security regulations. In cases where a woman is judged to be married or cohabitating she is not entitled to claim supplementary benefit. The assumption officially made is that where a man and woman sleep together the man will support her. Thus, at least in the case of women who are poor, the state insists that active heterosexuality cannot coexist with financial independence; nor can a man sleep with a woman without being assumed by the state to support her.

These regulations provide a striking example of the social control of sexuality in everyday life. More generally, it can be noted that coming to terms with personal feelings and cultural expectations regarding sexuality is a delicate part of the process of growing up. It involves timidity, anxiety and self-consciousness for both sexes. But for boys sexuality represents an extension of the masculine role – boys prove their masculinity (and reassure themselves of their attractiveness) by sexual exploit and adventure. The situation prescribed for girls is very different: girls are expected to be as sexually attractive as possible without being sexually active – femininity involves a suppression of sexuality. The strong demands placed on teenage girls by the media, peer groups and family to be attractive, combined with the strong condemnation of girls who are straightforwardly sexual, implies a built-in tension in the feminine role. It has been suggested by several writers that the appeal of 'romantic' magazines and films (with their emphasis upon courtship and glamour) is that these provide a way of resolving the contraction between being, as Willis (1977, p. 45) puts it, 'sexy but not sexual'. At the same time, Willis argues, the romanticism espoused by many working-class girls reinforces boys' sense of male superiority:

The contortions and strange [romantic] rituals of the girls are seen as part of their girlishness, of their inherent weakness and confusion. Their romanticism is tolerated with a knowing masculinity, which privately feels it knows much more about the world (Willis, 1977, p. 45).

Other authors – notably McRobbie (1978) – see romance as a lubricant which eases for girls the passage from adolescence to adulthood. The teenage working-class girls whom she interviewed did not have starry-eyed ideals about marriage; they see the realities of marriage through the experience of their neighbours, mothers and elder sisters, and many recognised the humdrum, exploitative and even brutal aspects of marriage. On the other hand, most of the girls expected to get married, seeing few alternatives for women within their own community. Romance offered the prospect of a little glamour, fun and attention before coming to terms with somewhat harsher realities.

Rape

At first glance cases of rape might appear to be far removed from everyday sexual encounters. The view of rape as an isolated act perpetrated by disturbed individuals is promoted by fictional accounts of rape and by sensational reports in the media which often give disproportionate attention to that small minority of rapists who are apparently 'psychopathic', and whose crimes seem like a spontaneous act provoked by the presence of an unknown (attractive) woman. Such an image of rape is at odds with analyses of rape cases in the USA and in Britain. Research indicates that few rapists are seriously disturbed, that many plan their crimes carefully, and that victims are often attacked by friends, kin or acquaintances within their own home. These studies have also disproved many of the most common myths about rape (that women enjoy rape; that only young, attractive women are vulnerable; that rape cannot succeed if the victim resists). From analysis of police files of rape cases over a five-year period, for example, Wright (1979) concluded that the widespread use of physical violence and of threats of injury or death meant that for most victims the rape was undoubtedly perceived as a 'life-threatening' situation.

When rape is analysed in terms of it relationship to cultural expectations and to the socially structured subordination of women in contemporary society – rather than being viewed as an idiosyncratic act by disturbed individuals – then we can begin to make some headway in understanding the incidence of rape and its social implications.

First, it can be suggested that the likelihood of rape may be enhanced by social pressures on men to 'prove themselves' and to adopt a dominant/ aggressive stance in their encounters with women. Such pressures may, in turn, be reinforced by the portrayal of women in the media, not as complex human beings, but as passive objects to be admired, enjoyed and 'consumed'. Finally, the double standard which embodies the notion that women who are sexually active (unlike similar men) are deviant and forfeit the respect of others should be considered; in many court cases the sexual history of rape victims has been discussed (and echoed in news reports), with the clear implication that women who engaged in sex voluntarily had no right to refuse their 'favours' to others, and placed themselves, in some sense, beyond the protection of the law. (This was dramatically apparent in 1979, when after the brutal murder of ten women alleged to have been involved in prostitution the killing of a girl of 'good reputation' prompted the announcement that the 'Yorkshire Ripper has claimed his first *innocent* victim'. The word 'innocent' is of course ambiguous; but many people complained that *either* the police and media were introducing information irrelevant to the crime (the women's sexual history), *or* they were implying that the earlier victims were in some sense guilty victims – as if murder were justified when the victim was a 'promiscuous' woman.)

The number of rape cases known to the police has been increasing in recent years. There is no way of determining whether the *actual* rate of rape is rising or whether, alternatively, in the light of increased publicity surrounding rape and the development of supportive networks to help victims to overcome their fears, more victims are reporting their rapes to the police. But whatever the actual (unknown) incidence of rape, the significance of rape may spread far more widely than its effects on individual victims. An argument pursued by Hanmer and Saunders (1984), and by Smart and Smart (1978) is that rape, and other forms of aggression against women (ranging from minor assaults to 'sexual harassment' – the frequent advances made by men to women in pubs, on the streets, or at work), act as implicit forms of social control upon women. This is not to say that all women are, or feel themselves to be, under constant threat, or that all women live in fear of sexual attack. On the contrary, most women learn from an early age strategies for insulating themselves from such dangers. At home with their families, shopping in town, at work, surrounded by people, they feel themselves (and rightly) to be, on the whole, safe. The forms of vigilance which serve as their protection become 'second nature' to women at an early age; this vigilance involves such things as care with clothing (not to appear too 'provocative'), care where they go (avoiding certain pubs and gathering places, avoiding walking alone at night), care what they do (lowering their eyes; avoiding hitchhiking or striking up conversations with strangers), and care to enlist wherever possible the protection of a man, be he brother or boyfriend, husband or father.

The pattern of rape and sexual assault

The Women's Safety Survey (Hall, 1985) collected questionnaires from 1236 respondents in London in 1982. The findings from this survey confirm earlier research reports on the patterning and the effects of rape and sexual assault.

1. Like other 'victim studies', the report shows that rape and sexual assault are more widespread than crime statistics indicate.
   Percentage of respondents who had been raped: 17 per cent.
   Percentage of respondents who had been 'raped' by their husband: 9 per cent.
   NB: these 'rapes' do not show up at all in criminal statistics, because rape in marriage is not classified as a crime.
   Percentage of respondents who had been sexually assaulted: 31 per cent.
   Percentage of raped women who had reported to the police: 8 per cent (of whom only 1 in 3 were glad they had done so).
2. In most cases, the offender is known to the victim – a casual acquaintance, a boss or supervisor, a friend or workmate, a family member, a neighbour. About one-half of sexual assaults, but only one-quarter of rapes, involved strangers.
3. The most common locations for rapes or sexual assaults, in order of frequency, are:
   a woman's own home
   a street or alleyway
   the assailant's home
   on, or waiting for, public transport.
4. Fewer than one woman in four felt safe or comfortable when out alone after dark. Many said that this fear affected their social life; one woman in five said fear of being out alone at night had restricted their choice of job. A sense of fear, and restrictions due to fear, were greatest for women on low incomes, and women without cars; 60 per cent of women chose improved public transport as a way of making the streets safer for women.

Thus women learn to behave in ways that minimise the chances of sexual assault and give a feeling of security and safety; but the crucial point is that these protective techniques involve a greater degree of restriction on the freedom of women than on the freedom of men. Women learn 'voluntarily' to limit their mobility, their travel, their territory, their range of encounters with other people; the alleged lack of adventurousness of women, their supposed timidity, is at least partly a result of conditioned responses to the atmosphere of physical danger of which they are warned from girlhood. They therefore have much less autonomy than do men. Coote and Gill (1975) have pointed out that rapists have a higher chance of being acquitted if the defence can argue that the victim lived an autonomous life: that she lived alone, for example, or went into pubs without a male escort. This suggests that the public find it more reasonable that women should accept

restrictions on their autonomy than that greater efforts should be made to
protect women from harassment or assault however they choose to live.
The notion that women should seek the protection of a man in order to be
safe is particularly interesting: it can be argued that the protection afforded
by a man is not merely a function of his (possibly) greater physical strength
but also because women 'alone' (even if in twos or threes) are considered to
be fair game for advances, aggressive or otherwise, from men – while
women with a man are more likely to be considered his 'property', and
therefore 'out of bounds'.

The aim of this section has been to explore the cultural expectations
surrounding sexuality in our society. It has been emphasised that (although
certain physiological drives may be innate) the ways in which human
sexuality are expressed are socially controlled and socially constructed.
Although the physiological basis of sexuality is given through our biology,
the way in which that potentiality is given expression (how, what, where,
with what obligations, and with whom) is *not* determined by biological sex.
The structure of sexual encounters must be seen in terms of the broader
relationships of women and men in our society.

5.7   EXPLAINING GENDER DIVISIONS

It may seem premature to attempt an explanation of gender divisions. After
all, systematic sociological research into this area is still in is infancy. The
task of describing the complex ways in which sex, gender and sexuality are
intertwined has only just begun. Although many aspects of male/female
relations that were previously treated as unproblematic have been subjected
to analysis, and in spite of the collapse of certain untenable stereotypes, the
complexity of men's and women's lives, and of the structures which
constrain them, have not yet been fully explored.

The social constructions of gender differentiation through socialisation

How far do parental actions, and the routine organisation of home life,
push little girls and boys in the direction of socially prescribed gender roles?
Gender-related expectations have been recorded at early stages in parent/
child relationships. Goldberg and Lewis (1972) found, for example, that
mothers of six-month-old infants expected their girl babies to be relatively
quiet, clean and restrained, while their boy babies were expected to be more
noisy and adventurous. Expectations such as these might, of course, be the
first stage in a self-fulfilling prophecy.

On the other hand, a persistent problem in this area of research is to
establish whether parents simply treat their children in a sex-stereotyped

fashion, or whether their actions represent a response to initial differences in behaviour between girls and boys. One reviewer notes

a tendency for parents to begin differential sex role socialization at a very early age, thus obscuring the nature – nurture issue. For example, it was found that newborn girls are spoken to and smiled at more than boys at feedings, and that boys are touched more than girls at this very early stage. It is hard to know whether these differences have been preceded by real differences in the infants themselves or arise through the transmission of sex role expectancies (Weitz, 1977, p. 64).

Parents may sometimes be unaware that they treat their sons differently from their daughters; at other times they may find themselves doing so against their own intentions. A set of interviews with feminist mothers revealed that – despite their avowed intentions to allow children to develop with minimal regard to conventional gender roles – boys (though less so girls) were often raised in sex-stereotyped ways (Van Gelder and Carmichael, 1975). The fact that mothers in this instance found less difficulty in encouraging their daughters to break free of stereotypical roles is consistent with a range of studies suggesting that 'tomboy' girls come in for less criticism, and less pressure to change, than 'cissy' boys. It is possible that, in so far as 'masculine' traits such as assertiveness are more highly valued, parents may be more distressed to see their sons 'stepping down' than their daughters 'reaching up'.

On the other hand, parents are often more protective of their daughters than their sons. Newson and Newson's (1976) study of child-rearing patterns mentions several respects in which 7-year-old girls may be more closely supervised than boys of the same age. Mothers were more likely to fetch daughter from school, less likely to allow daughters to roam outside or play in the street, and more likely to intervene when daughters became involved in 'unsuitable' friendships than in similar cases with sons. Protectiveness toward daughters appears to extend into adolescence. On the basis of interviews with Ealing schoolgirls, Sharpe (1976, pp. 213–14) comments:

Despite the so-called permissiveness of society today, girls are still kept under quite a strict family control which has consequences beyond the simple one of their protection. Parents fear for the safety of their daughters if they are out at night. But rather than equipping them with knowledge and confidence about the 'facts of life' many of them prefer a method of strict control.

This control – combined with the tendency to give daughters rather than sons domestic chores which centre on the home – may serve to restrict girls' range of experience and to limit their self-confidence.

There are many indications that sexual divisions are reinforced, rather than challenged, by current educational practice. As pointed out in Chapter 8, in spite of efforts to break down curricular barriers between the sexes in recent years, schooling continues to channel girls and boys towards different occupational niches. Moreover, the content of teaching materials, staffing arrangements in schools, and patterns of interaction in classrooms all tend to reinforce expectations of male dominance and of a gender division of labour. An analysis of British reading schemes in use in the 1970s (Lobban, 1975) found five central male characters for every one female; the author comments elsewhere (1976, p. 42) that the world portrayed in teaching materials is not only sexist but 'more sexist than present reality'.

The world portrayed within such books often has a counterpart in the staffing arrangements of schools. The overrepresentation of men among teachers of mathematics or science, and more generally in posts of authority, does little to undermine pupils' beliefs that scientific or technical subjects are 'unfeminine' and that women are unsuited to positions of power.

Classroom encounters, too, act as a venue where 'appropriate' relations between the sexes are constantly defined. Wolpe (1977) describes how teachers in a comprehensive school encouraged girls to adopt a coquettish manner with men, by, for example, advising them to smile when approaching a male member of staff. Teachers in mixed classes tend to devote a disproportionate amount of their time and attention to male pupils; this is partly a response to more demanding and often disruptive behaviour on the part of boys, who are in fact more frequently criticised for misconduct, but may lead unintentionally to neglect of girls and to the undermining of their confidence. Stanworth (1983) found that the apparent prominence of boys in A level classes led both sexes to underestimate girls' academic performance, and to regard boys as the more capable and more intelligent sex.

The family and schooling by no means exhaust the social agencies involved in the transmission of conventional gender roles. Our earlier discussion of sexuality pointed to the importance of adolescent peer groups in promoting and enforcing acceptable 'masculine' and 'feminine' behaviour. However, socialisation, and the promotion of gender-related views of the world, is an on-going process, and its very pervasiveness may make it difficult to pin down. The mass media, for instance, have been criticised for casting women mainly in domestic or sexual roles – important less in terms of what they do or say, and more in terms of whom they love or nurture. Partly in response to such criticisms women have increasingly been placed in starring roles, as detectives, doctors, and even newcasters; but as one of the newscasters, ITN's Anna Ford, pointed out at a news conference, these women are still presented more for their beauty than for other qualities, and are reacted to in those terms.

The pervasiveness of gender stereotyping is particularly apparent in the case of language. Phrases in common use – such as 'managers and men', or 'scientists and their wives', or 'athletes, some of whom were women' – convey the impression that workers, scientists and athletes are normally, typically, properly male. The use of the terms 'man' or 'mankind' when men *and* women are intended has similar effects. In one study (cited in Miller and Swift, 1979) American college students were asked to illustrate chapters of a forthcoming sociology textbook. Those who were given headings such as 'Industrial Man', 'Political Man' and 'Man and Society' overwhelmingly produced pictures of adult males. Other students, given headings like 'Industrial Life', 'Political Behaviour', or 'Society', offered illustrations of girls as well as boys, women as well as men.

While it is important to recognise the variety of influences by which individuals are socialised, the internalisation of gender roles by men and women constitutes only a partial explanation for the persistence of gender divisions. Three important reservations must be borne in mind.

First, some people have argued that our gender identities and our sexuality are so deep-seated that a thorough understanding must involve psychoanalytic explanations. Theorists such as Mitchell (1975) and Chodorow (1978) have tried to explore the complicated process of the construction of sexual identities through the psychological processes of interaction within the family.

Second, in looking at socialisation processes we have touched upon the family, schooling, peer groups, mass media and language. Some, but only some, of these processes create an expectation of inferiority or submissiveness in women, and of superiority or dominance in men. Others merely enhance *differences* between the sexes; and how those differences come to be evaluated as inferior or superior, or how they come to be unequally rewarded, requires another type of explanation, one venturing into the realm of the creation of ideology and the exercise of power.

Third, it is crucial to avoid adopting what Wrong (1980) calls 'the over-socialised conception of man' (*sic*). We must avoid the notion that people comply with convention, or that structures of inequality persist, because of normative commitment based on internalised values. The number of dissenting women (and men) would suggest immediately the error of such a view. Women and men who try to counteract in their own lives some of the aspects of sexual divisions which they find oppressive are confronted by structural obstacles and by forms of social control, many of which have been discussed in this chapter. It is precisely these obstacles, and forms of social control, which are challenged by collective campaigns, particularly those deriving from the Women's Liberation Movement. Many trade unions have also addressed themselves to issues of gender divisions; the massive TUC support in November 1979 for the campaign to resist restrictions on abortion was an example of an effort which extended beyond narrowly defined concerns with conditions and terms of employment.

Women and political power

One inhibiting factor in attempts to change oppressive aspects of gender divisions is the extent to which women have systematically been deprived of power. Of 635 MPs elected in the United Kingdom in 1983, only 23 (or 3.6 per cent) were women; this is one fewer than the number elected at the end of the Second World War. In 1984, women members constituted only 24.8 per cent of the British Medical Association, 16.5 per cent of the Institute of Bankers, 12.2 per cent of the Law Society, and 2.5 per cent of the British Institute of Management (EOC, 1985, Table 5.3, p. 88). At the end of 1984, at a time when 91 per cent of NUTGW members, 72 per cent of NUT members, and 67 per cent of NUPE members were women, women constituted only 11, 7 and 7 per cent respectively of full-time union officials (EOC, 1985, Table 5.4, p. 88). These statistics indicate the lack of formal power women have with respect to defining issues, influencing legislation and affecting the course of trade union struggles; they can be taken both as a reflection of, and a contributing factor to, women's subordination.

The apparent imperviousness to change of some of the practices and institutions which embody and reproduce male dominance is, in part, explained by the extent to which women are systematically deprived of power. However, there is, in turn a need to account for powerlessness itself. Theories that try to elaborate the fundamental structures underlying female subordination are very much in the process of development, and hence very incomplete; that is, perhaps, a reflection of how recently intellectual attention has been directed to the problem of gender divisions.

5.8   THE UBIQUITY OF MALE DOMINATION

The most promising attempts to construct a workable theory are those which attempt to take account of the ubiquity of male domination – its persistence through different historical periods and across different cultures – *and* its variety. Efforts are made to trace, on the one hand, the diversity of ways in which men exercise power over women (and the social and material circumstances that favour more or less rigid hierarchies) and, on the other, the course of sexual antagonisms – the forms of resistance mounted by women, and the circumstances in which such challenges are likely to be successful.

There are disagreements as to whether the male oppression of women has been characteristic of all human societies (and may, in some way, have been connected with the rise of civilisation or human society itself), or whether, on the other hand, an egalitarian sexual division of labour characterised the simplest human societies, with male domination only emerging under certain conditions. It is, however, fairly widely accepted that particular material and political changes served to increase the power of men *vis-à-vis* women: changes of decisive importance included, for example, changes in production techniques that denied women independent control over subsistence production, often combined with the reorganisation of women's labour around the family rather than the community or more inclusive kin-group; and, crucially, the emergence of the state, which consolidated and sustained the power of male heads of households over 'their' women and children. Anthropological and historical evidence suggests, then, that while most known societies have been characterised by female subordination, the rigidity of the hierarchical sexual division of labour became more acute as societies became more complex.

These considerations point to the conclusion that the systematic subordination of women in advanced capitalist societies involves two sets of interrelated structures. The first of these, patriarchy, is defined by Hartmann (1982, p. 447, n. 1) as 'a set of hierarchical relations which has a material base and in which there are hierarchical relations between men, and solidarity among them, which enables them to control women. Patriarchy is thus the system of male oppression of women.' Although it is recognised that some men are in a position to exercise more decisive power than others, the concept of patriarchy emphasises the benefits accruing directly to all men from the domestic, labouring, reproductive and sexual subordination of women.

The second structure implicated in the subordination of women in contemporary society is capitalist relations of production; these exacerbated the hierarchical nature of the sexual division of labour, and encouraged sexual antagonisms at the expense of class solidarity. One source of evidence that capitalism exploits and aggravates sexual divisions comes from anthropological research; studies of economic, social and political change in areas as different as the Dominican Republic, Columbia and Nigeria (see Reiter, 1975) indicate that in the process of capitalist penetration patterns of male domination over women become even more pronounced. Another source of evidence derives from historical analysis of changes in the sexual division of labour consequent upon the emergence of capitalism and the industrial revolution in England and the USA. In particular, Hartmann (1982) argues that in the transition to wage labour and the accompanying class struggle, patriarchy and capitalism were mutually reinforcing; each structure influenced the direction the other took. On the one hand, the actions of capitalists enhanced competition within the ranks of labouring people, and exploited (and reinforced) patriarchal relations within the family by offering women and children lower wage rates. On the other, male workers used trade-union organisation not only to protect their own position *vis-à-vis* capitalists but also to secure advantages over female workers, and to segregate women within the labour market so as to preserve patriarchal privilege at home. Hartmann (1982, pp. 468–9) concludes:

> The present status of women in the labour market and the current arrangement of sex-segregated jobs is the result of a long process of interation between patriarchy and capitalism. I have emphasised the actions of male workers throughout this process because I believe this to be correct ... Capitalists have indeed used women as unskilled, underpaid labour to undercut male workers, yet this is only a case of the chickens coming home to roost – a case of men's cooptation by and support for patriarchal society, with its hierarchy among men, being turned back on themselves with a vengeance. Capitalism grew on top of patriarchy; patriarchal capitalism is stratified society par excellence.

Hence the oppression or subordination of women in contemporary societies is neither simply an offshoot of the development of capitalism, nor to be understood independently of it. The dismantling of gender divisions would depend – if Hartmann's analysis is correct – on struggles both to transform the social relations of production and to construct radically new relations between women and men.

REFERENCES TO CHAPTER 5

Allen, S. and Wolkowitz, C. (1986) 'Homeworking and the Control of Women's Work', in *Feminist Review* (eds), *Waged Work*, London, Virago.
Barrett, M. and McIntosh, M. (1982) *The Anti-Social Family*, London, Verso.
Barrett, M. and Roberts, H. (1978) 'Doctors and their Patients', in Smart and Smart (1978).
Barron, R. and Norris, G. (1976) 'Sexual Divisions and the Dual Labour Market', in D. Barker and S. Allen (eds), *Dependence and Exploitation in Work and Marriage*, London, Longman.
Beechey, V. (1977) 'Some Notes on Female Wage Labour in Capitalist Production', *Capital and Class*, Autumn 1977, no. 3.
Beechy, V. and Perkins, T. (1987) *Women, Part-Time Work and Labour Markets*, Cambridge, Polity Press.
Benenson, H. (1984) 'Women's Occupational and Family Achievement in the US Class System', *British Journal of Sociology*, vol. xxxv, no. 1.
Blackburn, R. and Mann, M. (1979) *The Working Class in the Labour Market*, London, Macmillan.
Bland, L. *et al.* (1978) 'Women Inside and Outside the Relations of Production', in Women's Studies Group, Centre for Contemporary Cultural Studies (eds), *Women Take Issue*, London, Hutchinson.
Breugel, I. (1979) 'Women as Reserve Army of Labour', *Feminist Review*, issue 3.
Bunkle, P. (1984) 'Calling the Shots?', in R. Arditti *et al.* (eds), *Test-Tube Women*, London, Pandora Press.
Campbell, B. (1974) 'Sexuality and Submission', in S. Allen, L. Sanders and J. Wallis (eds), *Conditions of Illusion*, Leeds, Feminist Books.
Central Policy Review Staff (1980) *People and their Families*, London, HMSO.

Charles, N. and Kerr, M. (1986) 'Eating Properly, the Family and State Benefit', *Sociology*, vol. 20, no. 3 (August).

Chodorow, N. (1978) *The Reproduction of Mothering*, Los Angeles, University of California Press.

Coote, A. and Gill, T. (1975) *The Rape Controversy*, London, NCCL.

Coussins, J. (1980) 'Equality for Women: Have the Laws Worked?', *Marxism Today*, January 1980, p. 10.

Davis, A. (1982) *Women, Race and Class*, London, The Women's Press.

Delphy, C. (1984) *Close to Home*, London, Hutchinson.

Department of Employment (1974) *Women and Work*, Manpower Paper no. 9, London, HMSO.

Dobash, R. and Dobash, R. (1980) *Violence Against Wives*, London, Open Books.

Equal Opportunities Commission (1985) *Ninth Annual Report 1984*, Manchester, EOC.

Elston, M. and Doyal, L. (1983) *Health and Medicine*, unit 14 of the Changing Experience of Women course, Milton Keynes, Open University Press.

Finer Report (1974) *Report of the Committee on One Parent Families*, Department of Health and Social Security, London, HMSO.

Freeman, C. (1982) 'The "Understanding" Employer', in J. West (ed.), *Work, Women and the Labour Market*, London, Routledge & Kegan Paul.

Goldberg, S. and Lewis, M. (1972) 'Play Behaviour in the Infant: Early Sex Differences', in J. Bardwick (ed.), *Readings on the Psychology of Women*, New York, Harper & Row.

Graham, H. (1984) *Women, Health and the Family*, Brighton, Wheatsheaf Books.

Hall, R. E. (1985) *Ask Any Woman*, Bristol, Falling Wall Press.

Hanmer, J. and Saunders, S. (1984) *Well-Founded Fear*, London, Hutchinson.

Hartmann, H. (1982) 'Capitalism, Patriarchy and Job Segregation by Sex', in A. Giddens and D. Held (eds), *Classes, Power and Conflict*, Basingstoke, Macmillan.

Hartnett, O. (1978) 'Sex-role Stereotyping at Work', in J. Chetwynd and O. Hartnett (eds), *The Sex Role System*, London, Routledge & Kegan Paul.

Hope, E. *et al.* (1976) 'Homeworkers in North London', in D. Barker and S. Allen (eds), *Dependence and Exploitation in Work and Marriage*, London, Longman.

Land, H. (1972) 'Large Families in London', in E. Butterworth and D. Weir (eds), *Social Problems of Modern Britain*, London, Fontana.

Land, H. (1975) 'The Myth of the Male Breadwinner', *New Society*, October 1975.

Land, H. (1976) 'Women: Supporters or Supported?', in D. Barker and S. Allen (eds), *Sexual Divisions in Society*, London, Tavistock.

Land, H. (1986) 'The Unwelcome Impact of Social Policies on Women in the Labour Market', Paper presented to the conference on Work and Politics, Harvard University Centre for European Studies.

Lees, S. (1986) *Losing Out*, London, Hutchinson.

Lobban, G. (1975) 'Sex Roles in Reading Schemes', *Educational Review*, vol. 27, no. 3.

Lobban, G. (1976) 'Sex Roles in Reading Schemes', in Children's Rights Workshop, *Sexism in Children's Books*, London, Readers and Writers.

Low Pay Unit (1979) *The Hidden Army*, London, HMSO.

McIntosh, M. (1978) 'Who needs Prostitutes?', in Smart and Smart.

Macintyre, S. (1976) 'Who wants Babies?', in D. Barker and S. Allen (eds), *Sexual Divisions in Society*, London, Tavistock.

McKee, L. and Bell, C. (1983) 'Marital Relations in Times of Male Unemployment', Paper presented to the SSRC Workshop on Employment and Unemployment.

McRobbie, A. (1978) 'Working Class Girls and the Culture of Femininity', in Women's Studies Group, Centre for Contemporary Cultural Studies (eds), *Women Take Issue*, London, Hutchinson.

Martin, J. and Roberts, C. (1984) *Women and Employment*, Department of Employment, London, HMSO.

Mathieu, N-C. (1977) *Ignored by Some, Denied by Others*, London, Women's Research and Resources Centre.

Miller, C. and Swift, K. (1979) *Words and Women*, Harmondsworth, Penguin.

Mitchell, J. (1975) *Psychoanalysis and Feminism*, Harmondsworth, Penguin.

National Council for One-Parent Families (1981) *One Parent Families, Annual Report*, London, NCOPF.

Newson, J. and Newson, E. (1976) *Seven Years Old in the Home Environment*, London, Allen & Unwin.

Oakley, A. (1972) *Sex, Gender and Society*, London, Temple Smith.

Oakley, A. (1974) *The Sociology of Housework*, London, Martin Robertson.

Oakley, A. (1981) *Subject Women*, Oxford, Martin Robertson.

Oakley, A. (1987) 'From Walking Wombs to Test-tube Babies', in Stanworth, M. (ed.), *Reproductive Technologies*, Cambridge, Polity Press.

Oren, L. (1974) 'The Welfare of Women in Labouring Families', in M. Hartmann and L. Banner (eds), *Clio's Consciousness Raised*, New York, Harper & Row.

Pahl, J. (ed.) (1985) *Private Violence and Public Policy*, London, Routledge & Kegan Paul.

Phillips, A. (1983) *Hidden Hands*, London, Pluto Press.

Phillips, A. and Taylor, B. (1980) 'Sex and Skill: Notes Towards a Feminist Economics', *Feminist Review*, no. 6.

Pollock, S. (1984) 'Refusing to take Women Seriously: Side Effects and the Politics of Contraception', in R. Arditti *et al.* (eds), *Test-Tube Women*, London, Pandora Press.

Rakusen, J. (1981) 'Depo-Provera: the Extent of the Problem', in H. Roberts (ed.), *Women, Health and Reproduction*, London, Routledge & Kegan Paul.

Reiter, R. (ed.) (1975) *Toward an Anthropology of Women*, New York, Monthly Review Press.

Ritchie, J. and Barrowclough, R. (1983) *Paying for Equalisation*, Manchester, EOC.

Rowbotham, S. (1974) *Hidden from History*, London, Pluto Press.

Rubery, J. (1978) 'Structured Labour Markets, Worker Organisation and Low Pay', *Cambridge Journal of Economics*, vol. 1.

Sachs, A. (1978) 'The Myth of Male Protectiveness and the Legal Subordination of Women', in Smart and Smart (1978).

Savage, W. (1982) 'Taking Liberties with Women', *International Journal of Health Services*, vol. 12, no. 2.

Scott, H. (1984) *Working Your Way to the Bottom: the Feminization of Poverty*, London, Pandora Press.

Shacklady Smith, L. (1978) 'Sexist Assumptions and Female Delinquency', in Smart and Smart (1978).

Sharpe, S. (1976) *Just Like a Girl*, Harmondsworth, Penguin.

Smart, C. (1984) *The Ties that Bind: Law, Marriage and the Reproduction of Patriarchal Relations*, London, Routledge & Kegan Paul.

Smart, C. and Smart, B. (eds) (1978) *Women, Sexuality and Social Control*, London, Routledge & Kegan Paul.

Snell, M. (1979) 'The Equal Pay and Sex Discrimination Acts', *Feminist Review*, issue 1.

Stanworth, M. (1983) *Gender and Schooling*, London, Hutchinson.

Stanworth, M. (ed.) (1987) *Reproductive Technologies*, Cambridge, Polity Press.
Tiger, L. and Fox, R. (1974) *The Imperial Animal*, London, Paladin.
Titmuss, R. (1958) 'The Position of Women', in *Essays on the Welfare State*, London, Allen & Unwin.
Townsend, P. (1979) *Poverty in the United Kingdom*, Harmondsworth, Penguin.
Van Gelder, L. and Carmichael, C. (1975) 'But What About Our Sons?' *Ms.*, October 1975; cited in Weitz (1977, p. 62).
Wainwright, H. (1978) 'Women and the Division of Labour', in P. Abrams (ed.) *Work, Urbanism and Inequality*, London, Weidenfeld & Nicolson.
Warnock Report on Human Fertilisation and Embryology (1985) *A Question of Life*, Oxford, Basil Blackwell.
Weideger, P. (1978) *Female Cycles*, London, The Women's Press.
Weitz, S. (1977) *Sex Roles*, New York, Oxford University Press.
Westergaard, J. and Resler, H. (1976) *Class in a Capitalist Society*, Harmondsworth, Penguin.
Whitehead, A. (1981) '"I'm Hungry, Mum": the Politics of Domestic Budgeting', in K. Young, C. Wolkowitz and R. McCullagh (eds), *Of Marriage and the Market*, London, CSE Books.
Willis, P. (1977) *Learning to Labour*, Westmean, Saxon House.
Wilson, D. (1978) 'Sexual Codes and Conduct', in Smart and Smart (1978).
Wilson, L. *et al.* (1974) 'The Independence Demand', in S. Allen *et al.* (eds), *Conditions of Illusion*, Leeds, Feminist Books.
Wolpe, A.-M. (1977) *Some Processes in Sexist Education*, London, Women's Research and Resources Centre.
Wright, R. (1979) Paper presented to the British Psychological Society, London, December 1979.
Wrong, D. (1980) 'The Oversocialized Conception of Man in Modern Sociology', in R. Bocock *et al.* (eds), *An Introduction to Sociology*, London, Fontana.
Wynn, B. (1977) 'Domestic Subjects and the Sexual Division of Labour', in Schooling and Society Course Team, *School Knowledge and Social Control*, Milton Keynes, Open University Press.

6

Power and Politics

6.1 INTRODUCTION: THE STUDY OF POLITICS

Attempts to say what politics is may appear at first sight unnecessarily pedantic: we all 'know' what politics is about. In everyday popular usage, politics is seen as being about 'Parliament', 'the government', 'the parties', 'elections', 'voting', and endless debates and arguments which produce a month of yawns for every day of excitement. Thus, the common-sense view of what constitutes politics is the misleadingly limited and circular one of 'what politicians do'.

This view is particularly prevalent in stable liberal-democratic societies like Britain or America, where its validity often seems self-evident. But purely on a factual level, this view is highly limited, ethnocentric and lacking in historical perspective – politics is also about civil war, guerrilla movements, revolutions, military coups and assassinations, as well as about ballot boxes and speeches in the House of Commons or the Senate. All societies have some sort of political organisation or structure which does not necessarily take the form with which we are familiar in the West – a form which, in any case, is of only relatively recent origin. So, the apparently easy and straightforward exercise of defining what politics is requires more systematic attention if we are to understand political structures and processes sociologically.

Sociological analysis of politics requires, firstly, the study of political behaviour within a *social* context, the relation of politics to the entire social structure in which it is embedded. But more than this, it also involves the recognition that 'politics' is potentially present in *all* social relationships, in that politics essentially involves the *exercise of power*. As Worsley (1964, pp. 16–17) says: 'We can be said to act politically when we exercise constraint on others to behave as we want them to ... The exercise of constraint in any relationship is political.'

So, political behaviour is essentially 'power behaviour', not by any means confined to particular governmental institutions or forms, but present in any social situation. Thus, political decisions are being made, and hence power is being exercised, not only when taxation laws are changed by parliaments or when Nazis herd people into concentration camps, but also when parents forbid their daughter to attend an all-night party or when an employer sacks his workers. In this sense, then, almost all areas of social life

196

involve potential political elements, so the *politics* cannot be seen as involving merely 'what politicians do', but is to be seen as a *process involving the exercise of control, constraint and coercion in society*. Any unequal relationship has political dimensions, and since unequal relationships exist throughout social life, any search for patterns in social life must also involve a search for patterns in the distribution of power. A sociological approach to politics, then, implies the analysis of the operation of power in social contexts and relationships, and its consequences for social action and stability. Of course, while we all have some power, not all power relations are of equal significance, and we shall be discussing power relations at the societal level.

Power to most people seems distant and detached from their lives, 'not my concern'. But the very fact that individuals are often unable to see questions of power as permeating their lives is interesting in itself and raises the very important question of why they should accept domination and the limitations imposed on their lives by others.

At first sight, this may seem a foolish question – the obvious answer is that they may have no real choice: employees obey employers because they need to maintain income, peasants obey landlords because they must pay their rents and debts. They conform because of their *dependence* on others and because the powers that be may be able to impose *sanctions* on them: in other words, the powerful may be able to coerce the subordinates into compliance. But this does not necessarily *guarantee* the successful imposition of the will of the powerful, for although they have coercive resources at their disposal, 'naked' coercive power alone may not be sufficient to achieve compliance. They need to generate willing compliance. Hence, the powerful try to claim legitimacy for their power, so it is acknowledged and accepted in the eyes of their subordinates and institutionalised in social arrangements. Powerful groups in society attempt to influence the ideas of those below them through the dissemination of *ideology*, to persuade the majority that their subordinate position is normal and natural and that they, the powerful, have the right to command power and influence. Such claims may rest on a variety of foundations: that such a distribution of power has always traditionally existed, that it is a divinely ordained arrangement, that the holders of power possess intrinsic ruling skills or superior social status, or whatever.

In this way, then, unequal power relations persist not simply because of the weakness of subordinate groups, but also because of the *perceptions* and *expectations* which these groups have of their relationship with those holding power. These perceptions are not merely abstract, 'philosophical' ideas but are sociological phenomena in themselves, because they are socially constructed and sustained, and because they may shape the behaviour of subordinate groups and hence contribute directly and significantly to power relations and political stability. If a crucial question for sociologists is how conformity can be explained in a context of unequal power relations, then they have to understand the bases on which power is held and how individuals and groups 'see' their political roles.

So, in the first part of this chapter we will be concerned with analysing and explaining the way in which power is distributed in contemporary capitalist society, and with the political behaviour of the powerful and the powerless. Our major concern in the latter part of the chapter will be with the relationship between political consciousness and behaviour, and with the origins of political ideas and beliefs and their effects on political action – whether this be choosing who to vote for, or rising up in revolution.

6.2   THE RISE OF THE MODERN STATE

States and stateless societies

In our kind of society, political activities take place within the framework called the *state*, but the state is by no means a universal feature of all societies, nor has there always been a state in societies which today have one. In analysing the political organisation of primitive societies, anthropologists have generally found it useful to view political systems in terms of a continuum, with well developed states at one end, and stateless, or acephalous, societies at the other.

Although societies possessing statelike institutions can vary greatly, they tend to exhibit certain shared characteristics. Crucially there is always some kind of central authority which rules over a given territory and which has the power to force those over whom it rules to obey. However, this capacity to coerce is hardly ever directly achieved by the central authority, but by its delegation to the members of some kind of administrative machinery or other, e.g. to military, bureaucratic or religious functionaries. Also, there is usually some kind of established procedure for the transference of power through time, for state rule involves the continuity of office – leaders can be elected, or can claim divine appointment, or can inherit from their kin, and so on. Finally, the existence of the state usually implies the existence of structured inequality characterised by sharp cleavages between groups not only of prestige and wealth, but of power too. Political control, then, is ultimately achieved by the use of, or the possibility of the use of, force, with the control of the instruments of such coercion in the hands of the occupants of specialised and differentiated political statuses.

Forms of the state in capitalist society

The rise of capitalism in Western Europe is associated with the rise of centralised, specialised state institutions employing increasingly complex and sophisticated techniques of administration and social control. Paradoxically, however, this complex modern state has developed out of a feudal political structure which was extremely primitive in comparison with ancient centralised states such as those of Egypt or of the Incas.

As we saw in Chapter 2, the feudalism of medieval Europe was characterised by an extreme fragmentation of political power and production. Feudalism was based on the countryside, dependent upon agrarian production, with a dominant class of feudal lords monopolising economic and political control over localised areas. Whilst there was, theoretically, a hierarchy of allegiance from lower to higher lords and ultimately to the king, this was a fluid system of military alliances which allowed no stable centre of political power to exist. Ultimately based on conquest, the power of the local lord depended on his ability to obtain surplus labour or produce from his serfs, and on his ability to defend his area of land. Thus, larger states were only conglomerates of these local areas of domination, and the great empires of Eastern and Central Europe were little more than loose federations of principalities. Only with the pacification of large areas by dominant lords could wider trade and larger markets emerge. The decline of feudal arrangements was strongly associated with the rise of militarily successful monarchs supported by lords sufficiently powerful to claim dominance over large areas, and with the rise of towns as trading centres, which led to the development in importance of merchants and manufacturers. The independence of the town introduced an economic dynamism which undermined the rural base of feudalism, and paved the way for the emergence of new, economically powerful classes and a landless class of wage labourers.

Thus, by the sixteenth century in Britain and the seventeenth century in Europe, a far more centralised form of political domination emerged with the development of absolutist monarchies, which imposed laws and taxes over their territory and enforced them by the central monopolisation of the use of force. Clearly, this emergent central administration needed functionaries to run it, and initially these were powerful men, trusted as allies of the monarch. Gradually, they were replaced by administrators whose power depended only upon their official position and not upon their personal military power or wealth. Professional lawyers became more important as codifiers and modifiers of a recorded body of law, replacing arbitrary rule by nobles or local customary laws.

These features show the trend towards a *centralisation of power* and a *rationalisation* of politics. The state comes to be the only legitimate authority in a territory, and its administration increasingly operates on set principles and procedures. The trend to rational administration by officials culminates in bureaucracy and in the constitutional nation-state. As Poggi (1978, p. 93) defines it:

there is a unity of the State's territory, which comes to be grounded as much as possible by a continuous geographical frontier that is militarily defensible. There is a single currency and a unified fiscal system. Generally there is a single 'national' language ... Finally there is a unified legal system that allows alternative juridical traditions to maintain validity only in peripheral areas and for limited purposes.

However, this constitutional nation-state need *not* be democratic: European states became 'fully' democratic, that is, with votes for all citizens and free political association, only in the twentieth or the late nineteenth century. This development followed earlier struggles for representation within these states by the new economic groups, above all the bourgeoisie – the merchants, traders and manufacturers. However, such struggles came at different times with varying degrees of success. In all cases, the constitutional nation-state still aided the rise of capitalism because it maintained peace, protected property rights and contracts, protected foreign trade, and often regulated money as a means of exchange, all of which aided trade and the development of markets.

At the same time, the growing bourgeoisie could be threatened by this centralised state if it was not represented in it, and if the monarch tried to tax or regulate trade for his own purposes. In much of Europe, this led to struggles by the bourgeoisie (in alliance with other dissatisfied social groups) to gain political representation or to reverse a slide back to personal absolutism by the monarch. The seventeenth-century struggles in England are often seen as establishing the conditions for capitalist expansion through the winning of dominance for Parliament and the constitutional regulation of the monarchy. In France, the developments came later but perhaps went further with the French Revolution and the construction of a republic and the new constitution.

The contrast between English and German roads to capitalist development is highly significant. The English road gradually established the principles of representative liberal democracy, as first the commercialised land-owners, then the industrialists, and finally the working class gradually won access to state power and slowly established notions of individual citizenship and rights of political expression. This 'evolution' was punctuated by struggle and conflict, but there is still a marked contrast with the German route, where the political failure of the bourgeoisie led to a continuing 'bureaucratic absolutism' lasting until the end of the First World War. The central state made concessions to the growing working class and organised the growth of industrialised capitalism, but democratic institutions and principles were weak and had extremely shallow roots. Thus, in Germany and elsewhere in Europe, one road to capitalist development and expansion in the twentieth century was authoritarian and undemocratic, gaining its ultimate expression in fascism. In Germany, full liberal democracy has only been stabilised in its Western portion since the

Second World War; and this form of state is only now emerging in Portugal and Spain after the recent downfall of fascistic regimes. There is no natural and inevitable link between liberal democracy and capitalism, even though it is now the dominant form of regime in Western Europe. Elsewhere in the world, the establishment of capitalism has gone together with very different kinds of state.

Outside Europe and North America, capitalism has normally been imposed or 'grafted on to' a domestic economy by the expansion of the European economies. As producers of raw materials, as recipients of foreign goods, or as sites for the establishment of production, these nations have often experienced political domination as well as economic domination, with a variety of forms of regime imposed, ranging from imitations of the British constitution to foreign-funded military dictatorships. What is not surprising is the degree of instability characterising many such regimes, for they are not normally founded on the internal development of social and economic institutions, but on imported patterns instituted and run by foreign-sponsored elites dependent on the support of an external foreign power. Where politics is founded on the support of social groups in the society, these groups are frequently profoundly divided, not only by economic position but by language, cultures and territorial loyalty.

Thus, from the above discussion we can conclude that the state in capitalist society has no 'natural' or 'normal' form. Liberal-democratic regimes have developed slowly in America and in some European societies and have been stabilised in others only since 1945. It is not inevitable that these will always remain stable, or that liberal democracy will be established elsewhere in the world, particularly in nations with a peripheral position in the world economic system. What *is* established and growing, however, is the bureaucratic, centralised nation-state.

6.3   THE DISTRIBUTION OF POWER IN MODERN WESTERN SOCIETY: THE PLURALIST VIEW

One of the most distinctive features of Western pre-industrial societies was the grossly asymmetrical distribution of power. In feudal and absolutist Europe, power resided preponderantly in the hands of the barons and large landowners, while the mass of the population who formed the peasantry were merely passive pawns, acted upon rather than acting politically: the owners of the means of production monopolised power and effectively ruled unchallenged.

As we have just seen, the gradual development of commercial agriculture and the advent of industrialisation brought with them extensive and profound changes, spawning new systems of production, new socio-economic relationships and the emergence of new classes and interests, and while the French Revolution by no means gave 'power to the people', it seriously undermined the unquestioned legitimacy of power enjoyed by an aristocratic upper class.

The social, economic and political relations of nineteenth-century industrial society, then, rested less and less on the traditional norms and values of a feudal agricultural system: the new industrial bourgeoisie were keen to translate their economic power into political influence, while the industrial working class began to organise themselves to enhance the representation of their interests. In America and Britain and the rest of Europe (though by no means simultaneously or after an identical pattern), the industrial bourgeoisie came to occupy places in the legislatures, the right to vote was gradually extended, mass-based political parties emerged, and the right of groups of workers to organise occupationally for purposes of bargaining and representation was secured. Thus, a gradual process of democratisation was apparently taking place, the end-product of which would eventually be a system of liberal democracy, in which all classes and groups would have equal rights of participation and opportunity to influence – a 'democratic revolution', in fact.

As we shall see later in our discussion of Marxist views, such a picture has not been shared universally, but it did become the dominant model for portraying the social organisation of power in the West, in the form of *Pluralist theory*, most notably propounded by Dahl (1961), Riesman (1950), and others.

Pluralist democracy

The starting point for the pluralists is the equally forthright rejection of two opposing views of the political process, classical democratic theory and Marxist ruling-class models, as not corresponding to reality. On the one hand, pluralism denies the possible existence of any direct participatory democracy, since modern industrial societies are too large and too complicated for this to be remotely practical; while on the other, pluralists are equally insistent that a number of significant changes in the past century require that we reject notions of a dominant ruling elite, with a strong internal solidarity and shared interests opposed to those of the majority of subordinate citizens. The more accurate depiction of Western power structures is, they argue, that of 'pluralist democracy', in which a *diffusion of power* prevails, buttressed and safeguarded by a number of important mechanisms and institutions.

Now, if the pluralists' view is to hold water, they have to be able to reconcile their analysis of the power structure with the unavoidable facts that elites do exist in contemporary society and that most citizens are not directly involved in decision-making – that is, they have to demonstrate that something which can be meaningfully called 'democracy' and some diffused pattern of power can be identified in Western societies. Indeed, the essence of pluralism is an attempt by liberal theorists to develop, as they see it, a more realistic account of democratic society which accommodates these facts of political life, and which translates or modifies the more philosophical ideals of classical democracy into a practical theory of democracy. Rather than attempt to sweep the existence of elites under the carpet, pluralists recognise their existence in modern democracy, and in fact regard them as a *necessary and integral feature*. Thus, for them, the existence of elites does not compromise the idea of democracy but strengthens it, given certain conditions which we shall outline below.

Many non-Marxists would accept that the nineteenth-century Western capitalist class was the dominant and pre-eminent group socially, both economically and politically. But, for pluralists, such a description of the pattern of power is no longer tenable, since the power structures of modern societies are now crucially different from those of the eighteenth and early nineteenth centuries. Modern societies have developed into more complex structures characterised by increasing social differentiation, with a more heterogeneous network of social and occupational roles, and a greater proliferation of organisations whose members share common interests. The result of this, according to pluralists, is that interests in modern society have become progressively *diversified*, so that a greater number of groups with particular interests and political demands to be satisfied have come to make their presence felt in the political arena.

For the pluralist, power no longer resides in any one centre, and political resources are more widely distributed throughout society. This is not to suggest that a totally egalitarian society has come about: nevertheless, crucial changes have taken place, so that no single elite group exists in Western democracies, but a *variety of elite groups compete for power*.

The viability of democracy, then, is not compromised by the continued existence of elites, since for the pluralist the distinctive feature of liberal democracy is that it is a political system of *'open' power groups*, participating in the power game. The various elites are located in such institutional areas as business, government administration, politics (in the parliamentary sense), labour, education and culture, and draw their membership from various social strata on the basis of merit and regardless of class, sex, ethnic background, or whatever.

Thus, democracy is characterised as a system of *competing elites*, where no single group is able to secure a monopoly of power and manipulate the system consistently to its exclusive advantage. No monolithic unity exists, since elites are by and large non-overlapping in membership and are often in conflict with one another in policy preferences. Rather, there exists a system of 'strategic elites', which can influence decisions but *as separate* elites in their own distinctive social milieux, with their own values and interests and without overlapping memberships, thus minimising the possibility of an omnipotent oligarchy.

Furthermore, the very existence of a variety of elites competing to influence decisions safeguards against any narrow abuse of power. This is because the various elites serve as 'veto groups' able to exercise *countervailing power* against each other as and when necessary.

This multi-centred structure of power, then, is reinforced by the fact that power for the pluralists is essentially *situational* and *non-cumulative*. Elites have varying degrees of influence at different times and over different issues, their power being circumscribed and limited by the nature of the issue: sometimes an elite exercises power and sometimes it does not, depending on the issue. This assumption denies the possibility that power in one area of social life will give power elsewhere (for example, an automatic 'translation' of economic power into political power). Rather, politics and power are *tied to issues* which may be of greater concern to some elite groups than to others and which may produce differing opportunities and motivations for influencing a decision for some groups rather than others, depending on the nature of the issue. Certainly, one cannot assume that one group's interests will always prevail, and the Marxist emphasis on the prime importance of economic power resident in the hands of a small dominant economic class is also rejected, since there have supposedly occurred a number of significant changes in the economic arrangements of Western societies.

Private ownership is, allegedly, no longer as decisive a basis of power in modern society, for a variety of reasons. Firstly the state has come to play a greater part in the control of economic decisions than in the nineteenth century, and through the development of public ownership and nationalisation the principle of private ownership has been restricted and the 'capitalist class' consequently weakened in the 'mixed' economy. Secondly, in business and industry, there has occurred an increasing separation between ownership and control, since large-scale industrial organisations are now controlled by managerial specialists supposedly less preoccupied with maximising profit. And, thirdly, the growth of joint stock companies with very large numbers of shareholders invalidates the formerly crucial status of ownership. For these reasons, according to pluralists, we can dispense with the search for a dominant class characteristic of the nineteenth century.

But what guarantees do citizens have that power will not be abused? According to the pluralist, two important features of liberal democracy provide safeguards in this respect. First, there exists a *basic consensus* on norms and goals, so that there are no fundamental cleavages of values in society or in politics – hence there is no justification for assuming, as Marxist do, an opposition of group interests on a whole range of issues.

Secondly, such political systems provide a number of *fundamental safety mechanisms and devices* which are not evident in autocratic systems or where a ruling class consistently monopolises power. There exist the democratic mechanisms of *competitive mass political parties*, regular free elections, and the institutionalised opportunity for a multitude of *pressure and interest groups* to influence the process of political decision making. For Pluralists, all these inhibit the concentration and enhance the diffusion of power, so that no single group is able to secure a basis of power in order to suppress or deny effectively the demands of others. Let us examine more closely, then, the supposed virtues of these institutions.

Parties and elections: the Pluralist view

In democratic thinking, the *mass political party* is an integral element, a central institution linking individuals and groups with the formal power structure, representing and aggregating a wide range of (group) interests and policy platforms in the political process. The development of political parties in the mid-nineteenth century coincided with the growth of democratic ideologies and the concomitant electoral and parliamentary changes which were instituted in European and American political systems in that period, involving, particularly, the extension of participation in elections to increasing numbers of the population – most notably to the working classes spawned by industrialism. In Britain and elsewhere, this resulted in the creation of political parties on a national basis to organise and win mass support of voters, so that by the turn of the century the mass-based party had become a prominent feature of European political systems.

For the pluralist, parties make an important contribution to the diffusion of power in liberal democracy, serving as *secondary associations*, linking the mass of the people and the political elites. The mass party is regarded as a significant means by which popular interests, demands and grievances can be fed into the formal power structure to influence public policy. Additionally, parties have come to be the main source of recruitment for the political elites. This recruitment, it is argued, has increasingly manifested a *meritocratic* pattern: political elites have been rendered more socially heterogeneous, unlike in political systems where parties are absent and where ruling groups are drawn from traditional sources like hereditary ruling families, military personnel, and so on.

The existence of competitive parties allegedly acts as an important stabilising factor in democratic politics, since they commit and unite competing groups to the principle of orderly and open competition for power in elections and thereafter to the principle of majority decision by parliament. Thus, while conflict is accepted as a real and important element of the political process, it is formalised and acted out 'within the system', reinforcing the legitimacy of the idea of bringing power to bear through the appropriate democratic channels.

Pluralists, of course, would recognise that every elector is not and cannot be a member of a political party, but that for the vast majority a humbler and more passive role in the political process is preferred, limited to the opportunity to *choose* between these competing teams at regular intervals. However, parties are involved in the process, both at election times and between, of shaping, educating and clarifying public opinion: that is, they present the public with a choice between policies, by raising issues and taking stands on them. Thus, besides providing a formal opportunity for the populace at large to participate actively in the political game, a competitive party system generates a political awareness which allows the mass to confirm or veto at elections the holding of office by alternative political elites.

Such politicians are ultimately *dependent on votes*: thus, though they and not ordinary citizens normally initiate policies and issues, they have to be responsive to the majority and hence they will pursue vote-winning policies and not those which will lose them support. So, *accountability of decision-makers* is a key element in the pluralist perspective, and it is accorded greater priority than the lofty but unrealistic ideal of maximisation of participation built into classical democratic theory.

In fact, Dahl and others maintain that large-scale regular participation in decision-making is neither necessary nor desirable, and periodic participation is necessary only occasionally to legitimise the authority of decision-makers. The average citizen is neither well informed nor especially interested in politics and is more likely to espouse 'authoritarian' attitudes, and, Dahl maintains, extensive individual participation in decision-making is invalidated on purely practical grounds of efficiency. Thus democracy is *not* direct but *representative*, not 'government by the people', but 'government approved by the people'.

Parties and elections: a critique

There are, however, good grounds for questioning the extent to which parties and elections operate in the way Pluralists assert they do, particularly in providing competing and different teams with distinct programmes and philosophies. In Britain, for instance, the Labour Party is projected as committed to the equalisation of wealth, the extensive state provision of social and welfare services, central economic regulation, and public ownership; while the Conservative Party espouses the principles of free enterprise, minimum state intervention, the distribution of wealth by market economic forces, and the increasing of the 'national cake', so that individuals can make their own decisions regarding the provision of certain social services (e.g. medicine and education).

In practice, however, the degree of alternative choice offered is often *more illusory* than real, since fundamental differences in policy between, for instance, the major parties in Britain or in America are few, and on many issues they have moved increasingly closer together: in Britain, over the last twenty years, the Labour and Conservative parties have embraced immigration policies which have become increasingly similar in principle and practice, they have shared similar views on Britain's EEC entry and subsequent role, and both have adopted platforms stressing the necessity for 'responsible trade unionism.'

While the advent of Thatcherism in the Conservative Party, with its advocacy of monetarism, privatisation and aggressive anti-trade union policies, has undoubtedly heightened the differences between Tories and Labour in their strategies for managing the economy, it still remains the case that both parties (despite protestations about its 'unacceptable face') *largely accept as given the economic and social arrangements of capitalism.* As Lane (1976, p. 52) argues:

> The dominant political parties in Western democratic States do not differ much over *major* questions concerning the arrangements of capitalist societies. No large political party in stable democratic countries can be seen as a threat to the integrity of capitalist society.

Besides offering little choice to voters generally, parties also offer little opportunity to their mass members to influence affairs directly. The ideal of the political party as an organ of participation and a channel of communication does not appear to manifest itself in reality, since the mass-based parties of Europe assign *very limited participatory roles* to their mass membership. In the two major British parties, for instance, the members are inactive and largely ineffective and subordinate to the parliamentary teams which reign supreme and unencumbered by them. The party members have few, if any, real policy-making teeth, and any 'grass-roots' resolutions which do gain support at party conferences are not guaranteed adoption or inclusion in official party programmes or manifestos – rather, manifestos are drawn up for the approval of the mass membership by the parliamentary parties. Thus, Western parties are essentially 'parliamentary parties' unhibited by their mass members, whose major role is essentially that of acting as 'work-horses' for the party, particularly at election times, primarily in the task of 'vote-winning' for local party candidates.

Of course, it might well be argued that the interests of members and supporters of a particular party are still represented effectively by the parliamentary 'team', since, as we indicated earlier, a political party is seen by the pluralist as an amalgamation or aggregation of interests. But we must ask how realistically and effectively and in what sense do parties enhance the interests of their members and supporters. For instance, large numbers of Labour Party voters in Britain are of working-class background, and there is considerable evidence suggesting that working-class people form the bulk of those in favour of capital punishment, yet this 'interest' is in no way enhanced by the Labour Party.

We may well concede that the relations between parties in parliament and the electorate are not and cannot be as direct as this, but remain such that voters periodically choose teams of leaders, having been 'educated' by the debates conducted over political issues by these leadership teams. But again we must ask how extensive and profound a political education is provided by parties. Ideally, parties sensitise the public to issues and generate understanding. But it can be argued that this is a highly selective process, in which parties act rather more like *censors* of issues rather than straightforward suppliers. They are able, in the first place, to *define* what areas of potential controversy are to *become* public 'political issues': equally important, they are able to shape the climate in which the issue is to be debated; and they can also select and process what the public receives as 'political information'. It becomes, then, more difficult to sustain an image of parties as educators, as *merely* enlightening the public.

Moreover, politicians in Western capitalist societies are not a microcosm of society, but are predominantly drawn from the ranks of the middle and upper classes, with only a small minority of working-class origin. In the USA, despite the ideology of the American dream of rising 'from log-cabin to White House', Democratic and Republican politicians have long been massively bourgeois in origin and background. In Britain, the Conservative Party, traditionally an 'aristocratic' party, has remained solidly bourgeois and public-school educated: the 1979 Conservative government contained 24 members who had received their education at one school, Eton. The Labour Party began as a predominantly working-class party – all 29 Labour MPs elected in 1906 were of working-class origin – but like many of its European counterparts, its MPs have become progressively more bourgeois and less proletarian in the post-war era – in 1970 only four new Labour MPs out of 54 were clearly working class; and by 1974 only 89 MPs out of 319 (about 25 per cent) were of manual worker origin.

Pressure groups and politics: the Pluralist view

The inadequacies and shortcomings of political parties and elections may not deal the fatal blow to the pluralist case, since we have emphasised how they see pressure groups and interest groups as an equally (if not more) important mechanism for articulating the interests and preferences of groups in democratic societies, as 'translators' of 'raw' political demands into political issues. Ideally, the pressure group brings together those with interests or causes in common, in the hope of using their collective strength to transform demands into public policy. For the pluralist, the advent of democracy and diffusion of power go hand in hand with the rise of pressure groups and interest groups: in pre-industrial and pre-democratic society, such groups on any wide scale were essentially non-existent or at best only intermittent phenomena, since politics was the exclusive activity of a small minority.

In contrast, in modern Western society, according to pluralists, pressure groups provide an essential chain of influence for the mass of the population, allowing individuals and groups, should they so choose, to participate in political activity for the promotion of their interests, thus involving more people in the power game. They serve as 'secondary associations' between the mass and the political elite, enhancing democracy, and by virtue of their special concern with particular isues, they often have specialist knowledge and information to offer the political elite for consideration in decision-making. So, according to the pluralists, pressure groups both bring pressure to bear on decision-making and aid political elites in making policy decisions.

As we suggested earlier, an important element in the pluralist view of Western political systems consists in the idea that there exists a certain basic consensus about 'fundamentals': disagreement about large and fundamental issues of social life has declined, so that ideological conflict is becoming steadily less prominent. This implies that there are no longer highly charged debates over ideologies and issues, but rather that the politics of liberal democracy involves the progressive resolution of *specific* problems accommodating specific interests and demands – a politics of 'adjustment' – and that the widespread existence of pressure groups and interest groups reflects this.

In such a situation, a variety of autonomous groups and interests are able to share in the power game, supported by appropriate legal and institutional arrangements, such as the legitimate devices of 'lobbying' legislators and administrators, engaging in public opinion campaigns, supporting 'test cases' in the courts, and so on. Consequently, it becomes impossible for a political elite to promote its own policies and interests to the exclusion of those of other groups, or to see the state and political power as 'its' property (or that of a dominant class on whose behalf it may be governing).

Pressure group politics: a critique

This pluralist picture of politics has been subjected to attack on a number of fronts. First, it cannot be assumed that all groups have roughly equal potential for success in pressing their demands: pluralists may recognise that, in practice, some interest groups are more powerful and successful than others, but this is not strongly reflected in their highly optimistic ideas about degrees of equality in influence and benefit. There is no guarantee that simply because a pressure group shouts it will necessarily be heeded: success in influencing decision-making is far less likely to be determined by any abstract 'justice' or 'fairness' in a group's interests or demands than by a number of other considerations, such as its material resources, its position in society, and its size.

Certainly, a group with substantial resources of *wealth* and *personnel* has a significantly higher chance of getting itself heard: the Confederation of British Industry, for instance, can mount campaigns for the realisation of its interests on a scale not attainable by the vast majority of groups. Similarly vital are *ease and privilege of access* to formal decision-makers which a group enjoys: having 'friends in high places' is distinctly advantageous. While there is no guarantee that individuals of similar social background, attitudes and associations will necessarily think alike, the fact remains that in Western societies like Britain, the existence of an 'old boy network', whereby some groups appear more acceptable to formal decision-makers by virtue of their similarities in class and educational backgrounds and social intercourse, inevitably means that such groups' demands receive a far more ready ear.

But, of course, the pluralist might well suggest that the ultimate test is 'public opinion', that a group must convince the public at large that its demands are acceptable and 'in the public interest'. Here again, however, some groups are more successful and better able to present their demands as being in accord with 'the public interest' or 'the needs of the nation'. Such an exercise *is* more easily accomplished by business groups in capitalist societies (epitomised in the famous American slogan 'What's good for General Motors is good for America'), as a result of their image as creators of the nation's wealth and prosperity. Thus, their demands are more likely to be sympathetically received (and hence their interests more frequently realised) because they are consistent with the *dominant values* of capitalist society. It is important, of course, to ask where these values come from: pluralists see them as widely embraced voluntaristically by members of society – the product of a social consensus – while Marxists regard them as imposed, the product of ideological manipulation by the dominant economic class, the very class whose interests they best serve. Capitalist business groups have been remarkably successful in presenting their demands as providing benefits for all, while at the same time the demands of labour are frequently presented as 'inflationary', 'damaging to business confidence', 'holding the country to ransom', and so on. The pluralist assumption, then, that all citizens have potentially equal access to influence through the operation of interest groups is naively optimistic.

Perhaps an even more fundamental question is whether groups are equally free to *form*, or capable of forming, organisations to represent their interests. Deprived ethnic minorities such as blacks, the rural and urban poor, migrant workers, the old and the handicapped are much less likely to be able to develop organisational structures to enhance their interests, given both the lack of resources at their disposal and the lack of consciousness of having definite interests to be protected in an organised way. The poor are a classic case in point: even if groups like the Child Poverty Action Group mobilise pressure on their behalf, they have no real threats or sanctions they can bring to bear to force the hands of formal political decision-makers. Thus, governments are free to define welfare expenditure as a 'cost' which can easily be cut when public funds run short or are needed to give 'incentives' to the productive.

Pluralist liberal democracy quite simply appears to ignore the isolated, the less articulate, and the unorganised, attending to the claims of (some) organised interests, but giving very little attention to groups not located in traditional institutional spheres. This does not necessarily mean that some interest groups are omnipotent on each and every issue, but that unrepresentative concentrations of power do exist, so that the basic interests of these groups are not on the whole *significantly* compromised or subverted. Ultimately, then, pluralist theory devalues the fact that *inequality of opportunity to influence* is yet another aspect of the unequal distribution of *individual and group life-chances* in capitalist societies.

This leads us to a further difficulty with pluralism: while one may concede that opportunities to influence exist, these are frequently only available to groups whose demands and the methods they adopt to pursue them fall within the conventional and accepted 'rules of the game': lobbying MPs or Senators, assembling petitions, rallying public opinion, winning the backing of a political party, or approaching civil servants. Venturing beyond such tactics means that both the group's credibility and ability to influence may well be impaired by violating the bounds of what is considered a 'reasonable' method of attempting to influence decisions: the 'rules of the game' and the built-in assumptions and prejudices of politicians may *systematically exclude* some groups from influence and benefit.

The pluralist would interpret this commitment to the 'rules of the game' as a manifestation of the *consensus* which, they claim, characterises liberal democracies. Undoubtedly a set of societal values does prevail, but we must ask how far such an ideology is *imposed* by powerful groups, rather than voluntaristically embraced, *and whose interests* it serves best. Liberal democracies are not *merely* that: they are *capitalist* liberal democracies in which, as we suggested earlier, business interests profit from and sustain a dominant ideology of materialism, individualism and free enterprise.

A prevailing ideology exists which sets the boundaries within which decisions will be made, influencing the kinds of issues that may develop and limiting the range of possible policy options for consideration, so that a group in tune with this will have a significantly greater chance of influencing decisions. Within such a framework, a group's demands can be weakened or ignored by defining them as 'extremist', 'unpatriotic', or whatever, and the legitimacy of their challenge, or even a demand for basic rights, can be removed or headed off.

These observations lead us to consider a crucial weakness in Pluralist theory – its wholly inadequate conception of the *nature* of power.

The faces of power

As we have suggested, pluralists see power as being essentially situational, that is, tied to particular issues, so that, in order to discover whether power is concentrated in a single group or dispersed among several, we must study 'key issues' and *actual political decisions* – who is involved and who wins – to ascertain which group succeeds in having its policy preferences adopted in observable, open contests over policies. Dahl (1961) used such a methodology in a celebrated study of local community power in New Haven, USA: after a detailed examination of three areas of decision-making (political nominations, education policy, and urban development), he concluded that the political system of New Haven was one of 'dispersed inequalities' where power to determine policy was diffused and widely distributed among a variety of community elites, with no single group dominating and possessing cumulative power. His method of studying the process of active decision-making on key issues may appear sensible and straightforward, but, as Bachrach and Baratz (1963) have stressed, it is basically inadequate and reveals crucial weaknesses in the pluralist conception of politics and power. Dahl and others uncritically accept the *observable* political process as their object of study – that is, decision-making on 'issues' – but, as Bachrach and Baratz point out, this constitutes *only one* 'face of power' and completely ignores the equally important *second* 'face', '*non decision-making*'. Here groups have power to the extent that they may be able to *prevent or exclude* issues from becoming public and other groups from articulating their views and demands, so that power is often exerted, *and is just as real*, when groups can confine open decision-making and controversies to relatively safe issues. Thus, power is not just about decision-making but also about *managing* situations to prevent issues from arising for debate, about influencing the *definition* of matters for public debate. The pluralist preoccupation with 'key issues' automatically excludes those areas where controversy is subdued or prevent from reaching the surface in the 'private' face of power.

Thus, the pluralist researcher might well discover no obvious contests over, say, poverty or racial discrimination and (particularly in view of the pluralist equation of non-involvement with satisfaction) would completely miss the reality of a process whereby the interests of the poor and ethnic minorities had been 'organised out' of the political arena.

Now, while such criticisms are important, in one basic respect the pluralist account is not thoroughly challenged: Bachrach and Baratz take for granted that different groups are aware of their political needs and that non-decision-making is a conscious, deliberate strategy to exclude these groups. Power is still seen only as involving active, deliberate conflict –even if some acts deliberately prevent conflict from gaining expression. If Dahl rejects the notion of a conspiracy by one ruling group, Bachrach and Baratz merely show that the powerful can employ hidden ways of conspiring. Power may *also* benefit groups or classes unequally, *even though* neither the privileged nor the underprivileged fully understand or control this process of domination. It may be that those disadvantaged by political decisions do not realise it, and have no conscious political demands for grievances. The powerful need not exclude any challenge, for it has not arisen. At the same time, powerful groups may pursue policies which they genuinely believe to be in the communal interests but which *objectively benefit* some groups much more than others. Thus, while there may be no discoverable conflict or grievance, some groups systematically benefit at the expense of others.

We have to recognise, then, the notion of the *objective interests* of a group or class. That is to say, we must be able to judge as observers what will benefit or harm a group – *whether the group recognises it or not*. For example, we may judge that it is against the interests of citizens to be exposed to radiation, even if they do not recognise the problem as serious. The power of the owners of the nuclear reactor may be demonstrated by the fact that they can continue to run it without being challenged by those threatened by it.

Now this is a very different conception of power and interests to that of the models previously discussed. Steven Lukes (1974) calls this the '*third dimension of power*'. For pluralists, a group's interests are only its 'expressed preferences' – the demands the group actually is aware of and puts forward. Lukes defends the notion of objective interests as a necessary alternative, for we must be able to judge when power is being exercised, even in the absence of conflict. After all, power that is never questioned or challenged is the most potent of all.

This leads to a particular conception of power which asks '*who benefits?*' and *not* 'who takes or influences decisions?', and allows us to identify those social groups who benefit most from the routine, institutionalised, unchallenged exercise of power. A study of local power by Saunders *et al.* (1978) is illuminating here.

The study focused on Suffolk, a rural area which contains some of the most prosperous large farmers employing farmworkers at some of the lowest male wage-levels in the country. Here, apparently, was a clear basis for political conflict, but on examination Suffolk was noticeable for the lack of any real issues on which conflicts were visible, giving the impression of tranquillity, stability and harmony.

In fact, the farmers and landowners, although monopolising council positions, claimed to be community servants, engaged in disinterestedly discharging their obligations as councillors. They felt that two important planning policies, preservation of the environment and maintaining low rates, were in the interests of all and therefore desirable for 'the community'.

In housing, limitations on residential development to preserve the rural environment meant that private housing was scarce and costly and council house provision was restricted, with the result that agricultural workers were forced into 'tied' housing controlled by the farmers (the abolition of which farmers opposed because of the lack of alternative accommodation!). This further reinforced workers' dependence on their employers.

Similarly, the preservation of the environment restricted the introduction of new industries which might well have paid higher wages than farmers in competing for labour, thus benefiting farmers once more. The obsession with a low rates policy, moreover, meant that Suffolk has some of the poorest social service provision (in education, welfare, public transport, and so on) in the country: those lacking the means to pay for alternative private provision inevitably suffer more in these circumstances.

Now, while the *intentions* of councillors were not necessarily self-interested, the *effects* of their policy decisions were such that *their* objective interests were enhanced, while those of the agricultural working class were adversely affected. This 'non-politics of the status quo', as Saunders *et al.* term it, brought about the routine maintenance of the objective interests of an already advantaged group in the community.

The pluralist account of power: conclusion

The pluralist account of power suffers from major flaws. As we have suggested, it gives a bland, over-optimistic and uncritical account of decision-making in liberal democracies which fails to perceive many of the subtleties of the power game, and its very conception of the nature of power is inadequate. Its emphasis on observable events and issues as revealing power structures and processes simply gives inadequate attention to social structural factors which determine and constrain not only actual decisions and policies but the *definition* of the issues lying behind them. The study of the operation of power must encompass not just action by individuals or groups, in a vacuum, but the institutional and ideological frameworks in which action (and the absence of action) is embodied.

6.4   THE DISTRIBUTION OF POWER IN MODERN WESTERN SOCIETY: THE MARXIST VIEW

Long before the development and prevalence of Pluralist theory, many writers were unconvinced that a 'democratic revolution' had occurred or was imminent, despite changes which were taking place, maintaining instead that power was still effectively concentrated in the hands of a few, with little or no diffusion having occurred. One such view was expressed by Marx, whose basic ideas underpin many contemporary Marxist accounts.

Marx saw power relationships as being built into the very structure of society, whose principal feature is the existence of opposed classes. Thus, *relationships of class domination and subordination*, determined predominantly by the economic arrangements of society, are the central elements of the Marxist conception of politics and the distribution and operation of power.

We saw in Chapter 2 that Marx analysed social structures in terms of the *mode of production*, the central element of which is the particular form of the *relations of production*. For Marx, production is organised socially in ways which have always created classes with opposed interests and unequal resources of power: one class will dominate others through economic exploitation, with the relation of exploitation and domination merely taking different forms in different (pre-socialist) modes of production.

So, economic power and political power are inevitably linked through the prime importance which Marx attributes to the economic base of society in shaping social and political arrangements and forms. The possession of political power is the outcome of a group's relation to the means of production and the process of economic exploitation: the class controlling the means of production – the *dominant economic class* – enjoys effective political power and is of necessity a *ruling class*, and it is able to use that power to maintain and enhance its dominant position in society.

This equation of political power with economic power does not easily fit in with what is popularly regarded by the layperson as 'political power': that is, the power to legislate and enforce the law, to raise taxes, to declare war and so on. It is frequently taken for granted that these 'political' activities take place within a separate institution, the state, which is seen as being set above the conflicts and squabbles of the rest of society. It is an institution where a collective communal interest can be served: the state can pursue the common good and reconcile, or at least compromise between, opposed interests in society.

Marx's earliest works were directed vigorously against just such a view. He rejected the idea of the state serving as a neutral instrument of all the people, arguing that the ideals of justice, democracy and equality of political influence which such a view presupposed could only be an illusion while society itself was profoundly unequal. Since the important power relations were those built into the economic structure of society, politics in the state could never ultimately be anything other than *class politics*, because pre-socialist society was essentially a class society, based on an irreconcilable conflict of interests.

Under such circumstances it was impossible for the state to be impartial, satisfying the demands and interests of all. Rather, the political actions of the state were always to be understood as linked to the satisfaction of the economic interests of the dominant class in society. Thus Marx and Engels (1976, p. 486) wrote that, in capitalist society. 'The executive of the modern State is but a committee for managing the common affairs of the whole bourgeoisie.'

The State, then, gives the *illusion* of serving the general will, while in reality acting as a cloak for class interests. Attempts by the dominant class to cultivate a picture of the state as being above particular group or class interests constitute an *ideological strategy* to legitimise its own dominant position, and the state in turn involves itself in a constant exercise of legitimating the existing order through a variety of 'civil' agencies and institutions.

These attempts reflect a further fundamental feature of Marx's conception of power and class domination: while the economic relations of capitalism give the dominant class control over material forces and political power in society, they are also able to control ideas and beliefs. That is, they possess *ideological* power, whereby a set of *dominant values* (as we have suggested in Chapter 1) may be disseminated through major social institutions which justify or legitimate existing socio-economic and political arrangements, and hence their own dominant position. As Marx and Engels (1976, p. 64) say, 'The ideas of the ruling class are, in every age, the ruling ideas . . . The class which has the means of material production at its disposal has control at the same time over the means of mental production'.

In summary, then, Marx saw economic power as the basis for political power: the dominant economic class was effectively a 'ruling class', because the ownership of the means of production largely determines the distribution of political power.

The ruling class and beyond

The Marxist view that power is concentrated in a small dominant class should not surprise us too much. After all, power has been held by a minority in most societies, and various anti-democratic theories of 'natural leadership' or 'elite qualities' have celebrated the fact. What is more controversial is the Marxist claim that real democracy in politics cannot exist if there is fundamental inequality in the broader society. Economic and social subordination cannot coexist, say Marxists, with real political freedom. Liberal democracy may give us equal rights but it certainly does not give us equal capacity to exercise power or secure our interests. That capacity or effective power depends upon the distribution of resources – including wealth, influence, knowledge and status. Since it is easy to demonstrate how unequally these resources are spread (as we have done throughout this book), then it is natural to conclude that the most privileged social group is also the one with most effective political power.

Broadly speaking, this is a sound argument, but it leaves out of account the sheer complexity of contemporary politics in the modern state. This complexity undermines the credibility of any crude conspiratorial ruling class model – when Marx and Engels sloganised in the Communist Manifesto about 'the executive committee of the whole bourgeoisie' they offered only the simplest possible account of power. Such a model is often known as *instrumentalism*, where the state is a mere instrument wielded by a class. Even if there is a powerful minority – how is their power made effective? Do they always run the state? Are their class interests and political strategies always unified and unproblematic? In other words, what does the ruling class do when it rules?

The instrumentalist view of the capitalist state

Instrumentalism is the view that members of the dominant economic class actively exercise political domination. They use the state as an instrument:

by forming conservative governments
by occupying powerful positions in the state (such as in the Civil Service, the judiciary and the military)
by manipulating politicians and state officials.

A second dimension of traditional Marxism was the view that the economic 'base' directly shaped the social 'superstructure' including the state (a view often called economic determinism). Hence politics was a direct and simple reflection of the needs of the economy and the interests of the dominant class. More recent Marxists, while retaining this basic perspective, have tried to move away from a such a simple base-superstructure model.

Over the last decade or so, Marxist theories of the state have multiplied, addressing these questions in a variety of sophisticated ways (for brief summaries, see Jessop, 1977, McLennan *et al.*, 1984, or Coates, 1984, ch. 10). Central to all these new theories has been the concept of *relative autonomy*. This is the idea that the capitalist system makes possible – or even necessitates – an institutional separation between political state power and economic power. First, capitalist exploitation takes place through the impersonal and apparently fair economics of the wage contract, rather than through direct forcible means (as, say, in feudalism). Secondly, individual capitalist enterprises are competitive and normally cannot look beyond short-term self-interest. They therefore depend upon a central authority to do certain things on their behalf: they need a suitable legal and social framework for capitalist ownership, production and exchange, and they need some independent body to work out the collective interests of capital in general and then pursue suitable national policies. Thirdly, capitalists need a central body to control the working class. This may be done through force, or more subtly by gaining the loyalty of workers to the current system. The latter course may involve concessions, such as giving workers the vote, or founding a welfare state. These may be resisted by individual capitalists who do not perceive the collective benefits for capital of such stabilising compromises. Equally, there may be times when the system appears to be threatened by such concessions (workers' organisations seem too radical or welfare seems too costly) and then capitalists may force political changes.

If both workers and capitalists are committed to the current political system (such as liberal democracy) and they regard elected governments as *legitimate* (having the right to rule), then strains felt by capital are more likely to be solved by changes in policy rather than by a move to a new regime such as fascism or a military coup. Thus it is possible to serve the needs of capital within the existing political system, rather than destroying it, as long as class struggle does not get too severe, and challenges to legitimacy can be repressed.

While sharing these broad themes, there is a great variety of emphasis among current Marxist state theories. Two important variants are the *structuralist* and the *Gramscian* approaches. *Structuralist* theories (such as Althusser and the early Poulantzas) argue that the state in capitalist society inevitably has to function to sustain and promote capitalism. As long as some part of the bourgeoisie remains the dominant historical force, the outcomes of historical situations will favour them. Political outcomes are seen as corresponding to the current 'stage' of capitalism, or else as reflecting the 'balance of class forces' in the society. Either way, there is assumed to be a 'structural guarantee' that the state will serve the needs of the leading sections of capital. The result of the state's structural role is that the dominant class has its interests served, even if it does not actively rule. Many critics have complained about the quasi-functionalist tone of the structuralist argument – assuming that certain system needs will be fulfilled. If only for that reason structuralist theories should be treated with caution.

Gramscian state theory (drawing on the Prison Notebooks of the Italian Antonio Gramsci, written in Mussolini's gaols) goes much further in recognising the complexities of the process of politics and the struggles in the state over policies and strategies. Much stress is laid on divisions among the powerful, and their need to secure alliances. These occur through changes in the '*power bloc*' – that group of powerful organised classes and groups which together dominate the political arena. The Gramscian approach is also distinctive for its concern with '*hegemony*'. This concept refers to consent or acceptance of an ideology, a regime, or of a whole social system. Those attempting to gain hegemony in this sense must try to build consensus behind the ideas or social arrangements they wish to secure; full hegemony exists when a social order is accepted as natural and normal. A clear example of these processes was the attempt to build a consensus on basic political and economic goals after 1950. The framework of a welfare-state capitalism, offering full employment and rising living standards, was seen as a sound and achievable basis for political harmony – for a 'mixed economy' beyond class conflict. This attempted post-war settlement had some other conservative dimensions, as we shall discuss later, but it lasted in some form in Britain and elsewhere in Europe from 1950 to the early 1970s.

The Gramscian approach can be very illuminating, especially if combined with a broader focus on structural changes in the economy; recent events in Britain will be examined in this light shortly. First, however, let us evaluate the merits of the instrumentalist approach to our question: is there a ruling class?

Is there an active 'ruling class'?

(i)   Are powerful elites linked together with the propertied to form a dominant upper class?
(ii) Does this class always run the state and actively rule?
(iii) Does this class have a unity of interests, and an agreed political strategy?
(iv) How does the state link to other interests and demands in society?

A dominant upper class?

There is an upper class in Britain, socially closed, internally linked by social networks, and aware of itself as a social entity. This class overlaps sufficiently with the holders of powerful ('elite') positions to be called a ruling Establishment which holds the main reins of power. Evidence presented in Chapters 2 and 3 confirmed this. Social privilege and status are gained, we saw, through the twin routes of direct inheritance and elite education through private schools and ancient universities. Not only company directors, but others in elite positions are extremely likely to have social origins in the upper class, or else to have taken the elite educational route. Even positions with apparently meritocratic recruitment show these patterns; perhaps the most important politically are the senior civil servants. Public school products are vastly over-represented in elite positions, in proportion to their numbers, and the top six (Charterhouse, Eton, Harrow, Marlborough, Rugby and Winchester) provide pupils with the most glittering prizes of all.

The 1979 Conservative Government contained 24 Old Etonians. Among the Cabinet, 71 per cent were company directors and 14 per cent large landowners. In the 1970s, two-thirds of Conservative MPs held a business directorship.

Sources: D. Coates, *The Context of British Politics*, London, Hutchinson (1984, p. 236).

It may not be surprising that the 'party of property' recruits among the upper class, but the picture applies elsewhere. Two-thirds of Under-Secretaries and above come from public schools, and four-fifths of ambassadors (Scott, 1982, p. 165). An Oxbridge degree is almost compulsory. In addition, there is a significant trend to links with the business world, as civil servants move across into directorships (Coates, 1984, p. 236).

The patterns are clear, as Tables 6.1 and 6.2 indicate. But what does evidence on social origins actually prove? A crude instrumentalist view might argue that the upper class actively rules through all these powerful positions in the state – even if the government is formed by a party based in another class. The elites would be assumed to have goals and interests in common, which are actively pursued. Now this view may sometimes hold, but social origins do not entirely predict political goals, nor can a unity of aims be assumed.

However, it would be extremely surprising if the narrow common social origins did not have effects. The British upper class (and those of other capitalist societies) remains a self-recuiting and self-perpetuating stratum,

TABLE 6.1

	Percentage from Public Schools
Conservative MPs (1979)	73
Conservative Cabinet (1979)	86
High Court judges (1983)	79
Ambassadors (1983)	76
Senior army officers (1981)	80
Senior civil servants (1976)	69
Chairmen { Major clearing banks / Merchant banks (1983) / Insurance Companies } Directors of Bank of England	81

Sources: M. Moran, *Politics and Society in Britain*, London, Macmillan (1985) and C. Leys, *Politics in Britain*, London, Heinemann (1985).

TABLE 6.2

	Percentage from Oxford and Cambridge
Conservative MPs (1979)	49
Conservative Cabinets (1955–84)	73
High Court judges (1983)	80
Ambassadors (1983)	70
Senior civil servants (1983)	63
Chairmen {Major clearing banks, Merchant banks (1983), Insurance companies} Directors of Bank of England	68

Sources: M. Moran, *Politics and Society in Britain*, London, Macmillan (1985) and C. Leys, *Politics in Britain*, London, Heinemann (1985).

with shared economic interests and shared political and social outlook. Over the generations, this upper class has become highly experienced and sophisticated in the pursuit of its own general interests. Elite recruitment is a measure of social closure and self-awareness among the upper class. Moreover, it is by no means insignificant that the great majority of those in important positions share a common vocabulary, demeanour and social outlook, for this can not only facilitate communication and solidarity, but also insulate elite members from ideas or values which challenge their taken-for-granted orthodoxy. This shared cultural security remains, then, a valuable asset of the elite, but it may only be of background significance, for there are divisions of power and interest within the elite which may be more significant.

A unified ruling class?

Even if we consider simply those in elite positions, differences of interest are obvious. For example, senior ranks in the armed forces may compete (indirectly) for funds against university vice-chancellors; businessmen may desire tax cuts while civil servants hope to help the economy through some item of public spending. Clearly, the occupants of important positions have specific duties and interests relating to their area of responsibility. Only in times of crisis, or on the most fundamental issues, should we expect unity. However, some interests may be more fundamental than others, and the degree of overlap and linkage between elites should never be underestimated – once again the common class membership is significant.

One basic factor in the relative importance of different elites is dependence. To what extent are they dependent on the state (e.g. university vice-chancellors, chairmen of the BBC), and to what extent is the state dependent upon them (e.g. bankers, oil-company directors, major employers)? The relative power of different institutional links reflects the differing importance of parts of the economy, and the differing degrees of state dependence on them. The Department of Employment, closely working with trade unions in the past, is subordinate to the Department of Trade and Industry, which obviously has formal and informal links to employers. But pre-eminent in Britain is the Treasury, with its close ties to the Bank of England, and thence to the financial institutions. The relative power of these economic forces is reflected in the internal power structure of the state.

If, however, capitalist economic interests do predominate in policy-formation, we are still left with certain questions. How far are different sections of capital in harmony on policy strategies? Is it possible to override splits and conflicts among capital?

As we saw in the earlier discussion of the capitalist state's relative autonomy, Marxists argue that 'capital' cannot rule directly because no one capitalist has any real conception of the overall interests of their class. Individual firms compete, and 'fractions' of capital such as industry, banking, and agriculture may have divergent interests. For this reason, it is argued, the state and those who run it must have a 'relative autonomy' to generate overall political strategies and solutions. Obviously this opens up uncertainty in political processes, unless the outcome is somehow 'guaranteed' by the structure of social forces (as the more structuralist theories assume). We cannot accept that any such guarantees really exist. Instead, there is a process of change, as 'power blocs' are formed out of alliances of important social forces; politicians making policy have to either build acceptance in this power bloc or else recast it with some new alliance of social groups – which of course involves struggle and resistance. Coates (1984, p. 117) provides a clear account of the changing British power blocs; he emphasises, like Gamble (1985) and Longstreth (1979), the predominant place of financial capital in Britain through this century.

The changing composition of British power blocs is set out briefly in the box and, while open to debate, this list gives one version of the way different parts of the upper class came to rule at different times, and the way other classes were involved in ruling at certain points. This does not imply that there is no truth in speaking of a 'ruling class' since the very idea of the power bloc implies a ruling class model; however, power blocs do show how the whole class does not always rule, and how alliances are forged at various times with other social groups. The latter point is shown most clearly during wartime, and during the period of the post-1945 boom. Here the trade unions played a highly significant part in policy-making and in the running of incomes policies, industrial planning, and the like. Indeed, it has often been argued that the unions gained power considerably during the period of full employment, so that governments had to try to work with

---

British power blocs

Power blocs are ruling alliances of powerful groups, especially sections of the capitalist class.

Mid-C19	Liberal competitive capitalism, dominated by Northern industrial capitalists and the Whig section among land-owning aristocrats.
Early C20	Dominance of a few large landowners and capitalists. Increasing subordination of manufacturers to London-based financiers, merchants and shipowners.
1920s	Banking capital predominant, together with colonial capital, and coal and steel employers. Strategy of monetary control, unemployment and wage cuts.
1930s	Dominance of South consolidated with new consumer industries around London.
1939–45	Employers and unions cooperate with state planners in war production and plans for the welfare state.
1945–50	Labour government planners vie for control against employers, developers and external financial pressure. Welfare state and nationalisation consolidated.
1950s	Consensus on growth and employment policy, manufacturers coexist with revived financial capital.
1960–76	Growth policy conflicts with financial constraints from money markets. Growing common interests between financial capital and multinational producers. Repeated 'corporatist' attempts to sustain consensus through partial incorporation of employers and unions into state management of the economy.
1976–	Increased power for financial capital – dominant in anti-inflation policies. Decreasing capacity for governments to manage growth or sustain economic consensus; severe weakening of power of unions and manufacturing employers. Ever-increasing subordination of domestic economic policy to (a) international markets and corporations, (b) economic policies of stronger economies.

Source: Partly based on D Coates, *The Context of British Politics*, London, Hutchinson, 1984, p. 117.

unions in order to forestall opposition and control wage and price rises. Although usually limited to some areas of economic and welfare policy, these attempts at incorporation of the unions were often seen as part of a broader trend. This trend, often called *corporatism*, entailed the involvement of trade unions and employer organisations, together with the State, in collective deals on such matters as incomes policies and policies for economic growth. Although strong in some other Western nations (such as Sweden and Austria) this trend has been fitful and weak in Britain. Attempts to secure economic consensus have been undermined with monotonous regularity by efforts to weaken the unions and by restrictive economic policies such as spending cuts and high interest rates which aim to defend financial stability in the face of a falling pound or rising inflation. Such policies may help financiers but they hit both industrialists and workers through their squeeze on output.

Policies in the early 1980s were an extreme example, despite claiming to strengthen industry through the survival of the fittest. Policies against inflation brought major costs in plant closures and lost industrial capacity. Thus, there may well be differences of interest between sections of capital over the desirability of policies such as these, and the real effects certainly benefited some parts of capital at the expense of others. Thus, total unity among capitalists was neither natural nor inevitable.

In time of perceived crisis, however, these divergences of interest may be overridden by a common concern to defend the basic viability of the system. Unity is much easier then – and in times of war subordinate social groups may have a key role in the power bloc. But when capital seems threatened by 'the enemy within' (as Mrs Thatcher dubbed some trade unionists), such participation is not the favoured solution.

Real crisis occurs when the basic framework for capitalist activity appears to be under threat. Such basic preconditions of a capitalist order include legal protection of private property, labour contracts and market exchanges. In addition, the state must sustain a stable money system, and must prevent disorder (ideally through consent) among the working population. When any of these conditions are threatened, we can expect the upper class to unify behind harsh cures for serious ills.

For British capitalists, the early 1970s seemed to offer just such a fundamentally threatening environment. The stability of money, and markets was threatened by inflation. Conventional economic policy and state intervention seemed to worsen the problems. Trade union power was apparently great enough to challenge both employers and unsympathetic governments. The end of the post-war boom was signalled by the end of cheap oil in 1973–4. In such times were sown the seeds of the radical Conservatism of the 1980s. The goals of full employment, steady growth and expansion of welfare were steadily abandoned in the 1970s, and with them the possibility of a social consensus. The political strategy of the 'post-war settlement' lay in ruins, waiting for a new policy initiative to replace it.

Taking all this discussion into account, it is hard to retain faith in a simple instrumentalist view. Instead we are left with a number of pressing questions, summarised in the following list. We can now go on to see whether a Gramscian approach can help us understand power better.

How does the upper class rule?

(i) Are powerful elites closely linked to the dominant economic class?
(ii) What are the institutional links between the upper class and the state?
(iii) How far can groups within capital constrain or defeat policies which threaten them?
(iv) Are there effective ways for dominant groups to initiate policies and present them as serving the general needs of capital?
(v) Are there effective means of presenting these policies as being in the general, national interests of all citizens?

Hegemony and domination

How far can the Gramscian approach to politics provide better answers to these questions than instrumentalist theory? This section will apply the approach to contemporary Britain in order to judge. We already emphasised the ways in which there is a relative autonomy for those running the state, when policies and strategies are generated. This political process includes two key dimensions which deserve further discussion: first, winning agreement on policy within a power bloc, and secondly winning consent or acquiescence among the wider populace. These are two dimensions of hegemony; we can say that hegemony is fully achieved only if there is successful consensus-building among the powerful and/or the populace. If such attempts to build hegemony fail, policies may be implemented through force and fraud – just so long as the government can remain insulated from the consequences. Thatcherism provides a clear illustration of these processes.

The most fundamental form of hegemony is when 'moral and political leadership' is attained; here a form of regime and perhaps a whole world-view and way of life is established as normal, natural and 'ours'. In Gramsci's Italy, the Catholic Church held such a leading role. In Britain, and other societies with a plurality of churches, religion cannot bind citizens so securely. However, the monarchy has a special role in helping to legitimate (or defend as natural) aspects of the British social order. Notions of 'the British way of life' include not only liberal democracy but also monarchy, social hierarchy and some degree of capitalism. At this basic level the state in Britain has legitimacy even when particular governments or policies may be unpopular. However, this legitimacy has its limits – for example, the British state's authority in Northern Ireland is rejected by many there. As Gramsci knew only too well, all state hegemony is 'armoured with coercion', and radical or violent opposition will be met with forceful use of the state's monopoly of legitimate violence. Indeed, state violence may supplant any claim to legitimacy – as in South Africa, once the blacks rejected the legitimacy of constitutional devices such as making them citizens of 'independent homelands'. But if some mobilisation of consent is to be attempted, hegemony must be sought at two distinct levels: within the power bloc, and among the wider populace.

Hegemony within the power bloc. When a new strategy or major policy is proposed (e.g. Thatcherite Conservatism) support or acceptance must be mobilised among those with the power to resist – including elites within the state such as civil servants. Equally, it may be necessary to exclude hostile groups (in this case the trade unions) from the power bloc and find ways to weaken them. Ideally, those within the bloc will be persuaded that the policies are in the general interest of all the powerful groups. In this whole process there will be a changing balance of forces as groups are included, excluded, placated, and so on. At the same time the effects of the policies themselves will strengthen or weaken the power of particular groups.

The Thatcher years provide ample illustration of all these processes. The economic policies known as monetarism entailed very high costs in a context of world recession. Not only sacked workers paid the price; manufacturers were hit very hard from 1980 by reduced demand and adverse financial conditions. Was the upper class unified behind these policies? We saw earlier how the crises of the early 1970s unified capital behind drastic solutions to inflation and union power. As a result Mrs Thatcher took office with a free hand, due to her business backing as well as her big parliamentary majority. Within two years the Confederation of British Industry was voicing alarm – but they were placated and they allied with no alternative political group. Trade unions were weakened by unemployment, legislation and set-piece industrial battles. With the unions excluded from the power bloc and the industrialists mollified, the Thatcher governments could openly pursue economic policies oriented towards financial and multinational capital. Domestic industry was supposed to become leaner and fitter, so plant closures and lost capacity were a tolerable price.

As a strategy for helping capital be profitable (an 'accumulation strategy'), Thatcherism was only one possibility, and a very costly one at that. But financial capital actively promoted these policies, and industry had no effective means of proposing an alternative. As Leys (1985, p. 6) argues,

> (a) range of alternative 'accumulation strategies' exists in theory, but the practical possibilities are limited not only by the current balance of economic and political forces in a given country, but also by a much more complex and intractable web of norms and practices inherited from the past . . .

Popular hegemony. In liberal democracies the views of voters, expressed through votes, opinion polls, and direct political actions, cannot be completely ignored. If a degree of popular consent can be mobilised, the task of implementing long-term policies will be eased. If such consent is absent, then dissent must be suppressed and policies insulated from their consequences (for example, issues of poverty or joblessness must be made politically marginal). The 1980s saw major expressions of popular dissent in the urban riots of 1981, marches and demonstrations, protesting about mass unemployment as well as punitive policing. Yet the Conservative government overcame the unpopularity of Mrs Thatcher with the help of nationalistic support for the Falklands War, and won the 1983 election. Soon after, in a set-piece confrontation with the miners in their long and bitter strike, the government won a decisive victory over the strongest group in the working class. Their attempt to force a change in policy, and perhaps in government, was skilfully manipulated and suppressed.

In view of all this dissent, it is perhaps surprising that Thatcherism, with its massive effects on poverty and unemployment, should be seen on the Left as having gained popular support as an ideology. But one very influential theory suggested that Mrs Thatcher appealed to many voters through the rhetoric of 'authoritarian populism' (Hall and Jacques, 1983). Hall and others argued that Mrs Thatcher tapped a popular dissatisfaction with state intervention, taxation for welfare, and increasing collectivism. Instead she stressed self-help, competitive individualism, and increased inequality. Hall argued that Mrs Thatcher patched together old themes into a distinctive ideology of *authoritarian populism*, and that this struck a popular chord. Above all, this ideology breaks with the post-war settlement and its aim of creating consensus through state distribution of the fruits of economic growth. Attempts to build social harmony must be sacrificed in favour of harsh economic medicine and strong action to put down those who threaten social order by dissent or through union power.

Hall's insights are certainly illuminating, but there are problems with this analysis. It is very hard to prove that millions of people were really convinced by 'authoritarian populism'. The election victory could be explained by prosaic factors such as the divided opposition vote and the disarray of Labour in 1983. Even if millions of people opposed the policies between elections, their political expression was greatly weakened by the defeat of the unions and the lack of impact of demonstrations and riots. The suppression of dissent was taken to new heights; equally important was the capacity of the government to shrug off protests as mere criminality and deviance.

Thus even if popular hegemony is not secured – and Hall would not claim that consent was fully mobilised – this may not be fatal to the power bloc. One measure of the concentration of power is how insulated it is from popular dissent.

Conclusion

Our critical discussion of the distribution of power has led us to the conclusion that both orthodox pluralism and simple ruling-class models are quite inadequate for understanding the political process. However, we have argued that we can use the Gramscian notions of power bloc and hegemony to construct a more sophisticated ruling-class theory. This approach highlights the mobilisation and exercise of power, emphasising concentrations of economic and social domination. At the same time, we can recognise the complexity of the processes which link this pattern of social forces to actual political outcomes. In these processes the nature and history of political parties plays a role, as does the form and structure of the state (we shall examine the latter at the end of this chapter).

Despite what radical critics may say about the capitalist state, members of the upper class no doubt feel that politics has not always served them well, and they will point to the importance of social democratic and socialist parties. We have emphasised the limitations of this opposition politics, as well as the assured dominance of pro-capitalist policies. The politics of subordinate classes cannot be dismissed, though, and in the next section we examine the issue of working-class consciousness and political action in some detail.

6.5   POLITICAL CONSCIOUSNESS AND POLITICAL ACTION

Introduction

In both Chapter 2 and our preceding discussion of the distribution of power, we have demonstrated the persistently large inequalities in material resources and rewards, life-chances, opportunities to influence decisions, and symbolic rewards enjoyed by different classes in contemporary capitalist society. The most striking feature of this pattern is the systematically disadvantaged position experienced by the majority of the population, the working class. In terms of income, wealth, health, political power and the like, their middle-class and, more especially, upper-class counterparts enjoy significantly greater advantages, despite the social and political changes instituted in capitalist liberal democracies in the twentieth century.

As we have seen, Marx envisaged a situation in which capitalist society would become increasingly polarised into two warring and opposed classes, the bourgeoisie and the proletariat. The latter, gaining consciousness of their common interests and recognising the inherent conflict between their interests and those of the owners of the means of production, would rise up in revolution, destroy capitalism, and establish socialism. For Marx, such a transformation was *not* an 'automatic' certainty, since it depended on the development of a *revolutionary class consciousness* on the part of the proletariat, and while he felt that the contradictions of capitalism would generate such a consciousness, the transition of this class from a 'class in itself' to a 'class for itself' was essentially problematic.

This revolutionary class consciousness would involve the acknowledgement of a fundamental conflict of interests between those of their own class comrades and those of the bourgeoisie, coupled with the realisation of the pervasiveness of class relations and conflicts throughout all areas of social life and of the possibility of constructing a thoroughgoing alternative set of social, economic and political arrangements – in effect, a 'new society'. Workers attaining such a consciousness would act to do away with capitalism and its attendant social relations and establish socialist society.

In the century since Marx's death, Western capitalist societies have not succumbed to revolutionary transformation, but negotiated the twentieth century without the solidification of the working class into an active revolutionary force. The primary political activity of the latter is voting in national elections every four years or so, with working-class political action appearing to manifest itself within the constraints of the status quo; even in societies with strong communist parties, an apparent consensus seems to prevail. Thus, while we must not fall into the simple trap of assuming that capitalist liberal democracy is the only possible socio-political arrangement (after all, it is essentially a *recent* structural form and one which was 'laid aside' temporarily in fascist Italy and Germany), we can acknowledge its relative longevity. Moreover, we are still confronted with the fact that not only does the majority of the working class support 'parliamentary' rather than 'revolutionary' left-wing political action, but a substantial minority of this class gives its allegiance (at the ballot box, at least) to political parties committed to the maintenance of the existing social and economic arrangements of capitalism and its attendant inequalities. Are they, in fact, simply exhibiting 'false consciousness' in this behaviour?

The structural basis of working-class political consciousness

If we are to explore adequately working-class political action and consciousness in contemporary capitalist societies, we must attempt to locate these phenomena *structurally*, to examine the ways in which manual workers' perceptions are shaped by the organisation of capitalist society both materially and ideologically. Marx's own analysis attempted to do exactly this, but it is not sufficient to dismiss his ideas as 'wrong' or 'worthless', as do many commentators of the right, simply because the working class has not acted as a revolutionary force. His work has prompted a number of attempts to explain why a revolutionary consciousness has not emerged in the working class in capitalist societies.

Consciousness, images of society, and immediate social milieux

Lockwood (1966) has addressed himself to this problem. Like Marx, he argues that developing a revolutionary consciousness (or any other type of consciousness) implies seeing one's society in a particular light, but that actors do not all 'see' the 'same' society, class structure and patterns of inequality. Hence the investigation of actors' images of society and class structure may explain variations in response to the objective facts of inequality. The ideas which individuals have about the societies in which they live and the systems of inequality they experience may not correspond to objective, measurable inequalities, but they can and do have real consequences for action.

Lockwood argues essentially that images of society are largely the product of certain primary social relationships into which individuals are locked, so that *within* any class the *immediate social milieux* in which members of one class find themselves may not be identical. The most salient of these are the *residential* and *occupational communities* in which individuals are located, and he identifies three distinctive types of working-class environments which throw up their own images of society.

Proletarian traditionalism is typical of working-class groups living in homogeneous communities which are socially and occupationally isolated and characterised by large-scale industrial enterprise. These are typically communities with heavy industries and predominantly working-class populations with low rates of social and geographical mobility, conditions which generate a strong sense of shared work and community experiences. Thus, communities centred on mining, shipbuilding and dock work, employing large numbers of workers in similar jobs of a single-class character, exemplify most clearly Lockwood's proletarian traditionalism. The sense of community is reinforced by the mutual dependence the worker feels for his colleagues (given the often hazardous nature of such jobs) and by the sense of identity felt at 'doing a man's job', and is reflected in the amount of leisure time which is spent with workmates.

These distinctive community experiences, according to Lockwood, produce 'the most radical and class-conscious segment of the working-class', generating a distinct awareness of the class structure and of being 'proletarian', and give rise to a view of the world in which two classes stand opposed in an arena of conflict between 'us' and 'them'. Thus, proletarian traditionalists embrace a necessary commitment to collective action to defend and enhance their interests through their principled, solidaristic support of collectivist institutions like trade unions and socialist parties.

Deferential traditionalism characterises working-class groups living and working in more heterogeneous environments, in effect relatively more isolated from other members of the working class. Their work situations involve them in personal and particularistic relationships with middle-class employers, often of a paternalistic dependent nature. Agricultural workers in rural areas and workers in small-scale industries (e.g. family-run businesses) and in small towns are the obvious example of this working-class type. These particularistic communities where 'everyone knows one's place' generate an image of society as an organic whole, in which all play a necessary but not equally important part, so that inequality of reward is an inevitable and acceptable outcome.

These workers subscribe to a model of society as a legitimate hierarchy, with deference and trust accorded to social superiors by virtue of their possession of intrinsic skills for elite positions. There is, then, an awareness of a class hierarchy, but one which accepts it as legitimate and proper and involves neither antagonism towards superiors nor any desire to be their equals or to imitate them.

Lockwood's third group of manual workers are free of the traditionalist perspectives which distinguish their proletarian and deferential counterparts. The *privatised* manual worker lives in the community milieu of the housing estate and is involved in specialised but routine occupations which are well rewarded but lack autonomy and offer little intrinsic satisfaction. The classic example here is Lockwood and Goldthorpe's 'affluent workers', for whom work is a means to the end of money with little inherent reward: their low job involvement and instrumental attitude to work produce no strong attachment to workmates but manifest themselves in a privatised home-centred existence focusing on a preoccupation with their families and homes. Enduring fairly boring employment is the price they are prepared to pay for the financial rewards they desire for their families. Their community experience is lived out in less well established areas of the newer working-class housing estate, where neighbourhod relations are less cohesive and more loose-knit.

Such circumstances foster, according to Lockwood, a *pecuniary* image of society: these workers, although seeing themselves as working class, give greater salience to social divisions based on income and material resources, with status judged by personal possessions and conspicuous consumption. Their sense of collectivisn is more instrumental than solidaristic, so that their membership of trade unions and support for the Labour Party is less ideologically and emotionally founded than that associated with proletarian traditionalism.

Lockwood stresses that this type of worker is the product of the changes of the post-war period in the material circumstances (in the form of improved standards of living), in the nature of work (with the advent of new methods of production and new consumer goods industries), and in the living conditions (particularly the growth of housing estates in urban redevelopments) of sections of the working class. The decline of occupations and communities associated with proletarian traditionalism implies that the potential for radical class consciousness existing anywhere among manual workers has been steadily eroded.

Critics of Lockwood. Many studies have questioned whether Lockwood's three types are as clearly distinguishable and discrete as he suggests: do the workers he identifies posses coherent sets of social and political values and images of society? Cousins and Brown's (1975) study of Tyneside, Roberts *et al.*'s (1974) study of Liverpool, and Newby *et al.*'s (1979) study of East Anglian farm-workers were unable to find consistent class images among manual workers: while these workers shared an awareness of being working class, they often had more than one image of society and could not be easily located within Lockwood's scheme.

Even if we accept the existence of Lockwood's types, critics have questioned the link between proletarian traditionalism and any radical consciousness. Generally, it has been argued that the consciousness generated by proletarian traditional milieux may be *much more partial* and limited than Lockwood has indicated: they may well encourage occupational and community solidarity and consciousness, but not necessarily any *class* solidarity and consciousness, spawning very parochial conceptions of who constitutes the 'us' group, which may actually *inhibit* rather than encourage commitment to and recognition of shared interests with other manual workers generally.

Moreover, as Parkin (1971) and others have argued, factors other than immediate work and community milieux may shape manual workers' perceptions of society and their place in it, particularly the impact of the macro-structure of inequality and of ideological influences which transcend local environments. We cannot assume that the kinds of immediate and primary relationships in which workers find themselves will have *no* significance for their perception of society and their class images, but it may be equally misleading to give them primacy.

Parkin shares Lockwood's view that objective class position does not spawn an automatic and uniform class consciousness. Consciousness is structured according to individuals' exposure or access to '*meaning systems*', that is, to sets of ideas which interpret reality. For Parkin, members of the working class are differentially exposed to and touched by three meaning systems in varying degrees, and variations in exposure to these systems of meaning structure different types of working-class consciousness. Parkin differs from Lockwood initially, in that he stresses that meaning systems are formed at a more general societal level rather than through the relationships and experiences of the immediate milieux: that is, they are to be seen as directly related to the macro-structure of inequality and its class relationships and interests.

The dominant value system is 'a moral framework which promotes the endorsement of existing inequality' (Parkin, 1971, p. 81). There exists, then, a prevailing set of values and ideas subscribed to and propagated by the members of the dominant class which are successfully disseminated by the major ideological institutions, such as the education system, the mass media, and religious organisations, and which are embodied in Britain in the high esteem accorded to, for instance, the monarchy, the House of Lords, public schools, the ancient universities, and the military elite. These dominant values provide and sustain an 'official' interpretation of class inequalities, endorsing them as the legitimate arrangements of capitalist society, and members of all classes will subscribe to these values unless they find themselves in circumstances which act as a buttress against their influence:

> Members of the underclass are continually exposed to the influence of dominant values by way of the education system, newpapers, radio, TV and the like. By virtue of the powerful institutional backing they receive, these values are not readily negated by those lacking other sources of knowledge and information (Parkin, 1971, p. 92).

Thus, exposure to the dominant value system inhibits any radical class consciousness in the working class, not through coercive or other unsubtle methods but by fostering acceptance of status quo ideas and values, encouraging manual workers to interpret the world as legitimately arranged, to see that inequality is just, because higher reward is the result of talent plus effort; that the national interest and not group interests is what matters; that some are born to rule, and so on. This evokes either a *deferential* or an *aspirational consciousness* among manual workers: the former shares Lockwood's traditional deferential's world-view, while the latter sees an 'open' hierarchy with opportunities for self-advancement provided one has the ability to rise.

Parkin argues that it is only through exposure to the *radical value system* that an *oppositional consciousness* can emerge, one which emphasises the constant recognition of a division of society into inevitably conflicting classes and an unequivocal commitment to eliminating the existing capitalist reward structure. Such oppositional revolutionary values are the product of the radical socialist party, committed to 'a set of precepts . . . which are fundamentally opposed to those underlying the institutions of capitalism' (Parkin, 1971, p. 97). The absence of such parties, then, represents a crucial inhibitor to any radical consciousness and action among manual workers who are not able to generate an oppositional value system 'on their own'. Parkin and others maintain that the continued triumph of dominant values has been in large part the product of a progressive 'de-radicalisation' of European socialist parties and trade unions in this century and their consequent failure to provide a coherent alternative revolutionary ideology to the dominant value system of capitalism.

> Socialist parties were initially committed to abolishing the system of ownership and rewards of capitalist society and replacing it with a system based on equalitarian principles. All the major social democratic parties in Western Europe have now abandoned this aim (Parkin, 1971, p. 127).

They have come to embrace a commitment not to destroy and replace capitalism but to modify its inequalities. They have proved, however, singularly unsuccessful in this regard, in that the introduction of welfare state measures, changes in systems of education, and attempts at equalisation of economic reward have made no significant inroads into the unequal distribution of privilege. This is because these parties have gradually forsaken an 'egalitarian' version of socialism (that is, a commitment to the eradication of privilege and inequality) in favour of a 'meritocratic' version (that is, the alteration of the principles by which privileges are allocated), which is *far less threatening* to capitalism, since it does not question the basic legitimacy of the system.

This is well illustrated in the case of the British Labour Party, where reformism set in early, if not at birth. Miliband (1961), Lane and others emphasise that, from its inception, the Labour Party lacked a coherent radical critique of capitalism and a programme for working class liberation. It has consistently taken a piecemeal, *ad hoc* approach to social and political change as something to be realised through the established political machinery. This commitment to what Miliband calls 'parliamentarianism', alongside a desire to be seen as a responsible 'national' party fit for government, has meant that the Labour Party's potential role as a vehicle for radical working-class political expression has disappeared.

But, of course, not all manual workers are exclusively exposed to the dominant value system. While those living in socially mixed rural or urban communities, those working in close paternalistic relationships with their employers, and those who are weakly organised in trade unions or not unionised at all find themselves with little or no protection from dominant values, many more members of the working class have access to what Parkin calls the *subordinate value system*, generated at the level of the working-class community.

Parkin again differs from Lockwood here in stressing that this system of values should not be seen as exemplifying radical class consciousness or as providing the basis for opposition. Rather, it is better interpreted as 'a negotiated version' of the dominant value system, an adaptive rather than oppositional response to the status quo.

> The subordinate value system could be said to be essentially *accommodative*, that is to say, its representation of the class structure and inequality emphasises various modes of adaptation, rather than either full endorsement of, or opposition to, the status quo ... It would be misleading to construe the subordinate value system as an example of normative opposition to the dominant order (Parkin, 1971, p. 88).

Inequalities are seen as an unpleasant fact of life which, while neither recognised as legitimate nor enthusiastically accepted, do not produce wholesale repudiation or rejection. Thus, the subordinate value system allows manual workers to come to terms with the reality of inequality by accommodating themselves to it and by concentrating on improving their lot within the existing reward structure. The limited and adaptive nature of this value system is well reflected in trade-union activities which centre on attempting to win improved wages and conditions for members *without* advocating an alternative set of social and economic arrangements, 'but by working within this framework' (Parkin, 1971, p. 91).

Marx maintained that unions could serve as instruments for challenging the capitalist system of class domination, and as schools of solidarity generating consciousness for the class struggle, *provided* they retained a role as political movements, aiming and working to overthrow capitalism and its inequalities. Any commitment falling short of that would inhibit the growth of a revolutionary proletarian consciousness, since such a consciousness requires recognition of the necessity and possibility of supplanting capitalist production relations with those of socialism. Thus, organised manual workers' demands reflecting a truly socialist commitment would be oriented towards issues of *control*, towards questioning the *principles* of ownership, organisation and the system of power relations in production rather than being simply *economistic* in nature – that is, attempting merely to alter the worker's market position *within* the existing structure of capitalism by the pursuit of financial improvements and better working conditions. Such victories, while often involving bitter and protracted disputes, do not encourage a radical class consciousness. They reflect only a 'trade union consciousness', which, while producing some sense of unity, *is not in itself sufficient* for a radical consciousness, since it entails the acknowledgement of limited aims and lacks a coherent political programme for systematically questioning capitalism's fundamental assumptions and effecting its replacement.

Lane (1974) and others stress that this economistic and accommodative orientation to capitalism should not be seen as a recent one: Unions have *historically* adapted to capitalism with a socialist ideology essentially reformist in nature rather than with one advocating a radical dismantling of the system. This has largely been the consequence of unions seeing capitalism as involving a series of discrete 'problems' for workers and *not* as a *system*, the structural product of a historical process. This reformist orientation has its roots in the mid-nineteenth century when the 'aristocracy of labour' – the skilled upper strata of manual workers – were in the vanguard of the growth of the trade-union movement. These workers – relatively well paid, more 'respectable' and politically moderate – gained recognition for their occupational organisations and set the tone for the development of a reformist labour movement which rejected the idea of unions as tools of political change and produced no radical critique of capitalist society.

Economistic unionism, then, generates a collectivism limited in scope by its lack of independence from the dominant value system (particularly the values surrounding ownership, production and distribution). A trade unionism geared predominantly to the pursuit of control would be an altogether different proposition. As Giddens (1973, p. 206) says:

> Any sort of major extension of industrial conflict into the area of control poses a threat to the institutional separation of economic and political conflict which is a fundamental basis of the capitalist state – because it serves to bring into the open the connexions between political power in the polity as such, and the broader 'political' subordination of the working class within the economic order ... Union–management clashes involving economism are in principle reconcilable in a way which those over control are not.

Economistic orientations are reinforced and intensified by the *sectionalism* inherent in a movement composed of organisations whose individual role is the representation of the interests of workers in specific occupations rather than those of a whole class. This 'occupational' consciousness is partly inevitable, given the structural position of the worker in capitalism, but its political consequences may be fundamental and far-reaching in inhibiting the growth of any full-blown radical class consciousness. Trade Unions have traditionally been much concerned with guarding their status and maintaining differentials in reward in relation to other occupational groups at the expense of any massive class-based assault on capitalism. Roberts *et al.* (1974, pp. 97–8) stress that:

> Concern over differentials and relativities are as much part and parcel of shopfloor life and occupy as central a place in the history of Trade Unionism as the class struggle ... The factory, firm, and trade union are real entities with which ordinary workers can identify and ideas about a wider class struggle often cannot compete.

Now, for many political commentators of the Right, industrial action represents major threats to social stability, challenges to the system which attempt 'to hold the nation to ransom', 'to bring the country to its knees', and so on. It can be argued, however, that such action in the form of the strike does not represent an alternative to or departure from economism, but a mere extension or reinforcement of it, hence not threatening capitalism or escalating working-class political perspectives. In this view, strike action at best provides a support to trade-union consciousness, but has no necessary implications for a revolutionary working-class consciousness.

Industrial conflict tends to centre on specific industrial situations, to be *localised* in one sphere of production or plant, thus serving to narrow the workers' perception of 'them' to particular employers or particular management. The limitations of strike activity for consciousness are further compounded by the fact that the strike is basically an *economic weapon* which unions use in their bargaining role; and it is a device of fairly limited *negative* potential in the form of withdrawal of labour.

This highlights the fact that trade unions are essentially *defensive* organisations, concerned with attempts to limit exploitation within capitalism rather than to eliminate it, largely fighting a rearguard action with negative weapons like withdrawal of labour, work to rule and overtime bans. They are, as Lane and Roberts (1971) and Hyman (1975) have maintained, 'reactive', responding to the realities of the prevailing power relations of capitalism, 'because of the right accorded to management in capitalism to direct production and command the labour force' (Hyman, 1975, p. 97).

The discussion so far suggests, then, that the majority of the working class in Western capitalism, while exhibiting neither moral approval nor enthusiastic acceptance of the existing order, are not committed to full-blooded action to rectify inequalities and restructure social arrangements.

Mann too (1970, 1973) argues that we cannot successfully account for the lack of revolutionary class consciousness among manual workers either by crude Marxist explanations which attribute working-class compliance to the successful systematic dissemination of dominant values in a process of ideological manipulation by the ruling class, or by comfortable pluralist notions that a radical working-class consciousness has been dissipated by the development of a *value-consensus* resulting from the alleged economic and political changes in Western capitalist democracies.

Such interpretations must demonstrate a consistent commitment to dominant values on the part of the working class. But Mann argues that the working class have adopted, if anything, a response of *pragmatic acceptance* of their disadvantaged position in capitalism – an unenthusiastic, qualified, realistic response to their situation, where they are not convinced that capitalism and its attendant inequalities are morally legitimate, but where they accept it pragmatically as an everyday fact of life and perceive no realistic alternative.

Mann found that manual workers supported simultaneously both 'dominant' values and 'deviant' values, but these sets of values operate on different 'levels'. Manual workers appear more likely to endorse deviant values when they are related to concrete, everyday realities or when they are expressed in simplistic, unsystematically critical terms than if related to abstract political values. They are likely to concur with such statements as 'People in different classes share fundamentally similar interests' and 'Workers and managers should all work together for the common good' (supporting dominant values), while agreeing with 'The rich have always exploited the poor' and 'Managers should not have privileges like separate restaurants and car parks' (supporting deviant values, but on concrete issues or in a vaguely populist way).

He stresses that exposure to dominant values is a constant and never totally inescapable feature of working-class life, in which a number of important institutions – such as the education system and the mass media – are engaged in assailing manual workers with politically conservative values and attitudes, so that they cannot fail to absorb some elements of the dominant value system. But total ideological manipulation of manual workers does not ensue, because the more immediate settings in which the working class find themselves, such as the family, the work-group and peer-group experiences help 'deviant' critical values to breed. However, they are, according to Mann, of a rather 'raw' variety, not always articulated in the form of abstract principles which allow manual workers to grasp the *totality* of their subordination and disadvantageous position so as to generate a *systematic* critique of capitalist society.

Consequently, manual workers are confused by the clash between dominant and deviant values but are touched by both. As Blackburn and Mann (1975, p. 155) point out:

> If the workers in our sample are 'confused', then they have every right to be, for that is an accurate reflection of the reality that confronts them . . . This may not take us very far towards a theory of society, but it does enable us to make more sense of workers' thin images of society. For instead of viewing them as approximations to consistent and coherent images, we should regard them as attempts to grapple with the real contradictions of the workers' situation.

They emphasise that we should not find it surprising, given the contradictory cross-pressured circumstances in which manual workers find themselves, that they do not develop the cohesive and insulated subcultures and images of society of the kind outlined by Lockwood. Experiences in the work environment and in everyday life 'loosen' the potentially monolithic impact of dominant values, so that deviant values and the seeds of dissatisfaction are never completely absent: the ensuing pragmatic compliance leaves room for a 'latent class consciousness' to exist, in which inequalities are recognised, but with only a limited appreciation of the alternative social arrangements possible, so that opposition is at best spasmodic and partial.

An essentially similar position to that of Mann is taken by Hyman (1972, 1975) and by Westergaard and Resler (1975), though they tend to embrace a more 'optimistic' view of the potential for radical working-class action, while stressing the essentially *ambivalent* nature of working-class images of society. For Westergaard and Resler (1975, p. 403) there exists 'a common sense of grievance, a belief that the dice are loaded against ordinary workers', which, while not constituting any completely coherent ideology of dissent, contains the vital seeds of opposition to the capitalist system and its principles and practices. There are signs, then, of a *quasi-ideology* critical of the present social order, which should not be minimised or ignored, since its embryonic existence makes any notions about complete working-class incorporation *much* more open and problematic. The 'pecuniary' image of society, for example, allegedly embraced by Lockwood's 'privatised' workers, may be less straightforward than it appears, according to Westergaard (1970), who maintains that a pecuniary approach may not automatically produce an uncomplicated dilution of working-class consciousness. If workers are as instrumental in their work as has been claimed, committed to their job purely because of pay (the 'cash-nexus'), then their integration into capitalism is essentially partial and not total.

> The cash-nexus may snap just because it is *only* a cash-nexus; because it is single stranded ... And if it does snap there is nothing else to bind the worker to acceptance of his situation. ... The single stranded character of the 'cash-orientation' implies a latent instability of workers' commitments and orientations (Westergaard, 1970, p. 120).

The institutionalisation of class conflict and maintenance of working-class acquiescence then becomes conditional upon capitalism's ability continually to 'deliver the goods' to manual workers. Thus, in this view, it is not out of the question that working-class radicalisation might take place, particularly given certain changes and crises experienced by capitalist societies in the 1960s and 1970s, such as the decline of the traditional, particularistic, working-class community, escalating wage demands, shop-floor militancy, rising inflation and international economic recession, and falling rates of profit.

Ideological hegemony and the limits of incorporation

Thus far, we have argued that the main components of the labour movement, unions and socialist parties, have not provided a clear alternative ideology but have mediated the dominant ideology in a way that renders it acceptable. The result of this has been a gradual process of incorporation of the working class into capitalism and the continued hegemony of the dominant class, though we have questioned the extent to which either of these conditions has been rendered complete, and indeed whether *total* incorporation is in fact necessary for capitalism to survive.

It is tempting but misleading to see manual workers in capitalist society, both historically and contemporarily, as being faced with a straight choice between adopting economistic and accommodative orientations on the one hand or revolutionary action on the other, with the former gaining unambiguous preference. We must remember that there are both *practical and ideological pressures* guiding workers towards economism and away from wholesale radicalism.

First, manual workers are *not only* workers; they also have homes, families and leisure activities as elements of their everyday reality, and the routine and unsatisfying nature of most manual work does much to induce an instrumental approach to work, with only modest expectations of deriving any intrinsic benefit. Life outside work may be accorded greater priority and salience, and the daily grind of labour does not become a central life interest: work and the class struggle may at best represent only *one* dimension of manual workers' everyday reality.

Second, the realities of the worker's position in the capitalist industrial system make economism an essentially realistic response. As Mann (1973, p. 32) observes:

> Economism ... is rooted in the worker's very experience. ... Normally confronted by an employer who will budge on economic but not on control issues, the worker takes what he can easily get and attempts to reduce the salience of what is denied him.

But perhaps even more significant than these practical pressures is the *ideological climate* of capitalism. Hyman, for instance, argues that there exists a strong materialist ethos in capitalism which, systematically propagated by media advertising, persuades workers that the consumption of certain goods and services (washing machines, cars, holidays, or whatever) is the key to 'happiness' and self-fulfilment, so that it is not at all remarkable that economistic demands predominate.

Furthermore, the ideological hegemony of the dominant class is reflected in the way in which prevailing ideology regarding industrial relations and the structure of capitalist industry becomes ingrained in many workers' consciousness. These dominant values legitimise the principle of private ownership of the means of production and the organisation and operation of managerial authority, they stress the ultimate mutual interests of owners, managers and workers in the smooth running of the enterprise, and they sustain an unproblematic conception of the 'national interest', 'fairness' and 'reasonable demands', and of the kinds of action which threaten these absolutes (such as strikes).

As we observed earlier, these values are not easily resisted, and the majority of workers give them at least partial endorsement, since as Nichols and Armstrong (1976, p. 51) say: 'Workers are not born with a socialist consciousness. Nor is it something they naturally arrive at. Nor does the information to sustain them in alternative analysis automatically drop into workers' hands.' The practical effect of this is to blunt or reduce the possibility of a shared feeling of solidarity with other workers in the same structural position and hence to inhibit any *systematically* critical evaluation of capitalism. Thus, workers frequently condemn the industrial action of others (even within the same industry) as 'greed', 'agitation', 'trouble-making', and so on, even though they may regard their own demands and action as the legitimate expression of a grievance felt about their own employment conditions.

We cannot, however, ignore the fact that normative acceptance of existing social arrangements by the subordinate class has to be *achieved*, that is, to be continually reproduced. While we do not need to assume that the subordinate class are deliberately 'conned' into submission, we may regard the social relations of capitalist society and the constraints on change built into them as forming a taken-for-granted reality which is institutionalised in the routine assumptions and operation of capitalist enterprises, the mass media, the education system, the legal system and in the state itself. Under such circumstances, existing economic relations and property rights can come to appear immutable features of a 'natural' world, and this very 'naturalness' implies a moral rectitude for established arrangements.

There *are* limits to hegemony, if we mean by this a situation where both the dominant position of one class and the subordinate position of another are *totally* legitimated by normative acceptance by the subordinate class. We have attempted to show that the legitimacy of capitalist social and economic arrangements is not unambiguously accepted and hence that the incorporation of the working class is not unproblematic. Elements of working-class dissatisfaction and protest are present in capitalism, agreement with dominant social values is generally imprecise, ambiguous and even contradictory at times, and 'built-in' industrial conflict is a price capitalism has to pay. Workers see the inequalities of capitalism in education, housing, health, and so on. But as Nichols and Armstrong (1976, p. 59) observe:

> The real triumph of capitalist hegemony is seen in the fact that, for the most part, these workers do not affirm or deny its values. For them, capitalism is just part of an unalterable order of things (not necessarily a proper or just one). It is a world they did not choose, nor can make, nor can alter. Because of this, capitalism (like God) is not the sort of thing you should think about too much.

6.6 CLASS, POLITICS AND CHANGE

A consistent theme in our discussions so far in this chapter has been a recognition of integral links between *class* and *politics*, both in our consideration of debates about the organisation and distribution of power and about working-class political consciousness. At the same time, we have also cautioned against simplistic assumptions about the relationship between class position, class interests, political ideas/values and political action. Class divisions do not provide a ready-made agenda for class politics, so that there is a by no means perfect guarantee.that class *structure* will generate class *interests* and political *action*: the political values and behaviour of a particular class cannot simply be predicted or 'read off' wholesale from some model of the class structure – the links between class and politics are less straightforward than that.

Nevertheless such links do exist and have existed persistently over time, however imperfectly. In Britain, for instance, the connections between class interests and politics have historical roots in the long-established affinity between the upper and middle class and the Conservative Party, in the development of trade unionism and the Labour Party as vehicles of working-class industrial and political organisation from the second half of the nineteenth century, and in the pattern of electoral support enjoyed by the major political parties for much of this century. Numerous studies of voting behaviour over the decades demonstrated a consistent support for left-wing socialist and social democratic parties by the majority of the working class in European capitalist societies, and in Britain, at least for much of this century, class has constituted the single most important variable associated with voting. Roughly two-thirds of the working-class vote has regularly gone to the Labour Party, and this support was founded on a widespread (though by no means universal) view among those voters of the Labour Party as their 'natural' party and the guardian of working-class interests. The middle-class vote in Britain, moreover, has been traditionally even more class-cohesive than that of the working class, with only about 20–25 per cent at most of non-manuals deserting the 'party of their class' and voting Labour.

Class and politics in the post-war era

In the post Second World War era, the blossoming of welfare state systems, the gradual expansion of war-ravaged economies and modest improvements in standards of living encouraged in certain political and academic circles the view that the class politics of nineteenth century and pre-war capitalist societies was fast becoming an anachronism, and that the 'end of ideology' was just around the corner. Most notably, proponents of the 'embourgeoisement' thesis (see Chapter 3) in the early 1960s maintained that the death of class politics was imminent in West European societies, since rising standards of living were eroding the formerly solid class basis of politics, with so-called 'affluent' manual workers allegedly losing/giving up their traditional political attitudes and social values and no longer perceiving themselves as working class nor their interests as represented by left-wing socialist or Labour parties. Studies such as those of Goldthorpe *et al.* (1969) in Luton suggested, however, that the predicted demise of class politics was premature to say the least, with no appreciable weakening of levels of 'affluent' manual workers' electoral support for the Labour Party nor loss of confidence in the party as the political representative of their material interests. Other studies and election data, too, indicated that until the late 1960s some two-thirds of working-class voters identified with and voted for the Labour Party.

More recent evidence in the last decade or so, however, has suggested that electoral political support has become less predictable and more volatile, that party loyalty has become less stable, and more particularly that the old links between class and party loyalty have become more blurred and problematic – in other words, it has increasingly been suggested that a distinct process of *'class de-alignment'* in politics has occurred.

This has involved, on the one hand, a discernible increase in support for the Labour Party among non-manual workers during the 1960s and 1970s: in the 1964 General Election, for example, the Conservatives led Labour by 53 per cent among middle class voters but by only 35 per cent by 1979. But apparently more dramatically than this, the 1970s saw a significant decline in working-class support for the Labour Party, to such an extent that in the 1983 General Election, only 38 per cent of manual worker voters supported Labour, and only 39 per cent of trade unionists did so. This shift was particularly visible among skilled manual workers: even as late as 1974, almost twice as many skilled manual workers voted Labour as voted Conservative (49 to 26 per cent), but in 1979 their votes were almost equally divided between Labour and Conservative (42 per cent and 40 per cent respectively), and in 1983 more skilled manual workers voted Conservative than voted Labour (39 to 35 per cent).

If we are to entertain the notion that the established links between class and political loyalty have been undermined in recent years, as the class 'de-alignment' thesis implies, we need to consider two questions. First, is this merely a temporary hiatus in the 'normal' pattern of affairs, brought about by 'special' circumstances (for example, the effects of economic recession, the powerful if temporary appeal of Thatcherism, the Falklands factor, division and disunity within the Labour Party) which, once they disappear, will lead to a reversion to the 'norm' of class politics? Or does the process reflect more enduring and qualitative changes in the nature of class loyalties and political behaviour, such that a claim that 'class politics is dead or dying' can now be made with greater certainty and confidence? While the first of these possibilities may offer a superficial attraction in certain political quarters, it is sociologically more important to entertain the second question more seriously, since it necessitates analysis of the changing structure and culture of social classes in contemporary societies and hence raises important issues about changing patterns of class politics.

It is important to remember that class structures and classes within them are not static entities of eternal composition, neither in terms of the absolute numbers and proportion of a society's population they embrace nor in terms of their social mix. Neither are they immune from cultural changes. Our discussion in Chapter 3 has highlighted certain changes in the social and occupational structure and in social and cultural conditions and emphases which have had important implications of the way classes are constituted and which are therefore, obviously important in examining/considering the relationship between class and politics. This is *not* to say simply that class politics is dead or does not matter any longer, but that there have been changes in the reality of class and class experiences which may have significant political consequences.

As we have seen earlier in the book, one of the most visible changes in the post-war era, and particularly in the last twenty years or so, has been the emergence of a more complex occupational structure, with the rise of new industries, skills and occupations and changes in patterns of rewards. At the forefront of this process has been the significant decline of the once predominant traditional heavy manufacturing and extractive industries (such as mining, shipbuilding, metal production, heavy engineering, and docking), progressively giving way to the development of newer advanced technologies and industries such as car-making, light engineering, electronics, chemicals and so on, requiring fewer workers with different kinds of skills. At the same time, those working in the 'non-productive' service sector and those employed by the local or national State in the public sector have increased considerably, with the result that there have occurred shifts in the shape of the class structure and in the internal composition of classes which, while not signifying the end of class divisions or similar nonsense, do reflect the evolution of a more complex hierarchy, both between and within class boundaries.

In the case of the working class, this has manifested itself in a decline of traditional manual occupations and an overall contraction in the size of the working class base, paralleled by the growth of what has been called a 'new working class' (or more accurately, a new section/stratum of the working class). There has developed, then, a somewhat smaller, more heterogeneous and less unambiguously 'proletarian' group than in the nineteenth century or the first half of the twentieth century.

Alongside these occupational structural changes, there have also occurred cultural changes which have helped to reshape working-class behaviour patterns, expectations and aspirations and which appear to have had an impact on class and politics. The post-war era was marked by extensive programmes of urban redevelopment, with the gradual relocation of many working-class families from traditional urban working-class communities into new suburban housing estates and new towns. Additionally, the period of relative economic prosperity enjoyed by Western capitalist societies in the two decades after the Second World War – the 'post-war boom' – produced a revolution in patterns of mass consumption and leisure and entertainment with the increased availability of household consumer durable goods such as fridges, TVs, stereos, and cars and package holidays, and even home ownership. At the same time, the more overt signs of inequality which formerly distinguished manual workers' families from other people became less clearly visible, as better standards of living (most notably in health care, diet, clothes, and so on) became more commonly part of working-class experience as a result of welfare state provision and increased wages.

These occupational and cultural changes have undoubtedly influenced working-class people's experience of class, their aspirations and their material and political interests. Various studies, such as those of Goldthorpe *et al.* (1969) and Roberts *et al.* (1974), while dismissing simplistic notions of working-class economic and political embourgeoisement, have identified the changing contours of the working class and sections within it. Such studies pointed particularly to the increasing privatisation and home-centredness of sections of the 'affluent' manual working class, and more particularly to their more 'instrumental' commitment to trade unionism and the Labour Party. While such attitudes may have been sufficient to bind these workers to 'traditional' class political loyalties in the relatively prosperous period of the 1960s, the relatively more qualified/fragile nature of such a commitment has meant, in the changing socioeconomic circumstances of the 1970s and the early 1980s, that that political commitment could be more easily dislodged, even if not necessarily permanently. In Britain, for instance, at the 1979 General Election, 40 per cent of skilled manual workers who voted supported the Conservatives and in 1983, 39 per cent did so: Thatcherism and the New Right developed ways of appealing to sections of the working class (particularly those employed in the private sector) which attracted their support or at least loosened their commitment to the Labour Party. As Leys (1983, p. 140) observes:

> The old 'matrix' of working class life, which had included an increasingly automatic allegiance to the Labour Party, was breaking up. The changes of the post-war years had not made the workers 'middle class' but they had weakened the ties of tradition and place which underpinned the traditional sense of what it was to *be* 'working class' . . .
>
> In other words, what had changed were many of the historical connotations of working class life which had in the past so many *badges*, by reference to which workers knew they were, and were known to be, members of the 'working class'.

As we pointed out earlier, middle-class voting has been more class-cohesive than that of the working class, with the bulk of non-manual workers, by virtue of their family socialisation, work and educational experiences and opportunities, and so on, inclined towards the status quo and right wing or conservative parties. But as we suggested in Chapter 3, as a result of changes in the occupational structure, the middle class too is now more socially heterogeneous than formerly, and this has manifested itself in their political orientations. For many white collar workers in the marginal middle class, their jobs have been increasingly subject to a process of 'quasi-proletarianisation' as a result of the routinisation and de-skilling of much clerical work. Those employed by the State have in recent years been major casualties of government incomes policies which have limited wage increases, and they have been increasingly subject to the hitherto remote risk of unemployment as the result of large reductions in State expenditure in the public sector in the form of staffing cuts. While there is obviously no guarantee that such experiences have an unambiguously radicalising effect, they do appear to have had some effect on the traditional political loyalties of this section of the middle class.

In the past two decades or so, significant sections of the white collar middle class (most notably clerical workers and those working in the public sector) have increasingly identified with and aligned themselves politically with the labour movement, both in terms of increased unionisation and a willingness to take collective industrial action, and have been relatively more inclined towards parties of the left. We should not overemphasise the novelty or the extent of the political 'radicalism' of this minority. Many of them are people with working-class families of origin (and hence left-wing political loyalties) who have been the beneficiaries of the expansion of white-collar occupations of the post-war period. Also, many white-collar trade unions and their members have been, after all, industrially moderate and politically conservative and often anxious to defend themselves *against* economic parity with the manual working class. Similarly, many routine non-manual workers in Britain have aligned themselves more recently with the SDP/Liberal Alliance in preference to the Labour Party: in the 1983 General Election, 24 per cent of office and clerical workers who voted supported the Alliance and only 21 per cent voted Labour (Crewe, 1983).

Indeed, the rise of the Alliance clouds the issue of class and politics in Britain still further. In the 1983 election the Alliance gained 26 per cent of the vote, and while it is not easy to draw firm conclusions on the social composition of their supporters on the basis of one General Election, the Alliance did not draw its support predominantly from any one class, though it was relatively less popular among working-class people and had a stronger social base among those of non-manual clerical and professional background.

Although opinion poll data suggest that a proportion of Alliance support can be attributed to a negative 'protest' vote of dissatisfaction with the two major parties and to the sheer novelty of the SDP, the Alliance has proved positively attractive to a range of voters who have come to regard the Conservative and Labour Parties as too extreme and ineffective in their capacities to govern. Thatcherite Conservatism is seen as unacceptable in its rejection of the post-war 'welfare consensus' while the Labour Party's brand of socialism is seen as unworkable in its reliance on state intervention and its dependence on the political co-operation of powerful trade unions.

Class politics and non-class politics

As we have implied elsewhere both in this chapter and in Chapter 3, it is unrealistic to assume any spontaneous homogeneity of interests among members of a particular class, if only because the labour process itself in capitalism divides and fragments classes as well as providing certain potential conditions for a political unity of action. In the working class, for instance, even in the last century as well as more recently, differences in levels of skill, status and rewards cut across class unity and common political action.

In any case, as we also indicated in our discussion of working-class political consciousness, class membership is neither the sole nor necessarily the primary dimension of life experienced by ordinary people, it is merely one of several experiences that help to form their view of themselves, their society and their politics. This means, then, that class is experienced in a number of different ways. Most obviously, class membership and identity is mediated by gender, ethnic background, generation, region, and so on, and certain political and economic struggles and issues cut across class allegiances – gender equality, opposition to nuclear weapons and environmental conservation, for example. While participation in groups such as CND, the Women's Movement, Friends of the Earth, and so on largely involves the 'radical' middle class in professional, 'intellectual' and public sector employment and is often merely one element of a more general critique of the status quo on the part of those involved, they remain non-class 'radical' political causes. They cannot merely be seen as somehow secondary to the greater 'realities' of class politics; rather, they highlight the importance of a range of political issues and controversies which do not emanate simply from class divisions. Similarly, as Dunleavy and Husbands (1985) and others argue, there may be emerging in Britain a 'sectoral politics', a line of division not wholly independent of but cutting across class divisions and political interests, with people's involvement in the *public sector* or *private sector* both as *workers* (for example, whether or not one is employed by the State or by private enterprises) and as *consumers* of certain basic resources and services (for example, housing, transport, medical and health care) influencing their political loyalties and voting behaviour.

Given these observations, given the changes in the structure and location of occupations and the cultural consequences to which we have referred, and given the volatility of recent voting patterns, we cannot conclude that class is no longer influential in structuring political loyalties, beliefs and action. These depend to a significant though not exclusive extent on the experiences of the workplace, the home and immediate environments, and where these are lived out in a social context of material inequality and disadvantage, class politics are unlikely to disappear or recede insignificantly into the background. While Thatcherism in Britain may have been successful in effecting a partial shift to the right, it has also re-politicised economic life with social and economic policies which have increased inequality, created mass unemployment, attacked the rights of organised labour, greatly extended the powers of the police, and significantly reduced the provision of public and social services which were a key feature of the post-war 'consensus'. It may have severely weakened the power of the labour movement, it may have driven a wedge between the employed and the unemployed and between the North and South, but it remains highly open to question whether it has swept away class politics in the process.

6.7   THE CHANGING ROLE OF THE STATE

It has been argued that liberal democracy has developed into (in Lenin's phrase) 'the one best shell for capitalism' in contemporary Western Europe. At this stage, we can now ask why this form of the state seems so appropriate to capitalism, and whether there are any changes in the role of the state (particularly relating to the economy) which might undermine this form of government.

We argued earlier that the most stable liberal democracies were created by the defeat of traditional, rural-based plutocracies or autocracies, often through political revolution. The emerging bourgeoisie successfully removed previous restrictions on trade and manufacture and gained a great degree of economic freedom. At the same time, the state gradually involved itself in developments facilitating the establishment of capitalism, the most important of these being the gradual establishment of laws of property, contract and employment which differed significantly from their semi-feudal predecessors. Land and other productive assets became exchangeable commodities, owned by individuals who had the sole right to profit from the use or disposal of their property. Older regulations on wages, prices and employment conditions dating back to guild regulation and feudal rural ties were abolished, 'freeing' the worker and the employer to make a contract for the hiring of labour. In these respects, the state withdrew from intervention in economic activity to a position where it merely provided the legal and institutional framework. The more 'active' aspect of the state's role concerned military expansion to 'pacify' areas of the globe in order to open them to trade free from foreign competition. In addition, the state maintained and developed its monopoly of force, and used it to repress protest or rebellion against the emerging social arrangements.

These trends came to their heyday in Britain in the mid-nineteenth century with the *laissez-faire* state. Here the formal separation between economic activity and political rule reached its height. An ideology developed (far from dead today) where the whole society was seen to benefit from unfettered competitive capitalism. The state should therefore keep its distance and not 'distort' the hidden hand of the market or the vigorous expansion of capital. Out of this philosophy developed the claim that politics was 'above' the economy and could provide a neutral arena for representation of the national interest. As long as the subordinate classes agreed that economic growth and the expansion of empire were for the good of all, they could be accepted as citizens and allowed the vote and parliamentary representation. As we have seen, in Britain, and to a large extent elsewhere, the notion of the separation of 'economic' and 'political' issues was accepted by the working class in their *division* of the labour movement into the trade unions (with purely economic concerns) and the parliamentary party. Thus, the capitalist state came to claim legitimacy as the representative of all individual citizens, and not just the dominant class.

Governments were therefore faced with a more difficult task. Not only had they to generate strategies appropriate for profitable economic expansion, they also had to ensure that such strategies could command some degree of popular acceptance. The disciplines of unemployment, policing and strike-breaking may be one way of enforcing harsh economic remedies (in the 1920s and the 1980s), but one frequent alternative is to grant concessions and share out economic rewards. In an attempt to create legitimacy, concessions were gradually made, and the early part of this century saw the beginning of welfare and educational provision by most such states. Equally important in sustaining such legitimacy was the acceptance by workers' movements of the need for 'patriotism' to fight off competing European nations in the First World War. When (as in Germany) some workers rejected such compromises at the end of the war in uprisings and mutinies, the state acted to quell rebellion and secure the dominance of the social democratic parties over revolutionary rivals. For the communists, the capitalist state could never claim loyalty from the subordinate class, for it was necessarily a class state, serving only the dominant economic class. Real politics was class struggle, not shabby compromises over limited issues. In the crises of the 1920s and 1930s, political developments produced defeat for such movements, either through fascism or through the further incorporation of social democratic parties into the business of managing capitalism.

However, the latter solution was not fruitless for the working class. Major concessions were made with the development of welfare states, expanded education systems and protection for trade union organisation, and states came to accept the responsibility to intervene in the economy to sustain relatively full employment and steady growth. Through such measures governments attempted to harmonise political and economic interests in a new consensus after 1945.

In Britain the 'post-war settlement' lasted until the early 1970s, supported by the long international boom. It included progressive domestic policies for economic growth and welfare redistribution. However, the British 'settlement' also had highly conservative aspects, particularly in its international aspects. Costly military commitments in NATO and in the old Empire caused stress. Financial capital renewed its strength and freedom, regaining its constraining grip on economic policy. Time and again these financial constraints undermined policies for industrial growth. Simultaneously, internal stresses emerged in the settlement, but as long as it could be sustained, legitimacy was strengthened, because all classes were seen to benefit, and even those outside the labour market were aided by social provision. The state was drawn further and further into direct intervention in the economy through management of credit and money supply; through nationalisation and investment subsidies; through support for research and advanced technology; and above all through the fact that the state owned large sectors of industry and employed significant proportions of the work-force. While all this coincided with the long post-war boom, the political effects were largely beneficial; but counter-effects also emerged which have become most serious in those nations most hit by economic recession. As a result, the 'consensus politics' of the post-war period has come to appear more precarious and fragile.

The changes in the post-war state's role seemed to support such a consensus because the concessions made to the working class in such fields as health, education and regional aid often served the needs of expanding, technically based industry. A stable, healthy, educated work-force was clearly desirable. All this, however, is costly, and can come to seem to employers and their political representatives to be an intolerable tax burden. The pursuit of full employment and protection of workers' representation also created its own problems, since workers became significantly stronger at shop-floor level. (Full employment meant that strikes gained effectiveness, since no reserve pools of labour were available.)

While advances in wage levels and employment conditions could be powerfully defended, when growth falters there is strong pressure on union leaders to follow their social-democratic political rulers into wage-freezes, incomes policies and the like. Part of the post-war compromise involved the incorporation of union leaders into the formulation and implementation of such policies in order to 'manage' the economy. However, the unions are involved in such policy-making precisely because of their power (they cannot easily be excluded or forced to comply), but this power is fundamentally located at shop-floor level, where top-level compromises may well be rejected. In such circumstances, the union action either succeeds in changing unwelcome policy, or the unions become excluded from the arena of political policy. The limitations of union power may then become apparent as the right of managers and owners to impose redundancy or closure is met only by defensive union action.

Rapid changes in the British state have occurred during the 1980s. Domestically, the state became more centralised, more coercive, and more insulated from social pressures. Power was concentrated at the very peak through the Prime Ministerial office and the cabinet committees. The central state gained power through extensive controls on local authority spending, and even through the abolition of hostile elected councils. Policing became more centralised and more coercive in response to demonstrations, strikes, riots and peace protests. Trade Union resistance was decisively confronted and weakened. Those feeling the brunt of economic policies were marginalised and their votes contributed only to a weakened and divided opposition in the early 1980s. The post-war goal of social consensus was decisively abandoned as large parts of the population, divided, dispersed and powerless, became victims in a divided society. The condition for more economic 'freedom' was a stronger state, coercing those who sought to resist. Whether this legacy can now be broken, and opposition movements unified, depends upon all the dimensions of power we have discussed in this chapter.

REFERENCES TO CHAPTER 6

Bachrach, P. and Baratz, M. (1963) 'Decisions and Non-Decisions', *American Political Science Review*, vol. 57.

Blackburn, R. and Mann, M. (1975) 'Ideology in the Non-Skilled Working Class', in M. Bulmer (ed.), *Working Class Images of Society*, London, Routledge & Kegan Paul.

Bulmer, M. (ed.) (1975) *Working Class Images of Society*, London, Routledge & Kegan Paul.

Coates, D. (1984) *The Context of British Politics*, London, Hutchinson.

Cousins, J. and Brown, R. (1975) 'Patterns of Paradox: Shipbuilding Workers' Images of Society', in Bulmer (1975).

Crewe, I. (1983) 'The Disturbing Truth Behind Labour's Rout', *The Guardian* 13 June.

Dahl, R. (1961) *Who Governs?*, Yale University Press.

Dunleavy, P. and Husbands, C. (1985) *British Democracy at the Crossroads: Voting and Party Competition in the 1980s*, London, Allen & Unwin.

Gamble, A. (1985) *Britain in Decline* (2nd edn), London, Macmillan.

Giddens, A. (1973) *The Class Structure of the Advanced Societies*, London, Hutchinson.

Goldthorpe, J. *et al.* (1969) *The Affluent Worker in the Class Structure*, Cambridge University Press.

Hall, S. and Jacques, M. (1983) *The Politics of Thatcherism*, London, Lawrence & Wishart.

Hyman, R. (1972) *Strikes*, London, Fontana.
Hyman, R. (1975) *Industrial Relations: a Marxist Introduction*, London, Macmillan.
Jessop, B. (1977) 'Recent Theories of the Capitalist State', *Cambridge Journal of Economics*, vol. 1(4).
Lane, D. (1976) *The Socialist Industrial State*, London, Allen & Unwin.
Lane, T. (1974) *The Union Makes Us Strong*, London, Arrow.
Lane, T. and Roberts, K. (1971) *Strike at Pilkingtons*, London, Fontana.
Leys, C. (1985) *Politics in Britain*, London, Heinemann.
Lockwood, D. (1966) 'Sources of Variation in Working Class Images of Society', *Sociological Review*, vol. 14.
Longstreth, F. (1979) 'The City, Industry and the State', in C. Crouch (ed.), *State and Economy in Contemporary Capitalism*, London, Croom Helm.
Lukes, S. (1974) *Power: A Radical View*, London, Macmillan.
Mann, M. (1970) 'Social Cohesion of Liberal Democracy', *American Sociological Review*, vol. 35
Mann, M. (1973) *Consciousness and Action Among the Western Working Class*, London, Macmillan.
Marx, K. and Engels, F. (1976) *Collected Works*, London, Lawrence & Wishart.
McLennan, G., Held D. and Hall S. (eds) (1984) *The Idea of the Modern State*, Milton Keynes, Open University Press.
Miliband, R. (1961) *Parliamentary Socialism*, London, Allen & Unwin.
Moran, M. (1985) *Politics and Society in Britain*, London, Macmillan
Newby, H. (1979) *The Deferential Worker*, Harmondsworth, Penguin.
Nichols, T. and Armstrong, P. (1976) *Workers Divided*, London, Fontana.
Noble, T. (1975) *Modern Britain: Structure and Change*, London, Batsford.
Parkin, F. (1971) *Class Inequality and Political Order*, London, MacGibbon & Kee.
Poggi, G. (1978) *The Development of the Modern State*, London, Hutchinson.
Riesman, D. (1950) *The Lonely Crowd*, Yale University Press.
Roberts, K. *et al.* (1974) *The Fragmentary Class Structure*, London, Heinemann.
Saunders, P. *et al.* (1978) 'Rural Community and Rural Community Power', in H. Newby (ed.) *International Perspectives in Rural Sociology*, New York, Wiley.
Scott, J. (1982) *The Upper Class*, London, Macmillan.
Westergaard, J. (1970) 'The Rediscovery of the Cash Nexus', in R. Miliband and J. Savile (eds), *Socialist Register*, London, Merlin Press.
Westergaard, J. and Resler, H. (1975) *Class in a Capitalist Society*, London, Heinemann.
Worsley, P. (1964) 'The Distribution of Power in Industrial Societies', in P. Halmos (ed.), *The Development of Industrial Societies*, Sociological Review Monograph No. 8.
Who's Who (1981) London, Adam & Charles Black.

7

The Family

7.1 INTRODUCTION

The continued existence of every society depends, at a most fundamental level, on the reproduction of new generations of the population. Sexual relations between some women and some men, culminating in the birth of children, are an obvious necessity, but to satisfy the conditions for biological parenthood is not in itself enough. Human infants undergo a long period of maturation before they are capable of surviving by themselves, and during this period they require some form of protection and support. Moreover, an extended period of socialisation is necessary if children are eventually to become fully functioning members of society. In other words, children need not only biological parenthood but a form of 'social parenthood' – socialisation, protection and support – as well.

In our society, we have come to expect that sexual activity, child-bearing, maintenance and support of children, and socialisation will all be focused upon the institution known as the *nuclear family* – a domestic unit composed of a man and woman in a stable marital relationship, with their dependent children. A distinguishing feature of the nuclear family is that only two adults are involved in all the activities concerned with the reproduction of children: that is, one woman and one man are simultaneously sexual partners, biological parents and social parents, and the mechanism that links their various activities is the conjugal or marital tie.

Even in our own society, of course, the reproduction of children often takes place in different circumstances. Occasionally, for instance, we find *extended families*, where more than one generation of husbands and wives cohabit with their offspring; social parenthood in extended families may be more of a collective affair than is the case with the isolated nuclear family. A more common arrangement in Britain is the *single-parent family*, where a man, or more often a woman, carries out the tasks of social parenthood alone; in 1981–83 approximately 13 per cent of families with dependent children were single-parent ones (of which 11.6 per cent were lone mothers, and 1.4 per cent, lone fathers) (Family Policy Studies Centre, 1985). If we were to include under this heading those nuclear families where one of the adults opts out of parental responsibilities, the figure would obviously be much larger. In addition, 7 per cent of children under the age of 18 live with their mother and a step-father in families that have been 'reconstituted' by divorce and remarriage. Other differences from the nuclear family pattern are exhibited by *foster families*; here the roles of social parents are played for the children by two adults who had no part in the biological process by which children are born. Furthermore, some children, though obviously having, or having had, biological parents, nevertheless are socialised and supported in an institutional setting; children in local authority care or Dr Barnardo's Homes are obvious examples.

The multi-cultural character of contemporary Britain adds even further variety to this list; e.g. extended families of West Indian origin can range from those in which adult males dominate to those in which they are predominantly absent to those which, save for pre-adolescent boys, are exclusively female. British Asian families often exhibit considerable extension, as can Chinese and Malaysian ones; the collective parenting characteristic of multi-generational families is often substantially reinforced in these cases by the supportive features of close-knit, urban, community life.

So even in our society, the arrangement of kinship relationships we know as the nuclear family is certainly not the *only* way in which the reproduction of children is ensured. However, once we leave our world and look elsewhere, alternative patterns of child-rearing are even more marked. We can use both historical and cross-cultural evidence to demonstrate this.

Before the rise of industrial capitalism in Europe, the nuclear family did not occupy the privileged position it tends to be accorded today. Among property-owning groups, there was concern about inheritance and transmission of property and privileges, and about the social standing of their 'house', and for all classes, the family unit was an important economic unit, involved in the production of goods and services upon which survival depended. But the nuclear family was closely embedded in the community, and not regarded as a special private sphere set apart from the rest of the society.

In *Centuries of Childhood* (1973), Ariès points out that from the fifteenth to the seventeenth centuries the family did not occupy a special place in people's hearts and minds. People married and had children. But, as in other non-industrial contexts, marriage tended to be seen as an alliance, important for the connections it established with others, but hardly the central relationship in people's lives. Marriage did not have the religious connotations it later acquired; as Ariès (1973, p. 345) puts it, 'sexual union, when blessed by marriage, ceased to be a sin, but that was all'. Neither were children creatures around whom their parents' lives revolved. In many European countries it was common practice to send one's children away, at the age of 7 or so, to be 'apprenticed' – that is, to live for up to seven years in another house, where they would be expected to perform menial chores, to be instructed in manners and morals, and perhaps to learn the trade of members of the household. This was regarded as a more suitable preparation for adult life than a coddled existence in the bosom of one's own family. Thus child-rearing was not the prerogative of the child's biological parents and neither were families withdrawn from the wider community.

Ariès argues that the integration of the family into community life was reflected in housing, particularly that of comfortably-off citizens in the towns. Daily life centred on a series of social and business encounters, so that business life, social life and family life overlapped. Houses sheltered a shifting population of servants, apprentices, friends, employees, clergy and clerks, as well as the parents and children themselves; rooms were used interchangeably for eating, sleeping, entertaining and arranging business deals. Many people slept together in one room – parents, children, servants and friends alike. The home was definitely not, as we think of it now, a private place reserved for family and intimate friends; nor did the 'family' have the character of a private and privileged unit devoted to the working through of the conjugal relationship and the rearing of one's own children.

We can summarise this by saying that nuclear families in European history were less *privatised* – less detached from the wider society – than those of today. Since home and work-place were so often identical before industrialisation, child-rearing groups overlapped with productive groups. Children grew up and worked and played alongside a range of kinfolk, acquaintances and friends; socialisation was a sort of natural by-product of community life, rather than a specialised activity taking place in isolation from activities in the public sphere.

In pre-industrial Europe, then, family life was significantly different from the sort we are used to. If we now turn to look at evidence from primitive societies, we can see even greater differences.

Probably the most common kinship arrangements in simpler societies is a system of *unilineal descent*, in which descent groups consist not (as in the case of families in our society) of people related by both blood and marriage, but of blood relations only. Where descent follows *patrilineal* rules, membership of a descent group is acquired through the male line only. People become members of their father's descent group; such groups consist of generations of brothers and sisters, along with the children of the brothers. (The children of the sisters belong not to their mothers', but to their fathers' descent groups.) In the caste of *matrilineal* groupings, descent group membership is acquired through the female line. Here people become members of their mothers' descent group; matrilineal groups consist of generations of brothers and sisters, along with the children of the sisters. The crucial point is that in matrilineal or patrilineal descent systems people related by marriage are not considered as kin in the way in which people who are related by blood are. In contrast with our own society, the major kinship groupings are constructed by excluding marriage altogether.

It is usually the case, even in societies with unilineal descent, that the reproductive and child-rearing unit takes a form more similar to the kinds of families with which we are most familiar. Although descent groups consist only of the mother and her kin, *or* the father and his kin, people usually live, nevertheless, in domestic units based on a conjugal tie – as husbands and wives and children. Where residence follows *virilocal* rules, brothers remain in the descent group home and bring their wives to live with them; the sisters of the descent group eventually leave to marry men living in other descent group homes with *their* brothers. In the case of *uxorilocal* residence, sisters remain at home and import men from other descent groups as husbands, while their brothers leave to marry elsewhere. Residence arrangements such as these enable sexual partners to be in regular contact, while meeting the common cultural requirement that men and women must look *outside* certain categories of kin for their sexual partners. (Where unilineal descent prevails, marriage between members of the same descent group is usually forbidden.) Marriage outside the descent group has the additional advantage of enabling descent groups to establish alliances between their own and other such groups.

So although in unilineal descent systems kinship groups are made up of individuals drawn from only one side of the biological parent relationship, it is amost always the case that people live together as husband and wife in residence units in which some kind of conjugal tie features strongly, thus bearing a much closer resemblance to our own kind of family than the structure of descent groups would suggest.

The universality of the nuclear family?

The presence of residence groups such as these in unilineal societies has often been used as evidence to support the theory that the nuclear family *is* a universal social institution. This argument suggests that whatever the *formal* rules of kinship involved, all societies' child-producing and child-rearing arrangements will resemble nuclear family units. Often the argument is couched in functionalist terms.

In all societies, it is claimed, four basic functions must be performed: the reproductive function, involving conception and childbirth; the sexual function, or regular intercourse to ensure conception; the socialisation function, introducing children to their societies' culture; and the maintenance function, providing economic support and physical protection for children while they mature. It is further claimed that the most efficient arrangement for ensuring their performance is the nuclear family. Regularised sexual contact is said to be best achieved, and reproduction ensured, by the permanent residential attachment of men and women in marriage; the most satisfactory and convenient arrangement for child-rearing is for responsibility to rest with its biological mother; and support and protection of the mother and child is claimed to be most effectively provided by her husband – the child's biological father. Thus the argument is that, whatever the kin group looks like on paper, the requirements of child production and child-rearing mean that in practice the nuclear family will always form the basis of residence groups. Because the nuclear family is in this view best suited to performing functions that are essential for societal survival, it is claimed that the nuclear family *will* always perform these functions – that it will be a universal social institution.

However, there are often crucial differences between the organisation of residence groups in which members of unilineal descent groups live, and the organisation and functioning of our kind of nuclear family. First, there are societies where the conjugal tie is either absent or is not the basis for cohabitation; this happens in matrilineal societies that exhibit *natolocal* residence. Probably the best-known examples in the literature of societies with natolocal residence are the Nayar, the Menangkabau and the Ashanti. The Nayar were a warrior caste who lived in Malabar in South-west India. All Nayar men of fighting age were soldiers and thus away from home, either fighting wars or in barracks, except for brief periods of leave. For a substantial part of their lives, then, and particularly when their reproductive capacity was at its highest, Nayar men would not be available to be active husbands to Nayar women. Although a Nayar woman was always ritually married to a man from a descent group with which her kin wished to have an alliance, reproduction had to take place by other means. Having established an inter-group relationship in this symbolic fashion, the 'marriage' was then ritually dissolved, releasing the woman to bear children for her descent group through an institutional means not connected with marriage. Fox (1967, pp. 100–1) describes it thus:

> The impregnation of women was not a random affair – the woman was free to take as many as twelve 'lovers' or temporary husbands . . . [resulting in] relatively impermanent and non-residential unions . . . The number of lovers may seem rather large, but as many of them at any one time might be away on military duties, the large number gave some reserve strength to the task force. These men had visiting rights with their 'wives', and if one of the men on visiting found another's spear or shield outside the house, then he would go away and try again the next night.

In this method of reproduction the descent group – generations of brothers and sisters and the children of the sisters – coincided with the residence group; the roles of sexual partner, biological parent and social parent (played in the nuclear family by just two people) were far more widely distributed. The sexual relationship was not just restricted to two people: for any one person, a large number of members of the opposite sex (up to twelve for a woman, and any number for men) could be sexual partners. Although for purposes of legitimacy (to establish a child's correct caste origins) one of the woman's lovers was obliged to acknowledge biological paternity, paternity had no other significance and certainly no influence on child-rearing. Social parenthood was thus kept completely with the descent group, or, if you like, 'in the family'. Parenting was not restricted to individuals in a conjugal relationship, nor was it restricted to just *two* adults; parental roles were enacted not by spouses but by generations of siblings.

To put the contrast another way, among the Nayar, sex had nothing to do with marriage, and neither of these had anything to do with the domestic unit, whereas in societies with a nuclear family organisation it is expected that sex and biological parenthood will be based upon a conjugal relationship and that the domestic unit will be established through marriage.

The Menangkabau of Malaya and the Ashanti of Ghana operate similar reproductive arrangements: although in both societies men have permanent wives, they do not cohabit with them, but merely visit them for sexual purposes. So even in these less extreme versions of natolocality, despite the existence of a permanent conjugal tie, the fact that husband and wife do not cohabit has crucial implications for the links between biological and social parenthood. Once again, brothers and sisters form the descent group *and* the residence group, with husbands largely excluded from child-rearing.

Moreover, even in uxorilocal and virilocal domestic units in other unilineal societies where husbands or wives have got a residential foothold in the descent group, there are still significant differences between those child-rearing arrangements and those of the nuclear family. For one thing, they are often much larger units than our nuclear families, so that although a child's biological parents take most responsibility for its rearing, some aspects of social parenthood are attended to by other people. The fact of common residence encourages kin other than the biological parents to take a more active interest in child-rearing. Furthermore, it must be remembered that in unilineal societies only one of the biological parents belongs to the same descent group as their children; other members of that descent group may claim the right to a *greater* involvement with the children than the parent who is an 'outsider'.

Ideas about procreation in matrilineal and patrilineal societies often clearly reflect and support this separation of biological and social parenthood. In many matrilineal societies physiological paternity is either devalued or its role denied altogether. Among the Trobriand Islanders, for example, the biological father is considered to have no part in creating the child; he serves simply to 'open the way' for its eventual birth. The reverse ideology sometimes operates in patrilineal societies, with *women* considered to have no part in creating their own children. This is characteristic of the Tikopia of Polynesia, where the woman is just the 'shelter house' of the child. The Kachin of Burma extend such ideas into the arena of intrafamilial sexual activity; perfectly consistently, Kachin do not classify intercourse with one's mother as incest (she is not your mother after all) but adultery. (Many would argue that beliefs popular in our society about 'maternal instinct' constitute a similar ideological mechanism designed to justify *our* child-rearing arrangements, reliant as they are on women subordinating all other activity to the mother–child bond.)

In contrast to our own society, then, where it is expected that families will be formed on a marital tie, in unilineal societies the marital bond is not the basis for the establishment of descent groups or even residence groups: it is a mechanism by which a group otherwise defined reproduces itself. As Fox (1967, p. 40) puts it:

> The conjugal tie is variable. There are other ways of dealing with the problems of survival than by the institutionalisation of the conjugal tie, and when we see it firmly institutionalised we should ask why this is so rather than take it for granted.

This excursion into historical and cross-cultural studies clearly demonstrates that it is a considerable oversimplification to speak of the 'universality of the nuclear family'. There are in all known societies social units concerned with childbearing, with sexual activity and with the daily activities of eating and sleeping; but these social arrangements differ from one society to the next – in terms of the composition of the largest cohesive group, the composition of the domestic group, the links with the rest of the society, the authority patterns and division of labour within the 'family' – and these differences may often be dramatic.

> The family, particularly the nuclear family, can be seen, through comparative analysis, as just one very specific means of organizing the relationships between parents and children, males and females. It is not, as has so often been claimed, some kind of 'natural', instinctive and 'sacred' unit (Edholm, 1982, p. 177).

7.2 CHANGES IN FAMILY AND KINSHIP IN THE WESTERN WORLD

In Europe in the sixteenth and seventeenth centuries the production of most goods and services was organised on the basis of the household unit and usually involved the efforts of parents, children, and servants and all members of the household. Since the family unit produced most of the goods and services it needed to survive (and sometimes a little extra for sale in local markets), the family of this period was an independent commodity-producing unit – the basic unit of social production.

Over time smaller farming families and cottagers were displaced from their landholdings, with the result that families became more reliant on outside employment – often selling their services to larger landholders. But the most decisive change came from the late eighteenth century onwards, as production of goods became organised through workshops and factories. People left home each day to 'go to work', and earned wages by means of which they hoped to purchase the goods which formerly the family unit might have produced. This change is sometimes referred to as the 'separation of home and work-place'; from being an integral part of family life, work became a separate external activity.

A popular view of the consequences of such changes involves the proposition that the family has been 'stripped' of some of its functions. From being a unit of both production *and* consumption, it is said that the family has become a unit concerned solely with consumption. Goods and services are purchased primarily for the family unit and often consumed within the home, but the family no longer acts as a unit in the production of goods. Rather, individual family members sell their labour to employers who organise the process of production without reference to the family. In short, the family is alleged to have 'lost' the function of production, a change with profound consequences for the nature of family life. For example, the separation of home and work-place signified the general exclusion of women from social production; many women became, for the first time, 'just a housewife', with their husbands as the principal breadwinners.

There are other functions, too, of which the family is said to have been stripped. Recreation, for instance, is less clearly a family affair, especially where adolescents are concerned; recreational opportunities are offered by commercial organisations, from cinemas and discos to clubs and ski resorts, and are purchased on the open market rather than being 'manufactured' at home. Families are also said to have shed certain responsibilities for welfare, since specialised agencies now exist for the care of the sick and the elderly. Most children are exposed to formal schooling, which may at times contradict rather than reinforce the teachings of the family; while early childhood socialisation remains the province of the family, formal education has become the prerogative of school and college.

Now we must be careful about accepting too uncritically this essentially crude picture of the effects of industrialisation on family life. For one thing, long after wage labour became a prime source of income for most households, many families still continued to produce goods for domestic consumption. Even urban families in the early years of the twentieth century often supplemented their diets by keeping a few pigs or chickens, and growing their own vegetables on small plots. The almost absolute dependence of the family on purchased commodities which we experience today is a relatively recent development, coinciding not with the *emergence* of industrial capitalism, but with its *later* stages. Second, the exclusion of women and children from productive activity took place neither as quickly nor as decisively as many have implied. Many women and children were occupied in Britain with the production of goods for sale within their own homes right through to the last quarter of the nineteenth century – aspects of what was called 'domestic' or 'cottage' industry continued as essential contributions to the family income in many areas. Third, the notion that the family is a unit of consumption render invisible the daily work involved in transforming commodities into usable form: purchases must be carried home from the supermarket, carrots must be peeled and cooked, clothes require washing, mending and ironing, floors must be scrubbed. The work done by 'housewives' cannot simply be relegated to the status of 'consumption'. Finally, the idea that, with the rise of factory production, men kissed their wives and children goodbye and trooped merrily off to work, only rejoining their idle families at the end of the day, is completely mistaken. As Harris (1977, p. 86) points out:

> Industrialisation did not result immediately in a differentiation between domestic and industrial labour tied to gender, and the isolation of the family. On the contrary, all members of the family were employed in the factories and the mines, and women and children were only gradually excluded against the vigorous opposition of the factory owners and very often of the husbands and parents.

Sociologists have also offered objections to the view that the passing of leisure and welfare 'functions' into the hands of commercial agencies and state-controlled organisations has undermined the family as an institution.

First, writers such as Fletcher (1966) argue that the view of the multi-purpose 'pre-industrial' family is a fiction; the harsh realities of everyday life for the majority of people in pre-industrial, and early industrial, periods meant that most of the so-called functions such as welfare, education or recreation were largely neglected anyway – the struggle to earn a living under harsh conditions ruled out all but the most rudimentary forms of nursing, education or recreation. Second, sociologists such as Parsons (1959) assert that the family has become a more specialised institution, and that the loss of non-essential functions enables the family to perform its central responsibilities more efficiently, including basic child care. Third, Litwak (1960a, 1960b) and others point out that the family still lays a foundation for the performance of non-essential functions described above; the most obvious example is education, where the early training provided in the family is an important – even essential – foundation for success in the system of formal education.

Arguments such as these have been useful correctives to simplistic views about the waning significance of the family. However, in an effort to counteract popular notions about familial decline, some sociologists have promoted an equally one-sided view, that of the modern family as uniquely well adapted to meet the requirements of industrial society and the needs of individuals: the changes in family and kinship which resulted from the rise of industrial capitalism have been interpreted as the 'march of progress'. Fletcher, Parsons, Goode, Young and Willmott, and the historian Shorter are among those who appear to subscribe to a 'march-of-progress' model of family change in one version or another.

March-of-progress theories

These theories tend to isolate two aspects of change in family life as particularly significant. One of these is a marked alteration in relationships between the nuclear family and other kin – a move, that is, away from an emphasis upon extended kinship groupings and towards an emphasis upon conjugally based ties. The second is a radical change in the quality of the conjugal relationship; industrial capitalism is seen to have encouraged egalitarianism in marriage, a fundamental shift from pre-industrial society where the patriarch apparently reigned supreme. Furthermore, although the works of the writers mentioned above differ in emphasis and in subtlety, all tend to see the changes accompanying the transition from 'pre-industrial' to 'industrial' families as *advantageous*. Contradictions and strains inherent in contemporary family life are played down, and the focus is clearly upon the modern family as a vehicle for individual happiness and self-fulfilment, and for effective realisation of societal goals.

'March-of-progress' theorists

Young and Willmott

Perhaps the simplest description of the march of progress is provided by Young and Willmott in *The Symmetrical Family* (1973). They posit three distinct historical stages through which British families have passed. In stage 1 (the pre-industrial phase) the family was stable, it was centred on production, and the family members were linked by economic necessity; by virtue of his control over production, the father was undisputed master of the household. Stage 2 (from 1750 to 1900) is characterised as a stage of disruption, when the process of industrialisation threatened to tear the family apart. As home and work-place were separated, and family members became individual wage-labourers, the interaction between them was correspondingly less intense. Fathers were often absent from the family, driven out by overcrowding and forced out to work. Mothers assumed the burden of care and emotional support for the family as a whole, as well as responsibility for stretching the often meagre wages; the difficulties entailed in mothers' lot drove women in urban centres to seek the aid of female kinfolk, thus giving rise to new types of kinship networks from which men were by and large excluded.

Stage 3 began around 1900, and is still, according to Young and Willmott, spreading from the middle to the working class. Family and society have achieved a new equilibrium, and the family is once again stable after the disruptive effects of industrialisation – though its characteristics differ from those of the pre-industrial family. In the new 'symmetrical family' the conjugal pair and their children are very much centred on the home, and spend much of their time together there; the extended family counts for less in people's social horizon, while the nuclear family has pre-eminence; there is greater equality between women and men, and less role segregation by sex. Young and Willmott emphasise the 'mutual adaptation' between family and economy in the twentieth century. Cohesive families fuel the labour force of the industrial system, and the domestic goods available for use in the home provide a bond uniting family members:

> The more united family has provided the incentive for people to exert themselves in the new industrial system, and the new system has made the family more united by giving it some elementary rights in property (including the machines built to the scale of the smallest human group) which are held or at least enjoyed in common by its members ... After a long period at odds with each other, the family and technology have achieved a mutual adaptation (Young and Willmott, 1973, p. 271).

Ronald Fletcher

In *The Family and Marriage in Britain* (1966) Fletcher is concerned to demolish the popular notion that the family is in decline. The notion of a long-gone golden age of family life – with the parents and children gathered harmoniously around the fire in the evenings, with children respectful and obedient, with wife and husband secure in their traditional roles and sticking together through thick and thin – this vision is, according to Fletcher, an unrealistic stereotype.

To correct this romanticised picture, Fletcher emphasises negative aspects of the family in the pre-industrial and Victorian periods. For example, he documents in detail how the majority of families in pre-industrial England had to work unceasingly simply in order to survive, and how this, combined with lack of recreational or educational resources and poor housing conditions, made 'happy family life' on the scale described above virtually impossible. Again, looking at Victorian families, Fletcher emphasises that while the bourgeois Victorian family may have been cohesive, solidarity was often based on the tyranny of the father, the virtual enslavement of the mother ('a decorative bauble', in Fletcher's description), and the repression of the children ('seen and not heard'). Set against this backdrop, the twentieth-century family appears in Fletcher's work as a rewarding institution catering both for the satisfaction of societal needs and for individual self-realisation and autonomy.

Edward Shorter

In a somewhat similar vein, Shorter portrays the 'intimate life' of traditional European society (roughly, the late-sixteenth to late-eighteenth centuries) in wholly negative terms. In *The Making of the Modern Family*

(1977) Shorter asserts that courtship was based only on instrumental considerations: that the relationships between spouses were mainly contractual, with male peasants caring more for their animals than they did for their wives; that mothers were indifferent about their children's welfare; and that the community constantly interfered with family privacy, inhibiting the chances of loving interaction between family members.

Shorter argues that the emergence of capitalism broke the bounds of local economies, and hence freed family and community life from traditional constraints. This 'freedom' allowed 'natural' emotion to flourish; wage labour encouraged not only economic independence of young people from their kinfolk but also promoted individualistic values and, eventually, rising affluence. The immediate result was the first great *sexual revolution* (between 1750 and 1850), which began with pre-marital experiment among young people, and only later spilled over into the search for sexual fulfilment in married life; later consequences were equality of sexual and marriage partners, the emergence of maternal love, and domesticity or privatisation of nuclear families.

Shorter believes that capitalism brought about a variety of changes in values and attitudes which transformed the custom-ridden, unfeeling traditional family into the warm affectionate family of modern times. Like Fletcher, then, Shorter paints such a bleak picture of traditional family life that the changes allegedly wrought by capitalism are glorified in contrast. For example:

> The nuclear family was a nest. Warm and sheltering, it kept the children secure from the pressure of the outside adult world, and gave the men an evening refuge from the icy blast of competition. And as the nuclear family rose in the nineteenth century, women liked it too, because it let them pull back from the grinding exactions of farm work, or the place at the mill, and devote themselves to child care. So everyone huddled happily within those secure walls, serene about the dinner table, united in the Sunday outing (Shorter, 1977, p. 272).

William Goode

In *World Revolution and Family Patterns* (1963) Goode uses data from many different countries to try to isolate trends which he views as universal. Industrialisation seems usually to be accompanied, he argues, by a trend towards a 'conjugal family system' – relatively isolated nuclear families which retain links to grandparents and grandchildren – and to greater equality of status between husbands and wives. The development of free labour markets (where there are few constraints preventing individuals from selling their labour to a particular employer), he suggests, makes it possible for individuals to earn their living without the consent or co-operation of their kin. In Goode's analysis industrial capitalism resulted in greater individual freedom – by which he means primarily freedom from the authority of parents or of more inclusive kin groups. Economic independence provided the basis for the realisation of values of individual liberty; for example, Goode attributes the rising legal and political status of women in the West during the past fifty years to the extension to women of notions about individual freedom, though he adds that this was possible only when the precondition of *economic* independence was met.

Talcott Parsons

The theory most often associated with the question of the fit between industrial society and nuclear family systems is that of Talcott Parsons. His argument – that a nuclear family system is uniquely well adapted to the needs of an industrial society – has two prongs. First, he suggests that the economic differentiation which is so characteristic of industrial societies (the multiplicity of different occupations, with different incomes and life-styles attached) is incompatible with the maintenance of extended families but ideally served by the nuclear family. If the family is restricted to the small nuclear group with a single primary breadwinner who is also head of the family, Parsons argues, potential conflicts between members of an extended family working in different jobs are avoided – conflicts, for example, over where the family should live, or arising from a disparity in the incomes and life-styles associated with the occupations. Here Parsons is suggesting that only a nuclear family system eliminates economic differentation within the family and thus prevents the competitive elements of industrial wage-labour from undermining family solidarity; at the same time, the nuclear family is a small enough unit to be geographically and economically mobile, as an industrial economy demands.

The second part of his argument concerns the need to resolve a conflict between the values which underpin economic and 'public' activities in industrial societies and those which characterise family relationships. According to Parsons, families must inevitably be characterised by values such as *ascription* (an emphasis upon *who* people are) and *particularism* (priority for special relationships); for example, it is expected that parents should love and care for *their* offspring above all others, regardless of how 'successful' or 'attractive' these children are by public standards. However, Parsons argues, these same values are unacceptable and harmful in the public sphere; for example, in economic life, hiring, firing and promotion are supposed to take place according to individual merit only. In other words, for Parsons, the efficient operation of the public sphere depends upon constant application of the values of achievement and universalism – the opposite of those which characterise kinship relations.

Disruption would occur if kin obligations and occupational obligations overlapped – for example, where one member of the family was a supervisor and another a labourer in the same firm. Such conflicts are avoided, Parsons argues, by (i) segregating the nuclear family from other kin, and (ii) segregating the nuclear family from the public sphere (except for the father being the principal breadwinner). Intrusion of family values into work is thus avoided, and work values do not disrupt the solidarity of the family; people do not have constantly to choose between loyalty to kin and the impersonal standards demanded by their occupational roles.

From this analysis of the connections between family and economy, Parsons concludes that an arrangement whereby the nuclear family is structurally isolated from its kin is functional to the workings of industrial society. The norms governing family life dictate that our first and primary obligation will be to our spouse and dependent children. We *may* decide to care for ageing parents, or to take an unmarried brother into our home, but there are no clear-cut norms saying that we *should* do so – the decision is optional. The sort of relationship we establish with kin, other than our spouses and dependent children, is left largely to circumstances and personal choice.

Parsons's analysis of the 'fit' between family and society depends as much on the accuracy of his portrayal of the economy as on his portrayal of family systems, and it can be questioned on these grounds.

Is it the case, for example, that industrial economies 'require' of their labour force a higher degree of geographical mobility than other types of society? Certainly, at specific periods in pre-industrial Europe peasants and landless labourers were forced to move frequently in search of their livelihood, and the common image of pre-industrial populations as geographically static is grossly exaggerated. Moreover, in mature industrial societies it may well be the case that urbanisation reduces the necessity for geographical mobility, by making available to people a variety of jobs, resources or opportunities with a fairly narrow locality. Thus it is possible the contrast between a relatively static pre-industrial population and a relatively mobile industrial population has been greatly exaggerated. Also, the improvement of mass communications and transportation facilities which often accompanies industrialisation makes it possible for more people to work at a distance from their home – witness commuters – or to maintain close contact with kin who are geographically dispersed.

It is possible, too, that the emphasis upon *social* mobility is greatly exaggerated. First, social mobility of a short-range variety may have been more common in pre-industrial societies than simple typologies would lead us to expect. Second, there are more obstacles to social mobility than some would have us believe; 'achievement' and 'universalism' in the public sphere are paid lip-service but are mediated by the ability of privileged groups to translate their privilege into 'achievement' for their children – or, as in the case of the propertied upper class, to transmit their advantages to their children directly in the form of inherited wealth. In other words, in capitalist societies social mobility seems to be limited to a level which does not threaten the privileges of dominant groups, and it is not surprising that kinship plays an important part in this process. Lupton and Wilson (1959) show quite clearly how in British society kinship is used as a basis for recruitment to elite positions. The extent to which the economy 'requires' occupational selection on the basis of 'achievement' and 'universalism' can certainly be called into question.

However, these are criticisms of Parsons's model of the economy. What really concerns us here is his account of *family* structure and relationships; we will now look at this account, and those of the other 'march-of-progress' theorists, in the light of historical and comparative evidence.

The evaluation of 'march-of-progress' theories

There are two crucial sets of questions to be asked. First, we must consider whether such theories are, in broad outline, historically accurate. Have industrialisation and capitalism been the motor of family change, and have the changes taken roughly the form suggested by Parsons, Goode, Young and Willmott, Fletcher and Shorter? In detail, we may ask whether the rise of industrial capitalism in Europe resulted in (i) the attenuation of kinship ties, such that extended families of pre-industrial periods have given way to relatively isolated nuclear families in the present, and (ii) a marked change in conjugal relationships in the direction of greater equality between husband and wife, marked reduction in social distance between the conjugal pair, and a greater sharing of power and authority as well as of household and familial responsibilities. Second, we must consider whether it really is the case that the nuclear family of contemporary societies represents a marked *advance* of individual freedom and social effectiveness, a successful accommodation of family and society.

The accuracy of 'march-of-progress' accounts of family change

Relationships between nuclear families and their kinfolk: does industrialisation promote the attentuation of kinship ties?

One of the foremost sources of data on kinship in pre-industrial Europe is the work of the Cambridge Group for the History of Population and Social Structure, of whom Peter Laslett is a prominent representative. Laslett and his associates emphasise the use of quantitative data in the historical study of the family, and one of their primary sources of data is the quasi-censuses, or listings of inhabitants of communities, compiled in periods ranging from the sixteenth to the nineteenth centuries. After examining such data for one hundred English communities, Laslett launched a profound attack on the view that industrialisation brought about a decrease in average family size.

During the period surveyed, his data suggest, average household size in the communities analysed stayed fairly constant at approximately 4.75 persons per household; in other parts of Europe, too, from the late Middle Ages, the predominant form of household was the nuclear family plus servants, with even modest rural families having one female servant living in. As Laslett says: 'There is no sign of the large coresidential family group of the traditional peasant world giving way to the small, nuclear, conjugal household of modern industrial society' (in Laslett and Wall, 1972, p. 126).

This evidence fairly puts paid to the notion that the large, co-operative extended family household preceded the onset of industrialisation in Western Europe. However, the information available from quasi-censuses leaves certain ambiguities. For one thing it seems likely that, for a brief period of the family life-cycle, households may have accommodated other kin, such as grandparents or nieces and nephews, so that a form of extended family household was a common part of each person's experience. For another we do not know – and quasi-census data cannot tell us – whether the prevalence of nuclear family households in pre-industrial Europe was by choice (representing a normative ideal) or an unwelcome necessity, with factors such as patterns of landholding preventing people from living in an extended form which they might have preferred. Finally, this evidence tells us only about the household or residence group, but kin may co-operate with one another, and have close and privileged relationships, even though they do not live together. Nuclear families may, for all we know, have had a warm and vital interaction with kinfolk in nearby or even adjacent households in pre-industrial times – just as we find that nuclear families living in separate households today maintain close contacts with kin outside their home.

In *Family Life and Illicit Love* (1977) Laslett raises the possibility that households became more complex in the course of the industrial revolution. Indeed, a study of Preston in Lancashire, by Michael Anderson (1971), using census and other data for 1851, confirms this suggestion. Anderson notes that the proportion of Preston households in which kin other than the nuclear family members resided was higher than figures available for earlier centuries, or than statistics for twentieth-century Britain. Anderson suggests several factors which may have contributed to the willingness of nuclear families to 'take in' kinfolk. One such factor was the availability of work at more than subsistence wages for women in the cotton mills of Preston; it was financially beneficial for a family with young children to take in a relative, perhaps one from the surrounding rural area, who could be responsible for care of the children and day-to-day housekeeping, thus making it possible for the mother of the family to earn wages worth more than the cost of feeding and sheltering the relative. The presence or absence of kinfolk seemed to fluctuate with employment opportunities and wage levels in ways that implied how important these factors are in influencing family structure. Moreover, the better-paid factory workers, such as overseers, were more likely to have relatives in their homes of working age, suggesting that perhaps jobs were found for these relations by their Preston kin. Anderson's work thus raises the point that, far from inhibiting geographical mobility, kinship networks may facilitate it, by providing a base for newcomers to an area (in this case, probably, a base for rural people coming for the first time to industrial wage-labour) and contacts to assist them with settling in. Anderson's work underlines, too, the significance of kin as a resource to draw upon in meeting recurring life crises – temporary unemployment, homelessness, and so on. He emphasises clearly the effects of material conditions on the range of options that people have at their disposal in the use of kinship.

Kinship in contemporary societies. Post-war studies of Europe and America have demonstrated, in a variety of contexts, the continuing vitality of kinship ties, particularly those linking married couples to their families of origin. In Bethnal Green, the working-class urban community studied by Young and Willmott in the 1950s (*Family and Kinship in East London*, 1962) kinship networks constituted an important basis for community solidarity and sociability. Among married people interaction with kin was frequent and highly valued. Of married men with parents alive, 30 per cent had seen their father, and 31 per cent their mother, within the twenty-four hours prior to interview; of married women, 48 per cent had seen their fathers, and 55 per cent their mothers, within the previous twenty-four-hour period (Young and Willmott, 1962, p. 46). Here, as in the Ship Street area of Liverpool (Kerr, 1958), kinship interaction was skewed towards women. Mothers often helped their married daughters find accommodation, and provided regular assistance with baby-sitting, preparing tea for sons-in-law, taking clothes to the laundry or doing bits of shopping; they were the first source of help and advice in 'crises' such as illness or the birth of a child. Although there was some reciprocal aid in the form of loans or help in acquiring jobs between fathers, married sons, and adult brothers, Young and Willmott were in no doubt that the linchpin of the entire kinship network was the companionship and domestic help shared by mothers and their married daughters. Because of the residential stability of areas like Bethnal Green, a high proportion of people had kinfolk living within easy reach. Interaction and mutual aid was made all the more likely by the geographical proximity of kin; but, in addition, the affective and material significance of kinship ties may have contributed to the decisions of young married couples to remain as near as possible to their kin.

The relocation of many working-class families in new towns or overspill estates gave opportunity to consider the effects of geographical mobility on patterns of kinship behaviour. Young and Willmott's (1962) study of families from Bethnal Green who had resettled in the Essex estate of

Greenleigh appeared to bear out the view that geographical mobility attentuates kinships ties. Since people were relocated as nuclear family units, leaving most of their kin behind, mobility did indeed herald a reduction in interaction with kin; women seemed to experience particularly keenly the relative isolation from their mothers and sisters. Although some husbands could manage visits to kinfolk on their way to or from work in the East End of London, and although family reunions were arranged when possible, the major impression given by Young and Willmott is of the nuclear family drawing back on itself, from the community-centred life of Bethnal Green to the more privatised, home-centred life of Greenleigh. Goldthorpe and Lockwood's (1968a, 1968b, 1969) descriptions of the 'affluent workers' of Luton offered a similar theme of privatised nuclear families, with interaction with kin curtailed by geographical separation.

However, the attenuation of kinship ties should not be regarded as an inevitable effect of geographical mobility. In the first place, disruption of interaction does not necessarily imply the destruction of the relationship. For example, as Rosser and Harris (1965) note, kinship obligations are often so strong that people will extend hospitality and help to a visiting relative with whom they have only a slight acquaintance. Second, geographical separation becomes less of a barrier to interaction and help when standards of living are higher. In the Woodford area of London, for example, middle-class people were able to counteract the separating effects of distance by their greater access to cars and telephones, and by more spacious housing which made prolonged visits from relatives possible (Willmott and Young, 1971). Third, the geographical separation of nuclear families from their kin in new housing estates may be a temporary phase; if housing conditions permit, as the new residents pass through the family life-cycle, their children may grow up, marry and settle down near them, thus creating a new network of kin in the area. Willmott (1963) argues that at the time of its initial settlement in the 1920s and 1930s, Dagenham may have been much like Greenleigh of the 1950s; however, forty years on, to some of its residents it was 'like the East End reborn'.

Although studies of working-class kinship patterns have demonstrated conclusively that kinship networks can indeed flourish in urban industrial centres, it has sometimes been argued that only middle-class families, with their higher rates of geographical mobility, could provide a satisfactory test of the 'isolated nuclear family' hypothesis. Yet, as has already been pointed out in connection with the study of Woodford, the greater material resources of many middle-class families may make geographical separation from kin less of an obstacle to interaction than it would be for families who are less well off. For example, in Hubert's (1970) study of the north London suburb of Highgate, few of the couples interviewed had kin in the immediate area; nevertheless, both sentimental and practical involvement was strong, with mothers occasionally coming from abroad to help their daughters at the birth of a child. Moreover, the Highgate couples travelled frequently to see kinfolk, though they did so selectively; geographical distance was used as an excuse for failing to visit kin they did not like, while acting as no barrier to visiting kin of whom they were fond.

Studies by Sussman (1953) in New Haven, Connecticut, and by Bell (1968) in Swansea have observed that young middle-class couples assert strongly their autonomy from kin, and that kin in turn agree that the younger people should 'stand on their own two feet'. In both studies, however, parents provided their married children with considerable material aid, tactfully presented so as not to endanger the illusion of autonomy. Bell reports that even such extravagant assistance as central heating, a car or a house – though obviously of importance to the younger family's standard of living – might be delicately presented as Christmas or birthday gifts. Bell also makes the point that while geographical separation does not automatically rupture kinship networks, or prohibit mutual aid between kin, it does make day-to-day domestic help between mothers, daughters and sisters less likely; the balance of aid tends to shift (in families that are well enough off to make this possible) to the father/son or father/son-in-law relationship, and to financial rather than domestic help.

In reviewing the evidence from these studies, three additional points should be noted. First, the difference between middle-class and working-class families can easily be exaggerated. While Bell's research looked mainly at upper-middle-class families, Rosser and Harris's (1965) work in Swansea found little difference in kinship behaviour between those in their sample who were 'working class' and those who could be described as 'middle class'; for both strata the 'extended family' provided a focus of identity, and a living insurance policy, a resource that could be drawn upon – often the first resort – during times of unemployment, money shortage, bereavement, illness, and so on.

Second, while it has been emphasised that extended kinship networks can and do persist in the face of geographical mobility, it should also be noted that kin can and do actually *promote* both geographical and social mobility. As Anderson (1971) argued for nineteenth-century Lancashire, and Litwak (1960a, 1960b) for twentieth-century USA, kinfolk can provide a base for relatives who are newly geographically mobile; moreover, parents may actually help to finance the move of their married children to a more advantageous location or into a more promising career.

Third, the emphasis upon working-class and middle-class families should not be allowed to obscure the relevance of kinship ties to the cohesion of the upper class. For example, the intricate ties of blood and marriage between Cabinet Ministers, Directors of the Bank of England, and Directors of City banks and other powerful institutions traced by Lupton and Wilson (1959) offer some indication of the extent to which kinship links 'top decision-makers'.

The relationship of nuclear families to their extended kin: conclusions

From a consideration of this historical and contemporary evidence our conclusion must be that there is no simple pattern of extended families in pre-industrial societies, and nuclear families in industrial ones. Instead, we find from historical evidence that, prior to industrialisation in both Europe and America, the majority of the population lived in nuclear family units; the nuclear family was then, as it is today, an important domestic grouping. Furthermore, in terms of the composition of the usual coresident group, the evidence suggests that there has been continuity through from pre-industrial times to industrialisation. In advanced industrial societies extended kin relationships – particularly those between adult offspring and their parents – appear to continue to play an important part in contemporary family life. Such relationships may be disrupted by aspects of contemporary industrialism – e.g. by geographical relocation – but they appear capable of surviving this sort of temporary disruption; indeed, contrary to some views, such kin ties may facilitate geographical and social mobility by providing assistance for individuals and nuclear families who need it.

Conjugal relationships: has there been an increase in egalitarian marriage due to the effects of industrialisation and/or capitalism?

As we have seen, the 'march-of-progress' theorists have, by and large, argued that the later stages of industrialisation are marked by the rise of egalitarian marriage, in which the roles and power of husband and wife are more interdependent and less one-sided. For Young and Willmott (1973), for example, 'the symmetrical family' is one of the characteristics of the 'third stage' of British family development. Though 'symmetry' is not defined in a rigorous way, it seems to involve the gradual achievement of balance between the normative obligations of husbands and wives. The strongest indication of this is the erosion of the 'traditional' division of labour by sex; men are more involved in domestic work (housework, shopping and childcare) and women are more involved in paid work outside the home. The emergence of the symmetrical family is linked also to better standards of living, which make it possible for husbands as well as wives to focus more of their energies and aspirations on their homes and families, and to the demise of the extended family as a significant moral force in many people's lives, such that both men and women are thrown back more on each other's company and assistance in marriage. The image of a 'symmetrical family' brings to mind the popular notion of 'dual-career couples', where both husband and wife combine challenging careers with a deep commitment to their joint domestic life; and in fact, Willmott and Young argue explicitly that the symmetrical pattern is most characteristic of middle-class couples, but will, they predict, gradually 'trickle down' to husbands and wives in the working class.

Willmott and Young's arguments overlap with those of many other writers who emphasise changes in the emotional quality of conjugal relationships: Gavron (1968), Shorter (1977) and Fletcher (1966) all describe a trend towards greater closeness and intimacy in marital relationships – towards couples doing things together, rather than apart; towards sharing ideas and hopes and leisure activities; towards being friends and companions, as well as lovers and spouses. This sort of relationship is what is meant when writers refer to the modern companionate marriage; it is partly what is implied by the term joint conjugal roles.

In her influential study *Family and Social Network*, Bott (1957) identified two types of conjugal role-relationship – segregated conjugal roles and joint conjugal roles – which are perhaps most usefully imagined as the ends of a continuum, with numerous possibilities lying in between the two extremes. Where couples have segregated conjugal role relationships, husbands and wives inhabit separate and distinct social and working worlds, linked only by their reciprocal obligations and rights: each spouse has his or her own set of friends, and 'men's work' and 'women's work', inside and outside the home, are strictly differentiated. Within a joint conjugal role relationship, on the other hand, the demarcation between husband's world and wife' world is far less clear-cut. Husbands and wives do chores around the home interchangeably, and are highly flexible about which sex is responsible for which sort of task. They share most friends in common, entertain together, take their recreation together, and join together in the making of decisions.

Within her sample of London families, Bott found joint conjugal role-relationships to be more common amongst middle-class couples than amongst working-class ones. She explains this by reference to the impact of geographical mobility, and different types of social networks, on family life. Working-class couples, at the time she did her study, often lived in the same geographical area for much of their lives; their social network of friends, kin and acquaintances, built up over a lifetime, were generally tight-knit – i.e., the members of the network knew each other well and were in regular contact. Such a network could be influential in two ways in maintaining a traditional separation between men's worlds and women's worlds: first, the existence of such a network ensures that both husband and wife will have persons of their own sex to call upon for companionship or help with domestic tasks; second, the closeness of the network acts as a check, a form of social control, on the activities of the conjugal pair, and, by informal sanctions such as teasing, prevents the couple from drifting away from a 'traditional' division of labour. Hence, in Bott's views, the geographical stability of working-class families helped to maintain a tendency towards segregated conjugal role-relationships.

The opposite may be true, Bott argued, of middle-class couples: mobility (both geographical and social) scattered friends and acquaintances, and tended to leave middle-class couples with a loosely-connected network of friends. Under these circumstances, the more rigid demarcations regarding both tasks and leisure were likely to break down; husbands and wives would not be drawn away from each other by the attraction of a single-sex network, nor could they depend on their social network for companionship or assistance. Accordingly, husbands and wives more often came to rely upon other, and to construct a conjugal relationship in which 'jointness' – the sharing of activities and leisure – would be highly valued.

At first sight, applying Bott's framework to research done in Britain in the post-war decades would seem to support the march-of-progress contention of a strong trend towards egalitarianism in marriage. Both the study of a Yorkshire mining community, described below, and Tunstall's study of *The Fishermen* (1962), were conducted in communities dominated by one kind of manual employment, with low rates of mobility; these circumstances appear to generate strong single-sex networks and the kind of segregated relationships which Bott's theory would lead us to expect.

In *Coal is Our Life*, by Dennis, Henriques and Slaughter (1956), the relationship between spouses was described as highly contractual: that is, both husbands and wives had certain fixed and non-negotiable obligations, and being a good husband or a good wife consisted almost entirely in fulfilling these contractual duties. Husbands were expected to provide for their families, by giving a certain fixed proportion of their weekly pay packet to the wife as housekeeping money (her 'wages'). Beyond that it appears that little was expected of the husband. Wives were expected to use the housekeeping money and their own labour and ingenuity to provide a comfortable and harmonious home for husbands to seek refreshment in after a hard day at work. The wife's life, her schedule, was almost entirely dictated by the timing of the husband's commitments; whatever shift he was on, whatever time he returned home, she was expected to be waiting with a hot meal and a clean change of clothes.

Husbands spent most of their free time outside the home, at sports events or clubs with their male friends and workmates. Their commitment and loyalty to their workmates is portrayed as deep and overriding most other commitments; it stemmed partly from the experience of growing up together in the same community, and partly from their sharing of the arduous work of mining, in which not only the size of a man's pay packet but his very life might depend on the quick-wittedness and energy of the members of his work-team. Thus occupation is seen as a major influence on the type of friendships which cut across the conjugal relationship. The existence of segregated conjugal roles was reinforced by two other factors: first, the ideology that women, being 'incapable' of the difficult work of mining, are somewhat inferior beings not entirely worthy of the same respect as workmates; and second, the taboo against men showing (at least publicly) any display of tenderness towards women. The operation of this taboo during courtship resulted in many young men making up excuses to their friends for seeking out the company of women – excuses which reinforced the general disrespect for women, by suggesting publicly that they were only useful 'for one thing'.

However, since all industrial societies develop away from such a reliance on basic heavy industry, manual workers increasingly find themselves living in less homogeneous urban centres than those described by Dennis and his colleagues. Evidence from studies conducted in 'new towns', amongst people who have been geographically mobile, often show a greater home-centredness by men, and more privatised family life, which appears closer to Bott's joint conjugal role pattern.

For example, in Greenleigh, the new town housing estate to which many people from the East End of London were rehoused in the 1950s, Young and Willmott (1962) found that one immediate effect of the move was an increase in 'home-centredness', particularly for the men. The absence of their local public house, the lack of new friends and the reduction of spending money caused by more expensive rents and rates encouraged many husbands who previously spent a great deal of their leisure time outside the home with friends to rely instead on the company of their wives and children. The new houses, too, absorbed more time and energy, and encouraged many men into do-it-yourself projects around the home. Both husband and wife were cut off from their earlier closely knit networks; the isolated Greenleigh spouses were, accordingly, thrown back on each other both for company and for help with chores. This example seems most effectively to support Bott's assertion of a connection between mobility, networks and conjugal role relationships. It is confirmed further by Goldthorpe and Lockwood's 'affluent worker' studies, which suggest that workers in Luton, most of whom were geographically mobile and had young families, were relatively 'privatised', preferring to spend their leisure within the nuclear family and steering clear of close commitments outside.

But in spite of some support for the proposition that marriages are becoming more equal – and that this trend began amongst middle-class couples, and is filtering down – this view has been sharply challenged, on three major grounds: first, that it is not supported by empirical evidence about the division of labour in the household; second, that it ignores the distribution of power and authority in marriage; third, that it underestimates the impact on marital relationships of structured inequalities within society.

The division of labour in the household

Willmott and Young's own evidence in *The Symmetrical Family* regarding the household division of labour gives little reason for confidence in the idea that men and women increasingly take an equal share of responsibility for domestic life. They report, for example, that 72 per cent of married men in their sample 'help their wife' in the home in some way other than washing up at least once a week; included in that 72 per cent would be any husband who took his son on an outing on Saturday afternoon, or who made breakfast once a week – some indication of husbands' involvement in domestic tasks, but certainly not evidence of equal sharing. The interesting thing, in fact, is that less than three-quarters of husbands can meet even this loose criterion for participation in household work. Moreover, as Oakley has pointed out, the fact that husbands are seen by Young and Willmott to be 'helping' their wives indicates quite clearly where, in the authors' eyes and probably in the respondents' eyes, the responsibility for domestic work continues to lie. Oakley (1974, pp. 100–1) concludes:

> As long as the blame is laid on the woman's head for an empty larder or a dirty house it is not meaningful to talk about marriage as a 'joint' or 'equal' partnership. The same holds of parenthood. So long as mothers and not fathers are judged by their children's appearance and behaviour . . . symmetry remains a myth.

More convincing evidence than Willmott and Young's of the household division of labour has been amassed in recent feminist research. Hartmann (1981) summarises the results of a range of studies conducted in the United States in the 1960s and 1970s. She reports that women who are full-time homemakers average 50 to 60 hours a week on household tasks; their husbands, who do much of the gardening and car maintenance, average 11 hours a week. Where there are young children in the home, the work-load of full-time homemakers increases to 70 hours a week; their husbands spend, on average, 5 hours on childcare, but reduce correspondingly the time they spend on other household tasks. Women who are employed part-time or full-time tend to cut down on housework, but their total work-week (paid work and unpaid work combined) still increases substantially; the husbands of employed women participate more in housework than husbands of full-time homemakers, but their contributions in terms of time were small. Hartmann concludes that women are not, apparently, able to translate increased wage packets into decreased work weeks. Re-entry of married women into employment has extended women's responsibilities for 'men's work', but it has not been matched by an equalisation of husbands' responsibilities within the home.

This American evidence is matched by studies done in Britain of dual-career families – the type that might be considered, on the basis of Willmott and Young's argument, to exemplify the new symmetry in marriage. In a survey of over 400 couples, where both partners were doctors, Elston (1980) found that male doctors received far more help from their spouses than female doctors did. Some household responsibilities were jointly shared by a minority of couples, and the partners could afford in some cases to hire help with housecleaning or childcare. But the extent of asymmetry in spouses' contribution to the household is indicated in Table 7.1, which shows, for example, that while 85 per cent of doctor wives report doing the shopping themselves, only 1 per cent of doctor husbands so report.

TABLE 7.1

The division of labour in marriages where both partners are doctors

	Proportion of doctors reporting that they undertook the task alone	
	Female doctors (%)	Male doctors (%)
Shopping	85	1
Arranging social activities	39	4
Household repairs	10	71
Cooking	81	1
Housecleaning	51	1
Looking after sick child	80	2

Source: M. Elston, 'Medicine: Half our Future Doctors?' (1980, Table 5.2); adapted from M. Webb, 'The Labour Market', in I. Reid and E. Wormald (eds), *Sex Differences in Britain*, London, Grant McIntyre (1982, Table 6.22, p.146).

Rapoport and Rapoport's (1976) study *Dual Career Families Re-Examined* also focused upon couples where both husbands and wives had professional or business careers. They found that, although participants endorsed the dual-career pattern, the wife's career was seen as something she did primarily for her own satisfaction; both spouses placed upon the wife's shoulders the responsibility for dealing with any demands or problems created by her work – the problems, for example, of finding alternative childcare, dealing with sick children, doing housework or arranging for housework to be done. Husbands were tolerant of their wives careers, as long as those careers did not interfere with their own needs. On the basis of this evidence, Rapoport and Rapoport challenge the notion that equality – or even symmetricality – can be expected to spread from the top of the occupational hierarchy to the bottom. If wives whose careers are fulfilling and provide considerable status and income are still regarded primarily as housewives and mothers in their own households, what likelihood is there that things will be different for women in lower status, less well paid jobs? In fact, it can be argued, to the extent that women retain the bulk of domestic responsibility even when fully employed, the incentive to seek a career will be correspondingly reduced.

Power and authority in marriage

Dair Gillespie (1972) and Stephen Edgell (1980) are among those who insist that equality in marriage is most effectively assessed, not by the division of labour within the household, nor by the degree of 'closeness' couples display, but by references to the distribution of marital power – the relative capacity of each spouse to determine the course of their shared life. In *Middle Class Couples*, Edgell analysed processes of decision-making among salaried professional workers (scientists, academics, etc.) and their wives, most of whom were engaged in rearing children, and found clear evidence of a marked imbalance of power. Many of the decisions which couples think of as 'very important' – those, such as whether to move or how overall financial management should be organised, which provide a framework for other family activities – tend to be taken by husbands alone; husbands often 'consult' their wives, but in most cases the final decision, and the power of veto, is his. Some 'important' or 'very important' decisions – about holidays, or children's education – tend to be taken jointly by husbands and wives. No important decisions tend to be taken by wives alone. The areas of decision-making where wives have sole responsibility tend to be those – concerning interior decoration, children's clothes, or food purchases – which both spouses regard as relatively trivial. Edgell concludes from his research that, at least among professional couples at the child-rearing stage, husbands wield far more power than their wives. This power, he insists, is built into the marital relationship, in so far as the greater wage-earning capacity of husbands – particularly during the period of the family life-cycle when many wives are fully engaged in raising young children – gives husbands a leverage which they can draw upon when they wish to swing decisions in their favour. As Edgell explains:

> The husband, by virtue of his greater participation in the external economic division of labour compared to his wife, was able legitimately to avoid many household tasks and legitimately to dominate family life. To paraphrase Engels, the fact that not all husbands used their power does not in the least change the position of wives. The wife, by virtue of her relative exclusion from paid work and her major responsibility for the home and children, was consigned to economic and social dependence upon her husband (1980, p. 105).

Edgell's use of the term 'legitimate' to describe the power of husbands is echoed by Bernard, in *The Future of Marriage* (1982). Bernard observes that although women often possess a degree of power in marriage, their power is in many respects deemed deviant or illegitimate; for example, wives may apologise for being 'bossy' and try to disguise what little power they have by 'getting around him', 'making it seem like his idea' or 'leading from behind', while the wide currency of jokes about hen-pecked husbands and 'nagging' wives suggests how unacceptable it is for women to get their own way. By contrast, men's power in marriage is deemed to be legitimate, acceptable, part of the proper order of things; in most contexts, his power need not be hidden or disguised. Bernard points out that a variety of social institutions, including the church, the state, the divorce courts and the social security system, have traditionally conferred authority on men in marriage; it is not surprising, she concludes, that a large proportion of adults of both sexes treat husbands' power as legitimate. In so far as power is considered legitimate (and, Edgell finds, many wives do consider it legitimate, even if they contest some of its consequences), then husbands have not only the power to get their own way, but authority too.

The continuing importance of male authority in marriage is underlined by the (1980) study *Violence against Wives*. Wife assault is connected, Dobash and Dobash argue, to cultural expectations about male authority in marriage. Violent husbands, for example, swiftly resort to force when their wives do not provide for their needs (e.g., for a hot meal on the table) as quickly or in quite the way that the husband wants, or when wives question a husband's actions or opinions. An argument is ended, Dobash and Dobash found, when the man decides it should be; if the woman persists (if she continues, for example, to ask for housekeeping money) this is considered 'nagging', and provocation for an attack.

Dobash and Dobash insist that wife assault, far from being the action of a disturbed individual, is a mode of behaviour which has been considered legitimate through much of Western history. Legal, political and social support for husbands to exert authority over their wives has often extended to support for the use of violence to enforce his will. Although wife battering is now illegal in Britain, it is a commonplace occurrence; 25 per cent of the cases of violence that reached the Scottish courts in the years covered by the study were cases of wife assault. Moreover, societal reactions to wife assault indicate the extent to which it is still, today, tolerated. For example, in cases which reached the courts in 1978–9, the usual sentence was a fine of £5 to £10 – less, the Dobashes emphasise, than typical fines for many parking offences.

The study of wife assault is a sobering reminder of the extent to which the institution of marriage still provides a patriarchal framework for intimate relations. The fact that most husbands do not use their power in this way does not, as Edgell points out (1980, p. 105, quoted above) make that framework any less patriarchal.

In contrast to certain optimistic social theorists who claim that the nineteenth century patriarchal family has been superseded by a more democratic type . . . the present study provides abundant evidence of the survival of patriarchalism (Edgell, 1980, p. 68).

The impact of structured inequalities in society

Evidence of two kinds, then – of the household division of labour, and of the distribution of power and authority within marriage – suggest that modern marriages are far from equal. But, it can be argued, where march-of-progress theorists went most wrong was in underestimating the impact of the persistence of gender inequalities within society upon the relationships of husbands and wives.

Edgell, for one, contends that only if we look carefully at the impact of the wider sexual division of labour – which ties men to wage-earning, and women to domestic responsibilities – on the structure of family life can we understand decision-making processes in modern marriages. It is taken for granted, in capitalist societies, that employment takes precedence over all other activities, including the vital activities involved in organising a home and family. Therefore, men's involvement in wage-earning (and wives' and children's dependence on the continuation of the male wage) also gives men, their activities and their concerns priority over those of their children and their wives. In other words, many men are able to claim power in marriage, not as men, but as breadwinners: the middle-class husbands demand (usually successfully) that family and home life, and the interests of wives and children, be subordinated to the man's career. A good promotion opportunity for the husband is often considered to be enough of a reason to disrupt the wife's employment, interfere with children's schooling, uproot home and move away from family and friends.

Because of the precedence given to work over family life, and to men's work over women's, Finch (1983) found that the lives of wives in every social class tend to be structured around their husbands' jobs to an extent that is rarely reciprocated; a husband being asked to work late, for instance, is usually considered sufficient justification for keeping his wife waiting or cancelling joint social engagements. Wives' 'incorporation' in men's work, Finch argues, takes many forms, which include being expected to make crucial contributions to the performance of the husband's job: acting as receptionist, organising appointments, relaying telephone messages for doctors or tradesmen; typing reports and proofreading for academics; providing clients with sympathy and practical support for rural policemen or clergymen; entertaining and enhancing the public image of politicians or businessmen; serving customers and keeping the books for shopkeepers. In all of these capacities, Finch argues, wives are 'married to the job': they provide services, free, for employers; their daily life is structured around the demands emanating from the husband's work; and yet their services bring them no personal entitlement to security, promotion or income. The incorporation of wives in men's work may be an example of 'jointness' in marriage – after all, both partners are involved in the same project – but it is hardly an indication of equality.

Moreover, it should not be a surprise that in the majority of marriages, where wives are in paid employment, the husband's job still enables him to dominate the marriage. As Lupri and Symons (1982) emphasise in their critique of Willmott and Young, in few cases will employment give wives equal social power to that of their husbands, either in terms of income or in terms of security and prestige; gender divisions within employment (discussed more fully in Chapter 5) ensure the power husbands derive as 'primary breadwinners' is preserved even when wives are full-time employed.

Contemporary conjugal relationships: conclusions

It is highly likely that people in Western industrial nations have come in the course of this century to expect more in terms of intimacy, closeness and 'jointness' from marriage; that working-class families – or, at least, the men in those families – have become more home-centred; and that there has been a blurring of the boundary that divides the responsibilities of husbands from those of wives. But none of these changes are sufficient to demonstrate a strong trend towards equality in marriage. An emphasis upon intimacy or closeness in marriage can and does co-exist with marked inequalities of power and responsibility between husbands and wives. Joint conjugal roles – the sharing of friends and activities by spouses – have no necessary connection with equality either, as Bott herself pointed out. If joint conjugal roles arise because a wife is cut off from sources of support outside the marriage – if she becomes reliant on social contacts her *husband* brings home, and must join her husband in activities he chooses and initiates – then mutuality may represent a *decrease* in autonomy for the wife, *increased* dependence on the husband, and greater inequality.

Family change: conclusions. The 'march-of-progress' description of contemporary families as (i) relatively isolated from kin, and (ii) egalitarian, must be seen as greatly oversimplified. While changes have occurred in relationships with kin and with spouses, these changes cannot be summed up as representing a unilinear movement from extended to nuclear families, or from patriarchal to egalitarian ones. Nor can it be upheld that 'industrialisation' has been the principal cause of any such changes; on the contrary, industrialisation – described by Goode (1968, p. 322) as 'that ragbag of variables' – may take place in different ways, producing different effects and results for families.

Let us now turn to the second level at which this kind of approach to family change can be assessed: to what extent are 'the march-of-progress' theorists right in interpreting the kinds of changes they identify as *progress*?

The evaluation of family change

As we have seen, 'march-of-progress' theorists tend to emphasise the positive reciprocal influence between family and the rest of society; reacting against the pessimistic view that the family is in decline, such theorists have bent over backwards to emphasise the strengths of the modern family. It is seen as effective with respect to child-rearing (and all the more so, since certain non-essential functions have been catered for elsewhere), and as providing a refuge for emotional development for adults, a refuge characterised not by dependence on kin but by autonomy, and by egalitarian rather than patriarchal relationships between spouses. The evaluative character of this theory is fairly obvious: the familial institution is (reasonably) flourishing in modern societies, it is held, and this is beneficial for society.

Morgan (1975) points to four positions that might be argued with respect to the evaluation of contemporary families. Each position combines two elements: a judgement as to whether the family is or is not in decline, and a judgement as to the effects of the family's position on the rest of society. For example, it might be held that the family is weak, and that this is a major source of the ills of our society; or that the family is weak, and that this is to be applauded, since the decline of the family will bring a number of other benefits (freedom for children, perhaps, or for women). The former position is the one often taken by lay commentators, who wish to find a relatively easy explanation for social problems; the latter position is rarely articulated.

The 'march-of-progress' theorists tend, of course, to subscribe to the third of Morgan's four positions, arguing that the family is alive and well *and* that this is all to the good. While certainly the dominant view in the sociology of the family for some time, it should not be thought that *all* contemporary sociologists subscribe to it; for example, writers in the Marxist tradition, while agreeing that the family is relatively strong, complete Morgan's typology by tending to argue that this strength is to the *detriment* of most sectors of society.

The idea of progress: the Marxist critique

Most Marxist analyses draw attention to the ways in which families tend to encourage and reproduce hierarchical inegalitarian relationships, and to act as a safety-valve, dampening down discontent so that it is robbed of revolutionary content. In providing a place where children can be conceived, borne and reared in relative safety, the family is providing tomorrow's labour force. At the same time, by offering a centre for relaxation, recreation, refreshment and rest, the family helps to ensure that members of today's labour force are returned to work each day with their capacity to work renewed and strengthened. This is what is meant when it is said that the family reproduces labour power on a generational as well as a daily basis. The family also provides much of the motivation that keep workers at their benches. This happens again on a generational and daily basis. Children are taught the necessity of work and the basic forms of work discipline (punctuality, obedience) in the context of the family, though this is heavily supplemented by the school. Adult men and women are discouraged from 'dropping out' of the labour force, or from turning their backs on work which is less than fulfilling, by the expectation that *good* husbands/ mothers/parents must do their utmost to earn enough to buy their children and themselves certain comforts and advantages. Furthermore, this 'incentive' may be all the more compelling, the more that adults feel their own lives to be barren and want to 'live' through their children. The theme of the 'family-as-incentive' comes through in many studies in industrial sociology. In Beynon's *Working For Ford*, for example, a man describing his intense dissatisfaction with assembly-line work finally commented, 'I just close my eyes and stick it out. I think about the kids' (Beynon, 1973, p. 113).

The privatisation of family life is also seen as contributing to the survival of capitalist society. On the one hand, small and fairly self-sufficient family units offer an enormous market for the sale of domestic goods; competition between families with respect to consumption – keeping up with the Joneses – is, of course, encouraged by advertising. On the other hand, the privatisation of family life acts as a barrier to the development of strong, organised and collective opposition to the status quo. It undermines class consciousness, whether at work or in the neighbourhood, by emphasising that one's first loyalty is to the family; the struggles of workmates or friends must be neglected, if joining in would in any way penalise the family. Privatisation thus counteracts class solidarity and, further, reinforces the notion that goodness, or morality, or commitment, are personal matters, to be enacted on a private basis with one's family rather than on a public basis through efforts to create a better society: this, after all, is part of the implication of 'Charity begins at home'.

Finally, from certain Marxist perspectives, the family quells rebellious spirits in two other ways. Through socialisation of children and also through day-to-day relationships (parents and children, older child and younger child, men and women) people are inculcated into patterns of authority, obedience and power. Thus patriarchal relationships outside the family, or the habit of submission to the 'boss', have a foundation in family life. Second, to the extent that family life is satisfying and warm (for at least some of its members) it can help to sustain inegalitarian and unfree structures outside the family, by offering an escape from these and a chance of recuperation – and this will be all the more effective as a dampener of opposition in so far as people come to believe that the family *is* the only possible sphere of emotion, creativity and fulfilment.

Thus, in the Marxist tradition, although the family is seen as relatively strong, this strength is thought of as detrimental to the development of the individual and society. The strong family helps to preserve the fundamentally unsatisfactory and unliberating patterns of capitalism, and therefore serves to forestall the emergence of better, more enriching ways of life. The fundamental irony from this point of view is that the less fulfilling work and life in the public sphere is, the more desperately people cling to their one potential source of satisfaction, the family; but of course, by escaping to the family, they reproduce the very structures of inequality and powerlessness which made them seek refuge in the first place.

In most versions of the 'march-of-progress' theories, the emphasis is upon the fit between 'the family' and 'industrial society'. In Marxist theory, the emphasis is not upon industrialisation in general, but upon industrial *capitalism* and its effects. The nuclear family, at least in its more repressive forms, is thought to persist not because of its inherent advantages, or its effectiveness at satisfying human needs, but rather because of its general structural position in society – a position which helps to protect the status quo from unified challenge. Thus, from many Marxist positions, the solution lies not in any alteration to the family but in wider structural changes – in particular, the destruction of industrial capitalism.

For others, however, this offers no solution, as the real issues in the sociology of the contemporary family concern the consequences of an institutional coincidence of child-rearing and the conjugal relationship, which remains a basic feature of the nuclear family whatever the wider structural arrangements may be. Here we are concerned with representatives of the fourth of Morgan's possible evaluations of the contemporary family: that which sees the family as a weak institution in our society, but, because it considers that an alteration in our child-rearing arrangements is eminently desirable, does not bemoan this weakness. What are the characteristics of our sort of family which give rise to this position?

The idea of progress: an alternative critique

At the beginning of this chapter we argued that it is quite wrong to see every kind of child-rearing arrangement in the world as being like that embodied in the nuclear family, and that one of the principal peculiarities of a nuclear family-based system is the primacy of marriage – the conjugal tie – in the child-rearing unit. This has a number of significant consequences.

Where a society forms its child-rearing groups exclusively on the conjugal tie, the efficiency of such groups depends directly on the nature and performance of this tie: the family will be as strong as the relationship on which it is based. Now it seems clear that the strength of any conjugal relationship will depend on (among other things) the expectations held by the married couple: *why* people get married will be an important indicator of the potential strength of their marriage over time. Furthermore, the nature of these expectations will vary directly with the degree to which the institution serves the interest of individuals or of groups in a society. Let us explore these connections.

7.3 CONFLICT AND INSTABILITY IN FAMILY LIFE

The group aspect of marriage in non-industrial societies

Much of what we said at the beginning of the chapter demonstrated that in many kinds of non-industrial societies marriage serves *kin-group* interests. We argued that marriage is both a mechanism designed to provide a kin-group with its new members and also a major means of establishing alliances between such groups. In such societies, then, marriage has to be understood primarily as an institution designed to effect rights and obligations between groups of kin rather than individuals.

There are both structural and normative consequences of this. Since a marriage is an arrangement for and between kin-groups there are very many vested interests in its continuance and therefore many potential structural pressures on the individuals involved. In a patrilineal society, for example, where the children of a marriage belong to their father's group, it would be most unlikely that a groom's group would be happy to see a bride for whom they have paid a substantial bride-price wishing to leave her husband, at least if her child-producing days were not yet done. In any case, her own group would hardly be too pleased to be in danger of having claims made on them for the return of bride-wealth already consumed.

This is one of the reasons why divorce is often so difficult to obtain in a patrilineal society. The aim of patrilineal groups is to secure, via marriage, rights over the reproductive powers of a woman from another group: having effected this exchange and having handed over the bride-wealth, it is hardly likely they are going to hand the bride back. Sometimes, of course, there *are* no constraints which can be brought to bear on the individuals involved in order to avert a threat to the permanence of the conjugal tie. For example, what happens if one of the spouses dies before the groom's group has got its 'money's worth' out of the marriage? It is not surprising that on such occasions there are often contingency plans which can be put into operation, and these only appear bizarre if it is forgotten that patrilineal marriages are primarily designed to serve group, not individual, interests.

In the *levirate*, for instance, if a married man dies, his widow is taken over by one of his brothers. There need not be any new marriage: from the deceased's group's point of view, all that needs to be done is for one of its members to do what the dead man now cannot do – provide group heirs. The woman is still regarded as her dead husband's wife and any children she bears to his brother are still regarded as the dead man's. The structural definition of marriage as a group institution is quite clear here. The levirate is not only an expression of the principle that nothing has changed so long as the bride-wealth remains paid, but also that once a patrilineal group has obtained a woman her reproductive capacity belongs to the group, not to any particular individual.

The reverse patrilineal circumstance, of course, is where a man's wife dies prematurely (that is, the group gets a bad deal so far as her child-producing capacity is concerned). In this case, the arrangement – known as the *sororate* – is that the widower is entitled to a replacement wife, usually the dead woman's sister, from the group who received the bride-wealth. Once again the principle is clear: marriage is meant to serve the interests of the group, and so long as the group gets its money's worth the institution is doing its job.

In matrilineal societies, in contrast, divorce is often more easily available than in patrilineal ones. Marriage is just as much of a mechanism designed to serve kin-group interests here, so why should this be? The answer is simple enough. In matrilineal systems women reproduce for their *own* groups. There is no transference of their reproductive powers on marriage; instead, matrilineal marriage involves men from other groups being borrowed, more or less permanently, to do for their wives' brothers what they cannot do, for themselves – give them heirs. The group only loses out if a woman remains unattached, not if she changes husbands. Divorce is no problem for a matrilineal group (so long as remarriage is not long in coming), since a woman remains its heir-producer and her children remain its heirs *whoever* her husband is. Here, then, the group aspect of marriage is reflected less in constraints against the instability of a *particular* marriage so much as against descent group women remaining unmarried.

Probably the best-known method of ensuring that women remained married is that made famous by Hart and Pilling's (1960) account of life among the aboriginal Tiwi of North Australia. The method was devastatingly simple. In Hart and Pilling's words (1960, p. 14):

> The Tiwi took the very slight step from saying 'All females *should* be married' to saying 'All females *must* be married.' As a result, there was no concept of an unmarried female in Tiwi ideology, no need for such a condition in their language, and in fact no female in the population without at least a nominal husband ... all female Tiwi babies were betrothed before, or as soon as, they were born; females were thus the 'wives' of their betrothed husbands from the moment of birth onwards. For similar reasons, widows were required to remarry at the gravesides of their late husbands.

Clearly, these kinds of marital arrangements only appear strange if looked at from the point of view of our definition, that marriages link individuals. If marriage is understood as a structural mechanism primarily designed to serve group interests and establish relations between kin-groups run by men, they appear much less bizarre.

One of the consequences of marriage institutions whose primary purposes are child production (for the kin-group) and the establishment of alliances (between kin-groups) is that they tend to promote ideologies which subordinate individual well-being to the benefit of the group. In traditional China, for example, the family was treated as the most important institution and family life as sacred, yet people were taught that they were not to expect romance or happiness out of marriage, being told instead that at best they might achieve contentment and peace. The existence of such limited expectations acts as a mechanism preventing marital breakdown, of course: since people expecting little from marriage are less likely to be disappointed, the chances of marital stability are enhanced.

However, it is important not to confuse the notion of 'expectation' with that of 'choice': just because people learn to expect little from marriage does not mean that such expectations necessarily match their desires. Thus, although normative definitions such as these might promote 'societal integration' and 'stability', this does not mean that it is *therefore* promoting individual happiness. Moreover, such definitions operate much more in favour of men than women. In societies such as these, where the definition of women as primarily child-bearers and rearers is only one aspect of their subordination, it is not surprising that the consequences for them of the structural location of marriage are far more oppressive than for men. For example, where divorce is hardly possible, it is normally men who tend to have the freedom to take lovers and concubines, while women remain not only subordinate but shackled. In traditional China usually the only way in which women who refused to swallow the ideology could escape their kin-group obligations was to commit suicide, while in present-day India such a fate can meet even those who comply; the well-publicised cases of newly wed brides being burned to death by their husbands' relatives for failing to provide a sufficient dowry are dramatic manifestations of the general exploitation of women in such systems.

Marriage and divorce in Britain

In sum, then, in societies where marriage is subordinated to descent group interests, where there are strong structural constraints supporting it, and where individual men and women's expectations of their married life are undemanding and readily achieved, marital breakdown tends to be inhibited. In our society, however, the marital relationship is potentially much more fragile. Marriage still 'unites' two families, but (with the clear exception of the wealthy) such alliances have little social significance. We tend to view marriage as an arrangement between individuals, entered into for their mutual benefit. Moreover, in our society, the normative emphasis in marriage is upon the emotional and sexual gratification it may provide for the conjugal pair, not upon the heirs that may be provided for descent groups or the alliances that may be effected by the marriage.

What constitutes a 'successful' marriage in our society – with expectations of companionship and romance, as well as a harmonious domestic arrangement – is therefore arguably more difficult to achieve, and consequently more likely to be frustrated, than the objectives of a 'successful' marriage in other times and other places. The emphasis upon personal fulfilment through marriage may justify for many people abandoning an unsatisfactory relationship in order to pursue fulfilment with another partner. Moreover, in the absence of effective pressure from kin-groups, the decision whether or not to remain 'till death us do part' is clearly more dependent upon the circumstances and (fluctuating) emotions of the marital pair.

This may be part of the reason why divorce has been made more available in our society. Lacking the structural and normative constraints which inhibit dissatisfaction with, and severance of, the conjugal tie in other societies, we have instead developed a means of facilitating break-*up* when break-*down* is irredeemable. Not that it was always so, for recourse to divorce is, in Britain, a relatively new 'solution' to the problem of marital unhappiness. In Victorian times, for example, divorces cost on average £700–800 – an incredibly high sum – so it is hardly surprising that the great majority of divorces went to members of the gentry or to men in professional or managerial occupations. Quite simply, the ordinary *men* of Britain could not afford divorce, and sought rather cruder escapes (desertion, physical abuse of wife or children, relationships with mistresses or prostitutes) from unhappy marriages. For women in such marriages the options were even more limited. Their legal access to divorce was more restricted than that of men; for example, it was not until 1923 that it became possible for women as well as men to sue for divorce on grounds of adultery. More important, perhaps, the lack of state support for single-parent families, and the narrow employment opportunities which made it unlikely that a woman on her own could earn a living wage, meant that the great majority of women trapped in unhappy marriages had no choice but to endure them. They effectively remained the property of their husbands, and the marriage contract constituted a principal basis for their subordination.

The increasing availability of divorce in the twentieth century must be explained as much by increasing political and economic independence of women as by general changes in 'ideals' or 'attitudes' to marriage. During this century the grounds for divorce have been extended, and the costs of legal proceedings lowered, in such a way that divorce is less the monopoly of wealthy men. The 1970 Divorce Law Reform Act did away with the idea that one partner had to commit a matrimonial offence (for example, desertion or cruelty) and substituted the notion of 'irretrievable breakdown of marriage' as the sole grounds for divorce. Breakdown can be demonstrated simply by living separately (for two years if both parties wish a divorce; for five if one of them is opposed), though some of the old matrimonial offences can still be invoked as evidence of breakdown.

As laws and procedures regulating divorce have altered, the divorce rate has tended to increase by leaps and bounds; with each new piece of legislation making divorce more readily available, the rate has risen rapidly for a time before levelling off. Today there is one divorce in Britain for every three marriages. (In the USA the rate is one in two.) Many people have suggested that the higher divorce rates reflect an underlying increase in marital instability; the problem with this argument is that we have no way of knowing how many 'unstable' or 'unhappy' marriages existed before legislation made it possible to dissolve them in a public (and recordable) form. Some commentators have gone further, and argued that more permissive divorce laws in themselves *cause* marital breakdown. But we can certainly be sceptical of such a view, suggesting as it does that happily married couples can suddenly be persuaded to abandon their relationship, propelled by the attraction of a new divorce law. A more plausible explanation for rises in the divorce rate after the passage of a law is that unhappily married couples were for the first time given access to a legal solution to pre-existent marital problems; in other words, changes in divorce laws are less likely to cause marital breakdown than to provide new types of solution where breakdown has already occurred.

Contemporary marriage and child-rearing

With divorce now much more readily available than ever before, it might seem that we are lucky. People appear to get married because they love each other, and, if mistakes are made or feelings change, they can relatively easily go their own way to pursue the ideal of love once more.

But are our *children* so fortunate? What are the implications of our patterns of marriage for child-rearing? The outline of the argument so far is summarised in the box overleaf.

In sum, the more marriage links individuals, and the more men and women expect personal fulfilment in marriage, the more fragile the conjugal tie and the greater the need for a means to facilitate break-up. In contrast, the more marriage links kin-groups, and the lower the expectations of individuals (of both women, and husbands and wives), the greater the stability of the tie and the need for divorce reduced.

Since this is so, where child-rearing is based solely, and therefore relies exclusively, on the conjugal tie, it might seem logical to define marriage in

(1) Any society needs to produce children and rear its new members satisfactorily.

(2) Our society tends to do this by using marriage – the conjugal tie – as the sole basis of child-rearing units. In the contemporary nuclear family just two adults, *because* they are husband and wife, are responsible for all the activities associated with reproduction and child care.

(3) This is not inevitable or 'natural': it is only one way of organising things. For example, in an extended family context ties of descent, especially between mother and daughter, can be more significant for child-rearing than the conjugal tie. Other kinds of societies, though usually using some form of marriage, do not rely on it exclusively in the way we do. Ties of descent, whether patrilineal or matrilineal, and blood ties (particularly siblingship) are often as significant as marital ties so far as social parenthood is concerned, and sometimes much more important.

(4) However, if the child-rearing unit is based solely on the conjugal tie, with all responsibilities devolving on only two adults, then this unit can only be as strong as the tie on which it is based.

(5) What affects the strength of the conjugal tie? Although other factors can be significant, two crucial ones are the degree of male dominance and the expectations of the relationship between husband and wife. Marriage will tend to be strongest where wives rely for their survival on their husbands and where expectations of love or romance are absent. It will tend to be weakest where women do *not* have to be married in order to survive and where husbands and wives *do* expect to achieve emotional fulfilment in marriage.

(6) What affects the existence of these sources of stability? A major factor (though not the only one) is whether marriage serves kin-group or individual interests. Where marriage is primarily a mechanism for reproducing and linking kin-groups, individual interests – and particularly women's – tend to be subordinated in favour of the group. Where marriage primarily links individuals, both husbands and wives tend to be encouraged to expect individual fulfilment in marriage.

such a way as to lower the expectations of the individuals involved, thereby reducing the possibility of instability. Conversely, this might be less necessary where child-rearing is less dependent on the stability of marriage.

However, what *actually* happens is the *reverse* of this. It is in societies where marriage is an institution serving kin-group interests, where the expectations of marital partners are encouraged to be lower, and where the relationship is therefore inherently more stable, that satisfactory child-rearing is *not* dependent solely on marriage. In contrast, the performance of these roles *is* wholly dependent on the conjugal tie precisely in those societies – like ours – where the expectations of those about to be married are encouraged to be high. The irony is that it is precisely in *our* kind of society, where the institution of marriage is so inherently fragile, that we nevertheless *still* expect these unions to form stable, secure and efficient bases for child-rearing. In short, the normative bases of the two institutions of marriage and child-rearing in our society are completely contradictory.

Even given our definition of marriage they *could* still be stable and efficient, of course, but only if it could be somehow guaranteed that husbands and wives will always want to stay together all their lives, *and* that men and women who fall in love with each other and get married will always become good parents. However, since the only provisions we operate to ensure the former is to have a ceremony in which spouses say 'till death us do part' – hardly a guarantee of stability and permanence – and since we make no provision at all to ensure the latter, it is only surprising that conjugally based families do not fail more often than at present.

Not that we have any accurate indicator of the extent of such failures, for we cannot assume that husbands/fathers and wives/mothers who actually split their marriages/families up are the only ones who have not succeeded. For one thing, divorce is a solution which is still unequally available to men and women: state support for single-parent families is still too meagre and women still too discriminated against for separation to amount to anything other than a last resort for many married mothers. In any case, although our marriage practices can often spell disaster for child-rearing, it seems reasonable to assume that the demands of child-rearing can often have equally deleterious effects on the pursuit of our marriage ideals as well. Who knows how many husbands and wives would like to split up but are deterred because they are stuck with being father and mother to their children, and must therefore reconcile themselves to marital failure? Or again, who knows how many potentially successful marriages suffer because of the demands made on the couple by their parental responsibilities? These responsibilities impose just some of the practical strains and constraints which contribute to divorce.

Parenting and the contemporary family

However, it is not just the respective ideals underlying the family and marriage which contradict each other in our society. What about the position of women in our families? Traditional nations regarding the importance of the conjugal tie as the basis of the family unit assume not only that marriage will be lifelong and that husbands and wives will be good fathers and mothers but also that married women will above all else wish to spend a large part – if not the bulk – of their lives being full-time mothers.

This 'traditional' view regarding parenting is of fairly recent origin, even in British society, but is so much a part of common-sense thinking about the 'natural' role of women and the 'natural' way in which children should be raised that most of us find it difficult to imagine things being done differently. Yet child-rearing has *not* always had the character we take for granted, and we *can* find reasons why things changed.

Ideas about the nature of children have changed through the centuries, and so, too, have ideas concerning the proper relationship between parents and children. Modern families are often described as 'child-centred'. Viewed in historical perspective, the phrase is apt: not only because parents tend to spend so much of their time and energy on their children, but also because we tend to view the careful nurturing of the young, their protection and their education, and their emotional well-being, as the *raison d'être* of the family as an institution.

However, the family was not always viewed this way. As Ariès (1973) has shown, and as we pointed out at the beginning of the chapter, in pre-industrial Europe family life was much less private and much more a part of community life generally than it is for us. The same applies to childhood. Ariès (1973, pp. 395–6) puts the contrast clearly:

> Our world is obsessed by the physical, moral and sexual problems of childhood. This preoccupation was unknown to medieval civilisation, because there was no problem for the Middle Ages: as soon as he had been weaned, or soon after, the child became the natural companion of the adult.

This is not to say that people of the Middle Ages did not love their children; rather, the needs of the children were differently conceived, and hence the interaction of loving parents with their children was different.

The change from the Middle Ages to the contemporary relationship between parents and children occurred very gradually and is too complex to document in detail here. However, what we can notice is the significance once again of the removal of most productive activity from the home with the rise in factory production; this accelerated the isolation of children from the 'real world' (at least after various Factory Acts limited their labour) and encouraged the notion of them (as of women) as somehow uniquely familial creatures. In addition, their removal from most production, as well as the extension of formal schooling, probably reinforced views of the frailty and dependence of children by making them quite literally dependent upon their families for support for a longer period of time.

One of the results of these changed conceptions of childhood has been a systematic increase in the obligations of parents towards their offspring. These include: financial obligations (and not only food and ordinary clothing, but school uniforms, money for school meals, educational toys, journeys, pocket money, and so forth); fairly constant attendance, particularly during the first five years; and not just warmth, affection and protection from harm but also intellectual stimulation, exposure to new learning experiences, and so on. One consequence of this is that despite far lower fertility rates than in the nineteenth century, it is probable that parents, nevertheless, spend more time in active child care than used to be the case. Parental attention is made all the more urgent given certain of the changes, especially in the urban environment, which make a greater degree of autonomous play for children rather more dangerous – busy traffic, lack of commons or green spaces, high-rise flats, and so on.

If the obligations attached to parenting have increased, this burden has fallen disproportionately on women. 'Parenting' connotes an activity involving protection and socialisation, security and affectionate interaction, an activity which is clearly necessary for the physical, moral, emotional and intellectual development of any human child (though it need not, of course, be offered by *biological* parents). However, in our culture, the ideological emphasis is upon mothers: they are regarded as the correct, the logical and the natural people to provide the parenting. This emphasis is reflected in, and supported by, a number of beliefs regarding parenting which refer either to a child's need for its mother or to a mother's predisposition to mothering. For example, beliefs about the importance of breast-feeding clearly do this (though of course the provision of milk is only a tiny part of child care) as does a belief in the existence of a 'maternal instinct'. However, in more recent times the principal belief of this kind has been the widespread but rather vague notion that 'A child needs its mother.'

In Britain this idea has been a plank underpinning many aspects of state policy since the Second World War, including social work objectives (to keep the child with its mother if at all possible) and policies concerning institutional care for children in difficulties. Much of the theoretical backing for this idea came from the work of John Bowlby (1965, 1971, 1975), whose studies on how human beings form attachments, and how they experience grief or loss, have been widely quoted and misquoted in support of the notion of 'maternal deprivation'. Bowlby suggested that human beings have from infancy a predisposition to form a deep and overwhelmingly important attachment to one person – and that person will probably be the mother. Disruption of the relationship with the mother in childhood by, for example, prolonged separation will produce anxiety in the child and effects similar to grief for the loss of a loved one. This experience may colour the child's later emotional make-up, and may interfere with his or her ability to form emotionally stable relationships. Thus, in brief, 'maternal deprivation' in childhood is believed to have effects which are severe and lasting. Bowlby's work has, sometimes unreasonably, been read to imply that even temporary separations from the mother (e.g. leaving the child with a minder while at work) can 'scar' the child for life; in this form the notion of maternal deprivation has been used to castigate mothers even for working in paid employment, or for taking an occasional evening out. Mothering has, in other words, been interpreted as a 24-hour, 365-day-a-year, responsibility, with anything other than this being potentially damaging to the child's welfare.

Thus, reflected in and supported by these kinds of beliefs about the relationship between mothers and children, the conventional view is that only women can perform child-rearing properly and 'naturally'. Now while this may or may not be true (and we will refer to objections to it shortly), the fact remains that it is a view which is entirely incompatible with another contemporary belief – that women should have equality with men. Just as we noted contradictions in our ideal definitions of family and marriage, here we find two directly opposed conceptions of the role of women. So far as conjugally based child-rearing is concerned, we expect that women should get married, have children and devote themselves to raising these children. In contrast, so far as contemporary attitudes regarding women's rights are concerned, the demand is that women should have exactly the same opportunities in life – political, educational and, especially, occupational – as men. The contradiction here is plain to see: given our views about women's role in nuclear families, how is it *possible* for women to have the same opportunities as men? Leach (1968) portrays the conflicts clearly:

> As nuclear families become more isolated, the network of kinsfolk families becomes dispersed. The young mother can still talk to her Mum on the telephone, but she can't ask her to drop in for a few minutes to mind the baby. Ideas about the status of women have been changing; wives are now thought of as companions rather than servants to their husbands, but perhaps they are even more thoroughly enslaved to their children than before.
>   There is no easy solution. There is a genuine clash of interest between the right of a woman to be treated as a free and self-respecting individual and the right of her child to demand care and attention. But we don't get out of the difficulty by mouthing shibboleths about the eternal sanctity of the family. We have set ourselves noble ideals: social equality of men and women, permanence of the conjugal relationship, life-long love and cooperation between parents and children, but we have created a social system in which it is quite impossible for these factors to co-exist.

It is important to remember that these kinds of problems are not simply of academic interest. We must not forget that because we are talking about contradictions and tensions involved with our kind of family, we are also talking about resulting strains and pressures under which people in our society have to live out their lives as husbands and wives, fathers and mothers, and children. Unfortunately, however, because there has been little sociological interest in such issues we have little real evidence about the kind of consequences they have had for people's lives. Certainly there is a considerable body of literature devoted to the analysis of crisis situations in families – coping with the death of a spouse, for example, or with the birth of a severely handicapped child – and with the situation of 'problem families'. But what is less often acknowledged are the strains and tensions which, we are arguing, may well be a fairly routine part of life in 'non-problem' families.

For too long, in our view, many sociologists, eager to counteract superficial notions of the decline of the family, have unintentionally given substance to another myth, the myth of the happy family. Of course, it would be nonsensical to suggest that it is not *possible* for families to provide a haven of warmth and security while allowing an optimum level of individual freedom and contributing successfully to the socialisation of children – but whether they do or not is an *empirical* question. Thus, any adequate conceptualisation of modern families must ask questions about child neglect, battered wives, absentee husbands and problems people face in the transition from adolescence to adulthood – about what Morgan calls 'the dark side of family life' – *as well as* about the warm attachments which many people undoubtedly experience within the family. And in fact, when research into the contemporary family *has* been directed by concern with such issues, a very different picture from that painted by the 'march-of-progress' theorists often emerges.

The dark side of family life

One important facet of the dark side of family life is the incidence of marital violence that we have already discussed. Studies like that by Dobash and Dobash (1980) referred to above (p. 279) indicate that wife-beating is seen by many as an unremarkable extension of a husband's right to control his wife – both reflecting and resulting from the asymmetricality of marital relationships. Although the majority of battered women in the Dobash study left home to escape their husbands' violence, most were forced to return; major reasons for returning were the social stigma against a wife leaving her husband for *any* reason, lack of child-care facilities, and economic dependence on the husband. The disadvantages facing women in the wider society increase the likelihood that women will have to endure physical violence in marriage. Thus it can be argued that the persistence of wife-battering is not an idiosyncratic phenomenon but the predictable consequence of the inequality of the sexes and of the asymmetrical nature of marriage in contemporary society.

Inequalities of power within the family are not confined to the marital relationship of course; children can be treated by their parents not only with (more or less) love and concern but also with violence and abuse. Recent research (Straus, 1982) shows that however much we may wish it were not so, in contemporary families children can be just as vulnerable to physical assault as women.

Several psychiatrists have drawn attention to 'the dark side of family life', notably Laing. A typical problem of family life, and a recurrent theme in Laing's work, is the tension between a child's early dependence on its parents and its eventual strivings towards independence. Parents are often depicted as being highly ambivalent about letting go of the child in which so much of their energy has been invested. The striving for independence raises problems for the child, too. The family has defined for the growing child not only who he or she is but also, simultaneously, what *they*, the world outside, the others, are like; hence the child's sense of identity is so closely bound up with family relationships, and the sense of uncertainty about the outside world ('them') may be so deeply ingrained that breaking free is a highly traumatic process. In Laing's accounts, the process of socialisation is by no means a smooth process of gradually preparing the child to take its place in the adult world: on the contrary, interaction in the family involves all manner of confusions, ambiguities, uncertainties, even deceptions, to which the child is forced to adapt. This may be poor preparation indeed for an independent adult life. As Laing (1960, p. 189) says, 'the total family situation may impede rather than facilitate the child's capacity to participate in a real, shared world'. A central theme of Laing's writings, then, is that loyalty to the family often goes hand in hand with distrust of autonomy and of the outside world.

One serious objection that has often been raised against Laing's work is that his analyses of family life are based, in the main, on the study of schizophrenic patients. Indeed, part of Laing's argument is that many of the more bizarre symptoms of such patients may be understood if we know enough about patterns of interaction in the patients' families. Laing is not simply suggesting that families drive patients to madness; rather, he wishes to argue that familial relationships provide the grammar in which certain disturbances may be expressed. One of the useful aspects of Laing's writings is that since the families in question rarely involve instances of extreme child abuse, neglect or other sensational incidents, these analyses highlight the way in which fairly mundane patterns of family interaction can still confront the developing child or adolescent with severe tensions or contradictions.

However, while Laing's work is very sensitive to the tensions within family life, it fails to consider how these might be shaped or affected by the social context in which particular families are embedded. It is not clear, for example, how social class or ethnic differences, how property ownership or lack of property, or how the emphases of different historical periods, might influence the patterns of leaving home that have been described. In arguing that the family is an *experience* lived by its members, existing only through interaction, Laing may be underestimating the extent to which the family is given a particular structure and form by laws, welfare regulations, wage structures, and so on. To take a simple example, while it is certainly the case that parents have considerable room for discretion in the relationship they aim to construct with their children – and that no two parent–child relationships are likely to be identical – nevertheless the laws which specify that parents or guardians have a right to 'reasonable' physical punishment of a child sets a certain boundary upon the nature of parent–child interaction.

In some Scandinavian countries, in contrast to Britain, children have the same rights as others to protection from physical punishment, and the parental relationship does not override this right.

If it is the case that the process of seeking independence from the family which has reared a child often involves tensions, then we must ask why that is: why, for instance, are parents ambivalent about letting go of their children? Harris (1977) argues that the answer must be sought in terms of the progressively degraded character of contemporary life: the exclusion of most people from all but the most superficial involvement in political decision-making, and the gradual routinisation of the majority of jobs, as well as the attenuation of community ties, all tend to mean that men and women are progressively denied the chance for expression of their talents for creativity. This, Harris insists, is the backdrop against which the contemporary child-centred family must be understood. Disappointed and denied in other spheres, men and women load the family with great expectations – the family, it is hoped, will ease the frustrations of life, and will supply the solidarity, companionship and enrichment which are otherwise absent. While the ideology of privatisation, and the image of happy families promoted by the media, may help to encourage unrealistic expectations, the fundamental impetus, Harris suggests, comes from the inevitable frustration and disillusionment with public aspects of life in advanced capitalist societies. The recurring tensions of family life result from 'the attempt to realise within the family household the creative potentials of its members which are denied expression elsewhere' (Harris, 1977, p. 79).

Harris applies this analysis in particular to the emotional investment made by parents in their children; in an effort to compensate for disappointments in their own lives, parents try to live through their children, and to control them. This effort is, by and large, doomed. Ironically, the same division of labour which (by denying fulfilment) leads parents to seek satisfaction by controlling their children also denies parents the power to retain that control. In Harris's account (1977, p. 80) this is one of the central contradictions reflected in contemporary family life:

> the need to control and hence live 'through' one's children increases at the same time as the basis of this sort of control is eroded. The emotional demands made by parents upon children increase at the very point at which the children have least to gain from acceding to them. As a result the fulfilment of the parents becomes incompatible with the autonomous development of the children.

Harris's analysis suggests, then, that many of the agonies of child-centred families are the (more or less) predictable outcome of pressures upon the family in a society which identifies family as the *only* source of solidarity and fulfilment for the majority of the adult population.

7.4   THE FUTURE

It would seem that developments out of this present condition could occur in one of two ways: either our marriages could be modified in some way to make them a more suitable basis for proper child-rearing or different child-rearing institutions could be developed instead.

People who support the idea of a modification of marriage as a solution tend to see the problems we have outlined as stemming from a lack of commitment on the part of spouses which affects their performance as parents. Marriage, they say, should be taken more seriously, and once entered into should be difficult to abandon. The argument here, then, is that strictly limited opportunities for marital dissolution will discourage all but the most committed and will make the conjugal relationship, and therefore the parenting built upon it, more secure and effective. Proponents of such a position thus tend to support the establishment of quite definite constraints on divorce for those who get married and choose to be parents.

Pringle (1980), for example, proposes a two-tiered marriage contract. One tier, appropriate for spouses who do not wish to become parents, would be a loose arrangement, easily dissolved; the other tier would involve a contract legally binding for fifteen years, and would apply to those who intended to have children. At first glance this might appear to adequately solve at least two preconditions for a satisfactory solution; children would be guaranteed a permanent set of parents, and if people felt the pursuit of love more important to them than parenthood they could enter into the first kind of marriage instead. However, critics argue that if people enter the binding kind of marriage and *then* find out they are unsuitable for each other, they obviously have no recourse at all; therefore, it may well be that only those who want or expect companionship alone from their adult relationships will accept the risk and become parents. But in a world where love *can* be pursued elsewhere, how many of these people will there be, and *who* will they be?

The other kind of objection to this sort of 'solution' is that it makes no attempt at all to cope with the need for women's equality. Pringle, for example, stresses the importance of an equal division of labour in the family through role reversal by mother and father, either on a long-term or short-term basis. However, any solution that favours the retention of child-rearing as it is, *and* that bases child-rearing on the marital bond, necessarily involves making the traditional assumption that the people best made responsible for the social rearing of children are their biological parents, and that, in particular, women should be primarily responsible for raising their children.

Others reject this, insisting that there is no *necessary* reason why child-rearing should be based on the conjugal tie – why biological parents should always be the social parents. The argument here is that if marriage and the family no longer necessarily implied each other, this might free both institutions from the problems they presently pose for each other. Marriage could be about the 'proper' pursuit of love and, at the same time, children could be protected, since spouses who are unhappy together would no longer automatically be parents who are unhappy together. In addition, women would have a choice about whether to become social parents as well as biological parents.

Of course, this sort of argument is in direct opposition to notions such as 'maternal instinct' and 'maternal deprivation' which underpin popular views of parenting. Such notions have recently come under serious attack. However one defines the 'maternal instinct' – as, perhaps, the instinctive knowledge of what a child needs and how to provide it, or as the instinctive and overwhelming desire to have children, or as the instinctive and irresistible love for one's own child – there are always sufficient women who do *not* know how to care for a child, who do *not* wish to have a child, who do *not* love their children, to demonstrate that a universal notion of maternal instinct in women is a myth which occupies the same sort of ideological status in our society as beliefs about procreation do in patrilineal and matrilineal societies (see p. 258 above).

Moreover, there is considerable evidence which contradicts Bowlby's conclusions about maternal deprivation. Bowlby's work was thoroughly examined by Rutter (1972). Rutter takes Bowlby's point that children form early attachments on the basis of intense social interaction, but notes that interaction leading to stable attachments, play and physical care are three distinct activities which need not come from a single person. In Rutter's view, the evidence suggests that separation need not involve disruption of attachments – children can, and do, maintain close relationships with loved people during those people's absence; and they do so all the more successfully if play and physical care are adequate in the meanwhile. Finally, Rutter notes that the troublesome effects of separation from mother are mitigated by the presence of other familiar people, such as brothers or sisters. He argues that this indicates that the bond to the mother is not necessarily different in quality from that with other people with whom the child has intense interaction – and hence, the more people to whom the child is attached, the less chance of a sense of loss there is. Rutter (1972, pp. 124–5) concludes:

> Of course in most families the mother has most to do with the young child and as a consequence she is usually the person with whom the strongest bond is formed. But it should be appreciated that the chief bond need not be with a biological parent, it need not be with the chief caretaker, and it need not be with a female.

It is difficult to gauge the potential success of any kind of child-rearing arrangement which denies the need for any necessary connection between biological parenthood and social parenthood. Where such attempts have been made in the past, they have tended to generate the kind of horror-struck reaction usually only associated with revelations of incest. For example, the Oneida community, founded in New York in 1848, in which children were reared apart from their parents and whose inhabitants were therefore able to enter into complex sexual relationships with one another, encountered so much hostility from the surrounding society that it only lasted thirty years. Contemporary (but much less dramatic) equivalents – so far as child-rearing is concerned – are communes and the Israeli kibbutzim. Although in Britain and the USA, for example, communes have varied very considerably in character, they too have often adopted the principle that child-rearing should be communal, with the community as a whole taking corporate responsibility for looking after the children. In many cases, however, the continued recognition of ties of blood and marriage between spouses and their own children within the context of community life has meant that traditional notions of child-rearing as the responsibility of biological parents have often overwhelmed the ideal of corporate responsibility.

The same has also become true of an even more celebrated alternative child-rearing arrangement embodied in the Israeli kibbutz. The original notions here regarding parenthood were once again that biological parent–child ties should be lessened in favour of ties between children and the whole community. For example, in the early kibbutzim care of the children was in the hands of a communal nursery, and trained nurses and teachers took over many of the duties performed in the nuclear family by parents, who were encouraged to spend only Saturday and an hour or two each weekday with their children. Once again, however, the continued recognition of blood links as signifying special social relationships eventually began to undermine the ideal: as time passed, conjugal relations became well-established and three-generational ties developed (although recently, in some kibbutzim, extended collective child-care provision has reasserted the old ideals).

These apparent 'failures' have been used to support the idea that the nuclear family is universal – that any attempt to bypass or ignore the supposedly elemental ties between parents and children must be doomed. Whether this is a fair judgement seems open to question. It could well be argued that the commune/kibbutzim evidence serves not to prove that alternative child-rearing institutions *cannot* succeed, but that individuals already socialised into traditional values will find it difficult to reject these totally, especially where the alternative is practised at a micro level only, inside a wider society which is unhelpful or hostile.

In his Reith lectures in 1967, Edmund Leach (1968), as he says himself, 'aroused much public hostility' when he suggested that:

We should look carefully at experimental institutions, such as the Israeli kibbutz and the Chinese commune in which the local community takes over the parental support role which has been exercised in the past by the family. As in the case of Oneida, these experiments have not worked out very well but their problem is real. Sooner or later we shall have to devise some variation on the same theme ourselves.

Although it seems doubtful that the commune or the kibbutz should be held up as any kind of model for alternative child-rearing in an industrial society (while such units may work well where they are self-sufficient or constructed around the production of agricultural goods, they are probably too large to suit a world demanding a mobile work-force), it seems likely that Leach's conclusion is correct. The strains resulting from the institutional contradictions we have been describing make it unlikely that people subjected to strain will allow the institutions to remain the same. For example, the pressure for more nursery schools, and the growth of single-parent families and open marriages, might be interpreted as manifestations of the contradictions and the search for a proper solution.

However, such a solution will not come automatically. Social institutions producing strain, suffering and disadvantage have persisted long enough to show that the 'needs' of social groups will not necessarily be served and that 'social integration' will not emerge of its own accord. The isolated individualism that characterises the contemporary family is an enormous barrier to any mobilisation of collective demands for change. Social institutions do not emerge solely through deliberate choice but act back on people in expected ways; at the same time, understanding the source of our problems can permit deliberate change. Sociology has an important role to play in providing some of this understanding – above all, through emphasising that the nuclear family system is *not* natural, universal and inevitable.

REFERENCES TO CHAPTER 7

Anderson, A. (1971) *Family Structure in Nineteenth Century Lancashire*, Cambridge University Press.
Ariès, P. (1973) *Centuries of Childhood*, Harmondsworth, Penguin.
Bell, C. (1968) *Middle Class Families*, London, Routledge & Kegan Paul.
Bernard, J. (1982) *The Future of Marriage*, New Haven and London, Yale University Press.
Beynon, H. (1973) *Working for Ford*, Harmondsworth, Penguin.
Bott, E. (1957) *Family and Social Network*, London, Tavistock.
Bowlby, J. (1965) *Child Care and the Growth of Love*, Harmondsworth, Penguin.
Bowlby, J. (1971) *Attachment and Loss, vol. I*, Harmondsworth, Penguin.
Bowlby, J. (1975) *Attachment and Loss, vol. II*, Harmondsworth, Penguin.
Craddock, A. (1977) 'Task and Emotional Behavior in the Marital Dyad', in N. Glazer and H. Y. Waehrer (eds), *Women in a Man-made World*, Chicago, Rand McNally.

Dennis, N., Henriques, F. and Slaughter, C. (1956) *Coal is Our Life*, London, Eyre & Spottiswoode.

Dobash, R. and Dobash, R. (1980) *Violence against Wives*, London, Open Books.

Edgell, S. (1980) *Middle-Class Couples*, London, George Allen & Unwin.

Edholm, F. (1982) 'The Unnatural Family', in E. Whitelegg *et al.* (eds), *The Changing Experience of Women*, Oxford, Martin Robertson.

Elston, M. (1980) 'Medicine: Half our Future Doctors?', in R. Silverstone and A. Ward (eds), *Careers of Professional Women*, London, Croom Helm.

Family Policy Studies Centre (1985) *The Family Today: Continuity and Change*, Fact Sheet 1, London, Family Policy Studies Centre.

Finch, J. (1983) *Married to the Job*, London, George Allen & Unwin.

Fletcher, R. (1966) *The Family and Marriage in Britain*, Harmondsworth, Penguin.

Fox, R. (1967) *Kinship and Marriage*, Harmondsworth, Penguin.

Fox, R. (1975) *Encounter with Anthropology*, Harmondsworth, Penguin.

Gavron, H. (1968) *The Captive Wife*, Harmondsworth, Penguin.

Gillespie, D. (1972) 'Who has the Power? The Marital Struggle', in H. P. Dreitzel (ed.), *Family, Marriage and the Struggle of the Sexes*, New York and London, Collier-Macmillan.

Goldthorpe, J. H., Lockwood, D. and colleagues (1968a) *The Affluent Worker: Industrial Attitudes and Behaviour*, Cambridge University Press.

Goldthorpe, J. H. (1968b) *The Affluent Worker: Political Attitudes and Behaviour*, Cambridge University Press.

Goldthorpe, J. H. (1969) *The Affluent Worker in the Class Structure*, Cambridge University Press.

Goode, W. J. (1963) *World Revolution and Family Patterns*, London, Collier-Macmillan.

Goode, W. J. (1968) 'The Theory and Measurement of Family Change', in E. Sheldon and W. E. Moore (eds), *Indicators of Social Change*, New York, Russell Sage.

Harris, C. C. (1977) 'Changing Conceptions of the Relation between Family and Societal Form in Western Society', in R. Scase (ed.), *Industrial Society: Class, Cleavage and Control*, London, Allen & Unwin.

Hart, C. W. M. and Pilling, A. R. (1960) *The Tiwi of North Australia*, New York, Holt, Rinehart & Winston.

Hartmann, H. (1981) 'The Family as the Locus of Class, Gender and Political Struggle: the Example of Housework', *Signs*, vol. 6 (Spring 1981), pp. 366–94.

Hubert, J. (1970) 'Kinship', in E. Butterworth and D. Weir (eds), *The Sociology of Modern Britain*, London, Fontana.

Kerr, M. (1958) *The People of Ship Street*, London, Routledge & Kegan Paul.

Laing, R. D. (1960) *The Divided Self*, Harmondsworth, Penguin.

Laslett, P. (1977) *Family Life and Illicit Love in Earlier Generations*, Cambridge Univerity Press.

Laslett, P. and Wall, R. (eds) (1972) *Household and Family in Past Time*, Cambridge University Press.

Leach, E. (1968) 'The Family as an Instrument of Women's Enslavement', *Sunday Times Magazine*, 10 November 1968.

Litwak, E. (1960a) 'Occupational Mobility and Extended Family Cohesion', *American Sociological Review*, vol. 25.

Litwak, E. (1960b) 'Geographical Mobility and Extended Family Cohesion', *American Sociological Review*, vol. 25.

Lupri, E. and Symons, G. (1982) 'The emerging symmetrical family: fact or fiction?' *International Journal of Comparative Sociology*, vol. 23, no. 3–4.

Lupton, T. and Wilson, C. S. (1959) 'The Social Backgrounds and Connections of "Top Decision Makers"', *Manchester School*, vol. 27.

Morgan, D. H. J. (1975) *Social Theory and the Family*, London, Routledge & Kegan Paul.

Oakley, A. (1972) *Sex, Gender and Society*, London, Temple-Smith.

Oakley, A. (1974) *The Sociology of Housework*, London, Martin Robertson.

Pahl, J. M. and Pahl, R. E. (1972) *Managers and their Wives*, Harmondsworth, Penguin.

Parsons, T. (1959) 'The Social Structure of the Family', in R. Anshen (ed.) *The Family: its Function and Destiny*, New York, Harper & Row.

Parsons, T. (1964) *Essays in Social Theory*, New York, Free Press.

Parsons, T. and Bales, R. F. (1956) *Family: Socialisation and Interaction Process*, London, Routledge & Kegan Paul.

Pringle, M. L. K. (1980) *The Needs of Children*, 2nd edn, London, Hutchinson.

Rapoport, R. and Rapoport, R. (1976) *Dual Career Families Re-Examined*, London, Martin Robertson.

Rosser, C. and Harris, C. C. (1965) *The Family and Social Change*, London, Routledge & Kegan Paul.

Rutter, M. (1972) *Maternal Deprivation Reassessed*, Harmondsworth, Penguin.

Shorter, E. (1977) *The Making of the Modern Family*, London, Fontana.

Straus, M. *et al.* (1982) *Behind Closed Doors: Violence in the American Family*, New York, Doubleday.

Sussman, M. (1953) 'The Help Pattern in the Middle Class Family', *American Sociological Review*, vol. 18.

Sussman, M. and Burchinal, L. (1962) 'Kin Family Network', *Marriage and Family Living*, vol. 24.

Tunstall, J. (1962) *The Fishermen*, London, MacGibbon & Kee.

Webb, M. (1982) 'The Labour Market', in I. Reid and E. Wormald (eds), *Sex Differences in Britain*, London, Grant McIntyre.

Willmott, P. (1963) *The Evolution of a Community*, London, Routledge & Kegan Paul.

Willmott, P. and Young, M. (1971) *Family and Class in a London Suburb*, London, New English Library.

Young, M. and Willmott, P. (1962) *Family and Kinship in East London*, Harmondsworth, Penguin.

Young, M. and Willmott, P. (1973) *The Symmetrical Family*, London, Routledge & Kegan Paul.

8

Education

8.1 INTRODUCTION

On most weekdays in the 1980s, several million British youngsters will be sitting in schoolrooms under the watchful (or harassed) gaze of a teacher. Whether reading aloud in front of class, or waiting their turn for the big scissors, revising anxiously for a biology test, or hoping to 'have a laff' with their friends when the teacher's back is turned, each pupil will spend at least 15,000 hours of childhood and adolescence in school. Small wonder that formal education is regarded as a major agency of socialisation in advanced industrial societies. Socialisation is, however, a continuous process: individuals are subject to its influence before, alongside and after their school career. Education differs from other forms of socialisation in that it involves instruction which is deliberate, conducted within formal organisations set aside for that purpose, and relatively standardised; there is probably less variation in what children learn from schooling (whether through the official or the hidden curriculum) than in what they learn as a result of informal interaction with family, friends and workmates.

We tend to regard education as a necessary way of preparing children for adult life, in terms of certification (labelling people as 'eligible' for particular positions) as well as socialisation. Yet in many pre-industrial societies, young people learn by involvement in the life of the community, with deliberate, systematic instruction often confined to particular rituals. Ariès points to the marked contrast between our views of schooling and those prevalent in France and Britain in the Middle Ages, in his book *Centuries of Childhood*. Medieval schools were attended by individuals, at any age of their life and for any period of time. Education was a matter of *academic* learning; schools were not concerned with moral training or character building, nor were they specifically for the young. In fact, Ariès argues, the notion of 'childhood' as a special period of life requiring a systematic programme of training did not exist in medieval society. People passed from infancy – when little notice was taken of them – to full participation in adult life. From the age of 7, most young people were expected to work, learn or play alongside adults, and the performance of children and adults was evaluated by much the same standards. From the fifteenth century onwards, attitudes towards young people began to change, as did views on the nature of schooling. The emergence of a concept of childhood as a time of innocence and vulnerability seemed to justify the isolation of children from adult society in the specialised institutions of schools: 'Henceforth it was recognised that the child was not ready for life, and that he had to be subjected to a special treatment, a sort of quarantine, before he was allowed to join the adults' (Ariès, 1973, p. 396). Of course, the provision of schooling proceeded very slowly and selectively. Notions of the vulnerability of children did not prevent their employment on a wide scale in heavy, dangerous work in factories and mines. In Britain, as late as 1870, only 2 per cent of children aged 14, and 40 per cent of those aged 10, were receiving full-time education. Nevertheless, Ariès does help us to understand how culturally and historically specific many of our ideas of schooling are.

Ariès's research has had a great influence on many of those who argue for the abolition of compulsory schooling. Illich, for example, echoes Ariès when he writes, 'The school system is a modern phenomenon, as is the childhood it produces' (1973, p. 34). Both the spread of schooling, and the 'childhood it produces', are, in Illich's view, to be deplored; childhood robs young people of the right to be independent and responsible beings, and school compounds their indignity and degradation. Those who attend school are, in Illich's view, robbed of creativity, and taught to bow to the wisdom of others. Those who do *not* attend are still conditioned to doubt their own capacities:

> Half of the people in our world never set foot in school. They have no contact with teachers, and they are deprived of the privilege of becoming dropouts. Yet they learn quite effectively the message which school teaches . . . School instructs them in their own inferiority through the tax collector who makes them pay for it, or through the demagogue who raises their expectations of it, or through their children once the latter are hooked on it. So the poor are robbed of their self-respect by subscribing to a creed that grants salvation only through the school (Illich, 1973, p. 36).

While Illich's description of the experience of schooling accords with many of the criticisms offered by others, including those writing in a Marxist tradition, his solution (starting as it does with the transformation of individual consciousness) and his analysis (which takes little account of the relationship between schooling and economic and political power) are not so readily endorsed. Illich's view of the experience of school would not be shared by, amongst others, the Tuscan peasant children who wrote *Letter to a Teacher* (overleaf). Their argument suggests that the notion of children free to enjoy the benefits of adult life may be as much an idealisation as the idea that children cherish with delight their golden schooldays. Whatever faults we locate in schools, they also offer opportunities which might otherwise be absent

---

Letter to a teacher

Father Milani set up the School of Barbiana for peasant children who had been failures in the state schools. In this passage, pupils discuss the experience of studying seven days a week:

> There was no break. Not even Sunday was a holiday. None of us was bothered by it because labour would have been worse. But any middle-class gentleman who happened to be around would start a fuss on this question. Once a big professor held forth: 'You have never studied pedagogy, Father Milani. Doctor Polianski writes that sport for boys is a physiopsycho. . . .' He was talking without looking at us. A university professor of education doesn't have to look at schoolboys. He knows them by heart, the way we know our multiplication tables. Finally he left, and Lucio, who has thirty-six cows in the barn at home, said, 'School will always be better than cow shit.' That sentence can be engraved over the front doors of your schools. Millions of farm boys are ready to subscribe to it. You say that boys hate school and love play. You never asked us peasants (School of Barbiana, 1970, pp. 19–20).

8.2   EDUCATION SINCE THE SECOND WORLD WAR: EXPANSION AND CONTRACTION

While the Education Act of 1870 laid the groundwork for the provision of elementary or primary education for all children in England and Wales, it was not until the implementation of the 1944 Education Act that all girls and boys were entitled to a secondary education. Indeed, the decades immediately following the Second World War saw such a rapid increase in educational provision – in the USA, and many countries of Western and Eastern Europe, as well as in Britain – that some writers refer to the 'educational explosion' of the 1950s and 1960s. The minimum school-leaving age was extended from 14 to 15 years (in 1947) and raised to 16 (in 1971–2), but the proportion of people choosing to pursue their studies beyond this age hurtled upward; by 1971, 30 per cent of 17-year-olds were in full-time education in schools or colleges, compared with 2 per cent in 1902, 4 per cent in 1938, 18 per cent in 1961 and 22 per cent in 1966. The Robbins Report (1963) undermined the view that there was a finite 'pool of ability' – a limited number of people who could benefit from advanced education – and provided ammunition for the expansion of higher education. This expansion took place through the establishment of new universities and growth of existing ones, as well as through the conversion of colleges into polytechnics which could offer degree courses, and the founding of the Open University. In 1970, 17.5 per cent of 18-year-olds entered further or higher education on a full-time basis (compared with 1.2

per cent in 1900, 2.7 per cent in 1938, 5.8 per cent in 1954, and 8.3 per cent in 1960); another three million people enrolled for part-time day classes, evening classes or sandwich courses.

The 'educational explosion' reflected a commitment by successive governments of the time to educational growth. Underpinning this commitment were two major objectives. The first was to create a fairer educational system, and possibly thereby a fairer society, by giving greater opportunities to working-class children for advancement through education; widening access to secondary and higher education was seen as an important step towards a meritocratic society, based on equality of opportunity. The second objective was to use education more effectively to develop the skills of the nation's future labour force; from this standpoint, educational expansion and reform were seen as ways of exploiting the human resources on which national prosperity may depend. Since a large untapped reservoir of ability lay in the talents of working-class girls and boys, the two objectives were seen to be interlocked. Both the target of economic efficiency, and that of social justice, would be met, it was hoped, by educational reform.

Education in the 1980s

The expansion of opportunities – the hallmark of educational policy in the early post-war decades – was replaced in the 1980s by contraction. Government spending on education dropped from 6.3 per cent of public expenditure in 1975/6, to 5.2 per cent in 1983/4, with striking results for higher education. University places fell dramatically in the early 1980s, at the same time as the 18-year-old population approached a peak. By 1983/4, there was 7100 fewer male undergraduates in British universities, and 1400 fewer female undergraduates, than in the peak years of 1980/1 and 1982/3. Some of the qualified candidates who failed to get university places were initially absorbed by the polytechnics and colleges; but government proposals to reduce funding for public sector higher education means that student places there also face contraction. These cuts in educational provision – serious enough to be termed by Kogan (1983) an 'attack on higher education' – represent a clear abandonment of the Robbins principle, that higher education should be available to all those with suitable ability and attainments. The emphasis in the 1980s has been on 'content' and 'standards', rather than on access.

The growth of educational provision throughout the 1950s and 1960s was paralleled by an explosion of research within the sociology of education. The bulk of this research was aimed at monitoring the effects of educational expansion on equality of opportunity, and much of it was informed by a functionalist perspective. However, since the 1970s, many writers in the sociology of education have found a Marxist perspective useful for analysing the place of education in modern society. We will sketch these two competing accounts of the relationship between education, the economy and social equality, before examining evidence on this issue, since both perspectives draw upon similar bodies of data, but interpret them in radically different ways.

8.3   THEORETICAL PERSPECTIVES ON THE LINKS BETWEEN EDUCATION, ECONOMY AND SOCIAL EQUALITY

A functionalist account

From this perspective, the expansion of formal schooling is seen as a precondition for efficient economic growth and for the development of a meritocratic society. The changes connected with industrialism give rise to specific 'functional imperatives' – needs which must be met if society is to survive and prosper. The education system plays a crucial part in meeting at least three of these needs, performing three vital functions on behalf of society.

First, the education system is a vehicle for developing the human resources of an industrial nation. In pre-industrial society, the range of 'occupations' is relatively limited, and new recruits can usually learn all they need to know to do the job adequately by working alongside their parents or by apprenticing themselves to a skilled practitioner. But industrialisation brings with it marked changes in the occupational structure. New, highly specialised occupations emerge; the number of jobs requiring sheer muscle power is reduced by mechanisation; new forms of technology give rise to occupations requiring higher levels of human judgement and expertise; and the need for white-collar, technical, professional and managerial workers increases.

The expansion of mass schooling, and of higher education, is seen as a direct response to these changes. Through schooling, each new generation is provided with basic skills which will enable them, as the future labour force, to respond to complex technical instructions and to adapt to constantly changing occupational requirements. In addition, those children who are sufficiently clever and motivated can be instructed in the more specialised forms of knowledge necessary for work in professional, managerial or technical occupations. In sum, the provision of a highly developed system of education is a response to the general *technical* requirements of industrial production – the need for a labour force in which skills and talents are developed to the full, and matched to the complexity of jobs in a modern industrialised world.

Second, the fact that industrial societies have a multiplicity of occupations, with differing skill requirements and varied levels of responsibility, means that a sophisticated mechanism is necessary to select individuals according to their talents, and train them for the jobs they can most effectively fill. Education therefore has a vital selection or allocative function. As well as developing the talents of pupils, schools and colleges monitor or evaluate their performance by means of grades, school reports, references, and examinations. Educational attainments (reflected in grades or certificates) are widely used by employers to select the most able candidate for each vacancy. While education determines, then, through its selection function, who will be allocated to humdrum occupations, and who to the more rewarding posts, inequality is not a consequence of the education system itself but of the scarce distribution of skill in society, and of the necessity of attaching greater rewards to more demanding occupations so that individuals have the incentive to devote their energies to competing for these positions. But the selection of individuals through the education system ensures, more or less, that those who come to occupy the more highly rewarded jobs are those who deserve them on the basis of their greater achievement, and, presumably, their greater capacity.

In sum, schooling as we know it is taken (from a functionalist point of view) to be the 'inevitable' consequence of the general technical requirements of industrial production – requirements for technical training, and for allocation of 'the right man or woman' to the job.

Third, it is argued from a functionalist perspective that schooling contributes to the cohesion of society, by transmitting to new generations the central or 'core' values of that society. A standardised curriculum, at least in primary school, exposes all pupils – whether their parents were Jamaican, Irish or Polish, whether they are working class, middle class or upper class – to their 'common cultural heritage'; aspects of British history and political institutions, for example, will be discussed, and 'fundamental values', such as honesty, individualism, achievement orientation and a respect for parliamentary democracy will be imparted. The effect of the transmission of a core culture through the education system is to promote consensus on the basic values of the society, to ensure a fundamental level of agreement despite the diversity of individuals' life-experiences.

In recent years, the functionalist approach to education has come under attack from several quarters. The assumptions on which it is based appear to be highly problematic. Firstly, the degree of 'fit' between the technical and cognitive skills taught in school, and the technical requirements of efficient production, is far from clear; many pupils are well aware that the material on which they are examined and certified – be it algebra or Latin, sociology of education, or human biology – has little direct connection with the tasks which they undertake when they enter employment in a factory, shop, hospital or office. Berg, in *Education for Jobs: the Great Training Robbery* (1970), offers data which suggest that more highly qualified workers, in educational terms, are not necessarily more productive workers; educational certificates may be necessary to make you *eligible* for certain jobs, but it is unclear whether they make you *proficient* in those jobs.

Second, though schools do undoubtedly select certain pupils as successes or failures, and play a part in allocating them to unequally rewarded positions in the social structure, it is not clear whether the selection and allocation is related to some intrinsic merit of the pupils themselves, or to ascriptive characteristics such as their ethnic or social class backgrounds, or their sex. Some would argue that schools, in the main, *confirm* pupils in the status to which they were born, rather than acting as 'neutral' selection agents indifferent to the background of pupils. Moreover, the notion that the education system encourages pupils to compete for 'the glittering prizes', and hence raises their ambitions and aspirations, is contentious. In practice, many aspects of the education system (whether intentionally or not) seem to dampen down the aspirations of particular groups of pupils, persuading them that they have set their sights 'unrealistically high'.

Third, the notion of a core curriculum is difficult to sustain. Are the values and ideas promoted by the schools equally subscribed to, and equally emanating from, all sectors of society? As King, (1977, p. 3) puts it, 'There are many different ways of being British.' Many content-analyses of curricular materials show racist, ethnic, social class and sexist biases; moreover, it can be argued that the values and knowledge selected for transmission within schools will be more familiar, more compatible and more beneficial to some groups in society than to others. Within sociology of education, a renewed emphasis upon the curriculum in recent years has replaced the notion of 'transmission of core culture' with a question: how is it that, out of all the knowledge, ideas and values which are available in a society, only certain ones are selected? The question of the criteria behind the selection of *partial* curricula, and the question of which groups in society benefit most from a particular selection of knowledge, have come to the forefront.

A Marxist account

Partly in response to growing dissatisfaction with the prevailing functionalist account, many analysts have turned to conflict perspectives in search of a more adequate account of the relationship between education, economy and society. One of the best-known conflict models is that proposed by Bowles and Gintis, in *Schooling in Capitalist America* (1976). Bowles and Gintis, like the functionalists, see an intimate link between schooling and the economy; but, unlike the functionalists, it is the specific requirements of industrial *capitalism*, rather than the general needs of industrialism, which in their view shape the nature of educational systems.

The social relations of production under capitalism are characterised by rigid hierarchies of authority (shareholders and directors; managers; professional and technical staff; white-collar workers; manual employees), and by an increasing fragmentation of tasks. The diversity of occupations referred to earlier means that, apart from a small proportion of professional and executive personnel, the majority of the labour force are increasingly required to perform mundane tasks allowing small scope for initiative, responsibility or judgement. Because of the hierarchical pattern of work, and its fragmentation, most people have minimal control over what they do and how they do it. The explanation of this lies not in the demands of technology itself, but in the capitalist need to control workers more closely in the interests of greater profits.

Bowles and Gintis argue that schooling operates within the 'long shadow of work': that is, the education system reflects the organisation of production in capitalist society. For example, the fragmentation of most work processes is mirrored in the breaking up of the curriculum into tiny 'packages' of knowledge, each subject divorced from all others; lack of control over work processes is reflected in the powerlessness of pupils with regard to what they will learn in school or how they will learn it; and the necessity of working for pay when jobs seem pointless and unfulfilling in themselves is paralleled by the emphasis in schools on learning in order to gain good grades, rather than learning for its own sake. Therefore, Bowles and Gintis claim there is a *correspondence* between the nature of work in capitalist societies, and the nature of schooling.

While stressing those aspects of schooling that inhibit critical capacity and independent judgement, Bowles and Gintis (1976, p. 42) also point out that schools are not uniform in their patterns of organisation and instruction:

> But schools do different things to different children. Boys and girls, blacks and whites, rich and poor are treated differently. Affluent suburban schools, working-class schools, and ghetto schools all exhibit a distinctive pattern.

For example, in schools (or streams, or tracks) which cater largely for working-class children, the emphasis may be placed on docility, obedience, 'rule-following'; pupils may be closely supervised, and subjected to the same sort of discipline, and the same criteria for evaluation, which they will experience in their working lives in factories and shops. In educational institutions that cater for children from wealthy backgrounds, the emphasis will be on encouraging the leadership abilities considered suitable for a future elite. Thus, while it is not denied that schools teach a variety of technical skills and cognitive abilities, the emphasis in Bowles and Gintis's account is on the personality characteristics – particularly patterns of authority and control – that the schools foster and reward.

They also stress that capitalist societies are class societies; they are characterised by great and persistent inequality and by relationships of subordination and domination between social classes. These inequalities cannot be explained, they argue, by reference to the scarce distribution of ability or intelligence in the population; instead, the inequalities are the inevitable result of capitalist relations of production, in which the means of production are privately owned and all other people must compete in the market-place for rewards in the form of income. Thus class inequality is a *necessary* feature not of all societies, but of capitalist societies, and schools play an important part in transmitting inequality between generations. The occupations of future members of the labour force are to a large extent predetermined by the social class from which they come. The majority of girls and boys from working-class backgrounds, for example, are destined to follow in their parents' footsteps. Schools play a part in ensuring that this comes about, by assigning pupils to a school or track, or stream that is 'appropriate' to their future position in the labour force. There they will be socialised into the habits of thought and practice that will be required of them in their future work. In this way, schools take an active part in 'reproducing – or creating anew each generation – people who have been moulded in order to slot into their place in a labour force that is divided along lines of social class, sex and ethnicity.

At the same time that education creates the conditions necessary for recreating inequality, it also helps to legitimate that inequality: that is, education helps to justify in people's minds a system of inequality, and to reconcile them to their own position within it. How does schooling do this? As long as most people believe that education gives everyone a fair chance to prove their worth and as long as privilege and disadvantage are widely believed to stem from fair competition in the educational arena, then inequality *appears* to be justified by different levels of educational achievement. The successful ones view their privileges as a well-deserved reward for ability and effort, while subordinate groups are encouraged to 'personalise' their 'failure': they are encouraged, that is, to treat poverty or powerlessness as the inevitable result of their own individual limitations – lack of intelligence, ambition or effort.

A brief comparison of functionalist and Marxist approaches

Both functionalist and Marxist accounts have been criticised for positing too tight a fit between education and the economy, and for exaggerating the extent to which schools act as providers of a ready, willing and able supply of labour (Moore, 1984). Analyses of the content of education suggest that, in the period when education was expanding most rapidly, the relationship between school and work was relatively loose and unstructured; neither the functionalist emphasis upon technical skills, nor the Marxist emphasis upon socialisation for alienated labour, serve to account for the variety of purposes which schools served in the 1950s and 1960s (Finn and Frith,

1981). Curiously enough, since the 1970s, education has frequently been blamed for failing to provide the discipline and the technical skills which would fit young people for the labour force; in the context of rising youth unemployment, successive governments have trumpeted the necessity to make the education system more directly a servant of the economy. The state – by, for example, assigning responsibility for the education of 16–19-year-olds to the Manpower Services Commission – has taken a more direct hand in managing the transition from school to work. This emphasis upon training youth for work may be interpreted as an attempt to divert attention from the deep-seated changes in the economy which generate unemployment, and for which education cannot possibly offer a remedy (Clarke and Willis, 1984; Rees and Gregory, 1981). The recent recession has brought home the point that the expansion of education provides no guarantees of economic growth. But just as the economic boom of the 1960s cannot be attributed to the expansion of education, so too it would be unwise to blame education for the spectacular levels of youth unemployment in the 1980s.

The two competing approaches that have been outlined above are in fact similar in certain other respects. As structural approaches, both emphasise the macro-level of analysis – the relationship between education and other social institutions – and devote correspondingly less attention to the routine interactions of teachers and pupils in school. Both concentrate more on the structure of education than on its content, the curriculum. Both approaches tend to give enormous weight to the power of education to shape pupils' minds and their lives; the functionalist vision of pupils who eagerly compete to display to teachers their newly acquired technical skills would be as alien to many secondary teachers as the Marxist vision of pupils who have been moulded into conformity and docility. On all these counts, action theorists have been (as we shall see in a later section of the chapter) highly critical of both Marxist and functionalist views of education.

But if functionalist and Marxist approaches to education have emphases and weaknesses in common, they do differ radically in the way they conceive of the relationship between education and inequality. As Karabel and Halsey (1977, p. 35) explain: 'where functionalists have often viewed the educational system as offering opportunities for mobility for individuals, conflict theorists have generally stressed the role of education in maintaining a system of structured social inequality'. The next section examines evidence relating to this issue.

8.4 EDUCATION AND SOCIAL INEQUALITY: THE MERITOCRACY THESIS

Until the Second World War, education in Britain clearly had limited impact as a vehicle of social mobility. The education system did not provide a ladder of mobility but was, rather, 'the stamp put on the social character of individuals whose jobs and life-styles were predetermined by social origin' (Halsey, 1977, p. 176).

Educational reformers and sociologists alike saw the promotion of *equality of opportunity* in education as the key to a new, more open society – a meritocracy, in which people could move freely up and down the occupational hierarchy according to personal merit. In a meritocracy, the education system would act ruthlessly and impartially to allocate individuals to a station befitting their ability; being born into a humble home would be no barrier to success, and being born into a wealthy or powerful family no cushion against failure. In short, equality of opportunity in education would be the instrument for severing the old links between family background and adult success.

Before examining the evidence regarding the success or failure of this programme, we should note two points about the linked concepts of 'meritocracy' and 'equality of opportunity'. First, in most versions of the meritocratic thesis, social inequality is assumed to be a more or less inevitable outcome of individual differences in intelligence or talent, given the 'need' in industrial societies to offer incentives to those of higher ability. This assumption is the basis of the argument put forward by Herrnstein, in *IQ in the Meritocracy* (1973, p. 60):

> If virtually anyone is smart enough to be a ditch digger, and only half the people are smart enough to be engineers, the society is, in effect, husbanding its intellectual resources by holding engineers in greater esteem and paying them more.

The parallels with the functional theory of stratification, which is elaborated and criticised more fully in Chapter 2, are immediately apparent; what is also clear is that the meritocratic thesis addresses itself only to those rewards stemming from *occupational* position, and therefore completely ignores inequalities stemming from the distribution of wealth.

Second, a meritocracy is by definition a society with structured social inequality; all it promises is equal opportunity to compete for unequal power and reward. In a meritocracy the education system is not expected to eradicate privilege and disadvantage: it merely offers a new sorting mechanism for recruiting people to subordinate or dominant positions. In fact, several writers have argued that this limitation is part of its appeal: 'Education has always seemed one of the most acceptable ways of using the national wealth to provide opportunity for the poor without offending the comfortable' (Hodgson, 1973, p. 353).

Are modern industrial societies meritocratic?

A meritocratic society is one in which social rewards are allocated not according to ascribed characteristics, or accidents of birth, but according to talent. In a meritocracy, there are no social barriers to the translation of ability into educational achievement, and thereby into occupational success. Therefore, before any society can qualify as a meritocracy, the following two conditions have to be met:

(1) Occupational status and reward must depend solely on a person's academic achievement (perhaps in combination with other demonstrations of accomplishment); ascribed characteristics such as gender, ethnic origins or social class background must not have an influence on pay and prestige.

(2) Educational achievement itself must depend solely on merit; there must be equality of opportunity within education, such that the chances of success in school are the same for all those of similar ability, regardless of class origins, ethnic group or sex.

Is the distribution of occupational status and reward determined by educational achievement?

We must first make clear that we are only considering whether, *given* the existence of structured social inequality, access to privileged positions is determined by success in school; we are *not* suggesting that educational achievement might determine the structure of rewards. Education cannot transform us all into white-collar workers, nor can it eradicate the divisions between, for example, jobs with good pay and prospects and those without, or between occupations which last for a lifetime and those under threat of redundancy.

But how important is education in determining who gets what within the existing structure of rewards? Empirical evidence suggests that the 'returns' to education – that is, the financial and status benefits to be derived from qualifications – depend to a considerable degree on the ethnicity, social class background and sex of their holder. For example, after extensive analysis of data relating to the educational and occupational histories of American males, Jencks and his colleagues find that, although years of schooling affect the jobs men get, there are within each occupation vast income differences; men with equal educational achievement and similar occupations often earn vastly different amounts. They conclude, moreover, that these income differences are closely related to social class origins:

> men from high status families have higher incomes than men from lower-status families, even when they enter the same occupation, have the same amount of education and have the same test scores (Jencks *et al.*, 1973, p. 216).

The relatively small part played by education in the distribution of status and reward is further diminished if we look beyond the minority group of white males. Our discussions of gender divisions and of race relations earlier in the book documented multiple obstacles facing women and black people in the labour market; these obstacles persist even where educational levels are similar.

Returns to education by sex and ethnic group

In Britain in 1983, of adults in full-time employment, 69 per cent of men with degrees or equivalent qualifications had gross annual earnings of £9360 or more; only 44 per cent of women with identical qualifications were in that income bracket (*General Household Survey 1983*, HMSO, 1985, Tables 8.14 and 8.15). Among employed male adults with O-level qualifications, 61 per cent of whites, but only 42 per cent of West Indians and 29 per cent of Asians are in non-manual occupations; among employed female adults with no qualifications, only 51 per cent of whites, but 66 per cent of West Indians and 70 per cent of Asians, are in semi-skilled or unskilled manual jobs (Brown, 1984, Table 93, p. 199).

While educational qualifications increase the chances that their holders will secure good jobs and high incomes, *ascribed characteristics* continue to exert an influence on occupation and earnings, even among people who have reached identical educational levels.

To summarise our argument so far: the occupational structure, and the rewards available in society, are not determined by outputs from the educational system; furthermore, given an unequal structure of reward, educational qualifications do not determine an individual's success or failure. It follows (as emphasised by Jencks) that equalising educational achievement would not of itself equalise incomes (or other forms of reward). Equality of opportunity *within* education may be sought as a valuable end in its own right, but it would not guarantee even meritocracy, let alone equality, in society.

Is there equality of opportunity within education for children from different social classes?

Whether we measure opportunity in terms of access to educational facilities, or in terms of the results that pupils achieve, the overwhelming weight of evidence confirms that social class origins are strongly and clearly implicated in educational success or failure.

Class membership and educational achievement

Halsey, Heath and Ridge (1980), in a study of 8529 males educated in England and Wales, found that a boy from the 'service class' (employers, professionals, and managers), compared with a boy from the working-class, had:

40 times more chance of attending a public school
18 times more chance of attending a minor independent school
12 times more chance of attending a direct grant school
3 times more chance of attending a grammar school

Of all the types of secondary school, technical schools were the only ones to admit a respresentative cross-section of the male population. The pattern of unequal access to the more prestigious secondary schools remained, in the words of the authors, 'depressingly constant over time'. Despite the educational reforms of the post-war era, 'the likelihood of a working-class boy receiving a selective education in the mid 'fifties and 'sixties was very little different from that of his parents' generation thirty years earlier' (Halsey, Heath and Ridge, 1980, p. 203).

The degree of class inequality grows more severe as children move up the educational ladder. For example, a boy from the service class, compared with a working-class boy, had:

4 times more chance of being in school at age 16
8 times more chance of being in school at age 17
10 times more chance of being in school at age 18
11 times more chance of entering university

By comparing the oldest cohort of men in their sample with the youngest and most recently-educated cohort (see Table 8.1). Halsey and his colleagues refute popular notions that the working class have 'caught up' with other groups – or at least narrowed class differentials in educational attainment – over time.

During the period being analysed, the proportion of working-class boys entering university increased by 2 per cent, but that of boys from the 'intermediate class' (clerical workers, small proprietors, foremen) and from the service class increased by 6 per cent and 19 per cent respectively. The expansion of university places resulted in greater absolute gains for middle-class than for working-class men; differentials between the classes were preserved. Halsey and his colleagues (1980, p. 210) conclude:

the 1944 Education Act brought England and Wales no nearer to the ideal of a meritocratic society . . . Secondary education was made free in order to enable the poor to take advantage of it, but the paradoxical consequence was to increase subsidies to the affluent.

This conclusion is all the more persuasive because it is consistent with a range of over investigations, not only in Britain but in other capitalist countries as well. While there is, as we shall shortly see, disagreement about the *explanation* for persistent social class inequality in education, the *fact* of that inequality is not in dispute.

TABLE 8.1

Proportion of men from different birth cohorts attending university, by social class origin

Social class origins	Men born:		Improvement in chance of university education from older to younger cohort of men	
	1913–22 (%)	1943–52 (%)	(ratio)	(amount)
Service class	7.2	26.4	× 3.6	+ 19.2%
Intermediate class	1.9	8.0	× 4.2	+ 6.1%
Working class	0.9	3.1	× 3.4	+ 2.2%
All origins	1.8	8.5	× 4.7	+ 6.7%
Class advantage*	× 8 (1846 men)	× 8.5 (2246 men)		

*Class advantage: how many times more likely were service class men to attend university than working-class men, for each cohort.
Source: Adapted from A. Halsey, A. Heath and J. Ridge, *Origins and Destinations*, Oxford, Clarendon Press (1980, Table 10.8, p. 188).

A meritocracy, it will be remembered, is concerned not with equality *per se*, but only with equal opportunity – that is, equal results for those of similar abilities. Could it be that working-class children – while getting less out of the education system than others – get as much as they 'deserve' on the basis of their intelligence? Questions about the validity of IQ data will be pursued later in this chapter; for now, it is enough to point out that the educational disadvantages of working-class people persist even when their measured intelligence is identical to that of the middle class. For instance, in a classic longitudinal study of over 5000 primary school pupils in England and Wales, chances of being awarded a grammar school place were closely related to social class even when 'measured ability' was controlled; of children in the above-average ability band, 51 per cent from the upper middle class, 34 per cent from the lower middle class, but only 22 per cent from the lower working class were allowed entry to grammar school at the age of eleven (Douglas, 1967). It is not surprising, then, that the authors of *Origins and Destinations*, a more recent survey of opportunities in education, estimate that each year in the post-war period, 6000 fewer working-class boys went to selective schools than would have been expected on the basis of 'intelligence' alone (Halsey *et al.*, 1980, p. 209).

Is there equality of educational opportunity for girls and boys?

The study *Origins and Destinations*, discussed extensively in the previous section, represents a major attempt to determine whether changes in the British educational system have moved the UK closer to meeting meritocratic objectives. But as Blackstone (1980) points out, the researchers' capacity to answer the questions they posed was severely hampered by the restricted nature of their sample; because their analysis was limited to males, we learn nothing from this research about how educational opportunities for women have changed over time, nor about the impact of social class background on women's educational fates.

Thus we are forced to rely heavily upon official statistics in order to compare the educational chances of girls and boys. From these, it is clear that gender is a major influence on the amount and the type of education that pupils are likely to receive.

Gender and educational achievement

For the past twelve years, girls have slightly outstripped boys in terms of CSE and O level results; yet 53 per cent of A level passes went to boys in 1983, and it is men who constitute a large majority of students on advanced courses in further and higher education. In England and Wales in 1983, women comprised only 38 per cent of those enrolling for advanced courses in further education or in polytechnics. In British universities in 1983/4, six out of ten undergraduates were men. Women predominate in arts, literature and language courses at undergraduate level, but in universities they comprise only 33 per cent of those taking science degrees and only 9 per cent of those studying engineering and technology, and in polytechnics the proportions (31 per cent and 6 per cent) are even smaller. At postgraduate level, where almost seven out of ten students are men, women are in the minority in every subject with the sole exception of education.

While males and females receive differing amounts of education, the most remarkable way in which gender influences educational success or failure is in educational content. In spite of recent claims that girls and boys have access to the same range of subjects, outcomes are far from equal. The pattern of examination results at CSE level reflects the channelling of girls into domestic subjects, arts and languages, and boys into technical subjects, maths and 'hard' sciences (see Table 8.2); at higher levels, these divisions become even more marked. Thus, in spite of attempts to promote 'equal opportunities' in schools, girls and boys receive different amounts of education, pursue different courses of study, and are channelled towards different occupational niches. Patterns of attainment for males and females do not support the meritocratic claim that our education system is indifferent to gender.

It is worth emphasising that the gender distribution of achievement can not be explained in terms of 'intelligence'. The marked disparity in

TABLE 8.2

Selected CSE/GCE examination results, 1983, England and Wales

CSE subjects	Percentage of Grade 1 passes going to girls
Domestic subjects	97
Office practice	94
French	70
English	61
Mathematics	48
Physics	21
Technical drawing	5
A level subjects	*Percentage of passes going to girls*
Domestic subjects	99
Sociology	75
English	71
Maths	30
Physics	21
Computer Science	20
Technical drawing	3

Source: Derived from Equal Opportunities Commission (1985) *Ninth Annual Report 1984*, Manchester, EOC, Tables 2.1a and 2.1c, p. 58.

educational performance of girls and boys exists in spite of the fact that the average IQ levels of the two groups are virtually identical. This information alone should make us sceptical of claims that IQ is a strong determinant of patterns of educational success.

However, according to some studies, girls display greater verbal ability from an early age, while boys excel at visual-spatial tasks (for instance, visualising objects in three-dimensional space) which are thought to under-pin learning in scientific and technical subjects; but even these differences in specific skills are not sufficient to explain either girls' disadvantaged position in education, or the monopolisation by boys of scientific and technical courses. First, the differences related to sex are very small; they could make, at most, only a tiny contribution towards explaining the extent of the polarisation of girls into arts, languages and domestic subjects, and boys into science and maths (Fausto-Sterling, 1985). Second, these sorts of differences can in no way account for girls constituting a minority at postgraduate level even on courses, such as arts and languages, where their skills are allegedly superior to those of boys. Third, visual-spatial skills are themselves influenced by gender-related upbringing (by freedom of move-ment, for example, and by games such as model construction); differences between the sexes in visual-spatial scores have been shown in some studies to be readily eradicated by training in schools (Fausto-Sterling, 1985, ch. 2).

However, few schools offer such training; and it has been argued that in much of educational practice, the emphasis has been on compensating boys for areas of masculine weakness (by, for example, the provision of remedial reading) rather than on improving girls' performance relative to that of boys. While proposals to implement 'positive discrimination' on behalf of girls are often regarded with suspicion, positive discrimination has been widely practised on behalf of boys. Areas which retain 11-plus selection, for example, admit boys to grammar school on the basis of a poorer performance in the 11-plus examination than that required of girls (Weiner, 1985, p. 2). Were it not for this practice – if selection were more truly related to ability – then 30 per cent more girls than boys would go to grammar school.

Is there equality of educational opportunity for different ethnic groups?

An inquiry set up to investigate the education of children from ethnic minorities in British schools concluded in its 1985 report: 'Whatever the reasons, and they are certainly complex, West Indian children are not doing at all well in the educational system' (Swann Report, 1985, p. 60).

Among the evidence that impressed the members of the Committee was a pair of surveys of school-leavers conducted in the late 1970s and early 1980s. The principal findings of these surveys, summarised in Table 8.3, show quite clearly the relative failure in school of pupils of West Indian origin.

Ethnicity and educational achievement

In 1981/2, of school-leavers from the ethnic majority (or, more precisely, those whose origins were neither Asian nor West Indian), 13 per cent attained one or more pass at A level, and 9 per cent entered a degree course at university or college. For West Indian school-leavers, the comparable figures were 5 per cent and 2 per cent. Although black people are disproportionately concentrated in working-class occupations, these inequalities of educational outcome are not 'simply' the product of social class disadvantage; for a recent study carried out by Craft and Craft (1985) in an outer London borough shows clearly that, even with social class controlled, West Indian children fare less well in school than their white counterparts. Among middle-class pupils, for example, only 14 per cent of the white, but 31 per cent of the West Indian pupils, had a low performance in fifth-form examinations. Nor do the relatively poor performances of West Indian pupils result from a particularly high drop-out rate; on the contrary, West Indian pupils, especially girls, tend to stay at school longer than ethnic majority children, and are more likely to continue in full-time education of some sort after leaving school.

Differences in 'talent' are no more likely to account for the educational outcomes of West Indian pupils, than they do for working-class pupils or

TABLE 8.3

Educational achievement of school-leavers with different ethnic backgrounds

	West Indians		Asians		Other leavers	
	1978/9	1981/2	1978/9	1981/2	1978/9	1981/2
			(percentages)			
Got 5 or + higher grades at CSE or O level	3	6	18	17	16	19
Got higher grades in CSE or O level English Language	9	15	21	21	29	29
Got higher grades in CSE or O level Maths	5	8	20	21	19	21
Got one or more pass at A level	2	5	13	13	12	13
Went to university	1	1	3	4	3	4
Went to full-time degree course in college or polytechnic	1	1	5	5	4	5

Source: School-leavers' surveys conducted by DES in 1978/9 (six LEAs) and 1981/2 (five LEAs); reported in Rampton Report (1981), and Annex B, to Chapter 3, Swann Report (1985).

for girls. For one thing, the average differences in IQ levels between West Indian pupils and other pupils are very small when social class differences are controlled. For another – as we shall see in a later section of this chapter – there are reasons to be particularly wary of IQ results when comparisons are being made between groups who bring distinct cultural experiences to the testing situation.

In contrast to the experience of children of West Indian origin, the overall performance of children from Asian communities is, as Table 8.3 indicates, remarkably similar to that of pupils from the ethnic majority. In 1981/2, school-leavers of Asian origin lagged behind those of European origin only in terms of performance on English language examinations at CSE/O level, which in turn had a small effect on their chance of getting five or more higher grade passes. Thus, while ethnic origin is clearly linked to educational under-achievement for pupils of West Indian origin, it is not so linked for children of Asian origin as a whole. The 'ethnic minorities of Britain', sometimes considered as a homogeneous category, are in fact composed of distinct groupings, and each of these groups may have a unique relationship to the educational system.

Conclusion

The myth of meritocracy – the view that our schools stimulate individual talents and, without regard for ascribed characteristics such as social class or gender, reshuffle children according to ability – is one of the most cherished myths of our time. The overwhelming evidence is that the British education system, like that of many other countries, favours those who are already privileged, and puts further obstacles in the path of those who are disadvantaged.

While recognition of inequality of opportunity in education is an important step towards clearer understanding of the complexities of our society, it is only a beginning. Conventional measures of equality of educational opportunity (comparisons, for example, of the proportion of working-class to middle-class boys who reach university) tend to focus attention on that small minority of the population that arrives at the upper levels of the educational hierarchy. Such measures may, inadvertently, encourage 'elitist' research perspectives; they may distract attention from what might be happening to the majority of the population, who are condemned to inadequate forms of schooling. The weakness of a concern with equal opportunity is not that it expects too much, but that it expects too little.

8.5 EXPLAINING THE SOCIAL DISTRIBUTION OF ACHIEVEMENT WITHIN THE EDUCATION SYSTEM

Documenting inequality of opportunity in education is one thing; explaining why it is that children who are working-class, or black, or female are disproportionately among the 'failures' of the education system is quite another. We will examine, first, psychometric explanations which have had a powerful impact on popular thinking about education; and then we will consider sociological explanations focusing, in turn, upon cultural differences, material circumstances, and the impact of schooling itself.

Psychometric explanations: the impact of IQ

There is no doubt that some people perform certain tasks better than others. Some consistently lose at 'Monopoly', become tongue-tied in discussions, and write incomprehensible English essays, while others accumulate hotels on Park Lane, make fluent and forceful arguments, and are praised by teachers for original and stylish essays. We often summarise these differences by suggesting that some people are 'more intelligent' than others. But what does 'intelligence' actually mean? How useful are 'intelligence' tests in explaining performance in school, or in other areas of life?

To begin with, however we choose to define 'intelligence' – as a capacity for abstract thinking perhaps, or an ability to learn quickly and accurately – there is no method for determining or measuring individual differences in intelligence in isolation from what people may have learned to do through their upbringing and education. In other words, there is no way of measuring *innate* or inborn differences in intelligence. Imagine, for example, that we are investigating newborn infants, who have been less exposed than adults to the effects of the environment. We could measure differences in their eye movements, the frequency of their cries, the strength with which they grasp a nurse's finger; but there is no reason to suppose that the differences we record are in any way related to 'intelligence'. By the time our infants (or some of them) can take a few halting steps, utter words, or build towers of blocks, they will already have been exposed to a variety of environmental factors – ranging from the adequacy of their diet, to the way their parents handle them – which will have had important effects on their development. Not all the environmental factors to which children are exposed will be equally stimulating or equally likely to encourage 'intelligent activity'.

Poverty, for example, poses many obstacles to intellectual development; in an overcrowded house with open fires and poor sanitary facilities, infants may have to be confined to a cot or pram for much of the day to prevent them from exposing themselves to danger. Compared with other children who have carpeted floors to crawl on, safe toys, and a warm, comfortable physical environment, children in unsatisfactory housing may lack the 'psychological space' to explore the world around them, and thus to extend their skills and understanding. This example should serve to demonstrate that, while there *may* be such a thing as innate differences in intelligence, there is certainly no way of measuring such differences. At best, IQ tests (or tests of 'intelligence') measure the way that innate intelligence has developed in interaction with the environment.

Nevertheless, IQ tests have been widely employed in the past forty years as an aid to 'objective' assessment. By interpreting the results of such tests, skilled test administrators can conclude that, for example, Sarah performs better (gets more correct answers) than Rob; or that Sarah performs better than many people of her age group on the mathematical parts of the tests, while Rob's strength lies in the area of verbal skills. But what must be noted is that these results do not tell us about the *potential* of Sarah and Rob. On the contrary, IQ tests are measures of *performance* or *achievement*, and in this respect, they are no different from other examinations. An examination in A-level Sociology, for instance, measures your performance on a specific set of questions at a particular point in time, and not your capacity or potential to comprehend sociological issues or to adopt a sociological approach.

Furthermore, just as your performance on a sociology examination may

Race, heredity and intelligence

The issue of cultural bias in IQ tests is at its sharpest in controversies about race and intelligence. Jensen (1969) and Eysenck (1971) are among the psychologists who have claimed that the superior IQ scores of white Americans over black Americans are largely attributable to genetic differences between the two groups. This controversial claim stimulated an acrimonious debate, with important political and educational implications. It was reported in a recent court case that while only 10 per cent of California's school population are black, 25 per cent of pupils who are classified by IQ tests as 'mentally retarded' are black. The judge found that these pupils are segregated into 'dead-end' classes and given inferior teaching; this treatment causes them to lag further and further behind their schoolmates as the years go by. After hearing expert testimony from a variety of witnesses, Judge Peckham concluded that the reason for the disproportionately high number of black children in classes for the retarded was due to the use of 'racially and culturally biased' IQ tests which discriminated against black children. He deplored the unwarranted assumption of many educators that black children were intellectually inferior to whites, and saw this assumption as 'all the more invidious when "legitimated" by ostensibly neutral scientific IQ tests'. He banned the use of IQ tests on minority children, a ban later extended to all children in California (*The Economist*, 8 December 1979).

Whatever the details of this particular case, the judge's decision seems to be reasonable in several respects. First, the evidence for a largely genetic basis to group differences in IQ scores is highly unsatisfactory. Kamin (1977) has shown that most of the evidence used by Jensen and his supporters comes from studies with severe methodological shortcomings. Even Herrnstein – a supporter of Jensen in other respects – argues (1973, p. 118) that his information about black Americans is inadequate.

More fundamentally, we can question the *implications* of Jensen's emphasis on heredity. If we do not know precisely what IQ measures, or how IQ scores influence (or are influenced by) schooling, then the question of whether or not group variations in IQ are partly hereditary seems largely irrelevant. The objective of education is clearly not the raising or equalising of IQ scores *per se*; and it is equally clear that a group's comprehension and skills can be increased without any necessary alteration in IQ scores. The concentration on IQ may therefore distract us from more fundamental issues of learning and education. Furthermore, while some people have assumed that a large genetic component to IQ would necessarily entail the curtailment of educational spending on 'low IQ groups', or their allocation to less academic courses, or the withdrawal of funds from programmes of compensatory education, such suggestions should be seen as political judgements and contentious ones at that. Even if it were the case that certain groups were genetically disadvantaged in respect of IQ, *and* that IQ represented 'intelligence' – neither of which has been demonstrated – this could provide a powerful argument for devoting *extra* resources to developing these groups' potential to the full.

depend on a range of factors apart from your understanding of sociology (whether you care about the exam, how confident you are, whether you ate three Mars bars beforehand and gave yourself an upset stomach), so, too, performance on IQ tests reflects people's reaction to the test situation itself. This is especially important to bear in mind when comparing the average IQ scores of different social class or ethnic groups, whose experience and cultural values may diverge; for lack of familiarity with tests in which speed is required, distrust of the person administering the test, anxiety, or fear of failure, are examples of the many variables which, experiments have shown, can lower the IQ score of a group.

Complaints about IQ tests often focus on items which clearly discriminate against certain social groups. One notorious example (now removed from tests) required children to say which of three pictures showed the prettiest person; those who chose a black person, rather than a Caucasian, were counted as 'incorrect'. This item is clearly culturally biased, but the removal of such glaringly discriminatory questions does not in itself produce a 'culture-fair' or 'culture-free' IQ test. In fact, it is difficult to see how tests which *necessarily* draw upon people's familiarity with objects, shapes, words, and testing procedures – tests, that is, that draw upon cultural experiences that are more readily available to some groups than to others – can ever be 'culture-free'.

What, then, can we conclude about the relationship between IQ and schooling? Whatever IQ is, we can say with certainty that it does not *determine* an individual's educational achievement. Girls and boys with low childhood IQs can achieve excellent results in school, and even go on to college or university; this is all the more likely to happen, of course, if they receive support and encouragement from parents and teachers, or if their parents are sufficiently wealthy to buy them a place in an independent school. Conversely, people with high childhood IQ scores may, through lack of resources, motivation or effort, leave school with minimal qualifications.

On the other hand, there is, statistically speaking, a moderately high correlation across the population between IQ scores and education achievement – a reasonable likelihood that people who complete more years of school than others will also have somewhat higher IQ scores. But this correlation, like all statistical relationships, needs to be explained. One contributing factor may be that pupils with higher IQ are treated in such a way in school (for example, receiving more attention, being placed in higher streams or being awarded entry to selective schools) that their chances of success are enhanced; in other words, the success associated with high IQ may come from the expectations of teachers and the actions of schools, rather than from the abilities of the pupils themselves. Since, in addition, it is not at all clear to what extent IQ tests measure 'intelligence' apart from cultural skills and experience, an adequate account of the social distribution of achievement is unlikely to emerge from psychometric explanations. IQ tests tend to put a gloss of objectivity on differences between pupils that are, in fact, socially created.

As we shall see in the following two sections, sociological research over the last fifty years has produced a wealth of data concerning the relationship between social factors and pupils' educational progress. For clarification, we have categorised them into those that focus on the effect of home background and those that focus on school experience. But it must be emphasised that these aspects of experience cannot be seen in isolation. The social distribution of achievement depends upon the interaction between what the child brings (or fails to bring) to school, and what the school offers (or fails to offer) to the child.

The impact of home background: 1

Theories of cultural deprivation

While there is little evidence to show that children inherit from their parents by genetic transmission levels of intelligence which determine their academic future, many sociological researchers have been concerned to examine the impact on educational achievement of 'cultural inheritance' – that is, of the traits and values transmitted by parents to their children through the process of socialisation. The report of the Plowden Committee, for example, *Children and their Primary Schools*, identified parental attitudes as crucial elements in educational success, while Douglas's (1967) survey indicated that parental interest in education was a key factor governing children's chances of being awarded a grammar school place.

Findings such as these lend support to theories of cultural deprivation, which emphasise not innate differences in intellectual capacity, but the impact of values and attitudes internalised through the process of socialisation. Cultural deprivation theories assert that social groups who are educationally less successful than others may be bright enough, but lack the type of upbringing conducive to success in school. Working-class and black children may fail to acquire a range of values that underpin effective commitment to school – they may be less ambitious, less concerned with individual competition, less willing to prepare for the future, or less convinced of the value of a good education. In addition, their homes may not have provided them with the cultural experiences (good conversation, constructive forms of play, access to books and newspapers, travel) which help to nurture linguistic ability, stimulate curiosity and underpin the capacity to learn. In terms of both the experiences and the values provided by their cultures, black children and working-class children have been considered to be 'culturally deprived'.

While it does seem likely that a commitment to higher education will be less 'automatic' – that is, less a taken-for-granted fact of life – in white or black working-class families, and therefore, that such a commitment would require *more* effort (and more encouragement and support from teachers), certain reservations must be made about the connection between values and achievement that is alleged by theories of cultural deprivation.

First, it is important to examine critically the measures used to identify (for example) 'parental interest' or 'ambition' or 'emphasis upon the future'. Douglas, for instance, used a measure of *parental interest* that included teachers' comments on the parents' attitudes, and records of the number of times parents visited the school:

> The middle-class parents take more interest in their children's progress at school than the manual working-class parents do, and they become relatively more interested as their children grow older ... the most striking difference is that many middle-class fathers visit the schools to discuss their children's progress whereas manual working-class fathers seldom do so (Douglas, 1967, pp. 81–2).

As we have seen in other chapters, manual workers work longer hours than their middle-class counterparts, and they are less likely to be allowed time off with pay; the lesser 'interest' of working-class fathers may simply reflect this fact (as Douglas is aware). Thus the criterion used to measure attitudes may not so much indicate lack of interest, ambition, concern or encouragement by working-class parents for their children, but simply the constraints preventing translation of interest into practical help. What we might emphasise, rather than attitudes, is the social distribution of knowledge and power that may make it easier, for example, for middle-class parents to 'work the system', to hold their own in disagreements with middle-class teachers about treatment of their child, to fight sexual discrimination on behalf of their daughters, to know what books and periodicals to buy – and to have the money to buy them. The emphasis upon values and attitudes may, at its worst, produce an ideological cover for differences in material privilege: for instance, where it is alleged that parents displayed sufficient 'interest' in their children's education to 'scrimp and save' to send them to public school, we may note that, with independent school fees running, on average, at over £3000 a year, this kind of 'interest' is a luxury few parents could afford.

Second, it must be emphasised that ambitions and expectations may *reflect* pupils' levels of attainment in school, as well as influencing attainment. A study of secondary school pupils (Banks and Finlayson, 1973) revealed that the aspirations of unsuccessful boys and their parents moved downward as a result of their poor reports from school; the school does not merely receive inputs of children with varying levels of ambition, but plays a part, as we shall see later, in shaping that ambition. Furthermore, an investigation of students who had made their way to university from comprehensive schools argued that working-class children and parents,

Lack of ambition? Or different starting points?

Cultural deprivation theorists sometimes suggest that working-class children fail, in part, because of a lack of ambition. Boudon (1974) agrees that working-class children tend to aim for skilled manual, or clerical jobs, while middle-class children more often opt for professional or managerial occupations. But occupational ambition should be measured, he argues, not in terms of ultimate destination, but in terms of the size of the gap between your starting point and your objective. From the evidence, he concludes that working-class children are, if anything, more ambitious than the middle class; many working-class children want a job several steps up the ladder from that of their parents, while middle-class children aim for something/at a similar level to the work their parents do. It is not the values of working-class children – lack of ambition – which is the problem, but the class structure which forces them to begin at the bottom. Hence levels of ambition, like levels of parental interest, may reflect not cultural values but the material circumstances in which people live.

more than the middle class, look to the school for indications of how far the pupil should aim; as Neave (1975) points out, success at O level may trigger for working-class pupils the hope of a university career.

Indeed, some writers have argued that the very idea that black or working-class children are culturally deprived – unable, because of home background, to benefit from opportunities to learn – may give teachers and schools a reason and a justification for not really engaging those pupils, or for neglecting their needs; some of the most stringent critics of cultural deprivation theories (see Section 8.7) have argued that it is reactions such as these from teachers and schools, rather than any deep-seated propensity to under-achieve, which in the end explains the poor performance of black and working-class pupils.

We are not arguing that the cultural values of pupils and their families are of no significance for educational achievement, but rather that the generation of these values – their roots in the social and sexual division of labour – and the effects of school upon them, must be explored. It must be emphasised that attitudes towards education are not likely to be part of an arbitrarily acquired (and easily dropped) 'life-style', but are rooted instead in the shared experiences of working and community life. At the same time, we are particularly sceptical of those approaches which imply that child-rearing patterns result in children internalising rigidly established psychological traits, which then colour the whole of their school career. For example, it has been argued that working-class children and those reared in conditions of poverty may internalise a propensity to live for today, whereas their middle-class peers are taught to 'defer gratification' – to postpone current pleasures in order to reap greater rewards in the future.

This concept has been used in particular to 'explain' the greater proportion of middle-class children at college in the USA. Its limitations are readily apparent. To regard attendance at college by middle-class offspring as the result (and the indicator)' of their greater ability to defer gratification appears nonsensical as soon as we recognise that (i) the alternative may be humdrum labour – hardly a form of pleasure or enjoyment, and (ii) many, although not all, middle-class students may be subsidised by their parents to the extent that their standard of living and certainly their opportunities for gratifying leisure are better than those of many employed (or unemployed) working-class counterparts. In addition, continued attendance at school or college may itself be gratifying, if pupils are receiving praise, encouragement from teachers, and 'success'. The experience of working-class and black children may *create* a realistic refusal to wait for success which they doubt will be forthcoming. An experiment in the USA found that the tendency *not* to defer gratification was unrelated to social class or ethnicity, but arose as a reaction to unfulfilled promises: children who chose to wait a fortnight on the promise of getting two candy bars instead of one, but who were never given *any*, did not make the error of 'deferring gratification' the second time around!

While we have expressed reservations about the extent to which studies of values and attitudes can explain social class (or other) differences in achievement, other types of research into home environment, which focus on the acquisition of skills and socio-linguistic competencies, on experience and modes of social control, may have a more direct applicability to the problem. The socio-linguistic theories of Bernstein will be considered in the discussion of language and deprivation; for the moment, a simple example from the research of Bernstein and his colleagues may help to make the point. They find that, while many working-class mothers regard play and learning as separate activities (a view that may reflect the nature of manual occupations), middle-class mothers tend to view toys and play in general as vehicles for their children to 'find out about things'; it is possible that middle-class mothers enable their children to take explicit educational advantage from play.

This suggests that middle-class children may arrive at school with advantages in two respects: they may indeed have learned more as a result of their form of socialisation, and their expectations may be more in line with those of the school. School may greet them as an extension of home life, and they may appear to the teachers as more sophisticated; they may also – although this is a separate point – be more intellectually advanced. It is useful to conceive of the competencies and experiences that may be more prevalent in middle-class and upper-class households as *resources*, resources that are differentially distributed throughout the class structure, and that may be of concrete advantage to children who receive them;

inheritance, it has been said, can be 'cultural' as well as financial. (See the discussion of 'ruling class' in Chapter 6.)

However, a shortcoming of this type of formulation is that it tends to take for granted a single model of the 'educable' child – primarily white and middle class. The educational failure of certain groups is then 'explained' by the degree to which they deviate from this model. But instead of asserting that children who do not conform to the model are less well prepared for school, we could as easily argue that the school is unprepared for them – that the educational system is not oriented to their gifts and their needs.

One of the attractions of Bourdieu's theory of cultural transmission (see box below) is that his depiction of the family–school relationship appears to evade the dilemma described above (see, e.g. Bourdieu and Passeron, 1977).

Bourdieu: cultural capital

Each class, according to Bourdieu, possesses its own set of meanings or cultural framework, which is internalised initially through socialisation within the family; henceforth this *habitus* shapes perception, thought, taste, appreciation and action. Although one culture is not intrinsically superior to another, the power of the dominant class enables them to impose their own framework of meanings on others (and on the school) as the only legitimate culture. Through this capacity for *symbolic violence*, the dominant class succeeds in defining which topics are worthy of consideration, and the appropriate relationship to those issues – in effect, the dominant class defines what counts as 'intelligent' or 'knowledgeable' activity.

As pupils move up the educational ladder, those from the *dominated* class are progressively eliminated, or shunted into less prestigious forms of education; on the other hand, the *habitus* of children from the *dominant* class provides them with *cultural capital* which is translated into academic (and eventually, occupational) success. The education system acts 'neutrally', in the sense that it evaluates *all* pupils according to their mastery of, and their relationship to, the dominant culture. But those who have inherited a cultural capital that accords with the school will appear 'naturally' more gifted. Thus, schooling reproduces the relations of inequality between the classes; in the process, schooling validates the superiority of dominant classes, and confirms for the dominated their own worthlessness, their distance from 'what really counts'.

However, Bourdieu's theory also has its limitation. First, we are left with the unresolved difficulty of whether certain forms of knowledge or skill are superior in themselves, or whether (as is claimed) they appear superior *merely* because they are imposed. Second, as there are many different groups seeking to define the content of educational knowledge, we require a great deal more information about the processes by which powerful interests may be translated into educational programmes. Third, there are empirical questions about the usefulness of the notion of 'cultural capital'. Bisseret (1979) produces a strong case that in France, where the theory evolved, Bourdieu and his colleagues have not demonstrated the primacy of cultural capital over income in explaining educational success.

For England and Wales, Halsey, Heath and Ridge produced an ingenious analysis (1980, ch. 9) which reflects not only on Bourdieu's work, but on the cultural deprivation approaches we earlier discussed. They compared the educational impact of 'family climate' (cultural capital, plus parental values and encouragement) with that of the family's 'material circumstances'. Halsey and his colleagues found that both material circumstances and family climate influence whether or not a boy goes to a selective secondary school, and that the type of school attended has an independent effect on subsequent levels of achievement. But within any particular type of secondary school, for boys of identical IQ, family climate seemed to exercise no influence over a boy's success. Material circumstances did, however, continue to play a part in determining length of school career, examination results and so on: 'The results are clear. Cultural capital influences selection for secondary school, but thereafter its importance is minimal' (Halsey *et al.*, 1980, p. 200). This analysis suggests that equality within education might be furthered more by redistribution of wealth and power than by attempts to augment the 'cultural capital' of disadvantaged groups.

The impact of home background: 2

Income and material circumstances

Despite the elimination of fees in state schools, and the provision of grants for higher education, material inequality continues to play an important part in determining who is successful, and who less so, in the educational system. This is especially so at the extremes of the hierarchy of advantage: for the wealthiest children and the poorest, school career may depend as much upon parents' financial resources as on ability, attitudes or ambition.

In the first place, as David Bull (1980) has documented, there are quite stringent costs associated with the 'free' schooling received by the majority of pupils. These include the cost of transport and of outdoor clothing for journeys to and from school, of school uniform, and of meals, as well as expenses associated with the curriculum – books and equipment for studying at home, sports kit, materials for craft subjects, and in some cases, examination fees or fees for music lessons. These costs are a particular burden for the poorest families; the recorded instances of children being excluded from lessons, or having to miss school altogether because they lack the right clothing or equipment, are thought to be just the tip of the iceberg (Tunnard, 1979; Bull, 1980).

In addition, the cost of supporting offspring in the period between school-leaving age and higher education, when they become eligible for student grants, may be prohibitive for families on lower incomes. The authors of *Origins and Destinations* identify the lack of maintenance grants for this period of schooling as one of the major obstacles to equality of opportunity in Britain, contributing to the fact that three-quarters of their working-class respondents left school at the minimum school-leaving age, whereas three-quarters of the boys from the 'service class' stayed on (Halsey *et al.*, 1980, p. 202). The lack of grants may prove an even larger obstacle to working-class girls than to boys; many writers from Douglas and his colleagues onwards (1971, p. 47) have suggested that families who are financially hard-pressed may well give sons, rather than daughters, priority when it comes to financing post-compulsory education.

Inequality of educational provision

The cost to families of 'free' schooling is likely to have become more marked since the mid-1970s, in the face of cuts in government spending on education. Since parents with comfortable incomes are in a position to supplement the inadequate provision made by schools in their area, or to pay the fees for private schooling, the gulf between the standard of schooling available to the children of the rich and those of the poor, has increased. For example, spending on school books in state schools fell in 1984–5 in real terms by £5.1 million, while in the same year, in the independent sector, spending on school books doubled (Boseley, 1986). Within the state sector, Her Majesty's Inspectorate (1982) found that as a result of reduced expenditure the stock of library books and textbooks in over half the LEAs of England and Wales was unsatisfactory, while only five LEA out of 104 had tolerable levels of provision in all the major areas of educational resource. The report concluded that an increasing reliance by schools upon contributions from parents was leading to 'marked disparities' between the standard of schooling in affluent areas, and that available in areas serving the poor.

The impact of material circumstances on children's educational careers may stem, secondly, from adverse living conditions at home. Many childhood disadvantages – from unsatisfactory housing, to inadequate diet, to lack of access to pre-school playgroups or nurseries, to higher rates of illness, home accident and disease – are concentrated among families at the lower end of the income scale (Wedge and Prosser, 1973); not only will children born into poverty have fewer resources to buy educational materials, but their learning may suffer also from the adverse physical effects associated with poverty. Unsatisfactory housing, for example, has been shown to be associated with lower achievement in the primary school, and to have a more permanent impact on working-class than on middle-class children (Douglas, 1967). The National Child Development Study (Davie, Butler and Goldstein, 1972) revealed that children from over-crowded homes, who lack a quiet and private place to study, are, by 7 years of age, already nine months behind their school-mates in reading attainment.

Finally, under material circumstances we should also consider how much time pupils have available for schoolwork. The extent of the current market in child labour, recently explored by Finn (1984), which draws girls and boys into babysitting, shop work, paper rounds or warehousing, suggests that for many children there may be a conflict between schoolwork and paid employment. Among the 15-year-olds whom he questioned in Coventry and Rugby schools, 75 per cent had paid work experience, almost a third of those with jobs worked over 10 hours per week, and a substantial minority of pupils provided 'pocket money' entirely through their own earnings. While Finn does not measure social class origins, the heavier concentration of paid work among those he calls 'non-academics' suggests that the demands of casual labour may fall particularly heavily upon working-class pupils. Housework, too, tends to fall more heavily on working-class than on middle-class pupils, and far more heavily on girls than on boys (Griffin, 1985). From interviews with 180 pupils at Birmingham secondary schools, Griffin found that domestic responsibilities were one of the factors inclining some working-class girls towards leaving school at the first opportunity; full-time paid employment would raise their status in the household, and enable them to drop some of the domestic duties they found so onerous.

In sum, the inequalities in the wider society which generate poverty and low incomes, and heavier workloads for working-class people and for women, rebound on children's educational opportunities. But the same inequalities also generate great wealth and privilege. In the educational world, this is manifest in the private sector of education. Although the academic standards of independent schools tend to vary considerably, such schools may provide extra attention and supervision for flagging middle and upper class pupils, and a cushion against failure – at a price.

The impact of schooling: action perspectives on education

Until the 1970s, studies of educational achievement tended to assume that 'outputs' from the educational system (levels of achievement) could be explained simply in terms of the range of pupil characteristics – the intellectual, material and cultural 'inputs' – that pupils bring with them to school. But a sustained challenge has been mounted to this way of analysing education by sociologists working in social action traditions. Drawing upon the insights of symbolic interactionism, phenomenology and ethno-methodology, they insist that an 'input–output' approach to the explanation of the social distribution of achievement is misleading in two central respects.

First, the input–output approach does not give sufficient attention to the impact of schooling itself. Educational institutions have been treated, the critics cogently argue, as 'black boxes', the internal workings of which are obscured from the sociologist's view. To treat pupil characteristics (or, for that matter, structural features of the wider society, such as class relations) as the determining element in educational achievement means ignoring what goes on inside schools themselves. Social action theorists argue that analysis of the processes of interaction in schools is essential; and that sociology of education within the structural tradition has, curiously enough, closed its eyes to the actual process of teaching and learning. Consequently, the real contribution of *education* (as opposed to family life, or subcultural values) to the social distribution of achievement has been overlooked. As Keddie (1973) explained in her critique of 'the myth of cultural deprivation', we may, if we focus on the deficiencies of children, fail to notice the very real shortcomings of schools.

The second error of the input–output approach is to assume that pupil identities (such as 'less able' or 'culturally deprived') are fixed over time, and that they determine success or failure in school in the same way that hitting a billiard ball determines the way it will move. Rejecting this kind of starting point, those working in interactionist traditions stress instead the fluidity of the self. Success or failure is the product of a career moulded over a long period of time, the outcome of which is never certain. Moreover, action theorists insist upon the capacity of teachers and pupils for rational action based upon their own understanding of the experience of school. The 'failure' of working-class children, or of girls, or children of West Indian origin, they would say, is not *predetermined* by their abilities or their attitudes, nor by their place in the sexual and social division of labour. This failure has to be 'created' anew for each new generation of pupils, and in this act of creation the interactions of teachers and of pupils themselves will play an important part.

Schools, then, do not merely react to children with varying capacities and qualities in a neutral way; they play an active part in creating children who are more or less educable, more or less knowledgeable, and more or less manageable.

This is perhaps most obvious if we consider some aspects of the tripartite system, the division of secondary schools into grammar, technical and secondary moderns that was the typical arrangement in Britain until a decade ago. Opponents of the tripartite system criticised the inaccuracy of the 11-plus examination, which resulted in approximately 70,000 children being allocated to the 'wrong' type of school each year (Yates and Pidgeon,

1957), and pointed to the fact that these errors disproportionately penalised working-class children; this argument appealed strongly to meritocratic ideals.

The more crucial evidence to emerge, however, from often heated debates, concerned the ways in which the tripartite system placed a ceiling on the eventual performance of the *majority* of pupils, those who were allocated to secondary modern schools. Despite the existence of many excellent secondary moderns, the overall performance of their pupils was depressed by several factors: assignment to a secondary modern ('failure' of the 11-plus) led many pupils to lower their aspirations and ambitions, a reaction to the judgement made on their capacity, and to realistic assessment of what the school had to offer them; secondary modern schools often offered a less challenging curriculum, so that whatever pupils' *capacity* for academic work, their *opportunity* was restricted; such schools less often prepared pupils for, or even allowed them to sit, national examinations; many secondary modern schools suffered, in comparison with grammar schools, fewer resources, poorer facilities for special subject work, and fewer specialist teachers. Secondary modern pupils were indeed less successful by the end of their educational career than grammar school pupils; but with such a gap in provision and prestige, it is difficult to say whether differences in ability, or in educational advantage, account for inequality of results. Allegations that academic standards are lower within a comprehensive than a tripartite system often overlook the fact that comprehensive schools aim to cater for pupils who would otherwise be condemned to secondary moderns, as well as for that minority who previously entered grammar schools. (See Wright (1977) for a detailed analysis of 'standards' in the two systems.)

The main point is that schools can – and do – make a difference, not in terms of the extent of inequality in society, but in terms of 'who gets what' within the education system. Byrne (1976), for example, shows that the way local authorities allocate educational resources gives priority to the needs of 'academic' (disproportionately middle-class) pupils, to those in urban areas, and to boys, while providing less generously for the needs of less academic pupils, those in rural areas, and girls. Another study found that the higher the social class composition of an area, the more was spent on schooling – and the higher the average levels of achievement. The authors (Byrne, Williamson, and Fletcher, 1975) argue that broad social class differences in attainment may be accounted for (partly, we would say) by higher standards of resource-provision in largely middle-class area. This sort of evidence is regarded as controversial, especially as it seems to contradict findings that the differences in achievement between pupils who went to well-endowed schools in the USA, and those who went to poorly endowed ones, were not much greater than the differences between pupils *within* one school or school type. But the contradiction is less severe than it appears at first glance. As soon as we recognise that *within* a school (whether well endowed or poorly endowed) not all pupils are given the same treatment, or the same access to resources, we are part of the way to solving the problem. To put it crudely, working-class pupils (or black children, or girls) may be less favourably treated than others in a 'good' school, just as middle-class (or white, or male) pupils may be more favourably treated in a 'poor' one. Comprehensive re-organisation, and the gradual merging of single-sex into co-educational schools, makes it all the more urgent that researchers attend to the ways in which the experiences of working-class and middle-class, black and white, female and male, pupils may differ even within the same establishment.

Evaluation and surveillance are major features of virtually all class-rooms, from nursery class to undergraduate seminar. Even in the most 'progressive' infant classes, there exists what Bernstein (1977) calls an 'invisible pedagogy' – hidden criteria of judgement according to which some pupils will be approved of, and others regarded with pity or contempt. Teachers may, for instance, encourage the infant class to do 'whatever interests them', but they will not look with favour on children who are interested in talking dirty, or in setting fire to the Wendy house.

Though evaluation is an important feature of classroom encounters, teachers, as the study *Deviance in Classrooms* makes clear, do not always react in the same way to instances of rule-breaking. Their response depends, first, upon how they interpret the action (is it serious? will it spread?); and second, upon the view or 'typification' that they have developed of the pupil concerned (Hargreaves, Hestor and Mellor, 1975). Teachers tend to give the benefit of the doubt to pupils whom they already judge to be good, and to regard with scepticism good behaviour from those they believe to be bad. One result of this 'halo effect', as the process is called, is that pupils become typecast on the basis of earlier impressions – a boy who has been typed as a 'skiver', for example, may be suspected of cheating or copying when he hands in an excellent piece of work. Getting to know pupils, then, involves teachers in differentiating between the bright and the dull, the model pupil and the problem child. This process of differentiation has a bearing, in turn, upon the treatment pupils receive in the classroom. By analysing how teachers arrive at such judgements – by highlighting their activities as agents of differentiation – researchers have begun to show how teachers are implicated in the process of pupil failure.

There are two obvious ways in which teachers' judgements of pupils may have an impact on the social distribution of achievement. First, as several studies have shown, teachers' expectations can colour their assessment of pupils' performance; in Goodacre's (1968) study, infant school teachers rated children whom they thought came from a middle-class background as better able to read than those whom they believed to be from working-class homes; standardised tests did not, however, reveal such a marked difference in the reading level of these two groups of children. In cases such as this, teachers' assessments of pupils reflect their views of what middle-class and other pupils should be capable of, rather than their actual performance.

Second, teachers may, because of low expectations, make fewer attempts to stimulate pupils, or to overcome areas of weakness. It has been argued that the widespread use of IQ tests (on which, as we have seen, working-class children, and some black children, tend to do rather poorly) may well discourage teachers from stretching pupils to the full; some teachers, Pidgeon insists, 'will be satisfied with a relatively low level of achievement from many of their pupils simply because their test results tell them that the children are working "up to capacity" (Pidgeon, 1970, pp. 32–3). Class-room observation studies in a variety of settings testify that, on the whole, teachers do tend to give more of their time and energy to pupils whom they believe to be 'bright'; it may be partly the case that 'bright' children learn more than their classmates because of this extra attention.

In short, a process of stratification occurs within many classrooms, with teachers meting out different treatment to more or less favoured groups of pupils. By analysing interaction in three junior and three middle schools, Green (1985) was able to show that teachers who had highly ethnocentric attitudes differentiated sharply in their teaching behaviour between black pupils and whites. Boys of European origin were particularly favoured; they were given a lot more individual teaching time than their numbers would warrant, and plenty of opportunity to introduce ideas into the flow of discussion. West Indian girls and boys, on the other hand, received much less individual attention and considerably less praise and encouragement. Teachers tended to treat black children in a more restrictive way than others, issuing orders rather than encouraging them to express their feelings and ideas in class. This pattern of classroom interaction, Green argues, may, in turn, influence how pupils conceive of their own capacities; black pupils taught by highly intolerant teachers emerged with a lower self-image than either white pupils in the same class, or black pupils taught by teachers who were less intolerant.

As Green's research suggests, teachers' expectations may be directly translated into differential treatment in the classroom; this is particularly worrying in the light of studies which reveal that negative expectations of certain minority group pupils are widespread among teachers and heads in British schools. According to Brittan (1976), Allen and Smith (1975), Giles (1977) and Tomlinson (1979), many teachers expect West Indian pupils to be more badly behaved than white or Asian pupils, to be slower to learn, and to lack the long-term concentration and persistence necessary for educational success.

Nor is it only West Indian pupils who are likely to suffer from negative expectations. While teachers tend to expect pupils of Asian origins to be industrious, courteous and keen to learn, Asian girls may be typed as 'passive' or 'docile', in ways that lead to them being overlooked or underestimated in class (Brah and Minhas, 1985). In general, teachers' expectations for girls and boys tend to reflect the priority given to males in our culture. Teachers in secondary schools tend to prefer teaching male pupils, and expect boys to be more critical, more enthusiastic and more forthcoming than girls. Even in primary schools, where girls are usually recognised as better pupils than boys, the excellence of their work may be attributed by teachers to 'conformity' – a desire to please – rather than to creativity or intellectual promise (Clarricoates, 1987). Expectations – because they involve ideas about what 'such pupils' are 'really like' – enable ideologies about ethnic groups, social classes, and girls and boys to shape relations between teachers and pupils in the classroom.

Streaming: a self-fulfilling prophecy?

Studies of classroom interaction and the assumptions that underlie it indicate that classrooms are settings in which certain pupils are 'sponsored' for success, while others are nudged towards failure. This is vividly illustrated in Rist's (1970) study of an American kindergarten (similar to nursery school). When the pupils arrived, the teachers used information about home background, appearance and demeanor to divide pupils into three streamed workgroups. Those she guessed to be fast learners, the Tigers, were constantly shown signs of favour, such as being invited to the front of the room for 'show and tell', and they were seated at a table nearest the teacher where they could claim her attention more readily. The others, the Cardinals and the Clowns, were seated at tables further away. Because the Clowns and Cardinals had low-level workbooks and were expected to read as a group, there were few opportunities for individual children to demonstrate to the teachers their capacity to move to more advanced work. Rist argues that the teacher set in motion a 'self-fulfilling prophecy'; by predicting that the Tigers would be fast learners, and then by encouraging them and giving them signs of favour, the teacher almost ensured that the prediction would come true.

The notion of a self-fulfilling prophecy (which clearly has much in common with the labelling theory discussed in Chapter 11) implies that differences between 'dull' and 'clever' children, or 'good' ones and 'deviants', may be heightened, or even created, by classification. Pupils may gradually feel 'persuaded' to bring their own self-image in line with that of the teacher (what is the point of trying if the teacher *knows* you're hopeless at maths?). But even when pupils are resilient enough to maintain a good opinion of themselves, they may face – as did the Clowns and Cardinals – a withdrawal of the assistance that would enable them to prove their capabilities.

The impact of stratification is likely to be at its sharpest where pupils are divided into different bands or streams on the basis of 'ability'. The fact of being placed in a low stream may damage pupils' self-confidence, and discourage them from trying. Even where low stream pupils are not disheartened, teachers may expect little of them, and attempt less with them, than they would with others. This may be part of the reason why ability-grouping tends to boost the performance of top-stream pupils, but depress that of pupils in lower groups. And since streaming and banding are often linked to social class – the higher a pupil's social class background, the greater the chance of being allocated to the top stream – ability grouping may well play a part in the under-achievement of working-class pupils.

In his study *Beachside Comprehensive*, Ball (1981) indicates, like Hargreaves (1967) and Lacey (1970) before him, that ability grouping may also contribute to the formation of pupil subcultures opposed to the ethos of the school. The differentiation of pupils into three board bands of 'ability' on entry to Beachside encouraged a polarisation of values between pupils in the top and middle bands. Initially, both bands were described by teachers as pliable and a pleasure to teach, but by the second year, classes in the middle band were regarded as a 'disciplinary blackspot'. The higher record of detentions and absences among middle band pupils, their avoidance of extra-curricular activities and the fact that nearly half of them claimed to dislike school (see Table 8.4) are all signs, Ball argues, of the emergence of an oppositional culture. This 'anti-group culture' can be seen partially as a group response to failure; pupils appeared to dissociate themselves from the school that devalued their efforts. But of course, the subculture contributed to further failure; disorder in middle band classes disrupted the efforts of even those pupils who remained committed to the school.

When banding was abolished at Beachside, and pupils taught in mixed-ability classes, many of the behavioural and disciplinary problems that had previously been concentrated in the middle bands disappeared; lessons were far less often disrupted, and overall, far fewer pupils gave signs of disaffection with school. Yet differentiation of pupils did not disappear. Even within the mixed-ability classes, teachers continued to distinguish between 'bright' pupils, and those deemed 'average' or 'dull' – to sponsor some pupils for success, and to write others off as incapable. According to Ball (1981, p. 278), 'the stratification of pupils produced through the bands is condensed and reproduced within each mixed-ability form-group'. This stratification of pupils, Ball argues, seriously undermines the egalitarian objectives of comprehensive education; it means that even within the same classroom, pupils are offered sharply contrasting social and intellectual experiences, and propelled towards different sorts of fates.

By extending our understanding of the perspectives adopted by pupils and teachers in the classroom, and by showing how teachers may act – wittingly or unwittingly – as agents of differentiation, researchers working in social action traditions have helped to illuminate the impact of schooling itself on the social distribution of achievement. But one problem with this approach is the tendency to see the classroom 'in splendid isolation',

TABLE 8.4

Different bands, different worlds?
Comparison of top band (Mrs Culliford's form) and middle band (Mrs Tanner's form), second year cohort at Beachside Comprehensive

	Top band	Middle band
Teachers' stereotypes of each band	Academic potential Neat workers Bright, alert and enthusiastic Want to get on Rewarding	Not up to much Rowdy and lazy Cannot take part in discussions Not interested Unrewarding
Proportion of pupils from working-class homes	36%	78%
Proportion of teachers' time in class devoted to maintaining order	1.5%	12.5%
Average number of detentions, per pupil per year	0.4	3.8
Average number of absences per pupil in term 1	8.1	12.6
Average number of minutes spent on homework per pupil	47	16
Proportion of end-of-year subject tests graded at 50% or higher	58%	11%
Number of extra-curricular activities or club memberships, per class	43	10
Proportion of pupils who dislike school	13%	48%
Views held about each band by pupils in the other band	Brainy Unfriendly Stuck-up Arrogant	Thick Rough Boring Simple

Source: Compiled from Stephen Ball (1981) *Beachside Comprehensive*, Cambridge, Cambridge University Press, ch. 2.

divorced from wider processes of social control. Hence some researchers have tried, by combining structural and action approaches, to set classroom interaction within a broader framework. Sharp and Green (1975), for example, demonstrate that in Mapledene, an infant school where the child-centred philosophy puts a premium on allowing pupils to develop at their own pace, teachers used vaguely defined notions of the 'readiness' of

---

The cooling-out process

When Beachside Comprehensive (Ball, 1981) switched from banding to mixed-ability teaching, fewer pupils whom teachers regarded as 'not up to much intellectually' succeeded in retaining high ambitions; in other words, fewer pupils 'over-aspired'. This suggests that processes of stratification which are more subtle than streaming may be all the more effective at diverting opposition; where pupils can be persuaded that certain courses of action are not for them – where they can be induced to lower their sights, without being allocated to lower streams or failed in an obvious way – then they may be left with the conviction that it is not the 'system' that is at fault, but themselves. This has been termed the 'cooling-out process'; pupils who are cooled-out abandon their educational ambitions 'voluntarily', while believing that they have had a fair chance. Some educational practices do not serve simply to fail people, but to convince them that failure is an individual, rather than a structural problem

This brief account of the cooling-out process should not be taken to imply that academic staff consciously set out to 'con' particular pupils, or to legitimate a system of inequality. Rather, teachers do their job as best they can under conflicting pressures from pupils and parents, from colleagues and superiors, from local education authorities and employers. They try to uphold standards, while doing their best by their pupils. But – and here is the crux of the matter – notions of what pupils 'are' and what is best for them, views of what is possible and views about standards themselves, clearly influence the treatment that is accorded to individual pupils or to an entire class. Perceptions and expectations, beliefs regarding the nature of knowledge and academic standards – all of which have roots outside a teacher's individual consciousness – bridge the gap between 'good intentions' and 'bad effects'.

---

children for intellectual advance to justify inequality of treatment. All children, teachers claimed, are equally valued as individuals – but some are more 'ready', and it is these who commanded most of the teachers' time and attention. The child-centred philosophy allowed teachers to ignore children who were falling behind, on the grounds that they were not yet 'ready' for intellectual growth. But Sharp and Green refuse to see these patterns of interaction as an offshoot purely of the consciousness of individual teachers; instead, they argue, the constraints under which teachers operate – including not only the demands of classroom control in the face of a large numbers of pupils, but also the pressures even at an early age to classify pupils in the interests of eventual occupational placement – make it difficult for a teacher to do other than stratify, whatever her own philosophy and expectations might be.

Paul Willis (1977), also combining structural and action traditions, analysed the perspectives of a small group of working-class boys in secondary school. The 'lads' had little time for the qualifications and the good jobs to which the school claimed to hold the key. Drawing on the traditions of their working-class community, they scorned office jobs as soft and effeminate, and favoured 'real' knowledge with practical application over the abstract and irrelevant book-learning of the school. In resisting the school's attempt to control their actions and their thoughts, the lads perfected techniques for 'having a laff', for evading restrictive rules, and for maintaining group solidarity in the face of pressures for individual achievement. School became for them a kind of training ground to practice ways of remaining human in the factory jobs which they eventually expected to occupy.

Willis's analysis suggests, then, that disaffection from school and resistance to the ethos of the school is not merely a reaction to failure. Pupils come to school already equipped with class cultures; these enable (some of) them to see through the ideology of the school, and to find a rationale for challenging the school's authority and control. Nor is the eventual failure of pupils like 'the lads' merely a result of economic forces beyond their control, as structural theories of reproduction (such as Bowles and Gintis's correspondence theory) seem to imply. Schools, Willis suggests, are partially independent of economic forces, and so are their pupils; pupils act creatively, often in ways that contravene the expectations of the school. Thus schools do not simply 'reproduce' the social relations of capitalism; within schools, there is resistance, rejection, innovation and change. Pupils are not merely moulded by educational systems, they are busy rejecting and reshaping the messages that the school has to offer.

Many researchers have concentrated upon pupils who are overtly antagonistic to school – on non-conformists, like pupils in the middle band at Beachside Comprehensive, or on 'cultural critics' like Willis's lads – who may readily be viewed as dissenters from dominant values. But the division between conformists who want to get on, and non-conformists who want to have fun, is too simple to account for the variety of pupils responses that can be found in schools. Woods (1983) identifies eight modes of adaptation, ranging from optimistic compliance to outright rebellion. The most prevalent mode of adaptation for pupils is, he argues, 'colonisation'; such pupils are indifferent to the goals espoused by the school, but work the system for their own personal ends while 'keeping their noses clean'. The absence of overt antagonism, then, or even the desire to acquire qualifications, does not necessarily mean an uncritical acceptance of the authority of the school.

Moreover, as Fuller (1983) and Hargreaves (1979) have pointed out, there is a need to recognise the sociological significance of conformity itself. A greater understanding of the perspectives of pupils who cause the teachers few headaches would contribute to our understanding of the ways that people come to accept, with varying degrees of commitment, the dominant values and the constraints of the world around them.

8.6   WHAT DID YOU LEARN IN SCHOOL TODAY?

Our analysis so far suggests that education plays a powerful role in reproducing and legitimating patterns of inequality that characterise the wider society. But schools are knowledge-processing institutions, as well as people-processing ones. Too great an emphasis upon equality of opportunity may distract attention from the knowledge that is reproduced and validated through the schooling system – and from the way schools shape people's consciousness. What kinds of understanding, what world-views, are promoted by our schools? What aspects of reality are illuminated, and which obscured? An effective understanding of education depends upon knowing not merely 'who goes where', but 'who is taught what' – and when, and how, and why.

Classroom knowledge

In her study of the humanities department of a comprehensive school, Keddie (1971) found that teachers made distinctly different types of knowledge available to 'A', 'B' and 'C' stream pupils. They assumed, for example, that 'A' streamers did not require illustrations and examples, while 'C' streamers could *only* grasp issues in a concrete, descriptive way. Furthermore, while questions from 'C' streamers were viewed as attempts to disrupt the lesson, similar questions from the 'A' group were taken as confirmation of their thirst for knowledge. Keddie concludes from her observations that the pupils deemed 'bright' are not necessarily those with the greatest capacity for abstraction and generalisation (as many teachers assume) but rather those who are least sceptical of the teachers' definition of 'important' versus 'irrelevant' knowledge – those who, even when they do not understand the issues, are willing to 'accept the teacher's presentation on trust ... It would seem to be the failure of high-ability pupils to question what they are taught in schools that contributes in large measure to their educational achievement' (Keddie, 1971, pp. 151, 156). A similar conclusion arises from Sharp and Green's study of child-centred infant classes, where 'dull' or 'problem' children are often those who do not, of their own accord, involve themselves in activities considered important by the teacher. By contrast, 'The bright ones are the "biddable", easily controllable ones who are on the teacher's wavelength' (Sharp and Green, 1975, p. 121).

Many studies raise the possibility that schooling may involve a suspension of critical thinking, even (or perhaps especially) for successful pupils. Bowles and Gintis (1976), it will be remembered, argued that habits of thought and practice, such as submission to authority, discipline, and acceptance of the status quo, were in many ways more important outcomes of contemporary schooling than the fostering of cognitive skill. While this would be difficult to demonstrate, discussions of the 'hidden curriculum' provide some support. Attempting to take a pupils' eye view of the situation, for example, both Jackson (1968) and Hargraves (1972) argue that the pressures of evaluation lead many pupils to adopt a strategy of 'pleasing teacher'. Pupils develop a range of techniques for concealing ignorance or idleness (from guessing what teacher wants them to say, to mastering an appearance of rapt concentration that enables them to daydream undetected). While these individual adaptations indicate that pupils are still alive and well, and not 'brain-washed by the system', they may also inhibit learning, in so far as approval (or avoidance of punishment) rather than knowledge becomes the primary objective.

Nevertheless – surprising though it may seem after our emphasis upon stratification and achievement – pupils are exposed to knowledge in schools, and they do, sometimes, learn. The question of what they learn (or, as we suggested before, of who learns what) is pursued in studies of the official curriculum. There is, as Raymond Williams (1981) emphasises, a 'selective tradition' in educational knowledge; out of the vast stock of knowledge and skills available in a complex society – from ways of claiming benefit to motorcycle maintenance, from the thought of Marx to that of Mrs Thatcher – only a fraction is selected for transmission in schools.

What is selected, and what left out, has consequences for patterns of success and failure. In the study of physics or chemistry, for example, applications of science are often introduced only as an afterthought, examples are used which are more familiar to males than to females (e.g. combustion in a petrol engine), and textbooks and materials contain four illustrations of male characters for every one female (Samuel, in Whyld (ed.), 1983); this increases the sense of science as a 'masculine' area of study, and helps to explain why boys specialise in these subjects far more often than girls (Kelly (ed.), 1981; Smail, 1984).

What is selected for the curriculum, and what left out, also has consequences for social control. Schooling may help to sustain the status quo, not only by the stratification of pupils, but also by the images of society that it promotes. Hand's (1976) analysis, for example, identifies two themes that reverberate through the teaching of English literature: the dangers of revolutionary change (communicated through the ways that *Animal Farm* and *1984*, for instance, are analysed); and (through the pessimistic accounts contained in books such as *Lord of the Flies* and *Day of the Triffids*), despair about people's capacity for constructive social action. One of the main impacts of the English curriculum is, Hand argues, to give pupils the impression that the status quo is unchangeable – to suppress the systematic examination of possible alternative ways of organising the social world.

In a similar vein, examination of the content of science textbooks, and observation of science lessons, indicate that the existence of uncertainty and disagreement about important issues is disguised; knowledge is portrayed as external, objective – therefore unnegotiable – and the existence of conflict and disagreement is downplayed (Hine, 1977). As a result, the forms of 'knowledge' that come to be valued (consider *Mastermind*) may be those that appear to reveal uncontroversial facts, and in so doing suggest that the real nature of the status quo is fixed. (Certainly many sociology students initially complain that 'sociologists cannot agree even among themselves'; ambiguity seems to be experienced as threatening.)

Finally, the manner in which knowledge is taught and assessed in schools may encourage pupils to regard knowledge not as the evolving product of social activity, but as private property, to be acquired and hoarded: 'Children and pupils are early socialised into this concept of knowledge as private property. They are encouraged to work as isolated individuals with their arms around their work' (Bernstein, 1975, p. 97). These examples illustrate the ideological dimensions of the curriculum, and the way in which the organisation of knowledge may operate as a subtle and effective form of social control.

In the view of writers such as Young, Bourdieu and Bernstein, the organisation of knowledge in schools is closely bound up with the distribution of power in society. Knowledge is not merely organised in the sense that it falls into discernible patterns – it is *managed*. Powerful groups may be in a better position than others to impose their definition of educational knowledge – in short, to define the curriculum. For example, Nash (1972) found that 12 of the 14 most popular history textbooks in British junior schools omitted, in their discussion of South Africa, any mention of apartheid or of white supremacy; it seems likely that the textbooks would have looked very different if black communities in Britain were in a stronger position to define what would count as 'history'.

Moreover, knowledge is not only selected and managed, it is also stratified; subjects such as 'pure' sciences are accorded higher status than others such as Sociology or domestic science. High status knowledge, according to Young (1971), tends to be that which emphasises written (rather than oral) presentation, avoids group work, and is most unrelated to everyday experience. One implication of this, as Burgess (1984) points out, is that attempts to create more 'relevant' courses (attempts often reserved for pupils deemed 'less able') run against the grain; to pupils and to staff, relevant courses often seem like second-best. Moreover, the stratification of knowledge serves to promote a deference to 'experts' whose theoretical accounts must be taken on trust, and a corresponding devaluation of the knowledge which ordinary people create, acquire and apply in the course of their everyday lives; an example might be the demotion of knowledge that women pass on by word of mouth to the lowly status of 'old wives' tales'. Finally, where knowledge is stratified, possession of high-status knowledge may be used by powerful groups to validate their claims to moral and cultural superiority; such groups may have an interest not only in defining knowledge, but in restricting access to its more valued forms. One view of the way knowledge may be selected, managed and stratified is summed up below.

The management of knowledge?

I am the great Professor Jowett
And what there is to know, I know it
What I don't know isn't knowledge
And I am Master of this College.
(Halsey, in Hopper, 1971, p. 265)

The selective tradition of educational knowledge, and the links between curriculum and structures of power, make it impossible to sustain the functionalist view of education as a transmitter of 'our common cultural heritage'. But there are problems, too, with the assertion that powerful groups define the curriculum, and with the argument of some marxists that schools are simply involved in the reproduction of dominant ideology. For one thing, this ignores the efforts of parents, of the labour movement, of the women's and black movements, and of students themselves to influence the content of education. For another, groups with a vested interest in educational curricula include teachers and educational researchers – subject specialists whose careers are at stake. Moreover, since curricular change is a gradual process, some elements of the curriculum can only be explained by reference to groups who are no longer powerful. Hence the warning, put forward by Williamson (1974, p. 10):

It is not enough to be aware only of the fact that the principles governing the selection of transmittable knowledge reflect structures of power. It is essential to move beyond such suspicions to work out the precise connections.

The need to work out these connections is, perhaps, all the more urgent given the increasingly overt attempts by the state over the past decade to influence what is taught in schools and universities.

8.7 LANGUAGE, DEPRIVATION AND KNOWLEDGE

We have tried to emphasise that slogans about education reproducing inequality are insufficient; on the contrary, it is necessary to elaborate the processes linking the class structure (and patriarchy) to the school through its effects on individual pupils. Bernstein's theory of socio-linguistics attempts to do just that; his writings have had considerable influence on educational policy and practice, and have become the focal point for major controversy concerning the links between home, school, deprivation and inequality.

For Bernstein, social structure, especially class structure, generates specific linguistic forms; these forms in turn reinforce cultural differences, and help to channel behaviour into certain patterns. Bernstein suggests links between experiences at work, and community and family interaction, which influence the way in which children learn to relate to language. For working-class (especially unskilled or semi-skilled working-class) people, wage-labour involves slotting into prescribed work roles that minimise individuality, but may maximise solidarity with work-mates; these qualities are echoed in the cohesion, based on homogeneity of background and experience, that may characterise traditional working-class communities, and also in the family, where roles may follow traditional patterns and be fairly non-negotiable (called by him *positional families*). Modes of control over children in positional families lean towards commands with little explanation (Do it because I said so!), or towards 'positional appeals', involving reminders of the obligations and rights of mothers, fathers, boys, girls, older children, younger children, etc. (Daddy doesn't want to hear that sort of talk from little girls!) In short, rules are transmitted in such a way that children are reminded of what they share in common with others; children's similarity with others is constantly underlined, reinforcing the sense that what they feel, or see, or do, is what everyone in their group sees, or feels, or does. In Bernstein's view, these circumstances promote a particular relationship to language, in which language (speech) is understood as a way of enhancing solidarity; speech occurs against an assumption of shared experience with others, therefore minimising the felt need to make one's meaning explicit.

Briefly, the position of middle-class, especially professional, people is thought to generate a very different relationship to language. Relative autonomy in work, freedom to plan and organise tasks and schedules, combines with the lack of tight-knit community structure, to encourage a premium on individual development with reference to shifting standards and objectives. This is echoed, according to Bernstein, in *person-oriented* families, where greater discretion in role performance requires more frequent use of language to explore the meaning of individual actions in the face of ambiguity about appropriate behaviour. For the child in such a family, 'personal appeals', which emphasise individual motives and actions, and their consequences for other individuals, are likely to be the predominant mode of control (I know you don't like kissing Grandpa, but he is unwell, and it makes him very happy when you kiss him). Moreover, since middle-class parents may be more likely to punish for bad intentions than for bad consequences, children are encouraged from an early age to verbalise motives, and to express experience and emotion in verbal rather than other forms. These circumstances promote, in Bernstein's view, an understanding that language is the major means of expressing and interpreting emotion, and a vehicle for exploring and bridging the gulf between oneself and other people who are assumed to be different.

Bernstein identifies a *restricted code* (a form of speech in which meanings are relatively implicit, linked to a particular context, and particularistic) which can be fully understood only by those who have already shared the experience or emotion being verbalised. Restricted code is said to be more characteristic of the working class; although the middle class have access to this code, they tend to reserve it for use among peers (playmates, close friends or work colleagues). Against the restricted code, Bernstein sets the *elaborated code*, the usual mode of speech for the middle class. An elaborated code tends to make meanings explicit, to be universalistic in the sense that most English-speaking people can catch the meaning, and to be relatively independent of the context in which it is used. The differences between the two codes are not easy to grasp. An admittedly extreme example might be the difference between the speech of lawyers in a courtroom (elaborated code), and a chat with a best friend, where it is almost understood what is meant before it is said – where phrases like 'God!' or 'Same with George and me' can communicate a world of (implicit) meaning.

Bernstein's socio-linguistic theory

	Working class	Middle class
Social classes		
Family types	Positional	Person-oriented
Modes of control	Commands/ Positional appeals	Personal appeals
Speech codes	Restricted	Elaborated

Bernstein's argument is that lower working-class children, whose socialisation has given them easy access only to a restricted code, face several disadvantages in the schooling system. First, schools demand that children communicate in a universalistic way that can be understood by everyone, and this demand becomes more intense at the later stages of schooling. Children who have been reared with the restricted code are not used to projecting their separate experience, and their speech and written work will appear to teachers and middle-class school-mates as difficult to understand, incomplete, and inadequate. Second, the linguistic barriers between working-class children and teachers may compound misunderstandings.

Teachers who express emotions through purely verbal means may appear to the child as cold and unfeeling, while teachers may regard a child who speaks to them in restricted code (seen by middle-class people as suitable only for conversations with peers) as rude or aggressive. Third, while school represents to middle-class children an extension or refinement of earlier experience within the home, there are for working-class girls and boys severe discontinuities between home and school – discontinuities not only in language-use but also in modes of discipline, or ways of cementing personal relationships – with the result that success for working-class children does not merely involve learning more than they knew before, it means *unlearning* aspects of previous experience. Fourth, Bernstein emphasises that children cannot be taught elaborated code in the way they might be taught vocabulary: the use of restricted code is rooted, for working-class children, in the structure of their community and their family. They may feel uneasy with an elaborated code because it implies roles and relationships that are fluid and ambiguous, and that play upon a foundation of individual difference; the elaborated code is not simply *new* to many working-class children, it is an alien means of expression. Criticisms of restricted code seem to be attacks on the child's actual way of life.

The codes are not, in Bernstein's view, equivalent to differences in dialect, or accent, or vocabulary, nor are they simply arbitrary ways of speaking, which can be altered by providing models of 'good' speech. In order for working-class children to be judged successful in school, they must change their very identity, and radically alter a way of perceiving the world that is rooted in the realities of working-class life.

Since Bernstein's theory is so ambitious, embracing work relationships and forms of class solidarity, as well as modes of control and language-use both in home and school, it is not surprising to find that only fragments of the theory have as yet been put to the test. Questions remain as to whether there are two, or more, codes in the English language, whether codes are genuinely distinct from dialects, and whether the codes are actually linked to social class in the manner hypothesised. Years of further research might be necessary to produce a body of evidence that would finally support Bernstein's theory or lay it to rest.

Bernstein's views have often been counterposed to those of another sociolinguist, Labov (in Keddie, 1973). Labov examined the form of speech (called NNE or Negro Non-Standard English) used by some black children in the USA – children who, like those from working-class backgrounds, tend to under-achieve in the education system. He observes that children who are extremely reticent in a formal research setting become highly verbal when placed in a less threatening situation. More importantly, he concludes that though NNE differs from other forms of speech, it has a coherent inner logic and a complex structure, and is perfectly capable of being used to articulate complicated or abstract ideas. These observations have been taken to imply two fundamental deficiencies in work such as Bernstein's: first, the methodological error of eliciting speech from working-class people in formal contexts, which inhibit them from displaying their full range of verbal virtuosity; second, the false assumption that different forms of speech reflect superior or inferior patterns of cognition or reasoning. Labov's formulations are frequently claimed to be more promising than Bernstein's (Stubbs, 1976; Edwards, 1976). However, the debate does not end with this assessment; the controversy centring upon these figures extends into areas of educational research and educational policy, raising many questions of continuing importance for our understanding of education.

The argument that surfaced with the publication of *Tinker, Tailor* (Keddie, 1973) involved a telling condemnation of attempts to explain educational under-achievement by reference to children's cultural and linguistic heritage. Children in Britain and America have been identified as 'deprived' because of cultural or linguistic inadequacies in their upbringing, when in fact, Keddie and others contend, they are merely different – not inferior or superior, just different; the notion of cultural and linguistic *difference* replaces that of cultural or linguistic *deprivation*. The view that certain children are deprived is seen as not only mistaken but also politically reprehensible. They offer several reasons. First, to define the culture or language of working-class or black people as 'deprived' or 'inadequate' involves a lack of respect for those people, and an ethnocentric refusal to recognise their cultural richness and strength. Second, to suggest that children are deprived because of the inadequate heritage they have received from their family or community implies that these children are doomed to failure because of their *own* inadequacies – a position similar to that of 'blaming poverty on its victims' (see discussion of the *culture of poverty* in Chapter 4). Thus notions of cultural or linguistic deprivation may be similar in their effects to (equally mistaken) notions of the genetic inferiority of low-achieving groups.

Third, by locating the 'problem' in the family, a justification is produced for neglecting such children in schools. In illustration of this, Fuchs (in Keddie, 1973) describes how a teacher in a slum school was induced by her colleagues to stop worrying about the poor quality of teaching offered to the children, and to accept instead that they were already destined to fail. The notion of cultural or linguistic deprivation may trigger low expectations for children so labelled, leading to a self-fulfilling prophecy. Fourth, at the level of sociological research, an over-emphasis upon 'deprivations' which have their origin in family or community may limit research into the shortcomings of the schools themselves, where the real explanation for failure may well lie. Finally, we are urged to consider the possibility that the knowledge made available in school, which admittedly does not 'fit' with the orientation of many 'under-achieving' children, may be an inappropriate curriculum, favoured only because of its close association with dominant or 'mainstream' culture.

These criticisms of cultural and linguistic deprivation have been extended to include critiques of 'compensatory education' – the diverse programmes of remedial help, counselling, and 'educational enrichment' that were, in the 1960s and early 1970s, introduced ostensibly to improve the educational chances of young children who had been identified as 'deprived' or 'disadvantaged'. The charge was made that projects such as Headstart in the USA, and the Educational Priority Areas programme in England and Wales, were mistaken in aiming to 'compensate' for deprivation that did not exist. Moreover, they were denounced as politically misguided in so far as they institutionalised the 'deficit' view of working-class or black children, with the consequences that were outlined in preceding paragraphs.

The time has come to consider these arguments, to explore some of their implications, and to look at alternative views. While accepting some of these arguments (especially those concerning the failure to focus on inadequacies in the schools), there are others we reject: two issues seem to us to be central. The first concerns programmes of compensatory education. There are many valid grounds, in our view, for criticising the *particular* compensatory programmes of the past three decades. Many of the schemes were ambitious in outline, but inadequately implemented; not enough resources were made available; sometimes teachers were unclear about the objectives of the schemes, and unprepared for their part in the programme. Furthermore, many of the projects had a hit-and-miss quality, since there was little evidence available about the precise kinds of intervention that would most effectively help children in need. But in spite of these and other defects, the limited success of *certain* compensatory education programmes in no way demonstrates the inevitable failure of all such programmes to improve the skills of children in need. The principle of positive discrimination in favour of disadvantaged groups seems highly desirable; one of the remarkable features of our education system is that so much (at the level of national resources *and* classroom attention) is channelled towards a privileged few. However, to refer to positive discrimination (or even equal shares of resources) as 'compensatory education' may well be misguided. The issue is why schools do not, as part of the general run of things, orient themselves to the needs of children who do not fit a straightforward white middle-class model of educability.

'It is an accepted educational principle that we should work with what the child can offer; why don't we practise it? The introduction of the child to ... public forms of thought is not compensatory education – it is education' (Bernstein, 1971, p. 199).

The second issue concerns the educational implications of the view that groups of children who systematically underachieve are not 'deprived' but merely 'different'. One implication is that respect for the cultural heritage brought to school by working-class children, by girls, by children of Asian or West Indian origin in Britain, by black Americans, should be a basic tenet of education practice; this respect should be reflected in the books they and other pupils read and in the materials they study, while their view of the world should be a starting point for explorations of other issues. Our earlier discussion of causes of under-achievement indeed suggests the importance of reducing the discontinuity between home and school for many pupils.

More controversial suggestions to arise from the insistence on cultural *difference*, however, are for the provision of distinct curricula for children from working-class or ethnic minority backgrounds, and for the rejection by teachers of all efforts to 'substitute' their ideas for those of the pupils. These suggestions are certainly well-intentioned, but they could have unfortunate consequences. A consequence of special curricula for special groups could be to place children in 'educational ghettoes': that is, to confine their knowledge of the world to their immediate circumstances. Far from liberating them, this might foreclose options by denying them the chance to understand alternative realities. An insistence on equality of *cultural* status could distract from inequality of power and resource. Differentiated curricula could help disadvantaged groups to build 'positive identities and lots of pride' (Valentine, 1968, p. 151), while leaving unchallenged the structures of inequality and powerlessness that led to the devaluation of their culture in the first place.

What conclusions can we draw from this discussion of language, deprivation and educational achievement? First, we would argue that deprivation does indeed exist. Its source is not, as some have alleged, in the family, but rather in the class structure, the patriarchal structure and institutionalised racism which deny to many people not only a reasonable share of material resources and decision-making power, but also the chance to develop their capacities for learning.

Second, deprivation that has its roots in inequality cannot be 'defined out of existence' by simply insisting on the *cultural* equality of the privileged and the disadvantaged; it can only be tackled by a strategy that involves redistribution of effective power in society, as well as efforts to forge a more just and more liberating form of education. For schooling itself, this requires the recognition that education is about the development of skills and understanding. If that education is inadequate, it may be only marginally (as the peasant boy from the School of Barbiana remarked) 'better than cowshit'. The central questions raised by the sociology of education are about curriculum, pedagogy, and the relationship between society and schooling. In short, what kinds of skills can enable people to penetrate reality and increase their capacity for control over their world, *and* to what extent can these be realised or anticipated in present unequal society? While educational change cannot on its own transform that society, strategies for equality cannot afford to ignore the educational system. Arguments over knowledge and ideas are also arguments about the future of society.

REFERENCES TO CHAPTER 8

Allen, S. and Smith, C. (1975) 'Minority Group Experience of the Transition from School to Work', in P. Brannen (ed.), *Entering the World of Work*, London, HMSO.

Aries, P. (1973) *Centuries of Childhood*, Harmondsworth, Penguin.

Ball, S. (1981) *Beachside Comprehensive*, Cambridge, Cambridge University Press.

Banks, O. and Finlayson, D. (1973) *Success and Failure in the Secondary School*, London, Methuen.

Bates, I., Clarke, J., Cohen, P., Finn, D., Moore, R. and Willis, P. (eds) (1984) *Schooling for the Dole? The New Vocationalism*, London, Macmillan.

Berg, I. (1970) *Education for Jobs: The Great Training Robbery*, Harmondsworth, Penguin.

Bernstein, B. (1971) 'A Critique of the Concept of Compensatory Education', in *Class, Codes and Control*, vol. 1, London, Routledge & Kegan Paul.

Bernstein, B. (1975) 'On the Classification and Framing of Educational Knowledge', in *Class Codes and Control*, vol. 3, London, Routledge & Kegan Paul.

Bernstein, B. (1977) 'Class and Pedagogies: Visible and Invisible', in Karabel and Halsey (eds) (1977).

Bisseret, N. (1979) *Education, Class Language and Ideology*, London, Routledge & Kegan Paul.

Blackstone, T. (1980) 'Falling Short of Meritocracy', *The Times Higher Education Supplement* (18 January 1980) p. 14.

Boseley, S. (1986) 'Crisis Warning on School Books', *Guardian* (March 31).

Boudon, R. (1974) *Education, Opportunity and Social Inequality*, New York, Wiley.

Bourdieu P. and Passeron, J. C. (1977) *Reproduction in Education, Society and Culture*, London, Sage.

Bowles, S. and Gintis, H. (1976) *Schooling in Capitalist America*, London, Routledge & Kegan Paul.

Brah, A. and Minhas, R. (1985) 'Structural Racism or Cultural Difference: Schooling for Asian Girls', in G. Weiner (ed.), *Just a Bunch of Girls*, Milton Keynes, Open University Press.

Brittan, E. (1976) 'Multi-racial Education, 2: Teacher Opinion on Aspects of School Life', *Educational Research*, vol. 18, no. 3.

Brown, C. (1984) *Black and White Britain: The Third PSI Survey*, London, Heinemann.

Bull, D. (1980) *What Price 'Free' Education?*, London, Child Poverty Action Group.

Burgess, R. (1984) 'It's not a proper subject: it's just Newsom' in I. F. Goodson and S. J. Balls, eds, *Defining the Curriculum*, Lewes, Falmer Press.

Byrne, D. *et al.* (1975) *The Poverty of Education*, London, Martin Robertson.

Byrne, E. (1976) *The Rationale of Resource Allocation*, Milton Keynes, Open University Press.

Clarke, J. and Willis, P. (1984) 'Introduction', in I. Bates *et al.* (eds) (1984).

Clarricoates, K. (forthcoming, 1987) *Gender and Power in the Primary School*, Cambridge, Polity Press.

Craft, M. and Craft, A. (1985) 'The Participation of Ethnic Minority Pupils in Further and Higher Education', *Education Research*, vol. 25, no. 1.

Davie, R., Butler, M. and Goldstein, H. (1972) *From Birth to Seven*, London, Longman.

Douglas, J. W. B. (1967) *The Home and the School*, London, Panther.

Douglas, J. W. B. *et al.* (1971) *All Our Future*, London, Panther.

Edwards, A. D. (1976) *Language in Culture and Class*, London, Heinemann.

Eysenck, H. (1971) *Race, Intelligence and Education*, London, Temple Smith.

Fausto-Sterling, A. (1985) *Myths of Gender*, New York, Basic Books.

Finn, D. (1984) 'Leaving School and Growing Up: Work Experience in the Juvenile Labour Market', in Bates, I. *et al.* (eds) (1984).

Finn, D. and Frith, S. (1981) 'Education and the Labour Market', in Open University, *The State and the Politics of Education*, Milton Keynes, Open University Press.

Fuller, M. (1983) 'Qualified Criticism, Critical Qualifications', in L. Barton and S. Walker (eds), *Race, Class and Education'*, Beckenham, Croom Helm.

Giles, R. (1977) *The West Indian Experience in British Schools*, London, Heinemann.

Goodacre, E. (1968) *Teachers and Their Pupils' Home Backgrounds*, Slough, NFER.

Green, P. (1985) 'Multi-ethnic Teaching and the Pupils' Self-concepts', Annex B in *Swann Report* (1985).

Griffin, C. (1985) *Typical Girls?*, London, Routledge & Kegan Paul.

Halsey, A. H. (1977) 'Towards Meritocracy? the Case of Britain', in Karabel and Halsey (eds) (1977).

Halsey, A., Heath, A. and Ridge, J. (1980) *Origins and Destinations*, Oxford, Clarendon Press.

Hand, N. (1976) 'What is English?', in G. Whitty and M. Young (eds), *Explorations in the Politics of School Knowledge*, Driffield, Nafferton Books.

Hargreaves, D. (1967) *Social Relations in a Secondary School*, London, Routledge & Kegan Paul.

Hargreaves, D. (1972) *Interpersonal Relations and Education*, London, Routledge & Kegan Paul.

Hargreaves, D. (1979) 'Durkheim, Deviance and Education', in L. Barton and R. Meighan (eds), *Schools, Pupils and Deviance*, Driffield, Nafferton Books.

Hargreaves, D., Hestor, S. and Mellor, F. (1975) *Deviance in Classrooms*, London, Routledge & Kegan Paul.

Her Majesty's Inspectorate (1982) *The Effects of Local Authority Expenditure Policies on the Education Service in England, 1981*, London, DES.

Herrnstein, R. (1973) *IQ in the Meritocracy*, London, Allen Lane.

Hine, R. (1977) 'Political Bias in School Physics', in Open University, *School Knowledge and Social Control*, Milton Keynes, Open University Press.

Hodgson, G. (1973) 'Inequality: Do Schools Make a Difference?' in Silver, H. (ed.), *Equal Opportunity in Education*, London, Methuen.

Hopper, E. (ed.) (1971) *Readings in the Theory of Educational Systems*, London, Hutchinson.

Illich, I. (1973) *Deschooling Society*, Harmondsworth, Penguin.

Jackson, P. (1968) *Life in Classrooms*, New York, Holt, Rinehart & Winston.

Jencks, C. *et al.* (1973) *Inequality*, London, Allen Lane.

Jensen, A. (1969) 'How Much Can We Boost IQ and Scholastic Achievement?' in *Environment, Heredity and Intelligence*, Harvard Educational Review Reprint Series no. 2.

Kamin, L. (1977) *The Science and Politics of IQ*, Harmondsworth, Penguin.
Karabel, J. and Halsey, A. (eds) (1977) *Power and Ideology in Education*, Oxford, Oxford University Press.
Keddie, N. (1971) 'Classroom Knowledge', in M. F. D. Young (ed.), *Knowledge and Control*, London, Collier-Macmillan.
Keddie, N. (ed.) (1973) *Tinker, Tailor*, Harmondsworth, Penguin.
Kelly, A. (ed.) (1981) *The Missing Half*, Manchester University Press.
King, R. (1977) *Education*, London, Longman.
Kogan, M. (1983) *The Attack on Higher Education*, London, Kogan Page.
Lacey, C. (1970) *Hightown Grammar*, Manchester, Manchester University Press.
Moore, R. (1984) 'Schooling and the World of Work', in Bates, I. *et al.* (eds) (1984).
Nash, R. (1972) 'History as She is Writ', *New Society*, 3 August.
Neave, G. (1975) *How They Fared*, London, Routledge & Kegan Paul.
Pidgeon, D. (1970) *Expectation and Pupil Performance*, Slough, NFER.
Plowden Committee (1967) *Children and their Primary Schools*, London, HMSO.
Rampton Report (1981) *West Indian Children in our Schools*, Interim Report of the Committee of Inquiry into the Education of Children from Ethnic Minority Groups, London, HMSO.
Rees, T. and Gregory, D. (1981) 'Youth Employment and Unemployment: a Decade of Decline', *Educational Analysis*, vol. 3, no. 3.
Rist, R. (1970) 'Student Social Class and Teacher Expectations', *Harvard Educational Review*, vol. 40, no. 3.
Robbins Committee (1963) *Report on Higher Education*, London, HMSO.
School of Barbiana (1970) *Letter to a Teacher*, Harmondsworth, Penguin.
Sharp, R. and Green, A. (1975) *Education and Social Control*, London, Routledge & Kegan Paul.
Smail, B. (1984) *Girl-Friendly Science*, Schools Council Report, London, Longman.
Stubbs, M. (1976) *Language, Schools and Classrooms*, London, Methuen.
Swann Report (1985) *Education for All*, London, HMSO.
Tomlinson, S. (1979) *Decision-making in Special Education*, Ph.D thesis, University of Warwick.
Tunnard, J. (1979) *Uniform Blues*, Child Poverty Action Group, London.
Valentine, C. (1968) *Culture and Poverty*, Chicago, University of Chicago Press.
Wedge, P. and Prosser, H. (1973) *Born to Fail?*, London, Arrow Books.
Weiner, G. (1985) 'Equal Opportunities, Feminism and Girls' Education: Introduction', in G. Weiner (ed.), *Just a Bunch of Girls*, Milton Keynes, Open University Press.
Whyld, J. (ed.) (1983) *Sexism in the Secondary Curriculum*, London, Harper & Row.
Williams, R. (1981) *Culture*, London, Fontana.
Williamson, B. (1974) 'Continuities and Discontinuities in the Sociology of Education', in M. Flude and J. Ahier (eds), *Educability, Schools and Ideology*, London, Croom Helm.
Willis, P. (1977) *Learning to Labour*, Farnborough, Saxon House.
Woods, P. (1983) *Sociology and the School: an Interactionist Viewpoint*, London, Routledge & Kegan Paul.
Wright, N. (1977) *Progress in Education*, London, Croom Helm.
Yates, A. and Pidgeon, D. (1957) *Admission to Grammar Schools*, London, Newnes.
Young, M. F. D. (1971) 'An approach to the study of curricula as socially organised knowledge', in M. F. D. Young (ed.), *Knowledge and Control*, London, Collier-Macmillan.

9

Work

9.1 INTRODUCTION

For most employees work has a generally unpleasant quality. If there is little Calvinist compulsion to work among propertyless factory workers and file clerks, there is also little Renaissance exuberance in the work of the insurance clerk, freight handler, or department store saleslady ... Such joy as creative work may carry is more and more limited to a small minority (C. Wright Mills, 1953, p. 219).

It is often suggested that boring, mundane work is part of the price that people living in industrial societies have to pay for their high material standards of living. Moreover, it is argued, these standards can only be attained by the systematic utilisation of machine technology, and this requires both rational, bureaucratic forms of administration and a complicated division of labour. Consequently, *any* industrial society, because it *is* industrial, will incur certain costs – including the degradation of work – in order that sufficient surplus be produced to allow opportunities for leisure, diversification of interests and high mass consumption.

However, work and production are not just physical activities, they are social activities which can be organised in a variety of ways. Britain's industrialisation process – and that of most of Western Europe – occurred on a capitalist basis, a fact of crucial importance for understanding how work is organised and experienced.

In this chapter we shall examine the distinctive nature of capitalist social relations and the various strategies used by management to control labour and to justify that control. We shall also analyse the methods used by employees to resist this control, both at the point of production and in the wider society. Finally, we shall make a few brief observations about the possible future of work in societies such as ours.

9.2 THE CAPITALIST LABOUR PROCESS

General features: how is work affected by capitalism?

Capitalism means that much of the productive system is privately owned, usually concentrated in relatively few hands, and organised for profit.

Work has the status of wage-labour, and jobs are located within a labour market, where prospective workers must find employers willing to pay a wage or salary in return for the use of their skills, knowledge or physical strength. We shall argue that it is the *capitalist*, and not merely the industrial, nature of Western society that is primarily responsible for the way the organisation of work has developed.

Industrialisation involves basic changes in the structure of a society. A fundamental change is that, in industrial societies, most people become employees. This is in marked contrast to non-industrial societies, where three-quarters or more of the occupied population are either employers, self-employed, or family workers. The change to a society dominated by wage-labour is a relatively recent one which is associated with the emergence of the factory system of production, which became dominant in Britain as late as the nineteenth century.

The factory system developed alongside craft and domestic systems of production and took some time to supersede them – never replacing them entirely. The modern worker is often compared with the craftworkers of earlier centuries, so we must be wary of romanticising such workers' position. The craft system operated within a society marked by poverty, deprivation and brutal exploitation. There was, nevertheless, a difference in the nature of the relationship which existed between craft employers and employees, in that it was a *personal* relationship in which both employer and employee had mutual obligations much broader than anything expected today. Furthermore, the craftworkers owned their own tools and place of work, bought their raw materials and sold the finished product direct to the consumer. However, much more important was the skill and knowledge that they controlled:

> From earliest times to the Industrial Revolution the craft or skilled trade was the basic unit, the elementary cell of the labour process. In each craft, the worker was presumed to be the master of a body of traditional knowledge, and methods and procedures were left to his or her discretion. In each such worker reposed the accumulated knowledge of materials and processes by which production was accomplished in the craft ... The worker combined in mind and body, the concepts and physical dexterities of the specialty (Braverman, 1974, p. 109).

However, factory production was to involve basic changes in the social situation of *all* workers with far-reaching implications for craft skills and employment relations. It meant the concentration of labour in one workshop or factory and the separation of home and work. Workers were subject to the discipline of employers who required that they worked regular hours with regular intensity. Although legally free, they were subordinate and dependent both economically and socially.

The technical and social division of labour

The factory system also made possible much greater division of labour and specialisation as machine power was introduced. The introduction of the machine meant that greater amounts of fixed capital were required for manufacture, and that much factory work came to involve the performing of semi-skilled or unskilled tasks, fragments of the total process, in which the intrinsic satisfactions derived from the task itself and from the completion of a finished product were diminished. Increasingly employees lost a good deal of contact with their employer – sometimes *all* personal contact was severed. Finally, workers lost most of their rights over materials, tools, and the product of their labour.

The development of the factory system represents a division of labour between agriculture and manufacture which allows food and goods to be produced more efficiently. The *technical* division of labour and the development of new technologies are *potentially* liberating, in that both permit greater control over the environment and the possibility of producing a surplus. However, the technical division of labour – which separates work into specific tasks and which can create greater efficiency – is also accompanied by a crucial *social* division of labour between factory owners and those who work for them, and by the *intellectual* division of labour between manual labourers and clerks and administrators.

Through such divisions, the labour force is not just co-ordinated by the division of labour and rational production processes, it is also *controlled*. People at work have *power* exercised over them.

Controlling labour in capitalism

The reduction of labour power to the status of a commodity under capitalism has two very important implications for the nature of this control. The wages and conditions forming the basis of the employees' existence are a *cost* to the employer to be taken out of profits; consequently it is in employers' interests to resist improvements in these, just as employees are bound to press for them. Because employers must regard labour as a cost to be minimised, they will only employ people while it is profitable to do so. Therefore, workers are always at the mercy of economic and technological developments and constantly threatened by unemployment. Consequently, technological developments which cause redundancies are not always welcomed with enthusiasm.

Furthermore, when *marketable* skill becomes the basis of reward, it is imperative that workers who possess such skills attempt to control the conditions under which they are offered for sale. They must strive to maintain the scarcity and utility of their skills. Conversely, it is in the interests of capital to reduce its reliance upon skilled personnel, for skill is expensive. The simplest way of cheapening labour power is to break it up into its simplest elements and to divorce the labour process from special knowledge and training. In fact, the history of manual labour may be seen as a process in which workers have gradually lost control or possession of their knowledge and skills. (Arguably, the development of micro-computer technology poses a similar threat to intellectual skills.)

The same principle which breaks down work into routine and meaning-less tasks means that management, by organising and co-ordinating the fragments, can gain a virtual monopoly of knowledge and therefore control over the work process itself.

We shall see that as the approach to the study of work which puts the emphasis on the importance of understanding the capitalist labour process has developed, writers in this tradition have stressed not only *management* control strategies, but also *workers'* resistance to this attempted control, *and* the strategies that workers use against each other in order to obtain sectional advantages for their group.

9.3   MANAGERIAL THEORIES

Managers have developed their own accounts of, and justifications for, their actions which often bear little relationship to those provided by sociologists. These theories not only help justify and legitimise the function of management, but also provide explanations of worker motivation which, if highly ideological, also represent coherent attempts to come to grips with the capital/labour relationship. Managers are aware that when labour is sold in return for wages then what they buy is a *potential* to work which they must then direct and organise. Consequently the employer/manager is dependent – to a greater or lesser degree – on the motivations, attitudes and work orientations of the employee. Conflict may be endemic in the capital/labour relationship but it also depends upon *co-operation*. Managerial theory, then, has wrestled with understanding not only the basis for conflict, but the conditions which facilitate acquiescence or compliance with, managements' aims. One of the earliest of these attempts has become known as scientific management.

Scientific management

This theory is associated with the work of Frederick Taylor. An early management consultant, Taylor (1911) insisted that management should assume responsibility for deciding how work was to be performed, leaving to workers the task of obeying orders to the letter in order to gain maximum productivity at least cost. This was accomplished by offering financial incentives to workers and then specifying every detail of their work: when to load, when to rest, when to walk, the size of the shovel and the arc of the swing. Consequently, most of the Scientific Management studies of the 1920s and 1930s were concerned with finding the 'best' way of doing a job according to these prescriptions.

In *Principles of Scientific Management* Taylor (1967) argues that, left to their own devices, workers will do as little as possible and engage in 'soldiering' – working more slowly together in order to keep management ignorant of their potential. Similarly, left to plan their own work, workers' output is further lowered. They will do things in the customary way rather than the most efficient way. The solution is for management to 'relieve' workers of the necessity of planning their own tasks, particularly those with a mental component. Workers will learn from management how best to increase their output to the benefit of both. The best inducement, he believed, is *money* or *economic reward*. People are primarily interested in achieving a level of pay commensurate with the effort they have expended and expect a fair day's pay for a fair day's work; and piecework ensures that individual effort is rewarded.

In 1899 Taylor's methods were utilised at the Bethlehem steel-works where they were responsible for raising pig-iron production by almost 400 per cent per day. He did this by allying a range of financial incentives with a meticulously detailed analysis of what he regarded as the most technically efficient method of performing the work; what we now know as 'work study'.

Many of Taylor's assumptions – especially that people are primarily motivated by economic rewards – have since been questioned as oversimplifying the complex nature of human motivation. Similarly, exactly what constitutes a 'fair day's pay for a fair day's work' is subject to a continuous process of formal and informal negotiation between management and workers. Also, within a capitalist market, the price of labour depends upon a variety of factors such as scarcity, demand, economic conditions, and so on. However, the assumption most severely criticised was that people seek individual satisfactions in work, and necessarily value these above the satisfactions of solidarity with work-mates.

It is often argued that Taylor's methods of organising work 'failed' or that his ideas were superseded by those of the human-relations school that 'followed' scientific management. Others – such as Braverman (1974), as we shall see – have suggested that his techniques of work study have simply been refined and extended and his principles implemented in a range of settings, if in modified form.

The human relations school

Scientific management operated with a model of human motivation which stressed the 'rational', economically-motivated aspects of peoples' behaviour. The human relations school of management, on the other hand, sees people as being creatures of instinct or sentiments rather than rational, calculating economic beings, and attempts, via a variety of what Friedman (1977a) calls 'responsible autonomy' strategies, to harness this 'irrational' motivation in a manner beneficial to the firm. The best known and most influential group of theorists was the human relations school of Harvard and Chicago, represented by Elton Mayo.

Whereas Taylor's solution to worker resistance was to provide relatively high financial rewards and the satisfaction of operating at peak efficiency, the various psychological and sociological theorists that we can loosely term 'human relations' theorists have suggested a combination of: making the work itself more interesting (appealing to individual desires for sociability, security, challenge and variety); choosing workers who best fit in with the tasks required; and the sensitive and subtle exercise of managerial authority through the manipulation of sentiment – encouraging venom against competitors (especially foreign), 'counselling' non-co-operative workers, and encouraging a feeling of team struggle through the participatory and rewarded suggestion schemes, and the judicious payment of loyalty-inducing perks, such as company recreational facilities (Friedman, 1977a).

9.4   THE CRITIQUE OF MANAGERIAL THEORIES: LABOUR PROCESS THEORY

Braverman

The recent explosion of interest in the study of the labour process was sparked off by Harry Braverman (1974). Braverman claimed that the whole thrust of change in capitalism was towards deskilling the labour force and establishing control over the knowledge necessary for production. This process was well under way by the end of the nineteenth century, but its modern exemplar was, claimed Braverman, scientific management theory.

Braverman regards scientific management not as an objective 'scientific' study of the difficulties of performing and organising work in a complex society but as a means of *adapting* labour to the needs of capitalism and of *exerting control* over the labour process.

Although Braverman provides a range of stimulating insights into work in modern societies, we must not assume that employers' attempts to control the labour process in its entirety occurred without resistance, or that workers necessarily face management as isolated individuals. More-

Braverman's analysis of scientific management

Braverman claims that scientific management operated with three main principles which still operate today.

The first he calls the *dissociation of the labour process from the skills of the workers*, which, as Taylor himself observed, means that 'the managers assume ... the burden of gathering together all the traditional knowledge which in the past has been possessed by the workmen and then of classifying, tabulating and reducing this knowledge to rules, laws and formulae' (Taylor, 1967, p. 36).

The second principle he calls *the separation of conception from execution*. Here, the unity of the labour process is broken up by the capitalist, who separates mental from manual labour, and then further sub-divides both. Taylor argues that the full possibilities of his system 'will not have been realized until almost all of the machines in the shop are run by men who are of smaller calibre and attainments, and who are therefore cheaper than those required under the old system' (Taylor, 1903, p. 105). The study of work processes is reserved to management, who pass on to the worker simplified job tasks divorced from the overall logic of the process.

The third principle is *the use of the monopoly over knowledge to control each step of the labour process and its mode of execution*. Under 'ordinary' management the worker had become more skilled and knowledgeable than anyone in management, so the details of how work could best be done had to be left to him or her. By contrast:

Perhaps the most prominent single element in modern scientific management is the task idea. The work of every workman is fully planned out by management at least one day in advance and each man receives in most cases complete written instructions, describing in detail the task which he is to accomplish, as well as the means to be used in doing the work. This task specifies not only what is to be done, but how it is to be done and the exact time allowed for doing it ... Scientific management consists ... in preparing for and carrying out these tasks (Taylor, 1967, pp. 63, 39).

Braverman argues that the most important part of this process was not the written instructions but the systematic preplanning and pre-calculation of the labour process, which took away from workers the responsibility for conceiving, planning and initiating their work tasks thus leaving the imaginative tasks of creation to management.

over, we shall argue that management, in its attempts to gain control of the work-force, has proved to be both more sophisticated and more pragmatic than Braverman allows.

The critique of Braverman

(i) *Friedman's concept of 'responsible autonomy'*. Braverman's book sparked off a vast body of research into the labour process; inevitably this research has challenged, modified and refined some of his conclusions. In particular, more recent work by Friedman (1977a), Edwards (1979) and Crompton and Jones (1984) for example, while sympathetic to some of Braverman's ideas, has challenged the accuracy of his claim that de-skilling is a necessary and extensive part of the capitalist labour process.

Braverman argues that work is de-skilled not only to reduce labour costs, but also to achieve control of the worker. However, many critics have suggested that routinisation and fragmentation of the labour process, or 'de-skilling', is only one strategy by which such control may be achieved, and may, under certain circumstances, actually be counter-productive. For example, Friedman points out that, given the opposition that developed against Taylorism, managements have often adopted what he terms 're-sponsible autonomy' strategies which have avoided the direct control inherent in Taylorism. He (1977b, p. 48) defines responsible autonomy as:

> the maintenance of managerial authority by getting workers to identify with the competitive aims of the enterprise so that they will act 'responsibly' with a minimum of supervision.

So, groups of workers or individuals, are given a wider measure of discretion over the direction of work, with a minimum of supervision as a means of maintaining overall managerial authority. This is often a re-sponse, or accommodation to, levels of worker resistance to management strategies of control. Friedman, then, sees the forms of authority and control utilised by employers to be a product of confrontation and accommodation – the retention of craft workers after the 'technical' necess-ity for their skills has been eroded provides a good example – and the emphasis on the inevitable drive of capital to cheapen labour costs through increasing subordination and de-skilling is seen to be an uneven and complex trend. However, it is also recognised that resort to strategies of 'responsible autonomy' are unlikely to prove effective – indeed are unlikely to be tried – with workers whose whole experience of management has imbued them with a deep distrust of managements' motivations and practices. These are the workers who are likely – to use Edwards's term (1979) – to see relations with management as a 'contested terrain', where both sides constantly battle over the shifting frontier of control.

(ii) *Edwards's account of forms of managerial control.* Edwards, like Fried-man, suggests that management have at their disposal a variety of strategies for controlling workers. Whereas Friedman distinguishes between direct control and responsible autonomy, Edwards differentiates between direct or simple control, technical control and bureaucratic control. *Simple control* is where workers are personally controlled either by employers themselves or their representatives. Edwards sees 'simple control' as being more characteristic of the early stages of capitalist development, but suggests that it is likely to survive in small firms in the non-monopoly, or 'competitive' sections of the economy:

> These bosses exercised power personally, intervening in the labour process often to exhort workers, bully and threaten them, reward good performance, hire and fire on the spot, favour loyal workers, and generally act as despots, benevolent or otherwise (Edwards, 1979, p. 19).

Indeed, this type of direct control is widespread among the new casualised and part-time employment that is growing in the US and the UK.

Technical control, developed as a response to the problems of operating 'simple' control as the size of employing organisations grew and work-forces became more highly unionised. Technical control is defined as that which

> involves designing machinery and planning the work flow to minimise the problem of transforming labour power into labour as well as to maximise the purely physical based possibilities for achieving efficiencies (Edwards, 1979, p. 112).

This is seen as a qualitative advance on work that has been mechanised, or which is machine paced, in that such developments increase the productivity of labour without necessarily altering structures of control. Technical control, on the other hand, only emerges when the entire production process or large sections of it are based on a technology that paces and directs the labour process. The assembly line, when it was first introduced, provides a good example in that it relieved human agents such as supervisors of the responsibility of setting tasks, allowing them instead to merely enforce the apparently impersonal requirements of the technical structure:

> The work quota is no longer laid down, negotiated and imposed by a human authority which remains open to argument; it is ordered by the machine itself, imposed by the inexorable programmed advance of the assembly line (Bosquet, 1980, pp. 374–5).

Edwards would see computer-based technology as representing a further advance of technical control, although he would want to maintain the distinction between mechanisation/computerisation of particular tasks or groups of tasks, and machine direction of the whole labour process. The problem with the development of technical control, as Edwards sees it, is that it tends to create a homogeneous work-force by producing common pace and patterns of work. So in the process of solving the control problems of individual supervisors and work sections, conflict may be displaced and raised to a plant-wide level.

This is where *bureaucratic control* proves its efficacy. Companies have to find ways of simultaneously re-dividing the work-force, integrating it into a company structure, and gaining its loyalty. So, bureaucratic control is gradually introduced which has the effect of establishing the impersonal force of company rules as the basis for the regulation of work. Edwards uses the example of the Polaroid company to demonstrate the effectiveness of this divide and rule strategy:

> With eighteen different job families, three hundred job titles, and fourteen different pay grades, not to mention the dichotomy between the salaried and hourly workers, it might appear that Polaroid had gone far enough in dividing and re-dividing its workers. Not so: each job is now further positioned on the pay scale so that for any given job, seven distinct pay steps are possible . . . Polaroid has created roughly 2,100 individual slots for its 6,397 hourly workers. And that leaves out a number of ancillary means of sub-dividing workers – the seniority bonus, 'special pay' status, the incentive bonus and so on (Edwards, 1979, p. 134).

Polaroid, and other companies creating similarly complicated internal job-markets, not only create divisions among the work-force which inhibit the creation of a collective consciousness, but also help ensure that individual worker's careers are closely tied to that particular firm.

So, rather than placing the emphasis on Friedman's responsible autonomy strategies, Edwards suggests that managements have attempted to maintain control of the work-force by a variety of methods ranging from industrial realtions procedures, through bureaucratic rules which channel conflict into manageable and acceptable directions, and by using internal labour markets and dual labour markets (see ch. 6, pp. 343–5) to both generate commitment to individual companies and to divide and segment the working class.

(iii) *Labour market theories and de-skilling.* Many people have in fact argued that the de-skilling debate has to be situated within the wider analysis of labour markets. For example, 'dual' and 'radical' labour market theorists have suggested that control may be facilitated via the fragmentation, rather than the homogenisation of the labour force. These 'dual' and 'radical' labour market theories emerged in opposition to 'human capital' theories of wage determination – i.e. the theory that the returns to labour (wages) reflected the level of investment in the 'human capital' offered for sale such as training, education, and work experience etc. However, the various versions of labour market theory suggest that in reality the labour market is structured according to the particular requirements of employers rather than simply reflecting the 'quality' of labour available. It follows that some employers, particularly those operating in the 'secondary' or 'competitive' sector of the economy, will require cheap labour, docile because of its dependence, which can be easily taken on, and just as easily laid off, in response to short-term economic fluctuations. Women, and certain ethnic minorities, will often fit the bill admirably here. Other employers, particularly in the monopolistic, non-competitive sector, may require a more stable labour force, often 'skilled' by a process of adaptation to a particular technology or pattern of work organisation, which will be relatively protected from short-term fluctuations in the economy. Radical theorists argue that the structuring of the labour market is thus an element in capitalist control, for by dividing the labour force within and against itself, resistance to exploitation is rendered much less likely (Crompton and Jones, 1984).

Braverman's thesis is not invalidated by such arguments; they simply suggest that his account of capitalist control strategies was rather incomplete and one-sided.

Worker response to managerial control

A central criticism of Braverman is that he accepts far too readily that employers' attempts to control the work-force in its entirety occurred without resistance. As we have seen Taylor himself recognised the importance of 'soldiering' – i.e. workers' hiding from management the fact that they were capable of faster work – as a tactic for resisting management control, and this tactic survived his methods and was instituted against them. Workers do not face management as isolated individuals but very often as members of integrated work-groups with their own ideas about work-loads, pace and 'fairness'. Furthermore, they develop methods for resisting management encroachment upon these norms, and attacks upon their skills and jobs, which operate both at the point of production and at the broader societal level by means of trade unions and political parties. For example, several recent studies have revealed a considerable amount of resistance by craft workers to mechanisation in industries such as building, engineering, and textiles. This resistance could be quite successful in retaining both levels of skill and rewards. A key role was often played in this process by mechanisms of social exclusion. Penn shows how spinning and engineering workers were able to maintain structural support for their skills by retaining control over the use of machinery, and by a double means of exclusion. They were able to exclude management from complete control of the work process, and were also able to exclude other non-craft workers who represented a threat to their position (Penn, 1978, pp. 4–5).

We have suggested that employers may segment and divide the work-force in order to facilitate control, but we should recognise that the same tactic may be used by employees. Skilled workers, by attempting to control the supply of labour at the level of the firm and of society (thus resisting dilution of their skills by semi-skilled workers, or women, or immigrants entering the labour force), can themselves create segmentation in the labour market. This may help them to retain skills, since it reduces the employers freedom to interchange the work-force. The creation of separate labour markets for men and women is part of this process, of course.

However, it is not just skilled workers who are able to resist employers. Friedman points out that the material basis for worker resistance did not disappear with the spread of modern industry and the consequential partial erosion of skills. In fact the new situation often created the material conditions for successful and organised resistance by the semi-skilled and unskilled. Employers found it difficult to replace the increasing number of semi-skilled workers who had become proficient in the use of the new machinery, and stood to lose a lot of money if equipment stood idle for long. We shall in fact argue that even unintegrated, poorly or non-unionised workers, have 'weapons' at their disposal which may be used against management or which can serve as a protest against the work relationship and working conditions. These informal strategies may, in fact, prove more damaging to employer interests than more formalised methods of resistance such as strikes. Consequently, if official or unofficial union activity is curtailed by the fear of unemployment or by increasingly stringent legal constraints on union activity, as at present appears to be the case, recourse may more often be taken to these individualistic methods. Therefore, it may not necessarily be in the interests of capital to encourage these less easily 'controllable' forms of resistance. Let us now, though, look at more formal modes of worker resistance.

Collective bargaining

We have argued that one of the fundamentals of capitalism is that work has the status of wage-labour. Jobs are located within a labour *market*, and individuals wanting to work must first find an employer willing to pay a wage or salary in return for the disposal of their skills, knowledge or physical strength. Labour, under capitalism, is a commodity like any other, and its price depends upon conditions in the market.

Legally, of course, relations between employers and workers are governed by a contract of employment which, theoretically, is freely agreed between them. In reality, however, the notion of a free contract is dubious. The concentration of economic power in capitalism means that employers can virtually dictate the broad outlines of the employment contract. This contract is indeed free, in that people are not physically forced to work, but as we pointed out in Chapter 2 the alternative to not working for workers is very much more drastic than it is for employers.

Admittedly, market forces may occasionally work to the benefit of labour, with workers able to wring concessions from employers when their skills are scarce or in demand. Moreover, workers who organise themselves into unions or associations are far less vulnerable than isolated individuals.

This recognition of the inherent weakness of the individual worker and of the advantages to be gained by *collective* action lay behind the early development of the trade union movement, which helped workers offer or refuse their services collectively rather than individually. Consequently, it is often argued that collective bargaining lies at the heart of the trade-union movement as the means by which workers might counteract the power of the employer.

However, collective bargaining must not be seen as restoring a balance of power between workers and employers. For Hyman (1975) and Fox (1974), collective bargaining represents one way of challenging certain management decisions on issues which unions see as of immediate or special importance. But other equally important decisions could be challenged if they *did* possess decisive power. Most union/management disputes centre upon wages, or who does what work and under what conditions, or who should join what union – issues which are of obvious significance to both sides, but not ones which touch the fundamentals of the capitalist system. Most of the time trade unions are striving to effect marginal improvements in the lot of their members and attempting to defend them against arbitrary management action. What they do not do is to challenge management on such basic principles of the social and industrial framework as private property, the hierarchical nature of the organisation, the extreme division of labour, and the massive inequalities of financial reward, status, control and autonomy in work. Similarly, they have little or no say in decisions made within an organisation on issues such as management objectives, markets, capital investment and rate of expansion. Moreover, rarely do they challenge such principles as the treatment of labour as a commodity to be hired or dispensed with at the convenience of management.

In fact, although 'free collective bargaining' has provided a centrepiece of British trade union consciousness for over a century, and carries great emotional resonance as a slogan, it has always been something of a misnomer. The demands of trade union negotiators and their access to sanctions in pursuit of their objectives are subject to a variety of constraints and influences long before the two sides arrive at the bargaining table. However, in the traditional pattern of collective bargaining these prior constraints and influences are mainly covert rather than overt, and are not so complete as to eliminate all choice and unpredictability. 'The bargainers', says Hyman (1984, p. 217), 'do not merely engage in a predetermined charade'. In fact, the demand for free collective bargaining, represents a demand to preserve a limited area of autonomy, a margin of independent action, which – however circumscribed by the productive relations of capitalism and the ideological reflections of these relations – is of crucial importance in providing British trade unionism with what has long been regarded as its main reason for existence (Hyman, 1984).

However:

in the (present) political and economic context . . . even the traditionally limited sphere of trade union autonomy has cumulative effects (in terms of labour costs, restraints on managerial control of the labour process, obstruction to overall economic planning, disturbances to the 'confidence' of foreign and domestic financiers) which contemporary capitalism has a diminishing capacity to absorb. 'Free collective bargaining' may be regarded by trade unionists as a defensive and even conservative slogan, but its implications are increasingly disruptive and subversive' (Hyman, 1984, p. 217).

Our discussion of that most publicised area of industrial relations and most criticised area of trade-union activity – the strike – allows us to examine some of the developments which have turned traditional procedures of collective bargaining into potentially 'disruptive' and 'subversive' activities.

The strike

The strike is just one of a variety of 'weapons' that workers have at their disposal in combating management control, and just one indication of the extent of 'industrial' conflict. Other manifestations of conflict, or poor industrial relations, which might be said to emanate from the workers 'side', would include absenteeism, high rates of labour turnover, sabotage, pilfering, inefficiency, restriction of output, formal 'political' action, and so on. Employers might be said to utilise the lock-out, plant closures, sackings victimisation, blacklisting, speed-up, safety hazards, arbitrary discipline and, again, formal political action.

In fact, the very use of the term 'industrial conflict' may be questioned since it carries the implication that the industrial sphere may be isolated from the conflicts and tensions of the wider society. Conflict is built into the labour/capital relationship and strikes and other forms of industrial conflict may be seen as but one expression of wider class divisions in society. We shall argue that developments in industrial relations over the last decade or so, and the increasing involvement of the state in the industrial sphere, illustrate just how artificial the distinction between the industrial and the political has become.

Trends and patterns

What have been the major trends in British strike activity in recent years?

First, the official statistics show the total number of strikes rising to an unprecedented peak of 3906 in 1970; then declining, but for the next decade fluctuating around an average somewhat higher than in the 1960s. Despite rising levels of unemployment – normally associated with steep decline in the number of stoppages – in no year did the total fall below 2000. But from 1980 the number fell drastically, with the total for 1983 being the lowest since 1941. Since the late 1960s the number of workers involved has in

TABLE 9.1

British strike statistics: annual averages 1900–83

	Number of strikes	Workers involved ('000)	Striker-days ('000)
1900–10	529	240	4 576
1911–13	1 074	1 034	20 908
1914–18	844	632	5 292
1919–21	1 241	2 108	49 053
1922–25	629	503	11 968
1926	323	2 734	162 233
1927–32	379	344	4 740
1933–39	735	295	1 694
1940–44	1 491	499	1 816
1945–54	1 791	545	2 073
1955–64	2 521	1 116	3 889
1965–69	2 380	1 208	3 951
1970–74	2 885	1 564	14 077
1975	2 282	789	6 012
1976	2 016	666	3 284
1977	2 703	1 166	8 223
1978	2 471	1 041	9 405
1979	2 080	4 608	29 474
1980	1 330	834	11 964
1981	1 338	1 499	4 266
1982	1 528	2 101	5 313
1983	1 255	538	3 593

Source: *Department of Employment Gazette*, in R. Hyman, *Strikes*, London, Fontana, 1984.

almost every year been well above the average for the two previous decades. And the number of striker-days rose even more dramatically above the post-war norm, with peaks in 1972 and 1979, even in the 1980s the figure remains high by earlier standards (Hyman, 1984).

Secondly, in recent years the official trade union structure has become much more intimately involved in the conduct of disputes than was the case in the 1960s. It is still the case that, numerically most strikes start and end independently of the machinery of trade unionism outside the workplace; but the number of disputes involving outside union committees and officials has increased considerably, and it is strikes of this type which have assumed key political and economic significance in recent years (Hyman, 1984).

Thirdly, and of vital importance, has been the changing role of the state in British industrial relations, and the impact that this role has had upon the nature of conflict in industry. Government ministers, the courts and various statutory agencies have become far more actively and openly involved in shaping labour relations than ever before in peacetime. Consequently, as Hyman points out, the distinction between 'industrial' and 'political' issues, 'always artificial and misleading', has become increasingly unconvincing; with strikers themselves coming to regard their actions in a far more directly 'political' light than in the past.

Hyman argues that all these tendencies are interrelated. They stem partly from the developments affecting the whole capitalist world, partly from factors peculiar to the British context. Their cumulative effect, he suggests, has been to make it even less possible than previously to treat strikes as an isolated phenomenon: they can only be understood within a broader political economy of industrial relations.

It is clear that the trends in recorded strike activity in post-war Britain have been extremely complicated and uneven and that we cannot possibly go into all of them here. They would appear to be a reflection of underlying diversity and fluctuation in labour markets, the organisation of the labour process, the structure of capital, and the economic role of the state. However, it is clear that government involvement in industrial relations, particularly with incomes policies, has been of particular significance.

9.5   GOVERNMENT INVOLVEMENT IN COLLECTIVE BARGAINING

During the 1960s and 1970s collective bargaining was increasingly affected by broader economic and political developments. The rise in the number of strikes in the 1960s is primarily related to trends in workplace bargaining, but subsequent developments have owed a great deal to other influences. It is clear that changes in work-place bargaining created an increasingly fertile environment for strikes during the 1960s. The incidence of unofficial strikes was so high in Britain as to justify a Royal Commission, which produced The Donovan Report (1968). Donovan argued that the rise in the number of strikes was due to the progressive breakdown of the 'formal' system of industrial relations and the rise of the 'informal' system. He suggested that rising wage drift encouraged the fragmentation of bargaining while the growing number of shop stewards and the increasing volume of work-place bargaining contributed to the ability of workers to exploit the possibilities that this presented. British industrial relations have had a long tradition of strong organisation at work-place level, but it was only during the 1970s, with the unprecedented period of sustained full-employment after 1945, that the power of work-place organisations became firmly enough established to challenge management strenuously and frequently. One consequence was the emergence of the small unofficial strike which so concerned governments and academic commentators in the late 1960s. We shall return to this issue and what happened to work-place bargaining shortly; it must suffice to draw attention to the prediction made by McCarthy (1970) that the increase in strike frequency to 1970 showed no signs of abating, a prediction made when the increase was about to be reversed (Edwards, P. K., 1983).

The growth of the national strike

The most significant feature of strikes in the 1960s and 1970s was the re-emergence of the large official strike. it was this type of strike which had the greatest impact on worker involvement and days lost. Many of these strikes – although by no means all – occurred in the public sector and involved hitherto generally strike-free groups such as civil servants, teachers, and health service workers and local authority workers. It is generally recognised that this pattern can be related fairly directly to the incomes policies and other attempts to control inflation operating at the time, with workers being forced into action in the face of attempts to use the public sector to hold down wages. Various governments, in their attempts to get private employers to follow pay guidelines, have been particularly hard on public sector wage claims so it was not surprising that these workers increasingly engaged in strikes. Furthermore, the prevalence of national agreements meant that the strikes were conducted at the national level, and thus that they involved large numbers of workers. As we shall see, the decision – post-Donovan – of private employers to centralise bargaining at plant or national level was to exacerbate this trend.

The re-emergence of the large national strike in the 1970s was due to a variety of forces, with perhaps the large confrontations in the public sector around incomes policies being the most notable. These developments should not be viewed in isolation, however. Incomes policies should not be separated from the increased stress on efficiency in the public sector, for both reflected the growing pressure on the sector: the series of crises which affected the economy as a whole were felt particularly acutely here, with successive governments stressing the need to reduce deficits and fight inflation. The strikes of the 1970s cannot be understood outside this context. They provide a dramatic illustration of the way in which strike patterns have reflected broad economic and political pressures and not just the structure of bargaining. [It should also be borne in mind, of course, that most workers strike rarely – if at all – and that the great majority of strikes remain small and short.] (Edwards, P. K., 1983).

Similarly, it is impossible to discuss collective bargaining in the 1980s and the role of trade union activity in resisting management control of the work process, without making specific reference to the attempts of recent British Conservative governments to use monetarist policies to curb inflation. (However, similar 'experiments' were being conducted in the USA and continental Europe.) It was partly the proliferation of strikes among low-paid public sector workers during the winter of 1978/79, directed against the Labour government's incomes policy represented in the 'social contract', which swept the Conservative Party back into office on a wave of popular anti-union and anti-government feeling. The Conservative government was able to mobilise this sentiment in support of their policies to weaken the power of the trade unions and introduce radical anti-union legislation.

Coercive pacification

Recent Conservative governments, but particularly those dominated by Margaret Thatcher, have come to argue that most of Britain's economic problems are due to excessive State interference with the workings of the free market. In fact, the Conservative government which took office in May 1979 was committed to 'Rolling back the State' and allowing the market free rein, even if this increased economic costs, such as when profitable state industries were privatised. This support of the free market as a principle was a reflection of an individualistic philosophy which saw economic freedom as a condition of political freedom. Competition in a free market was seen as' a necessary cleansing agent capable of revitalising, not only British industry, but the whole of British society. Consequently the post-1979 Conservative administrations committed themselves to an economic and social strategy informed by a belief that most of Britain's problems were due to a combination of four main 'ills' with inflation as the result: over-powerful unions; weak government; an over-burdened public sector and, most importantly, profligate public-spending. The Government's actions in support of their principled objection to all four factors, had, as one consequence, a dramatic increase in the rate of unemployment, and as a corollary, an equally dramatic decrease in trade union influence and power.

So, while some people might see recent 'attacks' on trade unions by the Thatcher governments as evidence of a basic ideological antipathy to organised labour, they must also be seen as part of an integrated economic analysis and policy. The argument that strong trade unions constitute one element in Britain's recent economic difficulties is not exclusive to the political right, but has formed part of some Marxist analyses (see Mandel, 1978; Gamble, 1981). It has been argued, for example, that the profits of the private sector have been squeezed by the combination of intense foreign competition, preventing price rises, and strong unions, which have forced up wages. However, it is an analysis more readily associated with the political right which not only sees unionism as an infringement on individual liberties, and the growth of the closed shop has provided them with an important ideological weapon in this respect, but as also infringing on the operation of the free market. They see the trade unions as employing their monopolistic control over the supply of labour and their coercive powers, such as the right to picket, to force up wages beyond their 'natural' market level, thereby crippling the profitability of British industry.

According to this analysis, trade union power is an obstacle to company profitability and competitiveness, since it prevents them from reducing wages and shedding 'surplus' labour. Moreover, the argument goes, successive post-war governments have made the problem worse by their Keynesian full-employment policies which increased the unions bargaining power, and by their inclusion of union leaders as near equal partners in economic policy-making.

What was needed, therefore, was a drastic curtailment of union power and this is what the Conservative government set out to achieve, and in fact argued (with some justification) were mandated to do. Consequently, the government, from 1979 onwards, allowed unemployment to rise as a deliberate aspect of policy, thus exacerbating the problems created by structural changes already occurring. Moreover, union involvement in policy-making bodies was reduced: the days of 'beer and sandwiches at no. 10' were at an end. Most significantly, however, the government introduced legislation designed to undermine traditional union 'rights'. The Employment Acts of 1980 and 1982, for example, placed a variety of new restrictions on the rights of unions to organise. The definition of a 'trade dispute' was narrowed so as to rule out what many unions would regard as essential activities such as sympathy strikes and solidarity boycotts. The right to picket the customers and suppliers of an employer in dispute has been removed, thus removing one means of persuading other workers to offer assistance in the event of a dispute. The right to make agreements with employers on union membership has been curtailed: the necessity to ballot the membership every five years and the need to obtain 80 per cent majorities, now make it difficult to make closed shop agreements – further reducing the strength of the union. Moreover, the Trade Union Act 1984 made it a requirement, among other things, that unions ballot their members before each and every call for industrial action, and that they ballot their members every ten years on whether or not to have political funds. Many see this latter requirement as a deliberate attempt to weaken the Labour party and to destroy any concerted and broad-based opposition to the Conservative party itself.

This anti-union legislation was accompanied by attacks on individual trade unions, especially those operating in the public sector. There are many examples upon which we could draw, but perhaps the most significant were the withdrawal of union rights from workers at GCHQ and the plans which the government made to take on, and ultimately defeat, the National Union of Mineworkers.

The GCHQ affair

In January 1984 it was announced in the House of Commons that all civil servants working at the government communications headquarters, GCHQ, were to be deprived of their trade union rights. Union leaders were given 10 minutes warning of this announcement. With immediate effect, GCHQ staff were stripped of their rights under employment protection legislation, including the right to appeal to an industrial relations tribunal against unfair dismissal. The right to belong to a trade union was to be withdrawn from 1 March 1984. Union members who agreed to sign an official form surrendering their rights were to be paid £1000. People refusing to sign were threatened with dismissal. The government justified its action on the grounds that industrial action at GCHQ would constitute a threat to national security. (Manwaring and Sigler (eds), 1985)

Similarly, it has been argued that the miners strike of 1984–5 was deliberately engineered by the Conservative government as part of its policy of reducing public expenditure and of reducing the power of the unions in order to decrease wages.

The defeat of the NUM – one of the most powerful of the industrial unions – and the accompanying fragmentation and internal dissension which resulted in the breakaway of the rival Democratic Union of Mineworkers, demonstrates quite clearly that the political environment of collective organisation and action has been radically transformed in the 1980s. Not only is the level of strike activity lower than at any point since the Second World War, but each defeat – particularly those of the scale and nature inflicted on the miners – discourages other groups of workers from risking strike action. This negative demonstration effect is part of the process of what Hyman (1984) calls 'coercive pacification'; a process in which sustained mass unemployment allied to a governmental offensive have systematically undermined most workers' collective strength and confidence.

9.6 WORKER RESISTANCE

In 1960 Ross and Hartman advanced their thesis that strikes were 'withering away'. They suggested that violent, prolonged, bitter disputes were more typical of the early stages of industrialisation, and that as the working classes became more closely integrated into industrial/capitalist society there followed a decline in class conflict and hence a decline in strike activity (Ross and Hartman, 1960). However, as if to demonstrate the impossibility of predicting trends in industrial conflict, things changed abruptly in the 1960s as an array of unofficial strikes and other forms of

---

The 1984 miners' strike

In March 1984 the Coal Board announced its intention of closing 20 pits, reducing coal production, and losing 20,000 jobs – all over a twelve-month period. It was also intended to reduce employment in the industry by a further 50,000 jobs – closing 50 pits – over an eight-year period.

It has been recognised by successive governments since the inter-war period that the solidarity and industrial muscle of the National Union of Mine Workers represented one of the main sources of resistance to the power of capital, and that defeating the miners made the task of handling other unions, and other groups of workers, that much easier. It is also well known that the Conservative party had drawn up contingency plans for dealing with the unions, particularly those in the public sector, prior to taking office in 1979. A policy document had been drawn up by Nicholas Ridley MP – the 'Ridley Plan' – on methods of dealing with the nationalised industries. In 1983 Ian MacGregor, who had halved the work-force at British Steel during his period as Chairman, was appointed to chair the National Coal Board, with instructions to make the industry more 'economic'. This meant, of course, that the NUM would have to be 'taken on'. In 1981 the government was ill-prepared for such a task and had shelved plans for pit closures in the face of threatened strike action. However, by 1984, the propositions of the 'Ridley Plan' had put them in a much stronger tactical position. The plan had recommended that:

(a) Maximum coal stocks should be built up, particularly at the power stations.
(b) Contingency plans be made for the import of coal.
(c) The recruitment of non-union labour should be encouraged by the road haulage companies to allow the free movement of coal.
(d) Dual coal and oil-firing should be introduced in all power stations as soon as possible.

The 'Ridley Plan' also laid down that:

'There should be a large mobile squad of police equipped and prepared to uphold the laws against violent picketing'. (Manwaring & Sigler, 1985)

Many people would applaud the determination of government to protect citizens from intimidation and violence. Be this as it may, the defeat of the miners strike, and the role of the police in that process, has raised issues about civil liberties, police involvement in industrial relations disputes, and the drift towards a para-military style of policing, which will continue to be debated for many years to come.

---

work-place conflict destroyed even the illusion of industrial consensus. Although most of this activity was directed against the employer, a small, but significant, proportion might also be seen as stemming from dissatisfaction on the part of rank-and-file workers with the apparent incorporation into the state of official trade union leaders and organisational structures. (See Lane and Roberts: *Strike at Pilkingtons*, 1971, for a discussion of a strike that was as much against the official union structure.as it was against the Pilkington company.) Consequently – as unions became larger and more bureaucratic and increasingly part of the status quo – many workers became alienated from the very organisations supposedly established to represent and protect their interests. Therefore, worker resistance to management attempts at control and worker efforts to influence their immediate conditions of work at the point of production, assumed increasing significance. The struggle, at this level, was often led by shop stewards.

It should be borne in mind that national collective bargaining only provides the bare framework, leaving plenty of scope for local interpretations and modifications, the relevant location for which is the work-place. Here, the activities of shop stewards help fill the gaps left by the formal operations of the trade-union/management structure. Although shop stewards are often presented in the media as 'trouble-makers' and the instigators and leaders of unofficial strikes, most managements tolerate – if not actively encourage – their existence, recognising that they *prevent* more disputes than they cause by helping to iron out local difficulties. They also provide a means by which shop-floor workers can make their voice felt in an era of large-scale bureaucratised trade unions.

Nevertheless, shop stewards were often in the forefront of the struggles which produced such a high unofficial strike rate in Britain during the mid-1960s early 1970s. Not that Britain was alone in recording high levels of work-place conflict during this period; most of the industrialised world was affected. It was not just the scale of the action which impressed commentators, but its nature – with activity and demands showing a marked shift towards issues beyond wages. Case studies from various countries –France, Belgium and Italy for example – gave a wide range of examples of struggles over the control of line-speeds and piece-work, authority relations in the plant, challenges to job hierarchies and classification schemes, over general upgradings and so on (Thompson, 1983). There was, as Kumar notes, 'an increasing restlessness about the quality of working life and the nature of the job itself'. (Kumar, 1978). During this period, work place organisation and conflict, often led by shop-stewards, increased earnings at factory level, and eroded management control *at the point of production*. It was at this level that workers were often most effective in determining the conditions under which they worked.

Before we examine some of these techniques, and the extent of their effectiveness, we must examine the employment contract more closely. The obligations of employers are relatively precise and specific: they agree to pay a specified wage or salary, provide holidays, pensions and other fringe benefits, and to observe certain legal requirements. Here, their obligations to employees ends. On the other hand, the obligations on workers are imprecise and elastic. It is normally impossible for workers to agree to perform a certain amount of manual or intellectual labour, and employers never know how much work is available or how much labour they need at any particular time. Consequently, they need to be able to make flexible use of their labour force, and the contract of employment allows them to do just this. Rather than agreeing to expend a measured amount of effort, employees *surrender their capacity to work*; and it is the job of management, through its power of control, to transform this capacity into actual productive capacity. Here again the 'equality' of the employment relationship gives the employer the right to issue orders, while imposing on workers the duty to obey.

Yet there are limits to what employers can reasonably ask, and limits to what employees have to obey. The law often defines such limits (for example, through safety regulations), but an informal limit, tacitly acknowledged by manager and worker, often prevails, just as there is a tacit agreement about the level of effort which will be accepted by both as a reasonable equivalent for a given rate of wages. However, these understandings are imprecise and fluid, and such things as production speeds, manning levels, job allocations, performance standards, and the whole gamut of practices governing workers' relations with one another and with management, may depend upon a shifting set of understandings and traditions which are never identical in any two work situations. The power of employers may be substantial but they are still dependent, to a certain extent, upon their work-force. In most work organisations the commitment and co-operation of the most ordinary employee is necessary because constant supervision is impossible and a disaffected labour force can easily sabotage production. The vulnerability of employers to hostile action by employees increases as the work process becomes more technically sophistacted or the functions of the labour force become more strategic. As Hyman (1975, p. 26) puts it:

> in every work place there exists an invisible frontier of control, reducing some of the formal powers of the employer: a frontier which is defined and redefined in a *continuous* process of pressure and counter-pressure, conflict and accommodation, overt and tacit struggle.

It is at this frontier that workers are most successful in controlling their conditions of existence, though still remaining vulnerable to the forces of capital.

Management attempts to set certain goals for workers and expects a certain rate of work and quality of product for what is defined as 'a fair day's work'. These standards may be extremely rigid and be resented and resisted by workers. Beynon (1973, p. 135) shows how the imposition of these standards and the timing of jobs which often accompanies them, is questioned on both ethical and scientific grounds by workers subjected to them:

> They decide on *their* measured day how fast *we* will work. They seem to forget that we're not machines ... The standards they work to are excessive anyway. They expect you to work the 480 minutes of the eight hours you're on the clock. They've agreed to have a built-in allowance of *six minutes* for going to the toilet, blowing your nose and that. It takes you six minutes to get your trousers down.

However, in some cases workers deliberately avoid working to management's standards, if the machine allows and if they can do so without breaking their contract. Sometimes these 'restrictive practices' mean that workers' potential wages are cut. It is misleading to view this behaviour as sheer bloody-mindedness – rather, it represents an attempt by workers to exercise control over the work process and to carve out some autonomy for themselves. It is also a rational attempt to protect a job over which they only enjoy a very fragile hold:

> Workers who restrict their output, who 'malinger' at work, frequently justify themselves by their need to regulate the supply of labour. 'If we all worked flat out it would be dead simple what would happen. Half of us would be outside on the stones with our cards in our hands' (Beynon, 1973, p. 133).

Beynon points out that in car-assembly work the method of work and the strategic position of a particular section in the overall plant assist workers' attempts to make significant gains in job control. Similarly, market conditions affect workers' ability to influence control over line speeds, staffing levels and work allocation. During periods of market boom advantages may be pressed home. During one such period, Beynon found that the strategically placed small-parts section was able to establish staffing levels almost twice as high as those considered reasonable by management. But, as shop stewards recognised, such advantages are often shortlived.

The same applies in the case of demarcation disputes. The media and other commentators frequently publicise occasions when five people with different trades are involved in a simple task capable of being performed by any one of them. These disputes are frequently attacked for their triviality, but they have an entirely rational basis. It is perfectly understandable, given the insecurity of employment with which ordinary workers are faced, that they should attempt to establish some form of property rights in their jobs by drawing demarcation lines around them.

Escaping from the job and sabotage

It has long been recognised that workers suffering boredom or frustration do not always produce to their full potential, and this frustration may be expressed in a variety of ways which create problems for management. Wherever possible, workers will try to 'escape' from the job, and (as we have noted) absenteeism, job-changing and high labour turnover represent 'concealed' forms of industrial conflict. For example, in car-assembly work rates of absenteeism and labour turnover tend to be very high. Beynon observed high labour turnover at Fords, despite lack of alternative job opportunities and managerial policies rejecting men aged under 20 and preferring family men with mortgages. In 1966 the paint, trim and assembly plant lost 1140 manual employees out of a total labour force of 3200, in 1967 about 800, in 1968 1160 and in 1969 1800 (Beynon, 1973, p. 90).

Sabotage – in management's eyes – represents an equally damaging alternative to escaping from the job. Sabotage may be used as a tactic for winning better working conditions and as a means of control, but it may also arise out of sheer frustration and dislike of the work. It can be very expensive for management: 'In some plants worker discontent has reached such a degree that there has been overt sabotage. Screws have been left in brake drums, tool handles welded into fender compartments, paint scratched and upholstery cut' (*Fortune*, July 1970). Taylor and Walton tell of the half mile of Blackpool rock which had to be thrown away at one firm: instead of the customary motif running throughout its length, it carried the terse recommendation to 'Fuck Off' (in Cohen, 1971, p. 219).

Resistance (and co-operation) at the shop-floor level is a constant feature of the employment relationship, and, as we have emphasised, it takes a variety of forms. However, the *limitations* of this type of action need to be emphasised. Herding, for example, while recognising the necessity of, and reasons for, such shopfloor tactics, also comments that:

> Gains made in collective bargaining or through grievance processing and pressure tactics on the plant or shop level normally tend to strengthen the better situated plant, or the more strategic group within the plant at the expense of others (in Clarke and Clements, 1977, pp. 261–2).

Similarly, Hyman, while recognising the rationality of demarcation disputes, questions their long-term effectiveness, suggesting that 'It might show a higher level of rationality were workers to devote their collective energies to resistance to the employment status which condemns them to permanent insecurity' (1984, p. 139).

Nichols and Beynon, reviewing the methods open to process workers to control their work conditions, including sabotage, point out that:

> Jacko spoiling clean product, his mates practising their version of 'job rotation' [sharing out work and rotating jobs informally], regulating the size of their work teams and maximising the time they spend in the rest room – what these and other activities have in common is that they are entirely *covert*. They take place outside of established union–management relationships. The *significance of this is that while in certain circumstances management is prepared to turn a blind eye to them, it may also – quite arbitrarily and with a monopoly of right – choose not to do so* (Nichols and Beynon, 1977, p. 136, our emphasis).

It is clear, then, that attempts to control work, and to combat employers at the point of production are significant means of resistance available to workers. However, it is equally apparent that such piecemeal attempts at job-control, and even formal and informal union activity, lose their efficacy in the face of that everyday feature of contemporary capitalism, large-scale unemployment and redundancy. Worker resistance necessarily crumbles in the face of employer intentions to cease production altogether or to drastically reduce the work-force via the introduction of new technology.

Professionalisation: an occupational strategy

As we have seen Braverman was criticised for ignoring the fact that employers utilised a variety of strategies to control the labour process, and that employees also resisted that control in a variety of ways. He also failed to recognise that workers have themselves attempted to create segmentation in the labour market, not only to make it more difficult for employers to replace them, but also to protect their skills against usurpation by other workers. One group of white-collar workers have been particularly successful in this respect, and these are the professions. Professionals have been extremely skilful in carving out areas of the labour market in which they claim special competence and excluding all competitors.

A precise and unambiguous definition of a 'profession' is difficult. Most people could probably name occupations which they consider to be professions, without being able to abstract the general characteristics behind their choice, apart from a vague feeling that professions differ from mere 'jobs' in being more respectable, prestigious and highly rewarded.

Academic writers on the professions have faced similar problems in isolating *the* characteristics of professions. Millerson (1964) has amalgamated the most frequently mentioned characteristics into a model profession, without insisting that *all* professions will display *all* the characteristics. These include: skill based on theoretical knowledge; an extensive period of education; the theme of public service and altruism; the existence of a code of conduct or ethics; insistence upon professional freedom to regulate itself; and the testing of the competence of members before admission to the professions.

However, professionalism is not an in-built or fixed quality of particular occupations. Many occupations are constantly attempting to attain the status of a profession because they are aware of the advantages of doing so. In the USA, for example, undertakers have tried for years to achieve professional status in the eyes of the public. To this effect they have changed their name (to 'funeral directors'), emphasised their belief in service to the public, and have tried to insist on college degrees for entry to the occupation. Thus over the years an occupational group may attempt to move itself, with greater or lesser success, towards professional status.

Consequently, at any one time one may be able to distinguish between established, marginal and new professions.

To varying degrees, professions have been able to claim high status, high monetary and material rewards, and considerable autonomy, and there are conflicting sociological explanations of why they have been so successful in these respects. For many years the generally accepted interpretation of the professions was that provided by *functionalism*.

The functionalist interpretation of professionalism

Functionalists take as their point of departure the unique role of the professions in society and the special relationship that exists between the professional practitioner and the client.

They argue that work performed by professionals involves 'central values', such as health, justice and education, and is therefore of functional importance for all social groups. Consequently, this work commands both high material and symbolic rewards.

Furthermore, since the situations in which clients consult professionals are so crucial, and since professional expertise is so much greater than the clients, the latter, irrespective of their status, must be persuaded to submit unquestioningly to professional authority (to follow doctor's orders, for example).

However, this means that clients may be vulnerable to exploitation by the professional. Therefore, it is necessary that professions institutionalise various procedures and norms to *protect* clients. These protective mechanisms include: the socialisation of prospective professionals during the prolonged training period; a formal code of ethics; the ideal of public service; the disciplinary procedures of the profession; and, most importantly, the testing or qualifying process by which the competence of each professional is ensured.

Hence the functionalist interpretation claims to explain *both* the high status and high incomes accruing to the established professions, *and* (in addition) many of the specific characteristics of the professions.

An alternative interpretation: professionalism as control

The alternative view of the professions, as expressed, for example, in the work of Johnson (1972), claims that the characteristics of professionalism function as a means of occupational control and work to the benefit of *professional practitioners themselves* rather than the public. Similarly, the *image* of public service, altruism, and the disinterested pursuit of a vocation propagated by professions, is an *ideology*, used to *justify* the higher incomes and prestige of the professional.

Many of the long-established and most influential professions are those that have professional bodies which have a legal right to test the competence of prospective members. These, which Millerson (1964) calls the 'qualifying associations', include such bodies as the British Medical Association and the Institute of Chartered Accountants. They control the right of individuals to practise the profession and are able, by their control over entry, to control the number and type of practitioners in a particular field. Such control eliminates, or drastically reduces, competition from those who have not received the profession's seal of approval and creates an *artificial* shortage of practitioners. By controlling the supply of practitioners in this way the profession is able to command high salaries and comfortable working conditions for its members. As Ben-David (1964) puts it, commenting on the medical profession, 'control of entry into the medical societies boosts the income of doctors out of all proportion to that of comparable professions the same way as monopoly increases profit'.

One of the major implications of this perspective is the implicit parallel drawn between the occupational strategy of the professions and that of certain craft unions. Craft unions have traditionally attempted to control their market situation by insisting on long periods of apprenticeship for prospective craftsmen, and, by limiting the ratio of apprentices to journeymen, have been able to maintain an artificial shortage of craftsmen. Studies of apprenticeship claim that this is not very effective as a means of education, but *is* relatively successful so far as its regulatory functions are concerned. Liepmann (1960), for example, argues that apprenticeship regulates entry to the occupation, and protects jobs, by establishing demarcation lines between skills and by obtaining agreements with management to the effect that in a time of recession non-apprenticed labour is laid off before craftsmen. Moreover, 'skilled' craftsmen may use this fact to negotiate higher wages. As we shall see, professional associations use essentially similar strategies.

Some professions not only restrict entry to their occupations but, unlike craft unions, have secured a *legal* monopoly of the right to perform particular tasks. For example, it is illegal for a person not on the General Medical Council register to accept money for the diagnosis and treatment of medical problems. During the past century physicians in Britain have used their influence to ensure that many new medical occupations – dieticians, physiotherapists, chiropodists, for example – do not pose a serious threat to the dominance of doctors. Doctors have succeeded in obtaining legislation which ensures that professions 'supplementary to medicine' may only carry out treatment after prior diagnosis by a doctor, thus subordinating them to the authority of doctors. Lawyers, too, have retained a virtual monopoly over such areas as house conveyancing. Illich (1973) has referred to this process as 'occupational imperialism': a process of carving out an occupational territory and preventing even the competent outsider from practising the skill. So, while the practices of job demarcation and the closed shop by trade unions are often roundly condemned, essentially similar practices by professional bodies are accepted as the norm.

Again, then, the alternative interpretation of the professions presents this particular element of professionalism as a strategy protecting the interests not of the public but of the profession itself. In fact, the *Report on Professional Services* by the Monopolies Commission (1970) concluded that 'a number of the restrictive practices carried on by professional groups and justified on the basis of community welfare looked ... rather like arrangements for making life easier for practitioners at the expense of their clients'.

But how can the ethical codes and disciplinary procedures, characteristic of the professions, be explained using this alternative perspective? Three basic points are crucial.

First, professional ideology emphasises service to the client, but in fact the client is rarely given the opportunity to express satisfaction or dissatisfaction with the service received. Professionals usually insist that only fellow professionals are qualified to assess their performances, but their own ethical codes usually prohibt one professional from criticising another, at least in public.

Second, ethical codes are often concerned with preventing internal competition, rather than guaranteeing the quality of the service or protecting the public. Many professions, for example, restrict advertising so as to prevent attempts at fee-cutting which might adversely affect overall professional remuneration.

Third, studies by Carlin (1966) in the USA and Elliott (1972) in Britain reveal that the disciplinary committees of professional bodies deal mainly with cases where professionals have brought *adverse publicity* to the profession – being cited as co-respondent in a divorce case or being found guilty of drunken driving, for example – or where they have 'competed' with fellow practitioners. Few professionals are disciplined, and those that are tend to be the least influential.

Moreover, although most professional associations deny any affinity with trade unions, condemning many aspects of trade-union activity as 'self-interested', many professional associations do engage directly in collective bargaining, as well as acting as pressure groups lobbying Parliament for improvements in salary and working conditions. For example, the British Medical Association (BMA) tried to avoid all links with the trade-union movement and attempts to cultivate the image of doctors as neutral professionals. But its General Medical Services Committee negotiates very effectively with the National Health Service on behalf of doctors, and another organisation, the British Medical Guild (BMG), collects and administers a fighting fund for doctors in case of strikes or overtime bans. The BMG has no members, and is merely a puppet organisation used by the BMA for some of its trade-union-like activities.

We have argued, then, that all occupations seek to control the conditions under which they offer their labour; and professionals seek to do this as much as manual workers. Like trade unions, professions engage in collective bargaining, control entry to the occupation, and seek a monopoly of the right to practise so as to create a scarcity of licensed practitioners. In these ways the profession attempts to protect its skills and to improve its bargaining position in a market economy. As Parkin (1971, pp. 21–2) puts it:

> Although long and costly training is usually defended as an essential preliminary to ... professional work, there is little doubt that much of it is of little practical value and is simply a device for restricting the supply of labour. The persistent efforts of many white collar occupations to become professionalized may be understood ... as an attempt to enhance their market scarcity, and so increase their power to claim rewards.

And Johnson (1972) defines professionalism as a special means of occupational control whereby both the needs to be provided for, and the manner in which they are to be dealt with, are defined by the producer. At the same time, he argues, the notion of professionalism as involving public service and lofty ideals is still fostered, because it is an *ideology* which helps to justify the privileges of the professions. (For a discussion and critique of the functionalist approach, see Chapter 2.)

9.7   THE EXPERIENCE OF WORK: SATISFACTION AND FULFILMENT

Marx and alienation

The schools of scientific management and human relations both recognised that work in industrial societies was not very satisfying. However, their views of both what motivated workers and the satisfactions derived from work had their origins in management-inspired studies which were mainly concerned with fitting workers into a system of work over which they had little control. Marxists with an interest in the labour process, on the other hand, see humans as potentially creative creatures who express their basic humanity in and through work. This leads them to argue that the industrial worker is *alienated*, and that the source of this alienation is the structure and social relations of production under capitalism.

For Marx, alienation had four dimensions. First, workers in a capitalist society are divorced from the products of their labour. People put themselves into the goods they produce, but under capitalism the goods are then expropriated and sold for profit.

Second, the process of production becomes fragmented; labour becomes an uninteresting chore, meaningless, unfulfilling and unrewarding – a means to an end rather than an end in itself.

Third, at the social level people become alienated from others, as relationships come to be dominated by the market. Consequently the co-operative nature of human enterprise is corrupted.

Fourth, humans are alienated from their 'species being', for manual work is made mindless and uncreative. Capitalist production relations separates design and planning (mental labour) from routine manual labour, and reduces manual work to a bestial, inhuman level.

It should be stressed that Marx was not a critic of technological advance or of the machine. It was not the machine to which he objected but the way it was used under capitalism:

> Machinery considered on its own shortens the working time, whereas when it is used for capitalistic purposes it lengthens the working day; when on its own it is intended to lighten work, its capitalistic use increases the tempo of work; intrinsically it is a victory of mankind over the forces of nature, but used for capitalistic ends it employs the forces of nature to enslave men; on its own, it increases the operative's wealth, used capitalistically it impoverishes him (Marx, 1962, p. 465).

Thus Marx argued that the nature of work in capitalist societies – its fragmentation, specialised division of labour, confinement of workers to narrowly defined aspects of production – was alienating. But, apart from the physical and technological conditions of work itself, alienation also stems from the organisation of productive activity in a much broader sense. The social relations of production established under capitalism mean that workers are denied control over what is produced and why it is produced. Work is organised for profit rather than the satisfaction of collectively determined needs. Labour power becomes a commodity like any other.

Empirical studies of alienation

One of the most oft-quoted empirical studies of alienation in modern industrial society, by Blauner (1964), departs almost immediately from the framework established by Marx. Blauner, though believing that certain relationships and work arrangements are objectively satisfying, starts from the assumption that it is the technology itself, rather than the social relations of production within a capitalist economy, that is the 'cause' of alienation. He argues that not all workers are equally alienated, because they are exposed to a range of different technologies and then attempts to define 'alienation' in such a way that degrees and types of alienation may be *measured*. (The theoretical and methodological issues which this attempt at measurement raises are examined in Chapter 12.)

Blauner identifies four dimensions of alienation: powerlessness, meaninglessness, isolation and self-estrangement.

Individuals are *powerless* when they cannot control their own actions or conditions of existence.

Meaninglessness occurs when job specialisation and bureaucratisation reduce workers' organic connection with the work process and they experience difficulty in locating their contribution to it.

Isolation arises when workers feel no sense of belonging in the work situation and are unable or unwilling to identify with the organisation and its goals.

The final dimension, *self-estrangement*, stresses the *subjective* experience of work.

The individual gains no intrinsic satisfaction from work, is not involved or engrossed in the activity, and experiences boredom, monotony – even disgust.

Blauner, following his basic assumption about the importance of technology, then examines four different US industries, in order to assess how alienation varies with the type of technology. Printing is used as an example of craft technology, textiles as machine-tending, car production as assembly-line and chemicals as an example of continuous-process technology.

Although Blauner recognises the influence of three other variables on the level of alienation – the division of labour, the social organisation of the industry, and the economic structure within which it operates – he attaches overriding importance to technology.

> Since technological considerations often determine the size of an industrial plant they markedly influence the social atmosphere and degree of cohesion among the work force. Technology also structures the existence and form of work groups, in this way influencing cohesion. Even the nature of discipline and supervision to some extent depends on technological factors. And technology largely determines the occupational structure and skill distribution within an enterprise, the basic factors in advancement opportunities and normative integration (1964, p. 8).

Blauner concludes that the four industries he studied – *because* of their different technologies – produce very different alienating tendencies.

Alienation levels in *printing* were low because the craft technology allowed workers access to traditional skills and relatively high degrees of control over tools and techniques. The unique nature of the product makes standardisation difficult, and a strong union, together with steady demand for the industry's products, induces a sense of security. Consequently powerlessness, so far as employment conditions are concerned, is slight. Similarly, the skills necessary to produce high-quality printed products mean that printers have considerable control over the pace, quality and quantity of their work, and must be free to move around the print shop – so powerlessness in the work process is also slight.

Meaninglessness is reduced because the broad craft-training allows printers to appreciate their contribution to the whole productive process. Isolation is also low, not only because lack of pressure and freedom of movement allow friendships to be made in the course of work, but also because the work itself carries respect and status, both in the work-place and the wider community. Furthermore, the work is intrinsically satisfying and offers more than simply money, so the boredom and monotony characteristic of self-estrangement is seldom experienced.

The *textile* industry, on the other hand, employs a machine-tending technology producing standardised products for which there is a falling demand. The minimal skills required and the industry's concentration in the Deep South of the USA (where labour is cheap and plentiful) mean wages and unionisation levels are low.

The workers' control over the immediate work process is also minimal. The machine controls pace, output and the operatives' freedom of movement, so powerlessness is high. Meaninglessness is also quite high, because jobs are highly specialised, lack variety and involve only part of the process. However, the small size of many mills allows some workers to comprehend the full production process.

Social isolation, however, is fairly low because the industry's 'small-town' nature means that workers share common kinship and religious affiliations, and have personalised relations with management, which helps integrate them in their firms.

Similarly, self-estrangement is not as high as might have been expected given the lack of involvement implied in machine-tending; very few textile workers found their jobs dull or monotonous. Blauner suggests that they do not expect variety or interest in work and so do not define repetitive tasks as monotonous. However, textile work – especially for men doing what is regarded by them as 'women's work' for low wages – does not provide a favourable self-identity, and this encourages self-estrangement.

Blauner presents the textile worker as an example of the way objective tendencies to alienation may be overcome or lessened by the integration of work with family, religious and community life.

According to Blauner, the technology most likely to give rise to alienation is assembly-line technology, epitomised in *motor-car production*. The vulnerability of the car industry to fluctuations in the business cycle means that workers have little job security, and this powerlessness is only slightly offset by the existence in the USA of a strong car workers' union. However, in the work process itself powerlessness is at a maximum. The worker follows a set routine at an exhausting and constant pace; the line controls both the quantity and quality of the product with physical movement restricted to the few feet of one's 'station' on the line. Meaninglessness is encouraged by the standardisation of the product and extreme fragmentation of work tasks. The implications are brought home by Beynon in *Working for Ford*: 'In the last minute or so a man working on the high line ... in Fords ... has fitted a petrol tank into the shell of a car and is starting to fit another' (Beynon, 1973, p. 11). Under such circumstances a worker cannot take personal pride in the job or feel that a unique contribution to the final product has been made.

Isolation is also high because the line's speed, and the workers' separation from one another, inhibit conversation and the establishment of personal relationships. The social organisation of large, bureaucratically administered factories discourages any sense of loyalty to the company or its products – most car workers insist they would never buy their companies' cars – and encourages isolation. Car workers are likely to be self-estranged and experience their jobs as dull and monotonous. The work itself provides no source of satisfaction: it is merely a necessary evil and a source of income. In a study by Chinoy a worker remarks: 'The things I like best about my job are quitting time, pay day, days off, and vacations' (Chinoy, 1955, p. 85).

Blauner's final example is the continuous-process technology found, for example, in the *chemical* industry, which, despite, being the most highly mechanised of the four technologies surveyed, reverses the tendency towards alienation.

A key characteristic of this technology is that it restores the workers' sense of control over the work process. In chemical manufacture the raw materials flow through pipes from one stage of the process to another without being handled by the workers: temperatures, pressures and speeds are automatically regulated. It is the workers' responsibility to check that all is functioning smoothly, so that in contrast to the typical one-minute job cycle of car workers, chemical workers take a round of readings every two hours, checking perhaps fifty instruments in different places. According to Blauner, continuous-process production liberates workers from the rhythm of the machine, allowing them to set their own pace. It gives them freedom to move around the plant and to plan their own work schedule. Control is also restored in that they become free to use their own initiative. The jobs are much less standardised and repetitive than in mass-production industry, offering more interest and allowing workers to choose their own techniques and to experiment with different ways of doing the job. It also restores the meaningfulness of work. In assembly-line technology the work process is fragmented and workers cannot connect their fragment with the whole, but in automation meaning is restored in two ways. On the one hand, the workers gain an increased understanding of the overall process because they are no longer tied to specific work posts but can move around the plant and appreciate the complete sequence of operations. On the other, automation reconstructs the collective nature of work and encourages workers to think in terms of the whole rather than the part.

Blauner further suggests that in automated settings the work-team takes over responsibility for supervising the quality of work, consequently developing a more dignified and co-operative relationship with management. The dividing-line between manual and non-manual workers is broken down, encouraging the feeling of being part of a unified community.

Finally, because numbers of workers have been reduced to the lowest levels compatible with safety and efficiency (because output is determined by the equipment and not by worker effort, and profit is relatively assured by high demand for chemical products) employment is secure and unpressured. Management can afford to adopt a more humane approach – higher profit depending more on technological development than on increased exploitation of the workforce – in which greater account may be taken of workers' own needs. Hence powerlessness, meaninglessness, isolation and self-estrangement are all low.

In Blauner's account the different industries may be seen as stages in the development of technology, with the modern age characterised by continuous-process technology which increases the workers' control over the work process, checks the further division of labour and growth of large factories, and provides meaningful work in a more cohesive, integrated industrial climate.

Blauner's study, although a central one which stimulated further research, is flawed.

Undeniably the technology of an industry can affect the experience of work, but it has been argued that greater importance should be attached to the *organisation* of that technology. Hyman (1972, pp. 100–1) argues:

> whether the consequences of technology are in fact liberating or enslaving depends on *how* it is decided to use the machines and on *who* makes these decisions. To attribute unpleasant social consequences to inanimate machinery is to evade examining those *human* actions which – deliberately or by default – are in fact responsible.

Beynon's (1973) study of assembly-line car work supports this criticism. The technology of car assembly is internationally uniform, and yet levels of job satisfaction appear to differ from firm to firm and society to society. It is important to recognise that the *speed* of the assembly line is usually controlled by management. Consequently, workers wishing to maintain high standards of work may be prevented from doing so as much by management policy as the technique itself: 'The bad thing about the assembly line is that it keeps moving. If you have a little trouble with a job, you can't take the time to do it right' (Walker and Guest, 1952, p. 51).

Similarly, Beynon explains the *isolation* of Ford workers not only in terms of the technology but also in terms of management policies and the way in which manual workers are treated. One man pointed out the contrast between Ford executives and office workers, and the men on the assembly line: 'It's different for them in the office. They're *part* of Fords. We're not, we're just working here, we're numbers' (Beynon, 1973, p. 121).

Blauner, then, underplays the way in which power operates in the work-place itself and the importance that the workers' lack of formal control has for their experience of work. In addition, his contention that under continuous process automation the worker is no longer dominated by the technology but is liberated by it and allowed a new dignity, responsibility and sense of function has been questioned by more recent research, by Nichols and Beynon (1977) on the chemical industry and Gallie (1978) on oil-refining.

Both these studies stress that continuous-process technology requires *shift-work*, which imposes very real constraints on the workers' overall pattern of life. It is intensely disliked by those subjected to it and is seen as damaging to health, family and social life – dominating rather than liberat-ing.

Furthermore, both studies contradict Blauner's contention that automa-tion reduces the exploitation of workers, because management no longer has any need continuously to reduce staffing levels already reduced to levels compatible with safety and efficiency.

Similarly, Gallie suggests that – despite automation reducing much of the hardship and unpleasant features of traditional mass-production industry – Baluner's description of the typical work task was based on a very small section of the work-force, and that the tasks of most refining operatives were substantially less advantageous than he suggested. Nichols and Beynon, too, stress the negative side of chemical production for the majority of workers. They comment: 'as we walked around the site what struck us most strongly was ... the noise, the heat, the dust and the large number of men who were paid to hump one-hundred-weight bags of fertilizer' (Nichols and Beynon, 1977, p. 11).

Most work in the plant was unskilled 'donkey work' (ibid, p. 12) and not the demanding, dial-checking work emphasised by Blauner. Even control-room work – despite being easier than the humping and loading of sacks – was not so satisfying as Blauner implies. It was *not* teamwork – most of the control-room operatives worked alone – it *was* stressful, and it *was* noisy: 'You just listen to this noise. It's just a steady drone isn't it? Well, imagine having to sit in this hour after hour watching everything go OK' (ibid, p. 20).

Finally, both studies suggest that it is mistaken to see automation as *necessarily* leading to higher levels of satisfaction, social integration and more harmonious class relations. Automation is perfectly compatible with very different systems of power and organisation within the work-place and wider society, and these will help determine the relationships between managers and workers and the quality of the work experience.

Orientations to work

Technological-determinist and socio-technical systems approaches tend to attribute alienation or satisfaction in work to the effects of experiences of the work environment *on* the worker – that is, to a predominantly unidirectional process. However, it is possible for workers to find jobs boring and monotonous and yet be 'satisfied' with them if they do not believe they have the opportunity or right to enjoy work. Some workers may define an 'acceptable' or 'satisfactory' job as one which is reasonably well paid, clean and safe, only rejecting 'alienating' work if they expect to find interest, involvement and self-expression in work.

Such an attitude may indicate, therefore, that we need to consider the *orientations* which workers bring to their work. These may well vary from individual to individual in the same occupation, in such a way that reference merely to technological arrangements, and other work conditions, may be insufficient to explain workers' satisfaction or dissatisfaction. Reference to actors' orientations constitutes an important element of the *social action* approach to work satisfaction.

In Britain the 'affluent worker' studies conducted by Goldthorpe and Lockwood in Luton provide one of the best-known examples of this action approach (see also Chapters 3 and 12 for a further discussion of this work).

The affluent worker: industrial attitudes and behaviour

This study of car assemblers, process workers and machinists found that most of the workers bitterly disliked many aspects of their work – its monotony, pace, fragmentation, stifling of initiative, and so on. This, of course, would have been sufficient for Blauner to label these workers 'alienated' and to seek the primary cause in the technology employed (though, of course, this uniform dissatisfaction embraced workers in different types of technology). However, despite *disliking* the nature of the work, they were on the whole firmly attached to their jobs, having made few concrete attempts to find alternative work. How can this paradox be explained? Goldthorpe and Lockwood maintain that the explanation lies not only in the nature or conditions of the work itself but in the attitudes and values which the men brought to their work from outside. They argue that the Luton car workers came to work with an *instrumental* orientation, not looking to work for emotional, creative or social satisfaction but merely as a means for providing the wages which would allow them to live the kind of life they valued *outside* work. Work, then, is regarded as an *instrument* valued only for its use in satisfying other needs, a means to an end rather than an end in itself.

The affluent worker study, then, would appear to demonstrate that for some groups of workers work can be a depriving experience and yet still be tolerated in return for the extrinsic rewards in which they are primarily interested.

The value of Goldthorpe and Lockwood's contribution lies in their rejection of attempts to explain work behaviour and attitudes purely in terms of the working conditions themselves. Work-places are *not* closed systems, and attempts at explaining work behaviour *must* range outside the factory gates, and particularly beyond the influence of technology on worker behaviour and attitudes.

However, a one-sided emphasis on an action approach also has its danger, particularly in underestimating the force of objective and material constraints upon workers and in over-estimating the degree of *choice* they have in determining the conditions under which they have to work. As we have seen, Braverman argues that, objectively, the work that most people are asked to perform in capitalist societies is highly fragmented, offers little chance to exercise skill or initiative, and has, in his terms, been deskilled and degraded. As Blackburn and Mann observe:

> the *absolute* level of skill of all but the very highest jobs is – to say the least – minimal. Eighty-seven per cent of our workers *exercise less skill at work than they would if they drove to work*. Indeed, most of them expend more mental effort and resourcefulness in getting to work than in doing their jobs (Blackburn and Mann, 1979, p. 280, our emphasis).

Furthermore, various studies – Goldthorpe and Lockwood's among them – demonstrate that a high proportion of people actually *experience* work as tedious, monotonous and unfulfilling: that is, their subjective experiences are in line with the objective nature of the work.

Goldthorpe and Lockwood suggest that their workers willingly accept deprivation at work in order to satisfy their material aspirations in other spheres life. However, it is the *willing* nature of this acceptance that must be questioned. We must beware of seeing the identification of instrumental attitudes towards work as in any way a unique 'discovery'. Instrumentalism is better regarded as an *unsurprising* consequence of the capitalist organisa- tion of work, in which the survival and standard of living of an individual is dependent upon the selling of labour in an open and competitive market, and upon the kind of bargain that one can strike with an employer. The degree of choice that one can exercise given such a structure is necessarily limited.

9.8 UNEMPLOYMENT

'If there's one thing worse than alienating work, it's no work at all' (union official).

Although it is obviously important to discuss work satisfaction and alienation in industrial societies, it is equally apparent that for an increasingly large number of people in such societies, it is the *absence* of work which they find most dispiriting. Most of the advanced industrial societies of the West have experienced increasing rates of unemployment in recent years, and Britain is no exception. However, the rate of unemployment in this country continues to be very much higher than in most other major industrial countries. There are, of course, many and various reasons for the high rates which afflict the British economy, but we have implied that recent Conservative governments have used unemployment – as part of their monetarist policies – as an element in their strategy to weaken trade unions and discipline the labour force. It is appropriate, then, that we examine patterns of unemployment and some of the reasons – ideological and otherwise – advanced to explain them. We shall suggest that, serious though the problem of unemployment might appear, the official statistics consistently underestimate the full extent of the problem.

The pattern

Until recently economic policy relating to unemployment was guided by principles established by Beveridge in 1942, which assumed that governments had a responsibility for maintaining full or near-full employment. A fully employed society was defined as one in which 'those who lose jobs must be able to find new jobs at fair wages within their capacity, without delay'. This assumed that those registered as unemployed would simply be 'between jobs'; about 3 per cent of the labour force according to Beveridge. Immediate post-war developments seemed to indicate that Beveridge, if anything, had been too pessimistic.

Between 1948 and 1966, the average number of people on the unemployment register in the UK was approximately 350,000 – less than 2 per cent of the labour force. The mid-1960s saw a slight increase, with the recession of 1970–72 seeing the unemployment rate rise, briefly, above 4 per cent. During the 1975–8 recession, however, it exceeded 6 per cent and had hardly begun to fall below this level when the current recession began. Between July 1979 and July 1982 *registered* unemployment rose from 1.39 million (5.9 per cent) to 3.19 million – a numerically greater level than at the depths of the inter-war depression.

However, there is some evidence that, even during the 1950s – at least as far as male workers were concerned – longer-term unemployment was beginning to appear. At that time anything from one-fifth to one-quarter of the registered unemployed in the UK were likely to have been without work for over six months. During the 1960s this proportion rose to nearly one-third, continuing to rise throughout the next decade so that by July 1982 59 per cent of men on the register had been unemployed longer than 6 months.

One of the more serious features of the current situation is the growing proportion unemployed for more than a year. In 1955 only one in eight of the (177,700) people unemployed and registered for work had been so for more than a year. This proportion had almost doubled by 1980. By January 1985 more than one out of every five unemployed benefit claimants had been without work for over two years. Furthermore, in February 1986, the Manpower Services Commission announced that it expected that the increase since March 1983, in people unemployed for over three years would continue and that 'the best assumption for planning purposes remains a continuing high level of unemployment' (*Guardian*, 14 February 1986). Precise comparisons are difficult but the problem of long-term unemployment during the present recession is probably greater and geographically more widespread than it was during the inter-war years.

Until November 1982, when the counting system was changed, the statistics covered all unemployed persons registered at the Department of Unemployment as seeking work, capable of work, and available for work, whether or not they were entitled to unemployment benefit. Since then the 'unemployed' have been restricted to a computerised count of people entitled to unemployment benefit. This change effectively reduced the total stock of unemployed by about 6 per cent. The official statistics therefore understate the 'true' level of unemployment, given that there are always large numbers of people who are looking for work, particularly part-time work, who are not registered and who are unlikely to be eligible for benefit. Consequently, *Labour Research* – the monthly publication of the Labour Research Department – always gives two sets of figures: the official figure and the figure produced under the old system. So, the two sets of figures for August 1985 would be: 'new' 3,240,406, 'old' 3,640,354, or nearly 400,000 who would have been counted before the system was changed. This would raise the proportion of the unemployed from 13.4 per cent to 15 per cent.

Moreover, there are other forms of 'disguised' unemployment which do not, by definition, get into the official figures. The most significant 'absentees' are young people, 'old' people, and women.

Youth unemployment

Young people have been disproportionately affected by unemployment. In 1970 4.5 per cent of males under twenty were unemployed compared with 2.3 per cent of those aged 25 to 54; by 1982 these figures had risen to 28.9 per cent and 10.3 per cent respectively. Not only was the 1982 percentage much higher among youths in absolute terms, it has also increased at a faster rate than the 25–54 group. The other noticeable feature is the recent rapid increase in the unemployment rate among 20–24-year-olds.

How do we explain these developments? Suggestions that the high rates simply reflect the number of youngsters entering the labour market may be dismissed, for, as Ashton (1985) points out, the number of 16-year-olds entering the labour market peaked in 1979, i.e. before the very high levels of unemployment characterising the latest recession.

Similarly, it has been claimed that high wages have been a factor, and if only youngsters would accept lower wages unemployment would fall. No such link has been established. Various other explanations, none of which stands up to critical analysis, but having the common denominator of blaming youngsters for their unemployment – that they are irresponsible, and lack basic skills and discipline – are also advanced.

Youth unemployment is *usually* higher than that of adults, partly because youngsters are entering the labour market for the first time and consequently are more at risk from unemployment. Furthermore, many jobs entered on first starting work are unskilled and semi-skilled in the manufacturing and service sector, traditionally associated with high rates of labour turnover. Consequently, when young people leave these jobs, because they are temporary or casual, and/or boring and stressful, they are once more at risk from unemployment. Finally, in times of relatively full employment some youngsters may change jobs either to find variety or until they settle down, again placing themselves at risk of unemployment.

However, these factors do not explain the recent dramatic rise in youth unemployment. During recession employers stop recruiting and try to 'rationalise' their existing labour force, shedding staff on a last-in, first-out basis – again affecting young people. Furthermore, youngsters tend to be concentrated in a limited number of declining industries and occupations, not expected to provide increased employment opportunities when the economy improves. The new information technology also threatens clerical and typing jobs in commerce previously providing openings for young people. These, and other changes, are reducing the areas in the labour market where young people can compete (Ashton, 1985).

Disguised youth unemployment

The *official* figures on youth unemployment understate the extent of the problem. In the past, when youth unemployment was much less, one solution had been to raise the school-leaving age, thus removing substantial numbers of young people from the labour market. In the present recession, some youngsters are opting to remain at school, perhaps only temporarily delaying their appearance in the unemployment statistics. Recently, the methods most favoured by governments to remove large numbers of youngsters from the labour market and the statistics, have been the Youth Opportunities Programme and, currently, the Youth Training Scheme.

Since 1975, when youth unemployment first became a major political issue, the state has injected resources into various job creation, work experience and training schemes. Most of this effort has been directed towards the 16-year-old school leaver. In July 1983 over 50 per cent of these school leavers were either unemployed or on government-sponsored training schemes.

The Youth Opportunities Programme (YOP) was created in 1978 by the Labour government under the guidance of the Manpower Services Commission (MSC). Initially, 86,000 youngsters were involved, with 69 per cent of YOP trainees later finding full-time employment. The scheme was expanded in 1981, providing places for 180,000 young people. The same year, the Conservative government revealed its plans to begin operating a new Youth Training Scheme (YTS) by September 1983, under which unemployed school-leavers would be obliged to undertake a one-year period of post-school 'training'. This involved finding suitable placements for some 460,000 young people.

The basic premise of this programme was that youth unemployment had risen because of a sudden failure of youth to be suitable candidates for employment. However, this was merely to distract attention from much more basic deficiencies in the market economy. In fact, as Muncie (1984) points out, as the YOP expanded its 'success rate' noticeably declined, and by 1981 the number of trainees subsequently finding full-time employment had fallen to about 36 per cent. The largest element in the YOP, and its most criticised aspect, was the WEEP scheme (work experience on employers premises) which accounted for three-quarters of YOP places. Rather than providing secure future job opportunities, the scheme created an artificial demand for youth labour which was no longer profitable in market terms. Trainees were expected to work for up to six months with one employer, in return for a government allowance (£25 per week in 1983). Consequently the scheme was cheap to run, but allowed employers to replace paid employees with a succession of YOP trainees. By 1981 the MSC conceded that one in three positions created had lost a permanent worker a job. Moreover, the provision of six months free non-unionised labour meant that many employers took on YOP workers rather than employing school-leavers full-time.

Most young people found that WEEP only provided a temporary respite from the dole queue and that they were equally well off – if not better off – on supplementary benefit than a YOP allowance. Others questioned the dubious nature of the 'training' they received as cheap labour in menial jobs. Muncie concludes that the YOP made little difference to the amount of regular employment available to school-leavers, but that it had two clear political attractions: (a) it kept some 300,000 youngsters off the unemployment register each year and (b) it helped keep them off the streets, thus aiding social-control.

Partly in response to questions of social order, the government unwrapped a new training scheme designed to overcome the deficiencies of the YOP; the Youth Training Scheme (YTS), which replaced YOP in September 1983. This twelve-month training programme is directed at 16 and 17-year-old school-leavers. Its intention is to provide a permanent bridge between school and work by offering all young people under the age of 18 the opportunity either to continue in full-time education or to enter a period of work experience combined with related training and education. 'Trainees' will have their progress and achievements recorded in a personal profile, intended as a reference and recommendation for future employers. Hence, YTS is intended as a comprehensive scheme covering both employed and unemployed youngsters, seeking to influence industrial training as well as providing a scheme to cope with the unemployed.

However, the new scheme is also open to abuse by employers and its acceptance by employers and trainees depends on the level of grant that both parties eventually receive from the government. Moreover, there is no guarantee that all young people will receive a similar 'training'. 'All manner of types and levels of provision' will exist 'determined not by informed planning but rather by the accident of where they live and the short-term preferences of employers' (Muncie, 1984, p. 146). Muncie concludes that in the final analysis young people will be expected to display all the qualities that were formerly the products of experience when they are thrown onto the labour market after their year of training.

YTS thus remains a logical continuation of the government's and the MSC's attempts to provide a permanent structural resolution to the problem of youth unemployment by tightening control over school-leavers. YTS also persists in interpreting the problem of employment *for* young people as a problem *about* young people. As Muncie puts it:

> By insisting that the young working class now have special developmental needs, their exclusion from the labour market, their redefinition as trainees and their exposure to new forms of educational experience are spuriously justified.

Disguised unemployment among the 'old'

It is difficult to assess the numbers of older people 'missing' from the unemployment figures. The figure for the over-sixties must be regarded as an underestimate since, as a result of changes announced at the time of the 1983 Budget, most men aged 60 and over are removed from the official unemployment figures.

It is also difficult to estimate the numbers of older workers – willing and able to make a worthwhile economic contribution – who have been cajoled or frightened into accepting redundancy or early retirement. Hawkins (1984) suggests that it might be thought that older workers with long service would enjoy relatively strong protection against redundancy under 'last in, first out' arrangements. However, he argues, this does not appear to be the case, and in fact older workers are more likely to enter unemployment than any group other than the under-25s. The explanation lies in the availability of relatively attractive lump-sum redundancy payments for long-service employees, the possibility of early retirement and the reluctance of older workers to risk refusing an apparently generous offer. However, whereas many older workers in managerial and professional jobs may take early retirement on relatively favourable terms (i.e. lump sums and good pensions), losing interest in finding another job, those in unskilled or semi-skilled manual jobs may be compelled to enter unemployment with little more to live on than social security income, perhaps supplemented by a modest redundancy payment. They may be anxious to obtain work but find it virtually impossible to do so.

Disguised unemployment among females

The official statistics do not accurately reflect unemployment among women. Women who are made redundant have always been prone to disappear, without political or social embarrassment, back into the family. In many cases, indeed, women do not even need to be made redundant for the higher turnover of the female labour force resulting, for example, from pregnancy, means that the female labour force can always be cut, by non-replacement, without the expense of redundancy.

Moreover, although the propensity of females to register as unemployed is now much greater than it it was, for example, in the early 1970s, there is still a large minority of women who do not register. One estimate suggests that if women had the same propensity to register as men, about 350,000 would be added to the total of 906,000 unemployed women revealed by the July 1982 figures. With the recent rise in unemployment, many women have simply dropped out of the labour force.

Much of the growth in 'womens' jobs' in the 1970s, took the form of an increase in part-time employment in manufacturing and service industries, which attracted many married women. The service sector has ceased to grow since 1977 – declining in some areas – while the accelerated contraction in manufacturing has resulted in thousands of lost clerical and unskilled manual jobs for women in industries like engineering and motor-vehicles, with significant 'knock-on' effects on the service sector. Consequently, the *official* female unemployment rate passed 6 per cent in 1980 and exceeded 9 per cent in July 1982; the 'real' rate was probably very much higher. This figure is likely to go on rising with the continued application of microprocessor technology. In any service where large amounts of relatively simple information are handled considerable savings are likely to be made by displacing manual labour by microprocessor technology. Traditionally much of this labour has been performed by women who would seem to be particularly vulnerable to technological change in this area.

Unemployment and technological change

We do not intend in the limited space available here to analyse all the possible implications of the introduction into the work place of new technology, especially the new information technology (IT). Rather we shall limit ourselves (a) to a brief discussion of the possible effects of these technological changes upon employment levels, and the implications this may have for the 'disciplining' of the work-force and (b) whether the new technology will lead to further de-skilling and increased routinisation of work tasks.

Information technology

It is necessary to distinguish between product innovation and process innovation. Product innovation refers to the myriad new and improved products, such as word-processors and computer games, made available through the application of IT process innovation refers to the effects of IT in providing new ways in which existing products or services can be produced. It is process innovation which more usually leads to both increased unemployment and de-skilling.

It is difficult to generalise about the effects of the new technologies upon employment levels. On the one hand, as Wall (1985) points out, there are examples of new, fast-growing 'sunrise' industries grouped around the electronics sector, which seem to provide extra employment and output (the electronics industry now accounts for over 5 per cent of UK manufacturing employment and value added). On the other hand, there are many cases in which the application of IT seems to lead to the direct substitution of labour by capital. A report by the West German Commerzbank, for example, estimated that every robot employed in industry today replaces three workers on average, and that by the late 1980s the second generation of 'intelligent' robots, with heightened sensory powers, will each replace between five and ten workers in certain assembly jobs. In the service sector also, job losses are, and should continue to be, severe. The new automated system for clearing cheques in the city of London – CHAPS – has allegedly made the activities of 8000 messengers unnecessary and is jeopardising many other clerical jobs involved in routine cheque clearance (Wall, 1985).

It is clear then that new technology will provide one of the biggest challenges to trade unions throughout the 1980s and beyond. It has been introduced at a time when unemployment is already rising and when union membership is falling rapidly as a consequence. There seems little chance that, as in the past, high rates of growth in the economy will provide alternative job opportunities in an expanding service sector; it would appear that the very heart of trade union organisation at the enterprise level is under threat.

Colin Gill (1985) suggests that so far, faced with rapid technological change, the early experience of workers in Britain has been uneven. Some have experienced little dislocation and have adapted to technical change with little difficulty while others have been devastated by it.

> Whilst the 'quality of working life' movement of the early 1970s offered a move away from 'Taylorized' production lines, we now see fresh dangers that employers will seize upon their renewed bargaining power to introduce greater forms of degradation of skills and working life generally, not only on the factory floor but also in the office (Gill, pp. 138–9).

Gill's pessimism received support from the actions of the newspaper proprietor Rupert Murdoch in 1986. Murdoch used the introduction of new computer-aided printing techniques, not only to completely revolutionise the once highly skilled craft of printing (although the writing was already on the wall so far as printing was concerned), but also to completely undermine the print unions and impose a series of conditions upon the remaining workers – such as 'no strike' clauses – that they had little option but to accept.

Gill, echoing what many people have previously argued in response to technological determinism, points out that:

> The use of computer-based automation that trivializes work is both humanly tragic and technically unnecessary. An alternative direction that fully uses the extraordinary abilities that people possess requires a new vision of what technology can accomplish. This vision would not counterpose computer to people; it would not relegate human abilities to being taken over by an electronically controlled system. Instead, computers would amplify rather than eliminate the unique qualities that only humans can bring to production. The design of machines reflects social values as well as technical needs.
>
> The alternative is a much darker vision: the creation of a pyramid of skills that concentrates a few creative and meaningful occupations at the top, while the rest wind up with fewer skills and subject to new forms of monitoring and electronic control (p. 87)

Littler and Salaman suggest that the debate over the new technology and work contains two views of the future: a pessimistic and an optimistic view. The pessimistic view, associated with people like Braverman, emphasises that the employer's search for economic and technical efficiency within the capitalist framework of intense competition results in labour rationalisation, mass redundancy, and the restructuring of work towards more fragmented, routinised tasks. The optimistic view stresses that technological innovation results in more and better trained workers exercising increased autonomy in their jobs whilst the more arduous and repetitive tasks are assigned to machines. They quote the Japanese Robot Industry Association as saying that robots are 'tools for the liberation of mankind' creating enhanced leisure for all (Littler and Salaman, 1984). But, as they put it: 'The evidence so far does not encourage us to take the optimistic view'.

Indeed, optimistic predictions about micro-chip technology issuing in an 'age of leisure' – the twenty-hour week and substantial increases in holidays have been mentioned – would be amusing were not the implications of these, and other developments, so serious. Enforced idleness, redundancy and unemployment cannot, by any stretch of the imagination, be called *leisure*. There is no guarantee that under capitalism the fruits of technological advance will be shared out equally among the population, given that such technologies, and related developments, have had weakening effects upon traditional means of resistance.

This being said, we have to recognise that the relationships between technological innovation, social control and job satisfaction are very complex. Even in avowedly socialist societies the task of constructing satisfying and democratically organised work has hardly begun and remains a problem for the future.

REFERENCES TO CHAPTER 9

Ashton, D. N. (1985) 'Unemployment: Why Pick on Youth?', *Social Studies Review*, vol. 1, no. 1, pp. 36–40

Ben-David, J. (1964) 'Professions in the Class System of Present Day Societies', *Current Sociology*.

Beynon, H. (1973) *Working for Ford*, Harmondsworth, Penguin.

Backburn, R. M. and Mann M. (1979) *The Working Class in the Labour Market*, London, Macmillan.

Blauner, R. (1964) *Alienation and Freedom*, University of Chicago Press.

Bosquet, M. (1980) 'The Meaning of Job Enrichment', in T. Nichols (ed.) *Capital and Labour*, Glasgow, Fontana.

Braverman, H. (1974) *Labour and Monopoly Capital*, New York, Monthly Review Press.

Carlin, J. (1966) *Lawyers' Ethics*, New York.

Chinoy, E. (1955) *Automobile Workers and the American dream*, New York, Beacon Press.

Clarke, T. and Clements, L. (eds) (1977) *Trade Unions Under Capitalism*, London, Fontana.

Cohen, S. (ed.) (1971) *Images of Deviance*, Harmondsworth, Penguin.

Crompton, R. and Jones, G. (1984) *White-Collar Proletariat*, London, Macmillan.

Durcan, J. W. and McCarthy, W. E. J. (1972) 'What is Happening to Strikes?', *New Society*, 2 November, pp. 267–9.

Edwards, P. K. (1983) 'The Pattern of Collective Industrial Action', in G. S. Bain (ed.) (1983) *Industrial Relations in Britain*, London, Blackwell.

Edwards, R. (1979) *Contested Terrain*, London, Heinemann.
Elliot, P. (1972) *The Sociology of Professions*, London, Macmillan.
Fox, A. (1974) *Man Mismanagement*, London, Hutchinson.
Friedman, A. L. (1977a) *Industry and Labour*, London, Macmillan.
Friedman, A. L. (1977b) 'Responsible Autonomy versus Direct Control over the Labour Process', *Capital and Class*, No 1.
Gallie, D. (1978) *In Search of the New Working Class*, Cambridge University Press.
Gamble, A. (1981) *Britain in Decline*, London, Macmillan.
Gill, C. (1985) *Work, Unemployment and the New Technology*, London, Polity Press.
Goldthorpe, J. H., Lockwood, D. and colleagues (1968a) *The Affluent Worker: Industrial Attitudes and Behaviour*. Cambridge University Press.
Goldthorpe J H. (1969) *The Affluent Worker in the Class Structure*, Cambridge University Press.
Hawkins, K. (1984) *Unemployment*, 2nd edn Harmondsworth,Penguin,
Hyman, R. (1975) *Industrial Relations: A Marxist Introduction*, London, Macmillan.
Hyman, R. (1984) *Strikes* (3rd edn), London, Fontana.
Illich, I. (1973) 'The Professions as a Form of Imperialism', *New Society*, 13 September 1973, pp. 633–5.
Johnson, T. (1972) *Professions and Power*, London, Macmillan.
Kumar, K. (1978) *Prophecy and Progress: The Sociology of Industrial and Post-Industrial Societies*, Harmondsworth, Penguin.
Lane, T. and Roberts, K. (1971) *Strike at Pilkingtons*, London, Fontana.
Liepmann, K. (1960) *Apprenticeship*, London, Routledge & Kegan Paul.
Littler, C. R. and Salaman, G. (1984), *Class at Work*, London, Batsford.
McCarthy, W. E. J. (1970), 'The Nature of Britain's Strike Problem', *British Journal of Industrial Relations*, VIII, pp. 224–36.
Mandel, E. (1978) *Late Capitalism*, New Left Review Editions, Verso Books, London.
Manwaring, T. and Sigler, S. (eds) (1985) *Breaking the Nation*, London, Pluto Press.
Marx, K. (1962) *Das Kapital, Vol. I*, Harmondsworth Penguin.
Millerson, G. (1964) *The Qualifying Associations*, London, Routledge & Kegan Paul.
Mills, C. Wright (1953) *White Collar*, Oxford University Press.
Monopolies Commission (1970) *Report on Professional Services*, London, HMSO.
Muncie, J. (1984) *The Trouble with Kids Today*, London, Hutchinson.
Nichols, T. and Beynon, H. (1977) *Living with Capitalism*, London, Routlege & Kegan Paul.
Penn, R. (1978) 'Skilled Manual Workers in the Labour Process', Nuffield Paper, quoted in P. Thompson (1983) *The Nature of Work*, London, Macmillan.
Parkin, F. (1971) *Class Inequality and Political Order*, London, Paladin.
Ross, A. M. and Hartman, P. T. (1960) *Changing Patterns of Industrial Conflict*, New York: Wiley.
Taylor, F. W. (1903) *Shop Management*, New York, Harper & Row.
Taylor, F. W. (1967) *Principles of Scientific Management*, New York, Harper & Row.
Terry, M. (1983) 'Shop Steward Development and Managerial Strategies', in G. S. Bain (1983)
Thompson, P. (1983) *The Nature of Work*, London, Macmillan.
Walker, C. R. and Guest, R. (1952) *Man on the Assembly Line*, Harvard University Press.
Wall, S. (1985) 'Information Technology and Employment', *The Economic Review*, November.

10

Belief-Systems

10.1 INTRODUCTION

Most people live out their lives in a fairly stable pattern of daily encounters with others, whether in the home, at the shops, school or work. In these settings, actions can seem automatic and unthinking, and conversation accompanying them is normally carried out in terms of well-worn commentaries about the weather, the price of goods, the latest record, 'last night's result', 'the good news, the bad news', and so on. Much of the time these exchanges do not convey new information, since they are more devices for sustaining 'normal' patterns of social interaction. There is, then, a considerable amount of social 'patter' in 'public' that changes little from day to day, like the patter of the market tradesman. Everyday interaction tends to be most successful when 'short', 'sweet', and role-bound.

Despite its superficiality, the culture of everyday interaction in all societies bears the imprint of more articulate and critical social myths and ideologies, knowledges and beliefs, whether they be drawn from the institutions of religion, magic, science, politics, education as primary sources of ideas, or from secondary sources such as the media. In this chapter we examine the way in which these ideas are formed into what we call 'belief-systems'.

All people are more or less committed to a range of beliefs, attitudes, or opinions. Strongly held ideas are usually those that have been institutionalised among a body of like-minded people. The stronger and more persuasive a set of ideas becomes, the more it is likely to become an all-embracing system of belief and ideology governing members' actions and interpretations of the world. Some of the strongest belief-systems are those which have been formally instituted with specific ends in mind, such as the major religions or political philosophies of the world. Belief-systems work because the actors involved take account of others' ideas, intentions and behaviour. *What* we do and *why* we do it are comprehensible to others.

At the same time, however, one need not assume that accountability and comprehension necessarily imply social consensus. Given that in any society there are different groups with different social, economic and political interests, it is likely that specific belief-systems will be associated with each group. Specific ideas and beliefs may contradict other sets of beliefs, so that controversy and conflict develop between groups, as, for example, occurred in the struggle between religion and science in Europe in the eighteenth and nineteenth centuries. It would seem that science won the battle: it is said that we now live in a 'scientific age'.

Before proceeding further, however, we need to make some general comments on the concept of 'belief-systems'. First, to speak in terms of a belief-*system* is not to imply that the beliefs making it up are fully articulated, clearly worked out ideas ordered and arranged in a systematic, consistent fashion. Rather, people may hold beliefs without any clear reason why they do so (perhaps they are simply ideas that have been passed on by custom and tradition). Similarly, people may unwittingly hold contradictory beliefs simultaneously without this being in any way difficult or worrying for them. Second, to proclaim a belief is to assert that one holds something to be true. This may be an assertion like 'I *personally* hold X to be true, but don't require that you must as well'; or it could involve an assertion such as 'I believe that X is true, and you should as well'. As we shall see, the second assertion tends to figure more prominently in institutionalised belief-systems. Third, different belief-systems – say those of magic and religion – will invoke different criteria in measuring what is held to be 'right' or 'true'. If this is so, then sociology must not make any quick and easy judgements about the truth or falsity of belief-systems which are not based on the same type of assumptions that are used in 'modern' industrial society. In other words, we should not deride or denounce, say, witchcraft and magic as products of a 'primitive mind', expressions of stupidity and childishness. Instead, sociology should examine these belief-systems on *their own terms*, that is, in terms of the way they are used and described by *the very people who act* on them. This approach accepts that, as far as the actors who profess them are concerned, their beliefs do form a stable and rational set of ideas.

In short, then, belief-systems refer to those ideas that people hold to be right and true, which provide not only guides and rules for action, but also justifications for actions by which behaviour is made accountable to the self and to others.

Finally, as propositions that claim to be in some way true, beliefs imply access to 'knowledge': they can be treated as 'knowledge-claims', whether they be made generally or within the institutional contexts of science, magic, witchcraft, or religion. These institutions are deliberately established to give 'answers' to make the world (variously) accountable; they are also made up of people who claim to have special talents and abilities for discovering these 'answers' – 'scientists', 'magicians/witches', 'theologians'. If the 'layperson' accepts this expertise, then these knowledge-specialists are in a very favourable position, enjoying power, prestige and perhaps material reward. Clearly, however, this has important implications. 'Experts' may maintain ideas which support their position, refuse to consider. reject, or even squash non-orthodox, competing ideas from other groups outside the institutional framework who challenge the expertise and ultimately basic livelihood of the incumbent professional experts. Vested interests may then operate to varying degrees and with varying effects in belief-systems, indicating that what is accepted will depend on power relations as well as cognitive considerations. In as much as this is so, knowledge-claims may have ideological dimensions in serving the interests of different groups; we shall develop this point later, particularly in our consideration of the mass media.

10.2 MAGIC AND SCIENCE AS BELIEF-SYSTEMS

Although European anthropologists have long since distanced themselves from any covert beliefs about the white racial superiority, a considerable number of them did suggest that 'modern' – not so much 'white' – society is superior to, more evolved than, 'primitive' society. Some anthropologists, such as Frazer and Lévy-Bruhl, argued that primitive society's belief in magic, witchcraft, and totemic rites derived from the 'pre-logical' mentality of its people, a mentality that was essentially defective. It lacked the capacity to account for phenomena in terms of a logical, natural causality, a capacity enjoyed by people at a more developed stage of social and cognitive evolution: magic was seen to be crude, mistaken, suffering from inherent logical weaknesses that would be gradually acknowledged and displaced as 'primitive people' seek and are shown the way to modern 'rational' thinking.

Few, if any, anthropologists would subscribe to this (ethnocentric) evolutionary thesis today. The belief-systems of modern industrial society are no longer given a privileged position at the top of some evolutionary tree: instead, belief-sytems of whatever cultural origin are examined in their own right. Though they may be different from Western science in terms of *how* they account for the world, it is accepted that the account they use displays logical and rational characteristics just as Western science does. This change in perspective was in part due to the influence of the foremost British anthropologist of the last fifty years, Edward Evans-Pritchard (1902–73).

His major texts published in the 1930s are extensive ethnographies of three African tribes, the Nuer, Azande, and Bedouin, based on a number of years fieldwork living in their villages and camps and learning their languages. This use of participant observation was crucial: Evans-Pritchard insisted that one could only understand alien belief-systems by immersing oneself in their language, culture, and everyday activities. The anthropologist must seek out the assumptions and accounts of the world that underpin different systems, and be ready to accept that there is more than one way of constructing a rational and coherent belief-system. We can consider, for example, Evans-Pritchard's famous account of the Azande of Sudan in Central Africa.

Life among the Azande is built on a belief in witchcraft and magic. Whenever misfortune falls on someone, he or she consults a magic oracle which reveals the source of the witchcraft that has caused the mishap in the first place. To consult the oracle, a chicken is fed with a specially prepared potion ('benge') and is asked whether a particular person could be held accountable as the source of witchcraft. The diviner tells the potion to kill the chicken if the answer is 'Yes', and then, with a second chicken, to kill if the answer is 'No'. In the end the poison oracle provides an answer as to who is to blame for the misfortune. The sufferer can then go to the accused and publicly demand that the witchcraft stop. This public accusation is considered sufficient to prevent further trouble from the accused.

Witchcraft is not a source of great terror or fear for the Azande but is invoked as an everyday explanation for unaccountable events which are put down to the workings of 'fate' or 'chance' in the West. Witchcraft answers the question 'why *me*?', a question left unanswered in Western culture. Not all mishaps are attributed to witchcraft: as in any society, certain events are put down to technical incompetence – for example, cracks in pottery are seen to be caused by poor craftsmanship. Furthermore, the Azande are well aware that, for instance, there are diseases which make people sick, or that hippos may overturn boats and so cause people to drown. Yet the Azande asks, 'Why should *I* be sick while everybody else is well?'; or again, 'Why did the hippo attack *my* father, today, when he's been down the river a hundred times before?' Western science would simply say that it was coincidence that someone happened to meet an angry hippo in mid-stream on a particular day, and offer no further explanation. But the Azande are more curious than this and explain such apparently coincidental occurrences as witchcraft.

Witchcraft accusations – having been directed and confirmed by the poison oracle – are made against someone believed to be a jealous or envious neighbour. Normally, it is only neighbours who live together who accuse each other, since they are close enough physically and socially to envy one another, to quarrel, to compete and plan to hurt each other. The princes of the Azande, the Zande ruling class, are immune from accusations of witchcraft. At their personal courts, each prince owns an oracle which is used as final arbiter in maintaining peace and order, by confirming or rejecting witchcraft accusations made by one commoner against another after initial consultation with subsidiary oracles. Their immunity from witchcraft charges results primarily from the belief, reinforced by tradition and myth, that only they possess and control the magic of the major oracle whereby witchcraft may be detected. Such tradition and myth help to legitimate the privileges enjoyed by the aristocracy of Zandeland. The special status given to the knowledge-claims of the princes' oracles not only serves to maintain the social order but also the inequality of that order. As Evans-Pritchard (1967, p. 15) says, 'privileges invested in one class in society require the halo of myth'.

An accusation of witchcraft does not necessarily mean that the suspect will suffer great social opprobrium. The Azande believe that witchcraft is a *psychic* power emanating from a physical substance located in the intestines. A person may have witchcraft without using it intentionally to harm other people. This belief allows the accused to proclaim shock and amazement, to apologise and to promise that future bewitching will stop. This means that neighbours are encouraged to behave in an extremely courteous manner towards one another so as to minimise the likelihood of accusations. Hence, the belief in (non-deliberate) witchcraft ensures that good relations between neighbours in the homesteads can be maximised; small misfortunes can be accounted for, accusations made and acknowledged, and good will restored. As Douglas (1980, pp. 51–2) argues, 'The witchcraft belief-institution had a lubricating effect on community life. Grudges would not be allowed to fester . . . The air was cleared, and social life would go on.'

Major misfortunes, such as the death of a relative, are attributed to witchcraft being used in a deliberately malign manner by an evil witch. Deaths were, until stopped by British colonials, to be avenged by the death of the witch. When the witch was accused, he would be 'tried' by the final authority, the prince's poison oracle. He would be required to imbibe the poison ('benge'), and if death followed, the accusation was vindicated, and if not, the accuser would have to find another guilty party. If the accused refused to drink the poison, the court would administer it to a chicken to evaluate the charge, which (if proven) allowed the relatives of the deceased to spear the witch to death.

A correct accusation of witchcraft creates problems for the witch's kinsmen, since the Azande believe that witchcraft is inheritable, passing from male witch to son, or female witch to daughter. Hence, the immediate kin are suspected as witches. To allay witchcraft accusations against them, kin resolve to clear the name of their father or mother. This is done by the institution of the post-mortem, wherein the intestines of the deceased are examined by the court. If the court finds the accused to have been rightly charged and killed as a witch, his or her relatives may go so far as to deny that the person was a true member of their clan, that the witch was conceived and born illegitimately: if the mother is still alive she is forced to confess to adultery. This confession thus removes all suspicion of inherited malicious witchcraft from the living.

The Zande belief-system of magic and witchcraft institutions appears to serve two purposes:

(1)   It works to relieve anxiety created by worry and frustration over unforeseen and inexplicable events by pinning blame on an accountable member of the village.

(2)   Such accountability is typically required of people who are believed to be in competition, to be envious or spiteful: witchcraft accusations thus help to dissipate potential conflict between rivals and so reduce the level of enmity within the community. One cannot then dismiss Zande beliefs as 'foolish' or irrational: in many ways they are a reliable set of ideas that work well once one accepts certain assumptions.

Nevertheless, Evans-Pritchard recognised that Zande beliefs about witchcraft did not form a perfectly consistent body of ideas. Inconsistences do not undermine the Zande faith in witchcraft, because the analytical questions bringing them into relief are never considered by the Zande. Such questions would presuppose assumptions and a perspective that is no part of what Evans-Pritchard (1937, p. 338) calls 'the idiom of their beliefs': 'They reason excellently in the idiom of their beliefs, but they cannot reason outside, or against, their beliefs because they have no other idiom in which to express their thoughts.' Thus, for example, there would be no point in asking the Azande how a person can be proven innocent of witchcraft by postmortem when witchcraft is also believed to be present in all, and inheritable through descent. Again the Azande would laugh at a European who asked whether the poison would kill the chicken without any accompanying address. As Evans-Pritchard (1937, p. 315) says, 'If the fowl died they would simply say that it was not good "benge". The very fact of the fowl dying proves to them its badness.' Any such 'test', then, would actually reinforce rather than undermine the Zande belief-system. Within its terms, the Zande reason logically and coherently. If an oracle contradicted itself it would simply be said to have been addressed or prepared improperly, once again reaffirming the basic assumptions of the belief-system. These assumptions are used as interpretative resources, drawn on to account for the world, and establishing the point at which reasoning and further questions come to an end. As we shall see shortly, science itself relies on unverifiable assumptions, commitments towards certain perspectives that may encourage scientists to *ignore* evidence that appears to contradict their beliefs.

Evans-Pritchard's sympathetic treatment of the Zande culture not only made a more fruitful anthropology but also led to philosophical debate about the logical form of magic compared with that of science, and the sense in which *both* can be construed as belief-systems. Polanyi, for example, believes that it is possible to identify an idiom of belief operating at the heart of all scientific knowledge, albeit in a covert form. Implicit beliefs and assumptions have been screened from our eyes by the ideology of 'objectivism' in modern science, an ideology that insists that scientific truth is a matter of objectivity and not faith. This assumes that scientific theories are built on the observation of empirical 'facts' and the systematic consideration of evidence. Peering behind this curtain of 'objectivism', Polanyi (1958) brings to light a number of features common to both witchcraft and science.

There are, he says, three features working together to ensure that any belief-system is sustained as right and proper (for those who profess it) despite 'evidence' challenging its validity: their combination guarantees that questions, problems or issues not covered by the belief-system's assumptions will be 'unhesitatingly ignored'. First, Polyani points to the 'circularity' of the ideas that constitute any belief-system: each idea in the system is explained through reference to another idea, the validity of which is never doubted. This other idea, however, only makes sense itself through reference to the original idea. All languages as symbolic systems embody this circular aspect. Thus, for example, a dictionary presupposes a literary circularity of meaning and legitimation; the definition of a word may itself be explained in terms of the original word – 'marriage' may give 'wedlock' which in turn is defined as 'a state of marriage'. This circularity promotes the stability of a system of ideas and beliefs: if one belief is doubted, it is justified through reference to a different belief, which, if challenged subsequently, is justified in terms of the original belief. Hence, as Polanyi (1958, p. 289) says, 'So long as each doubt is defeated in its turn, its effect is to strengthen the fundamental convictions against which it was raised.'

Second, Polanyi suggests that all belief-systems hold in reserve a supply of 'subsidiary explanations for difficult situations'. For the Azande, for example, failure of the oracle could be accounted for in terms of incorrect use of the device; similarly in science, certain events or phenomena not conforming to expectation may be explained away in terms of some auxiliary hypothesis. Thus conflicting evidence is often discussed in science as 'anomalous findings', quirks of investigation that can be ignored. In physics or chemistry many experiments are designed to show constant relations between two phenomena, which can then be plotted as a straight-line graph. Sometimes, one point on the graph is consistently out of line with the rest: students may be told to ignore this apparent anomaly, which is frequently dismissed as the result of incorrect method at some point in the experiment, an explanation which an Azande student would find most appropriate!

Third, belief-systems reject alternative views of the world by refusing to grant any legitimacy to the assumptions on which rival conceptions depend. This may mean that new ideas challenging orthodox knowledge-claims are suppressed from their first appearance, and those making them denied any respectability within the community of 'experts'.

According to Polanyi, then, these three features explain how, in practice, contradictory evidence or inconsistent findings do not normally lead to the overthrow of a set of ideas, be it Zande magic or European science. Such evidence can be explained away, denied any validity and meaning, or simply ignored. Hence all systems of knowledge rest on basic premises which are sustained by virtue of actors' *commitment* to them as 'true': ideas are reaffirmed as much by faith and trust as they are by any 'methodologically correct' procedures: 'believing is seeing, as much as seeing is believing'.

Polanyi's commentary forces us to reconsider the way in which scientific knowledge-claims are certified as correct by scientists. Most importantly, we are required to abandon the customary view that regards science as an activity which, by unbiased, neutral observation, accumulates evidence from which the universal laws of nature are derived. It would seem, then, that an intrinsic feature of scientists' work is their selective inattention to evidence or knowledge-claims which do not conform to their picture of reality.

Recent contributions to the area known as 'the sociology of science' have extensively documented the way in which the production and acceptance of scientific ideas depend on social and cultural factors (see, for example, Mulkay, 1979). The growth of this area of sociological research was partly due to the influential work of Kuhn (1970). Kuhn (1972, p. 82) identified what he called 'the dogmatism of mature science', which he defines as 'a deep commitment to a particular way of viewing the world and of practising science in it'. As a scientific field such as physics becomes more mature or developed, as the number of practitioners increases, as education courses are established and textbooks produced, so those working and training within it adopt common ideological commitment to what it is 'to be a physicist and study physics'. This dogmatic commitment provides the scientist with 'the rules of the game', *what* is to be treated as a scientific puzzle and *how* it is to be solved. These rules constitute what Kuhn (1972, p. 93) calls 'the paradigm' of a scientific field or speciality:

> Their paradigm tells [scientists] about the sort of entities with which the universe is populated and about the way the members of that population behave; in addition, it informs them of the questions that may legitimately be asked about nature and of the techniques that can properly be used in the search for answers to them.

Kuhn's notion of paradigmatic science, can, then, be set against the misleading notion that scientists test their theories by collecting observable 'facts' which exist 'out there' in nature, awaiting observation and classification. Instead, scientists 'go out' armed with their respective paradigms seeking evidence, dealing with problems, that *confirm* it. As Kuhn argues, 'the challenge is not to uncover the unknown, but to obtain the known'. This clearly parallels Polanyi's concept of the 'circularity' of belief-systems, in as much as it suggests how scientific research operates in terms of a relatively closed system of ideas that are self-confirming. If counter-evidence to the paradigm does appear, it is typically ignored as an anomaly, and, says Kuhn, for good reason. An anomalous finding or unexpected discovery is, by definition, potentially subversive: it threatens to change the 'rules of the game' by which the paradigm works. Hence, the paradigm is a source of resistance to innovation in science. But if one stopped here, major innovations in science that have occurred – such as the shift from Newtonian to Einsteinian physics – would remain inexplicable. Kuhn explains that innovation takes place when anomalous findings become 'particularly stubborn or striking' such that they force scientists 'to raise questions about accepted beliefs and procedures'. When the paradigm consistently fails to deal with an increasing number of anomalous results, the scientific field experiences a period of major intellectual and social crisis, overcome by the formulation of a new paradigm.

Kuhn's analysis of the paradigmatic nature of science extends the general ideas raised by Polanyi. Polanyi was concerned to show how the *conceptual logic* of science is very similar in form to that sustaining the Zande belief-system; Kuhn indicates the way in which aspects of the *social institution* of science – textbooks, curricula, research communities – continuously sustain the conceptual commitments of its practitioners, guiding their activities, interpretations and accounts of the natural world, and reinforcing the stability of their scientific belief-system.

A commitment to a particular scientific interpretation of the world is therefore an ever-present interpretative resource that scientists use to justify their knowledge-claims, and encourages resistance to new ideas or 'deviant' interpretations. A considerable body of literature in the sociology of science examines the way in which non-orthodox knowledge-claims are received and evaluated by orthodox science (see, for example, Wallis, 1979). Case studies – for example, on parapsychology (Collins and Pinch, 1979), on acupuncture (Webster, 1979) – show how 'fringe' groups that threaten the conceptual and social status quo of science have been dismissed, but not on the basis of open-minded impartial scientific theorising and experiment: instead, many scientists have simply asserted from the outset that the existence of the kind of phenomena proposed is inconsistent with known reality, and therefore any findings, however carefully presented, must be the result of fraud or experimental error, and thus need not be taken seriously. Hence, as Mulkay (1979, p. 91) comment on parapsychology:

> For the critics of parapsychology, the central assumption that paranormal phenomena do not exist was never in question. Rather it pervaded and gave meaning to the whole armoury of formal arguments which they employed. It

ensured that, for these critics, every item of evidence and every claim of reasoning provided further grounds for rejection of the deviant views.

This once again draws our attention to the circulatory and self-confirming nature of orthodox science as an idiom of belief: as Polanyi argues, the stability of a belief system is apparent by 'the way it denies to any rival conception the ground in which it might take root'.

We see, then, that not only magic and witchcraft but also science can be regarded as belief-systems. We now want to focus attention on the institution of religion. As with science, we shall begin by comparing it with magic.

10.3   RELIGION

Religion may be said to be a system of belief about the individual's place in the world, providing an order to that world and a reason for existence within it. It has been institutionalised over the centuries, so that powerful religious organisations and ideas have arisen, like the Catholic, Islamic and Hindu churches. As such, it has a major influence in societies, affecting non-religious institutions specifically, such as the family or conjugal ties, as well as bringing about general social change, indicated by the great religious wars, the contemporary Islamic revolution(s), and so on.

We cannot merely define religion as a system of belief(s) that guides social action, since, as we have seen, this is also true of magic and science. One must go further and suggest that the beliefs are supported by a community which we call a 'church'. Moreover, a defining feature of religious belief has been said to be its concern to venerate 'the sacred', or the 'holy'. In 1945 the British anthropologist Radcliffe-Brown (1881–1955) defined religion as 'an expression in one form or another of a sense of dependence on a power outside ourselves, a power of which we may speak as a spiritual or moral power'. The dependency on supernatural powers is expressed in the importance of religious rituals, through which such powers are revered and supplicated, asked for direction, forgiveness, blessing, or vengeance. Durkheim's analysis of religion led him to define it as 'a unified system of beliefs and practices relative to sacred things, that is to say things set apart and forbidden – beliefs and practices which unite into a single moral community called a church all those who adhere to them' (1965, p. 47). Natural objects, such as minerals, animals, or plants are given a divine significance as symbols through which supernatural entities – gods, angels, or spiritual ancestors – are worshipped. Ritual is important in both reinforcing and expressing the solidarity of believers and establishing a distinction between what is to be treated as 'sacred' as opposed to 'profane' (the everyday, earthly concerns of life).

Though the veneration of 'the sacred' and the mystical is a hallmark of religious faith, something like this also goes on in magical rituals. Hence, it may be inappropriate to distinguish firmly between the two. Thus, Horton (1960) and Worsley (1968) argue that *religious* ritual may have a *magical* power for those taking part, and conversely, magical beliefs and actions normally presuppose some notions about gods, spirits, mystical forces, and so on. Those who maintain the distinction between magic and religion do so primarily because of their functionalist interpretation of belief-systems. That is, magic and religion are said to serve distinct functions in society, the former allowing the individual some control over events, the latter strengthening social values and attitudes through community ritual.

This functionalist perspective was developed in detail by Durkheim, principally in *The Elementary Forms of the Religious Life* (1912). He argues that belief in a supernatural realm cannot have any foundation in reality, since 'religious experience' has led to conceptions about 'the spiritual' which have 'varied infinitely'. The myths and 'imaginary forces' that religion creates are in fact inspired by the collective sentiment and shared morality of people in society. It is the *moral* order and not some mythical God that is held in reverence and awe by the individual. Although individuals may think that they are worshipping the divine, in reality the only thing that transcends individuals, that has a permanence outlasting them, is society itself: it is society that we really worship. Durkheim is interested in how religion 'binds people to society' through helping them to (i) understand the reality of social relations; (ii) communicate with other people; and (iii) establish obligations between people. Religion thus gives a 'sacred authority to society's rules and values'. In maintaining social solidarity religion is, for Durkheim, an essentially conservative force: when it fails to perform this function for social groups, new groups and new ideas emerge which become the new religions. Durkheim sees Nationalism and Communism, for example, as the new religions of industrial society, taking over from Christianity, giving the members of society an image of an ideal world. Politics and the rituals associated with it – flag-waving, parades, and doctrines – become the new form in which collective sentiments are symbolically expressed: collective ritual must be performed regularly to strengthen the moral codes and order of society. Thus the Durkheimian theory of religion suggests that religion, in one form or another, is a necessary and essential feature of society.

Durkheim's analysis of religion has a number of similarities to that developed by Marx. Like Durkheim, Marx believed that the 'supernatural' realm had no reality: God did not create mankind; instead, mankind had created God, as well as much of the physical world, and the social and political institutions that order it. But the illusion of religious belief turns all this upside down, making God (or gods) the supreme being, whose authority passes downwards through earthly rulers who order the affairs of ordinary mortals in 'the great chain of being'. Religion thus serves to legitimate the power and material advantage enjoyed by the dominant groups and rulers of society: rulers promote the myth that their position is given by God; hence 'the divine right of Kings'. Again, like Durkheim, Marx argues that religion serves a social function: it hides the real basis of power and exploitation in class society and hinders the development of class consciousness and a materialist politics that would show that the world is produced and reproduced through people's – not God's – labours. In hiding this reality, religion alienates people from their true selves, and yet is the means by which people can – albeit by delusion – escape the suffering and oppression brought about through the conflict of economic interest. It is in this sense 'the opium of the people'.

Both Marx and Durkheim, then, explain the origins and functions of religion in terms of *social* factors. But neither believed that one could reduce religious ideas to either purely economic or purely moral factors respectively. Both believed that once religion was institutionalised, it gained a relative independence from its underlying social bases. One cannot, for example, explain the opposition between Catholic and Protestant in Northern Ireland, or Jew and Palestinian in the Middle East, simply in terms of an economic or moral opposition between competing social groups.

This belief in the partial independence of religion from its material/social foundations was shared by Weber. As he says:

> However incisive the social influences, economically and politically determined, may have been upon a religious ethic in a particular case, it receives its stamp primarily from religious sources . . . [It] is at least usual that religious doctrines are adjusted to religious needs (Weber, in Gerth and Mills, 1948, p. 270).

Weber was interested in the way in which religious ideas varied and how they could effect social change rather than being simply a defence or justification of the status quo. His general concern was to explain the development of capitalism, which had only reached full maturity and dominated the world economy from within the social and economic climate of Western Europe. He examined the differing religious traditions of the West and the Orient and tried to show that the former was especially well suited to promoting the development of capitalism in the West, while the latter had the opposite effect in the East.

Weber showed that the ideas and practices of Protestantism were particularly conducive to capitalist development because of their general convergence with the 'spirit of capitalism' (Weber, 1952). He argued that the most significant feature of this spirit in Western Europe was the desire to be productive and accumulate riches continually. Elsewhere in the world, production was geared much more to the provision of exotic and luxurious material for immediate consumption. In the West, investment, hard work, and steady accumulation were seen as the correct and proper activities for working people: idleness and immoderate consumption of riches received harsh judgement. Such an attitude is by no means naturally adopted by individuals: people may just as easily produce sufficient for their needs and then stop working. Yet the continual accumulation through disciplined and controlled labour is a necessary condition for the growth of a truly capitalist economy. Capitalism could not have developed if the labour force worked erratically or only when they felt they needed to. Therefore, something peculiar to Western Europe must have encouraged people to work regularly, continuously, and in a disciplined manner. This, for Weber, was what he called the 'Protestant ethic', which found its most complete expression in the Calvinist doctrine.

The principle tenet of Calvinism is the belief in 'predestination': that God has selected those who are to be saved and those who are to suffer damnation. No individual can know whether he or she is one of the chosen few, nor can God's selection be altered in any way: salvation cannot be earned, but is given (or withheld) by God. Weber argued that those who believe in predestination are bound to suffer from 'salvation panic', a terrifying anxiety about whether one has been chosen, throwing the believer into psychological turmoil. In practice, the only way to cope with anxiety was to bend the Calvinist doctrine slightly, to believe that, like the good tree that cannot bear evil fruit, if one behaved in a Christian manner, performed 'good works', and was moderate in all, then these were *signs* that one had been elected for salvation.

Hence, the believer had to ensure that *everything* he or she did was for the 'greater glory of God' and a confirmation of election. Any slip, any brief lapse into immoderate or sinful behaviour was enough to show that one could not be among the chosen few, and that there would be eternal damnation. The pressure therefore to be highly disciplined and righteous in all one's daily activities was intense, with one's place of business or occupation being no exception. Here then we can begin to see the seeds of Weber's argument.

The Protestant ethic that derives from the doctrine of predestination demands the faithful to be diligent, disciplined, and fully committed to their 'worldly' obligations. The 'spirit of capitalism' encourages the view that hard work is an 'activity' which is good in itself, something to be admired as honourable and fruitful. Thus Weber believes that there is a convergence of attitudes and orientations here, an 'elective affinity' between the religious ideas of Calvinism and the spirit of capitalism, a reciprocal relationship only found in the society of Western Europe.

Weber's analysis illustrates one of his central beliefs about the relationship between ideas and the economic or material foundations of society. It is apparent that the 'ethic' is no simple reflection of the economic interests of any specific class group, nor even a direct mirroring of the capitalist spirit. Instead it derives from the rational solution to a psychological anxiety generated by belief in a religious doctrine. The solution – to behave as though one were chosen – had far-reaching consequences for other, non-religious, social institutions of capitalism.

Weber's thesis has been questioned on a number of points. For example, Samuelson (1961) points out that a number of places in Europe have had flourishing Calvinist communities yet have not been quick to develop along capitalist lines – Scotland is one case mentioned. Furthermore, the decisive role of the Protestant ethic in the growth of capitalism is challenged by some critics who argue that the accumulation of investment capital in, say, Britain, Holland, Huguenot France and New England, was as much the result of profiteering through trade, piracy, and plunder as it was of careful saving by frugal Calvinist craftsmen and traders. Marxists argue that the Protestant ethic served as an ideological legitimation of *laissez-faire*, free-market capitalism. Others question Weber's portrayal of Oriental belief-systems as obstacles to the development of capitalism, unlike Calvinism (Rodinson, 1977). Why is it, they argue, that a religion such as Hinduism could quite happily accommodate, even promote, the development of trade, a legal and monetary system, a division of labour, and yet apparently, as Weber claims, prevent further development in economic growth along capitalist lines? These critics suggest, then, that the lack of development in Hindu or Islamic societies must be attributed to factors distinct from the particular belief-systems of their respective religions, and so, by implication, cannot be explained in terms of their lack of a Protestant ethic.

While these criticisms must be taken seriously, and imply that continued historical and theoretical analysis is required if we are to understand the relationship between religious values and social change, Weber's analysis cannot be accused of being theoretically simplistic. He stated quite clearly that his thesis was *not* that Protestantism *caused* capitalism, but was one contributory factor in a highly complex process of economic and social change.

Rationalisation

One of the central features of this process identified by Weber is the dimension of *rationality* that underpins the Protestant ethic and the development of capitalism. Calvinists were being highly rational in seeking to maximise evidence of their 'calling' through adopting a disciplined and methodical approach to all their worldly concerns. Such an approach encouraged the likelihood of success, taken to be a clear sign of election. This rational religious ethic encouraged the Calvinist entrepreneur to be more and more calculating and efficient. This led to the growth of book-keeping, accounting, and an orientation that sought a continual, controlled return on investment. Hence the rationality of the religious ethic paralleled the rational characteristics of the organisation of capitalist enterprise.

Rationalisation of both religious belief and economic activity is the main feature of modern society in which the twin forces of rationalisation and intellectualisation lead to 'the disenchantment' of the world. The world becomes less and less an 'enchanted', mystical or 'sacred' place: all things in principle can be mastered by calculation, by reason. Weber insists that this does not imply an *increased* knowledge about the world, simply a different way of interpreting it. Nevertheless, this different interpretation has been seen to have great significance by a number of social theorists, some of whom argue that in as much as the 'holy', the sacred, and the mysterious no longer hold any meaning for members of a society, then that society can be said to be experiencing the process of 'secularisation'.

Secularisation

The argument that society is becoming increasingly secular seems fairly straightforward. 'Everyone knows' that religion is not as strong as it used to be. But clearly this begs the question as to how we are to measure the 'strength' of religion. Depending on the indices we use, a society could be defined as being more or less 'religious', or conversely, less or more 'secular'.

An account of the secularisation process depends on the definition of religion adopted in the first place. Many sociologists define religion, and hence secularisation, in *institutional* terms. Glasner (1977, p. 7) summarises this approach:

> The assumption is that, since a common usage definition of Christianity for example, is concerned with church attendance, membership and presence at rites of passage, these constitute significant elements of a definition of religion, and that any move away from this institutional participation involves religious decline.

Wilson (1966), for instance, defines secularisation as the process through which religious thinking, practice, and institutions 'lose their social significance'. He then provides 'statistical evidence of secularisation' for both English and American Christianity which measures 'the decline in organised religious participation'. While admitting that falling baptism and membership numbers in England may in fact be interpreted as people voting with their feet and seeking alternative religious vehicles, he still believes that such figures show how the institutionalised Christian *Church* is 'losing direct influence over the ideas and activities of men'.

Statistical information about membership of and participation in the Christian religion must be treated carefully, since it is provided by denominations – Catholic, Anglican, Non-Conformist – that use different criteria of membership. It is estimated that about 60 per cent of the adult British population are counted as members of the Anglican faith, roughly 30 per cent of the population split between Catholic and Non-Conformists (such as Methodists, Unitarians, etc.), with about 5 per cent belonging to small 'sects'. On average only 10–15 per cent of the adult population attend church on any one Sunday; baptism or 'christening' takes place in about 90 per cent of births, although the number baptised in the Anglican Church dropped from 623 per 1000 live births in 1885, to 531 per 1000 in 1962. Wilson comments that while institutional religious duties such as prayer, mass, and communion, have lost much of their importance for members of the Church of England and Roman Catholic Church, they still provide a number of ceremonial services that form the *rites de passage* for members, particularly marriage and burial. While the number of church weddings declined from the turn of the century till the 1950s, they are now much more constant and account for approximately 70 per cent of all marriages each year. Wilson argues that this need not be taken as a sign of renewed religious commitment among Church members: rather, Church weddings may give people a dramatic sense of occasion lacking in registry ceremonies. The continued use of religious funerals similarly need be no indication of religiosity: 'The control of funerals is so much more professionalised than the control of baptisms, confirmations and weddings that religious officiation becomes almost a matter of routine' (Wilson, 1966, p. 17).

Generally, however, the predominance of religious institutions has given way to new social institutions, in the realms of politics, education, social policy and morality, and the pulpit has lost out to the power of the mass media. Religions no longer wield the political or economic power that they once enjoyed, and have modified their doctrines in the face of pressure from secular society. Some sociologists, such as Parsons, claim that this process whereby the extent of the institutional influence of religion is narrowed, leads to a stronger church, since it is a purer one, less distracted by secular cares and so more able to concentrate on matters 'sacred'. This view may be challenged, however, in as much as such a process would seem more likely to increasingly isolate religious observance and participation, and the value on which they depend, from a widening majority of the population.

Wilson argues that the gradual development of 'denominations' within Christianity in competition and in conflict with the Church of England – such as Calvinism and Methodism – is an additional indicator of secularisation. Both these developments within Christianity have been linked to specific social strata and their experience of the early period of industrialisation. Calvinism, with its emphasis on election, was particularly suited as a religio-social ethic and belief-system to a privileged merchant class. Methodism, however, based on Wesley's doctrine that all were equal before Christ and were free to choose salvation, appealed to the 'new mass society' of industrial England, and, as Marx might claim, was perhaps better equipped as a theology to provide the poor working class with some relief from their suffering. Indeed, some of the early offshoots from the Anglican Church – the Adventists for example – expressed through their religious solidarity a critique of their poverty and suffering, although this was channelled into *religious* fervour rather than class protest against capitalism. Later, however, members of various denominational groups – especially the Non-Conformists – came to regard their lot in life as a necessary burden in the heavenly order of things. As Calvinism encouraged this ethic among the wealthier merchants, so Methodism, for different reasons, provided a corresponding work ethic and set of values that could bring 'dignity' to the working class, whose lives had been radically disrupted by the wage-labour demand of industrialisation. Indeed, to some extent Methodism became a vehicle of social mobility for some, in as much as a religious 'working person' was seen as a 'respectable person', a 'law-abiding person', above the 'common rabble' of the working class. But a religion closely associated with a subordinate group in the way Methodism was could, if tolerated, be an agency of *dissent* and *protest* against the dominant economic classes. Something like this occurred in the nineteenth century when a broad alliance of dissenters from within the ranks of the Methodists and the Liberal Party criticised the links between the Tory Party, the landed aristocracy and the 'established' Church of England.

The notion of an 'established' Church highlights the major distinction between a 'Church' and a 'denomination'. The 'Church' of England, for instance, claims to command loyalty and respect, not simply because people have chosen to become Anglicans, but also because they become members of a Church traditionally recognised as the national and ethnic religious body, formally regarded so by the state. A denomination, such as Roman Catholicism, need not have this political or social status, and is usually a smaller body within a broadly defined belief-system such as Christianity. A third type of religious organisation, the 'sect', is a highly exclusive group. All members are required to conform to clearly defined rules and regulations. Sects, such as the Jehovah's Witnesses or Christadelphians, do not typically have some form of ordained clerical or ministerial group at their head, being run instead by the laity themselves. The sect tends to reject any liaison or ties with the wider society, unlike an 'established church'. Stark (1967) has described the sect as 'typically a contraculture', indicating its tendency to reject the prevailing social values and norms. Wilson (1966, p. 181) describes the selective quality of the sect thus:

> Whereas the Church represents itself as the religious organisation of the nation or the society, to which men are come at birth as members, the sect regards membership as an achievement, proved by one's capacity to live up to certain standards. The sect member both chooses and is chosen.

As Churches appear to lose their institutional pre-eminence, they may in fact become more like sects, small and somewhat cut off from the dominant culture. Conversely, there are a number of religious groups that have now become considerably church-like but which were initially conceived as sects, such as the Quakers. These different patterns of development indicate that there is no simple chronological passage from Church to sect, or vice versa. Moreover, within particular social contexts, the *same* religious group may be perceived quite differently: thus the Mormons have a churchly status in America but a very sectarian one in Britain.

Secularisation has been characterised as a process accompanying the increasing rationalisation and industrialisation of society, and the expanding authority of the state over all areas of life, reflected by the separation of Church and state. Theorists like Parsons regard this separation as an expression of the increasing 'structural differentiation' of society, as it develops from a relatively simple to more complex form.

Even if one accepts that the religious institution has adapted to changes in its environment, one need not assume that the industrialisation process has the *same* influence on religious practice whatever society one examines. So, for example, while British institutional religious participation and membership has declined, the level of American religious practice is at least constant if not climbing. One explanation of this contrast has been given by Herberg (1967). He argues that three factors peculiar to the USA have encouraged sustained religious practice within the context of increasing urbanisation and industrialisation: the effects of massive immigration from Europe; the ideology of equality of opportunity; and the absence of an 'established Church' of any kind in the USA. Immigrants, and especially ethnic groups, shared in a religious community in which they found stability and identity in a vast, new, ever-changing 'land of opportunity'. At the same time, all religions enjoy the same social and legal status within the USA, there being no privileged established church. They are, then, a living reflection of the American dream of equality, freedom, and tolerance. Religious practice in America is a symbolic celebration of the urban, middle class, affluent community's life-style and values. Hence the American pulpit is a religious soap-box championing the values and standards of American society, a forum for preaching *secular* values. Thus it appears that a form of secularisation has occurred *within* American religion as a result of and not despite the sustained religious participation and affiliation. As Scharf (1970, p. 174) comments: 'In America there is secularisation within the churches; in England there is secularisation by withdrawal from the churches.'

Secularisation has also been explained in terms of the impact of science and technology on religious beliefs (see, for example, O'Dea, 1966, p. 82). The development of increasingly sophisticated technology means that human needs can be met only with greater ease, control and efficiency but

also to an increasingly higher standard. Thus if one believes, like Mali-
nowski, that human powerlessness and anxiety are the root cause of
reliance on religio-magical beliefs, then technological developments may
make religious faith redundant. 'Mysteries' can now be understood as
manageable 'problems', dealt with by the precision of scientific method
rather than the fervour of religious prayer.

The growth of science over the past fifty years has been massive, not only
in terms of the amount of money spent in the area, but also in terms of the
number of people, publications, and specialties that can be counted within
it. Large-scale research centres – the new 'cathedrals' of today – have
become the norm. The pace of scientific development and its application in
the industrial sector is encapsulated in Cooley's (1976, p. 76) comment that:
'In the 1930s machinery was obsolete in about twenty-five years, during the
1950s in ten years, and at the moment computerised equipment is obsolete
in about three to five years.' This process clearly threatens to make certain
machinery and many human skills obsolescent, and it has also meant that
more and more inventions are made and used by 'ordinary' people who
increasingly have less and less knowledge about how things work. Modern
science, then, plays a major role today as a system of ideas and understanding, but frequently only does so in a way that is quite baffling and
incomprehensible to laypersons. Yet the advance of science, while often
unintelligible for the individual, is nevertheless held to be the major
achievement of modernity. The predominance of the scientific culture is
suggested by the comment made by the editor of the journal *Nature* in the
1930s: 'My grandfather preached the gospel of Christ, my father preached
the gospel of Socialism, I preach the gospel of Science.'

Critique of secularisation

A number of criticisms have been made on the secularisation thesis, most of
which are discussed at length by Glasner (1977). We shall focus on two
aspects of the thesis: the first concerns the institutional decline in religious
participation and affiliation; the second, the alleged displacement of
religion by science.

We can question firstly the extent to which a drop in levels of institutional practices indicates a decline in religiosity. Could we not ask, as
Glasner (1977, p. 34) suggests, 'whether religion continues to flourish
outside the structures which have conventionally embodied it'? Might not
an extra-institutional religious commitment be possible, even in a highly
industrialised, scientific era, as suggested by the increasing importance of
sectarianism in today's society? Sects indeed demand a level of commitment
and involvement which would be 'above and beyond the call of duty' for
members of the traditional faiths.

Conversely, we could ask to what extent is public participation in religious institutions necessarily an indication of religious commitment? Thus, as Demerath (1965) argues, participation may not indicate any deep-rooted religious concern: elite members of a local community may feel obliged to attend Sunday services to sustain their image as public notables whose fortunes are blessed by God. Furthermore, we can also challenge the notion that there was some time in the past when religion was (institutionally) of central concern for the majority of the population of Western societies. Even using statistical evidence as a measure of religious concern, some studies (for example, Hill, 1964; Thomas, 1971) indicate that a past 'Age of Faith' is more myth than reality.

In short, the institutional definition of religion may be historically suspect and sociologically narrow. Some sociologists insist that a broader definition of religion is required. One of the broadest is given by Berger and Luckmann (1963), who claim that people only have a sense of identity, meaning and purpose in their lives because of a deep-seated religious dimension in their personal lives. According to Luckmann (1967), the decline in institutionalised religious practices has meant that personal forms of religion are beginning to emerge, and the 'specialists' and 'experts' of institutionalised religion (priests and theologians) are less able to control, interpret and speak with legitimate authority about this private religion. Whether or not this non-institutional private religion exists, we do need to look more carefully at activities that social actors regard with some sort of 'religious' significance – be it drug-taking, popular demonstration, political rallying, or rock music.

What, then, of the second aspect of the secularisation thesis, that science has dispelled the myths and irrationality of religion? Two issues need to be considered here. First, *has* religion really given way to science? As we have seen, much depends on how one defines religion, and possibly, on how one defines 'science', since one could argue that science is 'the new religion of today'. Second, even if we agree on a definition of religious belief, does the secularisation thesis propose that religion is weaker today than in the past, because people have consciously evaluated the relative explanatory powers of religion and science, and in the end have favoured the latter? If so, such a proposition would need to be challenged, since it implies that ideas and beliefs are judged independently of the social context in which they are found. As we saw with both magic and science, beliefs are sustained not so much for their conceptual veracity but because of the way they express and recreate the collective solidarity of various social groups – be they the Zande or the scientific community. Hence the shift away from a religious to a scientific interpretation of the world is as much a shift in the community in which one lives as it is in the ideas one has. This shift may occur very gradually, by meeting and living with a new group of people, and, crucially, *talking* to them in a language which has little reference to 'the sacred' or other conventionally defined religious dimension.

Nevertheless, science has of course developed as *an institution* over the past two hundred years. A principal reason for this growth has been its success in serving industrial development and profitability through techno-logical innovation. Industrial capitalism not only disrupted the long-standing pre-feudal and feudal traditions that had allowed stability for centuries, but it also initiated change of an order and at a pace never seen before. The division of labour that it set in motion meant that the task of discovery and invention was itself institutionalised, and the occupational role of being 'a scientist' was gradually established in academic, govern-mental and industrial contexts in Western Europe and America, most especially in Germany (Ben-David and Zloczower, 1962).

By providing answers to technical problems of industrialisation, the practical pay-off of science afforded it an ever-increasing prestige within administrative and economic circles, as it was, as Marx suggests, 'pressed into the service of capital'. This social and economic enhancement of the status of scientific inquiry, rather than any direct conceptual superiority it might have over religion, posed the real threat to the pre-eminence of religious orthodoxy and its specialists – the archbishops, clergy and theo-logians. Conceptually speaking, science and religion are, arguably, not necessarily incompatible, in as much as they pose different types of questions about, and give different answers to, the environment. Therefore, many scientists and many theologians may feel quite happy to sustain both religious and scientific conceptions of the universe. Indeed, over the last fifty years many theologians have sought to reassert the importance of religious ideas, not by debunking or attacking scientific discoveries, but by welcoming them as illuminating the immense knowledge behind the divine design of nature.

If anything, then, it was the development of science as a *profession* that may have led to a relative decline in the power of the established religions. Scientists have carved out an area of expertise for themselves which has claimed and received considerable material and symbolic reward through government and industrial patronage. Though public and private funding is crucial in sustaining the material viability of the institution of science today, the practitioners of science have sought to ensure that they be free from public scrutiny and control. The public or government are said to be unable to assess professional work competently. Whereas religious pro-fessionals, such as theologians and Popes, may be able to justify their claims on the basis of their privileged access to revealed truth or 'infallibi-lity', the 'imprimatur' of scientific knowledge-claims is in part a reflection of the exceptional degree of autonomy enjoyed by science, and the mystification of expertise this promotes.

Normally, in societies utilising belief in magic and witchcraft as a means of social control, as we saw with the Azande, the dominant groups – the monarch and princes – claim to have special powers and ultimate authority over the use of the magic, and as such, cannot be charged with witchcraft by subordinate diviners. In societies where religious institutions have been established with their respective experts and specialists, the latter try to ensure that religious ideas and beliefs which give them their *raison d'être* are under *their* control. Luckmann (1967, p. 66) points to 'The vested interests of the religious experts in the recruitment and training of their successors, in the exclusion of laymen from the "higher" forms of sacred knowledge and in defence of privileges.'

The institutionalised scientific enterprise has similarly created its own mythology: this is the notion that rewards only go to those scientists who have merited them by producing results which other scientists have evaluated and accepted through impartial, universally adopted criteria. Any inequality within the scientific community seems to be meritocratic: rewards and privileges only go to those who have fairly and honestly achieved them. Elite members of science can claim that their reputation 'speaks for itself'. Yet there are good grounds for questioning this view of the relationship between reward and the value of scientific findings: it appears that the value of knowledge-claims is much more dependent on the highly variable context of negotiation between competitor scientists than on any alleged standard criteria of evaluation. Thus some groups may be in a weaker 'negotiating position' because of their *structural* position in the institution of science: as Mulkay (1979, p. 26) says, 'women and the members of other social categories in science are systematically prevented from . . . establishing that their work is of high quality'. Thus while the low rank of women in science may be explained by participants in terms of the low quality of their work, we should not necessarily regard this as indicating objectively inferior work by female as compared with male scientists; instead, it is best regarded as an ideological justification for sexism in science. A similar type of argument applies with regard to the treatment given by scientific orthodoxy to deviant knowledge-claims that challenge the conceptual and social status quo, as suggested in the earlier reference to parapsychology and acupuncture.

These comments on the institutions of magic, religion, and science refer to the way in which elite practitioners *within* them can legitimise the privileges they receive over and against other members. In terms of their relationship to the wider society, professional experts, be they magicians, bishops, or scientists, will strive to ensure that the conceptual and social bases of their expertise will be publicly valued, either by restricting recruitment to their ranks or by mystifying their skills (see Chapter 9 on work). But dominant groups in society are not only, or even necessarily, constituted by trained 'experts' of one form or another. Thus there may be additional ideological resources that are drawn upon to help sustain the socio-economic status quo and cultural belief-systems, which may have their roots in religious or scientific conceptions of the world, but which have become generalised political conceptions about 'what's right and what's wrong', 'who should get what', and so on. Some of the more prevalent of these conceptions can be examined by considering the role played by the mass media in the construction of social ideologies in Western capitalism.

10.4 THE MASS MEDIA

What are commonly called the 'mass media' are those institutions which use the increasingly sophisticated technological developments of industrialism for the communication of ideas, for the purposes of information, entertainment and persuasion, to large-scale audiences, whether this be by means of newspapers, radio, television, books, magazines, advertising billboards, or whatever. Compared even with the nineteenth century, the mass media in industrial society have become hugely expanded both in terms of the *scope* of the audiences they reach and in terms of the *range* of the media available to those audiences.

Exposure to and consumption of media products has become an integral part of the daily lives of the majority of the members of Western societies, occupying a considerable proportion of their leisure time, and, as we shall suggest shortly, providing them to a considerable extent with their picture of social reality. Television, for instance, represents the major and most pervasive mass medium of today. It is the principal leisure activity of most adults and children, the 'organiser' of their entertainment and social life, missed when unavailable, and a source of information and ideas widely regarded as authoritative and trustworthy.

Given these high levels of exposure, the media constitute potentially strategic socialisation agencies, since they serve as sources of information and ideas for the large numbers of people consuming their products. As Golding (1974, p. 78) says, 'The media are central in the provision of ideas and images which people use to interpret and understand a great deal of their everyday experience.' More specifically, they represent an institutionalised channel for the distribution of *social knowledge* and hence a potentially powerful instrument of *social control* (as well as *social critique*) sustaining or challenging the status quo. As we have suggested elsewhere, there exists a variety of agencies disseminating ideas and values, and shaping actors' perceptions – the family, the school, the peer group, the ethnic group, and so on – so that the impact of the media on behaviour and attitudes cannot be seen as simple and unambiguous. For instance, the short-term effects of television on voting preferences during election campaigns appear limited, but its general long-term role in legitimating a system of parliamentary democracy may be much more fundamental and profound. Our discussion of the media, too, will focus not on the 'immediate' effects of media messages, but on their more pervasive role as a source of social knowledge, ideas, and beliefs for those exposed to them.

The media as providers of 'experience' and 'knowledge'

While modern industrial societies provide their members with access to a range of material resources, cultural artefacts and opportunities unavailable in former times, the nature of these societies is such that they are characterised by social differentiation and segregation, rather than sociological homogeneity and integration. This means that 'the world' has become much larger and more fragmented for most of us, no longer encompassed or measured solely by the immediate community in which we live. But this larger world is normally *not directly* experienced by us, despite greater national and international mobility. The media provide us with much indirect experience of events and processes happening beyond our own social experience. We increasingly 'know' more, and are encouraged to do so, through the mediated experiences of TV, films, radio, the press, books and magazines. The media have, then, become steadily more influential in defining 'reality', in encouraging a common image of society among its members. As Cohen and Young (1973, p. 342) observe:

> The mass media provide a major source of knowledge in a segregated society of what the consensus actually is and what is the nature of deviation from it. They conjure up for each group with its limited stock of social knowledge, what 'everyone else' believes.

The media and the construction of reality and consensus

But this view of the media as merely neutral or 'open' vehicles has received much critical sociological scrutiny. The mass media do not simply provide information and reflect a social world – rather, they *structure* it for us, not simply increasing our knowledge of the world but helping us to 'make sense' of it. Topics of conversation among workers, children at school, pub-drinkers and so on, are not only generated by what they have seen, heard, or read in the media, but the *content* and *context* of these conversations will be greatly shaped by media exposure. More fundamentally, the media represent the major means by which such individuals, groups and classes construct an understanding of the lives, meanings, and practices and values of *other* individuals, groups, and classes, and acquire a picture of how the whole of 'social reality' hangs together.

While there may exist in newspapers or in TV news an explicit propaganda position which deliberately aims to further particular views, ideas and values, such direct activity represents only a part of the media's influence. More subtle, less overt, but none the less important processes are

The pluralist view of the media

The popular image of the mass media – particularly of TV and the press - and one perpetuated by media personnel themselves, has a strong pluralist flavour about it. In this view, the media are important agencies within the democratic process of a 'free society', ensuring an unrestricted public airing of differences of opinion on issues of public interest and concern; in the ideal healthy democracy, the opportunity for free expression of a wide range of voices and opinions is a fundamental prerequisite. According to this pluralist conception, the media in Western societies contain a diversity of opinion and information, they are independent and not state-controlled institutions, presenting a variety of 'definitions of reality'.

Furthermore, the media allegedly act as neutral autonomous servants of the public: besides providing entertainment, they inform and educate the public and, more importantly, raise issues, act as watchdogs of the highest and lowest, and as guardians of the public interest against violation of generally accepted standards and patterns of behaviour, or abuse of power. The 'grilling' of politicians in TV interviews, the 'digging' of the investigative reporter, and the identification of disturbing new 'problems' all allegedly bear testimony to the media's public service role in social critique and democratic public enlightenment.

Such a view is buttressed by the argument that the media maintain above all the *sovereignty of the consumer*, attempting to satisfy consumer demand by 'giving them what they want', be it news, fiction or entertainment: the audience decides, and media owners and personnel respond to their wishes. Thus, any accusations that the media resort to a 'consensus' portrayal of the world are, according to this view, fundamentally misconceived, since the media are said to be merely *reflecting* ideas existing in society among the mass of the population, freely arrived at and accepted by them as 'sensible'.

at work in which implicit frameworks or guidelines for interpreting social reality, for 'making sense' of a problematic world, are provided, which encourage certain lines of thinking and perception, and discourage others. Reality, then, is constructed by imposing a *selective* framework which may exclude alternative interpretations or meaning systems.

One of the most important implications of this process is the media's reliance on an apparently prevailing *consensus* for the framework in which ideas and issues are presented, and in which action is interpreted: that is, they work within a climate of opinion which they themselves have played some considerable part in constructing – they both *utilise* a consensual image of society and help to *reproduce* it. This assumes that the majority of, if not all, members of society are in agreement on a wide range of norms, values and ideas, and therefore on what are 'reasonable' and 'acceptable' patterns of behaviour. The news media select and interpret events within the terms of this pre-existing consensus. This may not necessarily be consciously done – in fact, often in trying to be unbiased and objective, in attempting to examine a particular issue 'rationally', journalists, draw on consensual values unconsciously. As Hall *et al.* (1978, p. 55) observe of news reporting:

> This process of 'making an event intelligible' is a social process – constituted by a number of specific journalistic practices which embody (often only implicitly) crucial assumptions about what society is and how it works. One such background assumption is the consensual nature of society; the process of significa- tion – giving social meanings to events – both assumes and helps to construct society as a consensus. We exist as members of one society *because* – it is assumed – we share a common stock of cultural knowledge with our fellow men ... This 'consensual' viewpoint has important political consequences ... It carries the assumption that we also all have roughly the same *interests* in the society, and that we all roughly have an equal share of power in the society ... The media are among the institutions whose practices are most widely and consistently predicated upon the assumption of a national consensus.

Thus there supposedly exist no fundamental conflicts of interests between groups and classes; there are legitimate institutionalised means for resolving conflicts that do occur, and members of society enjoy equality before the law and equal access to decision-making opportunities by means of the conventional institutions of parliamentary democracy. Since legiti- mate political activity is seen to be conducted only through parliamentary democratic channels, the media tend to regard any activity going beyond this as not permissible, and its perpetrators as consequently less *credible* actors. Thus non-consensual opinions receive more critical attention, or no attention at all; where such dissenting views do appear, they are frequently made to appear peripheral, fanatical delusions, or mere fads; they are commonly portrayed as embracing a world view which is unreal and unnatural – literally a *misunderstanding* of reality. Thus in the news media, spokespersons expressing 'legitimate' opinions and values will be much less likely to have their basic assumptions questioned (because they echo the prevailing consensus), while those of 'non-legitimate' persuasion will be pressed to justify theirs. Those not operating within the rules of the game, that is, those who disregard the rules about what is considered 'reasonable' disagreement, are portrayed as marginal to, or outside the debate, because they are 'extremist' or 'irrational'.

Deviant values are regarded as restricted to a minority, and the likeli- hood of dissent being widely felt is generally perceived as too remote for consideration. As Westergaard (1977, pp. 110–13) observes:

> The possibility, for example, that large wage-claims, strikes and go-slows, direct action of other kinds, may reflect popular clamour for equity in a society where inequality is entrenched ... is not so much rejected as, simply, never more than momentarily entertained. When the media publicise dissent, in short, the effect of their interpretation is to minimise its sources and objects, to magnify its

fragmentation and incoherence . . . The eddies and currents of dissent in popular consciousness find virtually no representation in media interpretations of the world.

The media, then, constitute crucially important vehicles of basic social and political values, with a central role in creating and sustaining a consensus, and in structuring its *style*. Media personnel would probably maintain that they are merely portraying the world and its values 'as they are', and *reflecting* public opinion and conventional wisdom. This assumes that 'public opinion' is some supra-social entity in whose construction social actors play no part. But what comes to be accepted as conventional wisdom and public opinion is likely to be determined more by some actors and institutions than others – that is, opportunity to influence the production of ideas is unequally distributed.

But even at this point, those who regard the media as mere neutral and faithful reflectors of social reality might well point out that there exist some media outlets for non-conservative, even critical, social and political values (for example, in newspapers like the *Daily Mirror* and the *Guardian*, and in television documentaries and dramas). But in the 'popular' press this expression of 'alternative' values takes an essentially mild form, with support for a 'moderate' Labour party, but not one which might effect a thoroughgoing socialist challenge to the power of capital. The popular press

> takes a 'radical' editorial orientation no further than to a blend of vacuous populism with support for political moderation and social compromise . . . [they] blow a carefully tuned populist trumpet. Their tone is 'matey' and aspires to plain speaking; they pride themselves on talking for as well as to ordinary men and women . . . When they attack and 'expose', their targets are not the routine power of capital, property and profit in common affairs; occasionally, of course, business malpractice . . . but far more regularly officialdom (Westergaard, 1977, p. 103).

Furthermore, while the output of the media as a whole is not blatantly and uniformly consensual, it remains true that critical ideas and opinion do not amount to a *systematic* critique of existing social arrangements, but are essentially spasmodic and exceptional in their appearance. The critical character of the media is then severely restricted not so much by deliberate censorship – although this does occur – but by the routine practices of media production.

The manufacture of news

The dominant thrust of our argument so far has been that the media constitute a major source of knowledge and beliefs for members of industrial societies, helping to structure their perception of social reality and its constituent elements. One of the realms of media output particularly central to this process is that of *the news*. While it is a popular cliché that 'you shouldn't believe everything you read in the newspapers or see on TV', most people, reading the newspaper or watching a TV news broadcast, expect that they will obtain a picture of what significant events are occurring in the world, of 'what's happening'.

But as media researchers have increasingly observed, the news doesn't merely 'happen' – rather it is *made*, it is a *socially manufactured product*, the result of a social process with a distinct order to it. Thus items included in a TV broadcast or in a newspaper are not in reality the *only* events of that day, but are *defined* as 'news' by the media. In other words, the news is not merely a faithful account of events whose significance and interest is intrinsically obvious and unproblematic, but it is a socially constructed from of knowledge dependent upon a whole host of factors: media personnel's notions of what is important and interesting; the contexts in which the news is produced and the sources from which it comes, and so on. As Hall *et al.* (1978, p. 53) stress:

> The media do not simply and transparently report events which are 'naturally' newsworthy *in themselves*. News is the end-product of a complex process which begins with a systematic sorting and selecting of events and topics according to a socially constructed set of categories.

This process of selection – or 'agenda-setting' – does not occur randomly: on the contrary, it is the systematic product of a number of forces, as we shall see shortly.

Constraints on media news

What becomes 'news' is shaped not only by material and economic pressures, by cultural and normative constraints, but also by 'internal' organisational pressures within the media, which are equally potent contributors to the reproduction of the status quo. As Golding and Elliott (1979, p. 18) observe:

> The content of broadcast news portrays a very particular view of the world that we can label ideological ... This is not the result of a conspiracy within newsrooms or of the inadequacies, professional or political, of broadcast journalists. It is a necessary result of the structure of news-gathering and production, and of the routines and conventions built into broadcasting practice.

More specifically, the frameworks of perception which media news employs to interpret events and issues are partly 'internally' generated through editorial practices and procedures, technical restrictions, professional ideologies about journalistic objectivity and impartiality, and so on. A number of practical constraints, such as time limits (working against the clock), the desire to produce visually interesting material, pressures to obtain 'hot' news, as well as the standard size of a newspaper or length of a news broadcast, structure the need for a constant 'amount' of news to be regularly available, in more or less constant portions (foreign news, sports, industrial news, and so on) and often consigned to specific sections of the paper or programme. Therefore, for these reasons alone one cannot regard news reporting as merely recounting faithfully 'what happens in the world'.

The media operate with definitions of what is significant and 'newsworthy', with 'a set of institutional definitions and meanings ... commonly referred to as *news values*' (Hall, in Cohen and Young, 1973, p. 87). Journalists claim that their professional training, and expertly acquired 'nose' for a story, give them a special capacity for recognising what events and individuals are 'news' by virtue of their unusual or humanly interesting nature. Thus, for instance, stories which can be made dramatic and visually attractive (with suitably available photographs or film), those which can be reduced to the level of personalities and individuals, those which are immediate and presentable as completed accounts of discrete events or issues, those which are supposedly entertaining, quirkily diverting or titillating, or especially those which involve 'bad news' or the disruption of the normal pattern of events, are more likely to be considered newsworthy by media personnel.

As a result, certain areas of social life are given greater attention by the news media, and a particularly vital aspect of this agenda-setting process is the tendency for those in powerful and advantaged positions to be *more frequently consulted* for information and opinion. As Hall *et al.* (1978, p. 58) say:

> This is what Becker has called 'the hierarchy of credibility' – the likelihood that those in powerful or high status positions in society who offer opinions about controversial topics will have their definitions accepted, because such spokesmen are understood to have access to more accurate or specialised information on particular topics than the majority of the population.

While it would be too simple to suggest a conscious process of collusion between the news media and those in dominant positions in society as bringing about these circumstances, it is nevertheless the case that particular *structures of interpretation* are established which serve as given frames of reference within which issues can be 'naturally' located. Alternative interpretations have to be able to operate within this framework or have to face a struggle for recognition and legitimacy with the cards stacked heavily against them.

While it is obviously important to recognise the constraining effects and influence of technical and organisational aspects of media production on the nature of the end product, we cannot ignore or minimise a fundamental material constraint, that of the *pattern of ownership and control*. Quite simply, the media are big business, owned by or linked to some of the largest capitalist enterprises in society, so it would be surprising to find them adopting a consistently critical perspective on society and/or embracing a framework of interpretation and explanation at odds with that of the dominant value system – revealing social inequalities, offering radical solutions, and so on.

But the media are not a mere component of capitalist society: they are increasingly a part of capitalist commercial conglomerates. The growth of monopoly capitalism in the second half of the twentieth century is graphically reflected in the mass media, with their progressive concentration in the hands of a few large companies as a result of mergers and takeovers. In 1970, for instance, in Britain, five companies were responsible for 65 per cent of record sales, 70 per cent of paperback books, 78 per cent of cinema audiences and 71 per cent of daily newspaper sales, and the top five commercial TV companies accounted for 74 per cent of TV audiences.

Thus, the media have increasingly become parts of powerful capitalist interests through a steady concentration of control. There has occurred a progressive *interrelation* of different sectors of the media, with large corporations coming to accumulate control in several sectors simultaneously: in Britain, ATV for instance has interests not only in television but in feature films, commercial radio, theatres and music; Granada TV's television interests are supplemented by holdings in music, films, commercial radio, books and bingo; Thames Television, controlled by EMI, one of the world's biggest record producers, have sports facilities, films, commercial radio and theatres under its control.

The major motivation for this diversification and conglomeration appears to be the desire on the part of large enterprises to find ways of maintaining and expanding their profit potential. The acquisition of interests in a range of media outlets allows these companies to spread their risks, to minimise the possibility of being trapped in a sphere of the media which experiences a down-swing in popularity, and to cushion the effects of having to reduce their control in any particular media sphere as a result of possible government limitations on concentration. But such diversification also faciliates certain very profitable production strategies, one of which has recently become highly prevalent – that of the 'spin-off'. If a large organisation controls a variety of media outlets, then a single media product – say, a film – can generate a great variety of associated profitable 'spin-offs'. Audiences who have seen a film are persuaded to buy the book of the film, the special glossy magazine, the music from the sound-track, the book recounting the making of the film, and so on.

A number of important implications follow from the nature and pattern of media ownership. The goal of maximum profit and the need to maintain

The conglomeration of the British press[1]		
	Main British press interests	**Selected other media interests**	**Selected non-media interests**
Pergamon (Maxwell)	*Daily Mirror* *Sunday Mirror* *Sunday People* *Daily Record* *Sunday Mail* (Total circulation: 11.7 million)	Central Independent TV Rediffusion cablevision Pergamon Press International Learning Systems British Printing and Communications Corporation	E. J. Arnold (furniture) Hollis Plastics Paulton Investments Jet Ferry International (Panama) Mares Australes (Chile)
News Corporation (Murdoch)	*Sun* *News of the World* *The Times* *Sunday Times* *Times Educational Supplement* (Total circulation: 10.2 million)	Satellite TV Collins (Fontana) News Group Productions (New York) Channel Ten – 10 (Sydney) *Daily Sun* (Brisbane)	Ansett Transport (Australia) Santos (Natural gas – Australia) News-Eagle (Offshore oil – Australia) Snodland Fibres Whitefriars Investment
Fleet Holdings (Matthews)	*Daily Express* *Sunday Express* *Daily Star* *The Standard* Morgan-Grampian Magazines (Total circulation: 7.1 million)	TV-AM Asian Business Press (Singapore) Specialist Publications (Hong Kong) Capital Radio	JBS Properties M G Insurance Lefpalm Ltd David McKay Inc. (USA) (Trafalgar House)[2]
Reed Group[3]	IPC Magazines IPC Business Press Berrows Newspapers (Total circulation: approx. 12 million)[4]	Fleetway Publications (USA) Hamlyn Books Anglia TV A & W Publishers Inc. (USA) Européenne de Publications SA (France)	Crown Paints Maybank/Krever International (Bahamas) Reed Finance (South Africa) Reed Consolidated Industries (Australia) Consolidated Industries Holdings (Zimbabwe)

continued overleaf

The conglomeration of the British press–*continued*			
	Main British press interests	**Selected other media interests**	**Selected non-media interests**
Associated Newspapers (Rothermere)	*Daily Mail* *Mail on Sunday* *Weekend* Northcliffe Newspapers Associated South Eastern Newspapers (Total circulation: 5.3 million)	London Broadcasting Company Herald-Sun TV (Australia) Plymouth Sound Wyndham Theatres Harmsworth House Pub. (USA)	Blackfriars Oil (North Sea) Bouverie Investments (Canada) Burton Reproduction GmbH (W. Germany) Transport Group Holdings Jetlink Ferries
International Thomson Organization (Thomson)[5]	Thomson Regional Newspapers *Scotsman* Northwood Publications Whitehorn Press Standbrook Publications Illustrated Newspapers (Total circulation: 3.6 million)	Thomas Nelson Michael Joseph Radio Forth Thomson Publications (South Africa) Thomson Communications (Denmark)	Thomson North Sea Thomson Holidays Rym SA (Tunisia) Britannia Airways International Thomson Organisation – Canada (parent company)
Pearson Longman (Cowdray)	Westminster Press Group *Financial Times* *The Economist* *Northern Echo* (Total circulation: 1.8 million)	Longman Penguin Goldcrest Films Yorkshire TV Viking (USA) Morie Channel	Midhurst Corporation (USA) Whitehall Mining (Canada) Lazard Bros Royal Doulton Tableware Camco Inc. (USA)
British Electric Traction[3]	Argus Newspapers Illustrated Publications Model and Allied Publications	Capital Radio Thames Television Reditune GmbH (W. Germany) Communication	Eddison Plant BET Investments (property) United Freight Holdings (Australia)

The conglomeration of the British press–*continued*			
	Main British press interests	**Selected other media interests**	**Selected non-media interests**
	Industrial Newspapers Electrical Press (Total circulation: 1.4 million)	Channels Inc. (USA)	United Passenger Transport (South Africa) Almana-Boulton (Qatar)
Lonrho (Rowland)	*Observer* George Outram and Co. Scottish and Universal Newspapers (Total circulation: 1.3 million)	Radio Clyde Border TV Radio Ltd. (Zambia) Times Newspapers (Zambia) Gramma Records (Zimbabwe)	Whyte and Mackay Distillers Firsteel Group Consolidated Holdings (Kenya) Construction Associated (Zimbabwe) HCC Investments (South Africa)

Sources: *Who Owns Whom 1983*; Company Reports; Audit Bureau of Circulation (1983); Press Council; Independent Broadcasting Authority.
Notes:[1] All circulation figures exclude freesheets and controlled-circulation magazines. [2]Now an associated company, formerly the conglomerate parent company. [3]No dominant shareholder. [4]Excluding circulation of trade, technical and professional publications. [5]Not including North American chain of TV, radio and press interests. Source: J. Curran and J. Seaton, *Power without Responsibility: the Press and Broadcasting in Britain*, London, Methuen (1985).

advertising revenue, to attract the widest audience, to appeal to everyone and often no one, increase the likelihood of an attempt to find the 'lowest common denominator' at which to direct output. Furthermore, an equally vital consequence is implicit in concentration, as Murdock and Golding (1977, p. 105) point out:

Concentration limits the range and diversity of views and opinions which are able to find public expression. More significantly, it is those views and opinions representing the least powerful social groups which are systematically excluded by the process of concentration.

Thus the 'ownership and control of the means of mental production', as Marxists such as Miliband (1973, p. 203) put it, becomes increasingly concentrated also.

The Marxist view of the media

The Marxist view of the media is very different from that of media personnel and the pluralist conception to which we referred earlier, in emphasising that the media and their products cannot be seen outside the context of the material interests of capitalist society, its system of production, and relations of domination and control. For the Marxist, the media constitute a fundamental instrument of control possessed by the dominant class, who, besides controlling material production, also control the production of ideas through ownership of the communications media. The media serve, along with the family, the education system, religion, and so on, as part of the ideological apparatus used by the dominant class to reproduce the system of class domination.

The media, according to Marxists, systematically reproduce the ideology and so hegemony of the dominant class, and disseminate these ruling ideas into the consciousness of subordinate groups, thus shaping the form and impact of the value systems of these groups. They provide justifications and legitimations for prevailing socio-economic and political arrangements, excluding radical critiques and challenges to the system of material and power inequalities. Thus the presentation of a whole range of institutions, events and behaviour patterns in society (for example, patterns of inequality and poverty, deviants, women) is systematically distorted, since they take bourgeois capitalist society as their given base-point for interpreting social reality and for understanding social relations within it.

Ethnic relations, deviance and the media

A good illustration of our arguments about the socially produced nature of media news, and more particularly of its role in defining the issues and the scope and area of the debate, can be seen in the reporting of ethnic relations. Studies suggest that while the media do not necessarily encourage racial prejudice, their style of reporting defines the *presence* of ethnic minorities as an objective problem for society – that is, ethnic relations are a matter of the problems created by coloured people merely being here. Hartman and Husband's study (1974) found that in areas without large immigrant populations, children obtained their knowledge, ideas and opinions about immigrants predominantly from the media rather than through personal contact, and moreover, as a result of this exposure, immigrants were seen as causing trouble and conflict, as being a 'social problem' in themselves.

Coverage of ethnic minorities in the media tends to be disproportionately unfavourable, focusing particularly on the immediate social and political tensions of the presence of ethnic minorities, with little real analysis of their structural position – for instance, in the early 1970s, black 'mugging' received considerable media coverage, but the economic, social and educational deprivations of blacks did not. The absence of *background exposi-*

tion by the media of events and issues is particularly noticeable in the case of ethnic relations: in their reporting, the news media give little consideration to the long-term and more immediate historical contexts in which ethnic relations have evolved. As we have seen in Chapter 4 when discussing race relations, British colonial history has had crucial implications for the way in which those of Asian and African descent are perceived, though the widely exploitative nature of this period of British capitalist expansion is rarely discussed in the media. Perhaps even more pertinently, analysis of the *context* in which post-war immigration from the Commonwealth into Britain occurred is largely neglected in discussion of ethnic relations. Commonwealth immigration was encouraged by governments and employers to satisfy post-war demand for labour in jobs of low pay and inferior work conditions and hours; the media 'silence' on the economic functions of immigrant labour contrasts sharply with their frequently strident attacks on newly arrived groups of immigrants, such as Ugandan, Malawi and Kenyan Asians, or the dependents of already resident immigrants. Sensational and exaggerated headlines condemning their supposed exploitation of welfare services can only serve to generate negative connotations around those of minority ethnic background and to confirm their presence as a 'problem'.

This confirmatory effect also appears in the reporting of deviance and crime, where the media are crucial agents in the defining of groups as deviant, as violators of prevailing social norms. They shape the public knowledge about crime, and infuse that understanding with particular interpretations, so that the framework of what exactly constitutes 'the problem of crime' as a matter for public debate is set not by any objective criteria of frequency, seriousness, or whatever, but by the 'picture' of crime portrayed by the media. In Chapter 11 on deviance, we shall examine at greater length how the attachment of a deviant label to some actors and to some behaviour is very much a social process, with distinct implications for those on the receiving end and for their subsequent interaction with the rest of society: here we wish to emphasise that a particularly vital element of the media's role in this defining process serves to reinforce and sustain a dominant consensual morality.

As Cohen (1973), and Hall *et al.* (1978) have stressed, the media are frequently prime contributors to the creation of 'folk devils', around whom 'moral panics' take root, exaggerating the incidence of a phenomenon, increasing the likelihood of it being noticed, whipping up concern over its supposed epidemic proportions, and mobilising society against the perceived threat. This process of manufacturing 'folk devils' occurs particularly in periods of social, economic or political crisis or upheaval, and the responsibility for this state of affairs is directed at groups whose marginal structural position makes them ideal scapegoats. The exaggeration and stereotyping of their behaviour as 'mindless', 'wild' and irrationally founded simultaneously places them outside acceptable boundaries and depicts them as threats to social order, so that any explanation which locates their behaviour structurally, and critically analyses the contribution of existing social arrangements to their actions, is rendered irrelevant and easily dismissed.

Thus Teddy Boys, Mods and Rockers, Hippies, Skinheads, 'drug-takers' and 'football hooligans' have been prime targets for media identification as 'folk devils', and the subsequently created 'moral panic' has served to reinforce dominant social norms and to legitimise increased formal social control in the shape of 'law and order' campaigns.

The media and industrial relations

While such areas of behaviour are never far from the headlines of media news, pride of place in this respect is more regularly accorded to the reporting of industrial relations and economic affairs. In recent years, there has been a considerable amount of sociological investigation into the presentation of industrial and economic news, casting grave doubt on the notion that the news media present impartial and authentic records of events, of 'what's happened'.

The Glasgow University Media Group

The work of the Glasgow University Media Group has been the focus of major controversies in mass media research in Britain during the last decade. The Group's studies, which involve detailed analyses of the verbal and visual content of television news bulletins, have focused predominantly on the reporting of industrial relations and disputes. Their conclusions have strongly challenged the notion that this reporting presents an impartial, balance and even-handed account of such events. Rather, their results suggest a consistent, routinely biased presentation, through both words and pictures: employers and governments are portrayed favourably and positively, while workers on strike appear unfavourably and negatively as trouble-makers, disrupters of social harmony and threats to the 'national interest'.

Similarly their analysis of TV news coverage of the Falklands war emphasises how news bulletins relied very heavily on official sources of information, so that their presentation of the war was uncritically slanted towards the Government's interpretation of events and its justification of the conflict and of particular military action within it.

Both the BBC and ITV companies have consistently rejected the Glasgow group's analyses, and their work has been challenged by Martin Harrison (1985) who claims, on the basis of an analysis of printed scripts and transcripts of ITV bulletins, that the Group has been guilty of using evidence selectively and imprecisely to suit their thesis of media news bias. The Glasgow Group in turn, however, have suggested that Harrison's analysis is itself flawed, since he relied only on the ITV transcripts, which show significant discrepancies from their own video-recordings and transcripts.

The general conclusion to be drawn from such research is that trade unions, workers and strikers tend to be portrayed unfavourably as the root cause of national economic problems and under-performance, of industrial trouble and disruption, and of harm and inconvenience to the lives and interests of their fellow-citizens. Specifically, industrial relations tend to be discussed around notions of a unifying 'national interest', so that the range of images and interpretations employed by the media are contained within a set of *consensual assumptions* about the relations between capital and labour. Thus strikes are located within the context of their impact on *our* national economy, from whose smooth running we all benefit equally, and from whose disruption we all suffer equally, regardless of the disproportionate concentration of ownership of wealth and property and the unequal distribution of the capitalist cake. The state is presented as the neutral overseer of the national interest in handling the economy and in industrial disputes, working disinterestedly for 'the public good'; 'sectional interests' are equated with the shortsighted demands of greedy workers and/or the dubious political motives of a minority of activists, rather than as arising from the structure of inequality within capitalist society.

Accordingly, strikes are invariably 'bad news' and to be deplored, regardless of any inherent justice in the strikers' grievances or demands, or in the principles on which the action is based. They are always disruptive because they interrupt the production of goods and services that are equally beneficial to all. The 'national interest' is the ultimate barometer against which action is to be measured, so that trade union action is reported and analysed primarily within the context of national economic performance, its impact on trade and foreign customers, and only incidentally, *if at all*, within a framework which assesses the inherent validity or justice of their actions.

In fact, union leaders are invariably asked to provide justification for industrial action *vis-à-vis* society with little regard or consideration for the internal merits of their case. As a matter of *routine*, 'There is the constant assumption of the correctness of the managerial argument, that strikes achieve nothing and are basically irrational' (Walton and Davis, 1977, p. 129). Workers, then, can have little hope that their actions will be interpreted as matters of legitimate grievance, or still less as expressions of a fundamental conflict of interests in the work-place or the wage-labour relationship: their actions are more likely to be seen as disrupting the orderly patterns which management are seeking to maintain, as threatening national economic health, or as the misplaced, inexplicable blood-mindedness of workers led by the nose by minority elements.

Disputes and poor economic performance, then, unequivocally become problems caused by the *work-force* in a particular industry, with little reference to the inadequacies of management, investment strategies or international recession. The outcome of this is the distortion and simplification, not necessarily by conscious design, of industrial and economic matters in media news. A striking example in recent years has been the way in which the news media have tended to present inflation as unambiguously linked to wage increases, so that 'the problems of an economic system are thus reduced to the irresponsible actions of trade unionists' (Philo, Beharrel and Hewitt, 1977, p. 20). Yet, as these writers note, even *The Times* acknowledged that, during the first six months of 1975, average earnings rose by 6.1 per cent, while retail prices rose 17.3 per cent.

Now the successful dissemination of a particular explanation of a fundamental economic problem like inflation is not merely important for the way in which it attributes responsibility and to whom, but also for the acceptability and legitimacy accorded to *policies* for its *solution*. If wage rises are presented as 'causing inflation', policies controlling wage increases, irrespective of their effects on the distribution of wealth and patterns of inequality, may come to be regarded as right and proper, so that 'Rationality and hard "realism" are thus presented as being the prerogative of those who are in favour of wage restraint and of allowing unemployment to rise' (Philo, Beharrel and Hewitt, 1977, p. 13).

These processes of distortion and simplification are also manifested in the picture of the incidence and patterns of strikes presented in the news media, and in the *angle of emphasis* adopted in their interpretation. The *Bad News* team (Glasgow University Media Group, 1976) observed consistent 'over-reporting' of disputes in some British industries, notably car manufacture, and transport and communications, to the neglect of others, and a systematic tendency to report disputes with the emphasis on such themes as 'inconvenience to the public' and the 'threat to national economic interest'.

Furthermore, the partial nature of media news is reflected in the tendency to indulge in sensationalised reporting, which concentrates on *consequences* and *effects*, on incidents and personalities, at the expense of analysis of causes and of structural background and context. Thus interviews with commuters affected by a transport strike, films or photographs of jostling picket lines or of housewives in supermarket queues, are given greater prominence, not least because they correspond with 'news values' of what constitutes 'good television' or 'good copy'. While this may satisfy media personnel it frequently means that the real issues at stake in an industrial dispute become lost, and the dominant interpretation of strikes as disruptive and irrational, embraced by owners and managers, is sustained.

In fact, the importance of the internal construction and presentation of news items, while superficially appearing non-problematic, cannot be underestimated. The *Bad News* study points to the TV news media's tendency to seek 'facts' and information from official management sources, and to rely on workers to provide filmable 'events', while the *location* of filmed interviews may give authority to or discredit those involved: official spokespeople and management are far more likely to be interviewed in the quiet and comfortable surroundings of a studio or office, while workers' representatives more frequently have to put their case outside factory gates, surrounded by vociferous colleagues, background traffic, or whatever. Moreover, the *language* in which disputes are reported is an integral part of the framework of interpretation provided by the media. The use of such terms as 'moderates', 'militants', or 'extremists', of 'wildcat' or 'lightening' stikes, of 'violence on the picket-lines', constitutes a symbolic code which grants implicit legitimacy to managers' and owners' actions and opinions, while simultaneously denying it to those of the workers. But occasionally, of course, the news media are faced with the problem of high-status occupational groups involved in disputes but not fitting the stereotype of 'revolting workers'. In such circumstances these disputes receive rather different treatment, so that the grievances of, say, doctors are presented in a more sympathetic light, worthy of more legitimate consideration, and are reinforced by the use of more 'polite' language ('industrial action' rather than 'strike', 'representatives' rather than 'leaders', and so on).

Ultimately, then, our argument is that the news and the media generally present a systematically partial account of social reality, drawing on particular sets of values to interpret action and events. As we have stressed, it is neither merely a question of any deliberate, purposive, conspiratorial process of manipulation, nor a question of the expression of bias in *particular* news items or on the part of *particular* media personnel. More fundamental are the kinds of assumptions *regularly* invoked in interpreting the world, so that the content of the media is *organised around* particular explanations and solutions. In this sense the ideological character of the media resides in their creating and reinforcing acceptance of dominant social and political values, which take as given, and accord legitimacy to, the socio-political and economic status quo. The provision of this 'social knowledge' by the media serves to shape the ideas and beliefs and hence the consciousness of actors, and as such constitutes an important dimension of the mechanisms of social control in society.

10.5 CONCLUSION

This chapter has suggested that ideas and beliefs may not only be used to assist members of society in understanding their world, but also as resources serving a variety of groups. Since the structural position of these groups may be unequal, it is more likely that those in advantaged positions will obtain greater benefit from the successful dissemination and institutionalisation of a particular system of belief. As Evans-Pritchard (1967, p. 21) says 'any section of society enjoying special privileges, whether magical or otherwise, produces its own mythology, the function of the myth being to give sanction to the possession of the exclusive privileges'.

REFERENCES TO CHAPTER 10

Beharrel, P. and Philo, G. (eds) (1977) *Trade Unions and the Media*, London, Macmillan.
Ben-David, J. and Zloczower, A. (1962) 'Universities and Academic Systems in Modern Societies', *European Journal of Sociology*, vol. 3, pp. 45–84.
Berger, P. and Luckmann, T. (1963) 'The Sociology of Religion and the Sociology of Knowledge', *Sociology and Social Research*, vol. 47, pp. 417–27.
Cohen, S. (1973) *Folk Devils and Moral Panics*, London, Paladin.
Cohen, S. and Young, J. (eds) (1973) *The Manufacture of News*, London, Constable.
Collins, H. and Pinch, T. (1979) 'The Construction of the Paranormal', in Wallis (1979).
Cooley, M. (1976) 'Contradictions of Science in Advanced Capitalist Society', in H. Rose and S. Rose (eds), *The Political Economy of Science*, London, Macmillan.
Curran, J. and Seaton, J. (1985) *Power without Responsibility: The Press and Broadcasting in Britain*, London, Methuen.
Demerath, N. (1965) *Social Class in American Protestantism*, Chicago, Rand McNally.
Douglas, M. (1980) *Evans-Pritchard*, London, Fontana.
Durkheim, E. (1965) *The Elementary Forms of the Religious Life*, New York, Free Press (first published in 1912).
Evans-Pritchard, E. (1937) *Witchcraft, Oracles and Magic Among the Azande*, Oxford, Clarendon Press.
Evans-Pritchard, E. (1967) 'The Morphology and Function of Magic', in J. Middleton (ed.), *Magic, Witchcraft and Curing*, London, Natural History Press.
Gerth, H. and Mills, C. W. (eds) (1948) *From Max Weber: Essays in Sociology*, London, Routledge & Kegan Paul.
Glasgow University Media Group (1976) *Bad News*, London, Routledge & Kegan Paul.
Glasner, P. (1977) *The Sociology of Secularization*, London, Routledge & Kegan Paul.
Golding, P. (1974) *The Mass Media*, London, Longman.
Golding, P. and Elliott, P. (1979) *Making the News*, London, Longman.
Hall, S. (1973) 'A World at One with Itself', in Cohen and Young (1973).
Hall, S. *et al.* (1978) *Policing the Crisis: Mugging, the State, and Law and Order*, London, Macmillan.
Harrison, M. (1985) *TV News: Whose Bias?*, Hermitage Policy Journals.
Hartman, P. and Husband, C. (1974) *Racism and the Mass Media*, London, Davis-Poynter.
Herberg, W. (1967) 'Religion in a Secularized Society: the New Shape of Religion in America', in R. Knudten (ed.), *The Sociology of Religion*, New York, Appleton-Century.
Hill, C. (1964) *Society and Puritansim in Pre-Revolutionary England*, London, Secker & Warburg.
Horton, R. (1960) 'A Definition of Religion and its Uses', *Journal of the Royal Anthropological Institute*, vol. 9, pp. 201–26.
Kuhn, T. (1970) *The Structure of Scientific Revolutions*, University of Chicago Press.
Kuhn, T. (1972) 'Scientific Paradigms', in B. Barnes (ed.), *Sociology of Science*, Harmondsworth, Penguin.
Luckmann, T. (1967) *The Invisible Religion*, London, Collier-Macmillan.
Miliband, R. (1973) *The State in Capitalist Society*, London, Quartet.

Mulkay, M. (1979) *Science and the Sociology of Knowledge*, London, Allen & Unwin.

Murdock, G. and Golding, P. (1977) 'Beyond Monopoly – Mass Communications in an Age of Conglomerates', in Beharrel and Philo (1977).

O'Dea, T. (1966) *The Sociology of Religion*, Englewood Cliffs, N.J., Prentice-Hall.

Philo, G., Beharrel, P. and Hewitt, J. (1977) 'One-Dimensional News – Television and the Control of Explanation', in Beharrel and Philo (1977).

Polanyi, M. (1958) *Personal Knowledge*, University of Chicago Press.

Radcliffe-Brown, A. (1945) *Structure and Function in Primitive Society*, New York, Free Press.

Rodinson, M. (1977) *Islam and Capitalism*, Harmondsworth, Penguin.

Samuelson, K. (1961) *Religion and Economic Action*, London, Heinemann.

Scharf, B. (1970) *The Sociological Study of Religion*, London, Hutchinson.

Stark, W. (1967) *The Sociology of Religion*, London, Routledge & Kegan Paul.

Thomas, K. (1971) *Religion and the Decline of Magic*, London, Weidenfeld & Nicolson.

Wallis, R. (ed.) (1979) *On the Margins of Science*, Sociological Review Monograph No. 37, Keele University Press.

Walton, P. and Davis, H. (1977) 'Bad News for Trade Unionists', in Beharrel and Philo (1977).

Weber, M. (1952) *The Protestant Ethic and the Spirit of Capitalism*, London, Allen & Unwin.

Webster, A. (1979) 'Scientific Controversy and Socio-Cognitive Metronymy', in Wallis (1979).

Westergaard, J. (1977) 'Power, Class and the Media', in J. Curran *et al.* (eds), *Mass Communication and Society*, London, Arnold.

Wilson, B. (1966) *Religion in a Secular Society*, London, C. A. Watts & Co.

Worsley, P. (1968) *The Trumpet Shall Sound*, London, MacGibbon & Kee.

11

Deviance

11.1 INTRODUCTION: THE NATURE OF DEVIANCE

In our first chapter we pointed to a popular view which denies validity to sociological explanation by asserting the uniqueness and individuality of human beings – in simple terms 'we're all different' – so that generalisations about behaviour cannot be made. Furthermore, this recognition of individual differences is also reinforced by an *approval* of the fact: again, the casual observer often maintains that 'it would be boring if we were all the same', and generations of men and women have supported the principle of 'vive la différence!'

But by no means all the people we encounter who are 'different' from us are as easily accepted; foreigners, for instance, may cause us embarrassment and irritation by their peculiar inability to speak our native language or to abide by our 'sensible' practices like queueing, and some categories of people who are physically different through no fault of their own – whether by infirmity or deformity – can cause us to feel uncomfortable.

So, the toleration of differences between human beings is highly provisional, and this is equally so in the case of individuals and groups whose behaviour patterns generally – or particular aspects of them – differ from what is considered 'normal'. Such individuals or groups are engaging in 'deviant behaviour': that is, 'behaviour which somehow departs from what a group expects to be done or what it considers the desirable way of doing things' (Cohen, 1971, p. 9).

Assuming for the moment that there exists in a social group some set of shared expectations about what is 'normal' behaviour, we have here a conception of deviance as the violation of the accepted norms or social rules of a group or society, and of a deviant as someone who transgresses these (apparently) taken-for-granted standards. Thus nude-bathers, bank-robbers, alcoholics, suicides, shoplifters, adulterers, Marxists, tramps, rapists, 'tomboys', skinheads, feminists, murderers and female wrestlers are deviants because they indulge in behaviour which the rest of the society or group regards as socially different, odd, or undesirable.

Most people's direct experience of or contact with such individuals is often highly limited, yet despite this the reaction to them is invariably one of disapproval, fear, suspicion, hostility or outrage. Why is this? Essentially, deviants are disturbing because they disrupt our picture of reality by behaving in a way which questions our expectations of what 'normal people' do – 'normal people' only drink in moderation, 'normal' women do not indulge in anything so unfeminine as wrestling, 'normal people' *pay* for goods in supermarkets, and so on. Thus our social expectations about behaviour structure for us a conception of stable, orderly, understandable social life. Deviants are awkward people who disturb this, but by identifying them as 'deviant' we can place their behaviour in a category outside normality which makes it comprehensible to us and stabilises our perception of social reality.

Our observations so far on deviance have emphasised the reaction of others, and this in itself indicates one very important feature of deviance: what is regarded as deviance is very much a matter of *social definition* imposed by a community or by groups within that community. Thus a particular pattern of behaviour is not deviant *per se*, whether it be murder, lesbianism, belching, or whatever, but is defined as such by a social group. In the sociological sense, then, deviance is indeed *social* behaviour (despite being frequently described in everyday terminology as 'anti-social behaviour'), since it involves reaction by some actors to the behaviour of others with some kind of sanction such as social disapproval, ostracism, imprisonment or execution.

The socially defined nature of deviance is highlighted even further when we recognise that what is regarded as deviance in one society may not be so (or not so seriously regarded) in another: that is, deviant behaviour is often *culturally relative*. While sexual intercourse between black and white individuals is, in certain circles in Britain, merely frowned upon, in South Africa it is a criminal activity. Similarly, incest among those of high birth in Ancient Egypt was considered vital for the preservation of the lineage stock, while in modern societies such behaviour is both illegal and a matter of almost universal public revulsion.

Furthermore, within a particular society variations occur over time in what is held to be deviant or criminal: many activities regarded with disapproval in Victorian times (particularly for women) are now commonly accepted with little or no controversy – mixed bathing on beaches is a matter of comparative indifference to even the most ardent moralist in the 1980s. Similarly, professional boxing attracts considerable public interest, yet it was illegal in New York State as late as 1920.

Most societies, too, suspend or modify temporarily their definitions of deviance in particular contexts and circumstances. In Western societies killing is ordinarily regarded as the most serious of offences, but in the defence of the nation it may become an act of heroism and deserving of honour or reward, and even peacetime killing is hedged about with qualifications like 'self-defence', 'manslaughter', 'justifiable homicide', and so on. Similarly, in many pre-industrial societies and traditional rural areas in industrial societies, killing to avenge family honour may be a duty which members are expected to fulfil.

Deviant behaviour cannot be conceived as something which is absolute or universal but must be seen as socially variable and dependent on what a particular society or social group at a particular time defines as deviant.

Reference to the definitions and reactions of 'society' in the application of the label of 'deviance' to behaviour must not lead us into the trap of simplistically positing an unambiguous or voluntaristic consensus on what is considered normal or deviant in any society. There may exist a widespread consensus on what is deviant in certain spheres of behaviour, but no such straightforward agreement prevails in all other areas. While child-battering or bigamy would be unequivocally viewed as deviant by the vast majority of people in Western societies, other activities such as the consumption of soft drugs or the use of contraceptives before marriage evoke no clear-cut consensus as to the extent of their 'deviant' nature. Such examples as these may sensitise us, therefore, to the fact that the characterisation of some patterns of behaviour as deviant may ultimately depend on the ability of certain groups to *impose their definitions* of 'normality' and 'deviance' on the rest of society and hence to manufacture an apparent consensus about what is proper and improper behaviour.

In this chapter we concentrate our attention on two major areas of deviance: crime and suicide. While an analysis of such kinds of non-conformist behaviour is worth while by virtue of their intrinsically interesting nature, they also reflect very significant theoretical debates in sociology, particularly that between positivist and anti-positivist explanations of social phenomena.

11.2   EXPLANATIONS OF CRIMINAL BEHAVIOUR

If one accepts a conception of crime or deviance as being the behaviour of individuals who are not like normal or law-abiding citizens, then it follows that there must be some characteristics or propensities which mark off criminals or deviants from non-criminal or normal actors. Thus their behaviour can be seen as a sign or product of some personal or social trait(s) which make them different from the rest of society. Such a conception is certainly sustained in the mass media, where football hooligans, muggers, drug-takers and others are often portrayed as different to the point of being demoniacal. At best, many areas of deviant behaviour, and especially crime, are seen as *social problems*, about which something should be done, and a basically similar view has traditionally prevailed within the academic study of crime.

Positivist criminology

The study of crime has been a major meeting-point for several academic disciplines, all of which have taken the idea of crime as a 'social problem' as given: they have accepted that it is something which has to be eradicated or brought under control, and that any attempt to *explain* the phenomenon necessarily involves a commitment to a belief in the *application* of knowledge to practical ends. Thus criminology, according to this view, cannot be simply a matter of 'armchair theorising' but must involve putting analysis and explanation to use in developing policies and programmes to combat crime and to 'reform', 'resocialise' or 'treat' the criminal.

This correctionalist stance, with its prevalent emphasis on order and control, is a product of the fundamental assumptions underpinning much of the study of crime. The bulk of this study has been preoccupied with what Matza (1964) has called 'the search for differentiation', based on the premise that there is something 'wrong' with criminals or at least something very different about them as compared with law-abiding citizens, generating criminal behaviour and inhibiting conformity to conventional norms and legal rules. Thus 'criminality' resides in individuals or social groups and can be identified and explained by examining personal biography, background events or circumstances of criminals.

The criminal, then, is someone whose behaviour is *determined*, the product of some constitutional defect, of some physical or psychological condition or abnormality, or of some social circumstances or subculturally specific experiences. Such explanations of criminality have traditionally centred on the common principle that it is possible to identify causal forces or factors fundamentally distinguishing criminals from the rest of society: that is, that an explanation of criminal behaviour within a *positivist scientific tradition* is an attainable goal.

Gibbons and Jones (1975) suggest that we can broadly differentiate explanations into three types.

(1) *Biogenic explanations* of crime identify motivations to criminal behaviour in the physical or constitutional make-up of individuals. Thus early explanations which posited a link between criminality and physical degeneracy, or which ascribed criminal propensities to personalities or temperaments associated with particular body types or shapes, served as precursors to apparently more sophisticated explanations such as chromosome theories, in which criminality has been linked to the existence of an extra chromosome in the genetic constitution of some males.

(2) *Psychogenic approaches* identify a causal link between criminal

tendencies and psychological characteristics and processes. Freudians argue that very early childhood experiences which disturb or distort the development of a stable personality may result in later childhood and adulthood in anti-social tendencies in behaviour manifesting themselves specifically in criminal activity. Thus the causes of criminal behaviour lie in defective primary socialisation of the child, so that his or her innate anti-social motivations are not brought under control. Notably the failure to develop a warm, loving relationship with one or both parents – as the result of physical separation, deprivation, or harsh or inconsistent treatment – is seen as distinctly criminogenic, and subsequent criminal behaviour consti-tutes the 'acting out' of the feelings of guilt and frustration engendered by these early experiences.

Behavioural psychologists such as Eysenck (1970) suggest that criminal behaviour, like other patterns of behaviour, is the product of an indivi-dual's receptiveness to a process of psychological conditioning, and that a specific genetically determined personality type, the *neurotic extrovert*, is less conditionable and hence more prone to criminality than others. Deviant behaviour, then, is a product of the individual's psychological incapacity to response to the social training experienced in childhood and adolescence which conditions 'normal' individuals away from anti-social conduct.

Both biogenic and psychogenic explanations attempt to answer the questions 'What kinds of people commit crime?' and 'How do they get like this?' They attempt to identify types of 'maladjusted' individuals with some defects or pathological characteristics which predispose or impel them towards involvement in criminal activity.

(3) *Sociogenic theories*, on the other hand, see criminal behaviour as socially acquired and hence focus on the ways in which cultural and/or social structural factors are crime-producing. Thus social environmental influences or subcultural socialisation experiences in family, class and peer group make it likely that some social groups will be involved in criminal activity.

Now, while we can identify fairly easily, even from such a brief résumé as this, major points of divergence between these differing types of explana-tion, they share a fundamental similarity which we need to reiterate and bear in mind: that is, the belief that a meaningful distinction can be drawn between 'criminals' and 'non-criminals', and a commitment to the utility of formulating a theory to account for this distinction. This implies, then, that these types of explanation make certain assumptions about the phenomena under investigation – not only about the *actor* involved but also about the *behaviour* in which these actors engage.

They assume particularly that their criminal behaviour can be meaning-fully viewed as homogeneous and therefore subsumed under some single explanatory umbrella, and that the causes of this behaviour lie outside the actors' control in peculiar genes, defective personality, distinctive subcultural norms, or whatever. Individuals or groups commit offences because of the peculiar forces acting upon them.

In popular belief and in the eyes of the media, politicians, moralists, and indeed of many of those involved in what we may broadly call 'social work' with criminals, non-sociological explanations of criminal behaviour have held sway and continue to do so. While it is our task here neither to examine in detail such explanations nor to account for their relative popularity, we must briefly consider how and why sociologists have found them unsatisfactory and have felt the need for a sociological explanation of crime.

Most sociologists would reject non-sociological explanations of criminal behaviour as being inadequate and incomplete rather than for being necessarily 'wrong'. Fundamentally, the phenomenon under investigation – crimes – are unavoidably violations of *legal statutes*, which are not ethereal and absolute but are socially defined rules and hence part of social structural arrangements. Furthermore, even though crime may be individually enacted (which is not always the case anyway), we cannot assume that it is merely individually motivated. We must see criminals as located in a social structure and subject to specific conditions, opportunities and experiences, so that we must ask what it is about social structures which generate criminality and its preponderant incidence *within* certain groups in society. That is, criminal behaviour is not randomly distributed by genes or personality but follows a consistent *social pattern*, which must be explained by examining the different structural positions of criminals and non-criminals. While such explanations vary in emphasis on the key explanatory factors they identify, there is a basic acceptance of *social influences and social processes* as important in criminal behaviour. Before considering them in detail, however, we must examine the extent to which crime is socially patterned.

11.3　THE PATTERN OF CRIME

Evidence on any visible patterns and trends in criminal behaviour usually comes from official criminal statistics compiled annually in most societies. A distinction is usually made between 'serious' and 'less serious' crimes in these figures, with the former used as the major indicator of patterns and trends: in Britain, for example, 'indictable' offences (the more serious offences triable by jury) formed the basis of the official statistics until 1979, being subsequently referred to as 'notifiable' offences.

We shall present a detailed critique of these statistics later in the chapter, but at this stage we shall accept them more or less uncritically and merely suggest some of the difficulties to which they give rise. However, it is important to note at this stage that the figures refer only to crimes that are *known to the police* and are *officially recorded* as such. This means, of course, that they can be regarded neither as measures of any *actual level* of crime in society in any year nor as a perfectly accurate indicator of *patterns* and *trends* in crime, since many factors can influence the levels of recorded crime: better and more efficient policing, increased police resources, changes in the law, changes in public perception of both the police and the law, and so on.

With such cautionary remarks in mind, it is nevertheless safe to observe that crime has increased considerably during this century: the official statistics reveal steadily rising levels of recorded crime, so that by the 1980s in England and Wales, the police recorded more than 3 million offences (or one about every 8 seconds). The volume of crime recorded over the years is shown in Table 11.1.

TABLE 11.1

Indictable/notifiable offences known to the police (England and Wales)

	million
1963	0.978
1971	1.666
1973	1.658
1976	2.136
1981	2.964
1982	3.262
1983	3.247
1984	3.499

Source: Adapted from *Central Statistical Office Annual Abstract of Statistics* (1979) and *Social Trends* (1986).

Types of offence

Even though the rate of known crime appears to have increased, the general *pattern* of offences has remained remarkably stable over the years. As Figure 11.1 indicates, the vast majority centre on *property* offences, notably theft or other types of dishonesty involving property or money (such as handling stolen goods or fraud) and criminal damage or vandalism.

While dramatic bank robberies, lurid sex crimes and violent offences frequently make media headlines (since they fit journalistic criteria of 'newsworthiness' outlined in Chapter 10), they comprise a very small proportion of the total of recorded crime. But for this very reason popular confusion frequently abounds. Because the number of such offences is small, a modest numerical increase in reported crimes of violence is often distorted by the media into a spectacular *proportional* increase, and it is also

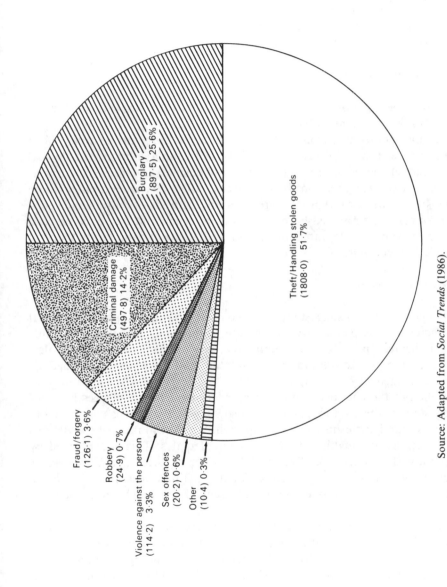

Source: Adapted from *Social Trends* (1986).

FIGURE 11.1 *Indictable/notifiable offences known to the police ('000s) England and Wales, 1984* possible that an apparent rise in such crimes may reflect not a more 'violent' society (a dubious description if historical comparisons are made) but a greater *willingness* to call in the police when violence does occur. Furthermore, while we obviously cannot regard violent crimes lightly, we need to be wary of sensationalism and to recognise that their typical form is not the 'mugging' of some defenceless old granny but a fight among friends, neighbours or relatives or a public brawl.

Geographical location

In most societies, crime rates appear to be significantly *higher* in *urban* areas than in rural areas, as Table 11.2 illustrates.

Various factors may contribute to this pattern. Large urban areas afford greater opportunity for criminal activity, with the availability of department and self-service stores, warehouses and business premises, cars, tower-block residences, and so on. In such areas, police resources are also more extensive, while in rural areas more informal methods of redress and social control may be employed both by victims of crime and by police officers, who may be more integrated into the immediate local community than are their urban counterparts.

Age and sex

The official statistics suggest that the two most striking and persistent social characteristics associated with crime are being *young* and *male*. As Table 11.3 indicates, in both sexes criminal activity appears to peak in adolescence and early adulthood, with roughly half of those cautioned or convicted aged 21 or under.

Although the age distribution of convictions across the sexes is essentially similar, the data in Table 11.3 also suggest that males commit more offences than females in all age groups, with an overall ratio of convictions and cautions of roughly 5 to 1 in favour of males. This is confirmed by longitudinal data in *Social Trends* (1986), which reported that among males born in 1953, nearly 1 in 3 (about 30 per cent) had been convicted of an indictable offence compared with 6 per cent of females born in the same year.

This sex ratio may indicate that females are simply significantly more law-abiding than males, although Self-Report studies (see p. 466) by Cernkovich and Giordano (1979) and Hindelang (1979) among others point to a smaller disparity between male and female offending than the official data suggest. Some studies have also suggested that the police and courts may be more 'chivalrous' in dealing with female than with male offenders and that the kinds of offences typically committed by females and the roles they play

TABLE 11.2

Crime rates per 100,000 population, by offence and area, USA, 1974

	Murder/ Manslaughter	Rape	Robbery	Aggravated assault	Burglary	Larceny	Car theft
Metropolitan areas	10.8	31.2	273.7	242.6	1652.6	2830.9	579.6
Other cities	5.7	13.4	54.2	175.9	1024.9	2543.5	209.6
Rural areas	7.6	11.6	20.4	111.5	693.2	808.3	93.8

Source: D. Gibbons, *Society, Crime and Criminal Careers*, p. 113 from FBI US Department of Justice: Crime in the US: Uniform Crime Reports 1974, p. 55, published by US Government Printing Office, Washington DC (1975).

TABLE 11.3

Offenders found guilty and cautioned by sex and age England and Wales, 1983

Age (years)	Males (000's)				Females (000's)			
	Found guilty	Cautioned	Total	%	Found guilty	Cautioned	Total	%
10–14	11.6	32.0	43.6	9.1	1.3	12.0	13.3	14.0
14–17	54.4	37.5	91.9	19.2	6.1	13.1	19.2	20.2
17–21	115.3	4.4	119.7	24.9	14.8	1.1	15.9	16.7
21 +	215.8	8.7	224.5	46.8	40.5	6.1	46.6	47.1
All ages	397.0	82.7	479.7	100	62.7	32.2	94.9	100

Source: Adapted from Central Statistical Office, *Annual Abstract of Statistics* (1985).

in criminal activities may not be as visible or as closely policed as those of males.

Moreover, as Shacklady-Smith (1978) and others have stressed, the law frequently operates in a highly *sexist* way by treating the sexual activities of girls as 'delinquent' when similar behaviour by boys is ignored, thus reflecting the dual standard of morality surrounding sexual behaviour which we noted earlier in Chapter 5. Young females are much more likely to be brought before the courts for 'status' offences (behaviour which, if engaged in by adults, is not defined by the law as criminal) such as 'running away', 'being in moral danger', or 'incorrigibility', which equally often are euphemisms for sexual behaviour. Thus their sexual 'deviance' is *over-emphasised*, even to the extent that their non-sexual delinquent activity is *ignored* by the police and courts.

Social class

The published statistics do not provide information on the social-class background of offenders, but other types of data would seem to indicate that a larger proportion of working-class people than middle-class people are convicted of crimes. Estimates based on such studies conclude that the sons of manual workers are four times as likely to be found guilty of offences as the sons of businessmen and professionals. Again, this does not *necessarily* mean that working-class boys and adults *commit* more crime than members of the upper and middle classes but that they are more likely to fall foul of the official judicial system. Their offences may be defined as more serious by police, magistrates and judges, and they are less likely to benefit from informal means of social control.

From the statistical evidence, then, it would appear that, generally, most crime is committed in urban areas against property by young, working-class boys. Consequently, much sociological research on crime has concerned itself with analysing and explaining the social pattern of juvenile delinquency, and, implicitly, with finding a *cure* for delinquency.

As we suggested earlier, sociologists traditionally started from the basic premise that the delinquent was not an isolated individual but was the product of a particular social world, and that criminal behaviour might best be explained by identifying the different structural positions of criminals. Consequently many sociological explanations have operated with the assumption that certain environmental conditions such as poverty, economic insecurity, poor housing, and so on, are more conducive to crime than other, more favourable conditions, and hence that most crime is committed by working-class people who are more likely to face these harsh social and economic conditions. Moreover, it has been claimed, the children of these families are more likely to be socialised into ways of coping with their environment which are criminal. Such assumptions led to the development of 'subcultural' explanations of delinquency.

11.4   THEORIES OF THE DELINQUENT SUBCULTURE

Traditional positivist sociological explanations take the view that delinquency is a social activity like any other, *learned* in association with others in much the same way that more conventional behaviour is learned. Furthermore, they suggest that certain norms, values and standards of behaviour become traditional among delinquent groups and are passed on and perpetuated within the group. That is, there exists a delinquent *subculture* in which certain types of delinquent or potentially delinquent behaviour are approved of or condoned. The more extreme versions of this thesis posit delinquent activity as a *requirement* for membership of the subculture.

We can broadly identify two competing conceptions of the nature of the relationship between the subculture and the larger culture which we can call 'independent' and 'reactive'. The *independent* conception sees the delinquent subculture as a discrete and self-contained set of norms and values which, while not consciously in opposition to the prevailing (largely middle-class) values of the wider culture, are the *independent* product of and solution to the group's particular way of life. The *reactive* conception, on the other hand, sees delinquent subcultural values and behaviour as a *response* to the values and opportunity structures which prevail in the wider society.

The 'independent' delinquent subculture

An example of the 'independent' variant in delinquent subculture theory is provided by Miller (1958), who argues that delinquency is, in fact, conforming behaviour. For Miller, delinquent activity is motivated by an attempt to live up to the values of the lower-class community itself and is not a reaction to, or turning away from, the values of the wider community. If a subculture exists, it does so only in the wider sense of there being different *class* subcultures, and one cannot suggest that the working-class subculture as a whole is committed to delinquency. Delinquency arises because young boys who are exposed to lower-class culture *over-conform* to its standards. By conforming to the norms of this culture they *automatically* violate middle-class norms, but this does not necessarily imply that these are maliciously or deliberately flouted.

   Miller supports this interpretation by arguing that lower-class life, in common with all distinctive cultural groups, is characterised by a set of 'focal concerns'. These focal concerns, together with their opposites, are:

(i)   a concern with trouble rather than law-abiding behaviour;

(ii)   toughness and masculinity rather than weakness and effeminacy;
(iii) smartness or achievement by mental agility as opposed to gullibility or achievement through routine;
(iv) excitement and thrill, as opposed to boredom and safety;
(v)   belief in fate, fortune or luck rather than control over the environment; and
(vi) autonomy and freedom, contrasted with dependency and constraint.

Miller argues that young males 'overconform' to the focal concerns of *adult* lower-class culture because of *status insecurity*, which occurs because lower-class culture is characterised by female-based households in which the significant relationships are between mature females and children. The children often have different biological fathers who may play an inconsistent and unpredictable part in the family, so that the family is not organised around the expectation of stable economic support provided by an adult male.

This type of household, Miller argues, generates delinquency, because the intensity of the mother–son tie creates an equally intense desire to demonstrate masculinity on the part of the boy. He is driven out into the adolescent street-corner group in search of the type of experiences his family cannot provide, and here he is more fully exposed to the focal concerns that *may* make him delinquent. His need to belong to the street-corner group and to gain and maintain status in it leads him to overconform to the values of lower-class culture, and to commit offences in so doing.

Miller has been criticised for appearing to stress the homogeneity of lower-class culture, which is, in fact, subject to wide regional and ethnic variation, with only blacks having any history of female-based households in the extreme form he describes. Furthermore, critics argue, his focal concerns are more likely to be found among the inhabitants of slums in large cities than elsewhere. Moreover, his reliance upon these concerns in his explanation has been criticised as tautological, in that they are *derived* from observing behaviour and then used to *explain* that same behaviour. He might well have done better to look in more detail at the structural factors giving rise to the focal concerns such as the prolonged instability of employment and the whole uncertainty of the lower-class way of life.

The delinquent subculture as 'reaction'

The 'reactive' conception of delinquent subcultures is illustrated by two explanations which, although different in emphasis and detail, can both be differentiated from that of Miller.

Cloward and Ohlin (1960) build on the foundations provided by Merton's (1938) reworking of Durkheim's concept of *anomie*. Merton argues that anomie results when there is a disjunction between the valued cultural goals of a society – in the American case, economic success – and the legitimate means of reaching such goals, such as hard work, education, or speculating on the stock market. Deviance is caused by the fact that large numbers of people at the lower levels of the social structure *accept* the dominant values and cultural goals but are unable to realise them by legitimate means, and so they 'innovate'. Thus, for example, if monetary wealth is stressed as the goal towards which each must strive, then it will be sought by illegitimate means such as robbery or fraud.

However, Cloward and Ohlin argue that not all boys who find their legitimate avenues for advancement blocked are able to utilise *illegitimate* means because these are not evenly distributed either; for instance, not everyone has the opportunity to learn how to crack safes. Moreover, the subcultural form which develops depends upon the illegitimate means available. According to Cloward and Ohlin, *criminal subcultures* devoted to theft, extortion and other means of securing an income are most likely to occur in more stable slum neighbourhoods which provide a hierarchy of criminal opportunity. Adult criminals exercise social control over the young to make them desist from expressive, non-utilitarian actions that might attract the attention of the police to their own activities. Similarly, *conflict subcultures* tend to arise in disorganised areas with high rates of geographical mobility and social instability that provide *no* organised hierarchy for criminal development. These boys turn to violence, gang warfare, the defence of 'turf', as alternatives. Finally, the *retreatist subculture* emerges as an adjustment pattern for those lower-class youths who have failed to find a position in either the criminal or the conflict subcultures because of lack of access to either legitimate or illegitimate opportunity structures. These 'double-failures' tend to move into a retreatist pattern of behaviour revolving around the use of drugs.

Our second illustration of a 'reactive' conception of delinquent subcultures is to be found in the work of Cohen (1955), who argues that Merton's innovation adaptation cannot account for the distinctive content of the delinquency of juvenile working-class gangs. Cohen points out that far from being an attempt to achieve material success by means of rationally calculated property theft much delinquency is *non-utilitarian*, *malicious* and *negativistic* in character. Boys do not steal in order to get their hands on valued objects, they steal for the hell of it, taking a malicious pleasure in the discomfort of others and in breaking the rules of middle-class society.

Cohen explains this by constructing an 'ideal type' of middle-class standards which he contrasts with the values of delinquents. He argues that subcultural values are at one and the same time in opposition to and a reaction to, those of the middle class. Cohen, then, reaches a conclusion which is almost diametrically opposed to that of Miller. How does he do this?

He maintains that a collective way of life – a subculture – develops when a number of people with a *common problem of adjustment* are in effective interaction. The common problem of delinquents derives from their working-class socialisation, which does not prepare them adequately for successful functioning in middle-class-dominated institutions such as schools, youth clubs and work-places. However, these institutions reward and punish the boys by reference to a middle-class set of standards: a 'middle-class measuring rod'. This set of standards or values stresses the virtue of ambition, the ethic of individual responsibility for actions, deferred gratification, the control of aggression, good manners, the importance of respect for private property and the enjoyment of wholesome recreation. Because the working-class boy is ill-equipped to measure up to these standards, he inevitably suffers disapproval, rejection and punishment. The delinquent subculture provides a way of *adjusting* to the resulting problem of status deprivation which lower-class youths share. This sense of deprivation stems not only from the negative evaluations of others but also from self-derogation: the working-class boy shares in the poor evaluation that others make of him. This is partly because there exists 'the democratic status universe', whereby everyone is expected to strive and everyone is measured against the same standard. But it is also because the boy's parents may have projected their own frustrated aspirations upon him, and because the existence of a certain degree of upward social mobility seems to indicate that it is possible to 'get on'. (That is, dominant values permeate through.)

According to Cohen, then, the young working-class male has partly accepted the values of the middle class as being a legitimate or even superior set of values. This creates status problems for him and a sense of ambivalence about his position in the world, for he not only knows that he is accorded low esteem in the eyes of the wider society but he also suffers from low *self-esteem*. Cohen's explanation of the nature of the boy's reaction to this feeling of inadequacy rests on the Freudian psychoanalytic concept of 'reaction formation'. (Basically this is an unconscious way of denying that which one really wants, exemplified by those disappointed in love claiming: 'I never fancied him/her anyway!') Cohen claims that the working-class boy has such a strong desire for status in the middle-class world – a desire which can only be frustrated – that the reaction formation is instituted against it. It is this which helps to explain the *content* and *spirit* of the delinquent subculture, as characterised by 'versatility, short-run hedonism and group autonomy'. Gang delinquency is an ambivalent denial of and opposition to the middle-class values and standards for which he has a grudging respect. The delinquent's conduct is right by the standards of his subculture *precisely because it is wrong* by the norms of *middle-class culture*, and his low status in the middle-class world is compensated by adherence to a different, antithetical set of status criteria which he *is* able to meet.

There have been many criticisms made of Cohen. Rabow (1966) questions the proposition that working-class boys accept middle-class success goals, and Short and Strodtbeck (1965) found little evidence that members of delinquent gangs reject either middle-class values or those who administer the middle-class measuring rod. Cohen stresses too strongly, it is claimed, the non-utilitarian aspects of delinquency, and his emphasis on malice and negativism leads him to miss some of the more 'positive' aspects of delinquent activity – much behaviour that is labelled 'delinquent' is not reactive or defiant but simply done for fun, for kicks. It is behaviour that, if engaged in by middle-class youngsters, would be called 'youthful high spirits'. He is also accused of relying too heavily on official statistics and therefore accepting too readily that working-class delinquency is more of a 'problem' than middle-class delinquency.

Perhaps the greatest flaw in Cohen's argument, however, is the rather crude distinction drawn between middle-class values and those which he claims characterise the delinquent subculture. His analysis, that is, is based upon a gross, undifferentiated concept of middle-class values and an equally gross and undifferentiated characterisation of those of the delinquent subculture. This is an issue to which we shall return.

How useful are 'subculture' explanations?

Our discussion so far has centred on the specific content and merits of particular subculture theories, but this should not be construed as implying that one merely has to 'choose the "best" one', for the *general* utility of explaining delinquency by recourse to subcultural theories has also been the subject of much criticism.

Various authorities question the stress that subculture theories put upon the existence of the delinquent *gang*. Much British evidence, for example, indicates that structured gangs with a leader, definite and enduring membership, and a territory are most unusual. Most delinquent acts are not committed by organised delinquent gangs but by small, fairly transient, loosely structured friendship groups. Scott (1956) found that when members of the teenage street-corner *groups* that he studied committed offences they did so as individuals, or with close friends or kin. Downes's (1966) study of East London supports this interpretation. Instead of utilising the concept of a subculture in which delinquency is a central norm, he sees working-class boys being led into delinquency by a process of 'dissociation' from the middle-class-dominated contexts of school, work and leisure. For the lower levels of the working class, *leisure* becomes a central goal – the only means of achieving self-realisation – and yet leisure opportunities open to them are dull and unexciting. Delinquency is the 'solution', providing the thrills missing from conventional leisure and life generally.

Similarly, Parker (1974) and Corrigan (1981) portray working-class adolescent delinquency as a much less highly structured and systematic activity than subculture theories imply: the working-class youths in their studies largely used delinquent activity to inject some 'action' into leisure lives which frequently involved standing around on street corners 'doing nothing'.

These findings represent a significant critique of subculture theories, for such theories *depend* upon the existence of permanent structured gangs, since it is only via such established gangs that the transmission of specific subcultural norms and values becomes a feasible proposition. If the gang is rare, or absent, then the idea of the subculture becomes difficult to sustain.

Matza's (1964) criticisms not only throw doubt on the validicity of subcultural accounts of delinquent behaviour and motivation but also raise important questions about the positivist assumptions underlying them. He argues that subcultural theories fall into the same trap as some orthodox positivist approaches in that they present a highly deterministic view of the subcultural delinquent and hence a distorted picture of delinquency.

The concept of delinquent subculture implies that working-class adolescents are committed to and organise their activities around the central value of delinquency so that illegal behaviour is widespread, collective, persistent and salient. Most working-class youth, however, do not engage regularly in criminal activity, and of those who do many apparently 'give it up' in early adulthood. How, then, can there exist delinquent subcultures of the type posited by Cohen, Cloward and Ohlin, and others?

Matza maintains that the over-deterministic assumptions of delinquent subculture theories generate a fundamentally erroneous portrayal of the nature of delinquent activity. He rejects the notion of the 'delinquent subculture' in favour of the less deterministic idea of the *subculture of delinquency*, in which the commission of offences, although common knowledge among a group of juveniles, is neither a condition of membership of the group nor a full-time activity of its members. In his view, adolescents *from time to time* act out delinquent roles rather than engage in permanent violation of the norms of conventional society. Their delinquency is casual and intermittent, they are predominantly occupied with the mundane, non-deviant activities of conforming society. They 'drift' into and out of delinquency periodically and temporarily without embracing it as a 'way of life'.

Law-breaking, according to Matza, results from the fact that male working-class adolescents' leisure time is peer-orientated and focused on asserting masculine identity and gaining acceptance by friends. They are under pressure to conform to the norms of the group because not to do so would threaten their position within it. So, when an activity is suggested which involves law-breaking, each individual adds his support, thinking that the others are in favour of it. However, Matza suggests that this is a 'comedy of errors', with each individual misapprehending the motives of all the others. These 'shared misunderstandings' are not challenged because adolescents want to appear 'one of the boys'. Their activities centre on delinquency not because of any fundamental value conflict with conventional society but because much adolescent activity is geared towards finding something to do, towards solving their 'leisure problem'. Leisure, if it is to be satisfying and exciting and at the same time a way of asserting toughness and masculinity, carries the risk of law violation.

Matza also rejects the 'absolutist' conception of values contained in subculture theories (in the form of 'conventional' societal values and 'deviant' subcultural values) in favour of a position which views commitment to values as a more problematic and relativistic process. Rather than assuming that law-abiding individuals subscribe unambiguously to a discrete set of values, he suggests that coexisting with the 'official' values of society are series of 'subterranean' values distributed throughout the various social classes and which, for the middle classes, find expression in leisure, sports and other ritual events. Values supposed to characterise delinquency, such as the search for excitement and masculinity, may be given expression on these occasions with social approval. British Rugby Union players who are predominantly middle and upper class regularly violate middle-class values and standards of behaviour relating to violence, drunkenness, obscenity, and so on, and yet this behaviour is often condoned as 'excusable high spirits', whereas similar activities by soccer supporters are condemned as 'hooliganism'.

Among working-class youth, Matza argues, this simultaneous acceptance of 'official' values and 'subterranean' values is also apparent, in that they often experience and express guilt over their law-breaking. But they, too, are able to call upon subterranean values which, particularly when activated at 'improper' moments, in inopportune circumstances and accentuated beyond an acceptable limit, take the form of delinquency. In Matza's view most rules are not categorical imperatives but qualified guides for action which are limited in terms of time, place, persons and social circumstances. The law itself recognises this with its allowance, for example, of 'justifiable homicide'. Similarly, one can avoid *moral* culpability for criminal actions if one can show that criminal intent was lacking.

He maintains that the male delinquent extends this by justifications for deviance seen as valid by himself but not by the legal system or society at large. These *techniques of neutralisation* allow the delinquent to justify his offences to himself in particular circumstances while knowing them to be wrong. By denying responsibility for his actions, by denying any real injury to the victim, by denying that the victim deserves consideration, by condemning those who condemn him, or by appealing to higher loyalties like 'family solidarity' or 'friendship', he deflects in advance the sense of guilt which in other circumstances may have inhibited or constrained him.

Thus Matza's overall critique of subculture theorists, and his own explanation of delinquency, may be described as weakly anti-positivist, in that he does not entirely abandon the search for the structural location of delinquency or its 'causes'. However, he does raise important questions about deterministic explanations of crime, about the provisional nature of rules and values, and about the meaning of action for both actors and the rest of society. Such questions form the basis for a more thoroughgoing anti-positivist critique – which we shall examine in detail shortly.

The official crime statistics: a critique

We have already suggested that the official criminal statistics may not in fact tell us very much about the patterns of crime, trends in crime or the type of person who commits crime. This does not mean that official statistics cannot be profitably used by sociologists but that the use made of them will have to differ from that made by traditional sociology and criminology. Much recent writing on deviance suggests that, rather than assuming that these statistics represent 'hard' data which tell us something 'real' about patterns of crime within a society, they should be seen as arising out of complex processes of social interaction between offenders, victims, members of the public and formal agencies of social control, and these processes *in themselves* constitute the real problem for sociological investigation. Thus official statistics on crime may only be useful in so far as they tell us something about the activities of official agencies and about the way 'crime', the 'delinquent' and the 'criminal' are socially constructed phenomena which emerge in 'solid' form from a variety of sifting and selecting processes.

Of course, once one accepts that the dimensions of crime cannot be measured accurately by means of the official statistics, then the validity of traditional theories purporting to 'explain' crime – including subcultural theories – must be called into question, as we shall see later in this chapter.

A major limitation of the statistics is that they concentrate, as we pointed out earlier, on the number of *crimes known to the police* and *recorded* by them as such (the CKP index). Considerable evidence indicates that this figure merely represents the tip of an iceberg and that the 'dark figure' of hidden or undetected crime is very much larger.

Two main methods have been utilised to highlight the limitations of the official statistics and to provide a rough indication of the 'dark figure' of crime. These are *self-report studies* and *victim surveys*.

Self-report studies usually involve asking people to volunteer their past illegal actions either in response to a questionnaire or interview. Various studies reveal that anything between 50 and 90 per cent of people admit some kind of illegal behaviour, whether trivial or serious, that could result in a court appearance. Wallerstein and Wyle (1947) found that 91 per cent of their sample of adults in New York admitted imprisonable offences, and even ministers of religion admitted an average of 8.2 offences committed since the age of 18! In Elmhorn's (1965) sample of Stockholm schoolboys 57 per cent admitted to at least one serious offence, and of these 93 per cent were not caught. The boys admitted to 1430 serious offences between them, with the culprit being known to the police in a mere forty-one cases, or 3 per cent of the reported total. Belson *et al.*'s (1975) study of London schoolboys found that 60 per cent admitted receiving stolen goods, 63 per cent had stolen from school, and more than half had stolen from a shop.

There may be problems with the validity and reliability of these self-report studies, of course. Respondents may exaggerate or under-report their delinquencies due to dishonesty, bravado or forgetfulness. Be that as it may, these studies nevertheless clearly demonstrate the partial nature of the statistics. Moreover, they also seem to indicate that middle-class individuals are just as likely to commit crimes as working-class people. While some researchers suggest that, on average, convicted offenders do seem to commit a greater number of *serious* offences than unconvicted self-reported offenders, these studies do throw into doubt unambiguous distinctions between 'criminals' and 'non-criminals' and particularly the assumption that working-class individuals have a virtual monopoly of criminal activity.

Victim surveys are designed to investigate the number of individuals who have been victims of crime. They too indicate that official statistics are an incomplete and unrepresentative sample of the actual amount of crime committed. Erickson and Empey's (1963) study of Utah found that only one-third of the burglaries that had been committed were reported to the police and only one-quarter of the rapes. A Washington study showed that 38 per cent of the surveyed population had been the victims of a serious crime within a year compared with the 10 per cent revealed by police statistics (US President's Commission, 1967).

Similarly the British Crime Survey's (1985) attempts to estimate unrecorded crime suggested that only about one-third of the offences uncovered by the survey were reported, with reporting rates varying considerably in different categories of offence: only about 1 in 10 sexual offences were reported, only about 1 in 5 domestic petty thefts, and 2 in 3 burglaries or attempted burglaries (see Table 11.4).

Such studies obviously also suffer from limitations, especially the diffi-

TABLE 11.4

Percentage of crimes reported to police for selected crime categories

	Per cent reported
Well reported crimes	
Theft of cars	99
Burglary with loss	87
Bicycle theft	68
Vandalism over £20 to the home	62
Wounding	60
Robbery	57
Less well reported crimes	
Attempted and no-loss burglaries	51
Theft from cars	44
Common assault	31
Theft from the person	31
Poorly reported crimes	
Theft in a dwelling	23
Vandalism over £20 to cars	30
Vandalism £20 or under to the home	19
Sexual offences	10
Vandalism £20 or under to cars	9

Source: M. Hough and P. Mayhew, *Taking Account of Crime: Key Findings from the 1984 British Crime Survey*, HMSO, 1985.

culty of remembering how often one has been 'victimised', though this would seem more likely to produce underestimation rather than the reverse. They also, of course, concentrate on crimes with *identifiable victims* and by definition provide no information on *crimes without victims* and *crimes against public order*. These different types of offence have a variable chance of becoming known to the police and appearing in the statistics.

The British Crime Survey (1985) suggested that only about 10 per cent of known crimes are discovered by the police themselves, the other 90 per cent being reported by the public. The vast majority of crimes with victims become known in the latter manner, but crimes in the other two categories usually have to be detected by the police themselves before they appear at all.

Offences are more likely to be reported, of course, if the victims are aware that they *have been* victimised, and this in itself may produce an underestimate of the 'real' amount of crime. We all 'lose' objects that may in fact have been stolen. Furthermore, some knowledge of the criminal law is necessary before we are *able* to define certain acts as crimes, and even then we may be reluctant to involve the police in matters we regard as 'trivial'.

In some cases the victim may not report an offence because of sympathy with the offender, who may be a relative or friend. Victims or witnesses may dislike or distrust the police and courts or may reside in a community where reporting crimes is considered deviant. Other communities, on the other hand, such as public schools, universities and army camps, provide their residents with 'institutional immunity' by operating internal systems of social control which often shield offenders and 'silence' victims. The private context of the family, too, often provides immunity for domestic violence in which women and children suffer physical abuse in silence, as our discussion of the 'dark side' of family life in Chapter 7 illustrates. Similarly, sexual offences against women such as rape are considerably under-reported as a result of the victims' unwillingness to expose themselves to the traumas of police investigation and the public examination of their 'morals' in court.

Much crime, too, is not reported because those who witness it (as well as those who perpetrate it) regard it as inconsequential, socially approved, or a legitimate 'perk'. The theft of stationery, pens, building materials, etc., from one's employer is often regarded in this way, as is travelling on public transport without paying.

Table 11.5 summarises the British Crime Survey (1985) data on reasons for non-reporting by victims.

The statistics for the second category of offences – crimes without victims – are *notoriously* unreliable as an index of the amount of crime of this type. These consensual crimes – such as prostitution, illegal abortion and supplying drugs – usually involve one party providing a service or good that another person requires. Consequently, few offences of this type would appear in the statistics at all were it not for the activity of the police themselves, and this in any case merely scratches the surface. For example, in Britain before the implementation of the 1967 Act legalising abortion under certain circumstances, the annual average number of illegal abortions known to the police during the period 1962–6 was 262. Unofficial estimates based on the reports of social workers and other welfare agencies put the 'real' annual figure at somewhere around 100,000.

A similar situation prevails with the third category of 'crimes against public order', such as drunkenness or disorderly conduct. Only a very small proportion of these are reported by the public, most becoming known through the activities of the police themselves. Hence, as with 'crimes without victims', clear-up figures for this group are virtually identical with figures of crimes known to the police, which again, represent only a small minority of the actual offences of this nature that are committed.

Even if a crime is reported or detected, there is no guarantee that it will be *recorded* by the police (the British Crime Survey estimated, for example, that the police record only about two-thirds of property offences known to them), or that it will be recorded as the type of crime originally reported or

TABLE 11.5

Reasons why the police were not notified, for selected offence categories

	Vandalism (%)	Theft from motor vehicle (%)	Burglary (%)	Bike theft (%)	Theft in a dwelling (%)	Other household theft (%)	Assault (%)	Theft from person/ robbery (%)	Other personal theft (%)	All offences (%)
Too trivial: no loss or damage	62	60	63	34	56	65	39	51	44	55
Police could do nothing	18	21	16	27	2	15	6	23	18	16
Inappropriate for police; dealt with matter ourselves	2	5	3	17	18	6	30	7	18	10
Fear/dislike of police	—	—	1	—	2	—	1	1	1	—
Inconvenient	1	3	1	2	3	2	2	4	3	2
Police would not be interested	9	4	10	9	8	9	6	2	2	7
Fear of reprisals	1	—	—	—	—	—	1	2	—	1
Reported to other authorities	1	1	3	—	5	1	3	5	12	3
Other; vague	10	11	13	12	7	10	15	10	9	11
Unweighted *n*	751	500	183	67	47	600	274	126	313	2882

Source: M. Hough and P. Mayhew, *Taking Account of Crime: Key Findings from the 1984 British Crime Survey*, HMSO, 1985.

detected. The police consistently make discretionary decisions about the recording of crimes and about whether to charge suspects, on what charge and on how many counts. Where 'clear up' rates are used as measures of police efficiency, the police may be less inclined to record all cases of offending in categories with traditionally low detection rates, and once suspects have been apprehended, the police may try to persuade them to admit to more crimes than they have been arrested for, or even to more crimes than they have actually committed. In return for a suspect's co-operation, they may promise to press for a lighter sentence.

The policies, priorities and activities of different police forces may vary from place to place as well as over time. In such circumstances, of course, the statistics will also vary. For example, Whitaker (1964, p. 30) notes that after the appointment of a new Chief Constable in Manchester, the recorded incidence of the crime of male importuning increased by 100 per cent over a four-year period. A change in police policy produced this dramatic increase, of course, and not thousands of new closet doors opening.

The police may also exercise their discretion in the light of what they know to be the priorities of later decision-makers in the judicial process. If they know that the local magistrates take a different line and that this is reflected in their sentencing decisions, then they may not 'waste' time arresting people who are likely to 'get off'.

Even if we were to regard the volume and pattern of known crime as a *sample* of all crime committed (an assumption which could be made with no confidence whatsoever, given our previous discussion), we would still face the major problem that the *clear-up rate* for known crime, besides varying considerably between offences, has rarely exceeded 40 per cent in recent years (see Table 11.6). Thus, while we may have data on some known offenders, the other 60 per cent of known offences may be committed by

TABLE 11.6

Clear-up rates by offence, England and Wales, 1984

	(%)
Violence against the person	74
Sex offences	72
Burglary	28
Robbery	22
Theft/handling stolen goods	35
Fraud/forgery	69
Criminal damage	23
Other	93
All notifiable offences	35

Source: *Social Trends* (1986).

very different criminal 'types' from those who come before the courts, *to say nothing* of the vast numbers of the perpetrators of *unrecorded* crime.

We have by no means exhausted all the possible influences acting upon the social construction of official statistics. Our analysis, however, does bear out the widely held view that the official statistics on crime, like most statistics, are not 'facts' to be accepted uncritically but are the product of dynamic social processes that involve the activities not merely of offenders but also of numerous decision-makers in the field of law and order. Consequently, sociological theories based upon such data must be regarded with considerable suspicion.

11.5 THE ANTI-POSITIVIST RESPONSE: LABELLING THEORY

We have seen how sociological theories of crime in the subcultural tradition have been the focus of considerable debate and criticism. Much of this criticism has questioned the 'internal' rationale and validity of these explanations, without necessarily questioning the *fundamental assumptions* of the explanations proposed. We must now turn our attention to an approach to crime and deviance which represents a significant departure from, and criticism of, traditional positivist explanations (both sociological and non-sociological) of crime and deviance. This perspective, drawing heavily upon symbolic interactionism, has variously been described as the 'labelling' approach (or simply 'labelling theory'), the 'interactionist' approach, or the 'social reactions' approach. Although there is no single theoretical position embraced completely by the various sociologists subsumed under such designations, there does exist an amalgam of themes and ideas which they share.

The critique of positivist criminology

The distinctive perspective of the exponents of the labelling approach stems from a fundamental criticism: they maintain that traditional positivist criminology employs erroneous assumptions about the nature of the phenomena of crime and deviance and about their explanation. Such theories, they argue, tend to see their subject-matter as straightforward, easily identifiable phenomena, as concrete, easily and more or less unambiguously 'known' to us – 'crime' is behaviour that violates the law, and 'criminals' are those who engage in this law-violating behaviour. By regarding their subject-matter as *objectively given* – out there, and amenable to observation – they too readily take it for granted: for labelling theorists such a stance cannot be justified.

The second major flaw in traditional criminology, according to this view, lies in the assumption that criminals are unambiguously *different* from non-criminals, and that it is possible to identify factors causing the differences in behaviour between them. This entails two difficulties. First, the kinds of behaviour falling under the umbrella of 'criminal' are massively wide-ranging. As Robertson and Taylor (1974, pp. 105–6) remark: 'It becomes difficult to regard crime as a behavioural constant when one is faced with such relatively diverse and novel behaviour as glue-sniffing, vandalism, industrial sabotage and football hooliganism.'

But according to labelling theory the search for causes is essentially misplaced for the second, even more fundamental, reason that it rests on *official statistics* of crime and on studies of *convicted criminal populations*; the former, as we have seen, cannot be taken as reliable indices of the amount of law-breaking, and the latter do not constitute a representative sample of those committing 'officially' known crimes, even disregarding hidden crimes. Self-report studies suggest that law-breaking among adults and juveniles is far more widespread than the official figures indicate – very few of us have not broken the law, and many of us do so frequently without these offences being officially known or recorded.

Thus, if everyone commits crime, it becomes difficult to sustain a qualitative distinction between 'criminals' and 'non-criminals', so that attempts to find universal causes of crime like abnormal chromosome structures, inadequate socialisation or distinctive subcultural value systems are inevitably misleading and fruitless. As Pearson (1975, p. 63) observes: 'When the blinds of positivism are pulled away, all men are revealed as potentially law-breaking. The commonsense gulf between "us" and "them", which is supported by positivist criminology to a considerable extent, is dismembered.'

The problematic nature of deviance

Labelling theorists suggest that crime (and any deviant behaviour) is to be best seen as *subjectively problematic*, since the relationship between the commission of a criminal act and the designation of that act and its perpetrator as 'criminal' is by no means a perfect one. Thus we need to ask why it is that behaviour in *some* contexts and engaged in by *some* people comes to be defined and processed as 'criminal', while other behaviour and actors experienced no such labelling. If anything, we should not be surprised at the amount of officially recorded crime but should concentrate our attention on how and why *so little* of the criminal activity which occurs is processed by the agencies of social control. We must abandon the search for 'causes' of crime in favour of an analysis of the *social processes* by which the behaviour of some individuals comes to be labelled as officially criminal and look at the ensuing *consequences* and implications for these individuals. Traditional criminology, despite occasionally recognising the inadequacy of official figures on crime, generally proceeded as if it were dealing with the whole 'class' of criminals (or at least a representative section of it), instead of recognising and treating as a primary the fact that official criminals constitute a *socially defined* population publicly labelled as 'criminal'.

So, a preoccupation with etiology – a search for causes – is to be dispensed with, in favour of an analysis of the processes of social definition of behaviour, of how some actors and their behaviour come, in certain contexts, to be labelled as 'criminal' or 'deviant'. We cannot categorise behaviour abstractly or non-contextually as criminal or deviant, since definitions of behaviour in those categories rests on a socially conferred judgement. Social rules and the persons and acts which become officially deemed as deviant from them are, then, *socially constructed* phenomena, emerging from the patterns of social interaction in a society. As Becker (1963, p. 14), perhaps the most renowned figure in the labelling tradition, says: 'Deviance is not a simple quality present in some kinds of behaviour and absent in others. [It] is not a quality that lies in the behaviour itself, but in the interaction between those who commit acts and those who respond to them.'

A major implication of such a perception is that the labelling perspective lays great stress on the *dynamic* processes of the labelling of behaviour as criminal or deviant, with the concomitant rejection of the idea that deviance can be seen as a 'present or absent' feature of behaviour. Thus the focus of investigation must be significantly extended to embrace a more micro-sociological perception of deviance and of the ways in which social meanings are imposed on behaviour within specific social settings.

In order to understand crime and deviance as problematic products of a process of social interaction we have to consider *all* the groups involved: rather than unambiguously concentrating on the deviant actor, we must also examine the *social audience* and its reaction to law-breaking, since labels are not automatically imposed on all law-breakers, and some escape labelling altogether.

We must see deviance as having two sides – behaviour and reaction – both of which are problematic but reciprocally and integrally interrelated. More specifically, we cannot understand social deviance *without* understanding social control, in the form of the response of the rest of society, and particularly that of the police and courts, to rule-breaking behaviour.

The study of crime or deviance, then, must encompass analysis of the law-breaker, the law-maker, the law-enforcer and the community at large. Traditional criminology tended to take social reaction for granted or at best to be studied as a discrete afterthought, and not as an integral element.

Similarly, official statistics, rather than being a means of research – that is, a resource providing data on the phenomenon to be studied – should be regarded as an *end* of research, a socially constructed phenomenon worthy of study in their own right. They may tell us more about the *activities of the agencies of social control* than about the extent and incidence of criminal behaviour. We shall consider these activities shortly, but we must first give some attention to labelling theorists' observations on *law-making*, since we have stressed how their approach emphasises a reorientation towards rules and social reaction in the social construction of deviance.

Labelling theorists argue that positivist approaches to crime and deviance tend to regard the norms and values of society as given and absolute, and hence fall into the trap (often unwittingly) of supposing that a consensus on values is more widespread than is the case with the 'norms of society', carrying misleadingly precise connotations of deviance and conformity. Labelling theorists argue that we should not adopt a position of *moral absolutism*, as positivist theories do, but should reject such a consensus view in favour of one of *moral relativism*, seeing rules and values as problematic, and not as societal 'givens'. (This is one reason why much work by sociologists within the labelling tradition has centred on behaviour on which no clear-cut consensus exists, such as drug-taking, gambling and homosexuality.)

But why *should* we adopt such a position? Their answer is that social rules and laws have to be seen as essentially *political products*: that some groups in society are capable of creating these rules and laws and hence of deciding what behaviour is regarded as deviant or criminal. Although many areas of illegal behaviour are popularly presented as a threat to widely held core values, laws are not an automatic reflection of 'the will of the people', nor are they invariably directed against behaviour which is universally believed to challenge fundamental social arrangements. Behaviour is often made illegal even when the majority may not regard it as deviant, criminal or terribly wrong: prohibition in the USA early this century was a classic example of laws often vigorously enforced which in no way commanded the support of the majority of citizens.

We need to understand, then, that definitions of 'criminal' and 'deviant' reflect the *power* of groups who have succeeded in having their ideas and values about normality, deviance and wrong-doing imposed on a society and established in social conventions and laws. Becker calls these rule-creators 'moral entrepreneurs' – individuals and groups with particular interests and the necessary resources to define and control behaviour as 'deviant' or 'undesirable'.

Thus, for labelling theorists, the establishment and enforcement of laws are very much bound up with the distribution of power in a society, so that some groups may be more likely to commit 'crime' because their behaviour is more likely to be defined as 'criminal' by those with power. Deviance, then, is 'a consequence of a process of interaction between people, some of whom in the service of their own interests make and enforce rules which catch others, who in the service of their own interests have committed acts which are labelled deviant' (Becker, 1963, p. 163).

Certain groups, then, are in a position to define the dominant social and legal values. But what about laws which exist to curb the behaviour of the powerful? Labelling theorists suggest that such laws are much less frequently activated, that the deviance of the more powerful is less publicly displayed, that these groups have the resources to shield their behaviour from exposure, and that their behaviour is much less heavily monitored by the agencies of social control. This inevitably leads us to a further important element of the labelling perspective – the problematic and selective nature of law enforcement.

Problematic law enforcement

Labelling theorists argue that the agencies of social control employ considerable *discretion* and *selective judgement* in deciding whether and how to deal with illegal behaviour which they encounter, so that an understanding of the organisational practices and perceptions of the police and the courts is fundamental to the study of crime. While such discretion might not be exercised in, say, cases of murder, most criminal activity is of a more mundane nature, in which police and court encounters with illegal behaviour do not result in all cases in similar action.

It is impossible practically and unwise tactically for the police to process *all* criminal activity. They come across all manner of illegal activities, but to deal with it all in a formal way would strain their resources beyond the limit. Tactically, relations with the general public are important, so that vigorous enforcement of laws not enjoying full public support may lead to loss of respect, hostility or lack of co-operation from sections of the community whose support they require. Hence full law enforcement does not occur, and 'criminal' labels are not universally bestowed.

Labelling theorists argue that the police operate in their work with *pre-existing conceptions* of what constitutes 'trouble', what 'criminals' are like, of what areas need heavy policing, and so on: that is, *stereotypical categories* shape their perception and structure their responses to behaviour which they encounter. Thus it may well be that a particular individual committing an offence will be arrested, charged, tried, found guilty and sentenced, while another may be ignored or merely cautioned for the (objectively) same act. Such selective discrimination, labelling theorists argue, may not so much depend on criteria connected with the nature of the *actual behaviour* as on police officers' personal biases and prejudices about certain groups and offences, their perception of the community's feelings about such offences, the family background of the offender, the latter's attitudes and appearance, and so on.

A good illustration here is a study by Piliavin and Briar (1964) of a police department in a large American city. They found extensive evidence of policemen exercising discretion in decisions about official action, largely based on officers' assessment of character from juvenile offenders' appearance, accent and attitude: those giving a positive impression on such counts were far less likely to be arrested and charged. The authors observe:

> The official delinquent, as distinct from the juvenile who simply commits a delinquent act, is the product of a social judgment, in this case a judgment made by the police. He is a delinquent because someone in authority has defined him as one, often on the basis of the public face he has presented to officials rather than of the kind of offence he has committed (Piliavin and Briar, 1964, p. 214).

Similarly, studies have shown that judicial decisions reveal selective patterns of conviction and sentencing, emphasising that, again, a process of social interaction is at work between offenders and the courts. Those involved in disposing of defendants have ideas about 'typical' offenders and the causes of their behaviour which are sometimes enshrined in the law. In Britain, for instance, the 1969 Children and Young Persons Act encouraged the setting aside of a custodial sentence – that is, a 'softening' of the labelling process – if the juvenile offender could be shown to come from a 'good' home background with supportive parents.

Police and court perceptions and practices, then, do not result in the uniform application of the law but often involve highly selective decisions. Thus we should not be surprised to find blacks and working-class people over-represented in the official statistics of crime, since they and their behaviour are more likely to fit law-enforcement agencies' perceptions of 'criminals' and 'crime', and they are less likely to be able to mobilise the material and social resources necessary to convince others that 'they're not like that'.

We have been emphasising how labelling theory is less interested in 'patterns' of crime and deviance than in the process whereby individuals come to be seen as deviant and labelled as 'outsiders'. As we have seen, the application of such public labels is frequently fortuitous, not necessarily dependent on the nature or gravity of the act but on the subsequent behaviour and/or social characteristics of the actor and the attitudes and perceptions of social-control agencies. Selective law enforcement is significant enough in itself, but it is even more important when one considers *what happens* to individuals labelled as 'deviant' or 'criminal'.

The process of labelling

In their view, the application of a deviant or criminal label to actors' behaviour serves essentially as a 're-ordering' mechanism with which to interpret satisfactorily action which may be perceived as dangerous, disruptive, alarming or unsettling. For example, two men seen walking hand-in-hand along the street disrupts many people's 'picture of reality', but the labelling of this behaviour as 'homosexual' and therefore deviant 'makes sense' of it and provides a set of interpretations for future encounters with these individuals. Thus the application of deviant labels is not merely a punitive response or an expression of disapproval but also an attempt by the social audience to produce a sense of order in social relations.

The major implication of this process rests on the fact that the attachment of a deviant label has important effects on how individuals are perceived by others, on how they come to regard themselves, and on the subsequent patterns of interaction between them and others, since the ascription of deviant or criminal status means that individual actors and the social group around them must accommodate themselves to a 'spoiled identity'. The critical point in this process is the public exposure of one's deviant activity. As Becker (1963, pp. 31–2) observes:

> One of the most crucial steps in the process of building a stable pattern of deviant behaviour is likely to be the experience of being caught and publicly labelled as a deviant ... Being caught and branded as a deviant has important consequences for one's further social participation and self-image.

. A process of *stigmatisation* occurs: getting caught leads to a re-evaluation of one's public identity by others, whereby one becomes labelled as a certain 'kind' of person, to be viewed and treated by others in the light of this label. A new status is accorded to the deviant, and the possibility of retaining a normal identity is made increasingly difficult. This is intensified by the fact that the label *oversimplifies* what the deviant 'is' through its *stereotyping and 'essentialising' effect*. It is not merely attached to his or her behaviour but to his or her whole being, so that he or she is seen as nothing but a deviant. This 'master status' takes over any other conception we may have of him or her or which he or she may wish to project. For instance, someone who has been sexually involved with children is not seen as a neighbour, a factory manager or a parent who has committed certain offences, but as a 'sex maniac' or 'pederast'. As Rock (1973, p. 32) says: 'Rule-breaking is not so much regarded as an ephemeral partial aspect of a person's self but as an indication of his essence. A deviant role is not just another role in a varied repertoire; it is a critical and revealing guide to a deviant *personality*.'

What deviants (occasionally) do becomes transformed into what they are: their whole identity and existence become questionable. But the re-ordering of present identity is not the only issue at stake – *past* behaviour may also come to be seen in a new (and inevitably negative) light, so that perfectly harmless behaviour is reinterpreted as having reflected sinister and deviant motivations. Similarly, *future* conduct is predicted as likely to be shaped by the present deviant identity – 'he won't change, they never do', or 'once a queer, always a queer', and so on.

Interaction now occurs within the context of the existence of a deviant label, and resisting its consequences becomes difficult, since it may not be possible to convince others that a continuing application of the label is not justified, that 'they've got it all wrong', and so on. Sustaining an alternative image in the eyes of others (and of oneself) is inhibited by the power of the deviant definitions which are being imposed, and the deviant's good intentions of behaving 'normally' may be subverted by the fact that the response of others in very practical ways reduces the chances of 'normal' behaviour – that is, the social support which may enable them to engage in such behaviour (and hence to resist the 'deviant' label) is now denied them. Imagine a 24-year-old male, living in a village, who has a 15-year-old girl friend with whom he has sexual relations: the public revelation of such activity brands him as an 'unlawful-sex' man (even 'kinky'), so that subsequent attempts to establish relationships with older females (i.e. 'normal' behaviour) may be constantly rebuffed, despite his attempts to reassure them that his sexual tastes are not deviantly narrow. He is thrown back, as it were, on younger females, thus 'confirming' his deviant inclinations.

The stigmatising effect, then, of the label places deviants outside conventional circles and sparks off a sense of uncertainty in them. They feel branded as 'deviant' despite their denials, and, put simply, become bad because they are defined as bad. That is, a *self-fulfilling prophecy* occurs, in which a self-image and subsequent behaviour result from the reactions of others: deviants are labelled and come to live up to this label, because their perception of themselves depends to a large part on the perceptions of others with whom they interact.

According to the labelling view, the long-term effect of this process is to lock individuals into deviant roles and project them along deviant courses or careers, by closing off legitimate opportunities and forcing them to resort to social groups which offer support but perpetuate their deviant activity, thus reinforcing and confirming an 'outsider' status and a negative self-image and precluding the possibility of a withdrawal from deviance. Thus society 'creates' deviance in the sense that the application of deviant labels may produce more deviance than it prevents. As Becker (1963, p. 9) says:

> Social groups create deviance by making the rules whose infraction constitutes deviance, and by applying those rules to particular people and labelling them as outsiders ... When the deviant is caught he is treated in accordance with popular diagnosis of why he is that way, and the treatment itself may well produce increasing deviance.

For the labelling approach, then, our focus of analysis must be on the ways in which the behaviour of certain actors comes to be defined as 'deviant' or 'criminal' and the effects of this labelling process on their future behaviour. We must recognise a difference *in kind* between what Lemert (1966) has called 'primary' and 'secondary' deviance and must concentrate our attention on the latter. Primary deviance comprises the widespread acts of deviant behaviour in which we all engage, but which in most cases do not lead to apprehension and public labelling. Lemert and other labelling theorists are not particularly interested in why individuals become involved in such activity: that is, they regard the study of the origins and 'causes' of this behaviour as of comparatively little value for two reasons.

First, a search for causes assumes, as we suggested earlier, a common thread running through illegal acts. Lemert argues that primary deviance arises from a variety of motivations and circumstances – a search for 'kicks', desire for gain, risk-taking, or whatever – which may be of such variation from one individual to another that any meaningful generalisation or all-embracing theory may well be impossible, or at best largely trivial.

Second, primary deviance entails *little implication* for the individual's self-image – it is behaviour engaged in without being incorporated into one's identity, but rather is accommodated easily into a favourable conception of oneself. Such acts are 'merely troublesome adjuncts of normally conceived roles . . . with only marginal implications for the psychic structure of the individual' (Lemert, 1966, p. 17).

It is only when social reactions in the form of public labelling occur that problems come about. Such processes may create numerous difficulties for deviants, forcing them to embark on a career of 'secondary' deviance, which is crucially distinct in evolving a *self-image* as a deviant. According to Lemert, a spiralling sequence of interaction between the deviant and the community in the form of progressive deviance and penalties ensues, so that the deviant becomes confirmed in a deviant role. Thus the process of what has been called *deviance amplification* is set in motion.

Undoubtedly the rise of labelling perspectives represents a major turning-point in the study of crime and deviance. Labelling theorists have been responsible for confronting many questions which traditional positivist explanations occasionally recognised but rarely made explicit: the problematic nature of the phenomenon of 'crime' and of the process of interaction involved in the definition of behaviour as such; the political and ideological implications of a correctionalist stance; the recognition of the value-laden implications of accepting an official definition of crime; and the stress on the role of power in the defining process. All of these have become central issues in the discussion of crime and deviance thanks to labelling theory.

But we must not assume that labelling theory has gone unchallenged, since it too has been the subject of much critical attention and has sparked off two distinctly divergent approaches to the study of deviance: on the one hand, an even stronger anti-positivist orientation in phenomenological and ethnomethodological approaches; and on the other, the development of a structuralist reaction in the form of recent attempts in 'radical' criminology to apply Marxist concepts and ideas to the explanation of crime and deviance. In this brief outline of the history of the study of deviance, then, the pattern of development of sociology is reflected in microcosm.

11.6   THE CRITIQUE OF LABELLING THEORY

Labelling theorists have received a variety of criticisms from a number of different perspectives. They have been accused of engaging in over-romanticised accounts of deviance which, in their concern to sympathise with the 'underdog', significantly distort the reality of crime. Thus their alleged over-concentration on marginal and often exotic forms of deviant behaviour has produced rich and varied insights into the 'grey' world of homosexuals, marijuana users, and others, but *at the expense of* a complete analysis of mainstream criminal offenders against property and the like. Young (1975, p. 68) says of the labelling perspective: 'Indeed it is engaged in an astonishing accomplishment – the development of a criminology that does not deal with property crime, and a criminology whose subjects live in a world not of work but of leisure.'

A number of critics, such as Akers (1967), Taylor *et al.* (1973) and Box (1971), also question labelling theorists' disregard of the origins of deviant behaviour. Such an omission, they maintain, places *too much emphasis* on the impact of the social reaction and hence on deviants' *present* experiences at the expense of a recognition of their *past*. This particular line of attack constitutes one of the underlying threads of a further criticism levelled at labelling theorists – that they have been guilty of *oversimplifying* the process of labelling, and particularly of minimising the *role of deviants themselves* in the defining process.

Such critics, along with Bordua (1970) and Gouldner (1968), argue that labelling theory tends to view deviants and criminals as rather too power-less and passive victims of labels about which they can do nothing. For Bordua, the deviant is portrayed as 'an empty organism or at least one with little or no autonomous capacity to determine conduct', they are 'men on their back ... more sinned against than sinning', a sharp and even contradictory contrast with the free-floating, self-willed primary deviant. Thus the *degree of choice* and *consciousness* of actors, and the *meaning* of their behaviour to them, is apparently devalued by the labelling perspective. And as Taylor *et al.* (1973) and Mankoff (1971) point out, we cannot rule out the possibility that deviants choose to continue in their behaviour simply because they find it *rewarding* in some way, 'because of a positive attachment to rule-breaking' (Mankoff, 1971).

Furthermore, critics argue, if the process of labelling is as simplified as it sometimes appears in labelling theory, then it should be uniform in its effects. Not only should it always produce negative consequences (secondary deviance) but, conversely, such consequences should only be produced by the application of the label. But is this always the case? Davis (1972) and Bordua (1970) suggest that the application of official deviant labels may well result in a *decrease* rather than an increase in deviant behaviour (as a consequence of the shock and shame of the experience). Similarly, it is possible that certain individuals or groups may take on a deviant identity and manifest all the features of a secondary deviant *without* any public labelling of their behaviour occurring – homosexuals, for instance, may see themselves as deviant prior to or in the absence of any public labelling experience simply by virtue of being *symbolically associated* with others so designated. And other deviants may *actively negotiate* labels for themselves in their interactions with others, by encouraging the application of deviant labels or adapting to the labelling process by employing 'techniques of neutralisation' (Sykes and Matza, 1957) or 'fighting-back' techniques (Rogers and Buffalo, 1974).

Much of the preceding critique of labelling theory thus centres on the dangers of not doing justice to the response of deviants and the *meaning* of their behaviour to them. The need to recognise and centralise the meaning of deviant acts to both actors and reactors has prompted the adoption of an even more micro-sociological and anti-positivist conception of behaviour in general and deviant behaviour in particular in the form of phenomenology and ethnomethodology. While a more detailed consideration of these approaches can be found in the last two chapters of this book we must examine briefly their general assumptions and procedures to appreciate their relevance for deviance study.

Phenomenology, ethnomethodology and deviance

Although phenomenological sociology and ethnomethodology share a number of common themes with the symbolic interactionist approach, which informs much of labelling theory, there are also significant points of departure between them. Phenomenology starts from the idea that the social world and interaction is essentially fragile and provisional, where the meaning of social situations and behaviour is not 'given' but has to be constructed by members. Stable social interaction rests on the possession of shared stocks of socially constructed knowledge: that is, 'social life' is a matter of the ways in which individuals create shared social meanings. The subject-matter for sociologists, then, is the subjective meanings of actors, and more especially the common-sense taken-for-granted knowledge of everyday life which they employ in effecting the 'practical accomplishment' called 'society'. Sociologists, however, must not *predefine* the members' world with their own concepts or 'second-order constructs', as opposed to the 'first-order constructs' employed by members, since one set of constructs is no more meaningful than the other – there can be no *special* status for sociological generalisations. Thus:

> The investigation of substantive areas should give primacy to the revealing of the shared meanings people attach to their situation, and the rules in terms of which they interpret their situation ... The sociologist's accounts are commonsense accounts, as are those of members, and share the same status as members' accounts as documents of practical reasoning (Phillipson and Roche, 1974, pp. 135, 139).

The study of deviance, from this point of view, is the study of the problematic nature and outcome of 'moral meanings' and their part in the 'production' of social order. Like labelling theorists, phenomenologists accept that deviance is constituted and made meaningful by social interaction, and they commend the former for questioning absolutist conceptions of legal and social rules and for pointing to the problematic and socially constructed definition of behaviour through public labelling and selective law enforcement. But in their view labelling analyses are not thoroughgoing enough. First, while labelling theorists stress the importance of actors' perspectives, they do not present and use members' meanings, but rather rely on *their own* sociological constructions of these meanings, or at least do not indicate clearly how these are derived from the first-order constructs of actors. Second, although they acknowledge the ambiguity of 'crime' and 'deviance', they still accept *official* definitions of deviance (even if they see them as selectively applied) and hence the idea that social norms as abstract rules exist as 'solid' and 'real' entities.

For the phenomenologist and ethnomethodologist the 'moral rules' involved in the production of deviance are inherently problematic and do not correspond (necessarily) with any social norms or 'surface rules', however selectively enforced. These moral rules require 'situation construction' for their use in everyday life, so that the interpretation of behaviour as 'deviant' does not depend on the application of some normative guideline but on certain 'common-sense' rules embracing notions of, say, responsibility, provocation, and so on – that is, it depends on methods of 'practical reasoning' and decision-making which are highly provisional.

The focus of interest in understanding deviance, then, should be on the *procedures* actors employ to make sense of problematic behaviour, on

> the procedures for arriving at formulations of character and biography, for accusing and excusing, for interpreting points of law in specific cases, for bringing

an action under the jurisdiction of a rule or law, for ascribing motives, for imputing responsibility, for assessing evidence, and the rest (Coulter, 1974, p. 131).

A number of ethnomethodological studies have demonstrated this preoccupation. Cicourel's (1968) study, for example, focuses on the 'background expectancies' and common-sense constructions employed by law-enforcement agencies, particularly police and social workers, in creating delinquents. He emphasises 'the negotiable character of who comes to be defined as "criminal"', a process which involves clarification of the ways in which formal legal statutes are linked by officials to concrete situations and cases to produce 'delinquents'. So, both official statistics and the 'delinquent' contained within them are artificially 'solid' phenomena of a highly provisional character which particularly conceal the ways in which the police and probation officers deal with cases and events by the use of 'typifications' or 'folk theories' of delinquents and their behaviour to produce a stable logical picture of 'delinquency'.

Similarly, Bittner's (1967) study attempts to show how police activities on 'Skid Row' are a matter of 'practical reasoning' in handling their everyday work with alcoholics. They act in accordance with the demands of the situation, regardless of whether this violates official legal statutes and recommended practices; these are merely *one* consideration, alongside protecting the alcoholics and preventing further trouble, which patrolmen employ in their work. The exigencies of the situation, rather than official rules and norms, prevail.

Radical criminology

Now, while a number of the criticisms made of labelling theory have been characterised by this kind of desire to develop an even more anti-positivist interpretation of deviance and crime, a very different development in the study of crime has sprung out of its analysis of *power*. A number of sociologists have attacked labelling theorists' failure to analyse systematically and fully the structures of power and interests at work in the making of laws and the definitions of 'criminals' and 'deviants'. Gouldner (1968) and Liazos (1972), for instance, maintain that while labelling theorists *raise* questions of power, they fail to deliver a sufficiently coherent and structurally based critique of the operation of the inequalities of power, so that their 'sociology of the underdog' remains a rather romanticised, pseudo-radical liberalism which pays too much attention to the *middle-level* agents of social control (the police, courts, etc.).

For these critics the essentially actor-dominated, mcirosociological level of labelling anaylsis, emphasising interaction, reaction and identity formation, devalues crucial *macrosociological* concerns and fails to expose the wider *economic and socio-political forces* operating in the construction and application of 'deviant' or 'criminal' labels.

This particular reaction to labelling analysis has been more fully reflected in the rise in recent years of a 'radical' or Marxist criminology, which, while accepting many of the insights of labelling theory, attempts to relocate the study of crime and deviance in a *structural* context, in the reality of existing social arrangements. The exponents of this perspective (who can be seen only loosely as a 'school') maintain that we can use Marxist frameworks for a theory of crime and deviance by analysing the ways in which particular systems of production and their attendant social relations in both contemporary capitalism and previous historical periods have generated attempts by the dominant class to order societies in specific ways. Thus today capitalist economic systems must be regarded as the central structural framework for analysing crime; in this view one crucial weakness of labelling theory is its neglect of 'master' structural institutions and its failure to recognise that the definition of behaviour as 'criminal' is inseparably bound up with questions of political economy. The potential radicalism in labelling theory is inhibited by a failure to produce a macro-social analysis of capitalist power structures and, particularly, a theory of the state.

Indeed, both traditional criminology – with its highly consensual view of social order and its correctionalism or liberal reformism – and labelling theory are guilty, according to Marxists, of continuing to accept *official definitions* of crime and deviance in their analysis, as this involves an acceptance of an existing social order by restricting analysis to a predefined range of subject-matter and inhibits the questioning of the propriety of other areas of behaviour. As Liazos (1972, p. 109) says:

> They concentrate their attention on those who have been *successfully* labelled as 'deviant', and not on those who break laws, fix laws, violate ethical and moral standards, harm individuals and groups, etc., but who either are able to hide their actions or when known can deflect criticism, labelling and punishment.

He recommends that we should be prepared to examine 'covert institutionalised violence' such as exploitation, poverty and imperialism. We must recognise, then, the *political dimension* of the definition of behaviour as 'criminal' and locate the ways in which the system of legal control regulating such behaviour is related to the structure of capitalism. In this sense capitalism 'creates' crime in its legal definitions; but it is also criminogenic in a more *direct* sense, in that the behaviour itself is an *integral product* of capitalist economic arrangements. It emanates from the class relations between a propertied and powerful class and the propertyless and powerless classes and is a product of the contradictions and inequalities of capitalism. Taylor *et al.* (1975, p. 34) maintain that

Property crime is better understood as a *normal* and conscious attempt to amass property than as the product of *faulty* socialization or inaccurate and spurious labelling. Both working class and upper class crime ... are *real* features of a society involved in a struggle for property, wealth, and self-aggrandisement ... A society which is predicated on the unequal right to the accumulation of property *gives rise* to the legal and illegal desire to accumulate property as rapidly as possible.

Crime, in this view, *is* determined, as the positivists say – their error, however, lies in their failure to locate their explanation in capitalism's effects on human nature. Radical criminologists stress how the designation of certain kinds of behaviour as 'criminal' is the outcome of the capacity of a dominant economic class to enshrine their definitions of 'crime' and 'deviance' in legal statutes, in definitions which simultaneously legitimise the status quo, proscribe activities which threaten the reproduction of capitalism, and conceal the inequalities of the capitalist system. As Pearce (1976, p. 81) says:

Concentrating on lower-class criminals ... is functional in maintaining the ... class system ... If the criminals are also the social failures ... then their criminality is caused by their *inadequacies* ... and the major social institutions are not exposed to critical assessment.

Thus the study of crime cannot be merely a matter of the uncritical analysis of behaviour which violates ('given') legal norms, since this fails to recognise the political dimension of the phenomenon of crime and perpetuates pluralist myths of impartial laws and an 'arbiter' role for the state. The legal system is an essentially coercive instrument which, while occasionally instituting some laws against powerful groups, is used to secure the interests of the dominant class against behaviour that threatens or disrupts them.

Ultimately, for radical criminologists the study of crime necessarily requires a theory of the state and the legal system in relation to particular systems of production and their attendant class relations and to the legitimation of these arrangements.

While a detailed critique of this approach is not possible here, there are undoubtedly important questions surrounding it which have to be recognised. Some critics, for example, question whether or how far *all* crime can be attributed to capitalism and whether or how far all laws operate in the interests of a dominant capitalist class. How does capitalism produce child abuse, for instance, and how does its prosecution by the law serve capitalist interests? The dangers of lapsing into a crude 'conspiracy theory' of the State and class and power relations are evident here, and some Marxist criminologists have recognised the necessity of theorising more fully and adequately the relation of law and crime to the State and class relations, in ways which view the legal system and agencies of social control as rather less mechanical 'instruments' of class domination.

11.7 WOMEN AND CRIME

A major omission in all the theories of crime and delinquency we have considered is their failure to address fully or at all the issue of *female* offending. Even if we accept that there is a disparity between levels of male and female law-breaking (though, as we observed earlier, Self-Report studies suggest that the gap may not be as large as official data indicate); it remains the case, as Smart (1976), Campbell (1981), Heidensohn (1985) and others have pointed out, that sociological approaches to crime and delinquency have seriously neglected gender variables and in effect, as in many other spheres of sociological theorising, have produced explanations of *male* behaviour while claiming to have explained behaviour generally.

Among the *subculture* theorists we have examined, only Cohen gives females any consideration at all, but in doing so, he fails to take their offencing seriously, defining it narrowly and explaining it simplistically. For Cohen, if the goal of young working-class males is to achieve status and material success, the goal of females is, in effect, to attract and catch men:

> For the adolescent girl as well as for the adult woman, relationships with the opposite sex and those personal qualities which affect the ability to establish such relationships are central in importance. It is no accident that 'boys collect stamps, girls collect boys' (Cohen, 1955, pp. 141–2).

Hence, while working-class male adolescents solve the problem of adjusting to their failure to achieve success by the collective solution of the delinquent subculture, young females make themselves sexually available, but in doing so they run the risk of being seen by the police, the courts and social workers as sexually 'delinquent'. Cohen thus presents a highly *sexist* interpretation which virtually equates female delinquency with sexual activity and give no systematic consideration to their involvement in non-sexual offending, to the patterns and processes of female peer group relations, or to the possible existence of female subcultures.

Labelling theorists similarly make no great attempt to incorporate gender variables into their explanations or specifically to consider in any systematic way the possibility of gender biases in the application of criminal labels or of the differential impact of labelling experiences on males and females. Given differences in gender role expectations and socialisation experiences of males and females in society, it seems likely, firstly, that agencies of social control may be less inclined to see females as fitting some criminal stereotype and hence less willing to attach a criminal label to them. Secondly, it may be that females, once caught and publicly labelled, may respond differently from males to the experience (for instance, feeling a greater sense of guilt and shame).

Radical criminologists, too, have said little about gender and crime: it may be, as they suggest, that capitalist social arrangements play a part in generating crime but, as Klein and Kress (1981) and others have argued, it cannot be assumed that men and women experience capitalism similarly, so that any adequate explanation of crime has to recognise the ways in which women are socialised into capitalist arrangements and the roles they perform within that system domestically, economically and sexually.

11.8   SUICIDE

Our discussion so far illustrates well how different theoretical perspectives in sociology have focused their attention on crime as a major area of deviant behaviour. The study of suicide too, has generated similar controversies, and we now turn our attention to these debates.

Only a small minority of people deliberately end their lives (only about 1 per cent of all deaths in Britain are officially classified as 'suicides'). This small minority may be regarded as deviant in terms of our earlier definition, in that their action goes against what is regarded as normal behaviour by other members of society. Indeed, it is important to remember that suicide and attempted suicide were *criminal* offences in Britain until 1961 – that is, they where *officially* defined as deviant. Not surprisingly, then, a wealth of sociological literature has been amassed over the years dealing with suicide as an example of deviant behaviour. The study of suicide raises in a readily accessible way many of the theoretical and methodological issues discussed throughout this book, and it spotlights once again the debate about the nature of social reality between positivism and interpretivism.

The divergence in these different approaches to suicide may be illustrated by the starkly different opinions of the worth of what is usually regarded as the 'classic' study of the phenomenon: *Suicide*, by Durkheim, first published in 1897. On the one hand, Selvin (1965, p. 113) claims that 'Sixty years after it first appeared in print, Emile Durkheim's *Suicide* is still a model of social research . . . few, if any, later works can match the clarity and power with which Durkheim marshalled his facts to test and refine his theory.' On the other, the ethnomethodologist Sacks (1963, p. 3) maintains equally categorically that 'in terms of the history of sociology nothing is more tragic than that Durkheim's *Suicide* should be conceived as a model investigation'.

In this section we outline the various premises about the nature of social reality and the sociological enterprise that lie behind these two very different assessments. We begin by presenting an uncritical account of Durkheim's *Suicide* which brings out its firm base in the positivistic tradition. We then briefly consider the kinds of criticisms that have been made by those operating from within the same kind of tradition. Finally, we turn to supporters of the interpretivist, anti-positivistic view, who fundamentally challenge the approach of the Durkheimian school.

Durkheim's theory of suicide

In Durkheim's time (the nineteenth century) there had developed a general intellectual movement seeking a scientific understanding of society. Just as the natural sciences, such as physics, proposed various laws of nature based on scientific observation, so the founders of modern sociology sought laws about society. Durkheim believed that if sociology were to be accepted as a science and an academic discipline in its own right, it must be able to establish that its own special area of investigation, 'society', exists as an object that can be studied and about which laws can be formulated. Sociology must be able to identify and account for *social* phenomena.

To demonstrate the existence of social phenomena, we must be able to identify, says Durkheim, processes which are consistent across a whole range and number of individuals but which cannot be reduced to or explained solely in terms of any one individual's expression of them. These processes allow us to identify a collectivity or society which is greater than its parts, the individuals who comprise it. Durkheim was claiming that society exists independently of its individuals, just as a football team is more than just eleven individual players. Members of society adopt its values, beliefs and traditions in common. This neither happens by chance, nor by individual members of society consciously deciding to support particular values and/or beliefs. Rather, Durkheim argues that these aspects of culture are products of collective interaction: individuals are constrained to adopt their culture precisely because they are members of that culture. So, for example, individuals may behave as members of a crowd or audience, they feel obliged to applaud or laugh at the 'right time', to conform to the feeling of the collectivity. The social group is then a social phenomenon since it can be seen to constrain individual behaviour. All such phenomena Durkheim called 'social facts' which can be observed by the sociologist: they comprise 'every way of behaving, fixed or not, capable of exercising an outside constraint' on the individual (Durkheim, 1964, p. 13). In *The Rules of Sociological Method* Durkheim (1964) argues that social facts must be regarded as *things* which can be observed existing at the level of the collectivity and are not reducible to the level of individual behaviour or meaning. It then follows that we can identify social (collective) phenomena by identifying situations of social constraint.

Now suicide is, according to a common-sense view, the most individual of actions. If Durkheim could show that, on the contrary, this act is influenced by the social collectivity, then his proposition that we can identify purely social phenomena has passed its most difficult test: that even in this most solitary and individual of acts something external to individual consciousness, namely 'society', has not only been a 'witness' to but also the 'director' of this tragic drama.

To test his general hypothesis, Durkheim sought evidence that would indicate the social nature of suicide. For this he turned to the statistics of suicide recorded for various societies and groups within societies. From these he could determine different *suicide rates* for different populations. Tables 11.7, 11.8 and 11.9 illustrate the suicide rates used by Durkheim, as well as providing more recent figures.

From his statistical analyses Durkheim drew three conclusions:

(i) Within single societies the incidence or rate of suicide remains remarkably constant over time, e.g. England, 1866–78.
(ii) The suicide rate varies between societies.
(iii) The suicide rate varies between different groups within the *same* society.

The crucial points for Durkheim were that (a) for any society the suicide rate remained constant over many years despite the fact that the individuals comprising it changed, and that (b) between different populations the rate varied considerably. How could such constancy and variation be explained?

TABLE 11.7

Rates of suicide per million

	1866–70	1871–5	1874–8
Italy	30	35	38
Belgium	60	69	78
England	67	66	69
Norway	76	73	71
Prussia	142	134	152
Denmark	277	258	255
Saxony	293	267	334

Source: E. Durkheim, *Suicide*, London, Routledge & Kegan Paul, 1970, p. 50.

TABLE 11.8

Differences in suicide rate across religions
(rates of suicide per million)

Protestant states	190
Mixed states	96
Catholic states	58
Greek states	40

Source: E. Durkheim, *Suicide*, London, Routledge & Kegan Paul, 1970, p. 152.

TABLE 11.9

Rates of suicide per million

	1951	1955	1959	1961
Australia	95	103	111	119
Italy	68	66	62	56
England and Wales	102	113	115	113
France	155	159	169	159
Ireland	26	23	25	32
Japan	183	252	227	196
West Germany	182	192	187	187

Source: World Health Organisation, *World Health Statistics Report*, no. 6, Geneva, 1968.

Having discussed and eliminated factors associated with climate, heredity, alcoholism and the seasons, Durkheim also had to rule out psychological explanations of suicide, which see individual mental states as more or less predisposing some individuals to the pathological states that lead to suicide.

Although Durkheim was prepared to admit that some individuals may have a psychological predisposition towards suicide, he rejected the view that suicide was governed solely by such a predisposition. By considering the variations in the suicide rate across different populations he found no significant correlation or connection between the mental state of individuals and the number of suicides. Psychological explanations of suicide do not then explain the variations in the suicide rate across different populations.

Durkheim was then able to offer a more adequate, sociological, explanation, built on two concepts upon which much of his general sociological perspective depended. These are his ideas of the '*social integration*' and the '*moral regulation*' of society. Durkheim believed that the order or 'harmony' of any society or group within society – such as the family or a religious community – depends on the extent to which it is 'integrated'. Although Durkheim's definition of 'integration' was somewhat vague, in general the concept describes the sharing of values, attitudes, beliefs and behaviour patterns among individuals in a social group: individuals are (more or less) dependent on their group membership for their social identity. The group provides an ordered world which guides individual action in such a way that it continuously renews the bond between members of the group. An integrated family is one in which individuals share values and expectations, and engage in behaviour that promotes the interests and 'order' of the family as a group.

Durkheim's other central idea, moral regulation, refers not so much to *how* groups or societies in general establish cohesion among their members but more to *why* this process occurs. According to him, individuals have human appetites and desires that, left unchecked, are limitless, so that society needs to restrain humans' unlimited, egocentric desires – otherwise they would be engaged in an endless and ungratified search for satisfaction. Thus Durkheim claimed that society functions to provide control over individual desires, such that individuals are satisfied with their position in society, by not only controlling the means through which satisfaction is to be achieved but also by socialising the individual into accepting that certain ends or goals rather than others should be pursued. In a sense, then, Durkheim believed that individuals only want those things that society tells them to want. While there could not be too much moral regulation in society, Durkheim argued that too much integration could have harmful effects; we shall see later how over-integration may promote the tendency to commit suicide.

Durkheim (1970, p. 44) defined suicide as 'every case of death resulting directly or indirectly from a positive or negative act performed by the victim himself which he knows will produce this result'. A positive act would be to hang oneself, for example. A negative act would be the captain who 'goes down with his ship'.

> Durkheim then offers the following proposition to account for the variation in the suicide rate: 'Suicide varies ... with the degree of integration of the social group of which the individual forms a part.' He follows this by attempting to demonstrate its validity by classifying suicide into three basic types: 'egoistic', 'altruistic', and 'anomic' suicides.

Egoistic suicides

These are the most common, according to Durkheim, and result from 'excessive individualism' among individuals with few social ties – that is, when individuals become detached from the values and expectations shared by those around them. Durkheim says that egoistic suicide is 'inversely proportional to the degree of integration to be found in the groups of which the individual is a part'. In other words, a low degree of integration gives rise to a high suicide rate, and vice versa.

Durkheim argued that particular religious, domestic (family and parental) and political ties act as social integrators and therefore as factors inhibiting egoistic suicide. For example:

(i) Single, widowed and divorced people are more prone to suicide than married people, and in turn, married people with children have even more immunity to suicide, which is strengthened as the number of children increases.

(ii)   There are higher suicide rates among Protestants than among Catholics and Jews, and a higher rate in predominantly Protestant countries than in predominantly Catholic ones. All condemn suicide equally strongly, so why should such variation occur? Durkheim's answer is that Protestantism involves a higher degree of religious individualism and is less dominated by a group morality. Protestants are given much more personal freedom in deciding how to express, both intellectually and behaviourally, their faith. The Catholic church, however, has a tightly woven set of beliefs and ritual practices to which the life of individual believers is closely bound. In other words, Catholics are much more protected from egoistic suicide because they are much more integrated into religious life. Similarly, Durkheim argued that Jews have a lower rate than Protestants because they have strong ethnic and family allegiances, and a history of persecution which has bound them together as a highly integrated group.

(iii)   In times of political turmoil – e.g. in war, revolution – there is a greater feeling of unity between people, a stronger sense of community: the struggle against a common crisis unites the population and hence increases individuals' immunity from egoistic suicide.

Altruistic suicides

These occur when individuals are *completely* immersed within their social group, so highly integrated that in effect the individual has little or no value. For example, the Hindu widow in India throws herself on the funeral pyre of her dead husband because it is expected of her by the social group, i.e. she is conforming to the demands of the society without regard to her self-preservation. Altruistic suicide is also found in armies, where the suicide rate is higher among officers than lower ranks. This is because officers are subject to a code of behaviour, or, more correctly, a 'code of honour'. It is honourable for officers to die for soldiers because they are responsible for their safety. Alternatively, they may commit suicide as the honourable thing to do because they have failed in their duty as officers. Durkheim sees this type of suicide as essentially obligatory: that is, the individual has little choice, since he or she has 'little value', but is part of a highly compact and integrated society. As Durkheim (1970, pp. 220–1) says: 'For the individual to occupy so little place in collective life he must be almost completely absorbed in the group and the latter, accordingly, very highly integrated.'

Anomic suicides

An 'anomic' situation exists when society's members have lost the normative order by which their behaviour and expectations are regulated. For some reason or other the established norms cease to operate. According to Durkheim, when the social order is disturbed an increase in the anomic suicide rate ensues. This influences society's capacity for moral regulation: when a society has lost its ability to regulate the moral order, when there is a lack of a clear definition of norms, individuals have little to guide them and no longer derive a sense of satisfaction about their position in the world. Desires and wants at these times are less disciplined, and so, Durkheim argued, 'deregulation or anomie' sets in. A period of social disorder may occur through economic disruption, such as a financial disaster like the Wall Street 'crash' of 1929, or times of sudden and extreme economic prosperity.

In conclusion, Durkheim argues that these three types of suicide (egoistic, altruistic and anomic) are related to one single social factor – the internal cohesion and integration of the social group. Thus the suicide rate in a society depends on the degree to which its institutions produce objectively identifiable states of egoism, altruism and anomie: 'The basic proposition that social factors are objective ... finds a new and especially conclusive proof in statistics and above all in the statistics of suicide' (Durkheim, 1970).

The 'internal' critique

Durkheim's theory and methodology, as well as many of his conclusions, have been subjected to detailed criticism over the years from within positivism. It is not our intention to examine all of these here, for most are relatively minor ones which do not question the overall adequacy of the assumptions behind Durkheim's pioneering efforts to use empirical data to support a theoretical explanation of the causes of suicide. For example, his student Halbwachs (1930) confirms the relationships that Durkheim establishes between suicide and family structure and suicide and religion, only adding that we should not see these variables as having an independent effect. He argues that several of the factors that Durkheim *isolates* as being associated with a high rate of suicide are in fact *combined* in the conditions of modern urban life, and that perhaps the major explanatory factor in suicide is the difference between rural and urban ways of life. Thus the higher rate of suicide among Protestants than among Catholics may be more a function of Protestants' *urban* location than any independent effect produced by the religion itself. Similarly, he argues, evidence indicating a higher suicide rate among the unmarried, divorced and those living alone could be attributed to a lack of integration in urban areas and the absence of friends or relatives willing and able to hide the evidence of suicide.

From the same kind of perspective Durkheim has also been criticised for not providing an adequate operational definition of one of his key concepts, social integration – without an adequate indicator of what integration is, it is hardly likely that different degrees of integration can be adequately assessed. Gibbs and Martin (1964) attempt to provide such a definition, suggesting that an integrated society exhibits stable and durable relationships and that these are most likely to occur when the individual has compatible statuses. Arguing that status integration exists when the individual's status in one role does not conflict with the status in another (for example, an individual can be said to have compatible statuses when educational status and occupational status are in alignment), they suggest that the suicide rate varies inversely with the degree of status integration. A variety of other criticisms from within a positivist tradition have also been levelled at Durkheim's work on suicide: for example, it has been claimed that Durkheim ignored contradictory data in his attempts to 'fit' the available data to his theory; that he misinterpreted, often deliberately, other theoretical contributions to the suicide debate; and that he dismissed far too readily the influence of non-social factors in suicide.

However, these kinds of criticisms proceed from a position which essentially accepts the validity of Durkheim's basic approach, only questioning the accuracy and adequacy of specific aspects of his analysis.

The 'external' critique: the interpretivist reaction

Interpretivists, on the other hand, provide what we can call an 'external' critique of the approach not only to Durkheim but of all those working in a positivist tradition. The work of Douglas (1967) and Atkinson (1978) exemplifies this kind of criticism.

Interpretivists, as we have pointed out in this chapter and elsewhere in the book, argue that the source of individual attributes and behaviour cannot be seen as external to individual actors, since social reality is consciously and actively created by individuals who *mean* to do things and who attribute meanings to the behaviour of others. Durkheim appears to deny this premise by arguing that suicide rates are social facts which can only be explained by reference to sociological categories of 'egoism', 'anomie', etc., and not by examining the way in which individuals make sense of the situations in which they find themselves by assigning meanings to them. Douglas argues that the social meanings of suicide should be the central concern of sociologists *and* that they were in fact central to Durkheim's *own* analysis; according to Douglas, Durkheim operated with an *implicit* theory of shared social meanings, and these meanings are the real causal agents in his findings.

For example, he stresses that Durkheim's argument that common morality reproves suicide is no more than an *assumption* on his part for which he provides no evidence; he simply assumes that common morality corresponds to his own morality. Similarly, in explaining the different relationship between non-marriage, marriage and suicide rates for men and women he again relies fundamentally upon his own common-sense interpretations of the differences between the masculine and feminine mind and social position which fit his theory but for which he again provides no evidence. In effect, then, Douglas argues, Durkheim contradicts his own rules of explaining social facts only by reference to other social facts.

So, for Douglas, the error in Durkheim's approach lies in its assumption that suicide is a unidimensional and unvarying form of behaviour just waiting to be discovered 'out there' by analysis of official statistics. According to Douglas, we must instead investigate the way in which these statistics are *themselves* socially constructed – an analysis of those processes of interpretation by which acts come to be *defined* as suicide.

How and why do such interpretations vary? Douglas argues that we must examine both the way in which different *societies* operate with different cultural conceptions of what sort of action constitutes suicide and also, within the *same* society, the way in which the interpretations of a variety of interested parties (often influenced by the wishes of the deceased) can transform a death into a suicide.

Douglas shows how the act of taking one's life, and in fact the very concept of 'death', may have very different meanings for the members of different societies. For example, among Trobriand Islanders attempted suicide is used as an acceptable sanction in matrimonial disputes and is 'meant' as an indictment of an offending spouse. Again, in Japan, suicide may be regarded as a *honourable* death, which contrasts with the shame accorded it under the Christian tradition.

The social construction of suicide

Douglas's most significant emphasis – and the focus of much of Atkinson's work – is on the way in which particular deaths within particular societies come to be defined as 'suicides'. Both agree that from an examination of this process it becomes clear that suicide, far from being a 'social fact', is instead very much the product of meaningful categorisation by officials investigating certain kinds of act, and that it cannot be assumed that these officials share the *same* meanings on which they base their interpretations. Officials, no less than all other members of society, necessarily operate with their respective stocks of common-sense knowledge which they cannot help but use to make sense of the reality which they encounter – in this case suspicious death. Let us examine more closely the implications of these interpretivist assumptions for the sociology of suicide.

In Western culture suicide is regarded as an unnatural form of death, and suspected cases have to come under the scrutiny of a wide range of officials, including doctors, the police and coroners. Consequently, what eventually appears as a 'suicide' in the official statistics results from a very complicated process of inference and the application of common-sense notions on the part of all the people involved in the process.

Furthermore, despite the fact that there may be some general agreement that 'intention to die' is in some way a necessary distinguishing characteristic of suicide, there are likely to be considerable differences of opinion among officials of different countries, and among officials of the *same* country, as to how such an intention may be inferred.

Both Douglas and Atkinson provide numerous examples of this. Douglas (1967, p. 185) cites an American coroner who refused to label a death as suicide unless a note was found with the body, while Atkinson (1971) shows not only that coroners can be crucially influenced by the *mode* of death – road accidents, for example, are very seldom classified as suicides, whereas hangings almost invariably are – but that they also often take into account other significant factors such as the location and circumstances of the death. There is, however, no consistency among coroners in their selection of those factors which they regard as significant indicators of the intention to die.

Furthermore, they argue, different coroners' offices – and indeed *all* the officials concerned – use different *search procedures* in their efforts to obtain evidence of *cause* of death, and different degrees of thoroughness in looking for indications of *intent*. For example, some officials approach more informants than others in their search for socially defined motives for suicide (such as unhappiness). These different informants thus add to the cumulative process by which suicides are socially constructed by using *their* own stocks of common-sense knowledge and assessments of the victim's character and state of mind in making their own sense of his or her action. One official may read private diaries and letters in the search for clues, whereas another official might define such actions as violation of basic rights of privacy that even the dead possess. There is, of course, no way of knowing whether the biases introduced into the statistics by these practices are systematic or random.

According to Douglas and Atkinson, whether the official cause of death is designated as 'suicide' or 'accidental' is very much a *social* product, the result of a complex interaction process involving the physical scene, the sequence of events leading up to the act, the significant others of the deceased, various officials such as doctors and the police, the public, and finally the official who must impute the 'correct' category. It is this final categorisation that produces an apparently 'solid' suicide out of what can in fact be a much more imprecise, and problematic, situation.

All of this clearly demonstrates the interpretivist emphasis on the way in which definitions of deaths as suicides are *social* constructions. Quite simply, the argument is that since the accomplishment of *all* social interaction necessarily involves the application of a meaning by one actor to the action of others, there can be no reason why things should be any different so far as the interaction between the living and the dead is concerned.

Yet interpretivists also emphasise that we should not think that the interpretative procedures employed by those whose job it is to apply a meaning to a death are the *only* meanings involved; like all other pieces of social interaction, the social construction of suicide is not simply a one-sided activity. Although (except in the case of suicide notes) suicides lack the usual means which actors employ to communicate meaning – language – this does not mean that individuals who have taken, or intend to take their own lives cannot *by different means* try to structure the interpretations of this act by others.

We suggested in our discussion of crime that interpretivists see individuals not just as passive recipients of labels but as having a role to play in actively negotiating their own identity, and so it is with suicide. For example, someone wishing his or her death to appear an accident can accordingly arrange the scene in order to influence those involved in the categorisation process to interpret things in this way. Furthermore, as Douglas argues, the individual may be aware that his or her action, if defined as 'suicide', is likely to be interpreted in two basic ways by the various other actors who become involved: they will either see the individual as the cause of (or 'responsible' for) his or her own actions, or will see him or her as having been 'driven' to it by circumstances or by other people. Douglas suggests that the individual therefore often attempts to place one of these two general constructions of meanings upon his or her action by employing various devices indicating to others how they should interpret the cause of the act. However, individuals cannot simply use *any* means of attempting this but must make use of those meanings *likely to be accepted by other members of the society*. He suggests that in the West the most common patterns of meanings of this sort are those involving 'revenge', 'the search for help', 'sympathy', 'escape', 'repentance', 'expiation of guilt' and 'self-punishment'. Consequently, Douglas argues that these societal conceptions of suicide must be studied, because they exert a crucial influence on both the actor and the other participants in the drama. This is not to say that individuals are necessarily successful in having their intentions defined in the way that they would like (of course, the *living* very often fail to do this in their interactions as well) but simply that all these considerations influence whether a death comes to be labelled as suicide or not.

If suicide is a matter of social definition, and if these definitions vary – if there is nothing 'out there' with the intrinsic meaning of 'suicide' – then the only course for the sociology of suicide is to analyse the meanings that the various actors involved in suicides attach to the world. Douglas argues that to do this an in-depth analysis of their words and actions, in all its qualitative detail, is required, and in fact by using such a method he is able to produce a provisional classification of meanings, ranging from 'transformation of the soul', 'escape', 'expiation of guilt', through to 'revenge'.

Conclusion

The study of suicide, then, encapsulates clearly the problem of 'structure' and 'action' in sociological analyses – of providing an explanation of social phenomena which takes sufficient account of structural forces acting on individuals, while at the same time doing justice to the meaningful choices and responses made by actors. While explanations like Durkheim's have been subjected to considerable criticism, it would be foolish to deny the influence of the social environment upon individuals and the reality of the structures within which they operate. A study of suicide which concentrates almost exclusively on the interpretative procedures by which individuals attribute meanings to the actions of others remains essentially partial.

At the same time, however, interpretivists are justified in insisting upon the recognition of individual motives for suicidal behaviour, since individuals do play an active part in creating their own social world through the meanings they employ in social interaction. Such a view provides a valuable counter to a model of humans in which a passive creature responds to the pulls and pushes of social forces in a mechanical and deterministic way.

A synthesis of theoretical perspectives which emphasise on the one hand 'structure' and on the other 'action' would seem, then, to be a necessary exercise for the explanation of suicide and, indeed, of any sociological phenomenon. Giddens (1977) makes some preliminary suggestions as to how this might be effected in the study of suicide, though he and others, such as Willis, have attempted to explore the dialectical relationship between structure and action in a more complete theoretical way elsewhere (Giddens, 1976; and Willis, 1977). For, in fact, the resolution of such issues is ultimately a theoretical and methodological, not substantive, problem. We now turn to such issues in our final two chapters.

REFERENCES TO CHAPTER 11

Akers, R. (1967) 'Problems in the Sociology of Deviance: Social Definitions and Behaviour', *Social Forces*, vol. 46, pp. 455–65.
Atkinson, J. M. (1971) 'Societal Reactions to Suicide: the Role of Coroners' Definitions', in S. Cohen (ed.), *Images of Deviance*, Harmondsworth, Penguin.
Atkinson, J. M. (1978) *Discovering Suicide*, London, Macmillan.
Becker, H. (1963) *Outsiders*, New York, Free Press.
Belson, W. A. *et al.* (1975) *Juvenile Theft: the Causal Factors*, New York, Harper & Row.

Bittner, E. (1967) 'The Police on "Skid-Row": a Study of Peace-keeping', *American Sociological Review*, vol. 32, pp. 699–715.

Bordua, D. (1970) 'Recent Trends: Deviant Behaviour and Social Control', in C. Bersani (ed.), *Crime and Delinquency*, London, Macmillan.

Box, S. (1971) *Deviance, Reality and Society*, New York, Holt, Rinehart & Winston.

Campbell, A. (1981) *Girl Delinquents*, Oxford, Basil Blackwell.

Cernkovich, S. and Giordano, P. (1979) 'A Comparative Analysis of Male and Female Delinquency', *Sociological Quarterly* (Winter), vol. 20, pp. 131–45.

Cicourel, A. (1968) *The Social Organization of Juvenile Justice*, New York, Wiley.

Cloward, R. and Ohlin, L. (1960) *Delinquency and Opportunity*, New York, Free Press.

Cohen, A. (1955) *Delinquent Boys*, New York, Free Press.

Cohen, A. (1965) 'The Sociology of the Deviant Act: Anomie Theory and Beyond', *American Sociological Review*, vol. 30, pp. 5–14.

Cohen, S. (ed.) (1971) *Images of Deviance*, Harmondsworth, Penguin.

Corrigan, P. (1981) *Schooling the Smash Street Kids*, London, Macmillan.

Coulter, J. (1974) 'What's Wrong with the New Criminology?', *Sociological Review*, vo. 22, pp. 119–35.

Davis, N. (1972) 'Labelling Theory in Deviance Research', *Sociological Quarterly*, vol. 13, pp. 447–74.

Douglas, J. (1967) *The Social Meanings of Suicide*, Princeton University Press.

Downes, D. (1966) *The Delinquent Solution*, London, Routledge & Kegan Paul.

Downes, D. and Rock, P. (1971) 'Social Reaction to Deviance and its Effect on Crime and Criminal Careers', *British Journal of Sociology*, vol. 22, pp. 351–64.

Durkheim, E. (1964) *The Rules of Sociological Method*, New York, Free Press.

Durkheim, E. (1970) *Suicide* (ed. G. Simpson), London, Routledge & Kegan Paul (first published in 1897).

Elmhorn, K. (1965) 'A Study on Self-reported Delinquency among Schoolchildren in Stockholm', in K. Christiansen (ed.), *Scandinavian Studies in Criminology*, London, Tavistock, pp. 117–46.

Erickson, M. and Empey, L. (1963) 'Court Records, Undetected Delinquency and Decision-making', *Journal of Criminal Law, Criminology and Police Science*, vol. 54, pp. 456–69.

Eysenck, H. (1970) *Crime and Personality*, London, Paladin.

Gibbons, D. and Jones, J. (1975) *The Study of Deviance*, Englewood Cliffs, N.J., Prentice-Hall.

Gibbs, J. and Martin, W. (1964) *Status Integration and Suicide*, University of Oregon Press.

Giddens, A. (1976) *New Rules of Sociological Method*, London, Hutchinson.

Giddens, A. (1977) 'A Theory of Suicide', in A. Giddens, *Studies in Social and Political Theory*, London, Hutchinson.

Gouldner, A. (1968) 'The Sociologist as Partisan: Sociology and the Welfare State', *American Sociologist*, pp. 103–16.

Halbwachs, M. (1930) *Les causes de suicide*, Paris, Alcan.

Heidensohn, F. (1985) *Women and Crime*, London, Macmillan.

Hindelang, M. (1979) 'Sex Differences in Criminal Activity,' *Social Problems*, vol. 27.

Hough, M. and Mayhew, P. (1985) *Taking Account of Crime: Key Findings from the 1984 British Crime Survey*, London, HMSO.

Kitsuse, J. and Cicourel, A. (1963) 'A Note on the Uses of Official Statistics', *Social Problems*, vol. 11, pp. 131–9.

Klein, D. and Kress, J. (1981) 'Any Woman's Blues: A Critical Overview of

Women, Crime and the Criminal Justice System', in T. Platt and P. Takagi (eds), *Crime and Social Justice*, London, Macmillan.

Lemert, E. (1966) *Human Deviance, Social Problems and Social Control*, Englewood Cliffs, N.J., Prentice-Hall.

Liazos, A. (1972) 'The Poverty of the Sociology of Deviance', *Social Problems*, vol. 20, pp. 102–20.

McClintock, F. and Avison N. (1968) *Crime in England and Wales*, London, Heinemann.

Mankoff, M. (1971) 'Societal Reaction and Career Deviance: a Critical Analysis', *Sociological Quarterly*, vol. 12, pp. 204–18.

Matza, D. (1964) *Delinquency and Drift*, New York, Wiley.

Merton, R. (1938) 'Social Structure and Anomie', *American Sociological Review*, vol. 3, pp. 672–82.

Miller, W. (1958) 'Lower Class Culture as a Generating Milieu of Gang Delinquency', *Journal of Social Issues*, vol. 14, pp. 5–19.

Morris, T. (1957) *The Criminal Area*, London, Routledge & Kegan Paul.

Parker, H. (1974) *A View from the Boys*, London, David & Charles.

Pearce, F. (1976) *Crimes of the Powerful*, London, Pluto Press.

Pearson, G. (1975) *The Deviant Imagination*, London, Macmillan.

Phillipson, M. and Roche, M. (1974) 'Phenomenology, Sociology and the Study of Deviance', in Rock and McIntosh (1974).

Piliavin, S. and Briar, S. (1964) 'Police Encounters with Juveniles', *American Journal of Sociology*, vol. 52, pp. 206–14.

Rabow, J. (1966) 'Delinquent Boys Revisited', *Criminologica*, vol. 4, pp. 22–8.

Robertson, R. and Taylor, L. (1974) 'Problems in the Comparative Analysis of Deviance', in Rock and McIntosh (1974).

Rock, P. (1973) *Deviant Behaviour*, London, Hutchinson.

Rock, P. and McIntosh, M. (eds) (1974) *Deviance and Social Control*, London, Tavistock.

Rogers, J. and Buffalo, M. (1974) 'Fighting Back: Nine Modes of Adaptation to a Deviant Label', *Social Problems*, vol. 22, pp. 101–18.

Sacks, H. (1963) 'Sociological Description', *Berkeley Journal of Sociology*, 8 pp.

Scott, P. (1956) 'Gangs and Delinquent Groups in London', *British Journal of Delinquency*, vol. 7, pp. 8–21.

Selvin, H. (1965) 'Durkheim's "Suicide": Further Thoughts on a Methodological Classic', in R. Nisbet (ed.), *Emile Durkheim*, Englewood Cliffs, N.J., Prentice-Hall.

Shacklady-Smith, L. (1978) 'Sexist Assumptions and Female Delinquency', in C. Smart and B. Smart (eds), *Women, Sexuality and Social Control*, London, Routledge & Kegan Paul.

Short, J. and Strodtbeck, F. (1965) *Group Process and Gang Delinquency*, University of Chicago Press.

Smart, C. (1976) *Women, Crime and Criminology*, London, Routledge & Kegan Paul.

Sykes, G. and Matza, D. (1957) 'Techniques of Neutralization: a Theory of Delinquency', *American Sociological Review*, vol. 22, pp. 664–70.

Taylor, I. *et al.* (1973) *The New Criminology*, London, Routledge & Kegan Paul.

Taylor, I. *et al.* (1975) 'Critical Criminology in Britain: Review and Prospects, in I. Taylor *et al.*, *Critical Criminology*, London, Routledge & Kegan Paul.

Taylor, I. and Walton, P. (1975) 'Radical Deviancy Theory and Marxism: a Reply to Paul Q. Hirst's "Marx and Engels on Law, Crime and Morality"', in I. Taylor *et al.* (1975) *Critical Criminology*, London, Routledge & Kegan Paul.

US President's Commission (1967) *Report on Law Enforcement and Administration of Justice*, Washington, D.C., US Government Printing Office.

Wallerstein, J. and Wyle, C. (1947) 'Our Law Abiding Lawbreakers', *National Probation*, pp. 107–12.

Whitaker, B. (1964) *The Police*, Harmondsworth, Penguin.

Willis, P. (1977) *Learning to Labour*, Westmead, Saxon House.

Young, J. (1975) 'Working Class Criminology', in I. Taylor *et al.* (1975) *Critical Criminology*, London, Routledge & Kegan Paul.

12

The Production of Sociological Knowledge: Theory and Methods of Research

12.1 INTRODUCTION: UNDERSTANDING SOCIAL REALITY

This textbook is full of information on the family, education, inequality, power, and so on. But where does this evidence come from, what assumptions lie behind it and how was it collected?

To answer these questions we need to understand the sort of techniques that sociologists use in the course of doing research. The research process itself is often full of conceptual and practical difficulties, and there is no simple rule-book that all sociologists must use to guide their fieldwork. Moreover, just as there are different theories about 'what is going on out there' (we have seen, for example, 'deviance' explained in very different ways by the subcultural and labelling approaches to crime), so different theorists tend to adopt different research methods in order to collect data to test their particular views on society. One might ask, 'Aren't some research methods better than others?' Unfortunately there is no simple answer to this question. The research method one adopts is likely to be tied to certain assumptions about how to observe and understand people's behaviour and ideas. Such assumptions can always be challenged by other sociologists who may in turn question the very methods one has chosen.

There is, for example, considerable debate about how we can 'get at' or measure working-class consciousness in capitalist society. Some sociologists have tried to measure this by conducting surveys of workers' general opinions about the industrial capitalist economy. Often they find little real sense of working-class hostility towards the economic status quo. But others argue that the very method used – the formal survey – and the nature of questions asked – very general and unconnected with workers' immediate experience – are bound to understate or distort workers' real attitudes towards capitalism. Thus, when the same workers are asked in a more informal way about their *own* working experiences, critical or oppositional responses to work are much more forthcoming. At first sight this might suggest that the latter, a more informal research technique with a rather different set of questions 'closer to home', is a better indicator of

class consciousness than the former survey method. However, other sociologists, who have a particular set of assumptions about what 'social class'
is, may say that this second method is not in fact measuring *class*
consciousness but merely levels of worker dissatisfaction: there is no reason
to assume that simply because one has discovered that workers complain –
even strongly so – about their working life one has shown that they have
thereby a growing sense of collective 'proletarian' opposition to the
capitalist system.

One can see from this example that the key difficulty in trying to get
sociologists to agree on a theory and method for research is that there is not
universal agreement about the character and shape of society, what it is one
is trying to measure and how it should be measured. Such dispute is not
peculiar to sociology: all disciplines in which questioning occurs will
experience this same uncertainty, including those in the natural sciences.
Witness, in this regard, the debate among natural scientists about how the
risks associated with exposure to background nuclear radiation are to be
identified and assessed. Disagreement over this results in the fact that
measures of the risk of cancer vary by a factor of ten between the USA and
UK, yet the models of risk assessment used in each country, though
different, are defended vigorously by Government scientists on each side of
the Atlantic. Does this mean, then, that workers in the American nuclear
industry are more protected – less exposed to the risk of radiation – than
workers in Britain? It all depends on the assumptions one makes and the
methods one uses to collect data on radiation levels. Uncertainty in science
crops up continually – even in the so-called 'hard' sciences like physics or
molecular biology – and indicates that 'facts' and 'theories' can always be a
matter of contention. Debate in natural science, sociology or whatever is
often ultimately a debate about definitions of reality. In very general terms
we can say that different models of reality, whether natural or social, will
lead to:

(i)   different propositions about *what reality is*,
(ii)   different ways of *establishing what can be accepted as real*,
(iii) different strategies for *validating our claims*, and
(iv)   different techniques for *collecting data about such claims*.

These four aspects of the investigation and understanding of reality figure
in *all* forms of knowledge, including the 'common sense' of everyday life.
They are respectively designated by four key terms: *ontology, epistemology,
methodology* and *methods*. These terms can be understood as follows:

(1)   *Ontology*. Ontological issues are concerned with being – i.e. with what
       is, what we believe to exist. Here, then, the question may be: 'What is
       the particular object of investigation or subject-matter of sociology?'
(2)   *Epistemology*. Epistemological issues are concerned with knowing –

i.e. what sort of statement will we accept to justify what we believe to exist?

(3)   *Methodology*. Methodological issues are concerned with the logic of inquiry – i.e. how are we to discover and validate what we think exists?

(4)   *Methods*. Issues of method concern the technique for collecting data – i.e. which specific techniques do we use to get at evidence which will support our propositions?

We can illustrate how these aspects differ from one another, and possible variants of each, by constructing two possible accounts about the existence of atomic particles. If one puts all the (a)s together and all the (b)s together one will get two very different accounts, each having its own internal logic.

Ontological dimension: An atom exists
    (a) in the fourth dimension
    (b) in observable form
Epistemological dimension: I know it exists
    (a) because a clairvoyant told me
    (b) because I can see it
Methodological dimension: I can validate what I know about atoms through
    (a) crystal-ball gazing
    (b) experimentation and deduction
Methods dimension: I should collect data on atomic particles through the technique of
    (a) visiting as many authentic mediums as possible
    (b) collecting as much quantitative data as possible.

The key point, then, is that having adopted a particular ontological and epistemological position it is likely that one will choose particular methodologies and methods to test out one's ideas.

In general, therefore, it would be reasonable to argue that different sociologists tend to choose those research methods and methodologies that suit their particular ontological and epistemological beliefs. We shall shortly be describing two very broad perspectives in sociology that have been associated with distinct research techniques. But the fact that there *is* such a wide range of often conflicting (and not merely competing) views means that it is difficult to produce an unequivocal, absolute definition of 'the sociological method' and the 'object' it is supposed to study. A few decades ago this uncertainty about what the chapter calls 'the production of sociological knowledge' was less apparent. At that time sociology was growing rapidly as a subject, receiving considerable support from government, partly because many thought this 'new', 'social science' would help the State to fashion more effective as well as more enlightened social policies. As part of this process in the UK, the government established the Social Science Research Council (SSRC) in 1966 with considerable funds to promote social science research in universities, research institutes, polytechnics, and so on. But at this very moment, when social science had established itself in public as a sound scientific discipline which could 'produce the goods', developments in sociological theory (principally about the relationship between structure and action and developments in neo-Marxism) led many practitioners into heated debate about the status and direction of the discipline. This debate continues today and, in the UK, has led to an increasing dissatisfaction with sociology in some corridors of power. The very public dispute among sociologists over the status of their work as well as the emergence of increasingly critical and radical research led to a gradual decline in full government support. The most recent casualty of this has been the SSRC itself, forced to change its name to the Economic and Social Research Council.

Note, here, the abandonment of the 'science' tag. Sociology and related disciplines were no longer – at least officially – to be regarded as social 'sciences', seen instead by the Education Minister of the day, Sir Keith Joseph, as non-scientific humanities subjects. One effect of this has been a steady erosion in Government funding for social research through its annual grant to the ESRC, which in 1985 feared for its own survival as general Government cutbacks in expenditure on research were made. There seem to have been at least two responses to this difficult political situation which British sociologists find themselves in. One has been the tendency to restore the discipline's scientific 'feel' by adopting an increasingly quantitative, mathematical approach which typically involves the use of computers for the statistical analysis of large-scale quantitative data. This research also tends to be in some way policy-oriented. It is this type of research which is most likely to be part of national social research programmes fostered by the ESRC which is increasingly, though not entirely, interested in work that can contribute to government policy-making.

The second response has been to proclaim the sterility of the debate over the past twenty years and simply 'to get on with the job' of doing sociology, drawing on a wide range of research methods without feeling one has to raise for (interminable) discussion questions about the sort of methodological assumptions their use implies.

Whatever trends develop from this situation, it is clear that today many sociologists are much more willing than perhaps they were in the past to draw on a range of research methods and collect a variety of types of data in the course of doing research. Thus, for example, Hammersley (1985) has recently stated that:

> One should use any data that are available, of whatever type, if they follow one to develop and test one's theory effectively.

Applying for a research grant in the UK

Many sociologists do research without obtaining funding, though this might mean that the research is limited in its fieldwork and scope. Those who do seek a grant to aid their research normally apply to bodies such as the Economic and Social Research Council, the Department of Education and Science, and so on. The competition for research grants is considerable and increasing as funding agencies' budgets are cut back. Those applying for funds must have a well-planned research proposal to submit which includes detailed costings. To give an idea of the sort of issues that a proposal needs to deal with, the following list of points must be considered by applicants to the ESRC:

RESEARCH PROPOSAL FORM
What are the objectives of the research?

How does it relate to other research in the same field that has either been completed or is going on now?

What contribution (if any) will the research make to the development of theory in the subject?

Are the results expected to have any general or specific practical applications?

Will the research make any contributions to methodology?

How will the research be done? What techniques will be used? What were the reasons which led to the adoption of these methods and techniques?

If the research involves gaining access to the facilities or data of institutions or organisations, what assurance can be provided that access will be obtainable?

Are there any ethical and/or confidentiality problems, and how would they be overcome?

What other practical problems are likely to be encountered when doing the research and what plans (if any) are there to overcome them?

How will the work be divided between the applicants, the research workers, and other staff employed on the research?

What will be the specific functions of the research workers and other staff? What type and level of training, experience and skills will be expected from the research workers and other staff?

Will anyone else be associated with or working on the research (apart from the applicant and research workers employed out of the award)?

How will the research be organised and phased over the duration of the award? In particular how much time will be allowed for writing up the results of the research?

How will the results of the research be disseminated?
Source: ESRC Research Proposal Form

Later on in this chapter we shall look at the way in which recent research combines a variety of methods. At this point, however, we shall outline the two major perspectives that have been the bases on which social research has been built. At the heart of these two perspectives lie very different views about what social reality is and how we should go about describing and measuring it. Much of the debate in the philosophy of social science has concerned the division between these two views, particularly in connection with the question 'Can sociology be a science?' These two bases we can simply call 'positivism' and anti-positivism'.

12.2 POSITIVISM

First, we need a basic outline of this perspective. In very simple terms positivism involves the following assumptions.

Reality is constituted of phenomena which are causally linked to one another. What is 'real' can only be demonstrated to be real by reference to *empirical* evidence of its existence. While other kinds of explanation obviously exist, they are not admissible for the positivistic scientist unless they are based on empirical – observable – evidence. So, although it may well be that God made the world in six days, this is not an acceptable positivistic scientific explanation since there is no empirical evidence to verify it.

The establishment of scientific knowledge thus involves the empirical explanation of how phenomena are linked to other phenomena – and can be expressed in the form 'if A happens, then B happens'. Now, according to the positivist ideal, science involves the uncovering of such cause-and-effect relationships between phenomena in reality that *always* hold true. Such *universal* statements are called *scientific laws*.

Such laws are indispensable for the positivistic scientist, since it is their existence which enables explanations of events to be arrived at. A famous example of Carl Gustav Hempel demonstrates this very clearly. Upon waking up one morning a man finds that his car radiator has burst. How is he to explain this event to himself? He does so by remembering that he left his car outside the garage the night before when the temperature had fallen well below zero, he had forgotten to put anti-freeze in the water, the radiator had been filled to the top and that the radiator cap had been screwed on tightly. What is crucial about such an explanation, argues Hempel, is that it rests on the man only choosing *certain kinds* of factors as relevant to his explanation and not others. Why, for example, did he not ask himself whether the moon had been full the night before, or whether someone was practising witchcraft against him, or whether it was the work of fairies? The answer for the positivist is that people are attracted by things they think relevant to an explanation by the existence of empirically based 'scientific' cause-and-effect statements about reality.

So, in Hempel's example, the only reason why factors such as the lack of anti-freeze in the water and the severe drop in temperature are chosen as relevant to the explanation is because the laws of physics – and especially the one which states that the volume of water expands when it freezes – make them so.

Furthermore, since for the positivist *explanation* is facilitated by the existence of such cause-and-effect statements, they are also the reason why events in the future can be *predicted* as well. To use Hempel's example again, it is only our knowledge of the laws of physics that enables us to predict the consequences of leaving a car outside on a freezing night without anti-freeze, etc.

So, for positivistic science, scientific laws or their equivalent perform the double function of allowing both explanation and prediction and as such are obviously crucial. Next, we must consider *how* such cause-and-effect statements about reality are established, and to do this we must look at what the positivistic scientist means by the *scientific method*. In simple terms, this involves the construction of as yet unproven cause-and-effect statements about reality, called hypotheses. These are then used to explain regularities in nature. The hypotheses can be built into a general theory which must then be able to predict other laws or regularities if it is to be acceptable.

Since much of the rest of this chapter is a discussion of the applicability of this kind of model of scientific method for the study of social behaviour, we ought first to look at the strategy for scientific research which it implies in more detail.

Positivistic methodology

It will help if we think of this as a methodology which consists of three separate stages:

(i)   a stage at which *reality* is defined
(ii)   a stage at which *validation* is made
(iii) a stage at which *explanation* is made

and look at the logic underlying each stage separately.

Definition of reality

(i)   *The categorisation of reality.* All reality has to be conceived of in such a way that it can be talked about – that is, it has to be categorised and its existence given a symbol of some sort. Most of these symbols make up the *language* that we use, for this is what a language is for – it enables us to refer to aspects of reality meaningfully. Normally in our everyday life the application of these linguistic symbols is unproblematic; we can interpret the vocal sounds others make when they speak 'our language' without having to stop and *self-consciously* make the connection between the sounds and their meaning. We do it without, apparently, thinking.

The language of physical and natural science may, however, be much more deliberate in its formulation, employing a very precise terminology which refers to certain aspects of reality in as clear and unambiguous a manner as is possible. Often, of course, the everyday symbols we all use may be adequate; so, for scientists and laymen alike, the terms 'rock', 'tree', etc. will do to talk about these aspects of the world. Sometimes, however, the common-sense meaning of a term may not be precise enough for science; for example, a chemist prefers to talk about calcium carbonate rather than chalk because it specifies more clearly the relationship between calcium and carbon than the term 'chalk' does. At other times, however, there are not everyday symbols available. Here the scientist has to *invent* a term – e.g. 'molecules', 'atoms', 'DNA'.

Scientists must, however, be able to show that the phenomena they describe are, in fact, 'real'. So, although a scientist 'knows' that theoretical constructs like pressure, volume and temperature have a *conceptual* reality, it is still necessary to provide *empirical* evidence of their existence so that they can be investigated. This process is called the *operationalisation* of theoretical concepts. It is carried out by translating these theoretical *variables* into *indicators* of their existence which are *observable* – perceivable by the senses; thus, for example, in the case of pressure we measure it by using the reading of a pressure gauge, while in the case of temperature we do so by using a thermometer.

(ii) *Hypothesis construction.* Having categorised reality so that it can be talked about meaningfully and having established indicators by which theoretical concepts can be examined empirically, scientists then proceed by hypothesising about relationships between the phenomena in which they are interested – their variables – in such a way that these are, in principle at least, capable of being tested.

Process of validation

Dealing with non-human phenomena the natural or physical scientist relies overwhelmingly on a single method – the *experiment*. Thus one tests the hypothesis 'if X exists, then Y is likely to follow' by setting up an experiment which makes X happen in order to see whether Y happens as a result. One must, of course, *control* the experiment in such a way that variables *other than* X cannot accidentally cause Y. For example, in order to see whether carbon dioxide is produced by the action of hydrochloric acid on calcium carbonate, a chemist will isolate these two variables in a bell-jar and collect any gas produced as a result. Furthermore, the chemist can measure how *much* carbon dioxide is produced by how *much* hydrochloric acid and calcium carbonate. Indeed, it is natural science's ability to *quantify* and *measure* cause-and-effect relationships between natural phenomena in this way that has proved so attractive to positivistic sociology.

Form of explanation

For the positivist scientist then, as we said earlier, reality is thus explained by the establishment of empirical evidence of the extent of cause-and-effect relationships between phenomena.

Positivism in sociology: an idealised account

A complete positivistic *sociology* will thus embrace not only the ontological/epistemological position we outlined earlier but will follow the logic of natural and physical science research methodology at each of these three stages.

Definition of reality

(i)   *Categorisation of reality.* First of all this means that like other scientists the positivist sociologist will seek to define and use terms clearly and unambiguously, to categorise reality meaningfully, and to allow concepts easy operationalisation so that they can be empirically investigated. (However, as we shall see when we examine the sort of critique made of positivistic methodologies by anti-positivists, compared with other sciences this is a task fraught with unique difficulties.)

(ii) *Hypothesis construction.* Having decided what the variables are and how they can be best investigated empirically, the positivist sociologist then hypothesises a causal relationship between these variables.

Process of validation

The next task is to measure these relationships by providing empirical evidence of the extent of their existence. As we have seen, for the natural or physical scientist this almost invariably means setting up an experiment to do so.

However, this type of physical manipulation of variables is usually impossible for the positivist-minded sociologist, not only for practical reasons – for example, how could one introduce the Protestant ethic and wait and see if capitalism is encouraged? – but also ethical ones: one would presumably find it morally reprehensible to test Durkheim's hypothesis about suicide by encouraging the development of those social conditions which he correlated with it. So, instead of physically manipulating variables, as in the classical experimental method, positivist sociologists typically construct *symbolic simulations* of experiments using statistical models. Indeed, the establishment of statistical relations between formally defined variables – such as age, sex or occupation – is probably the major source of evidence for testing hypotheses in positivist sociology. For example, the positivist may want to examine the relationship between occupation and voting behaviour. Accordingly, one variable X defines the particular jobs people may do, and another Y the way these same people vote. Experimentation involves measuring the extent to which an hypothesised relationship between these two variables exists. Other variables – such as social background, nationality, sex and education – are held *constant* so that only those actors with similar attributes in these respects are examined. Any correspondence between occupational status and voting behaviour is then measured. The results are typically reproduced in graphical or tabulated form (see Table 12.1 for an example).

TABLE 12.1

Class and vote in 1983: the class distinctiveness of the parties

	Conservative	Labour	Alliance	Others
Salariat	34	14	35	24
Routine non-manual	25	21	26	37
Petty bourgeoisie	12	3	5	2
Foremen and technicians	8	6	7	5
Working class	21	55	26	32
	100%	99%	99%	100%

Source: A. Heath, R. Powell and J. Curtice, *How Britain Votes*, Oxford, Pergamon, 1985.

Form of explanation

The logic underlying the positivist sociologist's explanation of social reality is, then, based on the desire to measure quantitatively the extent of a relationship between phenomena, and in so doing to match the rigour of the laboratory experiment in other sciences, and to provide general law-like propositions about social reality.

12.3   ANTI-POSITIVISM IN SOCIOLOGY

The positivist perspective, depicted in somewhat idealised fashion above, has been the subject of considerable debate within sociological theory. In this section we shall present the major alternative approach to the nature and explanation of society: anti-positivism. The term 'anti-positivism' is only a label we have devised for purposes of the discussion here. In your more general reading, as elsewhere in this book, the terms 'interpretivism' or 'social action theory' will frequently have been used to designate this alternative perspective. As with the preceding section, the following is only a general outline of the principal arguments involved.

The perspective in sociology we have called 'anti-positivism' has its primary roots in nineteenth-century German philosophy and social science. The more prominent German academics, particularly those writing at the close of the century, such as Sombart, Dilthey, Rickert and Weber, were all concerned in varying ways to distinguish the 'human' or 'cultural' sciences from the natural sciences. Dilthey (1833–1911), for example, believed that whereas the latter provide casual explanations of 'outer' events, human science (or 'life philosophy') is concerned with the 'inner' knowledge of 'meaningful conduct', or, as Sombart put it, with 'grasping the meaning' of an individual's experience of the world.

Max Weber placed probably the most influental emphasis on sociology's need to understand and interpret meaningful behaviour: for him sociology should develop the method of 'interpretative understanding'. The German term, *Verstehen*, denoting this technique, has been very closely associated with Weber, though he was not the first to develop it. (As we shall see later, Weber does not neatly fit into the anti-positivist perspective outlined below, however, for although he was concerned that sociology should examine the meanings lying behind social action, he nevertheless believed a positivistic type of explanation for such action to be possible.)

Anti-positivism: an idealised account

For anti-positivists the source of individual attributes and behaviour cannot be seen to be ontologically *external* to the individual actor, since for them social reality is consciously and actively created by individuals who mean to do things and who attribute meanings to the behaviour of others. Ontologically, then, social reality only exists as meaningful interaction between individuals. Hughes (1976, p. 25) gives the following broad description of the anti-positivist position:

> Human beings are not 'things' to be studied in the way one studies rats, plants or rocks, but are valuing, meaning-attributing beings to be understood as subjects and known as subjects. Sociology ... deals with meaningful action, and the

understanding, explanation, analysis, or whatever, must be made with consideration of those meanings that make the ordering of human action possible. . . . To impose positivistic meanings upon the realm of social phenomena is to distort the fundamental nature of human existence.

Positivist sociology is thus criticised for assuming that society can be described and understood according to an ontology and methodology that is committed to seeing social behaviour as an empirically evident, quantifiable, object of investigation. By implication, the preconceived categories devised by positivism to define social reality are rejected since they are not derived from any understanding of the subjective aspirations, meanings, values and language people have in everyday life. It is the latter, claim the anti-positivists, which must form the basis of sociological understanding. Unlike the positivist approach, then, the meanings and consciousness of the social actor are not seen as a problem to be overcome by a strict adherence to quantitative methods that 'objectively' measure social behaviour. Rather, sociology must treat the (subjective) meanings, values, beliefs and hopes of individuals as its principal data, its primary subject-matter.

Definition of reality

The anti-positivist discovers or 'discloses' social reality, not as the positivist does, by imposing observer categories on individual action but by being receptive to and accepting the actor's *own* perceptions and interpretations of the world fashioned through interaction with other actors. Since meaningful human communication depends primarily on language, this is obviously of central interest. Positivists are criticised for believing that it is possible, via the use of observer categories and theories, to provide an 'expert' account of the social world superior to the 'lay' accounts of actors. Instead, anti-positivists insist that the process of discovery in sociology can only involve the attempt to look at the world through the actors' eyes and make sense of it through the means they employ, since there *is* no more to the social world than this. Consequently, not only are the positivist's observational categories rejected but also any preconceived hypothetical statements about causal relations: the latter would impose a totally illegitimate structure on sociological research that would prevent an understanding of the actor's ways of seeing and interpreting the world.

Process of validation

Validity therefore involves *not* the measurement of alleged causal relationships between variables but the apprehension of the way individuals create reality in interaction with others. In order to contrast this enterprise with the *quantification* typically associated with positivism in sociology, this validating process is sometimes referred to as the establishment of *qualitative* data.

Form of explanation

Whether understanding reality as the actor sees it means that it is therefore capable of *objective explanation* is a matter of debate among anti-positivists. There are those who feel that once one has avoided imposing categories on the subject-matter at the discovery and validation stages and has understood the actor's way of looking at the world, one is then in a position to provide an objectively valid explanation of the nature of this socially constructed reality. Max Weber was an important exponent of this view (as we shall see in more detail in the final chapter). However, there are others who claim that such objectivity is impossible. These argue that sociologists are just other social actors trying to make sense of the world: they can only interpret, understand and attribute meaning to the world by virtue of the fact that they are capable of engaging in meaningful social interaction with other social actors. Although this capacity allows sociological understanding, there is no reason for assuming that such understanding provides a more objectively true account of society compared with competing accounts from others – be they sociologists or non-sociologists. From this point of view the only sort of explanations that sociologists can provide are *sub*jective: reflexive or retrospective accounts of how, as

TABLE 12.2

Positivism and anti-positivism – differences

	Positivist	**Anti-positivist**
Ontology/epistemology	Social reality exists as objective causal relations between phenomena	Social reality is a product of meaningful social interaction
Methodology (i) Defining reality	Observational constructs in order to hypothesise about causal relations between variables	Actor constructs
(ii) Process of validation	Testing of hypotheses by use of quantitative evidence	Understanding through the apprehension of qualitative evidence
(iii) Form of explanation	Empirically valid statement about law-like causal relationships between variables	Meaningfully intelligible descriptions of how social life is accomplished.

meaning-attributing individuals, they arrived at their particular understanding of some specific social situation. Ultimately, as we shall see later, this can result in the process of 'doing sociological research' becoming the actual topic of inquiry: that is, the research effort itself can be considered a legitimate source of data.

In Table 12.2 we summarise the main positivist/anti-positivist differences suggested above. These are very much idealised versions of positivism and anti-positivism, and in the 'real world' of sociology matters are often not so clear cut. We shall now assess the extent to which these perspectives are adopted by the major theoretical approaches established in contemporary sociology.

12.4 THE RELATIONSHIP BETWEEN THEORETICAL AND METHODOLOGICAL PERSPECTIVES IN SOCIOLOGY

Different theoretical approaches are more or less positivistic in the logic of their research strategy; we should not expect sociological perspectives to either completely embrace a positivistic methodology or completely embrace a non-positivistic one. If we think of the models we have construed as poles at either end of a continuum, we can properly understand the positions perspectives variously occupy along it by bearing in mind the distinction we have made between the logical stages of discovery, validation and explanation in methodology.

The structural perspective

Although there are a number of radically different structural theories in sociology – including structural-functionalism and Marxist structuralism – common to all is an analysis of society in terms of its structural properties and how these combine to form a social system. In more concrete terms this type of analysis may, for example, propose that the investigation of family life reveals the existence of a regular, systematic order governing the relations between and the behaviour of members in the kin group. It might then be argued that one can only understand observable aspects of family life – e.g. forms of residence and marriage – by seeing them as expressions of a more general system of kinship. More abstractly, whether dealing with the family, the economy, politics or systems of belief, an analysis of the overall system takes precedence over the examination of its constituent elements. The parts are to be explained in terms of the system, and not the system in terms of its parts: in other words, the system is seen as being greater than the sum of its component parts.

Much structural sociology may be characterised as positivist to a greater or lesser extent. Of major importance here is Durkheim's work and that area of research on which it has had great influence – the structural-functionalist school of Talcott Parsons that dominated American sociology from the 1930s to the end of the 1960s. Without denying that individual social actors have values, beliefs, motives and attitudes, the Durkheimian and later Parsonian analyses claim that these aspects of experience and meaning come from *outside* the individual. Individual attitudes and behaviour are first and foremost reflections or expressions of a non-individual collective culture which generates expectations, beliefs and practices. Thus the cultural system is regarded as *external* to individual consciousness, its structural components, in particular its institutionalised set of norms, constraining individuals to behave in a specific way. This type of analysis, therefore, assumes that social structures, as external determinants of behaviour, cannot be reduced to, or defined in terms of, discrete individual actions.

Durkheim's idea of the 'social fact' – a 'thing' that can be identified as external to individual consciousness, a phenomenon (like the suicide rate) that indicates the existence of wider social forces – clearly derives from the type of structural perspective outlined above. In developing Durkheim's analysis Parsons not only promoted and carried out research into the structural and systemic character of society, but did so having adopted with some amendments Durkheim's broad positivist methodology. For example, he states that sociological theory should concern itself with 'the formulation and logical relations of propositions containing empirical facts in direct relation to the observation of the facts and thus empirical verification of the propositions' (Parsons, 1937, p. 49). George A. Lundberg added to the positivist cause in American sociology by claiming that the quantitative methods common to natural science not only could but should be used in sociological research to establish an accurate and objective description of social phenomena. Thus, for example, for Lundberg, from a 'scientific' point of view, intelligence can be nothing else than that which intelligence tests measure. Here, then, actors' ideas, attitudes and beliefs may be counted as data but only as expressions of the external – and quantifiable – social reality.

As stressed earlier, since positivism and anti-positivism are not exclusive categories, but should be seen as the poles of a continuum, structural approaches can vary in their positivistic commitment. We can illustrate this variation by comparing the respective methodologies of two basically structural accounts about industrial attitudes and behaviour. These are: (1) Robert Blauner, *Alienation and Freedom* (1964); and (2) J. Goldthorpe and D. Lockwood *et al.*, *The Affluent Worker: Industrial Attitudes and Behaviour* (1969).

Blauner – 'Alienation and Freedom'

In this study of alienation in industrial work Blauner adopts a markedly positivistic methodology at all stages.

(i) *Defining the reality of alienation.* First, since alienation is a theoretical concept, it has to be given some means of being measured empirically:

> Alienation is a general syndrome made up of a number of different objective conditions and subjective feeling-states which emerge from certain relationships between workers and the sociotechnical settings of employment. Alienation exists when workers are unable to control their immediate work processes [he calls this *powerlessness*], to develop a sense of purpose and function which connects their jobs to the overall organisation of production [he calls this *meaninglessness*], to belong to integrated industrial communities [he calls this *isolation*], and when they fail to become involved in the activity of work as a mode of personal self-expression [he calls this *self-estrangement*] (Blauner, 1964, p. 15).

To put this another way, he is saying that if you measure:

(i)   the extent to which workers feel powerless in their work,
(ii) the extent to which they feel their work is meaningless,
(iii) the extent to which they feel isolated in their work, and
(iv) the extent to which they feel uninvolved in their work,

then what you are doing is measuring the extent to which they are alienated in work.

(ii) *Hypothesis about alienation.* Having operationalised his concept in this way, Blauner then hypothesises that the degree to which it will be experienced by individuals will be causally related to another variable – a material, or real-world phenomenon this time – the nature of the *technology* with which they work and the structure of their work roles. In the hypothesis, alienation is the *dependent* variable (the effect), while technology and work-role structure are the *independent* variables (the cause). Blauner (1964, pp. vii, 166) states:

> I attempt to show that the worker's relation to the technological organisation of the work process and in the social organisation of the factory *determines* whether or not he characteristically experiences in that work a sense of control rather than domination. ... His industry even affects the kind of social personality he develops, since an industrial environment *tends* to breed a distinctive social *type* [our emphases].

Process of validation. To test this hypothesis Blauner investigates worker attitudes in different sorts of industries with different sorts of socio-technical systems:

craft – printing
machine-tending – textiles
assembly-line – cars
process – chemicals

Having collected his data (and used other results for secondary analysis), he then attempts to see whether they indicate that the hypothesised relationship between the existence of a particular work structure and a level of alienation holds, as measured by his indicators.

Form of explanation. From his analysis Blauner (1964, p. 182) concludes that alienation in industry is to be seen as following 'a course that could be charted on a graph by means of an inverted U-curve', as shown in Figure 12.1. In other words, Blauner believes that at a certain stage of the development of technology (i.e. at the 'continuous-process' stage) mechanisation no longer dominates and alienates workers as before but rather allows workers to control their work process: 'The alienation curve begins to decline from its previous height as employees in automated industries gain a new dignity from responsibility and a sense of individual function' (Blauner, 1964, p. 182).

In general, therefore, workers' attitudes and behaviour are to be

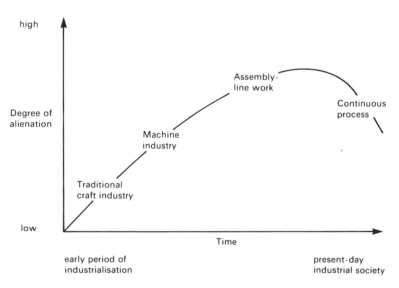

FIGURE 12.2

explained in terms of the structure of the work roles which they perform; change this, and attitudes and behaviour change also. In order to specify the sort of changes required, the sociologist provides a measure of the extent to which the specific structural factors cause the four aspects of alienation defined above. The correspondence between the ontological assumptions specified by Blauner's theoretical perspective and the logic of his research procedures is thus clear: social attitudes and behaviour are determined by external structural factors, and so the job of the researcher is to measure the strength of these determinants.

Goldthorpe and Lockwood et al. – 'The Affluent Worker: Industrial Attitudes and Behaviour'

In contrast to Blauner's approach, that of Goldthorpe and Lockwood is sometimes called 'weak actionism' since it is based on a theoretical perspective whose ontological position, while still essentially structural, allows much more causal status to actors' meanings and definitions of situations.

They argue that to understand industrial attitudes and behaviour one should not *impose* one's own understanding of reality on the individual workers but instead look at the way they perceive their world. They thus try to move away from using predefined categories – such as Blauner's 'power-lessness' – to classify an individual's experience of work. Rather, they try to understand the meanings the workers attach to their actions and the actions of others, meanings which arise from *both* their non-work and work roles and experiences. The first step in such research, then, they say, 'must be that of establishing empirically the way in which, in any given case, the wants and expectations which men bring to their employment, and the interpretation which they thus give to their work, shape the attitudinal and behavioural patterns of their working lives as a whole' (Goldthorpe and Lockwood *et al.*, 1969, p. 184).

However, they simultaneously want to examine the way in which this 'variety of meanings' is moulded, influenced or 'mediated' by structural factors, such as 'the workers' experience of both social and geographical mobility, their position in the life cycle, and their present patterns of family and community living'. Hence the second research stage involves

> demonstrating how any orientation to work which is in question is in fact socially generated and sustained. The values and motivations that lead workers to the view of work they have adopted must be traced back ... to typical life situations and experiences. In this way, therefore ... the necessity ... arises ... of explaining and understanding the social life which goes on within the enterprise by reference ultimately to the structure and processes of the wider society in which the enterprise exists (Goldthorpe and Lockwood *et al.*, 1969, p. 185).

As we shall see shortly, compared with the approaches of symbolic interactionism and, in particular, ethnomethodolgy, this has a positivistic orientation.

Here, then, is an attempt to allow for both structural determination of attitude and behaviour while also recognising the existence of 'action' – *meaningful* social behaviour. However, this is a task which produces both methodological problems and, as we shall see in more detail later on, problems of method.

Since in an ontology such as Blauner's, reality is *given* as an *external* structure, the methodological job of the sociologist is to conceptualise this structure, investigate its empirical indicators and produce quantifiable results. But if, albeit only in part, reality is not a *given* – if it is not just a question of conceptualising an objective reality but also of discovering the conceptualisations of actors which are a significant part of the reality itself – then new problems arise in both defining reality and validating what we have to say about it.

Definition of reality. Goldthorpe and Lockwood want to understand social actors' meanings of the world *as they affect and are affected by* the structure of society.

> Reality cannot be in any simple way reduced to positivistic statements about how the social structure causes workers to behave in certain ways. It must be a reality that is in part created by the intentions and meanings of the workers themselves.

So Goldthorpe and Lockwood's categorisation of the workers' 'world' and the hypotheses they make about it, must seek to integrate sociologically 'expert' concepts of the structure of that 'world' with the actors' own concepts of it.

Process of validation. Goldthorpe and Lockwood sought to produce generalisations about a relatively large 'population' of workers and, as is normally the case with large numbers, a survey technique was employed. While this method may be good at generating and handling a large volume of quantitative data, it is much less able to accurately portray the range, depth and quality of the subjective meanings of respondents. This results then in a tension in Goldthorpe and Lockwood's work: their partial anti-positivist commitment to the discovery of respondents' *own* definition of reality seems to run up against their positivistic process of validation, the structured survey.

Form of explanation. As was seen earlier, Goldthorpe and Lockwood, to use their own words, 'ultimately' locate the explanations for workers in 'the structure and processes of the wider society'. At the end of the day then there is a stronger commitment to explaining social action and the values

and motivations it expresses through reference to external social constraints, structural forces at work in society, than to the subjective
meanings of the actors themselves. It is this position that has been subject
to strong criticism from those sociologists who adopt a more keenly anti-
positivistic stance, such as Silverman (1970, pp. 184–5) who comments:

> By arguing that work orientations are determined by a combination of internal
> and external factors, one may miss the way in which people's view of themselves
> and their situation is the outcome of an *ongoing process*, i.e. never fully
> determined by one or another set of structural constraints but always in the act of
> 'becoming', as successive experiences shape and reshape a subjective definition of
> self and society.

This fundamentally anti-positivistic definition of reality as process rather
than as a static entity is the hallmark of the next theoretical and methodological approach we shall consider – symbolic interactionism.

Symbolic interactionism

The principal ontological claim of the symbolic interactionist is that reality
is not immutable or fixed but is constantly being recreated or 'achieved'
through the meaningful interaction of individuals; for the interactionist,
social actors are continually engaged in 'negotiating' the meaning of reality
with one another. Major representatives of this approach include Howard
Becker and Erving Goffman. Challenging the Durkheimian and Parsonian
analysis, these theorists criticise the view that behaviour can be perceived as
an expression of a rigid system of normatively defined statuses and roles.
Social identity is much more fluid – being built up and broken down as a
result of interaction; its development is analogous to that of an occupational career, with opportunities, dangers, success and failure. A classic
study adopting this perspective is Goffman's work *Asylums* (1968), in which
(among other things) he looks at the 'career' of mental patients and
prisoners in their respective confining institutions. These characteristic
interactionist concerns are examined more fully in the final chapter.

Methodology

Definition of reality. Given the interactionist's epistemological position that
social reality can only be known through understanding the point of view of
social actors, their meanings and definitions of their situations, a positivistic logic of discovery is not followed. That is, the construction of
hypotheses prior to investigation based on predefined observer categories is
replaced by research that asks much more open-ended questions: the usual
exhortation is for the researcher to 'tell it like it is'; such a research
enterprise is very often described as 'naturalistic'.

Process of validation. Once this initial exploratory research has been accomplished, interactionists are then normally more prepared to develop tentative hypotheses, though even these may be reformulated in the light of further evidence. To some extent, therefore, it is not unreasonable to suggest that in interactionist research, discovery and validation take place at one and the same time. The logic underlying this approach – often formally defined as 'analytic induction' – is that understanding can only emerge out of the continual interplay of theory and method in the field. Investigation is thus concerned with the deliberate search for disconfirming, or *negative*, cases, so that hypotheses can be continually refined.

The development of hypotheses and assessment of them against further evidence is one indication that interactionism is not *completely* free from positivist influence. A further indication is that interactionists often try to provide *proof* for their theories. The attempt to prove something presupposes that the subject-matter one is dealing with has an *objective* existence, and that one is capable of *demonstrating* this to be so.

Form of explanation. This positivist influence carries on through to affect the interactionist's form of explanation. Thus, although most research reports are largely qualitative in character, interactionists may claim support for their discoveries by using evidence of an implicitly quantitative nature. Phillips (1971, p. 137) makes a telling point here:

> all descriptions and analyses of behaviour are inevitably *both* qualitative and quantitative – although with observational studies the counting and measurement may be implicit. For instance, in observational studies there are assertions that a pattern of behaviour occurs *frequently, often, sometimes, seldom*, or in *many* different situations.

Moreover, *explicit* quantification is not entirely absent either. For example, in his study of college students – *Making the Grade* – Howard Becker numerically tabulates some of his data. We will return to these kind of points when we look in more detail at observation as a technique. Here we can conclude by quoting Cuff and Payne (1979, p. 173): 'It is not the case that structuralists measure, while interactionists do not. Interactionists merely tend to have a distate for certain ways of measuring.' So the symbolic interactionist goes some way down the anti-positivist road but stops short of its end. Farthest down this road, however, are ethnomethodologists.

Ethnomethodology

The term 'ethnomethodology' was coined by Harold Garfinkel. It is worth considering its two parts: 'ethno' refers to the stock of common-sense knowledge available to a member of society: 'methodology' refers to the methods or strategies which actors use in different settings to make their meanings understandable, or, in Garfinkel's terms, 'accountable' to others. These methods allow the successful accomplishment of everyday communication and activity.

Ethnomethodologists thus share the interactionists' view that social reality must be seen in terms of the on-going process of 'interaction' by which participants accomplish or achieve meaningful communication with one another. However, ethnomethodology does *not* share the view that the processes through which such interaction is accomplished can be *objectively* described and explained by the 'expert' sociologist. Unlike all those perspectives discussed above, ethnomethodology challenges the idea that sociology can provide some 'scientific', objective, account of social reality. The sociologist is seen as being just one more actor on the social stage, trying to 'make sense' of the social world. He or she is no more than a 'member of the world', not a privileged observer rendering 'true' accounts of that world.

Thus 'doing sociology' is regarded as just one more practical activity by which certain actors – who call themselves sociologists – make sense of their world in terms of a shared 'common' sense. The term 'common sense' is therefore not meant to denote an *inferior* form of knowledge: rather, it must be taken literally – that is, it signifies a meaning system which is common to, or shared by, certain social actors, whether they regard themselves as 'sociologists' or not. However, ethnomethodologists argue that there is one significant difference between the sociologist and the non-sociologist. This is that 'doing sociology' is (or should be) a self-conscious reflexive activity. Unlike the majority of social actors who take for granted or rarely examine the means by which they successfully achieve understanding, the sociologist can actively investigate the ways in which he or she accomplishes his or her accounts of the world. This does not mean that these accounts can be regarded as more objective than alernative ones, but it does mean that they can be treated as topics for investigation in their own right. So it is that sociologists who do not share the ethnomethodological perspective often find themselves and their theories subject to the scrutiny of ethnomethodologists. This can be particularly exasperating for those who believe that their theories are true or objective accounts about social phenomena. Ethnomethodological accounts usually involve the close examination of the way language is used to convey meaning in social interaction – language being the primary symbolic means by which individuals make sense to each other – although, since there are other means, e.g. non-verbal gestures and communications, these are sometimes the object of interest as well.

This tends to mean that the topic for other sorts of sociologist – say crime, or suicide, or mental illness – is important to the ethnomethodologist only in so far as it provides an arena in which to investigate the *real* topic:

the common sense mechanisms through which human beings observe, conceptualise and make meaningful the world they encounter in their everyday life.

Definitions of reality

Social reality is defined solely in terms of what people agree it to be: social actors are not treated as the 'respondents' observed by a sociological expert. Instead all, including the sociologists, are seen as 'members' of social exchange, negotiating and constructing a social reality.

Process of validation

Sociologists can never 'validate' in the positivistic sense their views on social reality: instead, say the ethnomethodologists, they should make every effort to explain their views and lay bare their meanings through a constant self-scrutiny of their attempts to interpret the world. If accepted by others – e.g. other ethnomethodologists – they might say their views have been successfully accomplished inasmuch as they have an intelligibility to other 'members'.

Form of explanation

Ethnomethodologists do believe that there is an 'order' of sorts underlying social action, but it is one which is seen only as being the creation of social actors, that needs constant work to be sustained in interaction. It is a perception of an order that we impose on our behaviour rather than any 'real' structured order 'existing outside' individuals as the positivist might believe. Social reality is explained then through reference to the dynamic exchange of meanings in social encounters.

12.5   INTERIM CONCLUSION

Besides significant methodological differences, the theoretical perspectives we have examined so far can be distinguished in terms of the relative causal status they each give to individual action compared with structural factors in constituting the social world. The relationship between individual consciousness and a 'wider' social reality – between 'action' and 'structure' – is often regarded as the crucial theoretical problem for sociology. We shall consider this issue in greater depth in the final chapter. Here, because of its implications for methodology, it is worth drawing attention to one of the more recent contributions to this debate, Anthony Giddens's *The Constitution of Society* (1985).

Giddens tries to unify the notions of structure and action by giving a causal status to each in the production and reproduction of social reality. Not surprisingly, such a synthesis challenges the theoretical division between 'hard' positivism and 'hard' anti-positivism, with their mutually exclusive ontologies, epistemologies and methodologies. To effect such a reconciliation requires going beyond the conceptual framework upon which each of the two perspectives is built.

Against the positivist position, Giddens argues that social reality cannot be envisaged in terms of a 'pre-given universe of objects', open to some 'independent' or context-free observer. Rather, it should be understood as the on-going product of actors consciously creating their world as historical agents. At the same time, however, he argues that actors are constrained by the structural conditions under which they live such that although 'men produce society' they do so 'not under conditions of their own choosing'. He is suggesting, in other words, that there is a dialectical relation between structure and action: on the one hand, 'structures are constituted by action', yet, on the other hand, 'action is constituted structurally'. Such a logic seeks to overcome the positivist/anti-positivist split. However, although Giddens has demonstrated that this unification is theoretically warranted, he has yet to specify the methodological procedures that would follow from it for purposes of empirical sociological research.

Some recent work by Paul Willis, presented in two books, *Learning to Labour* (1977) and *Profane Culture* (1978), adopts a theoretical position which, in many ways, comes close to that advocated by Giddens. Willis (1977) tries to explain why 'working-class boys get working class jobs'. Endeavouring to unite the processes of structure and action, he argues that while specific structural features of capitalist society work to restrict the educational, occupational and political horizons of working-class boys, certain boys themselves actively use such features as sources of meaning to create and recreate working-class culture and life-chances. This process occurs in a variety of ways and may be expressed in apparently insignificant behaviour. For example, Willis argues that it even occurs when the 'lads' – those boys who constitute the 'counter-school culture' – choose to smoke. His perhaps somewhat contentious point is that they 'seize upon' cigarettes – 'one of the three great consumer goods of capitalism' (the other two being clothes and alcohol) – in this way, not simply because it is against school rules, but more importantly because through it they can project themselves into the adult male world of the working class. This 'act of insurrection' thus allows them to separate themselves from the school and to overcome what they experience as the 'oppressive adolescence' of the school; but ironically, Willis argues, it is this very act of liberation which places them more firmly within the constraints of working-class culture.

According to Willis, then, the task for sociology is to examine the way in which people – as individuals or groups – respond to their structural conditions. His commitment to this type of analysis is evident when he writes that

In the case of job choice amongst the unqualified working class, for instance, we can *predict* final employment quite well from class background, geographical location, local opportunity structure, and educational attainment ... But ... to quote [these] larger factors is really no form of explanation at all. It does not identify a chain or set of causalities which indicate particular outcomes from many possible ones. It simply further outlines the situation which is still in need of explanation: *how* and *why* young people take the restricted and often meaningless available jobs in ways which seem sensible to them in their familiar world as it is actually lived (Willis, 1977, p. 172).

We do not intend to assess whether Willis's work answers this question successfully: this would require considerable theoretical discussion going beyond this chapter. The point that should be taken here is that many sociologists – like Giddens and Willis – are trying to break out of the often sterile debate between positivism and anti-positivism as competing explanations of social reality. As always, however, much remains to be done.

We shall now move on to consider the actual methods that competing theoretical perspectives typically employ to collect 'data' for their research. There are two types of sociological data: 'primary' and 'secondary'. Primary data are those which sociologists collect for themselves. Later on we will look at some of the characteristics of, and problems involved with, the two most often used methods for the production of primary data – asking questions in surveys, and observation. First, however, we will look at the chief source of secondary data for sociologists, which, while apparently unproblematic and neutral, is in fact a renowned arena for the confrontation between the whole range of epistemological positions we have just considered – official statistics.

12.6   OFFICIAL STATISTICS

Most sociology students will at one stage or another be confronted by statistical data. Textbooks, for example, often rely on social statistics describing population, births, deaths, marriages, income and wealth, etc., as documentary evidence to support various interpretations of the social order. The very mathematical, quantitative character of such statistics presented in graphs, tables and figures seem to give the data the scientific, incontrovertible status of being 'hard facts'. The use of social statistics in sociology is not just a recent phenomenon: early British sociologists in particular regarded them as important and necessary sources of information which could be used, both to bolster the scientific usage of the discipline in academic circles, and to develop informed social policy programmes designed to relieve poverty, illness, poor housing, and so on. The more renowned of these early pioneers include Charles Booth, Seebohm Rowntree, and Sidney and Beatrice Webb.

Following in this tradition contemporary British sociologists draw on a wide range of *official* statistics in their analyses. Official statistics are obtained from 'official' sources: that is, government agencies such as the Office of Population Censuses and Surveys (OPCS), and the Home Office. Moreover, the Government Statistical Service publishes more detailed information collected from these two sources in its *Annual Abstract of Statistics* and *Social Trends*.

There are a number of reasons why sociologists have been particularly reliant on official statistics as sources of data:

(i)   they are frequently the *only* available source of data in a particular area;
(ii) they are readily available, such that the researcher does not have to spend time or money collecting his or her own information;
(iii) they allow an examination of trends over time – e.g. divorce, crime and strike rates;
(iv) they allow inter-group comparisons to be made, e.g. middle-class and working-class family size, as well as international ones, e.g. suicide rates in different countries;
(v)   they allow 'before' and 'after' studies to be made – e.g. examining the effect that changes in legislation have on divorce patterns.

At the same time, however, there are a number of major drawbacks connected with the use of official statistics. First, they may draw on information which has been collected for completely different purposes than those which the sociologist has in mind. That is, official agencies are normally concerned with gathering statistics to assess specific government policies, and they are unlikely to reflect the particular research problems of the sociologist. Second, the categories used by agencies – the official definitions of households, income groups, or social classes, for example – may differ from those employed by the sociologist.

Apart from these two problems, a more fundamental theoretical issue arises which bears on the positivist/anti-positivist debate examined earlier. This concerns the sense in which statistics can be regarded as objective, 'factual' measures of social phenomena. With regard to this issue let us consider once again Durkheim's use of statistics in his classic study of *Suicide*.

Durkheim drew on information from both official and non-official sources to document the number of suicides occurring in different countries. Accordingly, by comparing such data he was able to prepare differing *suicide rates* (per million) for each country. Crucially, not only was there apparent variation between countries but each country's particular suicide rate appeared to be constant over a number of years. Durkheim believed that such regularity indicated that the suicide rate, and those factors (such as religion) which encouraged its variation, could be treated as 'social facts', objective evidence on which to establish a scientific, positivistic, theory of suicide.

However, those who are critical of Durkheim's positivistic perspective challenge, among other things, his statistical 'evidence': Douglas, in his book *The Social Meanings of Suicide* (1967), and Atkinson, in his work contained in *Discovering Suicide* (1978), argue that if one examines the ways in which individuals – in particular official agents such as coroners – identify acts as 'suicides', one discovers wide variation and inconsistency. Both argue that statistics such as the suicide rate cannot be regarded as objective measures of phenomena precisely because they are the result of complex social processes of meaning and interpretation which eventually define certain acts as 'suicide'. This means that the actual suicide statistics do not record acts which are identical, as Durkheim assumed. Suicide rates cannot, then, be compared since, as Douglas shows, officials use various definitions of suicide. Hence Douglas (1967, p. 235) comments that

> the first task is to examine the different forms of behaviour which a society labels 'suicide' in order to develop a classification of the different meanings associated with what superficially appear to be similar forms of behaviour.

Atkinson provides further evidence of the socially constructed nature of the 'fact' of suicide where coroners *infer intent to have committed suicide* by relying on a wide variety of criteria. Some regard the mode of death as an indicator of suicide – for example, it is conventionally assumed that hanging must be self-inflicted, whereas road deaths are not. The point is that the incidence of so-called 'suicides' is socially constructed. This can be further illustrated in cases of death occurring in more equivocal contexts: for example, in the case of a drug overdose one coroner might be prepared to record a suicide verdict, whereas another may regard the death as the result of a mistake, or absent-mindedness on the part of the person taking the pills.

Indeed, Douglas tellingly shows how Durkheim himself, in order to explain the 'social fact' of the distribution of suicide, also fundamentally relied on such subjective interpretations based on common sense. He argues, for example, that Durkheim was only able to arrive at an explanation of the variations in the suicide rates of, say, Protestants and Catholics, or of those who are single and married, by employing stereotypical images of how Protestants, Catholics, single and married people behave. That these images are gleaned from *his own personal* stock of common-sense knowledge is well illustrated by his characterisation of those female attributes which (in his view) make them poorer candidates than men for inclusion in the suicide statistics. For instance, according to Durkheim, divorced women kill themselves less often than divorced men because the inferior female intellect reduces the traumatic effects of sexual deprivation!

He thus argues that 'woman's sexual needs have less mental character because, generally speaking, her mental life is less developed'. The point here, then, is the crucial one that not only do processes of interpretation produce statistics but that explanations of statistics thus produced *also* rely on them; for anti-positivists, in fact, suicide statistics can only tell us about the living, not the dead.

The anti-positivistic perspective embodied in the work of Douglas and Atkinson therefore focuses attention on the inevitable role that meaningful interpretation plays in the construction of statistical information about reality, as, indeed, for anti-positivists, it does in the construction of all social reality. However, it should not be thought that the anti-positivist/positivist debate is confined to the use of statistics in sociological explanation. What we have tried to emphasise in this chapter so far is that it should be recognised that *any* decision about how sociological research should be carried out is ultimately a decision about epistemological commitment; as we shall see, decisions regarding specific primary-data collection methods are no exception.

12.7   THE LOGIC AND PRACTICE OF DATA COLLECTION

Asking questions: the survey

Before we see how epistemological commitment affects the choice of question-asking techniques, we ought to be aware of the range of such techniques which are available.

Respondents can either be asked questions which are written down – in a *questionnaire* – or presented verbally, i.e. in an *interview*. Interviews and questionnaires are almost invariably used in the context of a *survey*. The point of any survey of a population is to make comparisons between the responses to the questions asked so that a general statement about them may be made. Surveys vary according to the degree of *structure* involved, for questions can be asked, and answers elicited, in a more or less structured way. In interviews the degree of structure of questions can vary:

(1)   The most *structured* interview is the sort where the order and wording of the questions are predetermined and each respondent is asked exactly the same question in exactly the same way with the questions following the same order every time.

(2)   The *focused* interview, as its name suggests, is the sort where the questions are focused on particular topics but where the interviewer can choose the words he/she uses to ask them as well as the order in which they are asked. (Usually, then, this sort of interview *schedule* – as the list of questions an interviewer is to ask is called – simply lists

general areas of interest the interviewer is to get the respondent to talk about.)

(3)   The completely *unstructured* or *discovery* interview involves the interviewer simply engaging the respondent in conversation, and then following up particular points of interest as they develop.

Structure of responses

In general two types of question may be used:

First, 'closed-ended' questions provide a range of alternatives from which the respondent is asked to choose his/her answer. For example:

Question Please tell me how you voted in the last election:
Tory
Labour
Liberal
Other
Didn't

Second, 'open-ended' questions place no such structure on the answer and allow the respondent to reply in any way he/she likes. For example.

Question Why did you vote the way you did in the last election?

In a questionnaire sufficient space is left for a lengthy answer, while in an interview the interviewer will usually write down the reply verbatim.

Coding

The degree of structure of the response determines the ease with which it can be *coded*. The purpose of coding is to convert responses to questions into symbols which can be easily compared with one another. If a question is closed-ended, the codes can be attached to the range of alternatives during the construction of the questionnaire or schedule; this is called *pre-coding*. Thus, in the case of our earlier example of a close-ended question, the alternative responses would be pre-coded and the respondent (if included in a questionnaire) or interviewer asked to indicate the answer to the question by ringing the appropriate code in the following fashion:

Question Please tell me how you voted in the last election:
Tory   1
Labour   ②
Liberal   3
Other   4
Didn't   5

If a question is open-ended so that the response is not structured in this way, and if coding is desired, it has to take place after the questioning has finished. This makes things more difficult, so a list of codes for each question is not usually drawn up until a number of answers have been examined in order to see if any patterns emerge. Thus, for example, after looking at a number of answers to our other question, 'Why did you vote the way you did at the last election?', it might be discovered that nearly all of them fit into one or other of the following categories:

family always vote that way
like the political leader
like the policies
dislikes the others
will improve standard of living

A list of these codes is then drawn up and answers to the remaining questionnaires/interviews coded from this list (which can be added to if need be). The advantage of coding is that the responses can be transferred to a punch card – nowadays almost invariably a computer card – and almost any sort of comparison between different sets of responses can be made very easily.

Before we go on three further points need to be made.

(1)   Some open-ended questions produce results that cannot be coded, either because the range of responses is too diverse or because they are not unambiguous enough and it would be illegitimate to 'force' them into particular categories. Since such responses cannot be coded, it means that they cannot be statistically compared and generalised about in quantitative terms; any comparison of the responses to these sorts of questions thus usually takes a qualitative form, typically with verbatim extracts reproduced alongside as part of the results of the survey.

(2)   Where individual questions are unstructured – where the interviewer can ask a question as he/she sees fit – it is not only impractical but also illegitimate to make the sorts of quantified comparisons which coding and computation facilitate, since differences in the way questions are asked of different respondents may well be influential in producing differences or similarities in the answers.

(3)   The same restriction obviously applies to an even greater extent to an unstructured interview since it has to be seen as a social encounter of a qualitatively different status from all the others in the survey. As a result, not only can quantitative comparisons not be made for practical (coding) and epistemological reasons but even qualitative comparisons can be made only with the greatest of care.

Obviously, then, there is a direct relationship between the degree of structure of both questions and interviews in a survey and the possibility or legitimacy of comparison, generalisation and quantification of the results. Therefore, we should next consider the way in which surveys are designed to be more or less structured, and how the degree to which they are affects the sort of results they produce. It is here that we begin to consider the relationship between epistemological position and choice of question-asking technique.

Survey design

In designing research of any sort there are two important issues which need to be examined – those of *validity* and *reliability*.

Validity. What may be valid for one sociologist may be invalid for another: thus, the validity or 'truth' of positivist research may be dismissed by the anti-positivist because it is based on an entire approach the latter would not accept.

Reliability. This concerns not so much truth as *replicability*. For a technique of data collection to be reliable, it should produce results which are not affected by the process of collection. For a *survey* to be reliable it must be reasonable to assume that each time the survey is repeated and applied to the same respondents it will produce similar results.

Validity and survey design. Notions of validity in asking questions are intimately bound up with

(i)   the ease with which the responses to the questions can be compared, measured and generalised about, and

(ii)   the size of the population about whom such comparison, measurement and generalisation can be made.

Validity, comparison and measurement. In general, the more we think we need to understand the meanings of our actors, the less structured our questions and our interviews will have to be. Since this is so, it follows that the more we think we need to understand meanings, the harder it will be for us to compare, measure and generalise about the results of our questions:

(1) *Structure of questions*. For example, if you think that the response to a closed-ended question like

Question Do you think trade unions in Britain have got too much power?
Yes   1
No   2
Don't know   3

is a valid indicator of the respondent's attitude towards trade unions and/or the distribution of power in Britain, then it also means that your results about this topic from your survey population are going to be easily coded (pre-coded in this case, of course), compared and measured. If, however, less positivistically, you think that only questions like

Question What do you think about trade unions in Britain?
Question Who do you think has power in Britain?

are valid – i.e. are likely to allow the actor to tell you what he means – then your results can only be coded, and comparison and measurement made, with great difficulty.

(2) *Structure of interview*. The more one wants to understand the way the actor looks at the world, the fewer preconceptions or assumptions should be made about the general topic of inquiry. Hence unstructured interviews should be seen as unique events since the questions, their sequence, the emphases given by the interviewer and, in fact, everything other than the general focus of the interview can vary considerably from one occasion to the next. This means that it is very difficult to compare and measure the responses of different social actors gained through this technique. For these reasons, unstructured interviews are hardly ever used in survey research where coding and measurement are the primary aims except as an exploratory technique (to discover questions to ask, as, for example, when key informants are used in the early stages of research), or as a means of enabling investigation of a greater depth into areas of interest previously uncovered by more structured interviews. However, this sort of interview can be a major instrument of data collection where an understanding of actors' meanings is the primary aim and where coding and comparison are of minimal importance. The results of such research are usually reproduced in an almost wholly qualitative fashion. In sum, then, the desire to understand actors' meanings in survey research is inversely related to the ease with which coding, comparison and measurement of its results can take place.

Validity and number of respondents. Validity is also inversely related to the number of respondents of whom questions can be asked – for the more unstructured an interview, the more time-consuming it is, and the fewer the interviews that can be carried out.

These relationships concerning validity and survey design are represented in Figure 12.2.

Conclusion on validity and survey design. These factors concerning validity have a number of consequences for the practice of asking questions in social research:

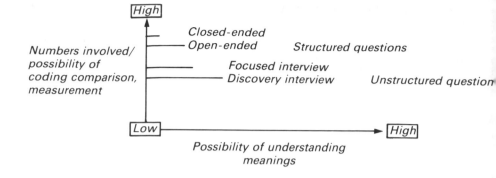

FIGURE 12.2

(i) The tail (method) can wag the dog (aim of the research). Here, while the inverse relationship between understanding and measurability is recognised by the researcher, the desire to come up with 'hard' quantifiable data which can be statistically manipulated in order to produce generalisations significantly reduces the likelihood of registering the subjective meanings of social actors.

(ii) Less extreme is the sort of compromise in what are known as 'attitude scales'. Essentially these are closed-ended questions about a respondent's attitudes which not only purport to get at his/her meaning but which are also, because of the structured nature of their responses, capable of easy coding and measurement. For example:

Question Which of the following comes closest to your point of view?

	Strongly agree	Agree	Neither agree nor disagree	Disagree	Strongly disagree
(a) You can be a good Christian without thinking about God and religion	1	2	3	4	5
(b) You can be a good Christian without being a Church member	1	2	3	4	5
(c) You can be a good Christian without attending Church	1	2	3	4	5

However well intentioned, anti-positivists usually dismiss such questions since they impose rigid observer categories on a respondent's view of reality and are therefore inevitably unhelpful so far as getting at real understanding is concerned.

(iii) The most usual result is that different *sorts* of question-asking takes place, with questions and interviews of varying degrees of structure being used, depending on the extent to which the need for an understanding of meanings is felt to be more important than a desire for quantification.

Reliability and survey design. If a survey is a short cut to observation, then sampling is simply a further short cut. Instead of asking questions of all the people in which we are interested we ask only a fraction of them. Reliable sampling is always concerned with representativeness. The more representative we can make our sample of the population we are studying as a whole in terms of the variables we think are important, the more reliable it is.

But sampling can be a rather difficult procedure. The document listing the parent population from which a sample is to be drawn is called a *sampling frame*. Obviously, the quality of the source of one's sample is crucial to the reliability of one's results, since the sample can only be as good as the frame from which it is drawn. For example, if an electoral register is not up to date, no matter how carefully a sample is drawn, it is not going to be wholly reliable or representative of the actual population concerned. Again, there can be real difficulties in drawing a reliable sample. Say we wanted to investigate students' perceptions of power in a college, and wanted to draw a 10 per cent sample. How can we make this representative? We could put the names of all students on pieces of paper, place them in a drum and draw out the requisite number. Or, better still, we could get a computer to select at random from student records. Or we could choose any other convenient way of obtaining a *random sample*. 'Random' thus does not mean haphazard here – it means that each unit in the parent population about whom generalisations are to be made has exactly the same chance of inclusion in the sample as any other unit. But randomness does not *necessarily* mean representativeness. Thus, drawing a simple random sample from our frame of the student population, we may end up with a disproportionate number of sociology students, or women, or part-time students. To get round such problems we can *stratify* our sample according to factors we believe may be relevant: for example, by full-time or part-time students, subject being studied, sex, or whatever. This would give us several different groups from which to draw random samples in porportion to their numbers in the parent population. Another term for such sampling is *purposive sampling*.

Another sort of sampling technique is *quota*, or *judgement*, sampling. This is a quicker and more convenient way of getting at a sample than other methods but is arguably the least reliable. Typically, before interviewing takes place, the major constituent categories in the population are defined –

e.g. categorisation by sex, age, occupation, religion, or whatever. Interviewers are then given a *quota* of respondents from each of these categories to contact, the size of the quota being determined by what it is believed (or, it is hoped, known) is the relative proportion of individuals in each category in the population as a whole.

Much depends on judgement here, however. First, it is exercised before respondent contact is made, in order to decide how many of whom will be interviewed; and second, it is exercised by an interviewer, who has to decide which individuals fit the predefined categories. It has been argued that the bias inherent in this sort of procedure goes a long way to explaining the variance and unreliability of public-opinion and political polls, and it is certainly the case that quota sampling is most effective when representativeness is not needed and where statements about particular groups are the only concern.

Some unusual sampling problems

I do not wish to dwell on the technicalities of sampling and questionnaire design, since they can be found in the conventional methods cookbooks, whose recipes I largely followed. As such, they are concerns which lie outside the expressed purpose of this book. However, some problems not customarily referred to can be highlighted briefly. Farm workers represent a highly scattered population, isolated and often socially invisible. The logistics of doing a survey are thus formidable: problems of creating a correct sampling frame, problems of contact, problems of travel, problems of interviewing as a piece of social interaction, all pile on top of each other. All sociologists believe that their own respondents present more difficulties than everyone else's, so I do not wish to overstate this; I merely wish to point out that the temptation to take some short-cuts was irresistible. In particular I sampled farms rather than farm workers, since I believed I could obtain a reliable sampling frame of farms (mistakenly, since the Ministry of Agriculture refused to co-operate and I was forced back on to the Yellow Pages) and then contact the workers via an employer. This was not only an administrative convenience, but probably also an administrative necessity. However, the result was that, in common with so many other sociological studies, I was taking the easy option of homing in on a captive set of respondents. So much sociological research takes place in an institutional setting – a factory, office, school, prison, hospital – whereby contact is made, especially with working-class respondents, via people in positions of authority over them. For despite our awareness of the 'Hawthorne effect' the practice continues, and we hope we can rectify any misconceptions of our purpose in the interview situation itself – but this in turn requires a careful and sensitive appraisal of the role required to obtain a sympathetic *rapport* with the respondent before data collection even commences.

Source: Howard Newby, 'Reflections on the Study of Suffolk Farm Workers', in Colin Bell and Howard Newby *Doing Sociological Research*, Allen & Unwin (1977).

Sometimes, of course, a clearly defined sampling frame is not easily available, for in some research – e.g. into deviance – there is no existing information about who constitutes the population (we shall look at Humphreys's problems in this regard later). One way around this is to construct a 'snowball' sample. One begins with a single informant or a few informants among the population in which one is interested and these help one to find more respondents: one contact leads to another, and each of these leads to still more respondents, and so on. Of course, there is no way one can check for bias here, and from this point of view purposive sampling is far better; however, a snowball is better than nothing and may often be quite appropriate if, for example, friendship or kinship networks are being investigated.

Survey implementation

Once satisfied with the design of a survey, the next problem is to implement it. The problems involved with survey implementation are of two kinds: (i) those concerned with making contact with the respondents; and (ii) those concerned with actually asking them questions.

Problems of contact. Although making contact might look straightforward enough, in fact it can be quite problematic. There are a number of issues involved.

Most importantly, the way in which the sociologist approaches respondents almost certainly defines his or her *role* in their eyes. It is impossible to have a *neutral* identity: any inquiring sociologist will inevitably be assigned a label of some kind. Consequently, where possible we must decide *in advance* the identity we wish to create for ourselves, one which will affect what we are doing least, and play the appropriate role accordingly. However, this is not always possible; sometimes, because we are ignorant of those whom we are studying, we do not know the most useful identity to present and this leads to more or less successful decisions being made on the spot.

No matter how diligent we are there are always those respondents we cannot contact: these are called *non-respondents*. This does not necessarily mean that they have refused to be interviewed but that, for some reason or another, we have been unable to get hold of them.

We need to be fairly certain that non-respondents are not a particular kind of person and that they thus do not differ in any fundamental way from respondents – i.e. that they are equally representative of the sample. The more non-respondents, the less likely this will be a valid assumption to make. A non-response rate of 10 per cent or less is suspiciously good, and in general less than 30 per cent is adequate in survey research. Above 40 per cent, problems of unrepresentativeness arise.

If we suspect real problems, we have two alternatives:

(i)   we can weight the replies for some non-respondents in a way which we think will counteract the bias in the sample (this is not very satisfactory); or

(ii)   we can replace non-respondents by others chosen in the same way as in the original sample (this is much better and, if done properly, involves drawing two separate samples of the same size so that if, for example, no. 83 in the sample proper is a non-respondent, no. 83 from the substitute sample is the replacement).

Problems with interviewing. Assuming we are able to make contact, we are then faced with problems involved with actually asking our questions. Again, these are of two kinds: (i) those concerned with the *design* of the interview schedule (as opposed to the content); and (ii) those concerned with the *interview situation* itself.

(i)   *The design of the interview schedule.* (The following points obviously also apply to the design of a questionnaire.) The questions must be asked sensibly and flow naturally rather than making sudden changes of direction or of area of discussion. Furthermore, because respondents often need to be 'warmed up', we do not start with awkward or embarrassing questions about details of the respondent's sex life, or his/her income or wealth. Instead we use easy and straightforward questions about variables like age, length of residence, marital status, etc., at the beginning and leave the more difficult questions towards the end, when the respondent is more relaxed. Questions must also be both intelligible and unambiguous. The only way to be sure of this is to try them out in what is called a *pilot survey*; this is usually carried out on respondents from the population under scrutiny not in the sample itself.

(ii)   *The interview situation.* Because the interview is itself an example of social interaction it can crucially affect the quality of the data collected. It is useful to see interviewing from a symbolic interactionist viewpoint. The researcher can define interviews in certain ways in order to reinforce the role he/she wants to play. Certain gestures, demeanours, tones of voice, the use of props like a briefcase or a printed schedule, the wearing of particular clothes, all serve to impose a certain definition of the situation on the respondent. From this point of view, then, because interviewing involves structuring our behaviour in order to achieve a required effect, it in fact involves doing no more than actors do in every social encounter in which they engage in everyday life, except that it is a self-conscious process.

However, it is this essential similarity between a social-research interview and a social encounter in everyday life that has led some sociologists to reject the type of data it produces. Their argument is that there is an invalidity inherent in the whole process of asking questions in social research which must cast fundamental doubts on the extent to which we can assume that a respondent's answers to questions actually reveal his or her behaviour and attitudes in everyday life.

The validity of the interview: the congruence of verbal responses and behaviour. We have seen that the primary assumption of the interview is that it is a short cut to observation and that with careful questioning answers given by respondents to questions about their past or future actions will correspond to how they did behave in the past or will behave in the future.

However, there is now much evidence to question the validity of this assumption and therefore the validity of the whole question-asking process in social research. This evidence seems to demonstrate that since asking questions of a respondent is itself an example of social behaviour, involving the meaningful interaction of two social actors, we therefore have to accept that the answers a respondent gives to a question may well be a direct function of his or her interaction with the interviewer rather than anything else, and that (as a result) these answers might not match his or her *actual* behaviour or attitudes.

One of the first demonstrations of this occurred when La Piere (1934) travelled across the USA with a Chinese couple, observing how they were treated by the proprietors at various rest and refreshment places like hotels, camping sites and restaurants. The couple visited 251 places, being accepted at all save one. Six months later, La Piere sent a questionnaire to each one, asking whether it would accept members of Chinese origin as guests: only *one* establishment said it would, a considerable discrepancy between what the respondents said they would do and what they actually did. Phillips (1971) documents similar discrepancies in an examination of a whole range of factors present in an interview situation that can affect the nature of the response elicited. He shows, for example, that the sex, age and race of the interviewer can influence the way a respondent answers questions, as can non-ascribed status characteristics like his or her assumed social status or religious affiliation. He demonstrates in particular how such factors are involved in the well-documented source of bias variously called the 'social desirability effect' or 'evaluation apprehension'. These terms refer to the way in which respondents seek the approval of the sort of person they imagine the investigator to be by answering in ways which may be far from the 'truth'. Hughes (1976) mentions another source of bias, referring to the evidence of a tendency among certain sorts of respondents to answer 'yes' or 'no' to questions irrespective of their content. He also points out that the relatively few attempts to check the accuracy of respondent reports after interviewing have demonstrated that even the response to fairly uncomplicated 'factual' questions cannot be assumed to be free from this sort of bias. For example, respondents have been found to give inaccurate replies with regard to whether they had voted or not, relied on social welfare, used birth-control techniques, and so on.

Of course, some of these discrepancies may well be due to 'faulty memories, attempts to "take a stab" at answering questions which are not fully understood' (Phillips, 1971, p.28), or a complete misundeerstanding of what is being asked. However, interpretivist sociologists stress that by far the more usual reasons for discrepancies stem from the fact that an interview situation is a *social* situation and thus, as in any social relationship, the action of one party to it will necessarily be a direct function of his or her interaction with the other. As Weber (1964) pointed out: 'Action is social in so far as, by virtue of the subjective meaning attached to it by the acting individual (or individuals) it takes account of the behaviour of others and is thereby oriented in its course.'

Given this emphasis, critics of the interview stress that it is, *like any other social encounter*, a potential source of bias, misinterpretation and fakehood. Indeed, Phillips argues that discrepancies between the words and deeds of respondents are not only *as* likely to occur in interview contexts as they are in everyday exchanges but even *more* so. This is because the respondents may be much more sensitive in the interview than in 'normal' interaction to how other people see how they maintain their self-image and respect while having to answer a number of unusually probing questions. This stress, which is not restricted to the interview but possible in *all* social encounters, may encourage an individual to give inaccurate or fake responses. According to Phillips, then, there are two general sorts of lie possible in any social encounter – one to avoid opprobrium, and the other to seek approval – and an interview is no exception.

For these sorts of reasons, critics such as Phillips argue that not only does the validity of the results of such social encounters have to be seen as very much in doubt but so does their *reliability*. Thus, however much care one takes to neutralise the effects of biases on the reliability of one's results, the *main* source of bias – that questions are asked in the context of some sort of social encounter – remains. Phillips concludes that the assumption that social research can be carried out without the researcher (or a representative) influencing what is obtained as data is preposterous. Yet this assumption does seem fundamentally to underpin survey research, at least in its most structured forms, and although it is a technique that has certainly experienced some decline in its popularity, there is evidence that this decline is rather less than significant: for example, more than 90 per cent of the papers in the *American Sociological Review* and the *American Journal of Sociology* in the mid-1960s had used survey-based material. Despite the sorts of serious objections which can be raised against the epistemology on which the technique is based, then, it does seem that at the present time, for many sociologists, the automatic response to coming across any area of ignorance about contemporary society is *still* 'let's do a survey'.

Observation

Subscribing to these objections to the interview involves acknowledging the anti-positivist position that because sociological understanding is essentially the understanding of actors' meanings, this can only be achieved by putting oneself in the actor's place and seeing "reality" as he or she sees it. Since this is so, participant observation is clearly a far less problematic research alternative for this viewpoint than asking questions.

However, it would be quiet wrong to assume that it is therefore a research tool *only* used by anti-positivists for wholly anti-positivistic purposes.

First, its use in no sense implies only the production of data of a totally qualitative character. (We made this point earlier when we referred to the often quite positivistic sorts of results produced by interactionists out of observational studies.)

Second, there is nothing inherently anti-positivistic in observation as a research technique; there is no *necessary* reason why it cannot be used to investigate causal relationships between variables defined in terms of observer categories. To make the same point a little differently: while the more committed one is to an anti-positivistic ontology/epistemology, the more one is likely, for reasons already mentioned, to doubt seriously the validity of the question-asking process and to tend to rely wholly on other methods like observation, this does not mean that all observers in sociological research are therefore anti-positivistic. On the contrary, as we shall see, all sorts of perspectives have made, and continue to make, use of it as a technique of data collection (whether on its own or in combination with other techniques). What matters is the *use* to which sociologists put observation.

Observer roles

The first question we must ask is: *how* is the researcher to join in and observe the actors under study? There is no easy answer, for everything depends on the particular situation being studied and the questions being asked.

The early 'Chicago School' sociologists, inspired by the interest in social problems of ex-journalists like Park and Burgess, characteristically concerned themselves with the open observation of the social fabric of the huge industrial metropolis that Chicago had rapidly become by the early years of this century. They simply pounded the streets and frequented meeting-places in an attempt to see the city in the raw: 'tell it like it is' was their watchword. This traditional approach is matched by the interests and techniques of the contemporary Chicago School, largely symbolic interactionists with a major interest in deviance.

One issue which is relevant with regard to observational research into any sensitive area of social life, but which is particularly so with regard to the study of deviance, concerns the extent to which observation should be *overt*, apparent to the actors under study, or *covert*, hidden from them. Supporters of covert stances in deviance research tend to argue that because of the very nature of the activities of their subject-matter, the latter would almost inevitably change their behaviour if they knew they were under observation.

The Chicago researchers have consistently rejected this sort of argument, however. As Douglas (1972, p. 6) points out:

> They believe the sociologist becomes a taken-for-granted presence – that is, *if* he establishes trust and rapport, which are, in any case, necessary to his being accepted at all or gaining entrée to the group. Moreover, the Chicago researchers generally argue that defining oneself as a member and trying to do secret research actually makes many things unobservable to a researcher. There are things that members would be willing to expose to a trusted individual who is not a member because he will not use the information against members to advance himself in the organisation, as ordinary members might do.

Ned Polsky, a renowned observer of various deviant activities, adopts a similar position to the Chicago School over the overt – covert issue. Talking about field research in criminality, he argues that you

> damned well better *not* pretend to be 'one of them', because they will test this claim out and one of two things will happen: either you will ... get sucked into 'participant' observation of the sort you would rather not undertake, or you will be exposed, with still greater negative consequences. You must let the criminals know who you are and if it is done properly it does not sabotage the research (Polsky, 1971, p. 122).

However, when describing the observational strategy for his study of homosexual behaviour in men's 'tea rooms' (rest rooms/public conveniences), Laud Humphreys (1970, p. 25) takes the opposite line on this issue:

> From the beginning, my decision was to continue the practice of the field study in passing as deviant ... there are good reasons for following this method of participant observation.
>
> In the first place, I am convinced that there is only *one* way to watch highly discreditable behaviour and that is to pretend to be in the same boat with those engaging in it. To wear a button that says 'I am a watchbird, watching you' into a tea room would instantly eliminate all action except the flushing of toilets and the exiting of all present. Polsky has done excellent observation of pool hustlers because he is experienced and welcome in their game – he is accepted as one of

them. He might also do well, as he suggests, in interviewing a jewel thief or a fence in his tavern hangout. But it should be noted that he does not propose watching them steal, whereas my research required observation of criminal acts.

The second reason is to prevent distortion. Hypothetically, let us assume that a few men could be found to continue their sexual activity while under observation. How 'normal' could that activity be? How could the researcher separate the 'show' and the 'cover' from standard procedures of the encounter? . . . a stage is a suitable research site only for those who wish to study the 'onstage' behaviour of actors.

Humphreys thus played an authentic homosexual role – as voyeur – which allowed him to participate without actually having to engage in homosexuality.

Indeed, William Foote Whyte, in his study of an Italian–American slum gang (*Street Corner Society*, 1943), admits that the actors' knowledge of his presence and intentions may well have changed their behaviour as a result. He quotes the gang leader, Doc: 'You've slowed me up plenty since you've been down here. Now when I do something, I have to think what Bill Whyte would want me to know about it and how I can explain it . . . Before I used to do these things by instinct' (Whyte, 1943, p. 301). As Hughes (1976, p. 119) points out, the implications of this comment are fairly obvious: 'a loss of spontaneity and an increase in self-reflection on the part of the actor concerning what he is doing and why, which may detract from the "naturalness" which the observer wishes to study'.

Another major issue to be decided by the observer concerns the extent to which he or she should *participate* in the activities of the actors under study. Whyte (1943, p. 304) shows how this decision was made for him by his subjects themselves:

a little later I had to face the question of how far I was to immerse myself in the life of the district. I bumped into that problem as I was walking down the street with the Nortons. Trying to enter into the spirit of the small talk, I cut loose with a string of obscenities and profanity. The walk came to a momentary halt as they stopped to look at me in surprise. Doc shook his head and said: 'Bill, you're not supposed to talk like that. That doesn't sound like you.' I tried to explain that I was only using terms that were common on the street corner. Doc insisted, however, that I was different and that he wanted me to be that way. This lesson went far beyond the use of obscenity and profanity. I learned that people did not expect me to be just like them; in fact, they were interested and pleased to find me different, just so long as I took a friendly interest in them. Therefore, I abandoned my efforts at complete immersion.

Ronald Frankenburg, when studying the Welsh rural community he called 'Pentrediwaith' (*Village on the Border*, 1957) was allocated an active role in the village of 'stranger', or 'outsider', which, while allowing him to become involved (he became secretary of the local football club, for example), nevertheless meant he could also remain sufficiently detached for an overall view of community life. According to Frankenburg, this is a genuine role in Pentre life (it was not just created to accommodate him) and, he says, is symptomatic of the need any small group or community has to find a means of preventing conflicts and disagreements between interests or groups being brought out into the open, thereby threatening the stability of social life. His argument is that in communities like Pentre 'strangers' or 'outsiders', located as they are outside any of the constituent groupings of the local social structure and therefore peripheral to any conflicts which may exist between them, can be used as scapegoats, in order that blame can be allocated and conflict channelled and contained.

There are literally hundreds more examples we could refer to, all demonstrating that the sorts of roles played by the participating observer can vary a great deal; in fact, the variation is only matched by the variation in the kinds of situations in which observation is used as a research technique.

The next question we have to consider is: How is observation practised? How do we arrive at our observation-based data?

The process of observation

Whether it is subscribed to be positivist or anti-positivist, an emphasis on the need to be involved implies that there is little 'common' sense between observer and observed which the sociologist can take for granted. From any ontological/epistemological standpoint, then, to choose participant observation involves seeing reality as initially unknown – and unknowable until the rules by which the actors play the game are learnt and understood. It thus involves seeing the social behaviour in a Welsh community or a modern urban township or a teenage gang or a hospital as just as immediately 'foreign' as the behaviour of a tribe in Africa obviously is.

Not surprisingly, then, all the normative texts stress the importance of immersing oneself properly before any legitimate conception of 'what's going on' can emerge. For example, Polsky (1971, pp. 126–7) exhorts the participant observer to

> initially, keep your eyes and ears open *but keep your mouth shut*. At first try to ask no questions whatsoever. Before you can ask questions, or even speak much at all other than when spoken to, you should get the 'feel' of their world by extensive and attentive listening – get some sense of what pleases them and what bugs them, some sense of their frame of reference, and some sense of *their* sense of language.

This bears out the point we made a little earlier – that observation as a technique should not be confused with a particular type of research methodology, for discovery is a problem for much if not most social research, positivistic or anti-positivistic, and observation at the outset is often the way ideas are first formulated for testing. This is often as true for positivists who write up their results according to the *logic* of the hypothetico-deductive method as it is for anti-positivists whose logic of research strategy – e.g. analytic induction – is more likely to match their practice. Thus although *reports* of positivistic enquiry generally claim that hypotheses have been constructed before any field work was done, this is hardly ever the case in practice, whether in natural or social science.

Whether observation is used by positivist or anti-positivist, how is one to judge that the interpretations of social activity are adequate and warranted accounts? Is it possible to *demonstrate* that the results of observation are objectively valid? Of course, there are those, ethnomethodologists for example, who deny the possibility of objective knowledge anyway and for whom the problem does not therefore exist. So far as less relativistic epistemological positions are concerned, it is sometimes assumed that the results of observation are completely qualitative, consisting of in-depth descriptions of social life and exhibiting no evidence of a desire to measure or quantify. But we cannot make this assumption, for however anti-positivistic the *stated* position of the researcher is, especially as regards discovery and validation, it is very often possible to discern more positivistic intentions when it comes to the provision of evidence *in order to explain*.

For example, it is common for quantitative data to be provided in order to supplement that gained through observation. Thus Humphreys followed up his role as voyeur with later interviews, selecting a sample of 100 of the participants in the tea-room encounters he had observed. He makes the purpose of this exercise quite clear: 'What verbal research is possible through outside interviews then becomes an independent means of verifying the observations' (Humphreys, 1970, p. 36).

So observation can be used, either by itself or with other methods, by sociologists espousing very different ontological and epistemological positions. This demonstrates once again that what matters is not the technique itself so much as the uses to which it is put (the questions it is used to ask), and this in turn confirms the importance of seeing sociological research as necessarily carrying specific theoretical commitments.

Problems of observation

What of problems involved with observation? We can identify two distinct kinds. For the positivistically inclined the problem is how the observer can remain objective in order to provide demonstrable proof, while for the anti-positivist it is how to get close enough to the actors to understand their meanings properly. We will look at each of them in turn.

Problems posed for objectivity because of the need for understanding via involvement. One of the more obvious objections to observation is that the participant does not know the extent to which the behaviour of those being observed has changed by his or her presence. We have already discussed some of the arguments used by supporters of overt and covert stances; ultimately, however, even completely covert role-playing by observers cannot *guarantee* that their actors are behaving as they would if they had not been present.

Another objection is that participant observation is always to some extent selective observation, because it is necessarily an account of reality from the point of view of the *particular* role the participant observer has chosen to play. This can have a number of implications for the validity of the research. For example, the role-playing observer can simply cease to be an observer and be 'captured' by his or her subject-matter – a process usually called 'going native'. A possible example of this would be the researcher working in a residential religious community abandoning the project in order to 'join up'. Less drastically, validity may be impaired if the sample chosen does not adequately represent the specific social group under investigation. Bell and Newby (1971) criticise Lloyd Warner's (1960) study of the American town he calls 'Jonesville' from this point of view, quoting Lipset and Bendix's (1967) point that, in his investigation into Jonesville's stratification system, nine-tenths of Warner's informants were upper middle class. According to Lipset and Bendix (1967, p. 162), this bias results in Warner's account of Jonesville stratification revealing only

> the perspective of the social climbers just below the upper crust of small town society. To people at this level class appears as a matter of interpersonal relations, manners, family and so on. It is not polite to suggest that class is a reflection of one's economic position.

In contrast, the only working-class informant Warner uses refers to class as 'purely a matter of income and power'. Here, then, is a picture of social reality which, because of the concepts and methods used, is incomplete and selective; as Bell and Newby put it, it is a 'social reality primarily as seen from the perspective of the higher strata'.

Even allowing for these problems of producing a valid account of the *particular* setting in which the observer is involved – the *internal* validity of the results – there remains the problem of the extent to which this account is applicable to behaviour *outside* of the particular setting in which it is being observed – *external* validity. That is, how *representative* are participant observation accounts? As Hughes (1976, p. 129) puts it:

> How can the observer be sure that the case he has studied, whether a military training programme, a street-corner gang, a group of workers in a factory or whatever are representative of the population about which the inferences are made?

Related to this is the further problem that the validity of participant observation accounts depends in part on their capacity to let the 'facts speak for themselves'. Normative prescriptions for participant observation have a tendency to exhort fieldworkers to have no preconceived notions, to have an open mind and to let reality present itself as it 'really is'.

However, as was suggested at the beginning of this chapter, 'facts' do not present themselves directly to us but rather are only meaningful as facts because they are an empirical representation of a theoretical model adopted prior to observation. Therefore, no one, however hard he/she tries to conform to Polsky's strategy of asking no questions and keeping his/her mouth shut, can avoid looking at the world selectively, if only because he/she is bound to have some preconceived idea of what constitutes a fact and what does not.

Where, then, does this leave the objectivity of the participant observer's findings? How do we establish that claims are demonstrably valid? In community studies in particular it is usually claimed that this can be done by replication, whereby one research report is checked by a different sociologist carrying out another study of the same community. However, the evidence from community studies' replication seems to suggest that ultimate validity is as impossible as is any separation of theory from methods or from findings. A famous example of this can be seen in the results of Oscar Lewis's restudy of Robert Redfield's account of life in Tepoztlan, a Mexican village.

Redfield's study was first published in 1930 as *Tepoztlan – A Mexican Village*; Lewis returned to Tepoztlan seventeen years after Redfield, producing his *Life in a Mexican Village* in 1951. The astonishing difference in their accounts is made very clear by Bell and Newby (1971, p. 76):

> The impression given of Tepoztlan by Redfield has a Rousseauan quality: relatively homogeneous, isolated, smoothly functioning, well-integrated with contented, well-adjusted inhabitants. The emphasis throughout his study is on the co-operative and unifying factors. He glosses over evidence of violence, disruption, cruelty, disease, suffering and maladjustment, poverty, economic problems and political schisms. Lewis, on the other hand, emphasises 'the underlying individualism of Tepoztlan institutions and character, the lack of co-operation, the tensions between villages within the municipio, the schisms within the village, the pervading quality of fear, envy, and distrust in interpersonal relations'.

Why such a dramatic set of differences? Although a number of reasons can be advanced, the most important is undoubtedly the selective influence of theoretical perspectives – the 'blinker-like nature of theory in fieldwork', as Bell and Newby put it. They continue:

> Redfield's theoretical orientation influenced the selection and coverage of facts and the way in which these facts were organised . . . Redfield was interested in the

study of a single social process: the evolution from folk to urban, rather than a well-rounded ethnographic account. The questions that he asked of his data were quite different to those asked by Lewis (Bell and Newby, 1971, p. 77).

Problems posed for understanding because of the need to be an observer. Obviously, the reason why the anti-positivist chooses participant observation as a research technique is because of the belief that there is no other way of understanding the principal subject-matter – the actors' definitions of their situation.

The unexpected effect of video as a research tool in a study of market traders

Our aim is to show how bargains, and related notions of worth, value, price and so on are constructed by market traders in their talk. The things that consumers take into account as the basis for making purchasing decisions are dealt with, managed and exploited in the pitcher's selling routines. Their rhetorical interventions between product and purchaser in one of the most elementary forms of economic exchange – selling in the market place – is taken to demonstrate that sales are fundamentally interactional accomplishments. ....

We have obtained a corpus of video and audio recordings of market pitchers (and fly pitchers) selling their products. We quickly encountered the extremely opportunistic selling skill of the pitchers. They welcomed and made use of the presence of the research team, with all its audio-visual hardware, by regularly announcing to their audience that advertisements were being made for a TV company:

(3) P: *all* we're gonna do tuh get us goin', (0.9) ah've got *all* sorts of oddments that ah'll charge yuh *coppers* for (0.5) for the *television* advert (0.5) right? We'll be on television (.) from *now* till Christmas, (0.6) so if yuh wanna get yer face on the box, now's yer chance.

Such references to the video equipment appeared to enhance both the pitchers' credibility and the bargain status of the goods. This was rather satisfying from a methodological point of view, not only as it facilitated data collection, but also because we became an integral part of the selling process itself. This entry into research quickly enabled us to build up contacts with the pitchers such that after a short time our presence (with, of course, the equipment) was requested for a Christmas perfume sales promotion, we were given 'trade secrets', and we were asked to pose as 'ricks' (front men/women) to 'get in on the action and find out what it's all about'.

Source: T. Pinch and C. Clark, 'Patter Merchanting', *Sociology*, May 1986.

Far from seeking to find ways to remain objective, then, the real problem for the anti-positivist is *how to become involved enough to understand*, not to worry about how to remain sufficiently detached. In fact, ultimately, the real problem faced by the anti-positivist observer is that, however hard one tries to see the world as the actor sees it, however involved one becomes, if the observer and his or her subject-matter are not one and the same person, then, as Hughes (1976, p. 132) puts it, 'there enters the possibility of bias and interpretation mediated by the observer's "uncleansed" experience which he must inevitably bring to the research setting'.

Some interesting anti-positivist solutions have been offered as a way out of this problem. For example, Phillips (1971) makes the point that this is exactly that same problem which is faced by social actors (ordinary people) in every social encounter with others. He argues that since this is so – since no actors in any social relationship can be finally sure of the validity of their understanding of others' behaviour since they are not those other people – participant observation-based social research as an activity is no different at all from social life: that is, the problems faced by an observer 'trying to understand' are no different from those faced by any actor trying to understand any other actor. For this reason Phillips suggests that the job of a social researcher should be .to become as much a part of the research setting as possible through participation and observation (to become as much like one of the actors as possible) and then report back, in a sense autobiographically, on his or her *own* experiences – on the problems encountered and the means of their solution, in coming to an understanding of the behaviour of others, in working out 'what was going on', in fact. The point here, then, is that since the process of arriving at understanding in social interaction is precisely what the everyday life of actors involves and is in fact what social life is about, then proper participant observation should be exactly that – *the observation of one's own participation.*

The theoretical consequence of Phillips's comments is that the possibility of objective knowledge by way of participant observation must by definition be denied. This kind of position is completely rejected by those who believe that worthwhile sociological knowledge can only be achieved through the participant observer being sufficiently detached in order to be objective. From this point of view, then, actually being the subject of the research finally denies any possibility of others being able to assess the validity of one's own analysis and 'reduces' the status of such an enterprise to the equivalent of writing novels and autobiographies.

To conclude this section, the diagram below (Figure 12.3) summarises the broad relationship between different theoretical approaches (which are more or less positivistic and the methods *typically* though *not exclusively* associated with each.

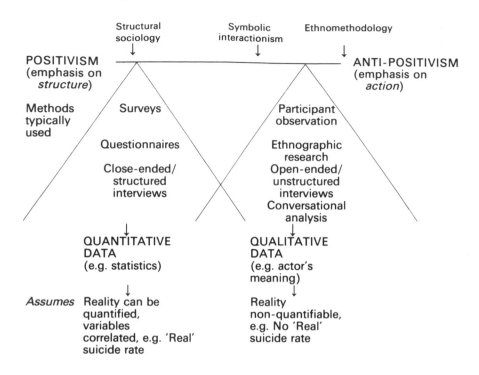

FIGURE 12.3   *A summary of the relationship between theory and methods*

12.8   CONCLUSION

The conflict of views over the specific issue of observation well illustrates the more general conflict in sociological theory and methodology that we have tried to make apparent throughout this chapter. Like any form of production, the production of sociological knowledge depends of course on the use of suitable tools. But, as we have seen, the same tools may be used to create very different images of social reality.

So where does all of this leave the practice of sociology? Having got this far and having seen the way in which the proponents of different epistemological and methodological positions oppose each other's strategies and procedures for research at virtually every turn, you may be forgiven for thinking that actually 'doing sociology', rather than writing about the difficulties involved with doing it, is well-nigh impossible.

Combining methods

From Eileen Barker, *The Professional Stranger: Some Methodological Problems Encountered in a Study of the Reverend Sun Myng Moon's Unification Church.*
The initial problem or impetus for carrying out research into the Unification Church (UC hereafter) was comparatively simple: why did people join and why did they stay in the movement? The problem was fairly sharply defined by the fact that few people outside the UC found it possible to believe that anyone who was fully in command of his or her senses could conceivably want to become, let alone remain, a 'Moonie'. I, too, found myself in a position where I could see no obvious attraction in what appeared by all accounts to be a bizzare, authoritarian sect, which held strange beliefs and whose members were ruthlessly exploited by a Korean gentleman who gave nothing but took all.

Immediately the basic problem was posed it became necessary to turn to methodological considerations. What should the answers to my questions look like? Did I want to seek an explanation of the membership in terms of the members' social backgrounds or their psychological make-up? Might the explanation lie in the contemporary scene – the society which the Church and the members rejected? Or would it be more fruitful to assume the clues lay hidden in the UC itself, in its beliefs and practices and, especially, in the methods or recruitment which it employed? Were members the victims of social or psychological forces over which they had no control? Was I to assume *anyone*, given a particular social context, could be a Moonie (was this brainwashing?), or could I sort out a potential pool of converts from other, 'no-way' types? Was I myself to remain objective, scientific and uninvolved or did I need to immerse myself in the 'world view' of Mooniedom and share the subjective feelings and experiences of a 'Moonie trip'?

There is in sociology a time honoured dichotomy between those schools that focus in interpretive understanding and those that stress more behaviourist, positivistic or scientific approaches. What was to be my approach? Should I perhaps become an ethnomethodologist and investigate the taken-for-granted Moonie world, or should I regard Moonies as rats and dispassionately watch them running about their mazes, dismissing from my mind any notions of meaning or conscious purpose that could not be covered by stimulus/response or the more sophisticated operant-conditioning models of behaviour? Or perhaps I should forget about individuals as such and search only for structures and functions at a societal level? Would I adopt a philosophical anthropology that assumed we are complicated but nonetheless determined, reacting robots: or are we free, initiating creators, capable of self determination? Whom would I believe when it came to descriptions of the Unification Church? Who was more trustworthy, the brainwashed Moonies themselves or the sceptical critics? Would I learn more as an outsider or an insider? What was the true reality and how could I get to know about it? Was I to be guided by fact or theory or both? But the, which theory, and how was I to get the facts?

I began to realize that there could be no one answer. Several of the perspectives seemed to be necessary while none was sufficient for my purposes. I was convinced that without having a methodology as scientific as possible one would be unlikely to produce a sociological contribution that

continued overleaf

would add anything to all the claims and counter-claims which already existed. But it also seemed that without *verstehen*, or in other words some kind of emphatic understanding, one could not hope to find one's data in the first – or in the last – place.

In the end I decided on three main lines of approach: in depth interview, participant observation and questionnaire. From the interview I hoped to understand the individual as an individual. Just over thirty interviews were carried out on the basis of a random sample of the membership. They were tape-recorded and usually lasted for between five and nine hours. The longest lasted for twelve hours. From the participant observation (that is, from living in UC centres and attending various courses), I hoped to observe the interpersonal level, and from the questionnaire I hoped to see patterns and relationships that I might suspect existed but about which I could only generalize from a large number of respondents. All the British members and several European and Amercian members were given a forty-one page questionnaire containing both 'open' and 'precoded' questions. The response rate was surprisingly high and around 450 cases were fed into the computer for analysis. Added to these were over 100 responses to a similar questionnaire, filled in by a control group, that is by non-UC members who were similar in age and background (class, education and religion) to the UC membership. This was a methodological necessity if I were to be able to assess the extent to which the phenomena I was analysing were peculiar to the UC members. A further 'sub-control' of around 1,000 cases was constituted from those who were interested enough to attend the Church's workshops but did not go on to join the movement. In the event these control groups produced some of the most interesting data of the study.

Of course, all three methods shed light on the other aspects in which I was interested. I certainly could not have produced the questionnaire if I had not first spent two years conducting a large number of interviews, living with members and undergoing the so-called 'brain-washing' process. All of this was necessary for the formulation of hypotheses to be tested by the questionnaire and for learning the language in which the questions were to be couched. And, of course, I did learn much about individuals and their interactions from the questionnaire, just as during the participant observation I could actually observe the individuals interacting with others, and I could try to judge the overlaps and differences between their presentation of self in an interview and in an actual social context. There was also a lot of library work, finding out what others had written about the UC and other similar and dissimilar groups, as well as reading press cuttings, anti-Church propaganda and the literature put out by the UC itself.

Source: The Open University (1981). Social Services: a Second Level Course. An Introduction to Sociology (D207 Media Booklet).

But this is only a valid conclusion if it is believed that sociology is, or should aim to be, a single-purpose endeavour – if it is felt that the debates we have been recording are symptomatic of a disordered discipline floundering around seeking some sort of unification of theoretical and methodological intent. But if it is accepted that reality is almost certainly much too complex for any particular human cognitive or intellectual system to apprehend wholly its workings, then it could be argued that the emergence of the multiplicity of 'sociological' approaches to the investigation of reality that has taken place over recent years and that we have been talking about in this chapter actually represents an *advance* for the subject.

This does not mean, however, that the individual sociologist can abrogate the need for making *a* choice; one must decide where one's sympathies lie and pursue one's work accordingly. Such a decision confronts those who work in all areas of research in both the natural and social sciences, and is based as much on analytical reasons for, as on personal commitment to, the greater explanatory power of one approach compared with others.

The existence of methodological diversity should not necessarily be seen as a sign of weakness in an academic discipline, therefore; in fact, it may well be in more danger if its practitioners fail to recognise, or deny, that these choices have to be made. This is not to say that, at present, the choices available are adequate, however. It should be clear from the discussion in this chapter that neither positivism nor traditional interpretivism alone can provide a sociology which adequately confronts the relationshp between structure and action; as we shall now see in our final chapter on sociological theories, the task of constructing such a sociology is far from complete.

REFERENCES TO CHAPTER 12

Atkinson, J. M. (1978) *Discovering Suicide*, London, Macmillan.
Barker, E. (1981) *The Professional Stranger* (OU Media Booklet), Milton Keynes, Open University Press.
Bell, C. and Newby, H. (1977) *Doing Sociological Research*, London, Allen & Unwin.
Bell, C. and Newby, H. (1971) *Community Studies*, London, Allen & Unwin.
Blauner, R. (1964) *Alienation and Freedom*, University of Chicago Press.
Comte, A. (1844) *Discourse on the Positive Spirit*, Paris.
Cuff, E. C. and Payne, G. C. F. (1979) *Perspectives in Sociology*, London, Allen & Unwin.
Douglas, J. D. (1967) *The Social Meanings of Suicide*, Princeton University Press.
Douglas, J. D. (1972) *Research on Deviance*, New York, Random House.
Durkheim, E. (1952) *Suicide*, London, Routledge & Kegan Paul.
Frankenburg, R. (1957) *Village on the Border*, London, Cohen & West.
Giddens, A. (1985) *The Constitution of Society*, Cambridge, Polity Press.
Goffman, E. (1968) *Asylums*, Harmondsworth, Penguin.
Goldthorpe, J. and Lockwood, D. *et al.* (1969) *The Affluent Worker: Industrial Attitudes and Behaviour*, Cambridge University Press.
Hammersley, M. (1985) 'From Ethnography to Theory', *Sociology*, vol. 19, no. 2, May 1985.
Heath, A., Jowell, R. and Curtice, J. (1985) *How Britain Votes*, Oxford, Pergamon Press.
Hughes, J. (1976) *Sociological Analysis: Methods of Discovery*, London, Nelson.

Humphreys, L. (1970) *Tea Room Trade*, London, Duckworth.
La Piere, R. T. (1934) 'Attitudes versus Actions', *Social Forces*, vol. 13.
Lewis, O. (1951) *Life in a Mexican Village*, University of Illinois Press.
Lipset, S. and Bendix R. (1967) *Class, Status and Power*, New York, Free Press.
Parsons, T. (1937) *The Structure of Social Action*, New York, Free Press.
Phillips, D. L. (1971) *Knowledge From What?*, Chicago, Rand McNally.
Pinch, T. and Clark, C. (1986) 'Patter Merchanting', *Sociology*, vol. 20, no. 2, May 1986.
Polsky, N. (1971) *Hustlers, Beats and Others*, Harmondsworth, Penguin.
Redfield, R. (1930) *Tepoztlan – A Mexican Village*, University of Chicago Press.
Silverman, D. (1970) *The Theory of Organisations*, London, Heinemann.
Warner, W. Lloyd (1960) *Social Class in America: the Evaluation of Status*, New York, Harper & Row.
Weber, M. (1964) *Theory of Social and Economic Organization* (ed. T. Parsons), New York, Free Press.
Whyte, W. F. (1943) *Street Corner Society*, University of Chicago Press.
Willis, P. (1977) *Learning to Labour*, Westmead, Saxon House.
Willis, P. (1978) *Profane Culture*, London, Routledge & Kegan Paul.

13

Sociological Theories

13.1 INTRODUCTION

There is no theoretical orthodoxy in contemporary sociology. The previous chapters in this book have all emphasised the diversity of theoretical approaches within the discipline, and they have all attempted to show that differences in concepts, presuppositions and theoretical orientations always produce significant differences in the explanations and accounts of social life offered by sociologists. Ultimately, it is misleading to separate off an area of concern called 'theory', for there can never be any such thing as non-theoretical sociology; no matter how descriptive, 'factual' or apparently 'obvious' sociological accounts may be, sociologists cannot avoid making theoretical assumptions and commitments in the course of their research. By now it should also be clear that many theoretical perspectives are mutually antagonistic and incompatible. We cannot assume that if we simply pursue an honourable compromise between all approaches we can thereby merge and synthesise them into one all-purpose, all-embracing theoretical extravaganza. As we shall see, some theoretical approaches may need to be rejected altogether – and these unacceptable ones are precisely those which have had the most securely entrenched dominance in the history of sociological thought.

That said, it must not be assumed that we have to abandon the quest for a synthesis of those theoretical elements which do appear to be partially acceptable; and we certainly should not jump to the conclusion that there are no criteria for choosing between theories and judging their validity. We saw in the previous chapter that issues of epistemology and methodology remain very problematic – we do not have final agreement on the philosophical grounds for judging the usefulness or uselessness of a particular theory. The quest for such acceptable criteria for knowledge-claims certainly continues, but in the meantime more limited criteria are available. This chapter will assume that provisional judgements of the quality of theories can be made on rational grounds – including standards such as internal coherence and breadth of applicability. This optimism is based on the belief that sociology can and must progress towards more adequate understanding, and that this increasing knowledge can enable people to reshape their society in order to create the conditions for greater fulfilment of human potential. This chapter will argue that sociology has a vital role to play in the active construction of a society better fitted to human needs and aspirations, for humans have the unique capacity to transform their own conditions of social existence. Indeed, people constantly attempt to do this by defending, adapting or transforming their society; a fuller knowledge of the social conditions of existence can only aid this process. What remains problematic, of course, is the goal and direction of such change. We shall see in the course of the chapter that while most great sociologists have been inspired by the concern to improve society, they have differed fundamentally in their definitions of the desirable relationship between humans and their society.

The bulk of the chapter is concerned with three distinct types of social theory which have been significant in the development of sociological thought: *positivist organicism*, where we are concerned with the theoretical approach that dominated for so long through the influence of Durkheim and the functionalists; *structural and historical sociology*, where the contributions of Marx and Weber are compared and contrasted; and *social action* theories of various forms are discussed. We then go on to examine the possibility of moving beyond these orientations to a more adequate general theory of human action in relation to social structures, and then finally to the issue of objectivity and value-commitment in the context of a discussion of the progressive and liberating potential of sociological understanding.

13.2   POSITIVIST AND ORGANICIST SOCIOLOGY

Organicism is one distinctive version of the holistic approach in sociology, and as such has exerted a dominant influence on sociology for several decades. Although highly contrasting ideas have existed at every stage, which have challenged (or formed a potential to challenge) the dominance of organicism and positivism, this fragmented opposition has only recently succeeded in breaking the claims to theoretical orthodoxy made by these approaches. Effectively, positivist organicism dominated sociology from the early nineteenth century until the early 1960s. The origins lie in the French tradition, but its more general dominance was assured when American sociology came to take the lead. European sociology in the early twentieth century was eclipsed by the massive growth of the discipline in the USA and so the triumph of the perspective was at its height when American functionalism reigned supreme. This functionalism had its deepest roots in the ideas of Emile Durkheim, who in turn extended and developed a general frame of reference inherited from his compatriot Auguste Comte. From Comte came the faith in organic social integration, and in the power of positivist science; uniting the whole stream of theoretical development was the concern for creating the conditions for a harmonious, orderly, integrated society. As we shall see, however, highly contrasting theories were available in American and German universities, and the socialist parts of Europe offered very different social analyses; we therefore need to consider how this perspective rather than others came to have such power. Although the intrinsic quality of an intellectual perspective is only one factor affecting its rise to power, our discussion starts with this aspect.

We saw as long ago as the opening chapter that the holistic perspective was indispensable for sociology – indeed, the reality of sociological explanations can be established by the demonstration that many phenomena (suicide, for example) cannot be completely understood without making reference to the characteristic of the whole social group and the broader social context. The notion that social phenomena cannot be adequately explained by the characteristics of individual actors lies at the heart of sociology. Since for a long period the *only* form of holism widely accepted was organicism, sociology appeared to have no alternative to the analogy. In the course of this section it will be argued that holism is vital, but organicism is a false and misleading version of it.

The distinctiveness of organicist holism lies in its most obvious feature: that a direct analogy is invoked between the living animal organisms and the structure of society. One underlying reason for the attractiveness of such an analogy is that biology as a life-science can thereby provide an exemplar for sociology as a science of the living society. Just as the characteristics of living organisms cannot be reduced to their chemical and physical composition (the organism has 'emergent properties' by virtue of its living organisation), the characteristics of society cannot be reduced to the nature of its component parts. The analogy thereby stresses the interlocking and mutual dependence of specialised 'organs', or elements, within the whole; the central guiding problem becomes the degree to which these parts are neatly and smoothly working together to ensure the 'health' or 'survival' of the social organism. At the broadest level, this leads to the central concern being the so-called 'problem of social order', for an organism is clearly not a real organism at all (or at any rate not a healthy one) if its component parts fight with one another, fail to operate, or drop off. This analogy *must* assume a fairly high degree of integration and co-ordination as 'normal', and it must in turn be able to specify the mechanisms or forces which sustain and reproduce this integration. As we shall see, in most cases this integrating force turns out to be *shared ideas* in one form or another.

Equally important in this general theoretical orientation was positivism. It will be recalled from the previous chapter that the appeal of positivism for social scientists lies in its enticing offer of readily accessible routes to certain knowledge, thus ensuring that sociological knowledge can claim the status of *science* and form the basis for production. Social engineering is therefore made possible, for the neutral scientist can provide the knowledge and tools necessary for social goals to be pursued. Unlike the philosophising, speculating and pontificating on social issues which had for centuries preceded the rise of positivism, the new positive science would provide *certainty* through *technical knowledge*. A vital element of such positivism is of course the presupposition that all events are caused, and that these causal relationships occur in regular ways which can be expressed in causal laws. In the field of social behaviour, this therefore implies that individual acts are not explicable by personal 'choices' or 'reasons' but by empirically identifiable external causes. It is an easy step to say that these external causes which derive from society are opaque to individual actors, and determine their behaviour. In the broadest terms, this accounts for the close compatibility of organicism and positivism; organicist approaches seek to *reveal* the 'true' causes of social phenomena by looking behind the naive accounts given by actors themselves, and disclosing the real explanations which lie at the *societal* level. The most familiar example, mentioned in several previous chapters, is Durkheim's account of suicide, which attempts to explain variations in suicide rates without any reference to the intentions or perceptions of actors, and which identifies social causes of suicide that are not 'visible' to the actors concerned. As we shall see, such explanations have come to be regarded as seriously inadequate in their wholesale rejection of the importance of the consciousness and perceptions of the actor; social action theories have led sociologists to regard positivistic social explanations as frequently anti-humanistic in their concern for 'external causes'. Having said that, we must not lose sight of the fact that the early proponents of positivism took its title seriously – they regarded it as a *positive*, progressive, constructive development allowing people to have true knowledge of the world for the first time. Equally important, nineteenth-century positivists were by no means as scrupulous about claiming value-neutrality as their twentieth-century successors – the pursuit of knowledge was for them inseparable from the use of such knowledge to reorder society on rational lines. The quest for the laws governing social organisation, once established as true, were regarded as clearly indicating principles for social reconstruction – society must be adapted (though not revolutionised) to conform to its ideal healthy condition. At the same time, this positive knowledge derived from a science of social *order* where the whole aim was to discover the conditions for harmonious organic integration. These themes run directly through the development from Comte to Durkheim to functionalism, and so we now turn to more detailed discussion of the way the elements are manifested in their particular theories.

Auguste Comte (1798–1857)

Auguste Comte (1798–1857)
Born: Montpellier, France, 1798.
Education: Ecole Polytechnique, Paris, 1814.
Career: Taught privately.
      Assisted H. Saint-Simon, 1817–24.
Main works: *Course in Positive Philosophy*, 1842.
      System of Positive Polity, 1851–4.

If Comte's birth coincides with the height of revolutionary change in French society, his mature work consists of an attempt to recreate order in that society through the application of true knowledge, as produced by science. The fact that Comte coined the label 'sociology' (previously he had dubbed the subject 'social physics') is not the only reason to regard him as the founder of modern sociology. As conventionally conceived, sociology differs from previous social thought by virtue of its rigorous scientific method and its commitment to holistic explanation; in his *Course in Positive Philosophy* Comte provided methodological prescriptions and theoretical conjectures which attempt to establish precisely these elements. All knowledge, he argued, must be founded upon experimentation or rigorous use of evidence. Knowledge had to be constructed out of the evidence from the senses, out of empirical data, even if there was a role for theoretical conceptualisation to make sense of this data. Truth, therefore, could never be attained through abstract speculation or pure intellectual philosophising. On the contrary, the laws which governed all events in the world (for all were caused in discoverably regular ways) were available to the rigorous observer. The scientist could then formulate these laws in order to subject them to test and verification (or disproof). All this of course was hardly new – British philosophy had said as much for nearly two centuries – but what *was* radical was the application of the positivist faith in discoverable laws to *social* phenomena. The implications were colossal, for positive sociological knowledge could offer the means for peaceful reconstruction of social order by the elite of enlightened scientists and intellectuals – social change need not depend upon revolutionary violence and the manipulation of the mob. As a result, Comte's work came to have an enormous appeal to intellectuals, whose confidence in their own ability to 'engineer' society was bolstered by some of Comte's more specific theories, especially those concerning social development. It should be no surprise to find that social change is explained by Comte in evolutionary terms, since this derives directly from the biological analogy and also implies gradual adaptation rather than transformation.

The evolutionary process Comte identifies develops through three stages of thought: theological, metaphysical and positive. This third stage brings the light of reason to the human mind, through the discovered truths of positivist science. It follows that those who know the truth about social life, the sociologists, should control things for the good of all. In particular, they can recreate moral order on a scientific basis through (as Comte argued in the *Positive Polity*) a new secular religion. Positivist knowledge gives scientists the authority and right to overcome conflict and prescribe the conditions for a healthy society.

General features of positivist organicism

Not only were Comte's 'laws' spurious, they exemplify the more general failings of theories which combine positivism and organicism:

(i)   The theories are ahistorical. They tend to employ simplistic schemes of 'stages' which are insensitive to historical complexity and diversity.

(ii)   Cultural change is emphasised rather than economic or political development.

(iii)   Organicism generally seeks general universal laws of social integration and social evolution. As a result these generalisations tend to be trite or vacuous.

(iv)   Moral order and normative consensus are seen as the keys to social integration, since shared values and norms are then taken to be the basic elements of social life.

(v)   The solution to social conflict and disorder therefore lies in the creation of a new secular moral unity within existing social structures.

We shall see that in differing ways both Durkheim and Parsons sustain these characteristic propositions, even though their theories are more subtle and persuasive than Comte's. Before moving on to them, however, we should consider the political philosophies which underpin sociological ideas.

Political values and early social theory

It has been argued (for example, by Nisbet, 1967) that these characteristics show the origins of sociology to lie in the classical conservative tradition of social thought, despite the liberal reformism of most sociologists. This claim is based on the contrast between the conservative vision of society and the liberal–individualist version. For the conservative (e.g. Edmund Burke's *Reflections on the French Revolution*) individuals have identity only by virtue of their social position in a hierarchy of social roles, and their position dictates their characteristics, social standing and degree of powerlessness or control. Individuals are civilised only in as much as social rules constrain their bestial selfishness. The key to human happiness, therefore, is a hierarchy of social control with tightly specified rules governing conduct. In complete contrast, the classical liberal view of humanity extols the virtues of unrestrained competition between individuals, and regards the rules and collective aspects of social life as merely the outcome of social contracts, or as the sum total of the individual characteristics of actors. The goal of imposing order by some central authority with specialist knowledge is not alien to the classical liberal, but is decidedly harmful (see Herbert Spencer's *The Man and the State*); only the outcome of competitive free action can be healthy and any modification can only induce ill-health in the collectivity of individuals. Equally, there is no consensus in society but neither is there any fundamental cleavage leading to fundamental conflict. The social organism is invigorated by internal turmoil.

It is clear from this comparison that the classical liberal position is profoundly anti-sociological in that it denies holistic explanations which deal with emergent properties of the social whole. (Despite being influenced by Comte, Mill regarded all social science explanations as ultimately reducible to individual psychology.) Sociology has also wished to stress the prior existence of society, and the extent to which actors are influenced by socialisation and by the constraints on them in their various social positions. At the same time, however, Nisbet is entirely incorrect to assume that sociology *must* therefore be committed to goals of social order, social control and moral integration. These distinctive emphases of positivist organicism certainly do have affinities with classical conservatism, but they do not by any means form the only intellectually viable alternative to the liberal individualism outlined above.

We might note in passing, moreover, that where sociology *was* founded on such a liberal philosophy in Britain by Herbert Spencer, this effectively led to the dissolution of any real sociological development until after 1945. American liberal individualism led towards the development of social psychology, as we shall see later, but British liberalism prevented the development of any real science of social life apart from anthropology.

Emile Durkheim (1858–1917)

Emile Durkheim (1858–1917)
Born: Lorraine, France, 1858.
Education: Ecole Normale Supérieure, 1879.
Career: Schoolteacher in philosophy, 1882–87.
       University lecturer, Bordeaux, 1887.
       Taught sociology and education, Sorbonne, Paris, 1902.
       Professor of Education and Sociology, 1913.
Main works: *The Division of Labour in Society*, 1893.
       Rules of Sociological Method, 1895.
       Suicide, 1897.
       Elementary Forms of the Religious Life, 1912.

The work of Durkheim is of far more significance for the development of sociology than that of Comte – in fact one of the prime motivations of Durkheim's project was the aim of establishing sociology as a credible and respectable academic discipline within universities. But more than this, Durkheim wished to apply sociological knowledge to social intervention by the state in order to recreate harmony. In these aims there is clearly a direct continuation of the legacy left by Comte. Just like his predecessor, Durkheim regarded himself as a progressive (even a socialist), pursuing reform guided by positivist sociological laws; the goals of these reforms were in each case oriented towards the traditional conservative concerns of moral consensus and stable hierarchy. Progress was towards order above all, rather than towards the emancipation of the individual human being.

Durkheim's earliest work was his doctoral thesis *The Division of Labour in Society* (1893), which provides a key to his earliest ideas on the problems of contemporary society and their possible solutions. In content, the book is purely speculative, imposing a grand conception of the evolution of social institutions reminiscent not only of Comte but also of the Enlightenment philosophers Montequieu and Rousseau. In this respect, it is remarkable to note the self-enclosed nature of French intellectual thought at this time. Durkheim was an exact contemporary of Max Weber, but the gulf between the philosophical and scientific ferment in Germany and the enclosed development of distinctive French ideas could hardly be more striking.

Durkheim's general thesis in *The Division of Labour* operates with the commonplace distinction (that sledge-hammer of the evolutionists) between 'traditional' and 'modern' society. The diversity and complexity of human civilisations is supposedly encompassed by this simple distinction, which stresses an evolution away from the *mechanical solidarity* characterising primitive societies, to the sophisticated *organic solidarity* which provides the basis for a new harmonious integration within industrial society. Primitive societies, he argues, were 'segmental', in that they were just the aggregation of kin-groups into clans and tribes, where these larger groupings had little real cohesion since each local unit could be self-sufficient as hunters or agriculturalists. Hence, like a worm, the society was divided into similar segments which could survive perfectly well if severed from one another. Even within these 'segments' social cohesion depended upon the power of rigid collective norms governing behaviour in every detail, so that total conformity was enforced; if any transgression did occur then revenge would be the basic social response. The primary source of conformity, however, was the shared consensus of norms and values, the *conscience collective* which was absorbed and reproduced by every member of society. For Durkheim, *mechanical solidarity* was a phrase which conveyed this rigidity and crudity of social form.

In deliberate contrast to the ideas of writers such Tönnies, Durkheim thus portrays 'traditional' primitive society not as an ideal, harmonious, integrated unity, but as a collection of fragmentary units emodying repressive conformity. Modern society, therefore, is not conceived as the fragmented breakdown of community portrayed by Tönnies, while contemporary society may appear to have this character in its current imperfect form, the evolution of society provides an underlying potential for more stable and sophisticated social cohesion. The key to this potential is the process of social evolution which takes the form of increased *social differentiation*, whereby society develops specialised institutions which deal with particular distinct areas of social life (e.g. religion, production). Just as the evolution of animals produces more sophisticated specialised organs to perform particular functions for the whole creature, society comes to develop a range of distinct institutions which deal more adequately with particular needs of the social whole. Just like anatomical organs, they are mutually dependent for their survival and correct functioning depends upon the healthy functioning of each other organ, and the maintenance of correct integration of all the organs. The potential, then, built into modern society is for *organic solidarity*. If the component parts of society can be induced to develop 'a lively sentiment of their mutual dependence' then the conflicts and crises so prevalent can be swept aside. Once again, a new *moral consensus* must be constructed to bring forth order; unlike that in primitive society, however, this moral order is flexible and adaptable to allow it to cope with the diverse social roles and positions in a complex society – the individual has more freedom within the social constraints. A prime task for contemporary sociology is therefore the construction of a new central civic morality which will be disseminated efficiently by a state education system. Durkheim was directly involved in the development of precisely these educational aims and techniques in his academic work and in advice given to the French government.

The primacy of value-consensus cannot be overemphasised for, like other organicists, Durkheim conceives of society as primarily a *moral order* constituted by the institutionalised norms and values. At the same time, however, social reform has to have an institutional basis. Durkheim identifies chaotic economic competition as the root of conflict and class struggle; as a result he advocates regulation of the economy and of the worker–employer relationship. He even suggests joint *corporations* or guilds to mediate between worker, industrialist and state.

Equally important, he argues, is the abolition of the *forced division of labour*, where inequality of opportunity denies individuals access to positions to suit their talents. Since unequal rewards should be given to different positions, and since education should be designed to 'get them' to like the idea of circumscribed tasks and limited horizons, then conflict will be created if individuals do not obtain suitable positions. All the other reforms are directed at overcoming the *anomic* division of labour, where economic life is characterised by *anomie* – that is, the lack of regulating norms. As we have seen elsewhere in discussing Durkheim's explanations of suicide (see Chapter 10 on deviance), he regards the lack of sufficient normative regulation as a key cause of social and individual ill-health. Without such norms, humans develop insatiable appetites, limitless desires and general feelings of irritation and dissatisfaction. Modern competitive market society encourages all of this and, despite its claims, condemns people to 'unfreedom'. The 'unfreedom', due to anomie, rests on the conservative assumptions about human nature discussed earlier – humans without normative constraint could only be uncivilised beasts, slaves of their own whims and passions. Individuals must be subordinate to society, they must play their humble part in the functioning of the social organism. The collective consensus may allow them some choice between roles, but once allotted their position they must conform or else become pathological deviants. As Durkheim (1974, p. 72) describes his vision of the correct relation between individuals and society:

> The individual submits to society and this submission is the condition of his liberation. For man freedom consists in the deliverance from blind, unthinking physical forces; this he achieves by opposing against them the great and intelligent force which is society, under whose protection he shelters.

Thus society is outside us and above us; it constrains us and shapes our lives and our physical responses. What is good for social integration is good for the individual. This emphasis on externality and constraint links directly to Durkheim's conception of scientific explanation as presented in *The Rules of Sociological Method* (1895), an essay which was, as Lukes says, 'at once a treatise in the philosophy of social science, a polemic and a manifesto' (Lukes, 1973, p. 226). The book showed all these qualities, for in it Durkheim developed conceptions of the subject-matter of sociology and of suitable methodology which were dictated by his view of science. Since sociology must be established as a scientific discipline (thus enabling social intervention on the basis of positive knowledge), then the conception of science must *dictate* methods and concepts.

The view of science adopted was, of course, a positivistic one – and a fairly crude positivistic one at that.

Deriving ideas from his contemporaries and teachers, Durkheim assumes that a particular science can only have the status of being a distinct discipline if it has a separate subject-matter not shared by any other science. At the same time, this subject-matter must be empirically accessible (which is why we must 'treat social facts as things'), and variations in the phenomena must be explained by causes which also lie within the scope of that particular discipline. These (false) assumptions led Durkheim to assert that sociology must become the *science of social facts*. These social facts can only be explained in terms of other social facts so that, for example, variations in suicide rates are social facts which must be explained by characteristics of the social group, such as lack of normative control. The claim that there are social facts, then, is important, for it establishes that there is a distinct level of social phenomena which are not reducible to individual characteristics or intentions – indeed they constrain the individual:

> A social fact is every way of acting, fixed or not, capable of exercising on the individual an influence, or an external constraint; or again, every way of acting which is general throughout a given society, while at the same time existing in its own right independent of its individual manifestations (*Rules of Sociological Method*, 1895, p. 13).

Although Durkheim accepted in principle that one could only observe the *effects* of social facts in their concrete mainfestations, as in legal codes or in individual acts of suicide, he nevertheless had a marked tendency to *reify* society and speak of social reality as a separate, detached realm from social action. He even writes of 'that conscious being that is society ... a *sui generis* being with its own special nature, distinct from that of its members' (*Rules*, p. 11). He often referred to social forces such as 'suicidogenic currents' which impose an external causal effect on individual action; this search for external causes is of course part of the general positivistic orientation.

His explicit account of this positive method is naively simple, for he simply advocates a search for correlations between phenomena which indicate *laws*. As long as we 'abandon our preconceptions' we can verify these laws with evidence. Once in possession of these laws, however, we are in a position to identify whether society is in a 'healthy' or a 'pathological' condition, and the sociologist must therefore prescribe the remedies required for social health. This latter assumption is clearly related to Comte's view of science. It demonstrates the distance between the optimistic positivism of the nineteenth century ('the true is the good and the natural'), and the hard-bitten positivism of the twentieth century, which drove a rigid distinction between truth and goodness. Social goals, it was argued, were based on values, and these values could not be derived from science. Such arguments are quite alien to Comte and Durkheim.

Although Durkheim assumes that the necessary starting-point for science is the proposition 'a given effect always has a single corresponding cause', he also accepts the usefulness of *functionalist* explanation. In the latter, phenomena are not explained by preceding causes (e.g. rainfall causes a flood) but by the *useful effects* of their existence. The central nervous system is explained, for example, by its integrating effects on the organism. Similarly, the explanation of the persistence of religion may be in the good effects of religious activity on the level of social integration. At the same time, Durkheim notes, the original causes of the phenomenon are a separate issue from the functions which cause its persistence. The link between the organic analogy and functionalist explanation is thus obvious – we explain elements of the organic whole by their good effects for the functioning of the organism. A closely linked assumption is that institutions only survive if they are useful for society. As in the functionalist theory of stratification (see Chapter 2), this can lead to a justification of existing institutions. This, as Merton (1949) pointed out, neglects the possiblity of negative effects (dysfunctions) or 'functional alternatives' where a societal need could be satisfied by another institution. Whether or not these modifications to functionalism are adopted, it is clear that the whole emphasis of positivist organicism centres on the integration (or lack of integration) of the social system, and the effects of social phenomena on this integration.

The organicist perspective is united with exemplary use of positivistic methods in Durkheim's study *Suicide*, which followed two years after the *Rules*. This study has been discussed at length elsewhere (in Chapters 11 and 12) but it is worth emphasising here the extent to which the book embodies Durkheim's methodological principles. Firstly, the methods used exemplify the emphasis on social facts, in that constant suicide *rates* are described, which are established empirically and statistically (even if later commentators criticise his dependence on offical statistics). Secondly, these rates concern *group* propensities to suicide and do not involve any attention to individual cases. Hence Durkheim can explain these social facts solely by other social facts – the propensity of the social group to normlessness, egoism or altruism that depends upon the organisation and culture of the group as a whole. Durkheim therefore sticks rigidly to his methodological precepts and attempts to exclude psychological and physiological explanations. Most commentators agree that this is productive only to the extent that it discloses the importance of social factors; it is, however, profoundly mistaken and misleading to attempt to divorce sociological explanations from other complementary ones. Suicide is a phenomenon which must be explained by a range of factors which fall within the fields of many disciplines; this in no sense undermines the scientific status of any one of these sciences. (For one recent attempt at constructing such an interdisciplinary account, see Giddens, 1977.)

Thirdly, the explanations of variations in suicide rates clearly embody the organicist concern for the social cohesion of the collectivity. If egoistic suicide derives from insufficient social integration, altruistic suicide is the result of an excess of it; moral regulation, in contrast, can only be too low (producing anomic suicide), for the 'fatalistic' form of suicide has only a shadowy existence. Thus the two dimensions of the social group that matter are social integration and moral regulation, and the element in society that most strongly influences both is the *moral order* – above all as embodied in religion.

In as much as society is ultimately constructed out of patterns of behaviour (in the organicist view), then norms and values are the ultimate basis of social life. Although related to other aspects of society, its culture remains the key dynamic force shaping individuals and governing their behaviour. Unlike the Marxists, organicists certainly do not regard culture and religion as mere ideologies justifying economic arrangements; instead religion is (as Durkheim put it):

> the most primitive of all social phenomena. It was the source, through successive transformations, of all other manifestations of collective activity: law, morality, art, science, political forms, etc. In the beginning all is religious (in Lukes, 1973).

Thus, one explains social organisations and cohesion by reference to a shared normative system (usually religious), common throughout the collectivity. Changes in this structure are not 'reflective' of changes elsewhere; instead, they are the prime movers of social adaptation. This view is common to all positivist organicists and is clearly opposed to all forms of Marxist economic determinism. As such, this approach directs our attention away from a concern with economic relationships, political and economic domination, or variations in class structure. The evolution of culture within the integrated organic society is seen as far more illuminating than the study of concrete structures of power, which vary in historical circumstances. Rather than historical analysis, organicism seeks the *universal laws* governing social order and social evolution.

This concern for the universal significance of religion led Durkheim towards his later ideas in *The Elementary Forms of the Religious Life* (1912). His views here lie outside our scope, but they lay the foundations for a tradition of speculative anthropology, which attempts to link the basic elements of social structure with the most basic elements in human thought – concepts such as space and time are seen as reflecting the structure of the group (e.g. Lévi-Strauss, *Totemism*). The general notion that shared ideas are a main integrating force in society is reflected in Durkheim's view of religion as the most basic of collective representations; 'Religion is, in a word, the system of symbols by means of which society becomes conscious of itself; it is the way of thinking characteristic of collective existence.' Religion must derive from something 'higher': for Durkheim this must be society. Even though modern society has lost its religious sensibility, Durkheim regarded the construction of a moral consensus to guide and constrain action as a vital necessity. Humans are more civilised to the extent that they can deliberately construct their own moral order and then live by it.

The rise of functionalism

In the course of the first half of the twentieth century, the general orientation developed by Durkheim came to be the predominant perspective in American sociology, and since that nation came to dominate the sociological scene, functionalism seemed for a while to be the only real theory in the discipline. By 1949, Kingsley Davis could claim that functionalism should not be seen as a separate perspective because *all* sociology was functionalist. This never was a valid claim, for although faculties and journals often gave this impression, there were always counter-currents and alternative perspectives surviving alongside. By the end of the 1950s functionalism was beginning to go on the defensive against increasing attacks from these counter-currents – although the criticisms ranged from social action theories to conflict theories with Marxist or Weberian roots.

In that first half of the century, however, functionalism provided a very general perspective which united many sociologists who wished to study the workings of society as a whole (so-called 'macrosociology'), and who wished to provide explanations of social phenomena without looking for answers in the intentions or consciousness of actors. Functionalism seemed to *reveal* the real significance of social institutions in terms of the way they aided the survival or health of the whole social organism.

One of the main areas for the early establishment of functionalism was the British school of social anthropology. Although British social scientists seemed unable to develop any real theories of the structure of modern societies (they concerned themselves with social philosophy or with the positivistic description of social problems) the Imperial connection did provide fascinating opportunities for studying alien preliterate societies. In these studies, the necessity of studying these societies as integrated interrelated structures was made clear by the weaknesses of grandiose speculative tours of 'primitive culture' by writers such as Frazer (*The Golden Bough*). In relation to this, anthropologists saw the need to study each society separately, on its own terms, as a functioning system. The lack of written history in these cultures encouraged the assumption that such primitive societies were stable, unchanging, and fully adapted for survival in their environment. With these assumptions, functionalist approaches (such as those developed by Radcliffe-Brown) are of clear relevance: we must ask how each social institution fits in with others to *serve the needs of the society* and sustain the harmonious integration which is deemed to be the norm. For example, even when conflict is observed, this is regarded as functional for integration if it is ritualistic and institutionalised. As an illustration, bitter arguments are a constant feature among the Makah tribe of American Indians, for they use scandal and gossip to question the purity of ancestry of other tribespeople; it can be argued that this apparently divisive behaviour actually strengthened the group by constantly reminding them of their shared ancestral identity.

Equally important, the functionalist perspective is lent support by the integrating power of shared cultural beliefs in the form of religion, magic and myth. The predominant importance of shared culture often appears self-evident.

These features of pre-literate societies are by no means always present in industrial societies, and so we may be sceptical about the applicability of functionalism; but even in 'primitive' societies this perspective only seems strong as long as we do not concern ourselves too much with change, with wars or with the dissolution of societies. Later anthropologists (including major figures such as Evans-Pritchard) have attempted to deal with these issues; moreover, the functionalists' assumptions of stability and integration have only been applied to modern society by anthropologists when they deal with old-established local communities. In the general European sociological context, few writers wished to transpose to modern advanced societies functionalist emphases on order, harmony, integration and societal health. This is scarcely surprising when one considers the history of twentieth-century Europe with its two world wars, genocide and clashes of class and ideology. What is remarkable is that American sociologists such as Parsons should agree with Durkheim that functionalist perspectives are the most illuminating for a contemporary world characterised by such events. For them, functionalism offered a universal perspective on social structure and in Parsons's case, a universal theory applicable to all areas of social life. Whilst not generated empirically, Parsons's theories pursue the general aim of constructing universal laws of society which are general enough to apply anywhere. Empirical studies should, he thought, validate the explanations generated by the theory.

Talcott Parsons (1902–79)

Talcott Parsons (1902–79)
Born: Colorado Springs, USA, 1902.
Education: Amherst College, 1920–4.
      London School of Economics, 1924–5.
      University of Heidelberg, 1925–6.
Career: Harvard University, USA, 1927–79.
Main works: *The Structure of Social Action*, 1939.
      Toward a General Theory of Action, 1951.
      The Social System, 1951.
      *Societies: Evolutionary and Comparative
      Perspectives*, 1966.

While Parsons's ideas were challenged and rivalled by those of other American functionalists (particularly Robert K. Merton), his enormously prolific output was very widely read and accepted as the most systematic and formalised functionalist theory. His significance for American sociologists was established in the 1940s, but his work began with *The Structure of Social Action*, which aimed to bring more modern European thought on social structure to American attention. In this work he purported to synthesise the European traditions, but the mix was heavily Durkheimian and was free of contamination by Marxian or socialist social theories. As his work developed, the functionalist themes were supplemented by cybernetics (the theory of the working of systems in general) to produce his most abstract and formalistic theory in *The Social System*. Here, Parsons argues that any system of action (a society, an institution, a small group, etc.) has general features, for in order to operate successfully as a system, certain *functional prerequisites* have to be fulfilled. These are, in ascending order of importance, (a) adaptation, (b) goal attainment, (c) integration and (d) pattern-maintenance. Correspondingly, within the social system as a whole, the most basic need is for (a), adaptation to the environment through economic activity, but this only provides the conditions for 'higher' aspects of social life. Actors pursue (b), socially shaped goals, in ways that are governed by (c), the norms and sanctions institutionalised in society; ultimately these goals and norms derive from (d), an overreaching cultural system of values, on which there is consensus. Thus the cultural system *controls* other aspects of society, and if we wish to explain social change we must look first at changes at the cultural level. For example, the civil rights riots by blacks in the USA during the 1960s were explained by Parsons in terms of the 'core American values' – equal citizenship rights, equal opportunity – being mobilised by the majority. Disparities of economic benefit and political power are systematically underplayed as features of the social world that might cause conflict or cleavage – even when Parsons does discuss power, it is not portrayed in terms of domination or oppression. Instead, power is seen as a necessary resource which members of society collectively agree to allocate to particular authority positions. The authority-holder then uses the power selflessly to satisfy particular collective needs.

Parsons clearly gives priority to the 'problem of social order' and suggests that this problem is solved at two levels. On the one hand, order in the sense of conformity by actors is maintained by socialisation and social control. His account of the personality places great emphasis on internalisation of socially given norms and values, rather than suggesting any more active process of negotiating or defining roles by the actor. Deviance does, of course, occur but this is generally suppressed by social control agencies. Occasionally, however, deviance in the form of innovation may aid the survival of the system of action because of some adaption to changed circumstances is needed for the social system. Any action system needs adaptive mechanisms to bring it back to *equilibrium* – and this need for structural integration is the second aspect of Parsons's solution to the problem of order. It is argued that the social system operates in such a way as to ensure that its functional needs are fulfilled and that social and system integration are sustained. The ideas of actors are far less important than the functioning and development of the system as a whole. Thus our key explanations lie at two levels – in terms of the cultural system and its effects on behaviour, and in terms of the functional needs of the system as a whole. Thus, the education system may be seen as socialising actors into the prevailing cultural order, but also interlocking with the economy and the political apparatus to aid the functioning of the society.

In addition, Parsons has to give some account of social change, and in his later work he developed the classic solution of the organicist perspective – evolution. Broadly, his evolutionary account lies within the tradition of 'structural differentiation', where modern societies are seen as becoming more complex and internally specialised. Predictably, the major stages of evolution are conceived in terms of cultural change, where modern industrial society is the peak of human achievement towards which earlier societies progressively led. The development of literacy, and then of formalised legal systems, mark the transitions between primitive, traditional and modern society. Thus, what characterises evolution is the development of more sophisticated culture; for those contemporary societies attempting to 'modernise', the problem is not one of economic or political subordination in a world-system, but is instead a question of developing the correct cultural values and orientations (see pp. 141–5). Once again, the organicist tradition betrays its ahistorical and uncritical approach to social development.

Evaluation of positivist organicism

The work of Parsons, then, displays the classic strengths and weaknesses of positivist organicism. He is not afraid to look at society as a structured, interrelated whole, or to attempt to reveal aspects of the operation of that social whole which are opaque to the actors making up the society. Such a perspective, however, can be criticised in three contrasting ways: it can be criticised for being *too* holistic and presenting a derogatory and inadequate account of social action, it can be seen as consistently underemphasising social conflict, and it can be regarded as presenting a false account of social structure.

Criticisms from social action perspectives

The first line of criticism became more insistent in the 1960s, as the old American tradition of symbolic interactionism and qualitative research attained a new prominence, partly through mergers with more philosophical European traditions such as phenomenology.

Their initial line of attack concerns the functionalist conceptions of the self, and of social action. These conceptions are shown to be overly deterministic, allowing individuals to display little or no creativity or originality, and providing little scope for actors to negotiate social situations and social identities. Holistic explanations came to be seen as falsely 'solidifying' social structure by attributing needs or even desires to 'society' as if it were a thinking being.

This leads us to their next line of attack, centring on the functionalist form of explanation. Action approaches rightly emphasise that functionalists commit the 'fallacy of misplaced concreteness': that is to say, society is treated as having a truly independent existence separate from its individual members. By accepting this criticism we do not have to deny a holism, but we do have to recognise that functionalism gives insufficient scope for the continuous development and change in society produced by social action. Such criticisms certainly apply to the perspective on social integration offered by organicists, for they undoubtedly stress the independent power of central values and social control mechanisms. Their account of socialisation seems to imply that the individual is simply a derivative product of the cultural system, and not a real actor at all.

Just as importantly, the structural explanations offered by functionalism *exclude* any connection with action. This is because the second level of functionalist explanation concerns not only conformity to norms, but also the *needs* of the social *system*. The theory claims to explain the persistence of institutions (e.g. the nuclear family) in terms of the functional needs of society, or in terms of the contribution of the institution to social *inte-*

gration. This only becomes truly explanatory if the functionalists propose that societies 'act' in such a way as to ensure that their functional requirements are met. Unless there are mechanisms which maintain social survival and integration, functionalist 'explanations' are not explanations at all. To really *explain* in functionalist terms, there must be some theory of *equilibrium mechanisms* which work at the societal level beyond the control (or intention) of any social actors. Functionalists generally fail to provide any real account of the nature of these mechanisms or how they operate independently of social action. Until they can actually demonstrate these things, functionalist accounts (of stratification, for example) will simply be fancy descriptions which tend to justify existing institutions. On the other hand, these criticisms must not be taken too far; action theories wrongly tend to suggest that *any* holistic explanations are inadmissable. It may be argued that structural explanations should not be abandoned altogether, even if the functionalist ones are unacceptable; but any alternative explanations must link up with social action theories, not deny them.

Criticisms from conflict theory

Critics such as Rex and Dahrendorf have accepted the view that models of society must give actors a great role in changing society, but their main emphasis rests on the assumption that social change is linked to actors' conscious activities. Members of society may produce change through individual decisions and actions, but more generally through their conflicts over issues of power and inequality. Functionalism both neglects change and overemphasises conformity – and the two are linked. Conflict theorists deny the assumption that there is a consensus of norms and values or that conflict is necessarily 'unhealthy' for everyone in society. Society may be divided into groups with conflicting interests so that shared general societal needs cannot be easily specified. The growth of conflict over civil rights and the Vietnam war only heightened such criticisms of conservative consensus theories in the 1960s.

Other critics however (e.g. Lockwood, 1964) have argued that these objections are insufficient, for they concentrate solely upon Parsons's first solution to the problem of order – the socialisation and enforcement of a consensus of values and norms. Those critics are quite right to criticise this aspect, for Parsons's account of social integration is mechanical and misleading. On the other hand, we must recognise the importance of the structural or system integration aspect of social order, for it is vital to know whether there are points of strain and incompatibility in the structure of society which might produce change. This level of system integration is not normally visible to actors and provides pressures and conditions for change which operate outside their consciousness. Thus changes in the basic structure of society (for example, during a period of transition from feudalism to capitalism) may create the conditions for social conflict and broader change in social institutions and social values.

The necessity for *structural* explanations (as well as those linked to social action theories) is therefore made clear, but *the terms in which structure is conceived* are quite different. In the positivist organicist tradition the basic building-material for society is cultural – that is, shared norms, values and world-views. While this aspect cannot be neglected, Lockwood and many other contemporary theorists would strongly reject the notion that the general structure of society and the causes and conditions for change can be located at the cultural level. In contrast, the basic structures of society are seen as concerning economic relations and broader relations of power and domination. The level of culture is instead linked to a concept of dominant ideology, which expresses the idea that consensus (if it exists at all) may simply be the forced or artificial dominance of ideas which justify and take for granted existing inequalities. Such an approach gives a central place to issues of stratification, economic power, political domination, and the organisation (and repression) of resistance from subordinate groups, and as such can be regarded as a *materialist* structural sociology. Such a sociology will concern itself with historical changes in the material structures of economic, political and ideological domination.

As we have seen, Durkheimian and functionalist perspectives give a subordinate role to such concerns; where they are discussed, it is in the context of an attempt to demonstrate how contemporary industrial society is potentially ordered, harmonious and integrated. These writers are 'optimistic' in the sense that they see 'modern' society as the culmination of previous evolution, and as potentially perfectible by fairly minor reforms introduced on the basis of positivist knowledge. There is no critique of exploitation or domination in contemporary societies – power and inequality are necessary as long as they are 'fair'. As a result, class conflict or clashes of ideas are pathological deviations from societal health. When these views are linked to the basic assumption that most institutions, most of the time, are functional for the needs of society and all its members, then we have a powerfully conservative social philosophy.

It is deeply ironic that the recent history of Europe should have allowed a brief American dominance in sociology, for that shift led to the dominance of theories which had little or nothing to say about the most pressing historical issues for the world. The apparent domestic security of America created a 'science of society' which had little or nothing to contribute to the understanding of war, revolution and fasicism, and had little room for the creative power of humans to destroy or liberate themselves by their own social actions. As a result, the positivist organicist perspective has lost all credibility through its production of misleading concepts and mistaken explanations, and its conservative political implications. The current task for social theory is to unite social action theory with a material historical account of social structure.

13.3 STRUCTURAL AND HISTORICAL SOCIOLOGY

Karl Marx and Max Weber

In contrast to the organicists' pursuit of integration in 'modern' society, the work of Marx and Weber is united by a determination to specify the historical origins, character and future of contemporary *capitalism*. The distinction lies in the recognition by Marx and Weber that capitalism is only one possible form of industrial society, and that the particular economic relationships which give this type of social structure its character are also vital for the understanding of other aspects of society. Marx extended this into a general principle of the primacy of economic relations over other aspects of social structure which was to apply to all unequal societies. Weber bitterly opposed any such general theory of history, and stressed the equal or greater importance of culture and politics. Despite these disagreements, they share the concern to distinguish *types* of social structure by specifying material structures (economic, ideological and political) and thus avoiding the search for ahistorical sweeping generalisations about the 'universal' features of society, or of 'modern' or 'traditional' societies. This sensitivity to specific historical developments and variations allows both Marx and Weber to have some account (however different) of the role of human actions in shaping history, even if neither approach can be seen as fully adequate. However, their conceptions of social action differ, as does their actual use of structural and historical explanation; consequently we must discuss the extent to which the ideas of Marx and Weber are ultimately compatible. We shall see that Marx does offer answers to the theoretical problem of system integration and the structural conditions for change, while Weber opposes this account as excessively mechanical. Instead, he regards political, cultural and economic structures as institutional frameworks in which social action takes place; ultimately, for him, historical outcomes are the result of the intentional motived acts of individuals. As a result, Weber gives less account of the 'internal dynamics' of structures than Marx.

Karl Marx (1818–83)

Karl Marx (1818-83)
Born: Trier, Rhineland, 1818.
Education: University of Bonn, 1835.
        University of Berlin, 1836-41.
Work: Editor, *Rheinische Zeitung, 1842.*
        Paris, 1843; Brussels, 1845; Germany 1848; London 1849-83.
Main texts: *Poverty of Philosophy,* 1847.
        Communist Manifesto, 1848.
        The Eighteenth Brumaire of Louis Bonaparte, 1852.
        Grundrisse (Outline of a Critique of
          Political Economy), 1857.
        Preface to a Contribution to the Critique of
          Political Economy, 1859.
        Theories of Surplus Value, 1862-3.
        Capital, Volumes 1-3, 1863-7.
        Critique of the Gotha Programme, 1875.

The influence of Marx on recent sociology can hardly be overestimated, but his work was not accepted as significant until almost eighty years after his death. Until sociology became more sensitive to political issues in the 1960s, academically respectable theorists paid little attention to Marx's work. Instead, his ideas have been elaborated and extended within socialist political movements which frequently condemned academic sociology as bourgeois ideology. As a result of this political engagement, Marxist theories have retained close contact with key issues of power and economic domination, and thus provide an alternative perspective for those sociologists who are commited to both historical structural analysis and intervention in social change. This does not mean, however, that sociologists with such interests have been uncritical of Marx's ideas or of the political developments within Marxism.

Perhaps the primary reasons for the great power of Marx's ideas lie in the timing of his work and in the way that he critically drew upon three diverse intellectual traditions – German idealist philosophy, French socialism and British political economy. Marx's theories responded to the establishment of capitalism in the middle years of the nineteenth century, through a critical rejection of all those sources; he rejected Hegel's idealist philosophy in favour of a materialist approach to history, and he attempted to put socialism on a scientific basis by specifying the conditions for socialism created by the structural weaknesses built into the capitalist economic system. As a result, his theory is original and wide-ranging, but also a product of a particular period in the history of a particular part of the world.

In his earliest writings, Marx displays his primarily philosophical training by engaging in abstract criticism of the philosopher Hegel, whose ideas dominated German intellectual life in the 1840s. For Hegel, the development of human society had to be seen as an uneven and fitful progress towards a state of true, full humanity. The ideal qualities of truth, reason and justice were only imperfectly embodied in the material world at any point in this evolution; but humans gradually recovered knowledge of their true nature through the development of theology and then philosophy. Hegel's system was a culmination of this development of Reason. As a result, once armed with Hegel's solution, the philosopher could subject the currently existing world to *critique* and discover within it the tendencies moving towards the full realisation of our true humanity. Philosophy was the means by which humanity might discover its real potential, while the state (as the home of law and justice) was the institution which demonstrated these higher qualities in contrast to mundane 'civil society'. Thus, despite its critical potential, Hegel's philosophy came to justify the existing Prussian state as the closest embodiment of Reason. Radical Young Hegelians – including the young Marx – accepted this role for the philosopher as all-seeing liberator, but wished to stress the critique of the contemporary state. While joining in this, Marx took things much further. Firstly, he drew upon the French socialist ideas which developed out of the French Revolution to suggest that the *proletariat* could be the 'universal class' that would actually bring the philosopher's critique to fruition through revolution. At this stage (1843–4) the role of this class is not derived from real economic analysis, but Marx does make the radical step of rejecting the notion that the state is the embodiment of Spirit or Idea, Hegel's force behind history. Instead, Marx came to see the state as a reflection of class relations in civil society, and he began to see these social relations as shaping human nature. This constitutes a complete rejection of idealism in favour of a *materialistic* explanation of history in terms of humans' practical actions within the constraints of particular social structures.

However, any imperfection in the structure of these social relations will necessarily create imperfection in people who cannot reach their ultimate human potential. There is no constant 'human nature' but there is a full, ideal human condition which is never reached until social relations are perfected. The faith behind Marx's vision is that society is perfectible by human action, given the historical circumstances which allow the movement to communism. In his mature work, Marx develops economic and political analysis of capitalism in order to provide understanding of the weaknesses in capitalism that will allow it to be superseded by a whole new social order – socialism. Lying behind this, throughout his work, is a vision of what humans could and should be if social conditions would allow, which is expressed in his theory of *alienation*. (Although first elaborated in his Paris Manuscripts of 1844, the basic ideas can certainly be found in his mature works such as *Grundrisse*, his preliminary notes for *Capital*.)

Alienation

The basis for this theory is the notion that what singles out humans from other species is the capacity to control nature by creative activity; they can work out a conception of what they wish to create and then put this into practice. Work can therefore be the expression of human intellect and creative capacity, unless it is *alienated*, by being (a) either concerned merely with survival, or (b) organised socially in such a way that work is debased and made into a burden. The conditions for true humanity are therefore the conditions which abolish alienated labour; these must include abundance, abolition of the current division of production into meaningless tasks, and a removal of all economic domination and exploitation. Alienation labour reaches its worst forms, Marx argued, with industrial capitalism, for here workers are tied to the machine in the performance of a meaningless task, only part of a larger process. They are forced to sell their ability to work (their labour-power) to the employer as a *marketable commodity*. Human creativity is therefore turned into an object, bought for the cheapest price. The product of this labour is owned and sold by the capitalist and so the harder workers labour, the more they are exploited by the capitalist. Therefore, since employers own the factory, the raw materials, the labour-power of their workers, and the product, they therefore claim the right to design and control the whole labour process so that the worker's creativity and intellect are constantly stifled and controlled by others (see also the discussion in Chapter 9).

Quite clearly, in order to overcome these aspects of alienation, the basic economic relations which create it must be abolished – by revolutionary means. The whole structure of society must be transformed:

> In a higher phase of communist society, after the enslaving subordination of the individual to the division of labour, and therewith also the antithesis between mental and physical labour, has vanished; after labour has become not only a means of life but life's prime want; after the productive forces have also increased with the all-round development of the individual, and all the springs of coopera-tive wealth flow more abundantly – only then can ... society inscribe on its banners: From each according to his ability, to each according to his needs! (Marx, *Critique of the Gotha Programme*, 1875).

Whether communist society really could sustain abundance through high productivity and still abolish alienation is a complex and contentious issue.

As Europe approached its year of revolutions in 1848, Marx became much more closely involved in practical politics through journalism and the Communist League, and he began to specify his account of social relations in terms of the *social organisation of production*. As we saw in Chapter 2, Marx came to see the structure of economic relations as the most basic and important element in society as a whole. We saw in the previous section that organicist social theorists regard economic activity as merely a mundane necessity facilitating the cultural structures which depend upon it; for Marx (and Engels) this dependance means that the rest of society – more or less directly – reflects these economic relations. The key to understanding a particular society is it predominant *mode of production* which consists of the tools and techniques (forces of production) and the compatible relations of production. The latter constitute *class relations* which in all non-communist societies produce an unequal structure of economic benefit and political and ideological domination. There is no 'common interest' or spontaneous 'consensus' at the level of social integration; fundamental class divisions are one aspect of the inherently unstable system – integration of the mode of production.

Conflicts take infinitely varied forms in society (e.g. religious or territorial) but they ultimately concern benefit or loss to different classes, and the conflicts have consequences for social relations, and hence class structure. In this broad sense then, Marx and Engels argue that 'the history of all hitherto existing society is the history of class struggles' (*Communist Manifesto*, 1848).

Behind these struggles, however, lie the *structural conditions for conflict*, and these derive from the structural features of the economic base. By 1859, Marx argues that 'The mode of production of material life conditions the social, political and intellectual life in general' (*Preface to a Contribution to the Critique of Political Economy*, 1859). Changes occur when structual strains emerge: 'At a certain stage of their development, the material productive forces of society come into conflict with the existing relations of production.' For example, the development of economic progress during the transition to capitalism in Britain came to be *held back* by feudal economic relations. As a result, Marx claims, these social relations must change: 'Then begins an epoch of social revolution. With the change of the economic foundation the entire immense superstructure is more or less rapidly transformed.'

The economic conditions for revolution in social institutions can, Marx claims, be known scientifically, but an apparent element of uncertainty is introduced by the fact that 'men become conscious of this conflict and fight it out'. We might thus conclude that this consciousness may vary, and that outcomes will be unpredictable, but Marx squashes such doubts by arguing that the consciousness of those struggling cannot be taken at face-value; they may delude themselves, and 'this consciousness must be explained from the contradictions of material life' – indeed 'mankind only sets itself such tasks as it can solve'. The main thrust of the *Preface* is, then, the emphasis on changes in the economic base, and these in turn produce ideologies which induce people to fight out social struggles – even if they do not fully understand the real consequences of these struggles. As it stands, this materialist conception of history certainly encourage us to regard the 'evolution' of the economic base as the key to social change – what Engels called 'the law of development of human history' – but we must qualify this in the context of other aspects of Marx's idea.

Firstly, this 'law' is only a general principle and we should not assume that all historical change can be reduced, simply and directly, to economic factors; on the other hand, the economic level is still seen as determinant in the last instance. In his historical essays, Marx showed no neglect of political and ideological factors but constantly related them to class interests and class divisions. However, no systematic theory is ever developed in general terms and so later Marxists have been led to produce widely varying elaborations which have often been mutually incompatible.

Secondly, the relationship between revolution and class struggle is problematic. We are accustomed today to regard revolution as a sudden seizure of political power, after which radical changes are made – and certainly Marx worked hard as a revolutionary for such a goal. However, the 'epoch of social revolution' Marx refers to in the *Preface* must mean the lengthy process of transformation of one mode of production (and related social structure) into another. According to Marxist historians of the transition from feudalism to capitalism in Britain, this took anything up to five hundred years – a very long revolution! Perhaps the answer is that revolutions as political crises are turning points made possible by the gradually emerging economic changes, which create new classes with an interest in breaking out of old institutional constraints – for example the emerging bourgeoisie extending its political and economic freedom in the French Revolution. The vital difference in the revolution that breaks out of capitalism rests in the fact that for the first time the subordinate class seize power instead of a new ruling class – and so class domination is abolished forever.

This simply raises once again the previous problem concerning ideology and politics, for we need to know not only the material conditions which make possible such change, but also how the working class is to take advantage of its historical opportunity. The material conditions are based in the tendency for capitalism to generate more collectivised and centralised forms of production through monopolies and banks. At the same time, this collectivised system cannot operate for the collective good because it is still tied to the logic of profit and capital accumulation. Eventually, the economy can progress no further until capitalist social relations are swept aside. However, we still need to know whether this consciousness develops inevitably, or whether there are powerful forces resisting the rise of revolutionary political action. Without better accounts of politics and ideology, we are in danger of viewing consciousness as a mere automatic side-effect of marital change. The continued survival of capitalism and the defeat of the West European Left have only intensified the pressure on Marxists to give an adequate theoretical answer to these questions. The problem of consciousness remains, however, and Marxists have been bitterly divided over this issue – especially over the role of Party leadership as opposed to 'spontaneous' class consciousness. Marx's own writings gave no real answer to this question, but the structure of his mature writings put so much emphasis on economic analysis that they encourage an almost exclusive concentration on the material conditions for change. The crisis and internal strains generated by capitalism create the conditions for the downfall of the system. Almost inevitably, the three volumes of *Capital*, plus *Theories of Surplus Value*, outweigh all other aspects of his theory, despite Marx's original intention to follow *Capital* with studies of landed property, wage labour, the state, international trade and the world market.

In the event, Marx died with only Volume I completed for publication and the broader studies were never begun. As a result, it is not surprising that orthodox Marxists have normally placed great emphasis on the economic theory of the weaknesses of capitalism such as the tendency of the rate of profit to fall. It is outside the scope of this discussion to evaluate Marx's economic theory of capitalism (the basic features are discussed in Chapter 2 on stratification), but we can see how the lack of similarly elaborated accounts of politics and ideology paved the way for crude economic determinism in some later Marxist ideas.

More generally, we can also see how the concern for the dynamics and contradictions of capitalism centres our attention on the economy as a separate institutional area of social life. This is possible in capitalism, for here economic activity operates with a logic and dynamic of its own through capital accumulation, expansion and competition. This is much less obviously applicable in pre-capitalist modes of production where economic domination is hard to separate from military, political and ideological relations. When this is the case, it is much harder to see a 'logic of development' for social structure deriving from the economic base. We need a much more complex account of the relations between economic, political and ideological aspects, even if economic relations are seen as the ultimate determinant of social relations. The work of recent structuralist Marxists such as Althusser has been oriented towards such an elaborate theory – though the adequacy of these theories can be disputed.

This leads us to the broader question of the nature of Marx's sociological explanations. If we need material structural explanations as one component of social theory, then we must see what can be drawn from his work.

While bearing in mind the dangers of over-simplified economic determinism, the concept of *mode of production* does provide a foundation for the analysis of *types* of social structure, and it does guide us towards explanations of broader aspects of social structure. The concept is one way to account for *system integration* (and non-integration) in material terms. We can distinguish, for example, capitalist or feudal societies as interrelated systems with particular structural features and dynamics (see Chapter 2 on class theory). We may also be able to show how potentials for change exist when the system itself generates internal strains or crises (above all, the contradictions of capital accumulation). As such, these structural accounts aim at being revelatory – they show systematic constraints and pressures on actors that those people will probably not understand or control. As Marx wrote, economic relations, once established 'are indispensable and independent of their will'. Despite all this, Marx's account of the rise of capitalist class relations stressed above all the deliberate creation of new economic relations by the capitalist gentry – so we must conclude that only when it is once established as a general dominant system does the capitalist system come to develop dynamics and tendencies that constrain the capitalist as much as the proletarian. At the same time, these structural features create the conditions for a recapture of human control by those who seek to transform the social structure. Thus there is a complex relation between human action and underlying social structures. The real causes lie at a level of structural causation which cannot be seen by looking at individual events or experiences. A theory is needed (as Marx offered in *Capital*) to give an account of the dynamic structures which lie beneath the surface. These structures are, however, constantly changing and developing in uneven, contradictory and crisis-ridden ways. They therefore constantly generate new possibilities for historical change and thus for intervention by groups of actors. This dynamic view of structure is entirely different from the tradition of organicist holism where the organic analogy inevitably produces a static conception of structure; change and development have to be artificially introduced through some notion of evolution.

Varieties of Marxism

For all these strengths in Marx's theory, the weaknesses and ambiguities within it have made possible a huge variety of differing academic and political approaches, all of which consider themselves Marxist. They are united in opposition to capitalism and in their goal of socialism, yet they are fundamentally divided in their content and emphasis.

First of all, we must distinguish between the orthodox Marxism of the Eastern Bloc and the diverse theories of 'Western Marxism' (Anderson, 1976). The academic Marxism of the West has become increasingly detached from any viable revolutionary struggle within Europe, to the point where some Marxist theories are so obscurely rarified that they only exist as the property of an intellectual elite. More positively, it can be said that recent theories have also been at the forefront of analysis of contemporary capitalism and its crises, whether these are economic, political, or ideological. As a result, mainstream sociology has been decisively moved in directions away from functionalism and empirical positivism. The older European tradition of philosophically grounded social critique gained great influence once more as German, French and Italian theorists helped launch the assault on positivism that swept through academic sociology in the 1960s.

Two different schools of theory contributed particularly to this assault – the Frankfurt School of critical theory, and the Parisian followers of Louis Althusser. The Frankfurt School found its roots in Hegelian philosophy and in their radical analysis of fascism's origins in bourgeois society (see Held, 1980). For the founders, and for today's thinkers such as Habermas, social theory has an obligation to reveal the potential in human society, so that actors can take charge of their future by understanding and overcoming their social constraints. This project has both structural and action dimensions as a result, but the main emphasis in Habermas's recent work has been on a philosophical search. He seeks a sure foundation both for truth and for the possibility of a just society. Habermas discovers this sure foundation in the inherent nature of communicative social action rather than in individual human nature. Thus social life contains within it the basis and the need for a better future. Other theorists in the school have been less optimistic; Marcuse, for example, has portrayed the demise of independent reason amongst workers because of the power of bourgeois ideology and institutions.

Althusserian approaches are anti-positivist on very different grounds. Althusser was implacably hostile to any 'humanistic' emphasis on social action and consciousness. His approach was an extreme example of structural social theory, where individuals are simply 'bearers' of the structural position they occupy. The shape of social structure and change is wholly determined by the complex and contradictory interlocking of the economic, political and ideological dimensions of the social formation, rooted distantly in the mode of production. This understanding is gained by abstract theoretical reasoning, intentionally divorced from empirical and historical study. As such it produced both disciples and bitter critics during the 1970s (e.g. Thompson, 1978). Amongst Marxists, one attraction of Althusserianism was its attempt to break with simple economic or class reductionism – that is, where Marxism simplifies and 'explains away' complex political and cultural phenomena. This need to break with the notion of simple determinism from the economic 'base' is at the heart of modern Marxist debate.

Nicos Poulantzas attempted to construct a more adequate Marxist account of the state and politics, drawing first on Althusser's ideas and then, more importantly, on those of the Italian Communist opponent of Mussolini, Antonio Gramsci. Poulantzas first tried to establish how the capitalist state functioned as the 'factor of cohesion of the whole social formation' guaranteeing the reproduction of capitalist society. This helped to found the Marxist debates on state theory. Poulantzas went beyond this (see Jessop, 1985) to emphasise the processes whereby various class fractions come to struggle for political and ideological dominance through the state, but he never finally broke with a class analysis of politics.

Gramsci's ideas have been extremely influential on recent attempts to understand culture and ideology. His concept of hegemony implies more than dominant values; it refers to a prevailing common-sense and way of life which is constructed as an unquestionable reality by dominant groups in the society. This has proved a valuable stimulus to recent work on the mass media and on Conservative political ideology (Hall and Jacques, 1983).

Sociology has also been greatly influenced by the more directly economic or historical writings of Marxists, above all in the areas of class formation and of international imperialism and dependence. These studies of domination and conflict have done much to correct the legacy of functionalism and its ancestors within sociology. However, Marxism has very real failings of its own. Basing sociology on Marxism alone would leave major gaps (not least the whole micro action sphere) and direct attention away from many key issues such as nationalism, patriarchy and militarism. Within Marxism, non-class relations are still down-played. Forces for change outside the economic system – whether working through the state or through warfare or through belief-systems – are still regarded as parasitic on the 'real causes' in capitalist economic relations. If we are to understand the inequalities and the dangers of the contemporary world, we need a broader analysis than Marxism has so far provided. One past attempt to provide an alternative was the work of Max Weber.

Max Weber (1864–1920)

Max Weber (1864–1920)

Born: Erfurt, Thuringia, 1864.
Education: University of Heidelberg, 1882.
            University of Berlin, 1884–5.
            University of Göttingen, 1885–6.
Career: Teaches Law, Berlin, 1892.
          Professor of Political Economy, Freiburg, 1894.
          Professor of Economics, Heidelberg, 1896.
Main works: *Methodological Essays*, 1902.
              Protestant Ethic and the Spirit of Capitalism, 1902–4.
              Economy and Society, 1910–14.
              Sociology of Religion, 1916.

Max Weber was a scholar of formidable accomplishment who through-out his work attempted to place modern capitalism in its historical context. Born into an academic family he pursued an intellectual career that spanned economic history, law, sociology, and philosophy. Despite psycho-logical illness he achieved a prolific output, but his body of work has often seemed to others to be fragmentary; Weber does not immediately appear to have any central organising theory to guide his work in the way that Marx did. However, certain guiding interests and theoretical perspectives *can* be seen as unifying the diverse themes within his work.

His first major concern was with the political paradoxes facing German society at the turn of the century. Weber was acutely aware that although Germany had become a strong capitalist state, the bourgeoisie had not succeeded in securing independent political power. As a result, Germany lacked democratic institutions; instead, traditional status groups such as the Prussian Junker aristocracy and their high-born functionaries in the army and state bureaucracies unified and ruled Germany. At the same time, the German working class was the most highly organised in Europe and was nominally Marxist. Weber was deeply committed to the pursuit of a liberal-democratic bourgeois regime, but was haunted by the threats from Marxism on the one side and all-powerful bureaucracy on the other. As a direct result, he engaged in passionate debate against the theories of Marx (or more precisely, the Marxists) while at the same time accepting that the contemporary world could only be understood by economic and historical analysis.

His other connected interest concerned the historical conditions for the rise of modern capitalism and science in the West. He posed the question:

> Through what combination of circumstances did it come about that precisely, and only, in the Western world certain cultural phenomena emerged which represents a direction of development of universal significance and validity? (*Origins of Industrial Capitalism in Europe*, 1920).

For Weber, science and modern capitalism were each part of an even broader cultural development: the *rationalisation process*. Unlike other areas of the globe, Western Europe developed from its Ancient civilisations in ways that gradually removed the influence of magic and supersition, and ultimately undermined the basis of spiritual faith. Instead, social institu-tions and individual action began to show more calculating, instrumental rationality. Law, administration and economic activity became formalised and rationalised, while the connected rise of science undermined the power of religious elites. Only in the West is there true science, and this new situation thereby allows us to look back at history and understand scientifically how we came to this position. The rise of this rational knowledge is, moreover, intimately linked to the rise of rational economic behaviour, institutionalised in the structure of modern capitalism.

For Weber, any pursuit of profit through exchange could be regarded as capitalistic, and so he saw most societies as containing some element of capitalist activity. In the modern West, however, the whole economy comes to be dominated by rational capitalism of a new form. The distinctive feature of this is the 'rational capitalist organisation of (formally) *free labour*'. These 'proletarians' are employed as propertyless wage-earners by an industrial 'bourgeoisie'. This employing class pursues capital accumulation (the continual growth of capital through profits) by using *rational calculation*, which Weber argues, is only possible with free wage-labour (as opposed to serfs or slaves). The emergence of this particular form of capitalism is thus 'the central problem in a universal history of civilisation'. It is with this question in mind that Weber embarks upon his vast comparative studies of economic, legal and religious institutions of countries outside the West; he is guided by the question 'Why was it in general that in those countries neither scientific nor artistic nor political nor economic development followed the path of *rationalisation* which is unique to the West?

At the most general level, the explanation Weber provides is in terms of the institutionalised world-views encouraged by other cultural traditions. The rulers and intelligentsia of other cultures are seen as being prevented from pursuing the road of rationalisation by the nature of the doctrines and intellectual orientations which they themselves produced. For example, the Buddhist monk withdrew from all worldly activity in order to achieve a spiritual elevation, while the Confucian Mandarin engaged in administration on the basis of highly traditionalistic and non-scientific literary knowledge. Only in the West did a cultural orientation emerge which favoured rationalisation. At one level, the non-theological philosophical thought of Ancient Greece and Rome bequeathed an intellectual heritage; this could later fuse with the worldly orientation of Judaic-Christian tradition to provide a basis for rationalistic art and science in the Renaissance. Later still, the Reformation sowed the seeds of a Puritan asceticism which, combined with the worldliness of Christianity, produced a transformation in economic behaviour (*The Protestant Ethic and the Spirit of Capitalism*). This came about because, Weber claimed, Puritanism demanded sober worldly activity – doing one's duty in a 'calling'. If this produced riches it was a sign of God's favour and demonstrated good work. However, this worldly wealth was not to be *consumed* (as the wealthy in non-capitalist societies and eras had all done) but instead the wealth must be reinvested to create the basis for further dutiful work. This was demanded, of course, by the ascetic nature of Puritanism – the demand that the godly should reject all earthly pleasures. This combination of asceticism with worldly work was seen by Weber as a unique cultural development, and one which fitted perfectly with capital accumulation: wealth is amassed but it is continually reinvested to accumulate further wealth. No other religious ethic had ever demanded this combination from the whole population of believers (rather than just from religious 'virtuosos'), none had revered worldly work so highly for its own sake. Therefore, Weber argued, the origins of modern rational capitalism must be seen in Western culture and above all in Puritain Protestantism.

This is not an appropriate context to judge the historical validity of Weber's thesis, even though it has stimulated a long and acrimonious debate among historians. We must concentrate on the form of explanation that Weber employs, and in outline this seems to be based on the opinion that general world-views have a crucial effect on the intentional motivated actions of individuals. These world-views derive most usually from the doctrines produced by religious elites who hold positions of intellectual dominance. Although the content of the ideas and the extent to which they are accepted may be influenced by economic or political interests, these cultural ideas must be accepted as independent causal elements in their own right:

> For those to whom no causal explanation is adequate without an economic (or materialistic as it is unfortunately still called) interpretation, it may be remarked that I consider the influence of economic development on the fate of religious ideas to be very important . . . On the other hand, those religious ideas themselves simply cannot be deduced from economic circumstances. They are . . . the most powerful plastic elements of national character and contain a law of development and a compelling force entirely their own (Weber, *Protestant Ethic*, p. 277, n. 84).

Weber goes on to suggest that the next most important factors are political and not economic; yet even so, he discounted the importance of any political move towards socialism. Even if Germany did move in a socialist direction, Weber argued, the rationalisation process could not be reversed. As a result, humanitarian goals (whether liberal or socialist) were doomed by inexorable and irreversible growth of rational bureaucratic administration. Sober instrumental calculation would dominate all social life and the individual would be stifled by the constraints of his role within the 'iron cage of bureaucracy':

> More and more the material fate of the masses depends upon the steady and correct functioning of the increasingly bureaucratic organisation of private capitalism. The idea of eliminating these organisations becomes more and more utopian (Weber, 1978, p. 988).

Utopian doctrines of all kinds were pathetic delusions, for rationalisation creates a world of technical efficiency and undemocratic administration that cannot be transcended; the sociologist must not fall prey to such illusions but instead face bravely the 'polar night of icy darkness' that is humanity's inevitable fate. The development of Western culture leads inevitably to a future which derides the very humanistic values which it earlier generated.

This dismal account of contemporary problems demonstrates the opposition to Marxist economic determinism in Weber's perspective, for he is clearly insistent on viewing culture as an independent factor. In consequence, one might think that this places Weber close to the positivist organicists with their stress on the primacy of cultural phenomena. This view cannot be sustained, for Weber always approaches 'culture' in a grounded, historical way as the ideas institutionalised in society by intellectual elites, and so it remains a materialist account of the role of ideas. More generally, it is impossible to reconcile Weber with the organicists because his conception of society is fundamentally different.

It is different because Weber regards social institutions as ultimately reducible to individual acts, although these intentional acts are shaped by this social context. Implicitly the grand historical studies connect with a philosophy of social action which stresses the deliberate intentions and motives of the individual actor (a view we will examine in the next section). As a result, Weber is led away from structural *explanations* in terms of the nature of the social system – a position which distances him from both Marx and the organicists. As we shall see from his approach to power and stratification, Weber only makes reference to social structure and types of social organisation in an *analytical* and descriptive manner – not in terms of structural explanations deriving from an account of the society as *system*.

One source of this perspective lies in his approach to history; Weber refers to the 'meaningless infinity of the world-process'. We only see pattern and order in this infinity of unique events by imposing ordering concepts (the *ideal types* – e.g. 'feudalism') and making comparisons. He rejects any notion of universal causal laws governing society, and is therefore certainly not a positivist. However, as a result of his view of history Weber resists making distinctions between different 'types' of society, and certainly does not attempt to offer analysis of the structural dynamics of any type of social structure. He may have described the basic features of capitalism and acknowledged that competition constrains the capitalist, but Weber makes no attempt to analyse the possible sources of crisis and change within capitalism itself. As a result, he displays a curiously fatalistic pessimism about the 'inevitablity' of being trapped in materialistic and bureaucratic capitalism. Since capitalism embodies rationality of technical means, it is inescapable. Curiously, progress ends, because Weber fails to acknowledge the potential for change generated by the failings of both capitalism and bureaucracy.

Similarly, his account of stratification fails to specify characteristic *sets* of class relations for particular types of society; instead we are presented with a confusing array of analytical concepts that are not even clearly separated from one another. Even though his concept of 'market capacity' is useful for understanding inequality in a market society (see Chapter 2), Weber confuses this account by including property as a form of market advantage, and by illustrating the theory with examples from societies such as Ancient Rome which were clearly not dominated by market relationships. These stratification concepts have achieved popularity because he refused to assume that property classes are the only real divisions, but his alternatives are undermined by the lack of any theoretical effort to distinguish and explain stratification *systems*.

Somewhat similar objections can be made to his account of power and legitimate domination (authority). Power is seen as the ability to achieve one's will, even against the resistance of others, while authority is seen as a phenomenon in which subordinates accept domination by another because they believe that the power-holder has a right to control them. All of this can be seen as excessively concerned with the subjective perceptions of actors, for (as we saw in Chapter 6) power may be institutionalised in objective economic and political relations – independently of the perceptions or wishes of those involved. This is not to suggest that such consciousness is normally absent, but we must pay attention to structures of domination which relate to the basic nature of particular social systems (such as feudalism); Weber generally fails to do this except at the level of historical description.

In summary, Weber's sociology displays a breadth of scholarship which must always remain instructive. However, his explanations of social change in terms of cultural development and actors' motivation would be much more plausible if they were developed in the context of theories of particular types of social structure and their dynamics. We shall see in the next section that Weber's methodology stresses social action in a way that seems to exclude structural explanation. Indeed, Weber claims that social phenomena can ultimately be described and explained in terms of individual motivated actions – which seems to preclude holistic theories. As a result of this, as well as his rejection of economic determinism, we can therefore argue that Weber's sociology must remain fundamentally incompatible with that of Marx.

We have argued in this section that structural explanations of some kind are a necessary part of sociology. As we shall see, however, it is by no means easy to reconcile structural explanation with the social action theories which have so far been produced. There is, at present, no simple compromise between them.

13.4 SOCIAL ACTION PERSPECTIVES

Despite all the other contrasts between them, positivist organicism and

Marxian sociology are united by a concern for holistic explanations. In each perspective, the stress is on explaining the causes and unintended consequences of action in terms of features of the social system external to the actor. As a result, the actions of the individual are seen as the effects of social forces (e.g. Durkheim's suicidogenic currents) or of structural constraints (e.g. competition between capitalist enterprises).

Social action theorists (as we saw in Chapter 12) have tended to regard such explanations as misleading in that they fail to take sufficient account of the *consciousness and intentions* of actors, and thus fail to show that the social work is a *meaningful construction* of its members. Actors, it is argued, are thinking, choosing beings who control their own actions through thought. This thought, furthermore, draws upon a stock of shared concepts and assumptions which are held in common by the actor's social group. So we should not look for external causes of behaviour, but instead should attempt to locate meaningful social action in its social context.

As we shall see, however, there are considerable variations in emphasis between particular theories within the social action perspective. We will begin with the widely influential American tradition of symbolic interactionism, then return to the European tradition of Weber and his phenomenological critic, Alfred Schutz, and finally show how the two strands can be seen to interconnect in ethnomethodology.

Symbolic interactionism

This action perspective has been widely influential – especially in the study of small-scale interaction, personality development, and deviant behaviour. It forms a central element in the tradition of qualitative research into the way actors negotiate situations and roles, and gain a social identity. Symbolic interactionism (SI) has come to emphasise the diversity of social roles and subcultures (e.g. how do you learn to be a marihuana-user?) and the way that social rules and social identities are constructed by actors through their interaction (e.g. how does a teenager come to be labelled as a criminal?). The fluidity and diversity of social life and the creative flexibility of social action are central themes of SI.

The origins of the perspective lie in the individualistic orientation of American social science as it developed at the turn of the century. As one might expect from the prevailing ethos of individualistic competition, early American social theories tended to concentrate on individualistic explanations of behaviour, or on moral constraints, neglecting material social structures. In reaction to the earlier emphasis on biologically predetermined behaviour patterns, theorists such as Cooley, Thomas and Mead came to pay much more attention to consciousness and to the social creation of the self. The characteristic approach (directly deriving from the psychology of William James) was on the unique capacity of the human being to develop conscious reflexive thought and symbolic communication. Human beings are not simply driven by innate programming or by learnt behaviour patterns; instead they monitor their own behaviour by conscious thought. This thought, however, takes place through symbols learnt in a social context largely through language. Though we also control our behaviour by reflecting upon our own actions, we can only know our own self, our social identity, through the responses of others. We come to know 'who we are' and 'what we should do' through our interpretations of the responses of others to our actions. Thus our personal identity is created through interaction, and our actions are shaped through our social interaction with others. These general notions develop in sophistication from Cooley's 'looking-glass self' to Mead's conceptions of the 'I' and the 'me', but they all begin from face-to-face interaction. While Cooley's work mainly portrayed society as an interlocking network of small groups, Mead did come to acknowledge more generally institutionalised roles and patterns. For Mead, the development of personality moved beyond a stage where the child responded to the demands of a 'significant other' (e.g. the mother) until the adult knew the demands of the 'generalised other' in the roles he or she played. At the same time, this world of roles remained flexible because actors could always renegotiate the nature of the roles through interaction.

George H. Mead (1863–1931)

Born: Ohio, 1863
Career: University of Chicago, 1893–1931.
Main tests (published posthumously):
    Mind, Self and Society, 1934.
    The Philosophy of the Present, 1959.
    The Philosophy of the Act, 1938.

Society, then, comes to be seen as interlocking interactions based on actors' perceptions and expectations of each other. The content of action depends upon the way actors come to define the appropriate patterns of action in the situation: as W. I. Thomas suggested, situations defined as real are real in their consequences. In other words, the nature of the social world ultimately depends on the shared definitions of roles and identities constructed through interaction. Thus, if 'definitions of the situation' (Thomas) and 'imaginations we have of one another' are the 'solid facts of society' (Cooley), then society changes as the definitions change through the interaction between socially created selves. However, some stability and continuity in society is created by socialisation and the institutionalisation of patterns of behaviour into roles. The work of Mead stresses the *social* construction of the self to the exclusion of the biological and instinctual elements that still figured in the work of Thomas. However, both self and society remain essentially fluid and adaptable:

> The individual is continually adjusting himself in advance to the situation to which he belongs and reacting back upon it. The self is not something that exists first and then enters into a relationship with others, but is so to speak, an eddy in the social current and so still a part of the current (Mead, 1934, p. 182).

The real strength of the symbolic interactionism approach lies not so much in its theoretical foundations as in the practical qualitative research that the approach has generated. Writers such as Hughes, Becker, Strauss and Goffman have all pioneered qualitative research methods that aim to 'get in where the action is' and 'tell it like it is'. In other words, we should try to understand the world as seen by our subjects – be they homosexuals, mental hospital patients or 'trainee' marihuana users. The task is to see how they make sense of the world and cope with alien and hostile powers such as the police or the staff of the mental hospital (Erving Goffman, *Asylums*); one therefore needs to use sensitive empathy and participant observation.

Very frequently, the concept of a 'career' guides SI accounts of the way a new social identity (as pot-smoker, physician, etc.) is negotiated. This will involve learning appropriate behaviour, applying initiative, or possibly resisting unwelcome labels being imposed by others. For example, a teenager caught stealing might try to resist the label of 'criminal'. However, undergoing the process of conviction and sentencing to a penal institution may impose such a social identity in the eyes of others. This labelling (and its consequences for employment), together with the skills learnt inside, may help produce an acceptance of the criminal self-identity by the person himself; this would be a completed 'deviant career' (see Chapter 10).

Generally, these qualitative methods are closely associated with sympathy for 'the underdog' and SI often appears as a manual for individual resistance to pressures from powerful social institutions, and a defence of the dignity and rationality of the individual actor.

For all the attractiveness and plausibility of this account of social life, certain problems remain. The first and most obvious is that social structures are neglected. Social institutions may be acknowledged as a backdrop to interaction but social systems and their related structures of economic and political power have only the most shadowy existence. Certainly, the claim that social life consists *solely* of actors' definitions is not sustainable. The consequences of class (for example) remain real, whether or not the actors define them as real, and the consequences of actions in a complex social structure may be outside the control or knowledge of any actors. In order to understand such consequences we need an account of the structure. However, it is unfair to direct these criticisms only at SI, for they may apply with even more force to other action perspectives. We can also question the adequacy of their notions of self and action since it might be argued that SI overemphasises the degree of conscious monitoring of action and manipulation of situations. Social life seems like a very consciously played game, and perhaps more scope should be allowed for unconscious drives and for social action which is less consciously 'controlled'. Again, though, this issue can also be raised with other action theories, as we shall see.

Despite these reservations, the SI perspective has provided an extremely valuable alternative to holistic theories – especially as it has coexisted with functionalism to produce some alternative to Parsons's over-socialised 'cultural dopes'. As we saw in Chapter 11, however, the *partial* nature of SI has now been generally acknowledged, in that it concentrates so heavily on face-to-face interaction.

Weber's theory of social action

The unique position of Weber's work was stressed in the earlier section on 'historical' and 'structural' sociology. Weber attempted to reconcile large-scale historical comparative studies with a methodology which began from the individual social act. Historical trends and social institutions are ultimately reducible to the unique individual actions from which they derive; at the same time, such actions have characteristic motives and goals which derive from the broader cultural context. The instrumental, calculating rationality of Western individuals derives from a much broader trend of historical development. At the level of abstract methodological statements, however, Weber does not succeed in clarifying this connection, for he concentrated on the problem of how to reconcile this concentration on social action with scientific sociological explanation. He tries to do this by systematising the use of *verstehen* (interpretive understanding) – the process by which the sociologist attempts to gain access to the meaning of action for the actor.

In defining action as 'human behaviour when . . . the agent or agents see it as subjectively *meaningful*' (1978, p. 4), Weber emphasises the *motive* present in the mind of the actor which is the 'cause' of the act. Thus, if we see a man chopping wood we may immediately recognise the act (direct *verstehen*). However, we also need to grasp the actor's motive by using empathy and rational judgement (explanatory *verstehen*). When we know the motive, we have explained the act, since 'to "explain", for a science concerned with the meaning of actions, is to grasp the complex of meanings into which a directly intelligible action fits by virtue of its subjectively intended meaning' (1978, p. 9). Weber distinguishes four types of motive: traditional conformity to habit, emotional rational behaviour oriented to an ultimate value (such as salvation), and rational behaviour oriented to a mundane goal (such as earning a living). Scientific explanation involves using *verstehen* correctly to discern the correct motive. We do this partly by locating the act in its context – we know that a woodcutter chops wood for rational reasons connected with pay. Generally, though, Weber's whole emphasis is on explaining actions by informed guesses about the actor's reasons for acting. This raises issues at two levels.

Firstly, Weber is often seen as trying to compromise with positivism to create a scientific sociology. It is quite clear that explanations in terms of actors' reasons are not at all compatible with the positivist search for external material causes which are empirically discoverable. Even with this perspective, it is difficult for positivists to ignore consciousness entirely, but they will amost certainly attempt to specify outside causes which determine the actor's choices. Weber did accept, in principle, that the choices were caused by social circumstances and by the personality of the actor. However, the causation was so complex that prediction was a practical impossibility. Causal laws were therefore unattainable, and so Weber's compromise with positivism was only partial.

More importantly, perhaps, Weber's theory has been regarded as an inadequate account of action since it remains excessively individualistic, failing to locate thought and action in any real social context. This may seem odd since Weber clearly does pay enormous attention to historical social structure, and to belief systems, as contexts for action; but it is true that the connection between these and action is never explained explicitly. This is very unfortunate, because critics of Weber's methodology – above all the phenomenologist Schutz – have radicalised action theory while at the same time abandoning Weber's historical and structural concerns.

Phenomenological sociology

Alfred Schutz, an Austrian philosopher and banker, is best known for *The Phenomenology of the Social World* (1934), a work in which he used the philosophies of Husserl and Bergson to criticise Weber's methodology and construct a radical account of the nature of social action.

In Schutz's view, Weber failed to give any real account of the way in which actions can only be constructed by drawing upon a shared set of social concepts, symbols and meanings. As a result he also presented an overly mechanical account of the relation between actions and reasons or motives.

We saw above that symbolic interactionists acknowledge shared definitions of situations and roles, and that they stress symbolic communication through language. However, they see these societal elements as built up out of interaction in a creative manner, whereas Schutz's emphasis is rather different. Instead, he argues that the 'life-world' is a precarious set of shared meanings available to the whole social group. It is a shared stock of common-sense knowledge, of taken-for-granted assumptions, about society, other actors, and the world. In this sense, the reality of social life is only created by these shared arbitrary assumptions and conceptions. However, the precarious fragility of this shared 'definition of reality' is not recognised by actors in normal circumstances, because they adopt the 'natural attitude' – that is, they see the world as solid, inflexible and constraining, even though it is really only a product of their shared ideas. It is only by a 'painful effort' that the phenomenologist can suspend this common-sense knowledge to see the real nature of social life. The basic structure of the social world can then be seen, Schutz claims, as resting solely upon 'acts of establishing or interpreting meaning'. Phenomenologists therefore claim that in as much as conventional positivistic sociology 'pretends' that there really is a constraining world of 'social facts', then it is suffering from the same common-sensical self-delusions as any ordinary member of society.

In contrast to other views of action, Schutz rejects the idea that single acts can be associated with identifiable motives. Instead, actors engage in a constant *flow* of action which takes place through a continuous use of 'recipe-knowledge' – practical knowledge of how-things-are-done. We do not constantly reflect on future acts and clarify a goal (though we do have long-term projects); we just use our common sense and do things. Only sometimes do we look back at an 'act' and give an account of our motives. In the course of our action we employ assumptions about society and how it works, and we use *verstehen* in a crude way to predict the action of others. We are therefore *all* amateur sociologists if we are successful social actors. Most important of all, we must understand the socially given meaning of an act in its context. This *socially given meaning* (e.g. of a gesture at an auction) is quite separate from any motive the actor might hold. All actors take part in a social collectivity which primarily consists of *a shared universe of meanings*. Our acts are 'meaningful' not because we have a particular intention or motive, but because other actors interpret our action as having symbolic significance. We act successfully when all share the same set of meanings – if we do not, then an itchy nose at an auction might produce an unwanted acquisition. The fact that we have bought a stuffed elephant has no connection with our intentions, but is a result of the socially given meaning of our act in the context of an auction.

Thus Schutz rightly emphasises the collective, *inter*-subjective nature of meaning, unlike Weber; however a greater problem now arises. Schutz, again unlike Weber seems to dissolve social life into a *purely* inter-subjective world. Social life becomes a 'mental event': we learn the importance of *shared* meanings, but we are left with no tools to understand social structure or unintended consequences. Our task is now limited to describing correctly the nature of social action. Schutz explicitly rejects any notion of *correcting* the accounts of the world given by actors – the sociologist might be more rigorous and logical than the lay actor but:

'Every social science takes as its goal the greatest possible clarification of what is thought about the social world by those living in it.' Such a conception of sociology removes any potential it might have for revealing the constraints upon action and thus aiding actors to overcome them. Indeed Schutz's assumption that the universe of meanings is shared by all (and collectively reproduced) comes remarkably close to the consensus which is the key to social order in organicist approaches. Schutz's society is not a 'moral order' but it is a collectivity of *meanings*, not material social relations.

Ethnomethodology

Ethnomethodologists could almost be called Schutz's shocktroops, for their general aim is to demonstrate the truth of his phenomenological arguments by practical experiments. Although only prominent since the mid-1960s, ethnomethodology has its roots in the fusion of symbolic interactionism and phenomenology. Harold Garfinkel is the founding figure and he is responsible for its title; as the previous chapter explained, he intended it to refer to the project of an ethnographic description and analysis of the methods used by actors to sustain social life. In other words, ethnomethodologists work from Schutz's claim that the social world is produced and reproduced by the practical actions of actors, on the basis of taken-for-granted assumptions.

Garfinkel (1967) developed ethnomethodology as a new answer to the 'problem of order'. Organicism had previously solved this by viewing 'moral order' as the guarantee of social integration, and Garfinkel was exposed to Parsons's version of this as a graduate student. He rejected it in favour of a search for the processes by which 'orderliness' emerges out of the flux of everyday life. These become the only legitimate focus of study. The task of ethnomethodology is therefore to expose the mundane everyday processes of social life as skilful accomplishments of the actors: whether one is a police officer dealing with a teenager, or party to a routine conversation, one is using knowledge, skills and taken-for-granted assumptions. The point is that we are, as lay actors, unaware of all this. Only a painful effort, a disruption, or an incomprehensible response from another will make us aware of how much we are taking for granted.

So when Garfinkel sent his students home to behave like boarders – polite, well-behaved and respectful – their families responded with incomprehension or even hostility. As in his other experiments, Garfinkel is arranging for 'background expectancies' to be violated so that the social setting ceases to make sense to the actors. Whilst not 'testing' or 'proving' hypotheses, these studies aim to demonstrate and illustrate ethnomethodological claims. Firstly, the disorientation felt by actors shows their dependence on taken-for-granted knowledge. Secondly, the work actors do in trying to impose order and sense on the disrupted setting ('Are you feeling ill? Is this some sort of game?') demonstrates how we all unwittingly use artful skills to sustain social meanings and interactions.

Thus ethnomethodologists seek appropriate methods to turn Schutz's 'natural attitude' into a researchable phenomenon, exposing the organised artful practices of everyday life. In this way, mundane interaction is treated as 'anthropologically strange' so that grounded observation and ethnographic description become the appropriate methods, together with the more specialised techniques of conversation analysis.

It may seem that these ethnomethodological insights are illuminating, if limited; they should simply be added to the range of sociological perspectives. This view is seriously mistaken, for ethnomethodology makes much more radical claims. In short, they claim that the processes they expose exhaust social reality – and any generalisations which go beyond are dangerously false. For the ethnomethodologist, the typologies and structural concepts of conventional sociology not only reify social processes, they merely reproduce the natural attitude of the lay actor that the social world is solid and constraining. Ethnomethodology dissolves away the patterns and regularities which are the focus of mainstream sociology; there are no social phenomena which are not open to transformation in the flux of everyday life. What is more, social action and understanding only really operates, they claim, in the particular social situation, since meanings are 'indexical' or context-bound. What is more, there is no guarantee that the ethnomethodological observer has achieved any detached objectivity, or neutral knowledge. Although they follow Schutz's notion of phenomenological detachment, they offer no real reason why this is objective: hence we may imagine a regress of ethnomethodologists doing an ethnographic study of ethnomethodologists doing a study . . . there is no coherent alternative to positivist epistemology being offered, just a vehement critique.

This critique of positivism was extremely influential in the late 1960s and early 1970s. A favourite focus for attacks was Durkheim's account of suicide, as Chapters 11 and 12 have shown. The ethnomethodological critique goes well beyond the point that Durkheim's explanations concern social circumstances to the exclusion of individual intentions or meanings. For them, the very patterns themselves are suspect because they are socially constructed records of decisions about deaths. The legitimate focus of study ceases to be the suicide itself, let alone 'causes' of 'patterns'. Instead we are directed to study only the processes by which deaths come to be defined as suicides through the common-sense judgements of coroners (Atkinson, 1978).

Such arguments radically transform the scope and aspirations of social understanding. We are only concerned with correctly identifying the nature of the processes; we are no longer attempting to provide propositions about the substance or content of action, since this involves illegitimate generalisation and reification. Not surprisingly, most mainstream sociologists are unwilling to concede so much to the radical action approach; a degree of mutual antagonism prevailed for some time. This hostility is redoubled for politically committed theorists by the stance of 'ethnomethodological indifference' which (like Schutz) refuses to correct or change actors' common-sense. Instead of revealing to actors the constraints on their freedom, ethnomethodology seeks merely to expose the most basic elements of social interaction. They are radical only in the sense that they claim this is the whole truth about social life.

Evaluation of social action perspectives

The general emphasis on social action is clearly important; sociology can no longer ignore the meaningful nature of social life, neither can it conveniently forget consciousness and motivation in a mistaken quest for general positivistic laws. Nor can we operate with rigid and simplified conceptions of action where motives precede actions, and where these motives are directly caused by external forces. It must be recognised that society is constantly reproduced and partly modified by the creative acts of individuals in unique social situations. Action theories are surely correct in their view that societies are continually transformed (though usually in a gradual way) by the innovative acts of individual members. Phenomenological approaches place a valuable emphasis on these processes and on the fact that these actions are created in terms of taken-for-granted assumptions characteristic of the particular society. From this it is revealed that the social world is a meaningful construction, created out of the interaction of its members. One profound consequence of this is that the social world is shown to be less solid and impenetrable than it seems to the individual lay actor. Action sociology exposes the potential fragility and *precariousness* of social reality. Instead of viewing society as a solid, fixed entity, we are made to recognise society as a changing flux created out of actors' shared perceptions and definitions (even if we do not accept that this is the *whole* truth about society). This emphasis is certainly a necessary rebuttal of the more 'mechanical' versions of social structure which have been commonplace in both organicism and Marxism (although we should also bear in mind that social arrangements have a good deal of stability in comparison with the power of most individuals). Social action theories are right to emphasise not only that the social world can be changed by actors, but that this is also a constant process.

As a result of this constant intentional and unintentional change, it is very hard to see how positivisitic conceptions of *laws* can be applied to social action or social structure. There do not appear to be invariable regularities which can be called laws; and where regularities do occur they are open to radical change by the accumulated effects of action. We have seen that we must attempt to specify the principles of organisation of *types* of society, *not* 'society-in-general'; even here there are no fixed laws, but characteristic structures of social relations which constantly generate change. The positivistic conception of sociology seems as unacceptable as the organicist account of structure and action. In general, then, social action theories provide a range of perspectives which are a necessary antidote to the more static and rigid conceptions of structure.

No current action theory, however, successfully combines a convincing account of social action with sufficient awareness of power, conflict and constraint. Schutz provides a better theory of action than either Weber or symbolic interactionism, but one totally detached from any real concern with social structure. Although SI does not provide any theory of system integration or disintegration, it does pay attention to individual responses to *constraints* from the social structure. Phenomenology and ethnomethodology abandon even this. Social life is conceived solely in terms of the negotiation of meanings and the practical accomplishment of routine activities. Society becomes a mere 'mental event' sustained only by the shared definitions and assumptions of actors. In the course of this chapter it has been emphasised that society is more than just this. However much individual citizens today may believe in the existence of liberty or equality, the real distribution of power and economic advantage will constrain their actions; whatever they may intend to do by acting, their actions will have unintended consequences. The nature of these consequences will depend upon the interlocking connections between parts of the social structure, and on the way the social system operates *as* a dynamic system. (For example, the cutting of wages by individual employers to protect their own profits might help to push the economy further into recession, and thereby threaten employers even more). Although perceptions of society certainly are used by actors in the course of their action, these perceptions are hardly reliable and they hardly constitute the sum total of social reality.

13.5 HUMAN ACTION AND SOCIAL SYSTEM

The most pressing theoretical task for sociology is to construct a theory of social life which acknowledges the fact that human activity embodies *both* social action and social structure simultaneously. Social structures do not inhabit a separate plane of existence, they can only exist through their manifestation in human action. These structures can therefore only be reproduced through such action, and as we have emphasised, social action is creative and innovative. Therefore, action not only *reproduces* structures, but continually *transforms* them to a greater or lesser degree. At the same time, such action takes place within a social system and suffers the *constraints* this imposes as well as employing the *resources* distributed through the social structure. Giddens (1976, p. 138) has expressed this two-way relationship in his conception of the 'duality of structure': 'Every act which contributes to the reproduction of a structure is also an act of production, a novel enterprise, and as such may initiate change by altering that structure at the same time as it reproduces it'. Here, and in *Central Problems in Social Theory* (1979), Giddens has made important contributions to the development of a unifying sociological theory.

Most sociologists have stressed the extent to which societies are reproduced rather than transformed; indeed the traditional 'problem of order' sought to explain how society ensured this reproduction. Traditional answers have been in terms of *socialisation* and *social control* (see the discussion in Chapter 1), but it is now clear that both these factors can be exaggerated. Organicism has tended towards an oversocialised conception where actors are simply 'cultural dopes'. Social control may be almost as important as socialisation for explaining the passivity of those who are relatively powerless but the threat of such coercion cannot be seen as the primary source of conformity. The pressures are far more widespread and subtle than this. Instead, we must explore the way that social action relates to an institutionalised structure of constraints and resources. That is, we must identify the way that power economic resources, and knowledge all constitute resources used by actors in their practical activity in society. Actors are therefore able to act with greater or lesser effectivness, depending on the extent to which they have access to these resources. At the same time, others may be able to impose constraints on action by holding more political power or authority, more economic power or resources, or by having better access to knowledge. Quite clearly, these constraints and resources are distributed in patterned ways – and our earlier chapters on politics, stratification and belief-systems all tried to show evidence for this unequal distribution.

Those chapters also emphasised the necessity to *explain* the patterns of constraints and resources, and it was argued that the explanation can be found in the *systems of social relations* which characterise different *types* of society. These structures of social relations can only be understood *as* systems and must be regarded as having their own special modes of operating and their own tendencies for dynamic development. For example, feudalism can be distinguished as a *type* of society with a certain basic structure of social relations revolving around the relationships between feudal lords, serfs and the clergy. Distinctive kinds of economic exploitation, relations of domination, and ideological control, all work together to form the particular distinctive social system of feudalism. Basic, relationships *cause* a distribution of constraints and resources: feudal lords hold a monopoly of force and demand surplus labour or surplus product, while the clergy hold a monopoly of knowledge. Thus we can see the underlying *system of social relations* as producing *structures of inequality* which both facilitate and limit the practical activity of actors (see Figure 13.1). The 'system' box relates to the system of social relations, while 'structure' represents the patterned distribution of constraints and resources which derive from the social system. In previous chapters we have also tried to show how groups can gain or lose in freedom or power as the class structure changes, as political concessions or initiatives are made, or as changes in knowledge and perception develop. For example, we saw how radical changes have occurred in the class position of the clerk, as the job has been de-skilled and feminised, and as some workers have organised in unions. Both the clerks and their employers have different resources they can draw upon to change or defend the clerk's position – in the end, of course, the clerk has more constraints and fewer resources for control. At the same time, the actions of the employer cannot be understood without using explanations derived from a theory of the nature of the social system: the employer may be a capitalist firm forced by competition to lower labour costs, but a liberal-democratic political system may allow union organisation and resistance. Equally, dominant ideology directed towards the workers may well encourage acceptance of the employer's authority as a 'fact of life'.

We can also see the need for a concept of *social system* if we look back at the contrast between Weber and Marx. For Marx, capitalist social relations come to form a system which generates inequalities and has its own 'laws of motion'. He writes at great length in *Capital* on the distinctive way this mode of production operates, and on the crises and possibilities for change that this social system generates by its own imperfect working. In contrast, Weber does not deal with societies as social systems, but only as structures of inequality and power. Weber provides many analytical concepts for describing the distribution of these things but never produces any complete theory of, for example, how capitalism continually generated inequality. Unlike Marx, Weber does not try to establish the structural conditions for social change in terms of changing economic relations, but emphasises the cultural conditions for the development of rationality in every sphere, including the economic. Of course, Weber paid enormous attention to power and conflict, but did not really link this to theories of the way different kinds of social system have interlocking institutions which work together as a whole. Marx, on the other hand, always looked for the roots of historical change in the social system (which in his view meant the mode of production). The social world was *not* static even though capitalism or feudalism (or whatever) had certain fixed system properties. This was because modes of production constantly developed and changed, generating problems, conflicts, and crises. There is therefore no such thing as a perfectly integrated system because: (a) systems may overlap with other systems (for instance, feudal and capitalist modes of production may overlap), and (b) even 'pure' social systems generate problems (for example, the falling rate of profit) and conflicts (especially between classes). Thus, unlike the organicist approach, this system perspective avoids the old split between 'theory of statics' and 'theory of evolution'. Social change and conflict is continuous, but these aspects derive from the underlying changes in the social system.

As we saw earlier, however, there are problems with Marx's approach. Many have questioned whether the structure of *economic* relations should be seen as the ultimately determining aspect of social systems. Whether or not economic determinism remains true 'in the last instance', social theories must work from the complex relationship between economics, political and ideological relationships. There is no smooth and perfect integration between them, so the relationship between the underlying social system and actual practical actions are dauntingly complex.

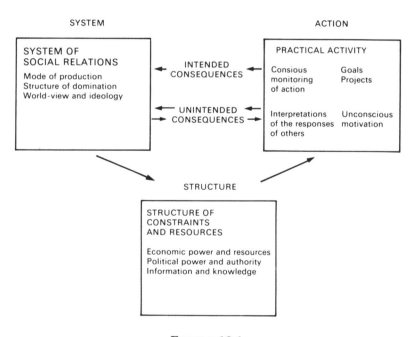

FIGURE 13.1

Figure 13.1 tries to show some of the simpler relationships. Within the 'action' box itself, some of the aspects of motivation and action are briefly suggested. Firstly, action should not be conceived as separate, rigid 'acts' which always have clearly defined motives behind them. Instead, the phenomenological approach rightly emphasises that individuals are constantly engaged in *practical activity* which takes place in a continuous flow of events; it is impossible to wrench acts out of their social context; and this context is defined in particular ways by the actors involved. In very different ways, both symbolic interactionism and phenomenology stress the inter-subjective quality of social life – actors negotiate definitions of situations and build up social identities. At the same time, this symbolic interaction involves the sharing of a universe of meanings taken for granted in the particular social group. Symbolic interactionists have convincingly stressed the ways in which these meanings can vary between groups and can be continually modified during the process of interaction. We should be careful not to assume (as Schutz seems to) that these shared meanings are uniformly available to actors with similar content – this shifts us back towards the 'consensus' theories which we rejected in organicism. We must thus acknowledge that *practical activity draws upon meanings which vary across society and are constantly negotiated*. We must also stress that action draws upon knowledge, information and perceptions of reality. These knowledge resources are unequally available to different groups of actors, and so the effectiveness of their intended actions will clearly be affected by this distribution. The 'structure' box in the diagram summarises these unequally distributed resources as 'information and knowledge'; in fact, of course, all actors employ some common-sense information and understanding about the world. The point is that reliable knowledge is unequally spread, and as Chapter 10 shows, institutions such as schools and the mass media are closely involved in the disemination of both true and false knowledge. Clearly, since all action draws on such knowledge, the role of science is crucial in that it produces the most reliable and legitimate understanding; the products of science must always have some effect on general practical action and so science can never be divorced from its involvement in everyday life. This intimate connection places a special responsibility on social science to modify the common-sense assumptions used in practical activity; if sociology can produce knowledge, then social actors can gain more control over their own social world.

The diagram also sketches in some aspects of the relationship between the *self* and social action. As the symbolic interactionists emphasise, actors have a unique capacity to monitor their own action reflexively. That is, they can be aware of what they are doing and modify it in the light of their interpretation of the responses of other people. If others react in a hostile manner (as the actor interprets their action) the actor can change his or her action to try to obtain a better response. At the same time, though, we must bear in mind some of the criticisms of SI. We must not assume that all action is as carefully monitored, and unconscious drives and motivations may be highly significant. At the same time, our action is often oriented to long-term goals or projects – such as being a good parent to one's child. Not only will these goals be chosen with the circumstances of socialisation and social control, but what it *means* to be a good parent is a socially constructed definition. For example, in post-war Britain, changes in female employment, family size, and so on, have produced a constant renegotiation of the meaning of motherhood for many women. This is partly in terms of the choices they make in their circumstances, but also in terms of the more general social norms and beliefs which are directed at women. There is a complex relationship (as we have seen in earlier chapters on sexual divisions and belief-systems) between these two aspects of practical activity, and also between them and the subconscious motivations attached to parenthood.

Action, then, is creative and innovative but it never takes place outside social contexts which involve (a) inequalities of power, knowledge and material resources as well as (b) socially constructed meanings, definitions and rules. These constraints upon action need not be recognised by the actor or consciously reflected upon. The circumstances constraining action may be just as opaque to the actors as the consequences for society of the things they do. Even though very often actors do wish to produce particular intended consequences, all actions have consequences which are unexpected and perhaps unrecognised. For example, the imprisonment of offenders may prevent future employment of the prisoner, expose them to professional criminals and disrupt the upbringing of their children. All this is likely to reinforce deviant behaviour rather than deter it. In addition, *the nature of these unintended consequences is not random – it depends upon the nature of the social system.* This cannot be otherwise, because every event has complex effects because of the patterned interrelations between actors and between social institutions.

This does not mean that all actions unwittingly reproduce the social structure, for the latter will be constantly modified by the effects of creative action. We must recognise, though, that an established social system, with established social structures of inequality, will normally possess a continuity which is only marginally affected by particular individual acts. The potential for change in societies depends upon the degree of system integration, and from this the degree of 'stability' in unequal structures of resources. As we have seen, the political, economic and ideological aspects of systems never fully integrate and indeed generate their own weaknesses and crises. There is always lack of integration, there is always a potential for dynamic change and conflict within society. Social action takes place in the context of social structures which are transformed as they are reproduced.

13.6 KNOWLEDGE, VALUES AND THE ROLE OF THE SOCIOLOGIST

Two basic goals characterise the project of constructing a science of society. The first is the true understanding of social life – that is, sociological knowledge which can claim the status of *truth*. The second is the goal of expanding human capacity to control our own future by the reconstruction or reform of society. The problem is to establish criteria for the validation of theories as true, while still allowing sociologists to be engaged in the struggle to create a better social world.

To many twentieth-century sociologists, such a combination of goals would seem absurd. It has become a matter of faith that sociological understanding must completely divorce itself from any connection with values – in order that it can claim the status of scientific knowledge. Truth has no connection with values, it is argued, because value-judgements such as 'coffee is nicer than tea' can never be regarded as true or false. Instead, they are personal commitments – neither correct nor incorrect. Therefore, it is argued, since science concerns itself only with *truth*, such judgements must be rigorously excluded from scientific accounts. Thus, when Hitler decided that the Jews should be exterminated, this was a judgement based on values, not empirically based theory, and so the scientist had no right to intervene. Many scientists, however, would be uneasy about conceding so much – can we really say nothing with certainty about the rights and wrongs of genocide? The study of society raises such questions acutely, and some answers must be found that are more adequate than simple moral neutrality for the scientist.

In fact, although early sociologists were committed to the pursuit of truth, they saw no conflict between this and the pursuit of the good society. For Comte and Durkheim, the whole point of seeking social scientific knowledge was to find the true principles for a good, ordered, integrated society. The laws of society show the natural and *correct* state to which it should conform; it cannot be doubted that Durkheim saw an extremely active role for the sociologist in creating the conditions for organic solidarity in modern society. This was not imposing the sociologist's values, but simply the pursuit of societal *health*. The latter concept conveys the notion clearly – science can specify a stable state which is also thereby desirable. For Comte, the sociologist-priests should rule; in Durkheim's view the educationalist and the reformer of the economy would create healthy order. Each of these writers, of course, held positivistic views of social science and each saw science as the major force for social progress. The two goals were inseparable until the developments in positivist philosophy during the twentieth century, when a great wedge was driven between truth and values. Before that, though, we should note that such a division was even more alien to Marx. For him it was inconceivable that sociological knowledge could be directed at anything but the criticism of prevailing institutions and the creation of ideal social relations. Anything else simply justified the existing society and thus could be nothing more than mystifying ideology. This clearly contrasts with the evolutionary reformism of the organicists and has only come to be an influential view within academic sociology during recent years. In general, sociologists have wanted to establish their discipline as scientific, and have therefore sought to conform to the dominant conception of science – that is positivism.

Even nineteenth-century positivism contained elements that threatened the progressive role of sociology. Here the source of knowledge is, of course, empirical observation; knowledge consists of generalisations about observed relations of cause and effect. As a result, speculative philosophy and theology are attacked for claiming knowledge without having any real empirical foundation for their pronouncements. Causes can only be discovered in *this* world: truth can only be produced by empirical observation of the material world. For example, Durkheim rejected any explanation of religious activity in terms of God or the supernatural, for these could have no place in rational science. Lurking within this epistemology, then, is a potential rejection of any ethical commitments, for these can never be justified empirically. It makes no sense to ask for material proof that genocide is undesirable – you either believe it or you do not. However, once absolute ethical standards (derived from God or wherever) are abandoned, we seem to lose any real grounds for making any rational decisions on moral or political issues. Fascist racialism becomes just another opinion, as good as any other.

These potential consequences of positivism were furthest developed within *logical positivism*, in the Vienna Circle in the 1920s. Here, scientists such as Mach and Carnap developed a toughened conception of positivism which rigorously excluded values from scientific knowledge. Their opposition to 'metaphysics' went so far that they condemned any statements which did not have direct empirical content (e.g. 'I think people should be kind') as literally meaningless and nonsensical. Statements involving values were thus non-empirical, senseless, and could only be mere emotional outbursts. Scientists must rigorously distance themselves from such distractions and concentrate on producing value-neutral knowledge. Thus two things become crucially, and dangerously, confused. Not only must value-judgements be excluded from scientific *statements* which claim truth, but the *scientist* must also be ethically neutral. This unwarranted claim is contained in the loose instruction to the scientist to 'be objective' – which fails to distinguish (a) the objectivity of knowledge from (b) the objectivity of the scientist in doing scientific work, or from (c) his or her moral responsibility as a citizen. Social scientists should not be 'biased', so it came to be assumed, they must be indifferent to ethical issues. As positivist sociology came to imitate the natural sciences more and more slavishly, the discipline became increasingly divorced from any ethic of social responsibility, let alone any commitment to social reconstruction. American sociology in particular became wedded to this principle of ethical non-responsibility; it reached its nadir in the notorious Project Camelot of 1964. This is worth discussing in detail.

Project Camelot

By the early 1960s American social science had successfully established an image of scientific and political respectability, and as Gouldner has argued (Gouldner, 1975), the commitment to value-neutrality was partly motivated by a desire to be seen as 'safe' and non-threatening to the established order. As Lundberg had proclaimed, social scientists were often technicians researching topics defined as 'problems' by others; usually they certainly were not social critics. Such self-defined roles encouraged the US Army to recruit social scientists for a huge research programme in Latin America, designed to discover the causes of social instability. In its natural concern for social order in the lower half of the continent, the Pentagon wished to discover the causes of revolt and remove them. In order to achieve this, they planned to spend up to six million dollars and recruit a huge team of political scientists and sociologists to work in the countries concerned. Their employer made the aims clear in a recruiting letter: 'The US Army has an important mission in the positive and constructive aspects of nation-building in less-developed countries as well as to a responsibility to assist friendly governments in dealing with active insurgency problems.' The aims were equally clear to the South American governments concerned, and they rapidly forced the abandonment of the project, with accusations of spying and covert intervention by the United States. All this came as a shock to those who agreed to take part, for they believed that they were aiding these countries by advocating policies such as land reform which would remove the need for revolution. It is a sad comment on social scientists that they could be so naive about the intentions of the powerful.

The furore surrounding Camelot added significantly to a growing tide of dissatisfaction with the dominant positivist functionalism. We have seen already how this was challenged on political as well as theoretical grounds; the 1960s saw a radicalisation of student politics and this was reflected (and led) by social scientists. A number of American writers instigated furious onslaughts on the bastions of establishment social science, few more so than C. Wright Mills and Alvin Gouldner. As we shall see, though, the debate was not always conducted at a particularly sophisticated level.

Mills (1970, p. 10), for example, states quite baldly that 'there is no way in which any social scientist can avoid assuming choices of value and implying them in his work as a whole'. On such a view the sociologist *must* have political and moral concern, and therefore 'value-freedom' is impossible. If this means, as Myrdal also argues, that we have competing sociological accounts based on opposed values, then that must simply be accepted. Sociologists must make their own stance clear and state their values openly. It is inconceivable that a scientist can or should be indifferent to ethics and politics, and so the goal of objectivity must be abandoned. These writers accept more of the conventional view than they realise, for they assume that value-commitment and scientific objectivity must always be incompatible. In doing so, they merely echo the view that Gouldner (1975, p. 4) summarises:

> The image of a value-free sociology is more than a neat intellectual theorem demanded as a sacrifice to reason; it is also a felt conception of a role and a set of (more or less) shared sentiments as to how sociologists should live.

Gouldner enters the fray in his usual apoplectic manner, arguing that this principle has dehumanised and demoralised sociologists: the fact-value distinction 'warps reason by tinging it with sadism and leaves it feeling smugly sure of itself and bereft of a sense of common humanity'. He claims that sociologists have betrayed themselves in this way only to buy a social and intellectual respectability; indeed he acknowledges that this 'did contribute to the intellectual growth and emancipation of our discipline'. This usefulness is long past, however. Today 'it has become increasingly the trivial token of professional respectability ... the gentleman's promise that boats will not be rocked'. The intellectual poverty of such a stance is only emphasised by the ritual references made to Max Weber's statements on objectivity, for Weber developed a position of more subtlety and complexisty than most contemporary writers. Very few of them acknowledge the significance of Weber's telling assertion that 'an attitude of moral indifference has no connection with scientific objectivity'. We need to pay more attention to the real nature of his contribution to the debate.

Weber certainly cannot be seen as adopting a simple positivist position on values. Instead he attempts an uneasy compromise with earlier views (especially those of Rickert) which emphasised the inescapable *relevance* of values to historical and social studies. Weber accepted Rickert's claim that history could only *select* from the seamless web of unique events. These made up what Weber later called 'the meaningless infinity of the world-process'; to discern order or significance in this chaos scientists have to impose pattern by selecting some aspects that they regard as relevant to the values of their time. Weber argued that particular cultural circumstances made some topics (such as the rise of capitalism) relevant for study at a particular time. In this sense scientific activity is guided by values. Unlike Rickert, Weber agreed with the principle that no values can be regarded as ultimately correct; despite this he was convinced that humans (especially scientists) must remain committed to the values they happen to accept. As a result, the scientist must also be a responsible citizen. Ethical and political responsibility cannot be shirked, for arguments over the *use* of knowledge inevitably involve value-judgements. Scientists should not pretend to have priority over any citizen in these decisions but neither should they withdraw from commitment on grounds of objectivity. Weber broadly accepted the view that *knowledge* must be cleansed of values, but the choice of subject-matter and the use of that knowledge are both areas where values must unavoidably be involved. Now this may seem to challenge the positivist position, and indeed it does contradict the simplistic postures adopted by many who followed him. However, it does not logically undermine positivism *if* (and only if) we still have objective-criteria for the testing of knowledge. Given neutral testing-procedures, it does not matter whether values affect our choice of topic, because any propositions we produce can be evaluated and modified against independent evidence. However, such a neat solution is dependent on the value-neutrality of this evidence and some of Weber's statements seem to undermine this – his logical solution is weakened by his worries about the availability of 'pure' evidence to prove or disprove our propositions.

Despite these nagging doubts, Weber succeeded in constructing a methodology which sharply distinguishes between the objectivity of *theories* and the value-neutrality of the *scientist*. The investigator cannot and should not be value-free in the choice of topic or the application of knowledge. The fact that Einstein later rejected the use of nuclear weapons in warfare does not invalidate the objectivity of his physics, and certainly does not harm his credentials as a scientist. We thus have a solution to the problems of objectivity available – but only on condition that we possess *neutral testing-procedures*. However, many critics of positivism have questioned the possibility of basing such tests on empirical data either (a) because sense-data are seen as dependent upon the theories and values used to interpret it, or (b) because non-positivist epistemologies often deny the relevance of empirical observations – many structuralist accounts, for example, seek to look 'beneath the surface' of concrete observable phenomena (such arguments were discussed in the previous chapter). In either case, empirical evidence will not be accepted as a neutral basis for testing-procedures and so the objectivity of knowledge will be under threat.

There are two possible responses to this threat. One is to accept the criticisms of empiricism and seek a new epistemology with new criteria for truth which still exclude values from theories. At the moment, such an epistemology does not appear to be available. A different response is to accept that values are inevitably built into all theories, *but* to then assert that some values are *correct*; on this view, truth will be reunited with 'the good', and the pursuit of knowledge will be the same as the pursuit of the correct values.

This second alternative sounds bizarre to those trained in positivist assumptions, but it is a position with a long philosophical history. Most obviously, theologians have confidently expounded the 'correct' ethical principles, while more recent political philosophers have defined some political principles and goals (e.g. democracy) as having an ultimate value. For the positivist in the twentieth century, such statements are metaphysical gobbledegook – entirely meaningless; the consequence of such a position is, however, that we have no rational basis for the discussion of ethical

and political goals. As argued above, positivists can only condemn genocide on the basis of 'emotional commitment' – and their feelings are
logically no more valid than those of Adolf Hitler.

In contrast to such a position, many thinkers have attempted to locate
the true goals of humanity in assertions about human nature – for example,
the belief that we are born free and equal forms the basis for modern
political constitutions in both capitalist and communist societies. Earlier in
this chapter, we saw how Marx's vision of human *potential* for free creative
labour implied that such a society was possible and desirable: human
nature is not fixed but it does embody *capacities* for creativity and control
of nature. For Marx, the task is to create a society where social relations
will allow such human capacities to develop to the full.

Marx's conception of humans can be criticised, of course, for his stress
on human creativity is tied directly to the control of nature in production;
and therefore linked to his stress on economic relations. We have argued in
the course of this chapter that as a result of this Marx does not provide a
satisfactory account of social action and consciousness. However, if we *do*
acknowledge the importance of these aspects of social life we are in an even
better position to see how sociology must be linked to human goals. This
link is unavoidable since humans are uniquely powerful creatures: they
have the capacity to transform their social world and thereby their own
nature. We have seen in the course of this book that humans constantly
change the social world as they reproduce it. Actors negotiate new ways of
acting and they consciously try to change things; yet at the same time, the
type of social system in which they are located imposes constraints upon
their action and produces effects of which actors are not fully aware. As a
consequence of all this, humans constantly seek knowledge about their
social environment and act upon it. The better their understanding, the
better they are able to reconstruct the social world. This means that by its
very nature as an attempt to understand rigorously social life, sociology has
a central part to play in the way in which actors come to control their own
future. Because of this, sociology cannot avoid being concerned with *both* a
quest for true knowledge *and* a struggle to reconstruct society. Sociology
can show how the human potential for creativity and self-determination is
held back by social systems which embody structures of domination and
inequality; this knowledge is inseparable from the struggle to liberate
human potential through the reconstruction of society.

REFERENCES TO CHAPTER 13

Anderson, P. (1976) *Considerations on Western Marxism*, London, New Left Books.
Atkinson, M. (1978) *Discovering Suicide*, London, Macmillan.
Durkheim, E. (1974) *Sociology and Philosophy*, New York, Free Press.
Garfinkel, H. (1967) *Studies in Ethnomethodology*, Englewood Cliffs, N.J., Prentice-
   Hall.

Giddens, A. (1976) *New Rules of Sociological Method*, London, Hutchinson.
Giddens, A. (1977) *Studies in Social and Political Theory*, London, Hutchinson.
Giddens, A. (1979) *Central Problems in Social Theory*, London, Macmillan.
Giddens, A. (1984) *The Constitution of Society*, Cambridge, Polity.
Gouldner, A. (1975) 'Anti-Minotaur', in A. Gouldner, *For Sociology*, Harmondsworth, Penguin.
Held, D. (1980) *Introduction to Critical Theory*, London, Hutchinson.
Hall, S. and Jacques, M. (1983) *The Politics of Thatcherism*, London, Lawrence & Wishart.
Jessop, B. (1985) *Nicos Poulantzas*, London, Macmillan.
Lockwood, D. (1964) 'Social Integration and System Integration', in G. K. Zollschan and W. Hirsch (eds), *Explorations in Social Change*, London, Routledge & Kegan Paul.
Lukes, S. (1973) *Emile Durkheim*, London, Allen Lane.
Mead, G. H. (1934) *Mind, Self and Society*, University of Chicago Press.
Merton, R. K. (1949) *Social Theory and Social Structure*, New York, Free Press.
Mills, C. W. (1970) *The Sociological Imagination*, Harmondsworth, Penguin.
Nisbet, R. (1967) *The Sociological Tradition*, London, Heinemann.
Thompson, E. P. (1978) *The Poverty of Theory*, London, Merlin.
Turner, R. (1974) *Ethnomethodology*, Harmondsworth, Penguin.
Weber, M. (1978) *Economy and Society*, University of California Press.

Author Index

Subject Index